Suzuki GSX1300R Hayabusa
Service and Repair Manual

by Matthew Coombs

Models covered

Suzuki GSX1300R-X, Y, K1, K2, K3 and K4 Hayabusa. 1299cc. 1999 to 2004

(4184-288)

© Haynes Publishing 2004

A book in the *Haynes Service and Repair Manual Series*

All rights reserved. No part of this book may be reproduced or transmitted in any form or by any means, electronic or mechanical, including photocopying, recording or by any information storage or retrieval system, without permission in writing from the copyright holder.

ISBN **1 84425 184 5**

British Library Cataloguing in Publication Data
A catalogue record for this book is available from the British Library.

Library of Congress Control Number 2004111805

ABCDE
FGHIJ
KLMNO
PQRST

Printed in the USA

Haynes Publishing
Sparkford, Yeovil, Somerset BA22 7JJ, England

Haynes North America, Inc
861 Lawrence Drive, Newbury Park, California 91320, USA

Editions Haynes
4, Rue de l'Abreuvoir
92415 COURBEVOIE CEDEX, France

Haynes Publishing Nordiska AB
Box 1504, 751 45 UPPSALA, Sweden

Contents

LIVING WITH YOUR SUZUKI HAYABUSA

Introduction
Suzuki – Every which way	Page	0•4
Acknowledgements	Page	0•8
About this manual	Page	0•8
Identification numbers	Page	0•9
Buying spare parts	Page	0•9
Safety first!	Page	0•10

Daily (pre-ride checks)
Engine/transmission oil level	Page	0•11
Brake fluid levels	Page	0•12
Clutch fluid level	Page	0•13
Coolant level	Page	0•14
Tyres	Page	0•15
Suspension, steering and drive chain	Page	0•15
Legal and safety checks	Page	0•15
Bike spec	Page	0•16
Model development	Page	0•17

MAINTENANCE

Routine maintenance and servicing
Specifications	Page	1•1
Recommended lubricants and fluids	Page	1•2
Maintenance schedule	Page	1•3
Component locations	Page	1•4
Maintenance procedures	Page	1•6

Contents

REPAIRS AND OVERHAUL

Engine, transmission and associated systems

Engine, clutch and transmission	Page	2•1
Cooling system	Page	3•1
Fuel and exhaust systems	Page	4•1
Ignition system	Page	5•1

Chassis components

Frame, suspension and final drive	Page	6•1
Brakes, wheels and tyres	Page	7•1
Bodywork	Page	8•1

Electrical system

Page 9•1

Wiring diagrams

Page 9•26

REFERENCE

Tools and Workshop Tips	Page	REF•2
Security	Page	REF•20
Lubricants and fluids	Page	REF•23
Conversion factors	Page	REF•26
MOT Test Checks	Page	REF•27
Storage	Page	REF•31
Fault Finding	Page	REF•34
Fault Finding Equipment	Page	REF•43

Index

Page REF•47

Introduction

Suzuki
Every Which Way

by Julian Ryder

From Textile Machinery to Motorcycles

Suzuki were the second of Japan's Big Four motorcycle manufacturers to enter the business, and like Honda they started by bolting small two-stroke motors to bicycles. Unlike Honda, they had manufactured other products before turning to transportation in the aftermath of World War II. In fact Suzuki has been in business since the first decade of the 20th-Century when Michio Suzuki manufactured textile machinery.

The desperate need for transport in post-war Japan saw Suzuki make their first motorised bicycle in 1952, and the fact that by 1954 the company had changed its name to Suzuki Motor Company shows how quickly the sideline took over the whole company's activities. In their first full manufacturing year, Suzuki made nearly 4500 bikes and rapidly expanded into the world markets with a range of two-strokes.

Suzuki didn't make a four-stroke until 1977 when the GS750 double-overhead-cam across-the-frame four arrived. This was several years after Honda and Kawasaki had established the air-cooled four as the industry standard, but no motorcycle epitomises the era of what came to be known as the Universal

The T500 two-stroke twin

Introduction 0•5

One of the later GT750 'kettle' models with front disc brakes

Japanese motorcycle better than the GS. So well engineered were the original fours that you can clearly see their genes in the GS500 twins that are still going strong in the mid-1990s. Suzuki's ability to prolong the life of their products this way means that they are often thought of as a conservative company. This is hardly fair if you look at some of their landmark designs, most of which have been commercial as well as critical successes.

Two-stroke Success

Early racing efforts were bolstered by the arrival of Ernst Degner who defected from the East German MZ team at the Swedish GP of 1961, bringing with him the rotary-valve secrets of design genius Walter Kaaden. The new Suzuki 50 cc racer won its first GP on the Isle of Man the following year and winning the title easily. Only Honda and Ralph Bryans interrupted Suzuki's run of 50 cc titles from 1962 to 1968.

The arrival of the twin-cylinder 125 racer in 1963 enabled Hugh Anderson to win both 50 and 125 world titles. You may not think 50 cc racing would be exciting - until you learn that the final incarnation of the thing had 14 gears and could do well over 100 mph on fast circuits. Before pulling out of GPs in 1967 the 50 cc racer won six of the eight world titles chalked up by Suzuki during the 1960s as well as providing Mitsuo Itoh with the distinction of being the only Japanese rider to win an Isle of Man TT. Mr Itoh still works for Suzuki, he's in charge of their racing program.

Europe got the benefit of Suzuki's two-stroke expertise in a succession of air-cooled twins, the six-speed 250 cc Super Six being the most memorable, but the arrival in 1968 of the first of a series of 500 cc twins which were good looking, robust and versatile marked the start of mainstream success.

So confident were Suzuki of their two-stroke expertise that they even applied it to the burgeoning Superbike sector. The GT750 water-cooled triple arrived in 1972. It was big, fast and comfortable although the handling and stopping power did draw some comment. Whatever the drawbacks of the road bike, the engine was immensely successful in Superbike and Formula 750 racing. The roadster has its devotees, though, and is now a sought-after bike on the classic Japanese scene. Do not refer to it as the Water Buffalo in such company. Joking aside, the later disc-braked versions were quite civilised, but the audacious idea of using a big two-stroke motor in what was essentially a touring bike was a surprising success until the fuel crisis of the mid-'70s effectively killed off big strokers.

The same could be said of Suzuki's only real lemon, the RE5. This is still the only mass-produced bike to use the rotary (or Wankel) engine but never sold well. Fuel consumption in the mid-teens allied to frightening complexity and excess weight meant the RE5 was a non-starter in the sales race.

Suzuki's GT250X7 was an instant hit in the popular 250 cc 'learner' sector

0•6 Introduction

The GS400 was the first in a line of four-stroke twins

Development of the Four-stroke range

When Suzuki got round to building a four-stroke they did a very good job of it. The GS fours were built in 550, 650, 750, 850, 1000 and 1100 cc sizes in sports, custom, roadster and even shaft-driven touring forms over many years. The GS1000 was in on the start of Superbike racing in the early 1970s and the GS850 shaft-driven tourer was around nearly 15 years later. The fours spawned a line of 400, 425, 450 and 500 cc GS twins that were essentially the middle half of the four with all their reliability. If there was ever a criticism of the GS models it was that with the exception of the GS1000S of 1980, colloquially known as the ice-cream van, the range was visually uninspiring.

They nearly made the same mistake when they launched the four-valve-head GSX750 in 1979. Fortunately, the original twin-shock version was soon replaced by the 'E'-model with Full-Floater rear suspension and a full set of all the gadgets the Japanese industry was then keen on and has since forgotten about, like 16-inch front wheels and anti-dive forks. The air-cooled GSX was like the GS built in 550, 750 and 1100 cc versions with a variety of half, full and touring fairings, but the GSX that is best remembered is the Katana that first appeared in 1981. The power was provided by an 1000 or 1100 cc GSX motor, but wrapped around it was the most outrageous styling package to come out of Japan. Designed by Hans Muth of Target Design, the Katana looked like nothing seen before or since. At the time there was as much anti feeling as praise, but now it is rightly regarded as a classic, a true milestone in motorcycle design. The factory have even started making 250 and 400 cc fours for the home market with the same styling as the 1981 bike.

Just to remind us that they'd still been building two-strokes for the likes of Barry Sheene, in 1986 Suzuki marketed a road-going version of their RG500 square-four racer which had put an end to the era of the four-stroke in 500 GPs when it appeared in 1974. In 1976 Suzuki not only won their first 500 title with Sheene, they sold RG500s over the counter and won every GP with them - with the exception of the Isle of Man TT which the works riders boycotted. Ten years on, the RG500 Gamma gave road riders the nearest experience they'd ever get to riding a GP bike. The fearsome beast could top 140 mph and only weighed 340 lb - the other alleged GP replicas were pussy cats compared to the Gamma's man-eating tiger.

The RG only lasted a few years and is already firmly in the category of collector's item; its four-stroke equivalent, the GSX-R, is still with us and looks like being so for many years. You have to look back to 1985 and its launch to realise just what a revolutionary step the GSX-R750 was: quite simply it was the first race replica. Not a bike dressed up to look like a race bike, but a genuine racer with lights on, a bike that could be taken straight to the track and win.

The first GSX-R, the 750, had a completely new motor cooled by oil rather than water and an aluminium cradle frame. It was sparse, a little twitchy and very, very fast. This time Suzuki got the looks right, blue and white bodywork based on the factory's racing colours and endurance-racer lookalike twin headlights. And then came the 1100 - the big GSX-R got progressively more brutal as it chased the Yamaha EXUP for the heavyweight championship.

And alongside all these mould-breaking designs, Suzuki were also making the best looking custom bikes to come out of Japan, the Intruders; the first race replica trail bike,

The GS750 led the way for a series of four cylinder models

Introduction 0•7

Later four-stroke models, like this GSX1100, were fitted with 16v engines

the DR350; the sharpest 250 Supersports, the RGV250; and a bargain-basement 600, the Bandit. The Bandit proved so popular they went on to build 1200 and 750 cc versions of it. I suppose that's predictable, a range of four-stroke fours just like the GS and GSXs. It's just like the company really, sometimes predictable, admittedly - but never boring.

Battle Cruiser

Back in the late 1990s the Japanese manufacturers fought the top-speed war not with lightweight superbike race-replicas but with giant beasts of bikes, or rather birds. Honda christened their high-speed monster, the CBR1100XX, the Blackbird, Suzuki's response had the usual collection of digits and letters – GSX1300R – and it also had a name: Hayabusa. This is a rare example of humour showing through in the nomenclature of Japanese motorcycles, because a *hayabusa* is a Japanese relative of the peregrine falcon, that fastest bird in the world, and one that presumably has been known to eat blackbirds. Naturally, this was never mentioned in any of Suzuki's publicity.

If the *hayabusa* is anything like the peregrine falcon, it is small, lithe and graceful. The Hayabusa is none of those things but it does share one vital attribute with its namesake, speed. When you take the motor from the GSX-R750, take it out to 1300 cc, wrap a massive twin-beam aluminium frame round it and clothe it in wind-tunnel developed aerodynamically efficient bodywork you get a very fast motorcycle. More to the point from a riding point of view, you get a quite astounding amount of torque – well over 90 ft-lb of it at 6750 rpm and well over 75 ft-lb down at 4000 rpm. Magazine dyno tests reported over 150 bhp at the back wheel. Not surprisingly, those same magazines were soon remarking on how startlingly quickly the Hayabusa got through rear tyres.

The really surprising thing about the Hayabusa was that it felt quite sporty to ride, Suzuki even launched it at a race track although they picked one with a long front straight – Barcelona. There is, of course, one other very noticeable thing about the Hayabusa apart from its speed, and that's its looks. No way could you call it a pretty bike; purposeful is about the nicest adjective you could use, and that's because its bodywork is the way it is purely for function, not for the sake of form. The clues are everywhere: the nose that's so pointy the headlights have to be stacked on top of one another, the flanks of the fairing protrude a long way forward, the big front mudguard that covers up as much fork leg as possible, the extension to the belly pan just in front of the back wheel, the big tail unit. All these are designed to cut drag to the lowest possible figure. To get the full idea you have to put a rider on the bike in a crouching riding position, then you can see how near to the ideal egg shape the designers have got. Of course, anything that sticks out is bad for aerodynamic efficiency so smaller components got the full treatment. Take the mirrors; they're longer front to back on the bottom than on the top to promote smooth airflow and, because they're like an upside down aerofoil, to reduce the tendency of the front wheel to lift. Even the mirrors' mounting arms get the same treatment. Aerodynamics was used to increase power as well. The pointy nose generated high pressure on its centreline so the air intakes were placed as close to the centre of the bike as possible and those indicator lenses in the mouths of the intakes are used to help force more air in and increase the ram-air effect.

The engine wasn't ignored, it was one of the first big bikes to use fuel injection and it had a slipper clutch – Suzuki called it a back-torque limiter – long before the big four-strokes in MotoGP were getting hot and bothered about how to manage their engine braking. As you'd expect from the biggest GSX, power delivery was simply breathtaking.

Suzuki's GSX-R range represented their cutting edge sports bikes

0•8 Introduction

GSX1300R-Y

GSX1300RZ-K3

GSX1300R-K4

The Hayabusa did what it was designed to do: go very fast in a straight line. The surprising thing was, it was also very good at doing all the other things a motorcycle is supposed to do as well.

Acknowledgements

Our thanks are due to V & J Superbikes of Mudford, Yeovil, who supplied the machine featured in the illustrations throughout this manual. We would also like to thank NGK Spark Plugs (UK) Ltd for supplying the colour spark plug condition photographs, the Avon Rubber Company for supplying information on tyre fitting and Draper Tools Ltd for some of the workshop tools shown.

Thanks are also due to Julian Ryder who wrote the introduction 'Suzuki – Every Which Way' and to Redcat Marketing who supplied model photographs.

About this Manual

The aim of this manual is to help you get the best value from your motorcycle. It can do so in several ways. It can help you decide what work must be done, even if you choose to have it done by a dealer; it provides information and procedures for routine maintenance and servicing; and it offers diagnostic and repair procedures to follow when trouble occurs.

We hope you use the manual to tackle the work yourself. For many simpler jobs, doing it yourself may be quicker than arranging an appointment to get the motorcycle into a dealer and making the trips to leave it and pick it up. More importantly, a lot of money can be saved by avoiding the expense the shop must pass on to you to cover its labour and overhead costs. An added benefit is the sense of satisfaction and accomplishment that you feel after doing the job yourself.

References to the left or right side of the motorcycle assume you are sitting on the seat, facing forward.

We take great pride in the accuracy of information given in this manual, but motorcycle manufacturers make alterations and design changes during the production run of a particular motorcycle of which they do not inform us. No liability can be accepted by the authors or publishers for loss, damage or injury caused by any errors in, or omissions from, the information given.

It is the policy of Haynes Publishing to actively protect its Copyrights and Trade Marks. Legal action will be taken against anyone who unlawfully copies the cover or contents of this Manual. This includes all forms of unauthorised copying including digital, mechanical, and electronic in any form. Authorisation from Haynes Publishing will only be provided expressly and in writing. Illegal copying will also be reported to the appropriate statutory authorities.

Identification numbers 0•9

Frame and engine numbers

The frame serial number is stamped into the right-hand side of the steering head. The engine number is stamped into the back of the crankcase. Both of these numbers should be recorded and kept in a safe place so they can be furnished to law enforcement officials in the event of a theft.

The frame and engine serial numbers should also be kept in a handy place (such as with your driver's licence) so they are always available when purchasing or ordering parts for your machine.

The frame number is stamped into the right-hand side of the steering head

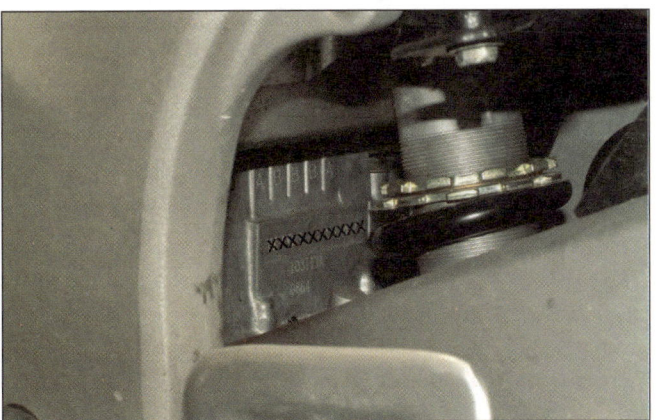

The engine number is stamped into the back of the crankcase

Identifying model codes

The procedures in this manual identify the bikes by model code and year. The model code (e.g. GSX1300R-X) is printed on the identification plate or label, which is located on the right-hand frame spar close to the steering head.

Model and code letter	Year
GSX1300R-X	1999
GSX1300R-Y	2000
GSX1300R-K1	2001
GSX1300R-K2	2002
GSX1300R-K3	2003
GSX1300R-K4	2004

Buying spare parts

Once you have found the identification numbers, record them for reference when buying parts. Since the manufacturers change specifications, parts and vendors (companies that manufacture various components on the machine), providing the ID numbers is the only way to be reasonably sure that you are buying the correct parts.

Whenever possible, take the worn part to the dealer so direct comparison with the new component can be made. Along the trail from the manufacturer to the parts shelf, there are numerous places that the part can end up with the wrong number or be listed incorrectly.

The two places to purchase new parts for your motorcycle – the franchised or main dealer and the parts/accessories store – differ in the type of parts they carry. While dealers can obtain every single genuine part for your motorcycle, the accessory store is usually limited to normal high wear items such as chains and sprockets, brake pads, spark plugs and cables, and to tune-up parts and various engine gaskets, etc. Rarely will an accessory outlet have major suspension components, camshafts, transmission gears, or engine cases.

Used parts can be obtained from breakers yards for roughly half the price of new ones, but you can't always be sure of what you're getting. Once again, take your worn part to the breaker for direct comparison, or when ordering by mail order make sure that you can return it if you are not happy.

Whether buying new, used or rebuilt parts, the best course is to deal directly with someone who specialises in your particular make.

0•10 Safety first!

Professional mechanics are trained in safe working procedures. However enthusiastic you may be about getting on with the job at hand, take the time to ensure that your safety is not put at risk. A moment's lack of attention can result in an accident, as can failure to observe simple precautions.

There will always be new ways of having accidents, and the following is not a comprehensive list of all dangers; it is intended rather to make you aware of the risks and to encourage a safe approach to all work you carry out on your bike.

Asbestos

● Certain friction, insulating, sealing and other products - such as brake pads, clutch linings, gaskets, etc. - contain asbestos. Extreme care must be taken to avoid inhalation of dust from such products since it is hazardous to health. If in doubt, assume that they do contain asbestos.

Fire

● Remember at all times that petrol is highly flammable. Never smoke or have any kind of naked flame around, when working on the vehicle. But the risk does not end there - a spark caused by an electrical short-circuit, by two metal surfaces contacting each other, by careless use of tools, or even by static electricity built up in your body under certain conditions, can ignite petrol vapour, which in a confined space is highly explosive. Never use petrol as a cleaning solvent. Use an approved safety solvent.

● Always disconnect the battery earth terminal before working on any part of the fuel or electrical system, and never risk spilling fuel on to a hot engine or exhaust.
● It is recommended that a fire extinguisher of a type suitable for fuel and electrical fires is kept handy in the garage or workplace at all times. Never try to extinguish a fuel or electrical fire with water.

Fumes

● Certain fumes are highly toxic and can quickly cause unconsciousness and even death if inhaled to any extent. Petrol vapour comes into this category, as do the vapours from certain solvents such as trichloro-ethylene. Any draining or pouring of such volatile fluids should be done in a well ventilated area.
● When using cleaning fluids and solvents, read the instructions carefully. Never use materials from unmarked containers - they may give off poisonous vapours.
● Never run the engine of a motor vehicle in an enclosed space such as a garage. Exhaust fumes contain carbon monoxide which is extremely poisonous; if you need to run the engine, always do so in the open air or at least have the rear of the vehicle outside the workplace.

The battery

● Never cause a spark, or allow a naked light near the vehicle's battery. It will normally be giving off a certain amount of hydrogen gas, which is highly explosive.

● Always disconnect the battery ground (earth) terminal before working on the fuel or electrical systems (except where noted).
● If possible, loosen the filler plugs or cover when charging the battery from an external source. Do not charge at an excessive rate or the battery may burst.
● Take care when topping up, cleaning or carrying the battery. The acid electrolyte, evenwhen diluted, is very corrosive and should not be allowed to contact the eyes or skin. Always wear rubber gloves and goggles or a face shield. If you ever need to prepare electrolyte yourself, always add the acid slowly to the water; never add the water to the acid.

Electricity

● When using an electric power tool, inspection light etc., always ensure that the appliance is correctly connected to its plug and that, where necessary, it is properly grounded (earthed). Do not use such appliances in damp conditions and, again, beware of creating a spark or applying excessive heat in the vicinity of fuel or fuel vapour. Also ensure that the appliances meet national safety standards.
● A severe electric shock can result from touching certain parts of the electrical system, such as the spark plug wires (HT leads), when the engine is running or being cranked, particularly if components are damp or the insulation is defective. Where an electronic ignition system is used, the secondary (HT) voltage is much higher and could prove fatal.

Remember...

✗ **Don't** start the engine without first ascertaining that the transmission is in neutral.
✗ **Don't** suddenly remove the pressure cap from a hot cooling system - cover it with a cloth and release the pressure gradually first, or you may get scalded by escaping coolant.
✗ **Don't** attempt to drain oil until you are sure it has cooled sufficiently to avoid scalding you.
✗ **Don't** grasp any part of the engine or exhaust system without first ascertaining that it is cool enough not to burn you.
✗ **Don't** allow brake fluid or antifreeze to contact the machine's paintwork or plastic components.
✗ **Don't** siphon toxic liquids such as fuel, hydraulic fluid or antifreeze by mouth, or allow them to remain on your skin.
✗ **Don't** inhale dust - it may be injurious to health (see Asbestos heading).
✗ **Don't** allow any spilled oil or grease to remain on the floor - wipe it up right away, before someone slips on it.
✗ **Don't** use ill-fitting spanners or other tools which may slip and cause injury.
✗ **Don't** lift a heavy component which may be beyond your capability - get assistance.
✗ **Don't** rush to finish a job or take unverified short cuts.
✗ **Don't** allow children or animals in or around an unattended vehicle.
✗ **Don't** inflate a tyre above the recommended pressure. Apart from overstressing the carcass, in extreme cases the tyre may blow off forcibly.
✓ **Do** ensure that the machine is supported securely at all times. This is especially important when the machine is blocked up to aid wheel or fork removal.
✓ **Do** take care when attempting to loosen a stubborn nut or bolt. It is generally better to pull on a spanner, rather than push, so that if you slip, you fall away from the machine rather than onto it.
✓ **Do** wear eye protection when using power tools such as drill, sander, bench grinder etc.
✓ **Do** use a barrier cream on your hands prior to undertaking dirty jobs - it will protect your skin from infection as well as making the dirt easier to remove afterwards; but make sure your hands aren't left slippery. Note that long-term contact with used engine oil can be a health hazard.
✓ **Do** keep loose clothing (cuffs, ties etc. and long hair) well out of the way of moving mechanical parts.
✓ **Do** remove rings, wristwatch etc., before working on the vehicle - especially the electrical system.
✓ **Do** keep your work area tidy - it is only too easy to fall over articles left lying around.
✓ **Do** exercise caution when compressing springs for removal or installation. Ensure that the tension is applied and released in a controlled manner, using suitable tools which preclude the possibility of the spring escaping violently.
✓ **Do** ensure that any lifting tackle used has a safe working load rating adequate for the job.
✓ **Do** get someone to check periodically that all is well, when working alone on the vehicle.
✓ **Do** carry out work in a logical sequence and check that everything is correctly assembled and tightened afterwards.
✓ **Do** remember that your vehicle's safety affects that of yourself and others. If in doubt on any point, get professional advice.
● If in spite of following these precautions, you are unfortunate enough to injure yourself, seek medical attention as soon as possible.

Daily (pre-ride) checks

Note: *The daily (pre-ride) checks outlined in the owner's manual covers those items which should be inspected on a daily basis.*

Engine/transmission oil level

Before you start:
✔ Take the motorcycle on a short run to allow it to reach normal operating temperature.
Caution: Do not run the engine in an enclosed space such as a garage or workshop.
✔ Stop the engine and support the motorcycle upright on its centrestand or an auxiliary stand. Allow it to stand undisturbed for a few minutes to allow the oil level to stabilise. Make sure the motorcycle is on level ground.

Bike care:
● If you have to add oil frequently, check whether there are any oil leaks from the engine joints, oil seals and gaskets. If not, the engine could be burning oil, in which case there will be white smoke coming out of the exhaust – see *Fault Finding*.

The correct oil
● Modern, high-revving engines place great demands on their oil. It is very important that you always top up with a good quality oil of the specified type and viscosity, and do not overfill the engine.

Oil type	API grade SF or SG
Oil viscosity	SAE 10W40*

*If you are using the motorcycle constantly in extreme conditions of heat or cold, other more suitable viscosity ranges may be used – refer to the viscosity chart to select the oil best suited to your conditions.

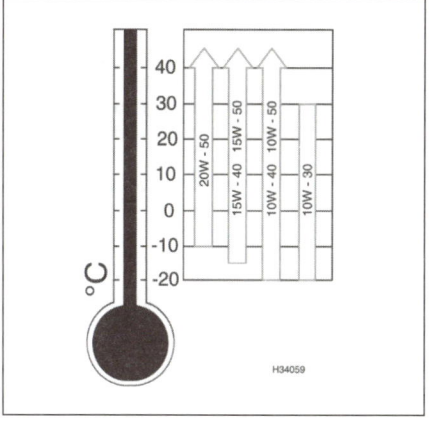

Oil viscosity chart: Select the oil best suited to your conditions

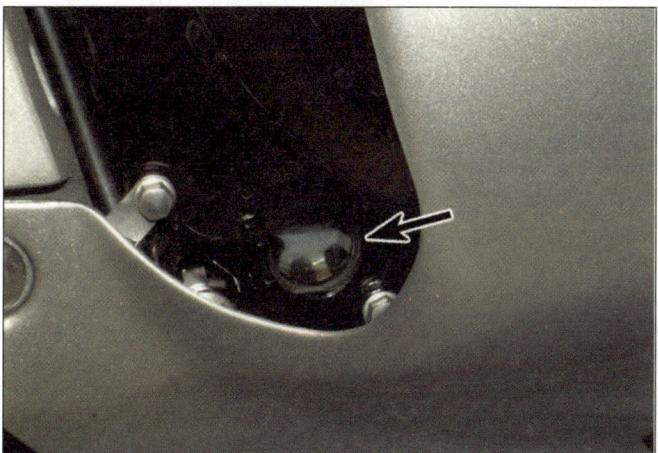

1 The oil level inspection window (arrowed) is located on the right-hand side of the engine – wipe it so that it is clean.

2 With the motorcycle vertical, the oil level should lie between the F (full) and L (low) level lines (arrowed) next to the window.

3 If the level is on or below the L line, unscrew the oil filler cap from the clutch cover. Check the condition of the O-ring and replace it with a new one if it is damaged, deformed or deteriorated.

4 Using a suitable funnel if necessary, top up the engine with the recommended grade and type of oil to bring the level almost up to the F line on the inspection window. Do not overfill.

0•12 Daily (pre-ride) checks

Brake fluid levels

> ⚠ **Warning:** Brake hydraulic fluid can harm your eyes and damage painted surfaces, so use extreme caution when handling and pouring it and cover surrounding surfaces with rag. Do not use fluid that has been standing open for some time, as it is hygroscopic (absorbs moisture from the air) which can cause a dangerous loss of braking effectiveness.

Before you start:

✔ Make sure you have the correct hydraulic fluid – DOT 4 is specified.
✔ When checking the fluid in the front reservoir turn the handlebars as required so the reservoir is level – support the motorcycle upright using an auxiliary stand if required. If topping up is necessary and you don't have a short or angled screwdriver that can fit between the reservoir and the windshield, slacken the screws with the reservoir clear of the windshield, keeping finger pressure on the cover until the reservoir is level again.
✔ When checking the fluid in the rear reservoir support the motorcycle upright on its centrestand or on an auxiliary stand.
✔ Wrap a rag around the reservoir being worked on to ensure that any spillage does not come into contact with painted surfaces.

Bike care:

● The fluid in the front and rear brake master cylinder reservoirs will drop as the brake pads wear down. If the fluid level is low check the brake pads for wear (see Chapter 1).
● If either fluid reservoir requires repeated topping-up there could be a leak somewhere in the system, which must be investigated immediately.
● Check for signs of fluid leakage from the hydraulic hoses and/or brake system components – if found, rectify immediately (see Chapter 7).
● Check the operation of both brakes before taking the machine on the road; if there is evidence of air in the system (spongy feel to lever or pedal), it must be bled (see Chapter 7).

FRONT

1 The front brake fluid level is visible through the window in the reservoir body – it must be above the LOWER level line (arrowed).

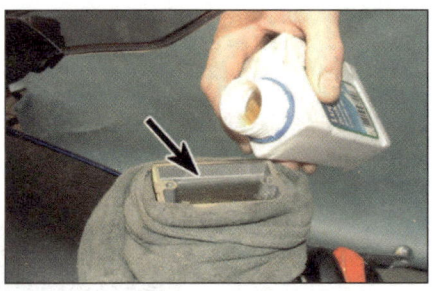

3 Top up with new clean DOT 4 hydraulic fluid until the level is above the LOWER level line, but not above the top level line (arrowed) on the inside of the reservoir front wall. Do not overfill and take care to avoid spills (see **Warning** above).

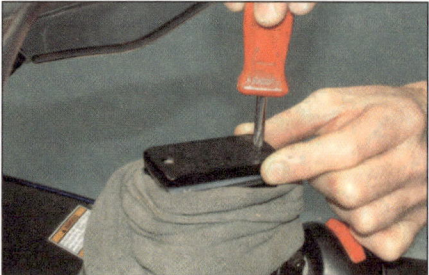

2 If the level is on or below the LOWER line, undo the two reservoir cover screws and remove the cover, diaphragm plate and diaphragm.

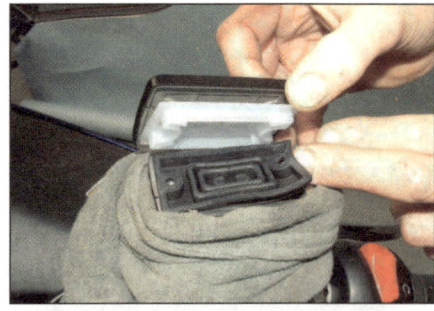

4 Ensure that the diaphragm is correctly seated before installing the plate and cover.

REAR

1 The rear brake fluid level is visible via the aperture in the right-hand side of the seat cowling – it must lie between the UPPER and LOWER level lines (arrowed). If the level is on or below the LOWER line, remove the seat cowling (see Chapter 8).

3 Top up with new clean DOT 4 hydraulic fluid until the level is above the LOWER level line. Do not overfill and take care to avoid spills (see **Warning** above).

2 Undo the two reservoir cover screws and remove the cover and diaphragm.

4 Ensure that the diaphragm is correctly seated before installing the cover. Install the seat cowling (see Chapter 8).

Daily (pre-ride) checks

Clutch fluid level

Before you start:
✔ Make sure you have the correct hydraulic fluid. DOT 4 is specified.
✔ When checking the fluid in the reservoir turn the handlebars as required so the reservoir is level – support the motorcycle upright on its centrestand or on an auxiliary stand. If topping up is necessary and you don't have a short or angled screwdriver that can fit between the reservoir and the windshield, slacken the screws with the reservoir clear of the windshield, keeping finger pressure on the cover until the reservoir is level again.
✔ Wrap a rag around the reservoir to ensure that any spillage does not come into contact with painted surfaces.

Bike care:
● If the fluid reservoir requires repeated topping-up there could be a leak somewhere in the system, which must be investigated immediately.
● Check for signs of fluid leakage from the hydraulic hose and clutch release cylinder – if found, rectify immediately (see Chapter 2).
● Check the operation of the clutch before taking the machine on the road; if there is evidence of air in the system (spongy feel to the lever), it must be bled (see Chapter 2).

> **Warning:** Clutch hydraulic fluid can harm your eyes and damage painted surfaces, so use extreme caution when handling and pouring it and cover surrounding surfaces with rag. Do not use fluid that has been standing open for some time, as it is hygroscopic (absorbs moisture from the air) which can cause a loss of clutch effectiveness.

1 The clutch fluid level is visible through the window in the reservoir body – it must be above the LOWER level line (arrowed).

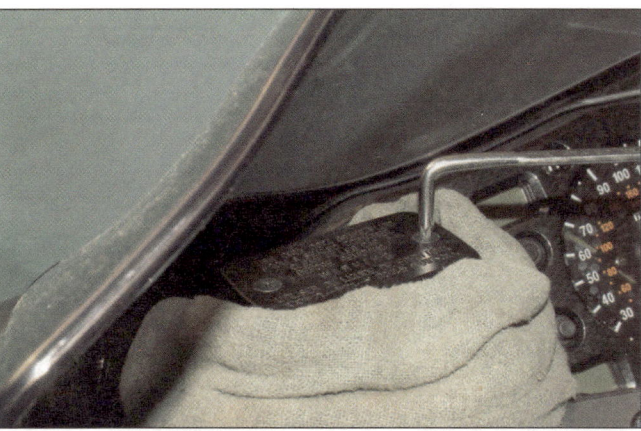

2 If the level is on or below the LOWER line, undo the two reservoir cover screws and remove the cover, diaphragm plate and diaphragm.

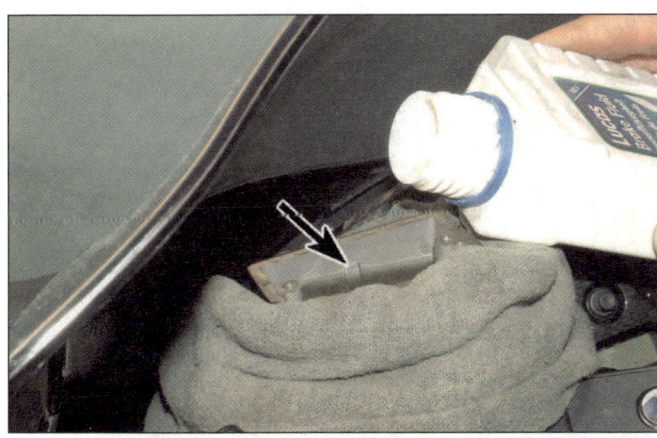

3 Top up with new clean DOT 4 hydraulic fluid until the level is above the LOWER level line, but not above the top level mark (arrowed) on the inside of the reservoir front wall. Do not overfill and take care to avoid spills (see **Warning** above).

4 Ensure that the diaphragm is correctly seated before installing the plate and cover.

0•14 Daily (pre-ride) checks

Coolant level

> **Warning: DO NOT remove the radiator pressure cap to add coolant. Topping up is done via the coolant reservoir tank filler. DO NOT leave open containers of coolant about, as it is poisonous.**

Before you start:

✔ Make sure you have a supply of coolant available (a mixture of 50% distilled water and 50% corrosion inhibited ethylene glycol anti-freeze is needed – do not use tap water, unless in an emergency, and then make sure it is soft water).
✔ Always check the coolant level when the engine is COLD. If the engine has been running allow it cool down fully before checking the level.
✔ Support the motorcycle upright on its centrestand or on an auxiliary stand. Make sure the motorcycle is on level ground.

Bike care:

● Use only the specified coolant mixture. It is important that anti-freeze is used in the system all year round, and not just in the winter. Do not top the system up using only distilled water, as the system will become too diluted.
● Do not overfill the reservoir tank. If the coolant is significantly above the F (full) level line at any time, the surplus should be siphoned or drained off to prevent the possibility of it being expelled out of the overflow hose (see Chapter 3).
● If the coolant level falls steadily, check the system for leaks (see Chapter 1). If no leaks are found and the level continues to fall, it is recommended that the machine be taken to a Suzuki dealer for a pressure test.

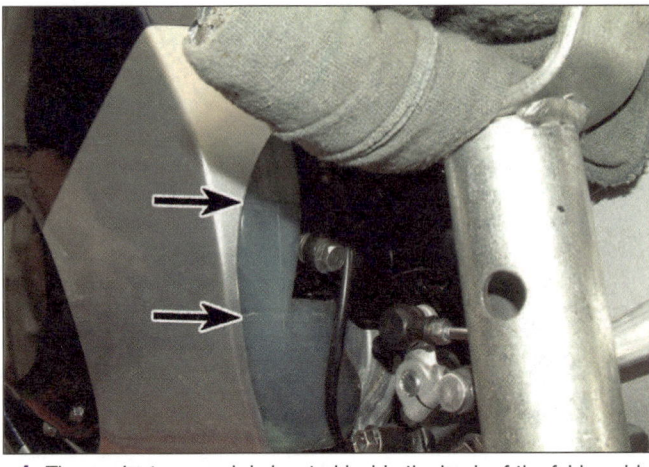

1 The coolant reservoir is located inside the back of the fairing side panel on the left-hand side. With the motorcycle vertical, the coolant level should lie between the F (full) and L (low) level lines (arrowed) on the reservoir.

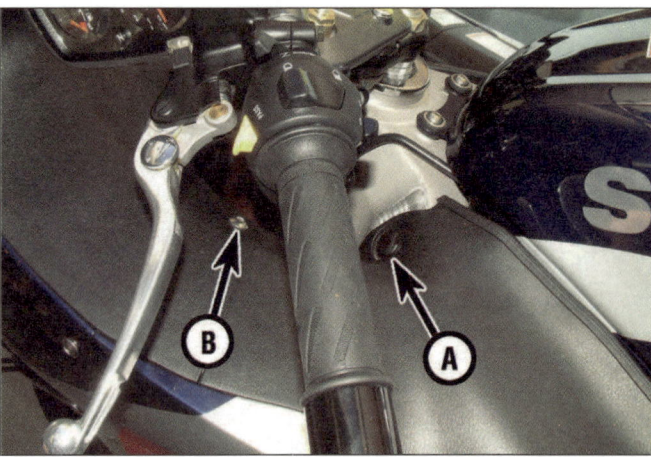

2 If the coolant level is on or below the L line, remove the trim clip (A) securing the top trim section of the fairing side panel at the front of the fuel tank and the screw (B) securing the middle of the section to the cockpit trim panel . . .

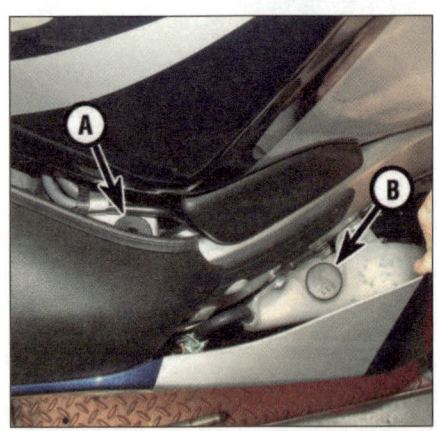

3 . . . then release the peg from its grommet (A) and carefully pull the panel away from the tank to reveal the top of the reservoir (B). If preferred, remove the fairing side panel completely (see Chapter 8).

4 Remove the reservoir filler cap.

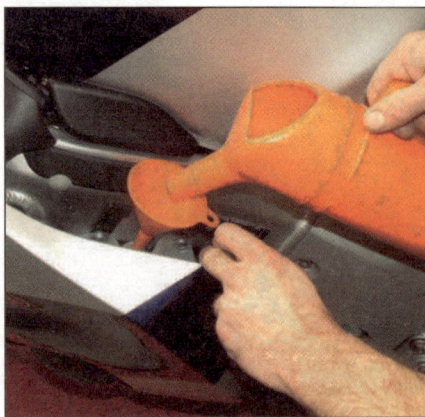

5 Top the reservoir up with the recommended coolant mixture to the F line, using a suitable funnel if necessary. Fit the cap. Locate the fairing side panel peg then install the trim clip and screw, or install the panel if removed (see Chapter 8).

Daily (pre-ride) checks 0•15

Tyre checks

The correct pressures:
- The tyres must be checked when **cold**, not immediately after riding. Note that incorrect tyre pressures will cause abnormal tread wear and unsafe handling. Low tyre pressures may cause the tyre to slip on the rim or come off.
- Use an accurate pressure gauge. Many forecourt gauges are wildly inaccurate. If you buy your own, spend as much as you can justify on a quality gauge.
- Proper air pressure will increase tyre life and provide maximum stability and ride comfort.

Front	Rear
42 psi (2.9 Bar)	42 psi (2.9 Bar)

Tyre care:
- Check the tyres carefully for cuts, tears, embedded nails or other sharp objects and excessive wear. Operation of the motorcycle with excessively worn tyres is extremely hazardous, as traction and handling are directly affected.
- Check the condition of the tyre valve and ensure the dust cap is in place.
- Pick out any stones or nails which may have become embedded in the tyre tread. If left, they will eventually penetrate through the casing and cause a puncture.
- If tyre damage is apparent, or unexplained loss of pressure is experienced, seek the advice of a tyre fitting specialist without delay.

Tyre tread depth:
- At the time of writing UK law requires that tread depth must be at least 1 mm over 3/4 of the tread breadth all the way around the tyre, with no bald patches. Many riders, however, consider 2 mm tread depth minimum to be a safer limit. Suzuki recommend a minimum of 1.6 mm on the front and 2 mm on the rear.
- Many tyres incorporate wear indicators in the tread. Identify the location marking on the tyre sidewall to locate the indicator bar and replace the tyre if the tread has worn down to the bar – some tyres have wear bars near the edge as well as in the centre.

1 Remove the dust cap from the valve. Check the tyre pressures when **cold**. Do not forget to fit the cap after checking the pressure.

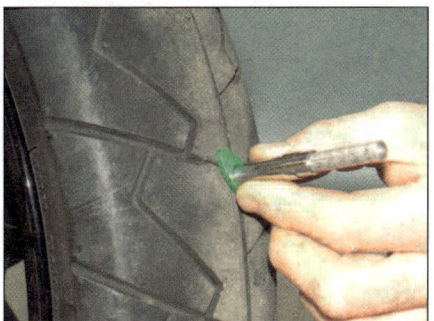

2 Measure tread depth at the centre of the tyre using a depth gauge.

3 Tyre tread wear indicator bar (arrowed) and its location marking (usually either an arrow, a triangle or the letters TWI) on the sidewall.

Suspension, steering and drive chain

Suspension and steering:
- Check that the front and rear suspension operates smoothly without binding (see Chapter 1).
- Check that the suspension is adjusted as required, where applicable (see Chapter 6).
- Check that the steering moves smoothly from lock-to-lock, and that there is no freeplay.

Drive chain:
- With the bike on its sidestand, check that the chain isn't too loose or too tight, and adjust it if necessary (see Chapter 1).
- If the chain looks dry, lubricate it (see Chapter 1).

Legal and safety checks

Lighting and signalling:
- Take a minute to check that the headlight, sidelight, tail light, brake light, licence plate light, instrument lights and turn signals all work correctly.
- Check that the horn sounds when the button is pressed.
- A working speedometer, graduated in mph, is a statutory requirement in the UK.

Safety:
- Check that the throttle grip rotates smoothly when opened and snaps shut when released, in all steering positions. Also check for the correct amount of freeplay (see Chapter 1).
- Check that the brake lever and pedal, clutch lever and gearchange lever operate smoothly. Lubricate them at the specified intervals or when necessary (see Chapter 1).
- Check that the engine shuts off when the kill switch is operated. Check the starter interlock circuit (see Chapter 1).
- Check that the centrestand (where fitted) and sidestand return springs hold the stand up securely when retracted.

Fuel:
- This may seem obvious, but check that you have enough fuel to complete your journey. If you notice signs of fuel leakage – rectify the cause immediately.
- Ensure you use the correct grade fuel – see Chapter 4 Specifications.

0•16 Bike spec

Weights and dimensions

Dimensions and weights
Overall length
    Switzerland models . . . . 2180 mm
    All other models . . . . 2140 mm
Overall width . . . . 740 mm
Overall height . . . . 1155 mm
Wheelbase . . . . 1485 mm
Seat height . . . . 805 mm
Ground clearance . . . . 120 mm
Weight (dry)
    X and Y models
        California models . . . . 216 kg
        All other models . . . . 215 kg
    K1 model onwards
        California models . . . . 218 kg
        All other models . . . . 217 kg

Engine
Type . . . . Four-stroke in-line four cylinder
Capacity . . . . 1299 cc
Bore . . . . 81 mm
Stroke . . . . 63 mm
Compression ratio . . . . 11.0 : 1
Cooling system . . . . Liquid cooled
Clutch . . . . Wet multi-plate with back-torque limiter and hydraulic release
Transmission . . . . Six-speed constant mesh
Final drive . . . . Chain and sprockets
Camshafts . . . . DOHC, chain driven
Fuel system . . . . Fuel injection
Exhaust system . . . . Four-into-two
Ignition system . . . . Digital electronic

Bike spec 0•17

Chassis

Frame type	Aluminium with engine as stressed member
Rake and Trail	24°12', 97.0 mm
Fuel tank capacity including reserve	
X and Y models	
California models	20 litres
All other models	22 litres
K1 model onwards	
California models	19 litres
All other models	21 litres
Front suspension	
Type	Oil-damped, coil sprung upside-down telescopic forks
Travel	120 mm
Adjustment	Spring pre-load, rebound and compression damping
Rear suspension	
Type	Single shock absorber with rising rate linkage, aluminium swingarm
Travel (at axle)	140 mm
Adjustment	Spring pre-load, rebound damping and compression damping
Wheels	Cast alloy, front 17 inch, rear 17 inch
Tyres	
Front	120/70-ZR17 (58W)
Rear	190/50-ZR17 (73W)
Front brake	Twin discs with six-piston opposed calipers
Rear brake	Single disc with two-piston opposed caliper

Model development

Suzuki GSX1300R-X, 1999

An in-line four cylinder liquid-cooled engine is fitted, with drive to the double overhead camshafts, which actuate the four valves per cylinder, by chain. The hydraulically-actuated clutch is a wet multi-plate unit with conventional springs. The transmission is a six-speed constant-mesh unit. Drive to the rear wheel is by chain and sprockets.

The lubrication system has a single rotor pump and a radiator-type oil cooler.

Fuel is supplied to the electronic injection system by a pump housed outside the fuel tank. The pump housing incorporates the fuel filter internally and the pressure regulator externally, and there is a strainer inside the tank and mounted on the fuel cock. The ignition system is fully electronic, with both fuel and ignition systems being controlled by a single engine control module (ECM). Each throttle body has a single butterfly valve and single injector.

The air filter housing incorporates an intake air control valve system that restricts air flow at low engine speeds. A vacuum-controlled butterfly valve in the air filter housing starts to open at a pre-set engine speed of 2500 rpm, and closes when the speed drops below 2200 rpm. A PAIR system reduces exhaust emissions by injecting air into the exhaust ports under certain engine conditions to ignite unburnt fuel and so reduce emissions. The control valve for the system is actuated by a vacuum from the throttle bodies.

The engine sits in an aluminium frame that uses the engine as a stressed member. Front suspension is by oil-damped upside-down telescopic forks with adjustable spring pre-load and both rebound and compression damping. Rear suspension is by aluminium swingarm acting via a three-way linkage on a single shock absorber. The shock absorber is adjustable for spring pre-load and both rebound and compression damping.

The front brake system has two triple opposed piston hydraulic calipers, and the rear brake system has a single opposed piston hydraulic caliper.

The frame supports a four-piece full-fairing and a one-piece seat cowling.

A steering damper is fitted as standard. A centrestand is available as an optional extra.

Colours available were copper/silver, black/light charcoal, and red/black.

Suzuki GSX1300R-Y, 2000

The crankcase breather arrangement was changed, doing away with the oil catch tank and increasing the size of the breather housing. Coincidental to this was a decrease in engine oil capacity.

Clutch spring length was increased and the spring support bolt length was increased in accordance.

The fuel feed and return hoses were changed and re-routed. The design of the fuel level sensor and low level warning switch was changed.

Colours available were blue/silver, black/light charcoal, and red/grey.

Suzuki GSX1300R-K1, 2001

The design of the cam chain tensioner was changed and the housing modified to receive an oil supply fed by hose from a union on the end of the front oil passage in the crankcase.

The fuel pump was changed from being externally mounted and positioned inside the fuel tank, again incorporating the fuel filter and pressure regulator, and also a mesh strainer and a new fuel level sensor and low level warning switch. The internal pressure regulator negated the need for a fuel return hose from the delivery rail on the throttle bodies, and consequently the supply hose and fuel delivery rail arrangement changed.

Colours available were blue/silver, black/light charcoal, and red/grey.

Suzuki GSX1300R-K2, 2002

The clutch plate arrangement was modified to incorporate an anti-rattle spring and spring seat. The clutch release cylinder piston and bore were reduced in diameter.

The exhaust system incorporated an oxygen sensor, which supplied information to the ECM and served to reduce exhaust emissions levels. The PAIR system control valve was actuated electronically via a solenoid valve that received its signal from the ECM.

Colours available were blue/black and silver/silver.

Suzuki GSX1300R-K3, 2003

The starter motor idle/reduction gear train incorporated a torque limiter to dampen the initial torque through it and so reduce stress on the individual components.

Colours available were blue/black, silver/silver and blue/silver. The special Z version (GSX1300RZ-K3) had a black frame, swingarm and disc centres.

Suzuki GSX1300R-K4, 2004

There were no significant changes for 2004, although Suzuki launched a limited edition model that comes in bright red with a black frame, swingarm and wheel centres, and carries special emblems.

Colours available were blue/black, black/purple and silver/blue.

Notes

Chapter 1
Routine maintenance and servicing

Contents

Air filter check and cleaning	2
Air filter renewal	20
Battery charging	see Chapter 9
Battery check	37
Battery removal and installation	see Chapter 9
Brake fluid level check	see Daily (pre-ride) checks
Brake master cylinder and caliper seal renewal	34
Brake fluid change	23
Brake hose renewal	26
Brake pad wear check	11
Brake system check	12
Clutch check	8
Clutch fluid change	24
Clutch fluid level check	see Daily (pre-ride) checks
Clutch hose renewal	27
Clutch master and release cylinder seal renewal	35
Coolant change	25
Coolant level check	see Daily (pre-ride) checks
Cooling system check	9
Cylinder compression check	29
Drive chain check, adjustment, cleaning and lubrication	1
Drive chain and sprockets wear check	10
Engine oil level check	see Daily (pre-ride) checks

Engine oil pressure check	30
Engine/transmission oil and filter change	21
Engine/transmission oil change	5
Front fork oil change	36
Fuel hose renewal	28
Fuel system check	4
Headlight aim check	39
Idle speed check and adjustment	6
Nut and bolt tightness check	14
Sidestand and starter interlock circuit	38
Stand, lever pivot and cable lubrication	15
Spark plug check and gap adjustment	3
Spark plug renewal	16
Steering head bearing freeplay check and adjustment	18
Steering head bearing lubrication	32
Suspension check	19
Swingarm and suspension linkage bearing lubrication	33
Throttle and fast idle cable check	7
Throttle body synchronisation	17
Tyre and wheel check	13
Valve clearance check and adjustment	22
Wheel bearing check	31

Degrees of difficulty

| **Easy,** suitable for novice with little experience | **Fairly easy,** suitable for beginner with some experience | **Fairly difficult,** suitable for competent DIY mechanic  | **Difficult,** suitable for experienced DIY mechanic | **Very difficult,** suitable for expert DIY or professional |

Specifications

Engine
Engine idle speed
   Switzerland models .... 1150 ± 50 rpm
   All other models .... 1150 ± 100 rpm
Spark plugs
   Standard type .... NGK CR9E, or Denso U27ESR-N
   Hotter type .... NGK CR8E, or Denso U24ESR-N
   Colder type .... NGK CR10E, or Denso U31ESR-N
   Electrode gap (all types) .... 0.7 to 0.8 mm
Valve clearances (COLD engine)
   Intake valves .... 0.1 to 0.2 mm
   Exhaust valves .... 0.2 to 0.3 mm
Throttle body synchronisation – max. difference between bodies ..... 20 mm Hg
Cylinder compression
   Standard .... 171 to 228 psi (12 to 16 Bar)
   Service limit .... 128 psi (8.8 Bar)
   Max. difference between cylinders .... 28 psi (2 Bar)
Oil pressure (at main oil gallery plug, with engine warm) .... 28 to 71 psi (2 to 5 Bar) @ 3000 rpm, oil @ 60°C

Miscellaneous
Drive chain
   Slack .... 20 to 30 mm with bike resting on sidestand
   Stretch limit (21 pin length – see text) .... 319.4 mm
Throttle twistgrip freeplay
   Opening (front) cable .... 2 to 4 mm
   Closing (rear) cable .... zero (no freeplay)
Tyre pressures (cold) .... see *Daily (pre-ride) checks*
Rear brake pedal height .... 55 to 65 mm
Gearchange lever height .... 50 to 60 mm

Recommended lubricants and fluids
Fuel grade
   European models .... Unleaded, minimum 91 RON (Research Octane Number)
   US models and Canada .... Unleaded, minimum 87 ((R+M) /2 method)
Engine/transmission oil type .... API grade SF or SG motor oil
Engine/transmission oil viscosity .... SAE 10W40 (but see *Daily (pre-ride) checks*)
Engine/transmission oil capacity
   X model
     Oil change .... 3.3 litres
     Oil and filter change .... 3.5 litres
     Following engine overhaul – dry engine, new filter .... 4.2 litres
   Y model onwards
     Oil change .... 3.1 litres
     Oil and filter change .... 3.3 litres
     Following engine overhaul – dry engine, new filter .... 4.0 litres
Coolant type .... 50% distilled water, 50% corrosion inhibited ethylene glycol anti-freeze
Coolant capacity (inc. reservoir) .... Approx. 2.95 litres
Fork oil type .... Suzuki L01 fork oil or equivalent
Brake fluid .... DOT 4, glycol-based
Drive chain .... Heavy motor oil (such as gear oil) or chain lubricant suitable for sealed chains
Steering head, swingarm and suspension linkage bearings .... Multi-purpose grease
Bearing seal lips .... Multi-purpose grease
Gearchange lever/rear brake pedal/footrest/stand pivots .... Multi-purpose grease
Brake and clutch lever pivots .... Multi-purpose grease
Throttle grip .... Multi-purpose grease or dry film lubricant
Front brake lever piston tip .... Silicone grease
Cables .... Engine oil or cable lubricant

Torque settings
Bottom yoke fork clamp bolts .... 23 Nm
Crankshaft end cap .... 11 Nm
Engine/transmission oil drain bolt .... 23 Nm
Main oil gallery plug .... 35 Nm
Rear axle nut .... 100 Nm
Rear brake torque arm nut .... 35 Nm
Spark plugs .... 11 Nm
Steering stem nut .... 90 Nm
Timing mark inspection cap .... 23 Nm

Maintenance schedule

Note: *The daily (pre-ride) checks outlined in the owner's manual covers those items which should be inspected on a daily basis. Always perform the pre-ride inspection at every maintenance interval (in addition to the procedures listed). The intervals listed below are the intervals recommended by the manufacturer for each particular operation during the model years covered in this manual. Your owner's manual may have different intervals for your model.*

Daily (pre-ride)
See *'Daily (pre-ride) checks'* at the beginning of this manual.

After the initial 600 miles (1000 km)
Note: *This check will be performed by a Suzuki dealer after the first 600 miles (1000 km) from new. Thereafter, maintenance is carried out according to the following intervals of the schedule.*

Every 600 miles (1000 km)
- ☐ Check, adjust, clean and lubricate the drive chain (Section 1)

Every 3500 miles (5500 km) or 6 months
Carry out all the items under the Daily (pre-ride) checks and the 600 mile (1000 km) check, plus the following:
- ☐ Check and clean the air filter element (Section 2)
- ☐ Check the spark plugs (Section 3)
- ☐ Check the fuel hoses, PAIR system hoses, EVAP system hoses (California models), and fuel system components (Section 4)
- ☐ Change the engine/transmission oil (Section 5)
- ☐ Check and adjust the engine idle speed (Section 6)
- ☐ Check throttle and fast idle cable operation and freeplay (Section 7)
- ☐ Check the operation of the clutch (Section 8)
- ☐ Check the cooling system (Section 9)
- ☐ Check for drive chain and sprocket wear and chain stretch (Section 10)
- ☐ Check the brake pads for wear (Section 11)
- ☐ Check the operation of the brakes, and for fluid leakage (Section 12)
- ☐ Check the tyre and wheel condition, and the tyre tread depth (Section 13)
- ☐ Check the tightness of all nuts and bolts (Section 14)
- ☐ Check and lubricate the stand pivots, lever pivots and cables (Section 15)

Every 7000 miles (11,000 km) or 12 months
Carry out all the items under the 3500 mile (5500 km) check, plus the following:
- ☐ Renew the spark plugs (Section 16)
- ☐ Check throttle body synchronisation (Section 17)
- ☐ Check the steering head bearing freeplay (Section 18)
- ☐ Check the front and rear suspension (Section 19)

Every 10,500 miles (16,500 km) or 18 months
Carry out all the items under the 3500 mile (5500 km) check, plus the following:
- ☐ Renew the air filter element (Section 20)
- ☐ Change the engine/transmission oil filter (Section 21)

Every 14,000 miles (22,000 km) or 24 months
Carry out all the items under the 7000 mile (11,000 km) check, plus the following:
- ☐ Check the valve clearances (Section 22)

Every two years
- ☐ Change the brake fluid (Section 23)
- ☐ Change the clutch fluid (Section 24)
- ☐ Change the coolant (Section 25)

Every four years
- ☐ Renew the brake hoses (Section 26)
- ☐ Renew the clutch hose (Section 27)
- ☐ Renew the fuel hoses, the PAIR system hoses, and on California models the EVAP system hoses (Section 28)

Non-scheduled maintenance
- ☐ Check the cylinder compression (Section 29)
- ☐ Check the engine oil pressure (Section 30)
- ☐ Check the wheel bearings (Section 31)
- ☐ Lubricate the steering head bearings (Section 32)
- ☐ Lubricate the swingarm and suspension linkage bearings (Section 33)
- ☐ Renew the brake master cylinder and caliper seals (Section 34)
- ☐ Renew the clutch master cylinder and release cylinder seals (Section 35)
- ☐ Change the front fork oil (Section 36)
- ☐ Check the battery (Section 37)
- ☐ Check the sidestand and the starter interlock circuit operation (Section 38)
- ☐ Check and adjust the headlight aim (Section 39)

1•4 Component locations

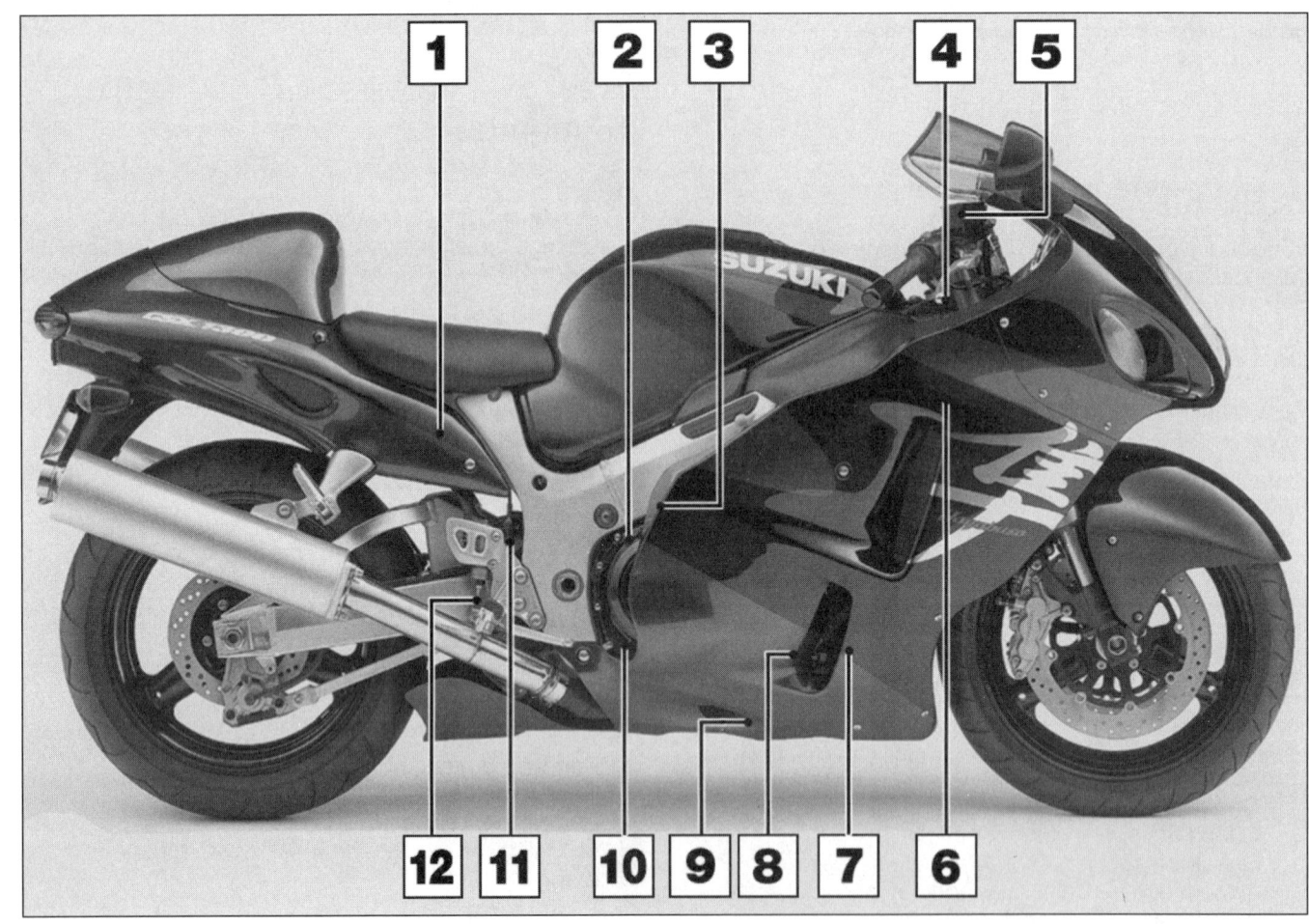

Component locations on right-hand side

1 Rear brake fluid reservoir
2 Engine oil filler
3 Idle speed adjuster
4 Throttle cable upper adjusters
5 Front brake fluid reservoir
6 Radiator pressure cap
7 Engine oil filter
8 Main oil galley plug for oil pressure check
9 Engine oil drain plug
10 Engine oil level window
11 Rear brake light switch
12 Rear brake pedal height adjuster

Component locations 1•5

Component locations on left-hand side

1 Choke cable upper adjuster
2 Clutch fluid reservoir
3 Steering head bearing adjuster
4 Air filter
5 Fuel filter
6 Battery
7 Drive chain adjuster
8 Main coolant hose-to-water pump joint
9 Coolant reservoir

1•6 Routine maintenance and servicing

1 This Chapter is designed to help the home mechanic maintain his/her motorcycle for safety, economy, long life and peak performance.

2 Deciding where to start or plug into the routine maintenance schedule depends on several factors. If your motorcycle has been maintained according to the warranty standards and has just come out of warranty, start routine maintenance as it coincides with the next mileage or calendar interval. If you have owned the machine for some time but have never performed any maintenance on it, start at the nearest interval and include some additional procedures to ensure that nothing important is overlooked. If you have just had a major engine overhaul, then start the maintenance routine from the beginning. If you have a used machine and have no knowledge of its history or maintenance record, combine all the checks into one large service initially and then settle into the specified maintenance schedule.

3 Before beginning any maintenance or repair, the machine should be cleaned thoroughly, especially around the oil filter, spark plugs, valve cover, body panels etc. Cleaning will help ensure that dirt does not contaminate the engine and will allow you to detect wear and damage that could otherwise easily go unnoticed.

4 Certain maintenance information is sometimes printed on labels attached to the motorcycle. If the information on the labels differs from that included here, use the information on the label.

Every 600 miles (1000 km)

1 Drive chain check, adjustment, cleaning and lubrication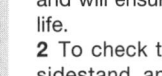

Every 600 miles (1000 km)

Check

1 A neglected drive chain won't last long and will quickly damage the sprockets. Routine chain adjustment and lubrication isn't difficult

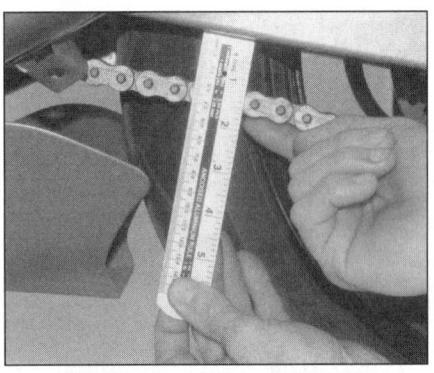

1.3 Measuring drive chain slack

and will ensure maximum chain and sprocket life.

2 To check the chain, place the bike on its sidestand and shift the transmission into neutral. Make sure the ignition switch is OFF.

3 Push up on the bottom run of the chain midway between the two sprockets and measure the amount of slack, then compare your measurement to that listed in this Chapter's Specifications **(see illustration)**. As the chain stretches with wear, adjustment will periodically be necessary (see below). Since the chain will rarely wear evenly, roll the bike forward so that another section of chain can be checked (having an assistant to do this makes the task a lot easier); do this several times to check the entire length of chain, and mark the tightest spot.

Caution: Riding the bike with excess slack in the chain could lead to damage.

4 In some cases where lubrication has been neglected, corrosion and galling may cause the links to bind and kink, which effectively shortens the chain's length and makes it tight. Thoroughly clean and work free any such links, then highlight them with a marker pen or paint. After the bike has been ridden repeat the measurement for slack in the highlighted area. If the chain has kinked again and is still tight, replace it with a new one. A rusty, kinked or worn chain will damage the sprockets and can damage transmission bearings. If in any doubt as to the condition of the chain, it is far better to install a new one than risk damage to other components and possibly yourself.

5 Check the entire length of the chain for damaged rollers, loose links and pins, and missing O-rings, and replace it with a new one if necessary. **Note:** *Never install a new chain on old sprockets, and never use the old chain if you install new sprockets – replace the chain and sprockets as a set. Refer to Section 10 for sprocket checks and chain stretch checks.*

Adjustment

6 Move the bike so that the chain is positioned with the tightest point at the centre of its bottom run, then put it on the sidestand.

7 On US and Canada models, remove the split pin from the rear axle nut. Discard it as a new one must be used.

8 Slacken the rear axle nut **(see illustration)**. Also slacken the nut on the bolt securing the torque arm to the rear brake caliper **(see illustration)**.

1.8a Slacken the axle nut (arrowed) . . .

1.8b . . . and the torque arm nut (arrowed)

Routine maintenance and servicing 1•7

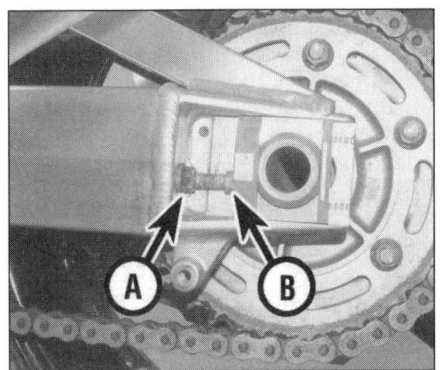

1.9a Slacken the locknut (A) and turn the adjuster bolt (B) as required

1.9b Make sure the adjustment markers are in the same position on each side relative to the index lines on the swingarm

1.13 Apply the specified lubricant to the overlap between the sideplates

9 Slacken the adjuster bolt locknut, then turn the adjuster bolt on each side evenly until the amount of freeplay specified at the beginning of the Chapter is obtained at the centre of the bottom run of the chain **(see illustration)**. If you are slackening the chain turn the bolts in then push the wheel forwards so the alignment markers contact the bolt heads. Following adjustment, check that the rear edge of each chain adjustment marker is in the same position in relation to the index lines on the swingarm **(see illustration)**. It is important the same index lines on each side align with the rear edge of the marker; if not, the rear wheel will be out of alignment with the front, leading to handling problems. If there is a discrepancy in the marker positions, adjust one of them so that its position is exactly the same as the other. Check the chain freeplay again as described above and readjust if necessary.

10 Tighten the axle nut to the torque setting specified at the beginning of the Chapter **(see illustration 1.8a)**. Recheck the adjustment as above, then check that the wheel runs freely. Tighten the brake torque arm nut to the specified torque setting **(see illustration 1.8b)**.

Make sure that the adjuster bolt heads are set against the alignment markers, turning them out slightly if necessary, then tighten the locknuts.

11 On US and Canada models fit a new split pin.

Cleaning and lubrication

12 If required, wash the chain in paraffin (kerosene) or a suitable non-flammable or high flash-point solvent that will not damage the O-rings, using a soft brush to work any dirt out if necessary. Wipe the cleaner off the chain and allow it to dry, using compressed air if available. If the chain is excessively dirty remove it from the machine and allow it to soak in the paraffin or solvent (see Chapter 6). **Caution: Don't use petrol (gasoline), an unsuitable solvent or other cleaning fluids which might damage the internal sealing properties of the chain. Don't use high-pressure water to clean the chain. The entire process shouldn't take longer than ten minutes, otherwise the O-rings could be damaged.**

13 The best time to lubricate the chain is after the motorcycle has been ridden. When the chain is warm, the lubricant will penetrate the joints between the sideplates better than when cold. **Note:** *Suzuki specifies a heavy motor oil (such as gear oil) or an aerosol chain lube that it is suitable for O-ring or X-ring (sealed) chains; do not use any other chain lubricants - the solvents could damage the chain's sealing rings.* Apply the oil to the area where the sideplates overlap – not the middle of the rollers **(see illustration)**.

 HAYNES HiNT *Apply the lubricant to the top of the lower chain run, so centrifugal force will work the oil into the chain when the bike is moving. After applying the lubricant, let it soak in a few minutes before wiping off any excess.*

 Warning: Take care not to get any lubricant on the tyre or brake disc/caliper. If any of the lubricant inadvertently contacts them, clean it off thoroughly using a suitable solvent or dedicated brake cleaner before riding the machine.

Every 3500 miles (5500 km) or 6 months

2 Air filter check and cleaning

Every 3500 miles (5500 km)

1 Raise the fuel tank (see Chapter 4).
2 Undo the screws securing the air filter and lift it out of the housing **(see illustrations)**.
3 Tap the filter on a hard surface to dislodge any large particles of dirt. If compressed air is available, use it to blow through the element, directing it from the outside (the side with the metal cage) to the inside so it is in the opposite direction of normal airflow.

2.2a Undo the screws . . .

2.2b . . . and remove the filter

1•8 Routine maintenance and servicing

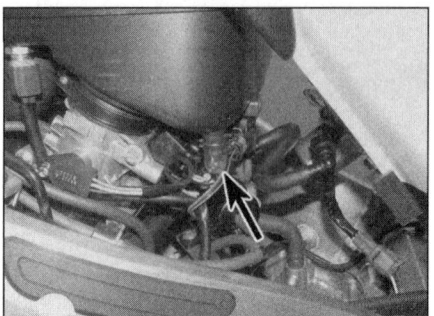

2.6 Water drain cap (arrowed)

3.3 Disconnect the wiring connectors (arrowed)

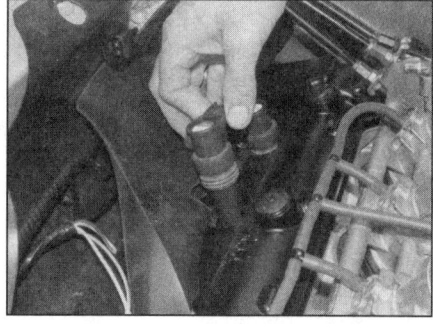

3.5 Pull the coil/cap off the spark plug . . .

HAYNES HiNT *If using compressed air to clean the filter, place a rag or a piece of card on the inside of the filter to prevent any dust and debris being blown from one side of the element into the other.*

Caution: *If the machine is continually ridden in dusty conditions, clean the filter more frequently.*

4 Check the filter for signs of damage. If the element is torn or cannot be cleaned, or is obviously beyond further use, replace it with a new one.

5 Fit the filter in the housing, making sure it is correctly seated, and secure it with its screws.

6 Release the clamp and remove the cap from the water drain on the underside of the air filter housing in the rear left-hand corner and allow any residue to drain from the housing **(see illustration)**. Refit the cap and clamp.

7 Lower the fuel tank (see Chapter 4).

3 Spark plug check and gap adjustment

Every 3500 miles (5500 km)

1 Make sure your spark plug socket is the correct size (16 mm) before attempting to remove the plugs – a suitable one is supplied in the motorcycle's tool kit which is stored under the seat.

2 Remove the air filter housing (see Chapter 4).

3 Disconnect the wiring connector from each combined ignition coil/spark plug cap, noting which fits where, and from the camshaft position sensor **(see illustration)**.

4 Lift the rubber cover up off the valve cover, noting how it locates.

5 Work on one plug at a time. Clean the area around the coil/cap seal on the valve cover before removing the coil/cap to prevent any dirt falling into the spark plug channel. Carefully pull the coil/cap off the spark plug **(see illustration)**.

6 Check the area around the base of the plug for debris and remove any found to prevent it falling into the engine when the plug is removed. Using either the plug removing tool supplied in the bike's toolkit or a deep socket type wrench, unscrew and remove the plug from the cylinder head **(see illustration)**.

7 Inspect the electrodes for wear. Both the centre and side electrodes should have square edges and the side electrode should be of uniform thickness – if not, they are worn. Look for excessive deposits and evidence of a cracked or chipped insulator around the centre electrode. Compare your spark plugs to the colour spark plug reading chart at the end of this manual. Check the threads, the washer and the ceramic insulator body for cracks and other damage.

8 If the electrodes are not excessively worn, if no cracks or chips are visible in the insulator, and if the deposits can be easily removed with a wire brush, the plugs can be re-gapped and re-used. If in doubt concerning the condition of the plugs, replace them with new ones as the expense is minimal.

9 Cleaning spark plugs by sandblasting is fine provided you blow them out with compressed air and clean them with a high flash-point solvent afterwards.

10 Before installing the plugs, make sure they are the correct type and heat range and check the gap between the electrodes **(see illustrations)**. Compare the gap to that specified and adjust as necessary. If the gap must be adjusted, bend the side electrode only and be very careful not to chip or crack the insulator nose **(see illustration)**. Make sure the washer is in place before installing the plug.

11 Fit the plug into the end of the tool, then use the tool to insert the plug **(see**

3.6 . . . then unscrew and remove the plug

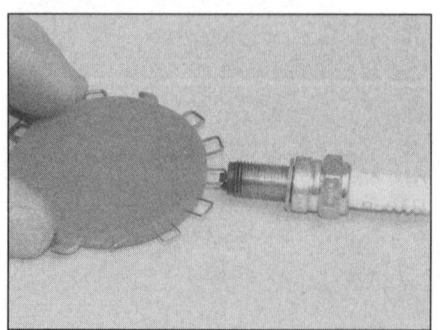

3.10a A wire type gauge is recommended to measure the spark plug electrode gap

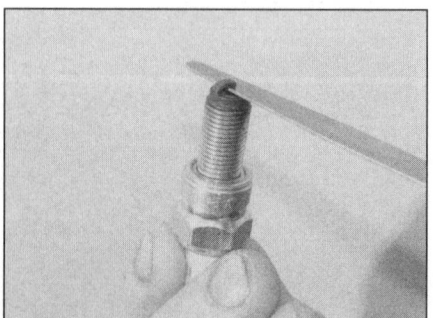

3.10b A blade type feeler gauge can also be used

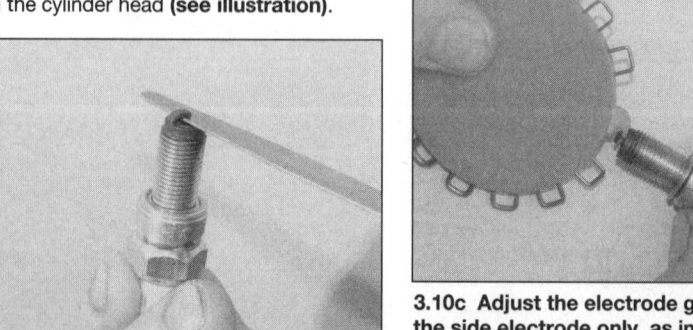

3.10c Adjust the electrode gap by bending the side electrode only, as indicated by the arrows, and be very careful not to crack or chip the ceramic insulator surrounding the centre electrode

Routine maintenance and servicing 1•9

illustration). Since the cylinder head is made of aluminium, which is soft and easily damaged, thread the plug as far as possible into the head turning the tool by hand. Once the plug is finger-tight, the job can be finished with a spanner on the tool supplied or a socket drive **(see illustration 3.6)**. If a torque wrench can be applied, tighten the spark plugs to the torque setting specified at the beginning of the Chapter. Otherwise, tighten them according the instructions on the box – generally if new plugs are being used, tighten them by 1/2 a turn after the washer has seated, and if the old plugs are being reused, tighten them by 1/8 to 1/4 turn after they have seated. Do not over-tighten them.

> **HAYNES HiNT** *You can slip a short length of hose over the end of the plug to use as a tool to thread it into place. The hose will grip the plug well enough to turn it, but will start to slip if the plug begins to cross-thread in the hole – this will prevent damaged threads.*

12 Fit the ignition coil/spark plug cap onto the plug, making sure it locates correctly **(see illustration 3.5)**. On completion of the job install all other components previously removed, not forgetting to reconnect the camshaft position sensor wiring connector **(see illustration 3.3)**.

> **HAYNES HiNT** *Stripped plug threads in the cylinder head can be repaired with a thread insert – see 'Tools and Workshop Tips' in the Reference section.*

4 Fuel system check

Every 3500 miles (5500 km)

> ⚠ **Warning:** *Petrol (gasoline) is extremely flammable, so take extra precautions when you work on any part of the fuel system. Don't smoke or allow open flames or bare light bulbs*

3.11 Thread the plug as far as possible by hand

near the work area, and don't work in a garage where a natural gas-type appliance is present. If you spill any fuel on your skin, rinse it off immediately with soap and water. When you perform any kind of work on the fuel system, wear safety glasses and have a fire extinguisher suitable for a Class B type fire (flammable liquids) on hand.

1 Raise the fuel tank (see Chapter 4).
2 On X and Y models check the fuel supply and return hoses and their connections for signs of leakage, deterioration or damage. Also check the tank, particularly around the fuel level sensor and fuel cock fittings. If there is leakage, remove the sensor or cock and replace the gasket or O-ring with a new one (see Chapter 4). Check around the pump assembly, particularly its unions and joints with the filter and the pressure regulator, for signs of leakage. If any is found, remove and disassemble as required and fit new O-rings (see Chapter 4).
3 On all other models check the fuel supply hose and its connections for signs of leakage, deterioration or damage. Also check the tank, particularly around the fuel pump assembly mountings. If there is leakage, remove the pump and replace the O-ring with a new one (see Chapter 4).
4 On all models check all the vacuum hoses, the PAIR system hoses, and on California models the EVAP system hoses (refer to Chapter 4 for details of these systems). Replace any hoses that are cracked or deteriorated with new ones.
5 Also check for signs of fuel leakage between the injectors, the fuel rail components and the throttle bodies. If there are, install new O-rings and seals as required (see Chapter 4).

6 Installing a new fuel filter is advised after a particularly high mileage has been covered. It is also necessary if fuel starvation is suspected, in which case perform a fuel pressure check (see Chapter 4). Suzuki do not specify a replacement interval. Check the condition of the inside of your tank – if it is old and there is evidence of rust, remove, drain and clean the tank, then clean the strainer and fit a new filter (see Chapter 4).

5 Engine/transmission oil change

Every 3500 miles (5500 km)

> ⚠ **Warning:** *Be careful when draining the oil, as the exhaust pipes, the engine, and the oil itself can cause severe burns.*

1 Consistent routine oil changes are the single most important maintenance procedure you can perform on a motorcycle. The oil not only lubricates the internal parts of the engine, transmission and clutch, but it also acts as a coolant, a cleaner, a sealant, and a protector. Because of these demands, the oil takes a terrific amount of abuse and should be replaced often with new oil of the recommended grade and type. Saving a little money on the difference in cost between good oil and cheap oil won't pay off if the engine is damaged. The oil filter should be changed with every third oil change (see Section 21).
2 Before changing the oil, warm up the engine so the oil will drain easily. Make sure the bike is on level ground. Remove the fairing side panels if required (see Chapter 8) – it is not essential as there is plenty of room to access the drain plug, but doing so negates the possibility of damage should your tool slip.
3 Position a clean drain tray below the engine. Unscrew the oil filler cap from the clutch cover on the right-hand side of the engine to vent the crankcase and to act as a reminder that there is no oil in the engine **(see illustration)**.
4 Unscrew the oil drain bolt from the bottom of the engine and allow the oil to flow into the drain tray **(see illustrations)**. Support the

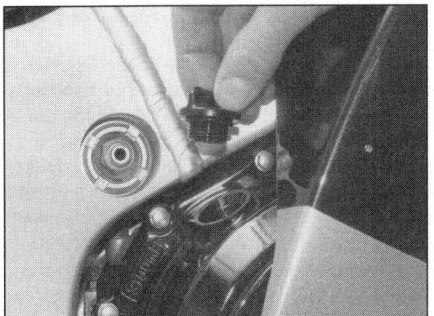

5.3 Unscrew the oil filler cap

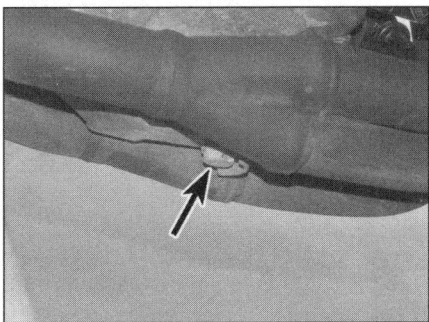

5.4a Unscrew the oil drain bolt (arrowed) . . .

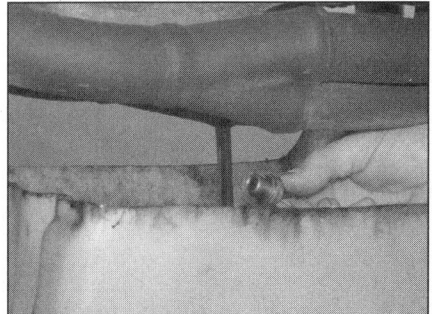

5.4b . . . and allow the oil to drain

1•10 Routine maintenance and servicing

5.4c Cut the old sealing washer off ...

5.4d ... and clean any particles off the magnetic tip (arrowed)

5.5a Install the drain plug using a new sealing washer ...

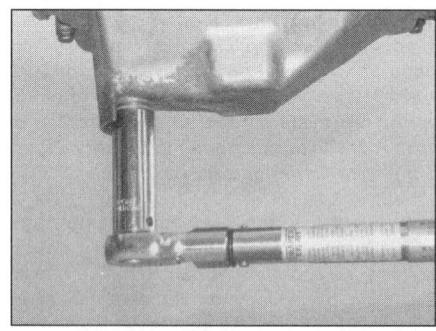

5.5b ... and tighten it to the specified torque

Note: *It is antisocial and illegal to dump oil down the drain. To find the location of your local oil recycling bank, call this number free.*

In the US note that any oil supplier must accept used oil for recycling.

> **HAYNES HiNT** Check the old oil carefully – if it is very metallic coloured, then the engine is experiencing wear from break-in (new engine) or from insufficient lubrication. If there are flakes or chips of metal in the oil, then something is drastically wrong internally and the engine will have to be disassembled for inspection and repair. If there are pieces of fibre-like material in the oil, the clutch is experiencing excessive wear and should be checked.

6 Idle speed check and adjustment

motorcycle upright while draining to allow as much oil as possible to escape. Check the condition of the sealing washer on the drain bolt and replace it with a new one if it is damaged or worn – it is advisable to use a new one whatever the condition of the old one. You will probably have to cut the old one off **(see illustration)**. Clean any debris off the magnetic tip of the bolt **(see illustration)**.

5 When the oil has completely drained, fit the bolt into the sump, preferably using a new sealing washer, and tighten it to the torque setting specified at the beginning of the Chapter **(see illustrations)**. Avoid overtightening, as it is quite easy to damage the threads in the sump.

6 Refill the engine to the proper level using the recommended type and amount of oil (see Specifications and *Daily (pre-ride) checks*).

Install the filler cap. Start the engine and let it run for two or three minutes (make sure that the oil pressure light extinguishes after a few seconds, and check that there are no leaks). Shut it off, wait a few minutes, then recheck the oil level (see *Daily (pre-ride) checks*). If necessary, add more oil to bring the level to the F line on the inspection window. Check around the drain plug and the oil filter for leaks. A leak around the drain plug probably means a new washer is needed. A leak around the filter probably means it is not tight enough.

7 The old oil drained from the engine cannot be re-used and should be disposed of properly. Check with your local refuse disposal company, disposal facility or environmental agency to see whether they will accept the used oil for recycling. Don't pour used oil into drains or onto the ground.

Every 3500 miles (5500 km)

1 The idle speed should be checked and adjusted before and after the throttle bodies are synchronised (balanced), after checking the valve clearances, and when it is obviously too high or too low. Before adjusting the idle speed, make sure the spark plugs are clean and the gaps correct, and the air filter is clean. If a valve clearance check is part of the service you are performing, do that first (see Section 22). Also, turn the handlebars from side-to-side and check the idle speed does not change as you do. If it does, the throttle cables may not be adjusted or routed correctly, or may be worn out. This is a dangerous condition that can cause loss of control of the bike. Be sure to correct this problem before proceeding.

2 The engine should be at normal operating temperature, which is usually reached after 10 to 15 minutes of stop-and-go riding. Place the motorcycle on its sidestand, and make sure the transmission is in neutral.

3 On X and Y models the idle speed adjuster is a knurled knob located on the right-hand side of the motorcycle inside the fairing side panel above the clutch cover **(see illustration)**.

4 On all other models the idle speed adjuster is a knurled knob located on the right-hand end of the throttle body assembly **(see illustration)** – raise the fuel tank to access it (see Chapter 4).

5 With the engine idling, adjust the idle speed by turning the knob as required until the speed listed in this Chapter's Specifications is

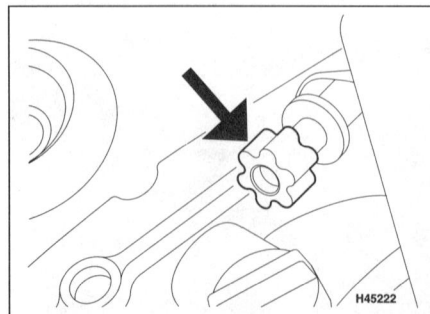

6.3 Idle speed adjuster (arrowed) – X and Y models

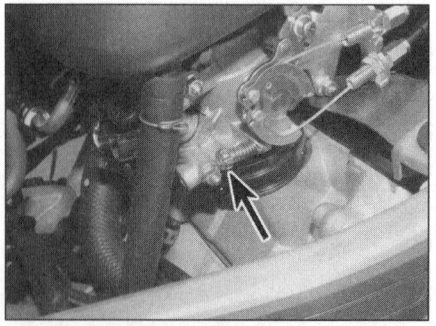

6.4 Idle speed adjuster (arrowed) – all other models

Routine maintenance and servicing

obtained. Turn the knob clockwise to increase idle speed, and anti-clockwise to decrease it. Snap the throttle open and shut a few times, then recheck the idle speed. If necessary, repeat the adjustment procedure.

6 If a smooth, steady idle can't be achieved, the throttle bodies may need synchronising (see Section 17), or there could be a problem with the fuel injection system (see Chapter 4). Also check the intake manifold rubbers for cracks or a loose clamp that will cause an air leak, resulting in a weak mixture.

7 Throttle and fast idle cable check

Every 3500 miles (5500 km)

Throttle cables

1 Make sure the throttle grip rotates smoothly and freely from fully closed to fully open with the front wheel turned at various angles. The grip should return automatically from fully open to fully closed when released.

2 If the throttle sticks, this is probably due to a cable fault. Remove the cables (see Chapter 4) and lubricate them (see Section 15). Check that the inner cables slide freely and easily in the outer cables. If not, replace the cables with new ones. With the cables removed, make sure the throttle twistgrip rotates freely on the handlebar. Install the cables, making sure they are correctly routed. If this fails to improve the operation of the throttle, the cables must be replaced with new ones. Note that in very rare cases the fault could lie in the throttle bodies rather than the cables, necessitating their removal and inspection (see Chapter 4).

3 With the throttle operating smoothly, check for a small amount of freeplay in the cables, measured in terms of the amount of twistgrip rotation before the throttle opens, and

7.3 Twist the throttle and measure the amount of free rotation

compare the amount to that listed in this Chapter's Specifications **(see illustration)**. If it's incorrect, adjust the cables to correct it as follows.

4 Freeplay adjustments can be made using the adjusters in the cables after they leave the throttle/switch housing on the handlebar. The front cable in the housing is the opening cable, and the rear is the closing cable. Loosen the lockring on the closing cable adjuster and turn the adjuster fully in **(see illustration)**. Now loosen the lockring on the opening cable adjuster and turn the adjuster in or out as required until the specified amount of freeplay is obtained (see this Chapter's Specifications), then retighten the lockring. Now, while holding the twistgrip in the fully closed position, turn the closing cable adjuster out until a resistance can just be felt – at this point all the freeplay between the outer cable and its socket in the adjuster has been taken up. Do not turn the adjuster out any further than the point at which the resistance is felt. Tighten the lockring.

5 If the adjusters have reached their limit, or if major adjustment is required, reset them so that the freeplay is at a maximum (i.e. the adjusters are fully turned in), then raise the fuel tank (see Chapter 4), and adjust the cables at the throttle body end. Slacken the

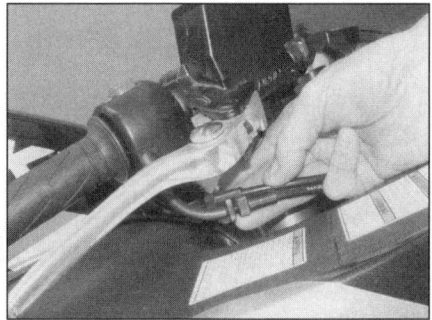

7.4 Slacken the adjuster lockrings and turn the adjusters as described

adjuster locknuts **(see illustration)**. Turn the adjuster on the closing (top) cable until there is no freeplay between the outer cable and its socket in the adjuster at the throttle end, as in Step 4. Now turn the adjuster on the opening (bottom) cable until the specified amount of freeplay is obtained (see Step 3). With the throttle held in the closed position check that the exposed section of the closing inner cable (between the end of the adjuster thread and the pulley on the throttle bodies) has about 1 mm of sideways slack **(see illustration)**, and if necessary turn the adjuster to achieve this – the cable should not be taut. Now tighten the adjuster locknut. Further adjustments can now be made at the throttle end. If the cables cannot be adjusted as specified, install new ones (see Chapter 4).

⚠️ **Warning: Turn the handlebars all the way through their travel with the engine idling. Idle speed should not change. If it does, the cables may be routed incorrectly. Correct this condition before riding the bike.**

6 Check that the throttle twistgrip operates smoothly and snaps shut quickly when released.

Fast idle cable

7 If the fast idle lever does not operate

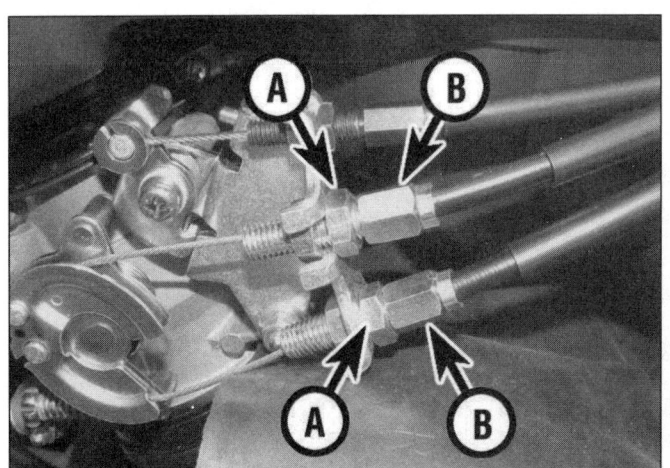

7.5a Slacken the adjuster locknuts (A) and turn the adjusters (B) as described

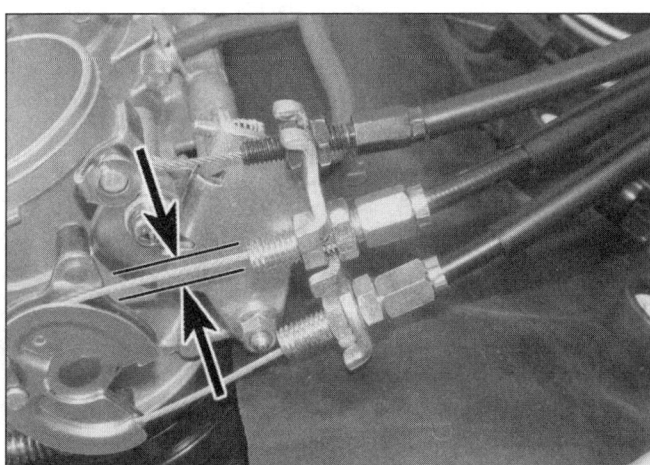

7.5b Check for 1 mm of sideways slack in the closing cable

1•12 Routine maintenance and servicing

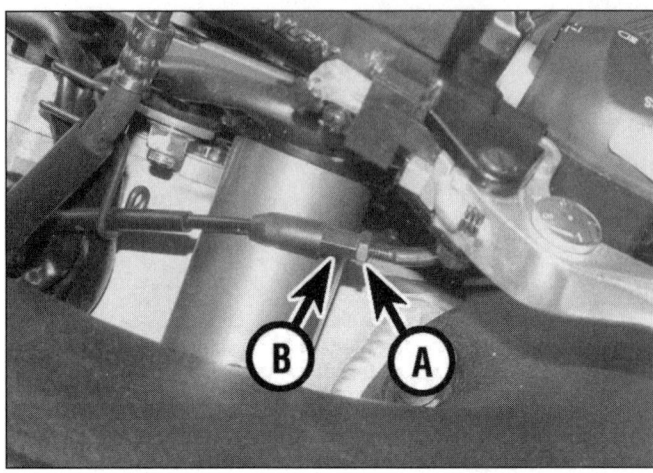

7.8 Fast idle cable adjuster locknut (A) and adjuster (B)

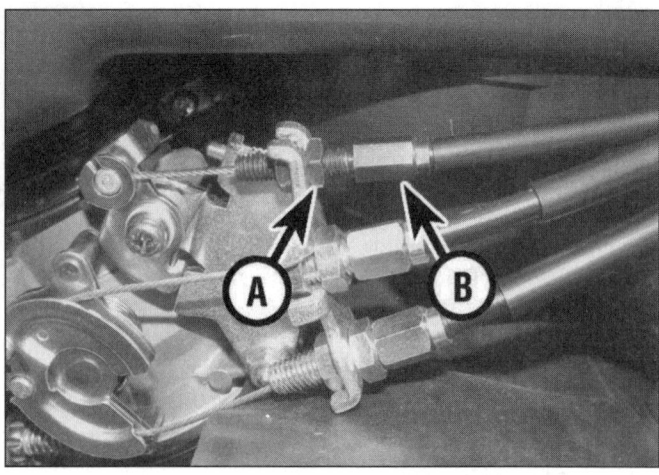

7.9 Cable adjuster locknut (A) and adjuster (B)

smoothly this is probably due to a cable fault. If necessary remove the cable (see Chapter 4) and lubricate it (see Section 15). Check that the inner cable slides freely and easily in the outer cable. If not, replace the cable with a new one. With the cable removed, make sure the lever is able to move freely in its guide channel. Install the cable, making sure it is correctly routed.

8 Raise the fuel tank (see Chapter 4). Operate the choke lever and check for a small amount of freeplay in the cable before the pulley mechanism on the throttle bodies actuates. Adjust it if necessary using the adjuster at the lever end of the cable. Slacken the locknut, then turn the adjuster as required until a small amount of freeplay is evident, then retighten the locknut **(see illustration)**.

9 If the adjuster has reached its limit, or if major adjustment is required, reset it so that the freeplay is at a maximum (i.e. the adjuster is fully turned in), then adjust the cable at the throttle body end. Slacken the adjuster locknut **(see illustration)**. Turn the adjuster in or out as required until there is a small amount of freeplay, then tighten the locknut.

10 Refer to Chapter 4 and check the fast idle speed, adjusting it as described if required.

8 Clutch check

Every 3500 miles (5500 km)

1 All models are fitted with an hydraulic clutch, for which there is no method of adjustment.

2 Check the fluid level in the reservoir (see *Daily (pre-ride) checks*).

3 Inspect the hydraulic hose sections and their connections for signs of fluid leakage, and flex them to check for cracking, deterioration and wear **(see illustrations)**. Also check around the release mechanism components (master cylinder on the handlebar and release cylinder in the front sprocket cover) for damage and leakage.

4 Change the clutch fluid every two years (see Section 24), and replace the hose and pipe assembly with a new one either if damaged or deteriorated, or every four years irrespective of condition (see Section 27). The master and release cylinder seals should be changed every few years, or if leakage from them is evident (see Section 35).

5 Check the operation of the clutch. If there is evidence of air in the system (spongy feel to the lever, difficulty in engaging gear, drag when in gear), bleed the clutch (see Chapter 2). If the lever feels stiff or sticky, overhaul the release mechanism (see Chapter 2).

6 The clutch lever has a span adjuster that alters the distance of the lever from the handlebar **(see illustration)**. Each setting is identified by a number on the adjuster, which must align with the arrow on the lever. Pull the lever away from the handlebar and turn the adjuster ring until the setting that best suits the rider is obtained.

9 Cooling system check

Every 3500 miles (5500 km)

 Warning: The engine must be cool before beginning this procedure.

1 Check the coolant level (see *Daily (pre-ride) checks*).

2 Remove the fairing side panels (see Chapter 8).

3 Check the entire cooling system for evidence of leakage. Examine each rubber

8.3a Check the hose (arrowed) as described . . .

8.3b . . . at each end

8.6 Clutch lever span adjuster – align the required setting number with the arrow on the lever

Routine maintenance and servicing 1•13

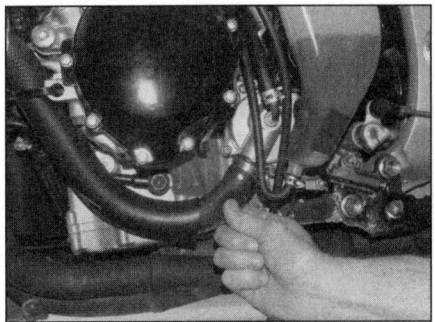

9.3 Check the hoses for evidence of cracks and deterioration

9.5 Check the drain hole (arrowed) for signs of leakage

9.8 Remove the pressure cap as described

coolant hose (including the hoses to and from the reservoir) along its entire length. Look for cracks, abrasions and other damage. Squeeze each hose at various points to see whether they are dried out or hard **(see illustration)**. They should feel firm, yet pliable, and return to their original shape when released. If necessary, replace them with new ones (see Chapter 3).

4 Check for evidence of leaks at each cooling system joint and around the pump on the left-hand side of the engine. Tighten the hose clips if necessary to prevent future leaks. If the pump cover is leaking, check that the cover bolts are tight. If they are, replace the O-ring in the cover with a new one (see Chapter 3).

5 To prevent leakage of coolant from the cooling system to the lubrication system and vice versa, two seals are fitted on the pump shaft. There is a drain hole in the pump body, which is just visible if you look up at the underside of the pump at the point just before it enters the crankcase **(see illustration)**. If either seal fails, the drain allows the coolant or oil to escape and prevents them mixing. If both seals fail, the oil and coolant mix to form a white emulsion. The seal on the water pump side is of the mechanical type which bears on the rear face of the impeller. The second seal, which is mounted behind the mechanical seal is of the normal feathered lip type. Both seals are available separately. If on inspection there is evidence of leakage from the drain hole, remove the water pump and replace both seals with new ones. Refer to Chapter 3 for details.

6 Check the radiator for leaks and other damage. Leaks in the radiator leave tell-tale scale deposits or coolant stains on the outside of the core below the leak. If leaks are noted, remove the radiator (see Chapter 3) and have it repaired or replace it with a new one.

Caution: Do not use a liquid leak stopping compound to try to repair leaks.

7 Check the radiator fins for mud, dirt and insects, which may impede the flow of air through the radiator. If the fins are dirty, remove the radiator (see Chapter 3) and clean it using water or low pressure compressed air directed through the fins from the inner side. If the fins are bent or distorted, straighten them carefully with a screwdriver. If the air flow is restricted by bent or damaged fins over more than 20% of the surface area, replace the radiator with a new one.

8 Remove the pressure cap from the radiator filler neck by turning it anti-clockwise until it reaches a stop **(see illustration)**. If you hear a hissing sound (indicating there is still pressure in the system), wait until it stops. Now press down on the cap and continue turning it until it can be removed. Check the condition of the coolant in the system. If it is rust-coloured or if accumulations of scale are visible, drain and flush the system and refill it with new coolant (See Section 25). Check the cap seal for cracks and other damage. If in doubt about the pressure cap's condition, have it tested by a Suzuki dealer or replace it with a new one.

9 Check the antifreeze content of the coolant with an antifreeze hydrometer. Sometimes coolant looks like it's in good condition, but might be too weak to offer adequate protection. If the hydrometer indicates a weak mixture, drain, flush and refill the system (see Section 25).

10 Install the cap by turning it clockwise until it reaches the first stop then push down on it and continue turning until it can turn no further. Start the engine and let it reach normal operating temperature, then check for leaks again. As the coolant temperature increases, the electric fan (mounted on the back of the radiator) should come on automatically and the temperature should begin to drop. If it does not, refer to Chapter 3 and check the fan and fan circuit carefully.

11 If the coolant level is consistently low, and no evidence of leaks can be found, have the entire system pressure checked by a Suzuki dealer.

10 Drive chain and sprockets wear check

Every 3500 miles (5500 km)

1 Check the entire length of the chain for damaged rollers, loose links and pins, and missing O-rings. Fit a new chain if damage is found. **Note:** *Never install a new chain on old sprockets, and never use the old chain if you install new sprockets – replace the chain and sprockets as a set.*

2 Remove the front sprocket cover (see Chapter 6). Check the teeth on the front sprocket and the rear sprocket for wear **(see illustration)**. If the sprocket teeth are worn excessively, renew the chain and both sprockets as a set.

3 Inspect the drive chain slider on the front of the swingarm for excessive wear and damage and replace it with a new one if necessary.

4 Measure the amount of chain stretch as follows:

5 On US and Canada models, remove the split pin from the rear axle nut. Discard it as a new one must be used.

6 Slacken the rear axle nut **(see illustration 1.8a)**. Also slacken the nut on the bolt securing the torque arm to the rear brake caliper **(see illustration 1.8b)**.

7 Slacken the adjuster bolt locknuts, then turn the adjuster bolts out evenly until the chain is tight, but not taut **(see illustration 1.9a)**. Measure along the bottom run the length of 21 pins (from the centre of the 1st pin to the centre of the 21st pin) and compare the result to the stretch limit specified at the beginning of the Chapter **(see illustration)**. Rotate the rear

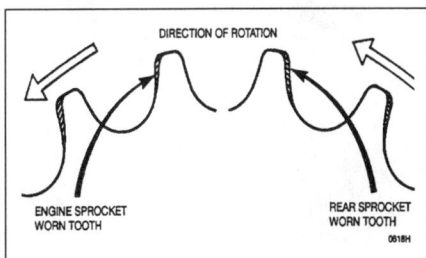

10.2 Check the sprockets in the areas indicated to see if they are worn

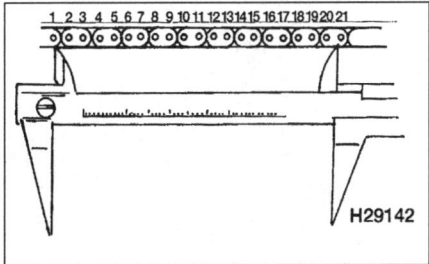

10.7 Measure the distance between the 1st and 21st pins to determine chain stretch

1•14 Routine maintenance and servicing

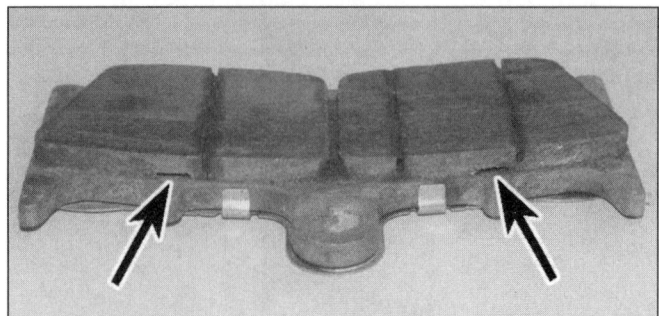

11.1a Front brake pad wear indicator cut-outs (arrowed). The grooves in the friction material also give a good indication of wear – shallow groove, nearly worn pad; no groove, worn pad

11.1b Rear brake pad wear indicator line (arrowed) – the centre groove can also be used (shallow groove, nearly worn pad; no groove, worn pad)

wheel so that several sections of the chain can be measured, then calculate the average. If the chain stretch measurement exceeds the service limit it must be replaced with a new one, together with new sprockets (see Chapter 6).

8 If the chain is good, reset the adjusters so that there is the correct amount of freeplay (see Section 1).

11 Brake pad wear check

Every 3500 miles (5500 km)

1 Each brake pad has wear indicator lines, grooves or cut-outs in the friction material that should be plainly visible from the most obvious vantage point, but note that an accumulation of road dirt and brake dust could make them difficult to see **(see illustrations)**. If the indicators aren't visible, then the amount of friction material remaining should be, and it will be obvious when the pads need replacing – if necessary remove the pad spring (front caliper) or cover (rear caliper), displace the caliper itself, or on the rear caliper use a mirror to view up into it, for the best viewpoint (see Chapter 7). **Note:** *Some after-market pads may use different indicators to those on the original equipment.*

2 If the pads are worn to or beyond the wear indicator or there is little friction material remaining, they must be replaced with new ones, though it is advisable to replace the pads before they become this worn. If the pads are dirty or if you are in doubt as to the amount of friction material remaining, remove them for inspection and measure the thickness of the material (see Chapter 7). Suzuki do not specify a minimum thickness, but anything less than 1 mm is worn. If the pads are excessively worn, check the brake discs (see Chapter 7).

3 Refer to Chapter 7 for details of pad removal and installation.

12 Brake system check

Every 3500 miles (5500 km)

1 A routine general check of the brake system will ensure that any problems are discovered and remedied before the rider's safety is jeopardised.

2 Check the brake lever and pedal for loose mountings, improper or rough action, excessive play, bends, and other damage. Lubricate the lever and pedal at the specified interval or as required (see Section 15). Replace any damaged parts with new ones (see Chapter 7).

3 Make sure all brake component fasteners are tight. Check the brake pads for wear (see Section 11) and make sure the fluid level in the reservoirs is correct (see *Daily (pre-ride) checks*). Inspect the hydraulic hoses and their connections for signs of fluid leakage, and flex them to check for cracking, deterioration and wear **(see illustration)**. If the lever or pedal is spongy, bleed the brakes (see Chapter 7).

4 Make sure the brake light operates when the front brake lever is pulled in. The front brake light switch, mounted on the underside of the master cylinder, is not adjustable. If it fails to operate properly, check it (see Chapter 9).

5 Make sure the brake light is activated just before the rear brake takes effect. If adjustment is necessary, hold the switch body and turn the adjuster nut until the brake light is activated when required **(see illustration)**. The switch is mounted on the inside of the rider's right-hand footrest bracket, just ahead of the master cylinder. If the brake light comes on too late, turn the nut clockwise. If the brake light comes on too soon or is permanently on, turn the nut anti-clockwise. If the switch doesn't operate the brake light, check it (see Chapter 9).

6 The front brake lever has a span adjuster that alters the distance of the lever from the handlebar **(see illustration)**. Each setting is identified by a number on the adjuster, which must align with the arrow on the lever. Pull the lever away from the handlebar and turn the adjuster ring until the setting that best suits the rider is obtained.

7 Measure the height of the top of the rear brake pedal in relation to the top of the rider's footrest and compare it to the height specified at the beginning of the Chapter **(see illustration)**. The height can be adjusted to bring it within the range, or to suit the rider's preference if different. Slacken the clevis

12.3 Flex the hoses and check for cracks, bulges and leaking fluid. Also check all connections for leaks

12.5 Hold the rear brake light switch body and turn the adjuster nut (arrowed) as required

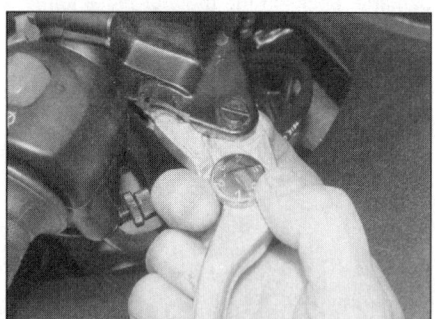

12.6 Brake lever span adjuster – align the required setting number with the arrow on the lever

Routine maintenance and servicing 1•15

12.7a Measure the rear brake pedal height and adjust if required

12.7b Slacken the locknut (A) and turn the pushrod using the hex (B) to adjust pedal height

locknut, then turn the pushrod using a spanner on the hex at the top of the rod until the pedal is at the correct or desired height **(see illustration)**. On completion tighten the locknut securely. Adjust the rear brake light switch after adjusting the pedal height (see Step 5).

13 Tyre and wheel check

Every 3500 miles (5500 km)

Tyres

1 Check the tyre condition and tread depth thoroughly – see *Daily (pre-ride) checks*.

Wheels

2 Cast wheels are virtually maintenance free, but they should be kept clean and checked periodically for cracks and other damage. Also check the wheel runout and alignment (see Chapter 7). Never attempt to repair damaged cast wheels; they must be replaced with new ones. Check the valve rubber for signs of damage or deterioration and have it replaced if necessary. Also, make sure the valve stem cap is in place and tight.

14 Nut and bolt tightness check

Every 3500 miles (5500 km)

1 Since vibration of the machine tends to loosen fasteners, all nuts, bolts, screws, etc. should be checked for proper tightness.
2 Pay particular attention to the following:
 Spark plugs
 Engine oil drain bolt
 Lever and pedal bolts
 Footrest and stand bolts
 Engine mounting bolts (refer to Chapter 2)
 Shock absorber and suspension linkage bolts; swingarm pivot bolt, nut and locknut (refer to Chapter 6)
 Handlebar clamp bolts and holder bolt nuts (refer to Chapter 6)
 Front fork clamp bolts (top and bottom yoke) and fork top bolts
 Steering stem nut
 Steering damper bolts
 Front axle and axle clamp bolts
 Rear axle nut
 Front and rear sprocket nuts
 Brake caliper and master cylinder mounting bolts, brake caliper body bolts, rear brake torque arm nuts
 Brake hose banjo bolts and caliper bleed valves
 Rear brake torque arm nuts
 Brake disc bolts
 Exhaust system bolts/nuts

3 If a torque wrench is available, use it along with the torque specifications at the beginning of this and other Chapters.

15 Stand, lever pivot and cable lubrication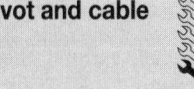

Every 3500 miles (5500 km)

1 Since the controls, cables and various other components of a motorcycle are exposed to the elements, they should be checked and lubricated periodically to ensure safe and trouble-free operation.
2 The footrests, clutch and brake levers, brake pedal, gearchange lever and linkage, and sidestand (and where fitted centrestand) pivots should be lubricated frequently. In order for the lubricant to be applied where it will do the most good, the component should be disassembled. The lubricant recommended by Suzuki for each application is listed at the beginning of the Chapter. If chain or cable lubricant is being used, it can be applied to the pivot joint gaps and will usually work its way into the areas where friction occurs, so less disassembly of the component is needed (however it is always better to do so and clean off all corrosion, dirt and old lubricant first). If motor oil or light grease is being used, apply it sparingly as it may attract dirt (which could cause the controls to bind or wear at an accelerated rate). **Note:** *One of the best lubricants for the control lever pivots is a dry-film lubricant (available from many sources by different names).*
3 To lubricate the cables, disconnect the relevant cable at its upper end, then lubricate it with a pressure adapter (but note they don't fit well on flanged cable ends) and aerosol lubricant, or if one is not available, using the set-up shown **(see illustrations)**. See Chapter 4 for the fast idle and throttle cable removal procedures.

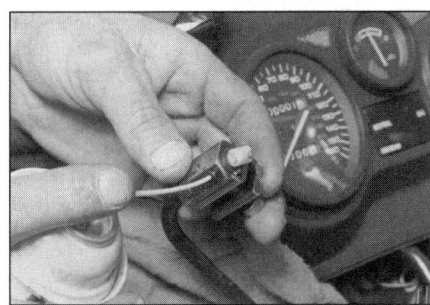

15.3a Lubricating a cable with a pressure lubricator. Make sure the tool seals around the inner cable

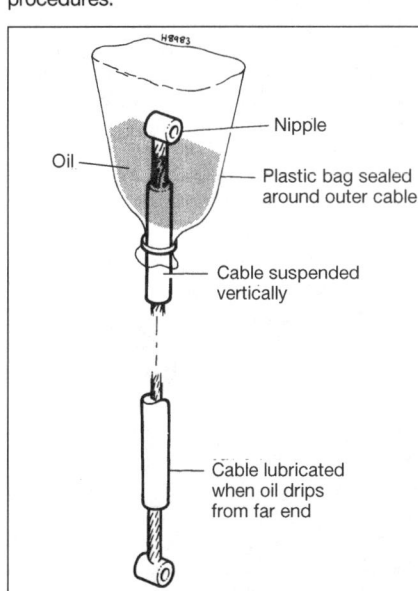

15.3b Lubricating a cable with a makeshift funnel and motor oil

1•16 Routine maintenance and servicing

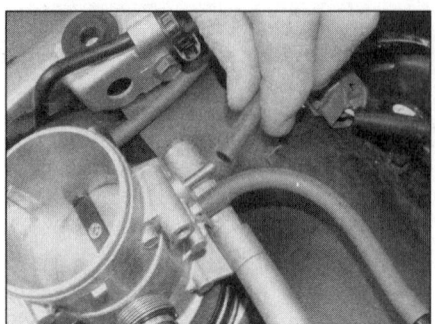
17.6a Disconnect the hose . . .

17.6b . . . and fit a cap over the union

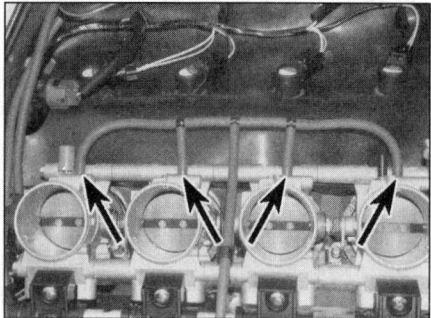
17.6c Disconnect the IAP sensor hoses (arrowed)

Every 7000 miles (11,000 km) or 12 months

Carry out all the items under the 3500 mile (5500 km) check, plus the following:

16 Spark plug renewal

Every 7000 miles (11,000 km)

1 Remove the old spark plugs as described in Section 3 and install new ones.

17 Throttle body synchronisation

Every 7000 miles (11,000 km)

⚠ **Warning:** *Petrol (gasoline) is extremely flammable, so take extra precautions when you work on any part of the fuel system. Don't smoke or allow open flames or bare light bulbs near the work area, and don't work in a garage where a natural gas-type appliance is present. If you spill any fuel on your skin, rinse it off immediately with soap and water. When you perform any kind of work on the fuel system, wear safety glasses and have a fire extinguisher suitable for a Class B type fire (flammable liquids) on hand.*

17.7 Connect the gauge hoses to the correct unions for your model – K2-on models shown

⚠ **Warning:** *Take great care not to burn your hand on the hot engine unit when accessing the gauge take-off points on the intake ducts. Do not allow exhaust gases to build up in the work area; either perform the check outside or use an exhaust gas extraction system.*

Note: *The throttle bodies must be synchronised with the air filter housing removed. To prevent dirt being drawn into the engine, it is suggested that you cut circles out of an old pair of tights (or similar material) which can be fitted over the air intake on each throttle body and secured with an elastic band.*

1 Throttle body synchronisation is simply the process of adjusting the butterfly valve linkage so each throttle body passes the same amount of fuel/air mixture to each cylinder. This is achieved by measuring the vacuum produced in each intake duct. Throttle bodies that are out of synchronisation will result in increased fuel consumption, increased engine temperature, less than ideal throttle response and higher vibration levels. If a valve clearance check is part of the service you are performing, do that first (see Section 22).

2 To synchronise the throttle bodies you need a set of vacuum gauges or calibrated tubes to indicate engine vacuum. The equipment used should be suitable for a four cylinder engine and come complete with the necessary adapters and hoses to fit the take-off points.

Note: *Because of the nature of the synchronisation procedure and the need for special instruments, most owners leave the task to a Suzuki dealer.*

3 Start the engine and let it run until it reaches normal operating temperature, then check that the idle speed is correctly set at 1150 rpm, and adjust it if necessary (see Section 6). Stop the engine.

⚠ **Warning:** *The engine and throttle bodies will be hot. With the restricted access to the screws, great care must be taken not to burn yourself while synchronising the carburettors.*

4 Raise the fuel tank (see Chapter 4). Remove the air filter housing (see Chapter 4). On X, Y and K1 models, remove the intake air temperature (IAT) and intake air pressure (IAP) sensors from the air filter housing and reconnect them to the wiring loom (see Chapter 4). On all later models only remove and reconnect the IAT sensor.

5 On X, Y and K1 models, disconnect the vacuum hose for the vacuum transmitting valve (VTV) from the left-hand vacuum take-off union on the No. 1 (left-hand end) throttle body, then block the hose using a suitable plug (see illustration 17.6a). Also disconnect the vacuum hose for the PAIR system solenoid valve from the left-hand vacuum take-off union on the No. 4 (right-hand end) throttle body, then block the hose using a suitable plug. Remove the blanking caps from the left-hand vacuum take-off unions on the Nos. 2 and 3 (inner left- and right-hand) throttle bodies.

6 On all K2 models onwards, either disconnect the vacuum hose for the vacuum transmitting valve (VTV) from the left-hand vacuum take-off union on the No. 1 (left-hand end) throttle body, then block the union using a suitable cap **(see illustrations)**, or alternatively fit a hose clamp onto the hose and leave it attached to the union. Disconnect the vacuum hoses for the IAP sensor from the right-hand vacuum take-off unions on the nos. 1 and 4 (left- and right-hand end) throttle bodies and from the take-off unions on the Nos. 2 and 3 (inner left- and right-hand) throttle bodies **(see illustration)**.

7 Connect the gauge hoses to the vacuum take-off unions **(see illustration)**. Make sure they are a good fit because any air leaks will result in false readings.

8 Start the engine. If using vacuum gauges fitted with damping adjustment, set this so that the needle flutter is just eliminated but so that they can still respond to small changes in pressure.

Routine maintenance and servicing 1•17

17.9 Checking and adjusting throttle body synchronisation

17.10 Synchronisation adjustment screws (arrowed)

9 The vacuum readings for the cylinders should be the same, or at least within the maximum difference specified at the beginning of the Chapter **(see illustration)**.

10 If the vacuum readings differ by more than the specified maximum difference, adjust the throttle bodies by turning the synchronising screws situated in the throttle linkage between each throttle body until the readings are the same **(see illustration)**. **Note:** *Do not press hard on the screws whilst adjusting them, otherwise a false reading will be obtained.* First synchronise the No. 3 body to No. 4 using the right-hand synchronising screw until the readings are the same. Then synchronise No. 1 body to No. 2 using the left-hand screw. Finally synchronise Nos. 1 and 2 bodies to Nos. 3 and 4 using the centre screw.

11 When the throttle bodies are synchronised, open and close the throttle quickly to settle the linkage, and recheck the gauge readings, readjusting if necessary.

12 Remove the vacuum gauges.

13 On X, Y and K1 models, remove the blanking plugs from the VTV and PAIR system vacuum hoses and connect them back to their unions, and replace the blanking caps on their unions (see Step 5 for locations).

14 On all K2 models onwards, connect the vacuum hoses for the intake air pressure (IAP) sensor to their unions (see Step 6 for locations). Either remove the blanking cap from the VTV hose union and fit the hose back on **(see illustrations 17.6b and a)**, or remove the clamp from the hose, according to your method.

15 Remove any material used to cover the throttle body intakes, then install the air filter housing, not forgetting to fit the IAT and IAP sensors, and lower the fuel tank (see Chapter 4). Run the engine and adjust the idle speed by turning the throttle stop screw (see Section 6) until the idle speed listed in this Chapter's Specifications is obtained. Check the throttle position sensor setting and adjust it if necessary (see Chapter 4, Section 12).

18 Steering head bearing freeplay check and adjustment

Every 7000 miles (11,000 km)

1 The steering head bearings can become dented, rough or loose during normal use of the machine. In extreme cases, worn or loose steering head bearings can cause steering wobble – a condition that is potentially dangerous.

Check

2 Remove the fairing side panels (see Chapter 8). Remove the steering damper (see Chapter 6).

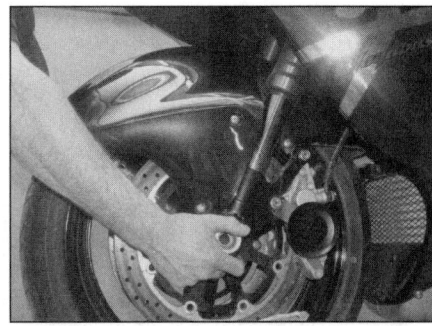

18.5 Checking for play in the steering head bearings

3 Support the motorcycle on its centrestand or on an auxiliary stand and raise the front wheel 20 to 30 mm off the ground using a jack, placing a block of wood between the jack head and the engine.

4 Point the front wheel straight-ahead and slowly move the handlebars from side-to-side. Any dents or roughness in the bearing races will be felt and the bars will not move smoothly and freely. Again point the wheel straight ahead, and tap the front of the wheel to one side. The wheel should 'fall' under its own weight to the limit of its lock, indicating that the bearings are not too tight. Check for similar movement to the other side. If a spring balance (graduated so that it can accurately measure between 100 and 600 grams) is available (they are not expensive, and provide an easy and accurate way of setting the bearings), attach one end to the outer end of the rubber grip on one of the handlebars **(see illustration)**. With the steering straight ahead, pull on the balance and check the reading at which the handlebars start to turn. If the reading is below 200 grams, the steering head is too loose, if the reading is above 500 grams the steering head is too tight. If the steering doesn't perform as described, and it's not due to the resistance of cables or hoses, then the bearings should be adjusted as described below.

5 Next, grasp the bottom of the forks and gently pull and push them forward and backward **(see illustration)**. Any looseness or freeplay in the steering head bearings will be felt as front-to-rear movement of the forks. If play is felt, adjust the bearings as described below.

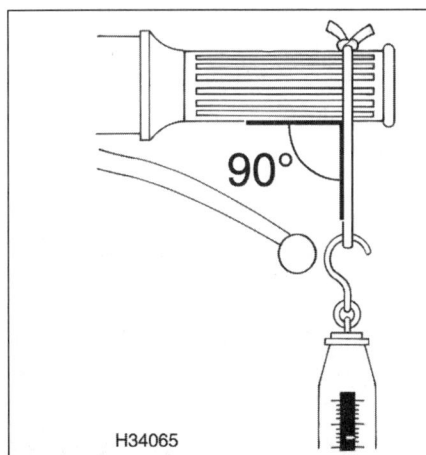

18.4 Checking the bearing loading with a spring balance

> **HAYNES HiNT** *Make sure you are not mistaking any movement between the bike and stand or jack, or between the stand or jack and the ground, for freeplay in the bearings. Do not pull and push the forks too hard – a gentle movement is all that is needed. Freeplay in the forks themselves due to worn bushes can also be misinterpreted as steering head bearing play – do not confuse the two.*

1•18 Routine maintenance and servicing

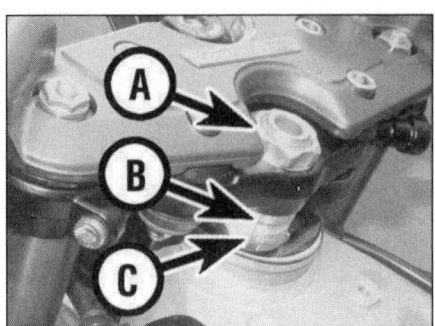

18.7a Steering stem nut (A), adjuster locknut (B), adjuster nut (C)

18.7b Slacken the bottom yoke fork clamp bolts (arrowed) on each side

Adjustment

6 First perform the check as described above. If adjustment is necessary cover the fuel tank in plenty of rag – this should prevent damage should a tool slip. To be absolutely certain, raise or remove the fuel tank (see Chapter 4).

7 Slacken the steering stem nut and the fork clamp bolts in the bottom yoke **(see illustrations)**.

8 Using a C-spanner or a drift located in one of the notches, slacken the adjuster locknut (the top nut) **(see illustration 18.7a)**. Now slacken the adjuster nut slightly until pressure is just released, then adjust and set it until all freeplay is removed, yet the steering is able to move freely as described in Steps 4 and 5. The object is to set the adjuster nut so that the bearings are under a very light loading, just enough to remove any freeplay, but not so much that the steering does not move freely from side to side as described in the check procedure above. If you have the spring balance, set the adjuster nut so that the steering starts to move at a load of around 350 grams. Turn the steering from side-to-side a few times, then re-check the setting.

9 If the bearings cannot be correctly adjusted, disassemble the steering head and check the bearings and races (see Chapter 6). *Caution: Take great care not to apply excessive pressure because this will cause premature failure of the bearings.*

10 Tighten the adjuster locknut tightly against the adjuster nut while making sure the adjuster nut does not turn with it. Tighten the steering stem nut to the torque setting specified at the beginning of the Chapter **(see illustration 18.7a)**. Now tighten the fork clamp bolts in the bottom yoke to the specified torque **(see illustration 18.7b)**.

11 Check the bearing adjustment as described above and re-adjust if necessary. On completion remove the jack from under the engine.

12 Install the fuel tank if raised or removed (see Chapter 4), the steering damper (see Chapter 6), and the fairing side panels (see Chapter 8).

19 Suspension check

Every 7000 miles (11,000 km)

1 The suspension components must be maintained in top operating condition to ensure rider safety. Loose, worn or damaged suspension parts decrease the motorcycle's stability and control.

Front suspension

2 While standing alongside the motorcycle, and with it off the stand and upright, apply the front brake and push on the handlebars to compress the forks several times. See if they move up-and-down smoothly without binding. If binding is felt, disassemble and inspect the forks (see Chapter 6).

3 Inspect the area below and around each dust seal for signs of oil leakage, pitting and corrosion, then carefully lever the seals out using a flat-bladed screwdriver and inspect the area around the fork seal **(see illustration)**. If leakage is evident, the seals in each fork must be replaced with new ones (see Chapter 6). If there is pitting in the tubes within the extent of fork travel, you should consider replacing them with new ones as it will eventually cause the seals to fail. If there is evidence of corrosion between the seal retaining ring and its groove spray the area with a penetrative lubricant, otherwise the ring will be difficult to remove if needed. Press the dust seal back into place on completion.

4 Check the tightness of all suspension nuts and bolts to be sure none have worked loose, applying the torque settings at the beginning of Chapter 6.

Rear suspension

5 Inspect the rear shock absorber for damage and fluid leakage and tightness of its mountings. If leakage is found, the shock must be replaced with a new one or rebuilt by a suspension specialist (see Chapter 6).

6 With the aid of an assistant to support the bike, compress the rear suspension several times. It should move up and down freely without binding. If any binding is felt, the worn or faulty component must be identified and checked (see Chapter 6). The problem could be due to either the shock absorber, the suspension linkage components or the swingarm components.

7 Support the motorcycle on its centrestand if fitted or on an auxiliary stand so that the rear wheel is off the ground. Grab the swingarm and rock it from side to side – there should be no discernible movement at the rear **(see illustration)**. If there's a little movement or a slight clicking can be heard, inspect the tightness of all the swingarm and rear suspension mounting bolts and nuts, referring to the torque settings specified at the beginning of Chapter 6, and re-check for movement.

8 Next, grasp the top of the rear wheel and pull it upwards – there should be no discernible freeplay before the shock absorber begins to compress **(see illustration)**. Any freeplay felt in either check indicates worn bearings in the suspension

19.3 Check the inner tube and seals as described

19.7 Checking for play in the swingarm bearings

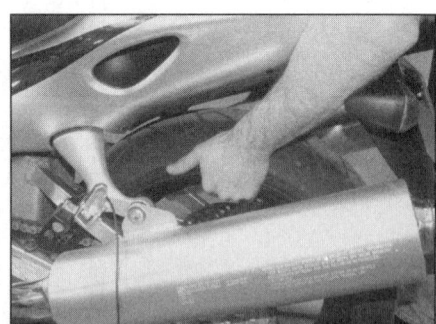

19.8 Checking for play in the rear suspension mountings and linkage bearings

Routine maintenance and servicing 1•19

linkage or swingarm, or worn suspension mountings. The worn components must be identified and replaced with new ones (see Chapter 6).

9 To make an accurate assessment of the swingarm bearings, remove the rear wheel (see Chapter 7) and the bolt securing the suspension linkage assembly to the swingarm (see Chapter 6). Grasp the rear of the swingarm with one hand and place your other hand at the junction of the swingarm and the frame. Try to move the rear of the swingarm from side-to-side. Any wear (play) in the bearings should be felt as movement between the swingarm and the frame at the front. If there is any play the swingarm will be felt to move forward and backward at the front (not from side-to-side). Next, move the swingarm up and down through its full travel. It should move freely, without any binding or rough spots. If there is any play in the swingarm or if it does not move freely, remove the swingarm for inspection of the bearings (see Chapter 6).

Every 10,500 miles (16,500 km) or 18 months

Carry out all the items under the 3500 mile (5500 km) check, plus the following:

20 Air filter renewal

Every 10,500 miles (16,500 km)

Caution: If the machine is continually ridden in wet or dusty conditions, the filter should be replaced more frequently.

1 Refer to the procedure in Section 2 and replace the air filter with a new one.

21 Engine/transmission oil and filter change

Every 10,500 miles (16,500 km)

⚠️ **Warning:** *Be careful when draining the oil, as the exhaust pipes, the engine, and the oil itself can cause severe burns.*

1 Refer to Section 5, Steps 2 to 5 and drain the engine oil. If not already done, remove the right-hand fairing side panel (see Chapter 8).

2 Now place the drain tray below the oil filter, located on the front of the engine. Unscrew the filter using a filter socket such as the Suzuki special tool (Pt. No. 09915-40610) or a commercially available equivalent along with a suitable size extension and tip any residual oil into the drain tray **(see illustrations)**. Discard the filter – oil disposal centres will accept the old filter. Note that due to the position of the oil cooler the socket extension has to be the correct length to be of any use. If you only have a long extension, use a universal drive with it to create the necessary angle.

3 Smear clean engine oil onto the rubber seal on the new filter and thread it onto the engine until the rubber seal just contacts its mating surface **(see illustrations)**. Now tighten the filter by two full turns (or by the number of turns specified on the filter itself or its packaging), but note that on the model we worked on the filter became very tight after 1½ turns, and did not leak, so it is worth using some discretion when applying the 2 turn specification as it is not worth damaging the new filter. **Note:** *Do not use a strap or chain wrench to tighten the filter as you will damage it. If you do not have a filter socket you can tighten the filter by hand, but make sure it is tightened by the number of turns specified or it may leak.*

4 Refer to Section 5, Steps 6 and 7 and refill the engine to the proper level using the recommended type and amount of oil.

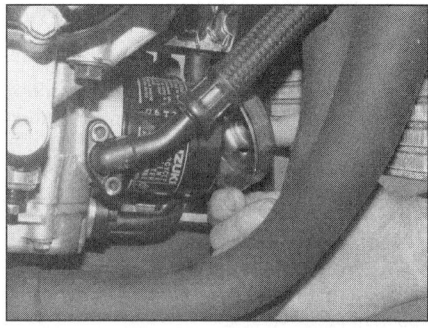

21.2a Unscrew the filter using a filter removing tool – the special socket shown . . .

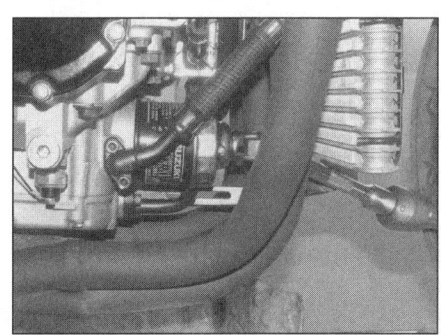

21.2b . . . with a socket extension and universal drive if needed is the easiest . . .

21.2c . . . and allow the oil to drain

21.3a Smear clean oil onto the seal . . .

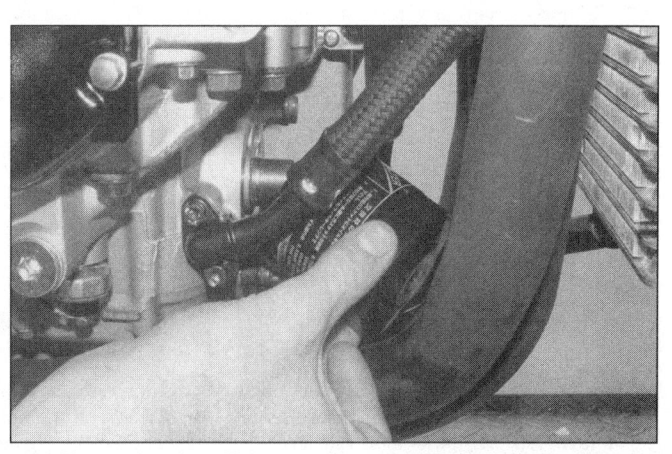

21.3b . . . then install the new filter and tighten it as described

1•20 Routine maintenance and servicing

Every 14,000 miles (22,000 km) or 24 months

Carry out all the items under the 7000 mile (11,000 km) check, plus the following:

22 Valve clearance check and adjustment

Every 14,000 miles (22,000 km)

Check

1 The engine must be completely cool for this maintenance procedure, so let the machine sit overnight before beginning.
2 Remove the right-hand fairing side panel (see Chapter 8). Remove the spark plugs to allow the engine to be turned over easier (see Section 3).
3 Remove the valve cover (see Chapter 2).
4 Unscrew the crankshaft end cap and the timing mark inspection cap from the starter clutch cover **(see illustration)**. Check the condition of the O-ring and sealing washer and discard them if they are damaged, deformed or deteriorated, but note that new ones should be used as a matter of course.
5 Make a chart or sketch of all valve positions so that a note of each clearance can be made against the relevant valve.
6 Turn the engine using a socket or offset ring spanner on the starter clutch bolt, turning it in a clockwise direction only, until the line on the starter clutch aligns with the notch in the timing mark inspection hole **(see illustrations)**. Now, check the position of the notch in the left-hand end of each camshaft. If the notch on the intake camshaft is facing down and the notch on the exhaust camshaft is at 8 o'clock, then No. 1 cylinder is at TDC on the compression stroke **(see illustration)**. If the notch on the intake camshaft is facing up and the notch on the exhaust camshaft is at 2 o'clock, then No. 4 cylinder is at TDC on the compression stroke **(see illustration)**. If the marks are not positioned as required for the cylinders being checked, turn the crankshaft through 360° (one complete turn) until the line on the starter clutch again aligns with the notch in the timing mark inspection hole.
7 With No. 1 cylinder at TDC on the compression stroke, the following valves can be checked:
a) No. 1, intake and exhaust
b) No. 2, exhaust
c) No. 3, intake
8 With No. 4 cylinder at TDC on the compression stroke, the following valves can be checked:
a) No. 2, intake
b) No. 3, exhaust
c) No. 4, intake and exhaust
9 Insert a feeler gauge of the same thickness as the correct valve clearance (see Specifications) between the base of the camshaft lobe and the follower of each valve and check that it is a firm sliding fit – you should feel a slight drag when the you pull the gauge out **(see illustration)**. If not, use the feeler gauges to obtain the exact clearance.
Note: *The intake and exhaust valve clearances are different.* Record the measured clearance on the chart.
10 Rotate the engine through 360° until the line on the starter clutch again aligns with the notch in the timing mark inspection hole **(see illustration 22.6b)** and measure the valve clearance of the remaining valves using the method described in Step 9. **Note:** *Turn the engine in the normal direction of rotation (clockwise) only, viewed from the right-hand end of the engine.*
11 When all clearances have been measured and charted, identify whether the clearance on any valve falls outside the specified range. If any do, the shim must be replaced with one of a thickness that will restore the correct clearance.

Adjustment

12 Shim replacement requires removal of the camshaft(s) (see Chapter 2). There is no need to remove both camshafts if shims from only one side of the cylinder need replacing. Place rags over the spark plug hole and the cam chain tunnel to prevent a shim from dropping

22.4 Remove the crankshaft end cap (A) and the timing inspection cap (B)

22.6a Turn the engine clockwise using the timing rotor bolt . . .

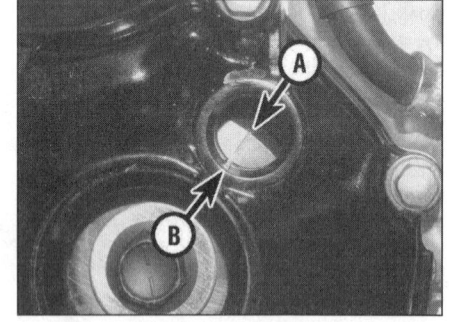

22.6b . . . until the line (A) aligns with the notch (B)

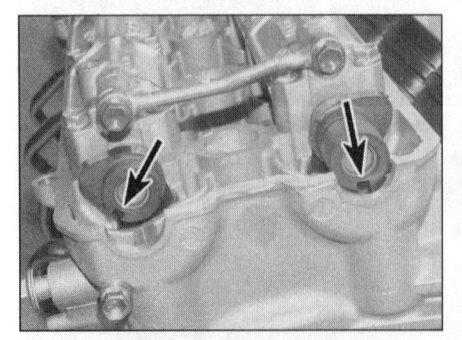

22.6c With the notches positioned as shown No. 1 cylinder is at TDC on compression

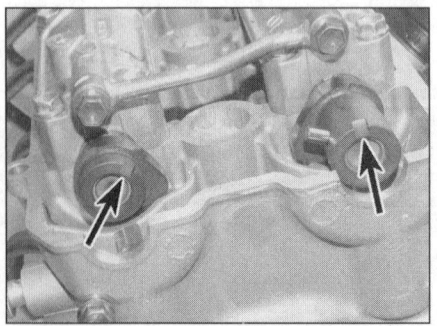

22.6d With the notches positioned as shown No. 4 cylinder is at TDC on compression

22.9 Insert the feeler gauge between the base of the lobe and the top of the follower as shown

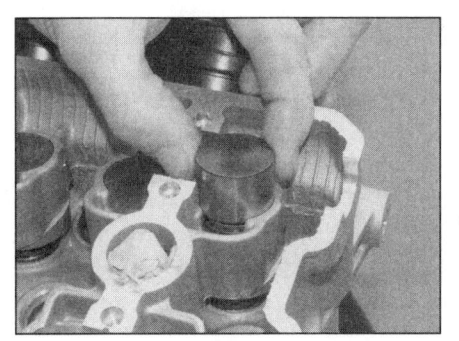

Routine maintenance and servicing 1•21

22.13a Carefully lift out the follower using grips, a lapping tool or a magnet...

22.13b ... and retrieve the shim from inside it ...

22.13c ... or from the top of the valve

into the engine on removal. Work on one valve at a time to prevent the possibility of mixing up the followers, which must be returned to their original location. If you want to remove more than one shim and follower at a time, store them in a marked container or bag, denoting which cylinder and which valve the follower and shim are from, so that they do not get mixed up.

13 With the camshaft removed, remove the cam follower of the valve in question, then retrieve the shim from the inside of the follower **(see illustrations)**. The follower is best removed with a magnet or using the suction created by a valve lapping tool, but fingers may suffice, and long nosed pliers can be used with care – do not grip the follower tightly as you could score it. If the shim is not in the follower, pick it out of the top of the valve spring retainer using either a magnet, a screwdriver with a dab of grease on it (the shim will stick to the grease), or a very small screwdriver and a pair of pliers. Do not allow the shim to fall into the engine.

14 A size mark should be stamped on one face of the shim – a shim marked 265 is 2.65 mm thick **(see illustration)**. If the mark is not

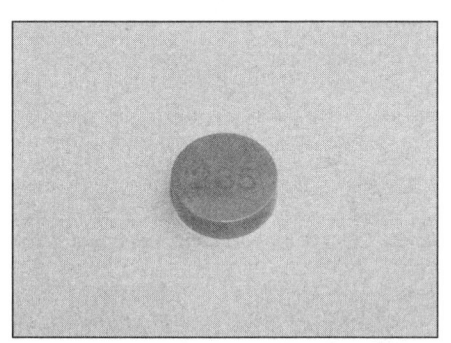

22.14a The size is marked on the shim ...

visible measure the shim thickness using a micrometer **(see illustration)**. It is recommended that the shim be measured anyway to check whether it has worn. Shims are available in 0.05 mm increments from 2.30 to 3.50 mm. If the shim thickness is less than its denomination, this must be taken into account when selecting a new shim.

15 Using the appropriate shim selection chart, find where the measured valve clearance and present shim size values intersect and read off the shim size required

22.14b ... check its thickness using a micrometer

(see illustrations). *Note: If the existing shim is marked with a number not ending in 0 or 5, round it up or down as appropriate to the nearest number ending in 0 or 5 so that the chart can be used.* *Note: If the required replacement shim is greater than 3.50 mm (the largest available), the valve is probably not seating correctly due to a build-up of carbon deposits and should be checked and cleaned or resurfaced as required (see Chapter 2).*

16 Obtain the replacement shim, then lubricate it with molybdenum disulphide oil (a

MEASURED VALVE CLEARANCE	PRESENT SHIM SIZE (mm)																									
	2.30	2.35	2.40	2.45	2.50	2.55	2.60	2.65	2.70	2.75	2.80	2.85	2.90	2.95	3.00	3.05	3.10	3.15	3.20	3.25	3.30	3.35	3.40	3.45	3.50
0.00 - 0.04 mm			2.30	2.35	2.40	2.45	2.50	2.55	2.60	2.65	2.70	2.75	2.80	2.85	2.90	2.95	3.00	3.05	3.10	3.15	3.20	3.25	3.30	3.35	3.40
0.05 - 0.09 mm		2.30	2.35	2.40	2.45	2.50	2.55	2.60	2.65	2.70	2.75	2.80	2.85	2.90	2.95	3.00	3.05	3.10	3.15	3.20	3.25	3.30	3.35	3.40	3.45
0.10 - 0.20 mm	SPECIFIED CLEARANCE/NO ADJUSTMENT REQUIRED																								
0.21 - 0.25 mm	2.40	2.45	2.50	2.55	2.60	2.65	2.70	2.75	2.80	2.85	2.90	2.95	3.00	3.05	3.10	3.15	3.20	3.25	3.30	3.35	3.40	3.45	3.50	3.50	
0.26 - 0.30 mm	2.45	2.50	2.55	2.60	2.65	2.70	2.75	2.80	2.85	2.90	2.95	3.00	3.05	3.10	3.15	3.20	3.25	3.30	3.35	3.40	3.45	3.50	3.50		
0.31 - 0.35 mm	2.50	2.55	2.60	2.65	2.70	2.75	2.80	2.85	2.90	2.95	3.00	3.05	3.10	3.15	3.20	3.25	3.30	3.35	3.40	3.45	3.50	3.50			
0.36 - 0.40 mm	2.55	2.60	2.65	2.70	2.75	2.80	2.85	2.90	2.95	3.00	3.05	3.10	3.15	3.20	3.25	3.30	3.35	3.40	3.45	3.50	3.50				
0.41 - 0.45 mm	2.60	2.65	2.70	2.75	2.80	2.85	2.90	2.95	3.00	3.05	3.10	3.15	3.20	3.25	3.30	3.35	3.40	3.45	3.50	3.50					
0.46 - 0.50 mm	2.65	2.70	2.75	2.80	2.85	2.90	2.95	3.00	3.05	3.10	3.15	3.20	3.25	3.30	3.35	3.40	3.45	3.50	3.50						
0.51 - 0.55 mm	2.70	2.75	2.80	2.85	2.90	2.95	3.00	3.05	3.10	3.15	3.20	3.25	3.30	3.35	3.40	3.45	3.50	3.50							
0.56 - 0.60 mm	2.75	2.80	2.85	2.90	2.95	3.00	3.05	3.10	3.15	3.20	3.25	3.30	3.35	3.40	3.45	3.50	3.50								
0.61 - 0.65 mm	2.80	2.85	2.90	2.95	3.00	3.05	3.10	3.15	3.20	3.25	3.30	3.35	3.40	3.45	3.50	3.50									
0.66 - 0.70 mm	2.85	2.90	2.95	3.00	3.05	3.10	3.15	3.20	3.25	3.30	3.35	3.40	3.45	3.50	3.50										
0.71 - 0.75 mm	2.90	2.95	3.00	3.05	3.10	3.15	3.20	3.25	3.30	3.35	3.40	3.45	3.50	3.50											
0.76 - 0.80 mm	2.95	3.00	3.05	3.10	3.15	3.20	3.25	3.30	3.35	3.40	3.45	3.50	3.50												
0.81 - 0.85 mm	3.00	3.05	3.10	3.15	3.20	3.25	3.30	3.35	3.40	3.45	3.50	3.50													
0.86 - 0.90 mm	3.05	3.10	3.15	3.20	3.25	3.30	3.35	3.40	3.45	3.50	3.50														
0.91 - 0.95 mm	3.10	3.15	3.20	3.25	3.30	3.35	3.40	3.45	3.50	3.50															
0.96 - 1.00 mm	3.15	3.20	3.25	3.30	3.35	3.40	3.45	3.50	3.50																
1.01 - 1.05 mm	3.20	3.25	3.30	3.35	3.40	3.45	3.50	3.50																	
1.06 - 1.10 mm	3.25	3.30	3.35	3.40	3.45	3.50	3.50																		
1.11 - 1.15 mm	3.30	3.35	3.40	3.45	3.50	3.50																			
1.16 - 1.20 mm	3.35	3.40	3.45	3.50	3.50																				
1.21 - 1.25 mm	3.40	3.45	3.50	3.50																					
1.26 - 1.30 mm	3.45	3.50	3.50																						
1.31 - 1.35 mm	3.50	3.50																							
1.36 - 1.40 mm	3.50																								

22.15a Shim selection chart – intake valves

1•22 Routine maintenance and servicing

MEASURED VALVE CLEARANCE	PRESENT SHIM SIZE (mm)																							
	2.30	2.35	2.40	2.45	2.50	2.55	2.60	2.65	2.70	2.75	2.80	2.85	2.90	2.95	3.00	3.05	3.10	3.15	3.20	3.25	3.30	3.35	3.40	3.45	3.50
0.00 - 0.04 mm					2.30	2.35	2.40	2.45	2.50	2.55	2.60	2.65	2.70	2.75	2.80	2.85	2.90	2.95	3.00	3.05	3.10	3.15	3.20	3.25	3.30
0.05 - 0.09 mm				2.30	2.35	2.40	2.45	2.50	2.55	2.60	2.65	2.70	2.75	2.80	2.85	2.90	2.95	3.00	3.05	3.10	3.15	3.20	3.25	3.30	3.35
0.10 - 0.14 mm			2.30	2.35	2.40	2.45	2.50	2.55	2.60	2.65	2.70	2.75	2.80	2.85	2.90	2.95	3.00	3.05	3.10	3.15	3.20	3.25	3.30	3.35	3.40
0.15 - 0.19 mm		2.30	2.35	2.40	2.45	2.50	2.55	2.60	2.65	2.70	2.75	2.80	2.85	2.90	2.95	3.00	3.05	3.10	3.15	3.20	3.25	3.30	3.35	3.40	3.45
0.20 - 0.30 mm	SPECIFIED CLEARANCE/NO ADJUSTMENT REQUIRED																								
0.31 - 0.35 mm	2.40	2.45	2.50	2.55	2.60	2.65	2.70	2.75	2.80	2.85	2.90	2.95	3.00	3.05	3.10	3.15	3.20	3.25	3.30	3.35	3.40	3.45	3.50	3.50	
0.36 - 0.40 mm	2.45	2.50	2.55	2.60	2.65	2.70	2.75	2.80	2.85	2.90	2.95	3.00	3.05	3.10	3.15	3.20	3.25	3.30	3.35	3.40	3.45	3.50	3.50		
0.41 - 0.45 mm	2.50	2.55	2.60	2.65	2.70	2.75	2.80	2.85	2.90	2.95	3.00	3.05	3.10	3.15	3.20	3.25	3.30	3.35	3.40	3.45	3.50	3.50			
0.46 - 0.50 mm	2.55	2.60	2.65	2.70	2.75	2.80	2.85	2.90	2.95	3.00	3.05	3.10	3.15	3.20	3.25	3.30	3.35	3.40	3.45	3.50	3.50				
0.51 - 0.55 mm	2.60	2.65	2.70	2.75	2.80	2.85	2.90	2.95	3.00	3.05	3.10	3.15	3.20	3.25	3.30	3.35	3.40	3.45	3.50	3.50					
0.56 - 0.60 mm	2.65	2.70	2.75	2.80	2.85	2.90	2.95	3.00	3.05	3.10	3.15	3.20	3.25	3.30	3.35	3.40	3.45	3.50	3.50						
0.61 - 0.65 mm	2.70	2.75	2.80	2.85	2.90	2.95	3.00	3.05	3.10	3.15	3.20	3.25	3.30	3.35	3.40	3.45	3.50	3.50							
0.66 - 0.70 mm	2.75	2.80	2.85	2.90	2.95	3.00	3.05	3.10	3.15	3.20	3.25	3.30	3.35	3.40	3.45	3.50	3.50								
0.71 - 0.75 mm	2.80	2.85	2.90	2.95	3.00	3.05	3.10	3.15	3.20	3.25	3.30	3.35	3.40	3.45	3.50	3.50									
0.76 - 0.80 mm	2.85	2.90	2.95	3.00	3.05	3.10	3.15	3.20	3.25	3.30	3.35	3.40	3.45	3.50	3.50										
0.81 - 0.85 mm	2.90	2.95	3.00	3.05	3.10	3.15	3.20	3.25	3.30	3.35	3.40	3.45	3.50	3.50											
0.86 - 0.90 mm	2.95	3.00	3.05	3.10	3.15	3.20	3.25	3.30	3.35	3.40	3.45	3.50	3.50												
0.91 - 0.95 mm	3.00	3.05	3.10	3.15	3.20	3.25	3.30	3.35	3.40	3.45	3.50	3.50													
0.96 - 1.00 mm	3.05	3.10	3.15	3.20	3.25	3.30	3.35	3.40	3.45	3.50	3.50														
1.01 - 1.05 mm	3.10	3.15	3.20	3.25	3.30	3.35	3.40	3.45	3.50	3.50															
1.06 - 1.10 mm	3.15	3.20	3.25	3.30	3.35	3.40	3.45	3.50	3.50																
1.11 - 1.15 mm	3.20	3.25	3.30	3.35	3.40	3.45	3.50	3.50																	
1.16 - 1.20 mm	3.25	3.30	3.35	3.40	3.45	3.50	3.50																		
1.21 - 1.25 mm	3.30	3.35	3.40	3.45	3.50	3.50																			
1.26 - 1.30 mm	3.35	3.40	3.45	3.50	3.50																				
1.31 - 1.35 mm	3.40	3.45	3.50	3.50																					
1.36 - 1.40 mm	3.45	3.50	3.50																						
1.41 - 1.45 mm	3.50	3.50																							
1.46 - 1.50 mm	3.50																								

22.15b Shim selection chart – exhaust valves

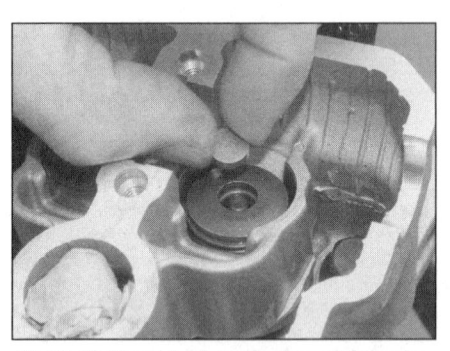

22.16 Fit the shim into the top of the valve with the size mark up

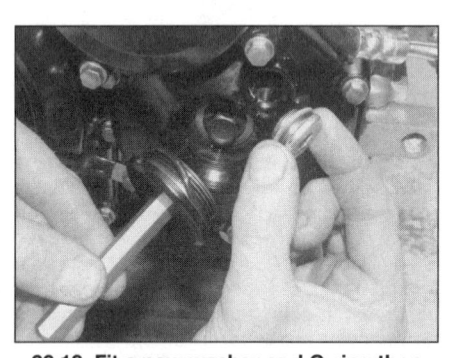

22.19 Fit a new washer and O-ring then install the caps

50/50 mixture of molybdenum disulphide grease and engine oil) and fit it into the recess in the top of the valve spring retainer with the size mark facing up **(see illustration)**.

17 Check that the shim is correctly seated, then lubricate the follower with molybdenum disulphide oil and install it onto the valve, making sure it fits squarely in its bore **(see illustration 22.13a)**. Repeat the process for any other valves which require adjustment, then install the camshafts (see Chapter 2).

18 Rotate the crankshaft several turns to seat the new shim(s) **(see illustration 22.6a)**, then check the clearances again.

19 Install all disturbed components in a reverse of the removal sequence, referring to the relevant Chapters. Install the timing inspection cap using a new sealing washer if required, and the crankshaft end cap using a new O-ring if required – smear the O-ring and the cap threads with grease **(see illustration)**. Tighten the caps to the torque settings specified at the beginning of the Chapter.

20 Check and adjust the idle speed and throttle body balance (synchronisation) (see Sections 6 and 17).

Every two years

23 Brake fluid change

Every two years

1 The brake fluid should be replaced at the prescribed interval or whenever a master cylinder or caliper overhaul is carried out. Refer to the brake bleeding section in Chapter 7, noting that all old fluid must be pumped from the fluid reservoir and hydraulic hoses before filling with new fluid.

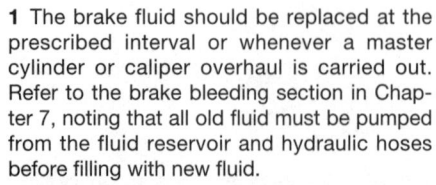

> **HAYNES HiNT** *Old brake and clutch fluid is invariably much darker in colour than new fluid, making it easy to see when all old fluid has been expelled from the system.*

24 Clutch fluid change

Every two years

1 The clutch fluid should be replaced at the prescribed interval or whenever a master cylinder or release cylinder overhaul is carried out. Refer to the clutch bleeding section in Chapter 2, noting that all old fluid must be pumped from the fluid reservoir and hydraulic hose before filling with new fluid.

25 Coolant change

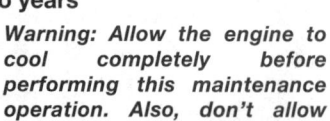

Every two years

⚠ *Warning: Allow the engine to cool completely before performing this maintenance operation. Also, don't allow antifreeze to come into contact with your skin or the painted surfaces of the motorcycle. Rinse off spills immediately with plenty of water. Antifreeze is highly toxic if ingested. Never leave antifreeze lying around in an open container or in puddles on the floor; children and pets are attracted by its sweet smell and may drink*

Routine maintenance and servicing 1•23

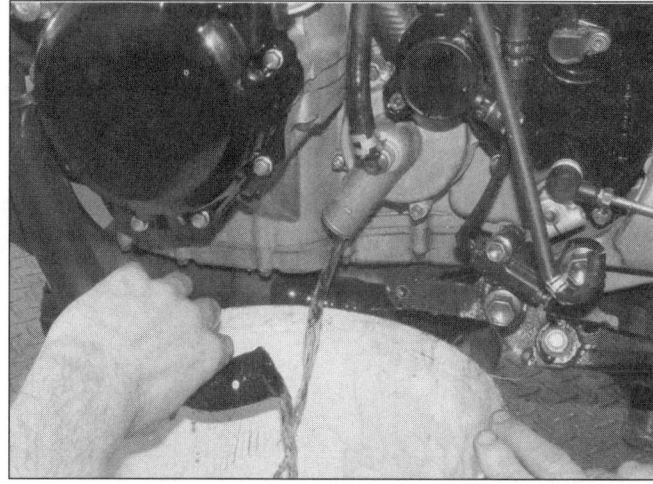

25.3a Slacken the clamp...

25.3b ... then detach the hose and allow the coolant to drain

it. Check with local authorities (councils) about disposing of antifreeze. Many communities have collection centres which will see that antifreeze is disposed of safely. Antifreeze is also combustible, so don't store it near open flames.

Draining

1 Remove the fairing side panels (see Chapter 8).
2 Remove the pressure cap from the top of the radiator by turning it anti-clockwise until it reaches a stop – **(see illustration 9.8)**. If you hear a hissing sound (indicating there is still pressure in the system), wait until it stops. Now press down on the cap and continue turning the cap until it can be removed. Also remove the coolant reservoir cap.
3 Position a suitable container beneath the water pump on the left-hand side of the engine. Slacken the clamp on the main hose to the water pump, then detach the hose and allow the coolant to completely drain from the system **(see illustrations)**.
4 Remove the coolant reservoir cap. Release the clamp and disconnect the hose from the bottom of the reservoir and allow the coolant to drain into the container **(see illustration)**. When the reservoir is empty, flush it out with clean water, then reconnect the hose.

Flushing

5 Flush the system with clean tap water by inserting a garden hose in the radiator filler neck. Allow the water to run through the system until it is clear and flows out cleanly. If the radiator is extremely corroded, remove it (see Chapter 3) and have it cleaned by a specialist.
6 Fit the coolant hose onto its union on the water pump and tighten the clamp.
7 Fill the cooling system with clean water mixed with a flushing compound. Make sure the flushing compound is compatible with aluminium components, and follow the manufacturer's instructions carefully. Fit the

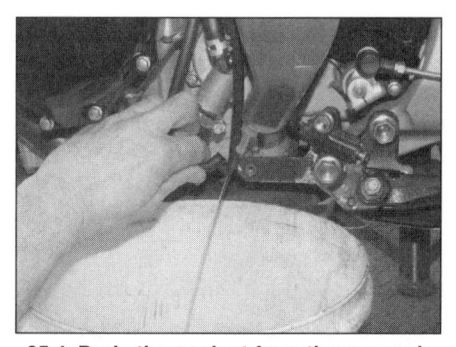

25.4 Drain the coolant from the reservoir as well

radiator cap and the reservoir cap.
8 Start the engine and allow it to reach normal operating temperature. Let it run for about ten minutes.
9 Stop the engine. Let it cool for a while, then cover the pressure cap with a heavy rag and turn it anti-clockwise to the first stop, releasing any pressure that may be present in the system. Once the hissing stops, push down on the cap and remove it completely.
10 Drain the system once again.
11 Fill the system with clean water and repeat the procedure in Steps 5 to 10.

Refilling

12 Fit the coolant hose onto its union on the water pump and tighten the clamp.
13 Fill the system via the radiator filler neck with the proper coolant mixture (see this Chapter's Specifications), until it reaches the base of the neck **(see illustration)**. **Note:** *Pour the coolant in slowly to minimise the amount of air entering the system.*
14 When the system is full (all the way up to the base of the radiator filler neck), tilt the motorcycle from side to side and allow any trapped air to escape. Top the radiator up to the base of the filler neck. Do not fit the pressure cap.
15 Start the engine and allow it to idle for 2 to

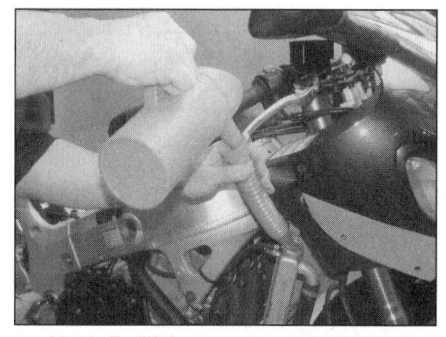

25.13 Refill the system as described

3 minutes. Flick the throttle twistgrip part open 3 or 4 times, so that the engine speed rises to approximately 4000 – 5000 rpm, then stop the engine. This process will bleed any trapped air bubbles from the system. Wiggle the bike about again to free any trapped air bubbles.
16 If necessary, top up the coolant level to the base of the radiator filler neck, then install the pressure cap. Also top up the coolant reservoir to the FULL level mark (see *Daily (pre-ride) checks*).
17 Start the engine and allow it to reach normal operating temperature, then shut it off. Let the engine cool then remove the pressure cap as described in Step 9. Check that the coolant level is still up to the base of the radiator filler neck. If it's low, add the specified mixture until it reaches the base of the filler neck. Refit the cap.
18 Check the coolant level in the reservoir and top it up if necessary.
19 Check the system for leaks. Install the fairing side panels (see Chapter 8).
20 Do not dispose of the old coolant by pouring it down the drain. Instead pour it into a heavy plastic container, cap it tightly and take it into an authorised disposal site or service station – see **Warning** at the beginning of this Section.

1•24 Routine maintenance and servicing

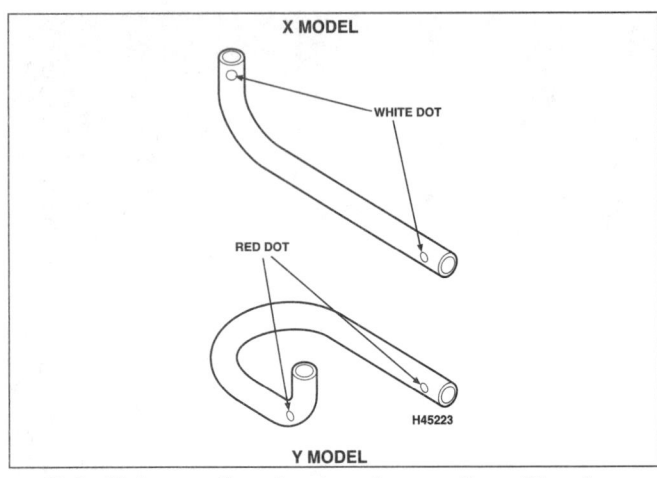

28.3a Make sure the return hose is correctly positioned . . .

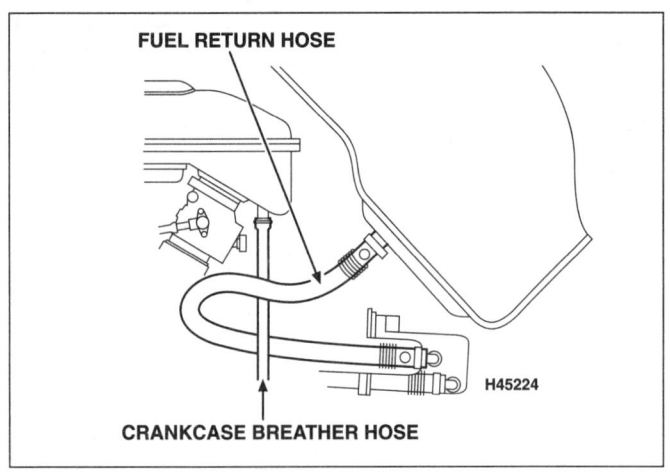

28.3b . . . and routed

Every four years

26 Brake hose renewal

Every four years

1 The hoses deteriorate with age and should be renewed regardless of their apparent condition. Refer to Chapter 7 and disconnect the brake hoses from the master cylinders and calipers. Always replace the banjo union sealing washers with new ones.

27 Clutch hose renewal

Every four years

1 The hose deteriorates with age and should be renewed regardless of its apparent condition. Refer to Chapter 2 and disconnect the hose from the master cylinder and release cylinder. Always replace the banjo union sealing washers with new ones.

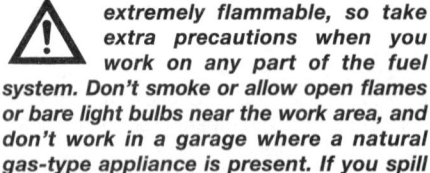

28 Fuel hose renewal

Every four years

⚠ *Warning: Petrol (gasoline) is extremely flammable, so take extra precautions when you work on any part of the fuel system. Don't smoke or allow open flames or bare light bulbs near the work area, and don't work in a garage where a natural gas-type appliance is present. If you spill any fuel on your skin, rinse it off immediately with soap and water. When you perform any kind of work on the fuel system, wear safety glasses and have a fire extinguisher suitable for a Class B type fire (flammable liquids) on hand.*

1 The fuel system hoses should be renewed at the first signs of cracking or hardening, or at the specified interval regardless of their apparent condition. This includes all the vent and drain hoses, and the vacuum hoses. You should also renew the PAIR system hoses, and on California models the EVAP system hoses (see Chapter 4).

2 Remove the air filter housing (see Chapter 4). Disconnect the hoses, noting the routing of each hose and where and how it connects (see Chapter 4, referring to the relevant Section). It is advisable to make a sketch of the various hoses before removing them to ensure they are correctly installed.

3 Secure each new hose to its unions using new clamps (where fitted). On late X and all Y models, make sure the white (X model) or red (Y model) dot marks face the left-hand side of the engine **(see illustration)**. On all X and Y models route the hose round the crankcase breather hose as shown **(see illustration)**.

4 Run the engine and check for leaks before taking the machine out on the road.

Non-scheduled maintenance

29 Cylinder compression check

1 Poor engine performance can be caused by many things, including leaking valves, incorrect valve clearances, a leaking head gasket, or worn pistons, rings and/or cylinder walls. A cylinder compression check will help pinpoint these conditions and can also indicate the presence of excessive carbon deposits in the cylinder heads.

2 The only tools required are a compression gauge and a spark plug wrench. A compression gauge with a threaded end for the spark plug hole (10 mm dia.) is preferable to the type that requires hand pressure to maintain a tight seal. Depending on the outcome of the initial test, a squirt-type oil can may also be needed.

3 Make sure the valve clearances are correctly set (see Section 22) and that the cylinder head fasteners are tightened to the correct torque setting (see Chapter 2).

4 Refer to *Fault Finding Equipment* in the Reference section for details of the compression test. Refer to the specifications at the beginning of the Chapter for compression figures.

30 Engine oil pressure check

1 The oil pressure warning light should come on when the ignition (main) switch is turned ON and extinguish a few seconds after the engine is started – this serves as a check that the warning light bulb is sound. If the oil pressure light comes on whilst the engine is running, low oil pressure is indicated – stop the engine immediately and carry out an oil level check (see *Daily (pre-ride) checks*).

2 An oil pressure check must be carried out if

Routine maintenance and servicing

the warning light comes on when the engine is running yet the oil level is good (Step 1). It can also provide useful information about the condition of the engine's lubrication system.

3 To check the oil pressure, a suitable gauge and adapter (which screws into the crankcase) will be needed. Suzuki provide the components (Pt. Nos. 09915-74520 (hose), 09915-74540 (adapter) and 09915-77330 (gauge)) for this purpose, or one can be obtained commercially. You will also need a container and some rags to catch and mop up any residual oil that gets lost in between removing the main oil gallery plug and installing the gauge. Check the engine oil level after installing the gauge and replenish if necessary *(see Daily (pre-ride) checks)*.

4 Remove the right-hand fairing side panel (see Chapter 8).

5 Unscrew the main oil gallery plug, located on the right-hand side of the engine just above the oil pressure switch, and swiftly screw the gauge assembly in its place **(see illustration)**. Discard the sealing washer on the plug and obtain a new one.

6 Warm the engine up to normal operating temperature – Suzuki specifies 10 mins at 2000 rpm in the summer, and 20 mins at 2000 rpm in the winter.

7 Increase the engine speed to 3000 rpm whilst watching the gauge reading. The oil pressure should be similar to that given in the Specifications at the start of this Chapter. Stop the engine.

8 Unscrew the gauge assembly and immediately install the oil gallery plug using a new sealing washer, tightening it to the torque setting specified at the beginning of the Chapter.

9 If the pressure is significantly lower than the standard, either the pressure regulator is stuck open, the oil pump or its drive mechanism is faulty, the oil strainer or filter is blocked, or there is other engine damage. Also make sure the correct grade oil is being used. Begin diagnosis by checking the oil filter, strainer and relief valve, then the oil pump (see Chapter 2). If those items check out okay, chances are the bearing oil clearances are excessive and the engine needs to be overhauled.

10 If the pressure is too high, either an oil passage is clogged, the relief valve is stuck closed or the wrong grade of oil is being used.

11 Check the oil level (see *Daily (pre-ride) checks*). Install the fairing side panel (see Chapter 8).

31 Wheel bearing check

1 Wheel bearings will wear over a period of time and result in handling problems.

2 Support the motorcycle upright on its centrestand or on an auxiliary stand, and support it so that the wheel being checked is off the ground. Check for any play in the bearings by pushing and pulling the wheel against the axle **(see illustration)** – turn the steering to full lock to keep it steady when checking the front wheel. Also spin the wheel and check that it rotates smoothly.

3 If any play is detected in the hub, or if the wheel does not rotate smoothly (and this is not due to brake or transmission drag), remove the wheels and check the bearings for wear or damage (see Chapter 7). If in doubt replace them with new ones.

32 Steering head bearing lubrication

1 Over a period of time the grease will harden or may be washed out of the bearings by incorrect use of jet washes.

2 Disassemble the steering head for re-greasing of the bearings. Refer to Chapter 6 for details.

33 Swingarm and suspension linkage bearing lubrication

1 Over a period of time the grease will harden or dirt will penetrate the bearings.

2 The suspension is not equipped with grease nipples. Remove the swingarm and suspension linkage as described in Chapter 6 for greasing of the bearings.

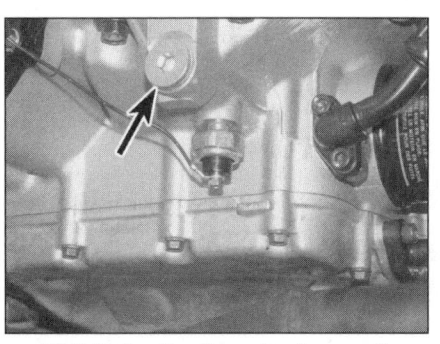

30.5 Main oil gallery plug (arrowed)

31.2 Checking for play in the wheel bearings

34 Brake master cylinder and caliper seal renewal

1 The seals will deteriorate over a period of time and lose their effectiveness, leading to sticking operation or fluid loss, or allowing the ingress of air and dirt. Refer to Chapter 7 and dismantle the components for seal renewal.

35 Clutch master cylinder and release cylinder seal renewal

1 The seals will deteriorate over a period of time and lose their effectiveness, leading to sticking operation or fluid loss, or allowing the ingress of air and dirt. Refer to Chapter 2 and dismantle the components for seal renewal.

36 Front fork oil change

1 Fork oil degrades over a period of time and loses its damping qualities. Refer to the fork oil change procedure for your model in Chapter 6. The forks do not need to be completely disassembled.

37 Battery – check

1 All models are fitted with a sealed MF (maintenance free) battery. **Note:** *Do not attempt to remove the battery caps to check the electrolyte level or battery specific gravity. Removal will damage the caps, resulting in electrolyte leakage and battery damage.* All that should be done is to check that the terminals are clean and tight and that the casing is not damaged or leaking. See Chapter 9 for further details.

2 If the machine is not in regular use, remove the battery and give it a refresher charge every month to six weeks (see Chapter 9).

38 Sidestand and starter interlock circuit

1 Check the stand springs for damage and distortion. The springs must be capable of retracting the stand fully and holding it retracted when the motorcycle is in use. If a spring is sagged or broken it must be replaced with a new one.

2 Lubricate the stand pivots regularly (see Section 15).

3 Check the stand and its mount for bends and cracks, and that the bolts and nut are tightened to the correct torque settings (see

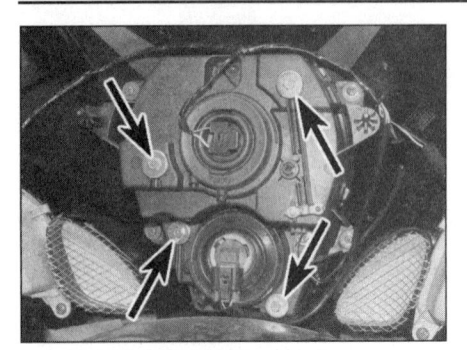

39.2 Headlight adjustment screws (arrowed)

Chapter 6). If necessary stands can often be repaired by welding.

4 Check the operation of the starter interlock circuit by shifting the transmission into neutral, retracting the stand and starting the engine. Pull in the clutch lever and select a gear. Extend the sidestand. The engine should stop as the sidestand is extended. Also check that the engine cannot be started when the sidestand is down and the engine is in gear, and that the engine stops if a gear is selected with the engine running and the sidestand down. If the circuit does not operate as described, check the various switches (sidestand, gear position and clutch) and the diodes in the circuit (see Chapter 4 for the gear position switch and Chapter 9 for other components).

39 Headlight aim check

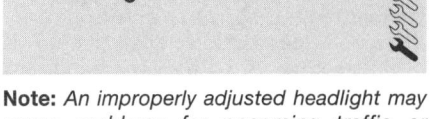

Note: *An improperly adjusted headlight may cause problems for oncoming traffic or provide poor, unsafe illumination of the road ahead. Before adjusting the headlight aim, be sure to consult with local traffic laws and regulations – for UK models refer to MOT Test Checks in the Reference section.*

1 The headlight beams can adjusted both horizontally and vertically. Before making any adjustment, check that the tyre pressures are correct and the suspension is adjusted as required. Make any adjustments to the headlight aim with the machine on level ground, with the fuel tank half full and with an assistant sitting on the seat. If the bike is usually ridden with a passenger on the back, have a second assistant to do this.

2 Horizontal adjustment of the low (dipped) beam is made by turning the adjuster screw on the bottom left of the upper beam unit **(see illustration)**. Vertical adjustment is made by turning the adjuster screw on the top right of the unit. Access the adjusters by removing the cockpit trim panels (see Chapter 8), and if required for better access the instrument cluster (leaving the fairing in place, but removing the windshield if required).

3 Horizontal adjustment of the high (main) beam is made by turning the adjuster screw on the top left of the lower beam unit **(see illustration 39.2)**. Vertical adjustment is made by turning the adjuster screw on the bottom right of the unit. Access the adjusters by removing the panel from the underside of the fairing – it is secured by six trim clips.

Chapter 2
Engine, clutch and transmission

Contents

Alternator	see Chapter 9
Balancer shaft assembly	24
Cam chain, tensioner blade and guide blades	10
Cam chain tensioner	9
Camshafts and followers	8
Clutch	16
Clutch check	see Chapter 1
Clutch master cylinder	17
Clutch release cylinder	18
Clutch release mechanism bleeding	19
Component access	2
Connecting rods	29
Crankcase inspection and servicing	26
Crankcase separation and reassembly	25
Crankshaft and main bearings	28
Cylinder block	13
Cylinder compression check	see Chapter 1
Cylinder head removal and installation	11
Cylinder head and valve overhaul	12
Engine removal and installation	4
Engine disassembly and reassembly – general information	5
Gearchange mechanism	21
General information	1
Idle speed check	see Chapter 1
Main and connecting rod bearing information	27
Major engine repair – general information	3
Oil cooler	6
Oil and filter change	see Chapter 1
Oil level check	see Daily (pre-ride) checks
Oil pressure switch	see Chapter 9
Oil sump, strainer and pressure regulator	23
Oil pump	20
Pistons	14
Piston rings	15
Running-in procedure	33
Selector drum and forks	32
Spark plug check	see Chapter 1
Starter clutch	22
Starter motor	see Chapter 9
Transmission shaft overhaul	31
Transmission shaft removal and installation	30
Valve clearance check	see Chapter 1
Valve cover	7

Degrees of difficulty

Easy, suitable for novice with little experience	**Fairly easy,** suitable for beginner with some experience	**Fairly difficult,** suitable for competent DIY mechanic	**Difficult,** suitable for experienced DIY mechanic	**Very difficult,** suitable for expert DIY or professional

Specifications

General

Type	Four-stroke in-line four cylinder
Capacity	1299 cc
Bore	81 mm
Stroke	63 mm
Compression ratio	11.0 : 1
Cylinder identification	1–2–3–4, from left to right
Firing order	1–2–4–3
Camshafts	DOHC, chain driven
Clutch	Wet multi-plate with back-torque limiter and hydraulic release
Cooling system	Liquid cooled
Transmission	Six-speed constant mesh
Final drive	Chain and sprockets

Camshafts

Intake camshaft lobe height
    Standard .... 36.780 to 36.848 mm
    Service limit .... 36.48 mm
Exhaust camshaft lobe height
    Standard .... 35.480 to 35.548 mm
    Service limit .... 35.18 mm

Camshafts (continued)
Camshaft runout (max) .... 0.10 mm
Camshaft bearing oil clearance
   Standard .... 0.032 to 0.066 mm
   Service limit .... 0.150 mm
Journal diameter .... 23.959 to 23.980 mm
Journal holder internal diameter .... 24.012 to 24.025 mm

Cylinder head
Warpage (max) .... 0.20 mm

Valves, guides and springs
Valve size
   Intake valve .... 33 mm
   Exhaust valve .... 27.5 mm
Valve clearances .... see Chapter 1
Stem diameter
   Intake valve .... 4.975 to 4.990 mm
   Exhaust valve .... 4.955 to 4.970 mm
Guide bore diameter .... 5.000 to 5.012 mm
Stem-to-guide clearance
   Intake valve .... 0.010 to 0.037 mm
   Exhaust valve .... 0.030 to 0.057 mm
Stem deflection (max – see text) .... 0.35 mm
Seat width .... 0.9 to 1.1 mm
Head thickness (min) .... 0.5 mm
Radial runout at head (max) .... 0.03 mm
Stem runout (max) .... 0.05 mm
Spring free lengths (min)
   Outer spring .... 35.1 mm
   Inner spring .... 45.2 mm

Cylinders
Bore diameter
   Standard .... 81.000 to 81.015 mm
   Wear limit .... see Piston-to-bore clearance
Taper (max) .... 0.05 mm
Ovality (max) .... 0.05 mm
Warpage (max) .... 0.20 mm
Cylinder compression
   Standard .... 171 to 228 psi (12 to 16 Bar)
   Service limit .... 128 psi (8.8 Bar)
   Max. difference between cylinders .... 28 psi (2 Bar)

Pistons
Piston diameter (measured 15 mm up from skirt, at 90° to piston pin axis)
   Standard .... 80.975 to 80.990 mm
   Service limit .... 80.880 mm
Piston-to-bore clearance
   Standard .... 0.020 to 0.030 mm
   Service limit .... 0.120 mm
Piston pin diameter
   Standard .... 19.995 to 20.000 mm
   Service limit .... 19.980 mm
Piston pin bore diameter
   Standard .... 20.002 to 20.008 mm
   Service limit .... 20.030 mm
Piston pin-to-bore clearance
   Standard .... 0.002 to 0.013 mm
   Service limit .... 0.05 mm
Connecting rod small-end internal diameter
   Standard .... 20.010 to 20.018 mm
   Service limit .... 20.040 mm
Piston pin-to-connecting rod small-end clearance
   Standard .... 0.010 to 0.023 mm
   Service limit .... 0.06 mm

Piston rings
Ring thickness
  Top ring .... 1.17 to 1.19 mm
  2nd ring .... 0.97 to 0.99 mm
Groove thickness
  Top ring .... 1.21 to 1.23 mm
  2nd ring .... 1.01 to 1.03 mm
  Oil ring .... 2.01 to 2.03 mm
Ring-to-groove clearance (max)
  Top ring .... 0.18 mm
  2nd ring .... 0.15 mm
End gap (free)
  Top ring
    Standard .... 7.3 mm (approx)
    Service limit .... 5.8 mm
  2nd ring
    X model
      Standard .... 8.1 mm (approx)
      Service limit .... 6.4 mm
    Y model onwards
      Standard .... 11.4 mm (approx)
      Service limit .... 9.1 mm
End gap (installed)
  Top ring
    Standard .... 0.08 to 0.20 mm
    Service limit .... 0.50 mm
  2nd ring
    Standard .... 0.15 to 0.30 mm
    Service limit .... 0.50 mm

Clutch – X, Y and K1 models
Friction plates (see illustration 16.30a for identification)
  Quantity
    Type A 8
    Type B 2
  Thickness
    Type A
      Standard .... 2.92 to 3.08 mm
      Service limit .... 2.62 mm
    Type B
      Standard .... 3.72 to 3.88 mm
      Service limit .... 3.42 mm
  Tab width
    Type A
      Standard .... 13.85 to 13.96 mm
      Service limit .... 13.05 mm
    Type B
      Standard .... 13.90 to 14.00 mm
      Service limit .... 13.10 mm
Plain plates (see illustration 16.30a for identification)
  Quantity
    Type A 7
    Type B 2
  Thickness
    Type A .... 2.0 mm
    Type B .... 2.3 mm
  Warpage (max) .... 0.10 mm
Spring free length
  X model
    Standard .... 24.88 mm
    Service limit .... 23.70 mm
  Y and K1 models
    Standard .... 28.96 mm
    Service limit .... 27.60 mm

Clutch – K2 model onwards

Friction plate (see illustration 16.30b for identification)
  Quantity
    Type A 8
    Type B 1
    Type C 1
  Thickness
    Type A
      Standard .... 2.92 to 3.08 mm
      Service limit .... 2.62 mm
    Type B and C
      Standard .... 3.72 to 3.88 mm
      Service limit .... 3.42 mm
  Tab width
    Type A
      Standard .... 13.85 to 13.96 mm
      Service limit .... 13.05 mm
    Type B and C
      Standard .... 13.9 to 14.0 mm
      Service limit .... 13.1 mm
Plain plate (see illustration 16.30b for identification)
  Quantity
    Type A .... 5 to 8 (standard 7)
    Type B .... 1 to 4 (standard 2)
  Thickness
    Type A .... 2.0 mm
    Type B .... 2.3 mm
  Warpage (max) .... 0.10 mm
Spring free length (min) .... 28.96 mm

Clutch release mechanism

Clutch fluid type .... DOT 4
Master cylinder bore ID .... 14.000 to 14.043 mm
Master cylinder piston OD .... 13.957 to 13.984 mm
Release cylinder bore ID
  X, Y and K1 models .... 38.100 to 38.162 mm
  K2 model onwards .... 35.700 to 35.762 mm
Release cylinder piston OD
  X, Y and K1 models .... 38.042 to 38.075 mm
  K2 model onwards .... 35.650 to 35.675 mm

Starter torque limiter – K3 and K4 models only

Slip torque range .... 33 to 52 Nm

Crankshaft and main bearings

Main bearing oil clearance
  Standard .... 0.016 to 0.040 mm
  Service limit .... 0.08 mm
Main journal diameter .... 39.976 to 40.000 mm
End-float .... 0.055 to 0.110 mm
Thrust bearing thickness
  Right-hand bearing .... 2.425 to 2.450 mm
  Left-hand bearing .... Selective fit ranging from 2.350 to 2.500 mm
Runout (max) .... 0.05 mm

Connecting rods and big-end bearings

Big-end side clearance
  Standard .... 0.10 to 0.20 mm
  Service limit .... 0.30 mm
Big-end width .... 20.95 to 21.00 mm
Crankpin width .... 21.10 to 21.15 mm
Big-end bearing oil clearance
  Standard .... 0.032 to 0.056 mm
  Service limit .... 0.08 mm
Crankpin diameter .... 37.976 to 38.000 mm
For connecting rod small-end specifications see under 'Pistons'.

Lubrication system

Oil type, viscosity and capacity	see Chapter 1
Oil pressure (at main oil gallery plug, with engine warm)	see Chapter 1

Selector drum and forks

Selector fork end thickness	4.8 to 4.9 mm
Pinion groove width	5.0 to 5.1 mm
Fork-to-groove clearance	
Standard	0.1 to 0.3 mm
Service limit	0.5 mm

Transmission

Primary reduction ratio	1.596 : 1 (83/52T)
Final reduction ratio	2.352 : 1 (40/17T)
1st gear ratio	2.615 : 1 (34/13T)
2nd gear ratio	1.937 : 1 (31/16T)
3rd gear ratio	1.526 : 1 (29/19T)
4th gear ratio	1.285 : 1 (27/21T)
5th gear ratio	1.136 : 1 (25/22T)
6th gear ratio	1.043 : 1 (24/23T)

Torque settings

Alternator oil jet	5 Nm
Balancer shaft cover bolt	10 Nm
Balancer shaft holder bolt	10 Nm
Cam chain stopper bolt	14 Nm
Cam chain tensioner blade pivot bolt	10 Nm
Cam chain tensioner cap bolt	
X and Y models	8 Nm
K1 model onwards	23 Nm
Cam chain tensioner mounting bolts	10 Nm
Cam chain tensioner oil hose banjo bolts – K1 model onwards	12 Nm
Cam chain top guide bolts	10 Nm
Camshaft holder bolts	10 Nm
Camshaft holder oil pipe bolts	10 Nm
Clutch cover bolts	10 Nm
Clutch hose banjo bolts	23 Nm
Clutch master cylinder mounting bolts	10 Nm
Clutch nut	95 Nm
Clutch pressure plate bolts	10 Nm
Clutch release cylinder bleed valve	7.5 Nm
Clutch spring holder bolts	23 Nm
Connecting rod bolts	
Initial setting	35 Nm
Final setting	67 Nm
Coolant inlet union-to-cylinder block bolts	10 Nm
Crankcase bolts	
Crankshaft journal 9 mm bolts	
Initial setting	18 Nm
Final setting	32 Nm
6 mm bolts	
Initial setting	6 Nm
Final setting	11 Nm
8 mm bolts	
Initial setting	13 Nm
Final setting	26 Nm
10 mm bolts	
Initial setting	28 Nm
Final setting	50 Nm
Crankshaft end cap	11 Nm
Crankcase oil pipe	
Banjo bolt to lower half	28 Nm
Union bolts to upper half	10 Nm
Cylinder block nuts	10 Nm

Torque settings (continued)

Cylinder head bolts
    10 mm bolts
        Initial setting .... 25 Nm
        Final setting .... 52 Nm
    6 mm bolts .... 10 Nm
Cylinder head oil hose-to-banjo bolts .... 20 Nm
Engine mounting bolts
    Adjuster bolts .... 10 Nm
    Adjuster bolt locknuts .... 45 Nm
    Front and middle mounting bolts .... 55 Nm
    Upper and lower rear mounting bolt nuts .... 75 Nm
    Spacer pinch bolt .... 35 Nm
Gearchange mechanism centralising spring locating pin ...... 19 Nm
Gearchange mechanism cover bolts .... 10 Nm
Gearchange selector drum cam plate bolt .... 10 Nm
Gearchange stopper arm bolt .... 10 Nm
Oil cooler hose bolts .... 10 Nm
Oil pump bolts .... 10 Nm
Oil strainer bolts .... 10 Nm
Oil sump bolts .... 10 Nm
Oil sump breather tube bolt .... 10 Nm
PAIR system pipe nuts .... 10 Nm
Piston oil jet bolts .... 10 Nm
Selector drum and fork retainer screws .... 8 Nm
Selector drum cam plate bolt .... 10 Nm
Sidestand bracket bolts .... 95 Nm
Starter clutch bolt .... 55 Nm
Starter clutch cover bolts .... 10 Nm
Starter idle/reduction or torque limiter gear cover bolts ..... 10 Nm
Timing mark inspection cap .... 23 Nm
Valve cover bolts .... 14 Nm

1 General information

The engine/transmission unit is a liquid-cooled in-line four cylinder, fitted across the frame. The engine has four valves per cylinder, operated by double overhead camshafts. The camshafts are driven by chain off the right-hand end of the crankshaft.

The engine/transmission unit is constructed in aluminium alloy and the crankcase splits horizontally. The crankcase incorporates a wet sump, pressure fed lubrication system, and houses an oil pump gear driven off the clutch housing. The water pump is driven off the oil pump via an interconnecting shaft. The one-piece forged crankshaft runs in five main bearings. The left-hand end of the crankshaft carries the alternator rotor. The ignition timing triggers are incorporated in the alternator rotor. The right-hand end of the crankshaft carries the starter clutch.

The clutch is a wet multi-plate and is gear driven off the crankshaft. The transmission is six-speed constant mesh. Final drive to the rear wheel is via a chain and sprockets.

2 Component access

Operations possible with the engine in the frame

The components and assemblies listed below can be removed without having to remove the engine/transmission assembly from the frame. If however, a number of areas require attention at the same time, removal of the engine is recommended.

    Valve cover
    Cam chain tensioner
    Camshafts
    Cam chain and blades
    Clutch
    Oil pump
    Gear position switch
    Starter clutch and idle/reduction gears
    Water pump
    Alternator
    Crankshaft position sensor
    Gearchange mechanism
    Clutch release cylinder
    Starter motor
    Oil pressure switch
    Oil sump, strainer and pressure relief valve
    Balancer shaft

Operations requiring engine removal

It is necessary to remove the engine/transmission assembly from the frame and separate the crankcase halves to gain access to the following components:

    Cylinder block
    Cylinder head
    Pistons
    Connecting rods
    Crankshaft
    Balancer shaft
    Transmission shafts
    Selector drum and forks

3 Major engine repair general information

1 It is not always easy to determine when or if an engine should be completely overhauled, as a number of factors must be considered.
2 High mileage is not necessarily an

Engine, clutch and transmission 2•7

indication that an overhaul is needed, while low mileage, on the other hand, does not preclude the need for an overhaul. Frequency of servicing is probably the single most important consideration. An engine that has regular and frequent oil and filter changes, as well as other required maintenance, will most likely give many miles of reliable service. Conversely, a neglected engine, or one which has not been run in properly, may require an overhaul very early in its life.

3 Exhaust smoke and excessive oil consumption are both indications that piston rings and/or valve guides are in need of attention, although make sure that the fault is not due to oil leakage.

4 If the engine is making obvious knocking or rumbling noises, the connecting rods and/or main bearings are probably at fault.

5 Loss of power, rough running, excessive valve train noise and high fuel consumption may also point to the need for an overhaul, especially if they are all present at the same time. If a complete tune-up does not remedy the situation, major mechanical work is the only solution.

6 An engine overhaul generally involves restoring the internal parts to the specifications of a new engine. The piston rings and main and connecting rod bearings are usually renewed during a major overhaul. Generally the valve seats are re-ground, since they are usually in less than perfect condition at this point. The end result should be a like new engine that will give as many trouble-free miles as the original.

7 Before beginning the engine overhaul, read through the related procedures to familiarise yourself with the scope and requirements of the job. Overhauling an engine is not all that difficult, but it is time consuming. Plan on the motorcycle being tied up for a minimum of two weeks. Check on the availability of parts and make sure that any necessary special tools, equipment and supplies are obtained in advance.

8 Most work can be done with typical workshop hand tools, although a number of precision measuring tools are required for inspecting parts to determine if they must be renewed. Often a dealer will handle the inspection of parts and offer advice concerning reconditioning and renewal. As a general rule, time is the primary cost of an overhaul so it does not pay to install worn or substandard parts.

9 As a final note, to ensure maximum life and minimum trouble from a rebuilt engine, everything must be assembled with care in a spotlessly clean environment.

4 Engine removal and installation

Peg spanners are required to slacken and tighten the adjuster bolts and their locknuts on three of the engine mounting bolts. If the Suzuki service tool (Pt. No. 09940-14990) is not available, suitable ones will have to be fabricated either from a piece of steel tubing, or better still by cutting old sockets. The advantage in using sockets is that a torque wrench can be applied when tightening, which in the case of the adjuster bolt is important. Note that as there are three different sizes required which means cutting up three different sockets (27 mm, 22 mm and 14 mm), it is probably worth buying the Suzuki tool.

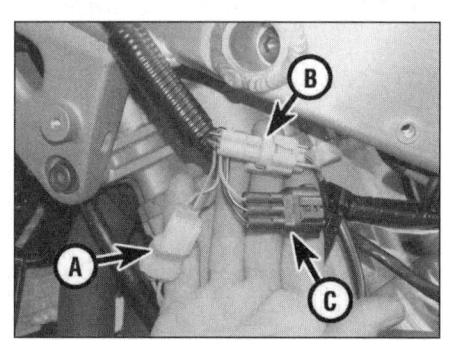

Caution: The engine is very heavy. Engine removal and installation should be carried out with the aid of at least one assistant; personal injury or damage could occur if the engine falls or is dropped. An hydraulic or mechanical floor jack should be used to support and lower or raise the engine.

Note: *The engine upper and lower rear mounting bolt nuts are self-locking, and Suzuki specify that once removed they should not be reused. It is best to order new ones before starting work in case there is any delay in obtaining them.*

Removal

1 Support the bike securely in an upright position on its centrestand if fitted or using an auxiliary stand. Do not use the sidestand to support the bike, firstly as it does not provide enough stability, and secondly as it is best to remove it for extra clearance. Work can be made easier by raising the machine to a suitable working height on an hydraulic ramp or other suitable platform. Make sure the motorcycle is secure and will not topple over (also see *Tools and Workshop Tips* in the Reference section).

2 If the engine is dirty, particularly around its mountings, wash it thoroughly before starting any major dismantling work. This makes working on the engine much easier and rules out the possibility of caked on lumps of dirt falling into some vital component.

3 Remove the fairing side panels and the bottom panel (see Chapter 8).

4 Remove the rider's seat (see Chapter 8). Disconnect the negative (–) lead from the battery (see Chapter 9).

5 Drain the engine oil and remove the oil filter (see Chapter 1).

6 Drain the coolant (see Chapter 1).

7 Remove the fuel tank, the air filter housing and the throttle bodies (see Chapter 4). Plug the engine intake ducts with clean rag.

8 Remove the oil cooler along with its hoses (see Section 6).

9 Remove the radiator along with its hoses (i.e. detach the hoses from the thermostat housing and water pump instead of from the radiator) (see Chapter 3). Also remove the coolant reservoir (see Chapter 3).

10 Remove the exhaust system (Chapter 4).

11 Remove the oil cooler and radiator mounting brackets – each is secured by two bolts **(see illustration)**. Note which way round they fit.

12 If required remove the PAIR system control valve (see Chapter 4). If you prefer to leave the valve in place, on K2 models onwards disconnect the wiring connector **(see illustration)**.

13 Trace the wiring from the oil pressure switch on the right-hand side of the engine and disconnect it at the connector, noting that

4.11 Unscrew the bolts (arrowed) and remove the brackets

4.12 PAIR control valve wiring connector (A), sidestand switch wiring connector (B), speed sensor wiring connector (C) – K3 model shown

2•8 Engine, clutch and transmission

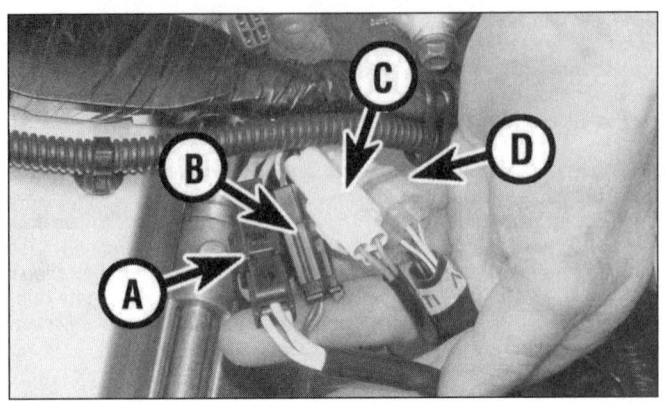

4.13a Alternator wiring connector (A), crankshaft position sensor wiring connector (B), gear position switch wiring connector (C), oil pressure switch/oxygen sensor wiring connector (D) – K3 model shown

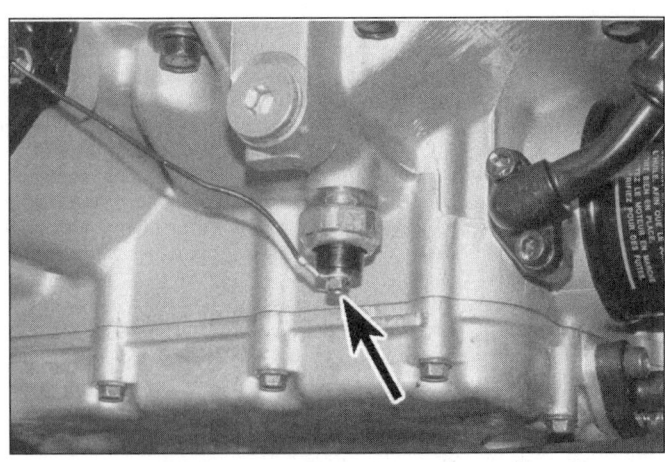

4.13b Oil pressure switch wiring screw (arrowed)

on K2 models onwards the connector is common with the oxygen sensor sub-loom **(see illustration)**. If preferred you can undo the screw securing the oil pressure switch wire to the switch, then free the wiring, on K2 models onwards including the oxygen sensor sub-loom wiring, from its clips and leave it attached to the loom – if you do this, note the routing of the wiring and coil it out the way **(see illustration)**.

14 Pull back the rubber boot covering the starter motor terminal, then unscrew the nut and detach the lead **(see illustration)**. Secure the lead clear of the engine. Remove the starter motor now if required (see Chapter 9), or do so after the engine has been removed if necessary. If you do not remove the motor now unscrew the bolt securing the earth lead and detach the lead, positioning it clear of the engine.

15 Trace the gear position switch wiring from the top of the clutch cover, freeing it from any ties and noting its routing, and disconnect it at the connector **(see illustration 4.13a)**.

16 Trace the alternator and crankshaft position sensor wiring from the alternator cover on the left-hand side of the engine, freeing it from any ties and noting its routing, and disconnect it at the connectors **(see illustration 4.13a)**.

17 Trace the wiring from the sidestand switch, freeing it from any ties and noting its routing, and disconnect it at the connector **(see illustration 4.12)**. Feed the wiring down to the switch. Unscrew the two bolts securing the sidestand bracket and remove the complete stand assembly **(see illustration)**.

18 Disconnect the wiring connector from the engine coolant temperature sensor, which is on the back of the cylinder head on the left-hand side.

19 Disconnect the wiring connector from each ignition coil and from the camshaft position sensor **(see illustration)**. Carefully pull the coils/caps off the spark plugs. Release the trim clip securing the rubber heat shield to the frame on the right-hand side then fold the shield up and out of the way.

20 Remove the front sprocket (see Chapter 6). If required withdraw the clutch pushrod from the engine **(see illustration)**.

21 At this point, position an hydraulic or mechanical jack under the engine with a block of wood between the jack head and engine **(see illustration)**. Make sure the jack is centrally positioned so the engine will not topple in any direction when the last mounting bolt is removed. Raise the jack to take the weight of the engine, but make sure it is not lifting the bike and taking the weight of that as well. The idea is to support the engine so that there is no pressure on any of the mounting bolts once they have been slackened, so they can be easily withdrawn. Note that it may be

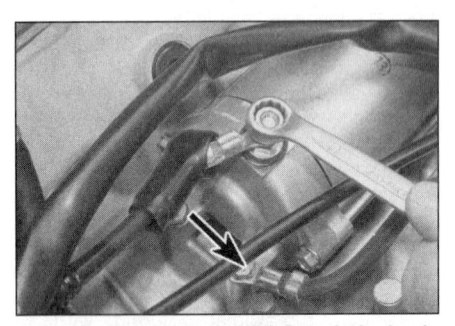

4.14 Unscrew the nut and detach the lead. If you are not removing the motor unscrew the bolt and detach the earth lead (arrowed)

4.17 Unscrew the bolts and remove the stand assembly

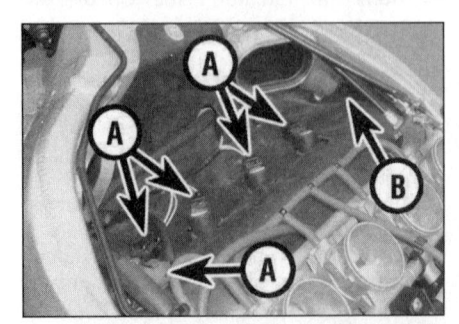

4.19 Disconnect the wiring connectors (A), then remove the coils/plug caps. Release the trim clip (B) and lift the shield

4.20 Withdraw the pushrod now if required

4.21a Support the engine using a jack as shown

Engine, clutch and transmission 2•9

4.21b Front mounting bolt (A), middle mounting bolt (B), upper rear mounting bolt (C), lower rear mounting bolt (D)

4.22 Unscrew the front bolt (arrowed) and the middle bolt on the left-hand side

4.23a Slacken the pinch bolt (arrowed) . . .

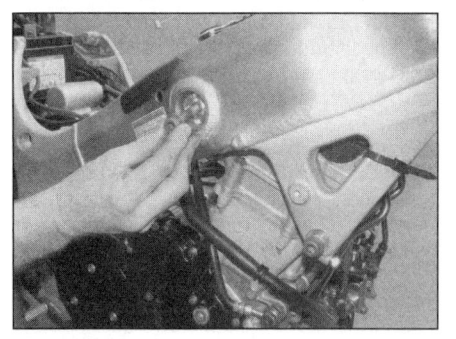

4.23b . . . then unscrew the bolts

4.25 Unscrew the nuts on the rear mounting bolts

4.26 Thread the locknuts off the adjuster bolts if required

necessary to adjust the jack as some of the bolts are removed to relieve the stress transferred to the other bolts **(see illustration)**.

> **HAYNES HiNT** *After removing each engine mounting bolt, make a note of its location and fit any adjuster, locknut, nut or spacer that goes with the bolt back onto it, in the correct order and way round – this ensures that everything can be reassembled with ease later on.*

22 Unscrew the front and middle mounting bolts on the left-hand side **(see illustration)**.
23 Slacken the pinch bolt clamping the front mounting bolt spacer on the right-hand side **(see illustration)**. Unscrew the front and middle mounting bolts on the right-hand side

(see illustration). Push the spacer for the front mounting away from the engine until the flange contacts the frame.
24 Slacken the locknut on the middle mounting adjuster bolt on the right-hand side using the Suzuki tool or a suitable peg spanner (see **Tool Tip** above). The locknut can remain loose on the adjuster bolt, or it can be removed if required. Now unscrew the adjuster bolt so it is flush with the inside of the frame.
25 Unscrew the nuts on the right-hand ends of the upper and lower rear mounting bolts, counter-holding the bolt heads on the left-hand side if necessary **(see illustration)**.
26 Slacken the locknuts on the upper and lower rear mounting adjuster bolts using the Suzuki tool or a suitable peg spanner (see **Tool Tip** above). The locknuts can remain loose on the adjuster bolts, or they can be removed if required **(see illustration)**. Now

unscrew the adjuster bolts so they are flush with the inside of the frame.
27 Check that the engine is properly supported by the jack, and have your assistant ready holding the engine. Withdraw the upper rear mounting bolt from the left-hand side and remove the two spacers that fit between the engine and frame on each side **(see illustration)**.
28 Check that all wiring, cables and hoses are well clear of the engine and frame. Withdraw the lower rear mounting bolt from the left-hand side, then carefully lower the engine on the jack, manoeuvring it as required so the drive chain can be slipped off the end of the output shaft **(see illustrations)**. When the jack is fully lowered, lift the engine off it, remove the jack, and manoeuvre the engine out of either side of the frame.
29 If required remove the spacer from the front mounting on the right-hand side (if you don't, tighten the pinch bolt so it holds the

4.27 Withdraw the upper rear bolt and remove the spacers

4.28a Withdraw the lower rear bolt . . .

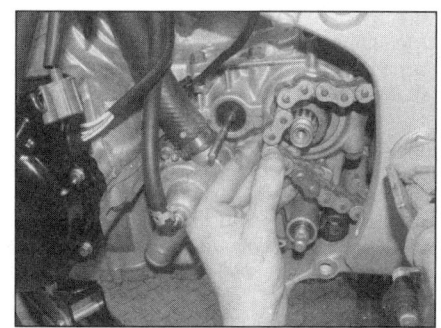

4.28b . . . then manoeuvre the engine so the chain can be slipped off the shaft

4.29 Remove the adjuster bolts if required

spacer in the mount). Remove the adjuster bolts from the frame **(see illustration)**.

Installation

30 Fit the adjuster bolts into the frame, threading them in from the outside until they are flush with the inside – the 39 mm adjuster is for the middle mount on the right-hand side, and the 43 mm adjusters are for the upper and lower rear mounts **(see illustrations 4.29 and 4.21b)**. If removed fit the spacer for the front mounting bolt on the right-hand side into the frame, making sure the flanged end is on the inside – push the spacer all the way in so the flange is against the frame.

31 Manoeuvre the engine into position under the frame and lift it onto the jack. Raise the engine, taking care not to catch any part of it on the frame or to trap any wiring, and loop the drive chain around the output shaft as early as possible **(see illustration 4.28b)**. Raise and move the engine as required to align the lower rear mounting bolt holes. When the holes are aligned slide the lower rear mounting bolt (the shorter of the two long bolts) through from the left-hand side and into the adjuster bolt **(see illustration 4.28a)**.

32 Raise the jack further as required until the remaining mounting holes align.

33 Slide the upper rear mounting bolt through from the left-hand side and into the adjuster bolt, locating the spacers between the engine and frame on each side as you do **(see illustration 4.27)**.

34 Install the front and middle mounting bolts (45 mm long) for the left-hand side and tighten them finger-tight **(see illustration 4.22)**.

35 Tighten the three adjuster bolts evenly and a bit at a time to the torque setting specified at the beginning of the chapter, using the Suzuki tool or suitable peg spanners as on removal. While tightening them make sure the engine is pressed against the left-hand side of the frame and that the left-hand spacer for the upper rear mounting bolt is tight between the engine and frame.

36 If removed, thread the locknuts onto the adjuster bolts **(see illustration 4.26)**. Tighten the locknuts to the specified torque using the Suzuki tool or suitable peg spanners as on removal. It is advisable to make a reference mark between the adjuster bolt and the frame to make sure it does not turn as the locknut is being tightened.

37 Tighten the front and middle mounting bolts on the left-hand side to the specified torque setting **(see illustration 4.22)**.

38 Push the spacer for the front mounting bolt on the right-hand side against the engine. Install the front and middle mounting bolts on the right-hand side and tighten them to the specified torque **(see illustration 4.23b)**.

39 Fit new nuts onto the left-hand ends of the upper and lower rear mounting bolts and tighten them to the specified torque, counter-holding the bolt heads to prevent them turning **(see illustration 4.25)**.

40 Tighten the pinch bolt clamping the front mounting bolt spacer on the right-hand side to the specified torque **(see illustration 4.23a)**.

41 The remainder of the installation procedure is the reverse of removal, noting the following points:

- Use new gaskets on the exhaust pipe connections.
- Apply a suitable threadlocking compound to the sidestand bracket bolts and tighten them to the specified torque **(see illustration 4.17)**.
- Clean any corrosion off the clutch pushrod and smear the rod with grease **(see illustration 4.20)**.
- When fitting the gearchange linkage arm onto the shaft, align the slit in the arm with mark made on the shaft, and tighten the pinch bolt.
- The radiator and oil cooler brackets fit with the ledge along the bolt hole section at the bottom, and the longer bracket is for the oil cooler **(see illustration 4.11)**.
- Make sure all wires, cables and hoses are correctly routed and connected, and secured by any clips or ties.
- Refill the engine with oil and coolant (see Chapter 1).
- Adjust the throttle cable freeplay.
- Adjust the drive chain (see Chapter 1).
- Start the engine and check that there are no oil or coolant leaks. Adjust the idle speed (see Chapter 1).

5 Engine disassembly and reassembly – general information

Disassembly

1 Before disassembling the engine, thoroughly clean and degrease its external surfaces. This will prevent contamination of the engine internals, and will also make working a lot easier and cleaner. A high flash-point solvent, such as paraffin (kerosene) can be used, or better still, a proprietary engine degreaser such as Gunk. Use old paintbrushes and toothbrushes to work the solvent into the various recesses of the casings. Take care to exclude solvent or water from the electrical components and intake and exhaust ports.

⚠ **Warning: The use of petrol (gasoline) as a cleaning agent should be avoided because of the risk of fire.**

2 When clean and dry, position the engine on the workbench, leaving suitable clear area for working. Make sure the engine is stable – some strategically placed blocks of wood under the crankcase or engine covers will help support it and keep it stable while you work. Gather a selection of small containers, plastic bags and some labels so that parts can be grouped together in an easily identifiable manner. Also get some paper and a pen so that notes can be taken. You will also need a supply of clean rag, which should be as absorbent as possible.

3 Before commencing work, read through the appropriate section so that some idea of the necessary procedure can be gained. When removing components note that great force is seldom required, unless specified (checking the specified torque setting of the particular bolt being removed will indicate how tight it is, and therefore how much force should be needed). In many cases, a component's reluctance to be removed is indicative of an incorrect approach or removal method – if in any doubt, re-check with the text.

4 When disassembling the engine, keep 'mated' parts together (including gears, cylinder bores, pistons, connecting rods, valves, etc. that have been in contact with each other during engine operation). These 'mated' parts must be reused or replaced as an assembly. It is worth obtaining a large sheet of card and marking it according to the layout of the engine so that parts can be placed on it and stored in relation to their position in the engine as they are removed.

5 A complete engine/transmission disassembly should be done in the following general order with reference to the appropriate Sections.

Remove the valve cover
Remove the cam chain tensioner and camshafts
Remove the cylinder head
Remove the cylinder block
Remove the pistons
Remove the clutch
Remove the oil pump
Remove the gear position switch (see Chapter 9)
Remove the starter clutch and idle/reduction gears
Remove the cam chain and blades
Remove the starter motor (see Chapter 9)
Remove the alternator rotor (see Chapter 9)
Remove the water pump (see Chapter 3)
Remove the gearchange mechanism
Remove the sump, oil strainer and pressure regulator
Remove the balancer shaft
Separate the crankcase halves
Remove the crankshaft and the connecting rods
Remove the selector drum and forks
Remove the transmission shafts/gears

Reassembly

6 Reassembly is accomplished by reversing the general disassembly sequence.

Engine, clutch and transmission 2•11

6.2a Unscrew the bolts (arrowed) securing the hose on each end of the cooler

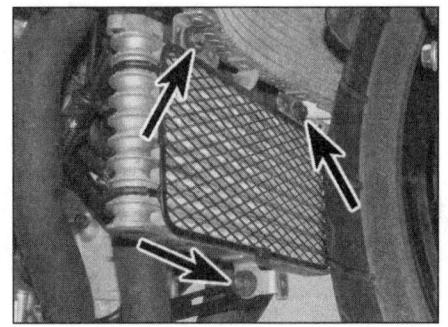

6.2b Oil cooler mounting bolts (arrowed)

6.3a Oil hose banjo bolts (arrowed) – engine end

6 Oil cooler

Note: *The oil cooler can be removed with the engine in the frame. If the engine has been removed, ignore the steps which do not apply.*

⚠ **Warning:** *The engine and exhaust must be completely cool before carrying out this procedure.*

Removal

1 The cooler is located on the front of the engine. Remove the fairing side panels (see Chapter 8). Drain the engine oil (see Chapter 1).
2 To remove the cooler without its feed and return hoses, unscrew the bolts securing each hose union to the cooler and detach the hoses **(see illustration)**. Discard the union O-rings as new ones must be used. Unscrew the cooler mounting bolts and remove the cooler **(see illustration)**. Note the spacers in the mounting grommets.
3 To remove the cooler with its feed and return hoses, unscrew the bolts securing each hose union to the engine and detach the hoses **(see illustration)**. Discard the union O-rings as new ones must be used **(see illustration)**. Unscrew the cooler mounting bolts and remove the cooler **(see illustration 6.2b)**. Note the spacers in the mounting grommets. Note the routing of the hoses between the exhaust downpipes **(see illustration)**.
4 To remove the hoses but leave the cooler in place, unscrew the bolts securing each hose union to the engine and cooler and detach them **(see illustration 6.2a)**. Note the routing of the hoses between the exhaust downpipes. Discard the union O-rings as new ones must be used.

Inspection

5 Remove the mesh guard, noting how it locates.
6 Check the cooler fins for mud, dirt and insects which may impede the flow of air through it. If the fins are dirty, clean them using water or low pressure compressed air directed from the inner side. If the fins are bent or distorted, straighten them carefully with a screwdriver. If the air flow is restricted by bent

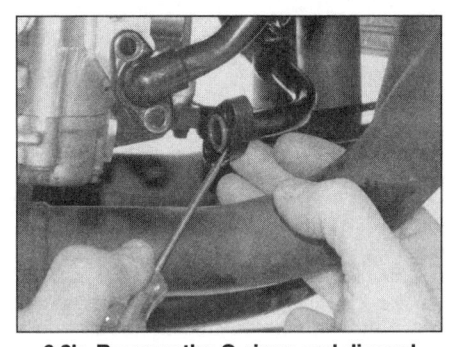

6.3b Remove the O-rings and discard them

or damaged fins over more than 20% of the surface area, replace the cooler with a new one.

Installation

7 Installation is the reverse of removal, noting the following:
● Make sure the hoses are correctly routed with the left-hand hose between the Nos. 1 and 2 cylinder downpipes, and the right-hand hose between the Nos. 3 and 4 cylinder downpipes.
● Check the condition of the cooler mounting grommets and replace them with new ones if they are damaged, deformed or deteriorated. Make sure the spacers are in the mounting grommets.
● Always use new O-rings smeared with grease on each hose union.
● Tighten the union bolts to the torque setting specified at the beginning of the Chapter – the longer bolts are for the left-hand hose unions.

6.3c Note the routing of the hoses between the pipes

● Fill the engine with the correct quantity of oil (see Chapter 1).

7 Valve cover

Note: *The valve cover can be removed with the engine in the frame. If the engine has been removed, ignore the steps which do not apply.*

Removal

1 Remove the fairing side panels (see Chapter 8).
2 Remove the fuel tank and the air filter housing (see Chapter 4). Unscrew the bolt securing each fairing side panel bracket to the frame, noting how they locate and how the left-hand one holds the clutch pipe **(see illustrations)**. The brackets are marked L and R so you can't mix them up.

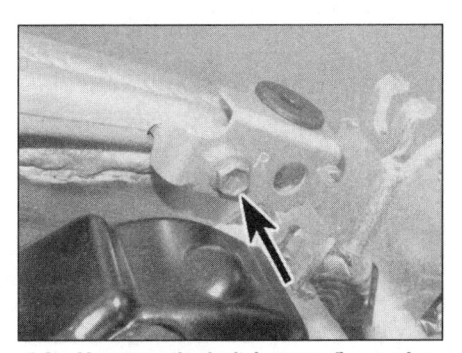

7.2a Unscrew the bolt (arrowed) securing the bracket . . .

7.2b . . . noting how the left-hand one holds the clutch pipe

2•12 Engine, clutch and transmission

7.4 Unscrew the bolts (arrowed) . . .

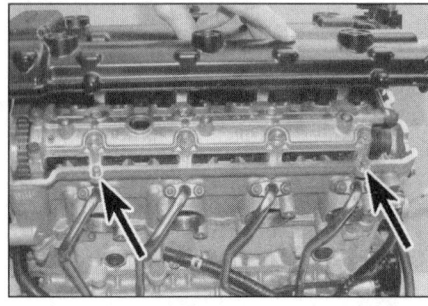

7.5 . . . and remove the cover. Note the dowels (arrowed)

7.7a Make sure the gaskets locate in the grooves

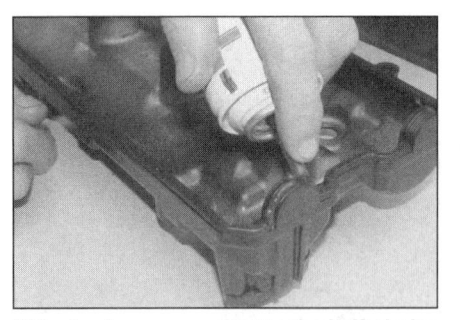

7.7b Apply some sealant to the half-circles

7.9 Smear the washers with oil and tighten the bolts to the correct torque

3 Disconnect the wiring connector from each ignition coil and from the camshaft position sensor **(see illustration 4.19)**. Carefully pull the coils/caps off the spark plugs. Disconnect the horn wiring connectors and draw the wiring through the hole in the rubber heat shield. Detach the coolant overflow hose from its union on the radiator filler neck and draw it through the hole in the rubber heat shield. Release the two cable ties securing the shield. Release the trim clip securing the shield to the frame on the right-hand side. Remove the shield, noting how it fits and that it is marked L and R on each side of its top surface to denote its orientation.
4 Unscrew the valve cover bolts **(see illustration)**. Remove the washers with the bolts if they are loose in the cover. Check their condition and replace them with new ones if required.
5 Lift the valve cover off the cylinder head and manoeuvre it away **(see illustration)**. If it is stuck, do not try to lever it off with a screwdriver. Tap it gently around the sides with a rubber hammer or block of wood to dislodge it. Remove the rim gasket and spark

plug hole gaskets and discard them as new ones should be used. Remove the two dowels from either the cover or the cylinder head if they are loose. Remove the camshaft position sensor if required (see Chapter 4).

Installation

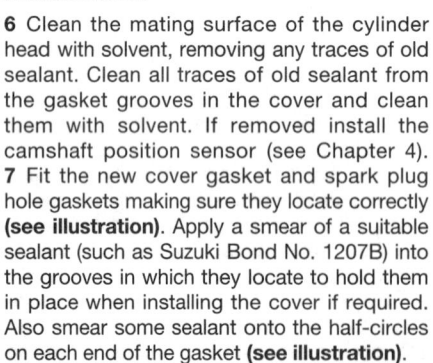

6 Clean the mating surface of the cylinder head with solvent, removing any traces of old sealant. Clean all traces of old sealant from the gasket grooves in the cover and clean them with solvent. If removed install the camshaft position sensor (see Chapter 4).
7 Fit the new cover gasket and spark plug hole gaskets making sure they locate correctly **(see illustration)**. Apply a smear of a suitable sealant (such as Suzuki Bond No. 1207B) into the grooves in which they locate to hold them in place when installing the cover if required. Also smear some sealant onto the half-circles on each end of the gasket **(see illustration)**.
8 Fit the dowels into the cylinder head or cover **(see illustration 7.5)**.
9 Position the valve cover on the cylinder

head, making sure the gaskets stay in place. Smear the washers, using new ones if necessary with clean engine oil and fit them onto the cover bolts **(see illustration)**. Install the bolts and tighten them to the torque setting specified at the beginning of the Chapter.
10 Install all other components previously removed.

8 Camshafts and followers

Note: *The camshafts and followers can be removed with the engine in the frame. The camshaft holder bolts are strengthened and must not be replaced by a weaker bolt. The bolts are identified by a 9 on the head. If new bolts are required, make sure you obtain the correct ones from a Suzuki dealer.*

Removal

1 Remove the valve cover (see Section 7).
2 Remove the spark plugs to allow the engine to be turned over easier (see Chapter 1).
3 Unscrew the crankshaft end cap and the timing mark inspection cap from the starter clutch cover **(see illustration)**. Check the condition of the cap O-ring and sealing washer and discard them if they are damaged, deformed or deteriorated, but note that new ones should be used as a matter of course.
4 Turn the engine using a socket or offset ring spanner on the starter clutch bolt, turning it in a clockwise direction only, until the scribe line on the starter clutch aligns with the notch in the timing mark inspection hole and the number 1 arrow on the exhaust camshaft

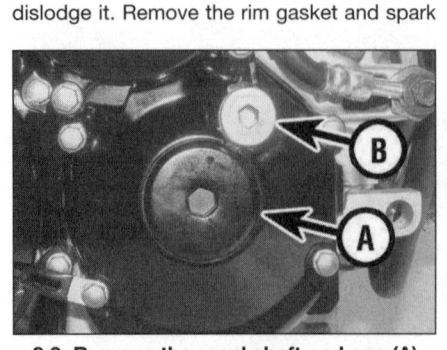

8.3 Remove the crankshaft end cap (A) and the timing inspection cap (B)

8.4a Turn the engine clockwise using the timing rotor bolt . . .

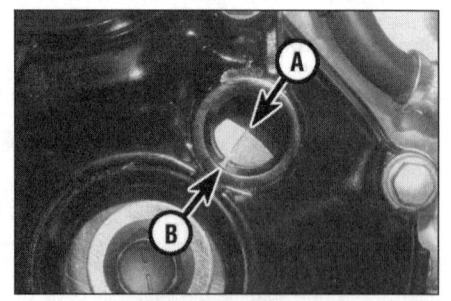

8.4b . . . until the line (A) aligns with the notch (B) . . .

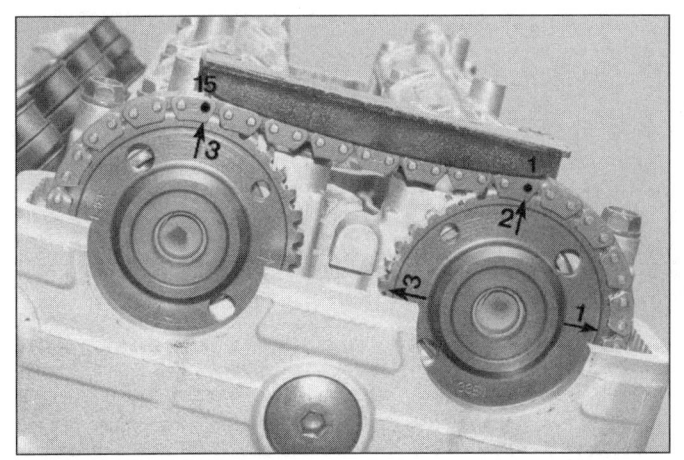

Engine, clutch and transmission 2•13

8.4c ... and the sprocket markings are aligned as described

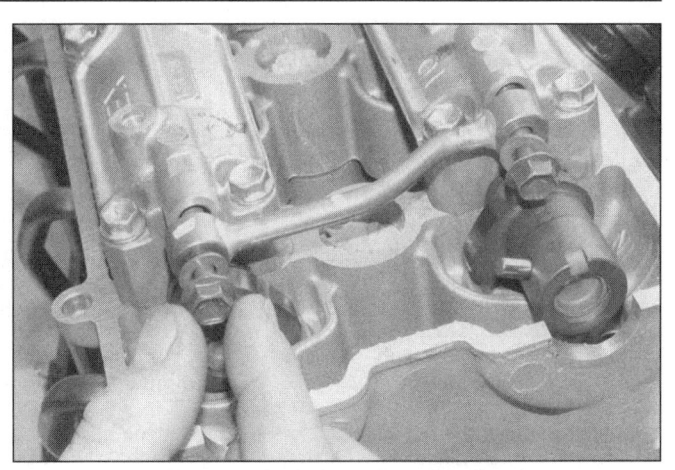

8.6 Unscrew the bolts and remove the pipe

8.8a Unscrew the camshaft holder bolts (arrowed) ...

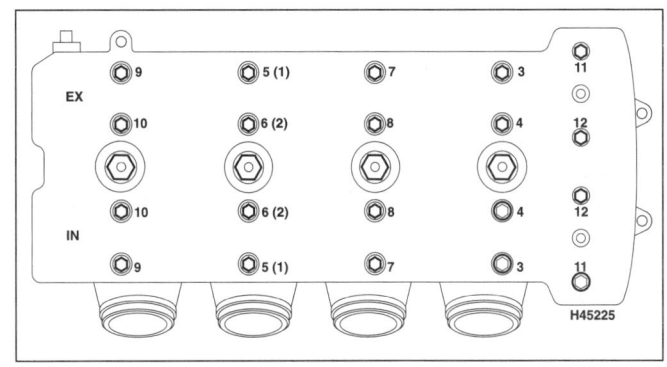

8.8b ... in a reverse order of the TIGHTENING sequence shown

sprocket points forwards and is level with the top surface on the cylinder head **(see illustrations)**. **Note:** *Turn the engine in the normal direction of rotation (clockwise) only, viewed from the right-hand end of the engine.* If the number 3 arrow is pointing forwards (it should be pointing backwards as shown), turn the engine clockwise through 360° until the scribe line again aligns with the notch – the number 1 arrow will now be correctly positioned. This is how the camshafts must be positioned for installation later.

5 Remove the cam chain tensioner (see Section 9). Remove the top cam chain guide (see Section 10).

6 Unscrew the two oil pipe bolts, noting their different lengths, and remove the pipe, noting which way round it fits **(see illustration)**. Discard the sealing washers as new ones must be fitted.

7 Before disturbing the camshaft holders, check for the identification markings. The intake camshaft holder is marked IN, and the exhaust camshaft holder is marked EX. These markings ensure that the holders can be matched up to their original camshaft on installation. If no markings are visible, mark your own using a felt pen.

8 Working on one camshaft at a time, but starting with the exhaust camshaft if removing both of them, unscrew the holder bolts evenly and a little at a time in a reverse of the numerical sequence marked on each holder until they are all loose **(see illustration)**. While slackening the bolts make sure that the holder is lifting squarely away from the cylinder head and is not sticking on the locating dowels. Note that the bolts above the No. 2 cylinder are marked with two numbers – this is because they must be slackened twice in the sequence while all others are slackened once. *Caution: If the bolts are carelessly loosened and the holder does not come squarely away from the head, the holder is likely to break. If this happens the complete cylinder head assembly must be replaced; the holders are matched to the cylinder head and cannot be replaced separately. Also, a camshaft could break if the holder bolts are not slackened evenly and the pressure from a depressed valve causes the shaft to bend.*

Remove the bolts, then lift off the camshaft holder, noting how it fits **(see illustration)**. Retrieve the dowels from either the holder or the cylinder head if they are loose. Slip the cam chain off the sprocket and lift the shaft out of the head **(see illustration)**. The camshafts are marked for identification. The intake camshaft is marked 'IN' and the exhaust camshaft is marked 'EX' **(see illustration 8.26a)**.

9 While the camshafts are out, either let the chain rest on the stopper bolt shaft, or wire it to another component to prevent it from

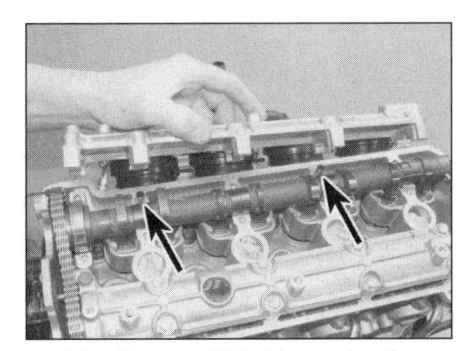

8.8c Remove the holder, noting the dowels (arrowed) ...

8.8d ... then remove the camshaft ...

2•14 Engine, clutch and transmission

8.9 . . . and the half-ring retainers

8.10a Carefully lift out the follower using grips, a lapping tool or a magnet . . .

8.10b . . . and retrieve the shim from inside the follower . . .

dropping. Remove the two bearing half-ring retainers from the cylinder head or from the bearings on the camshafts, noting how they fit **(see illustration)**.

10 If you are removing the followers and shims, obtain a container which is divided into sixteen compartments (or two divided into eight), and label each compartment with the identity of a valve location in the cylinder head, for example the intake camshaft, left-hand valve for the No. 2 cylinder could be marked I-L-2. If a container is not available, use labelled plastic bags. Lift each cam follower out of the cylinder head using either a magnet or the suction created by a valve lapping tool, though fingers may suffice, and long nosed pliers can be used with care – do not grip the follower tightly as you could score it **(see illustration)**. Retrieve the shim from either the inside of the follower or pick it out of the top of the valve, using either a magnet, a small screwdriver with a dab of grease on it (the shim will stick to the grease), or a screwdriver and a pair of pliers **(see illustrations)**. Do not allow the shim to fall into the engine. Store the follower and its shim in its correct compartment in the container, or in its labelled bag.

11 Cover the top of the cylinder head with a rag to prevent anything falling into the engine.

Inspection

12 Inspect the bearing surfaces in the camshaft holders and cylinder head and the corresponding journals on the camshafts. Look for score marks, deep scratches and evidence of spalling (a pitted appearance). Check the oil passages for clogging.

13 Check the camshaft lobes for heat discoloration (blue appearance), score marks, chipped areas, flat spots and spalling. Also check the lobe contact surfaces on the cam followers (refer to Section 12 for other follower checks). Measure the height of each lobe with a micrometer and compare the results to the service limit listed in this Chapter's Specifications **(see illustration)**. If damage is noted or wear is excessive, the camshaft must be replaced with a new one.

14 Check the amount of camshaft runout by supporting each end on V-blocks, and measuring any runout using a dial gauge. If the runout exceeds the specified limit the camshaft must be renewed.

> **HAYNES HiNT** *Refer to Tools and Workshop Tips in the Reference section for details of how to read a micrometer and dial gauge*

15 Next, check the camshaft journal oil clearances preferably using Plastigauge (but note that if none is available the oil clearance can be obtained by measuring the journal diameter and holder/head bore as described in Step 19, then calculating the difference, though this method is not as accurate). Note that Plastigauge comes in two different sizes, graded according to a range of clearances it can measure – make sure you order the correct one according to the oil clearance figure specified.

16 Check one camshaft at a time. Clean the camshaft and the bearing surfaces in the cylinder head and camshaft holder with a clean lint-free cloth. Fit the bearing half-ring retainer into its groove in the cylinder head **(see illustration 8.9)**, then lay the camshaft in its correct location in the head (see Step 8) **(see illustration 8.8d)**, making sure that the lobes are not contacting the followers (if not removed) or valve stem ends – if they are the shaft will turn as the holder bolts are tightened which will disturb the Plastigauge and lead to a false reading.

17 Cut strips of Plastigauge and lay one piece on each journal, parallel with the camshaft centreline. Make sure the camshaft holder dowels are installed. Install the holder and tighten the bolts evenly and a little at a time in the correct numerical sequence as marked on each holder (and tightening the bolts above No. 2 cylinder twice in the sequence as indicated), making sure the holder is pulled down squarely onto the dowels, to the torque setting specified at the beginning of the Chapter **(see illustrations 8.8c, b and a)**. While doing this, don't let the camshaft rotate, or the Plastigauge will be disturbed and you will have to start again.

18 Now unscrew the camshaft holder bolts evenly and a little at a time in a reverse of the numerical sequence, and lift off the holder.

19 To determine the oil clearance, compare the crushed Plastigauge (at its widest point) on each journal to the scale printed on the Plastigauge container. Compare the results to this Chapter's Specifications. If the oil clearance is greater than specified, measure the diameter of the camshaft journal with a micrometer **(see illustration)**. If

8.10c . . . or from the top of the valve

8.13 Measure the height of each camshaft lobe with a micrometer

8.19a Measure the diameter of the journal with a micrometer

Engine, clutch and transmission 2•15

8.19b Measure the journal housing diameter with a bore gauge

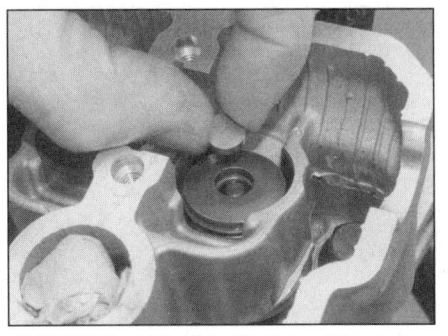

8.22 Fit the shim into the top of the valve with the size mark up

8.24 Fit each retainer into its groove

the journal diameter is less than the specified limit, replace the camshaft with a new one and recheck the clearance. If the clearance is still too great, or if the camshaft journal is within its limit, replace the cylinder head and holders as a set with new ones. If required the holder/cylinder head bore sizes can be measured with the camshafts removed and the holder tightened down, using a small bore gauge and micrometer, comparing the results to the specifications **(see illustration)**.

> **HAYNES HiNT** *Before replacing camshafts or the cylinder head and journal holders because of damage, check with local machine shops specialising in motorcycle engine work. In the case of the camshafts, it may be possible for cam lobes to be welded, reground and hardened, at a cost far lower than that of a new camshaft. If the bearing surfaces in the cylinder head are damaged, it may be possible for them to be bored out to accept bearing inserts. Due to the cost of a new cylinder head it is recommended that all options be explored.*

20 Check the condition of the bearing on the sprocket end of each camshaft, referring to *Tools and Workshop Tips* (Section 5) in the Reference Section. If the bearings are worn, new camshafts must be installed as the bearings are not available separately.

21 Check each camshaft sprocket for wear and damage, replacing the camshaft with a new one if necessary – the sprockets are not available separately. If the teeth are worn, check the drive sprocket teeth and the cam chain and its tensioner and guide blades as well (see Sections 9 and 10). If wear this severe is apparent, the entire engine may need to be disassembled for inspection.

Installation

22 If removed lubricate each shim with molybdenum disulphide oil (a 50/50 mixture of molybdenum disulphide grease and engine oil) and fit it into its recess in the top of the valve spring retainer with the size mark facing up **(see illustration)**. Take care to ensure each shim and follower are returned to their original location or the valve clearances will be incorrect.

23 Check that the shim is correctly seated, then lubricate the follower with molybdenum disulphide oil and install it onto the valve, making sure it fits squarely in its bore **(see illustration 8.10a)**. Repeat the process for all other valves.

24 Fit the bearing half-ring retainer for each camshaft into its groove in the cylinder head **(see illustration)**.

25 Make sure the bearing surfaces in the cylinder head, on the camshafts and in the holders are clean, then liberally apply molybdenum disulphide oil (a 50/50 mixture of molybdenum disulphide grease and engine oil) to each of them. Also apply it to the camshaft lobes and the followers.

26 Check that the cam chain is engaged around the sprocket teeth on the crankshaft and that the crankshaft is positioned as described in Step 4. Keeping the front run of the cam chain taut (and making sure you do not turn the crankshaft by pulling on it too hard), lay the exhaust camshaft (identified by EX) **(see illustration)** onto the cylinder head, positioning the camshaft so that the arrow marked 1 on the sprocket points forwards and is flush with the top of the cylinder head mating surface, and the arrow marked 2 points vertically upwards **(see illustration and 8.4c)**, and making sure the bearing retainer locates into the groove in the bearing, and engage the chain on the sprocket teeth.

27 Make sure the exhaust camshaft holder dowels are in position then fit the holder (marked EX) **(see illustration)**. Tighten the holder bolts evenly and a little at a time in the numerical sequence marked on the holder, and tightening the bolts above the No. 2 cylinder twice in the sequence as marked, to the torque setting specified at the beginning of the Chapter **(see illustration 8.8b)**. Whilst tightening the bolts, make sure the holder is being pulled squarely down and does not bind on the dowels, and that the bearing is locating correctly on its retainer. **Note:** *The camshaft holder bolts are of the high tensile type, indicated by a 9 mark on the bolt head. Don't use any other type of bolt.*

Caution: *The camshaft is likely to break if it is tightened down onto the closed valves before the open valves. The holders are likely to break if they are not tightened down evenly and squarely.*

28 With all bolts tightened down, check that the valve timing marks still align (see Steps 4 and 26). Now secure the chain to the sprocket

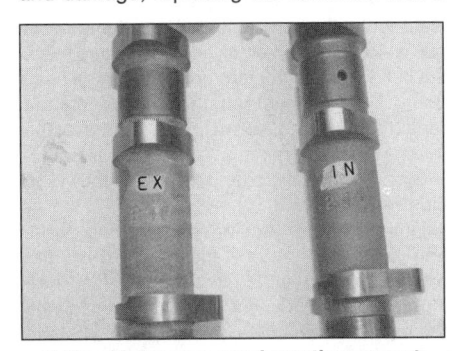

8.26a Make sure you have the correct shaft for the side being worked on

8.26b Install the camshaft aligning the timing marks as described

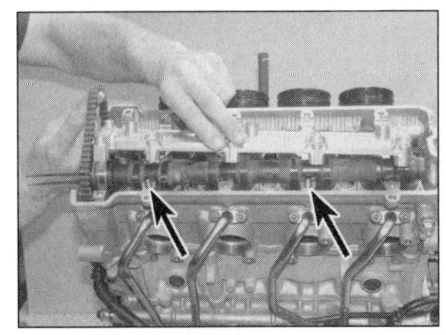

8.27 Locate the holder on the dowels (arrowed)

2•16 Engine, clutch and transmission

8.29 Secure the chain to each sprocket using a cable tie

8.31 Tension the cam chain as shown and recheck the timing marks

8.37 Fit a new washer and O-ring then install the caps

using a suitable cable tie inserted through the hole in the sprocket and around the chain as shown – this ensures the chain cannot jump teeth round the sprocket **(see illustration 8.29)**. Check that the camshaft is not pinched by turning the crankshaft a few degrees in each direction while holding the rear run of the chain taut.

Caution: If the marks are not aligned exactly as described, the valve timing will be incorrect and the valves may strike the pistons, causing extensive damage to the engine.

29 Starting with the cam chain pin that is directly above the arrow marked 2 on the exhaust camshaft sprocket, count 15 pins along the chain towards the intake side **(see illustration 8.4c)**. Lay the intake camshaft (identified by IN) onto the cylinder head, engaging the chain with the sprocket so that the arrow marked 3 on the sprocket points up and aligns with the 15th pin in the chain, and making sure the bearing retainer locates into the groove in the bearing **(see illustration 8.8d)**. When you are certain that the pin count between the sprockets is correct, secure the chain to the sprocket on the intake camshaft using a cable tie as before **(see illustration)**.

30 Make sure the intake camshaft holder dowels are in position then fit the holder (marked IN) **(see illustration 8.8c)**. Tighten the holder bolts evenly and a little at a time in the numerical sequence marked on the holder, and tightening the bolts above the No. 2 cylinder twice in the sequence as marked, to the torque setting specified at the beginning of the Chapter **(see illustration 8.8b)**. Whilst tightening the bolts, make sure the holder is being pulled squarely down and does not bind on the dowels, and that the bearing is locating correctly on its retainer. **Note:** *The camshaft holder bolts are of the high tensile type, indicated by a 9 mark on the bolt head. Don't use any other type of bolt.*

31 With all bolts tightened down, press on the rear run of the cam chain via the tensioner hole to take up any slack and check that the valve timing marks still align (see Steps 4, 26 and 29) **(see illustration)**. Check that the intake camshaft is not pinched by turning the crankshaft a few degrees in each direction while holding the rear run of the chain taut.

32 Install the cam chain tensioner (see Section 9). Check again that all marks are correctly aligned, then remove the cable ties securing the chain to the sprockets.

33 Rotate the engine clockwise through two full turns (720°) and re-check that the valve timing marks are correct.

34 Check the valve clearances (Chapter 1) and adjust if necessary.

35 Install the top cam chain guide (see Section 10). Fit the oil pipe using new sealing washers, making sure the white paint mark on the pipe faces up, and tighten the bolts to the specified torque setting – the longer bolt fits on the exhaust side **(see illustration 8.6)**. If the cylinder head has been removed, pour approximately 50 ml of the specified engine oil into the oil pockets in the head.

36 Install the valve cover (see Section 7). Install the spark plugs (see Chapter 1).

37 Install the timing inspection cap using a new sealing washer if required, and the crankshaft end cap using a new O-ring if required – smear the O-ring and the cap threads with grease **(see illustration)**. Tighten the caps to the torque settings specified at the beginning of the Chapter.

38 Check the engine oil level and top up if necessary (see *Daily (pre-ride) checks*).

9 Cam chain tensioner

Note: *The cam chain tensioner can be removed with the engine in the frame. If the engine has been removed, ignore the steps that do not apply.*

Caution: Once you start to remove the tensioner bolts, you must remove the tensioner all the way and reset it before tightening the bolts. The tensioner extends itself and locks in place, so if you loosen the bolts partway and then retighten them, the tensioner or cam chain will be damaged.

Removal

1 If the camshafts are not being removed, before removing the tensioner follow Section 8, steps 1 to 4 to align the valve timing marks, then secure the cam chain to the sprockets using cable ties inserted through the holes in the sprockets and around the chain as shown **(see illustration)** – this ensures the chain cannot jump teeth round the sprockets while the tensioner is out, which is quite likely if you don't secure them.

2 On K1 models onward unscrew the oil hose banjo bolt and detach the hose from the tensioner **(see illustration)**. Discard the sealing washers as new ones must be used.

3 Slacken the tensioner cap bolt slightly **(see illustration 9.2)**.

4 Unscrew the tensioner mounting bolts and withdraw the tensioner from the engine, noting which way up it fits **(see illustration 9.2)**. Do not rotate the engine with the tensioner removed.

5 Remove and discard the gasket as a new one must be used on installation.

9.1 Secure the chain to the sprockets using cable ties

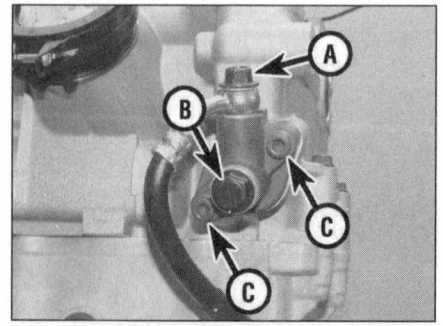

9.2 Oil hose banjo bolt (A – K1 models onward), tensioner cap bolt (B), tensioner mounting bolts (C)

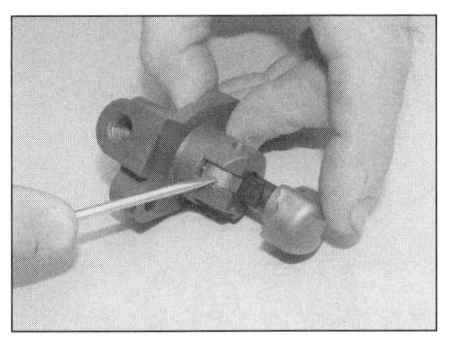

Engine, clutch and transmission 2•17

9.8 Release the ratchet and make sure the plunger moves smoothly and freely

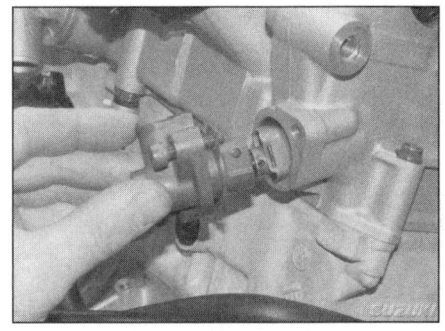

9.17 Install the tensioner using a new gasket

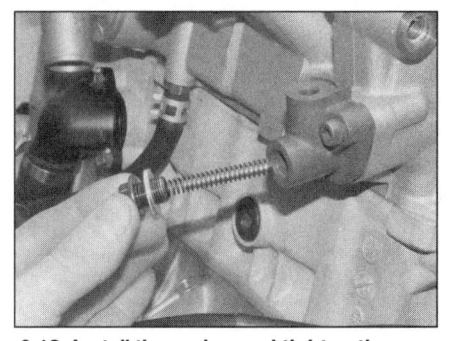

9.18 Install the spring and tighten the cap bolt

Inspection

6 Clean any remnants of old gasket off the tensioner body and its mating surface on the cylinder head. Examine the tensioner components for signs of wear and damage.

7 On X and Y models unscrew the cap bolt. Discard the sealing washer as a new one must be used. Insert a flat-bladed screwdriver into the slot in the end of the tensioner, and turn it clockwise to retract the plunger. A special tool (Pt. No. 09917-62430) is available which keeps the tensioner locked in its retracted position, rather than having to hold the screwdriver to prevent the plunger extending itself. Release the tensioner by turning the slotted end anti-clockwise with a screwdriver, or by removing the special tool, and check that the plunger moves freely in and out of the tensioner body.

8 On K1 models onward unscrew the cap bolt and withdraw the spring. Discard the sealing washer as a new one must be used. Release the ratchet mechanism and check that the plunger moves freely in and out of the tensioner body **(see illustration)**.

9 If the tensioner or any of its components are worn or damaged, or if the plunger is seized in the body, the tensioner or faulty component (if available separately) must be replaced with a new one.

Installation

X and Y models

10 Ensure the tensioner and cylinder block surfaces are clean and dry.

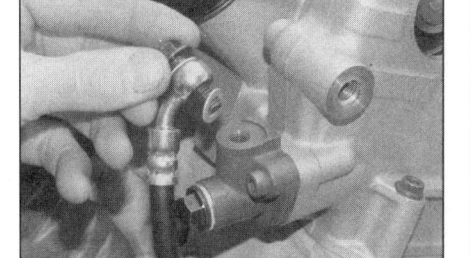

9.19 Connect the oil hose using new sealing washers

11 If not already done, unscrew the cap bolt. Discard the sealing washer as a new one must be used. Insert a flat-bladed screwdriver into the slot in the end of the tensioner, and turn it clockwise to retract the plunger. A special tool (part No. 09917-62430) is available which keeps the tensioner locked in its retracted position, or alternatively hold the screwdriver to prevent the plunger extending itself.

12 Place a new gasket on the tensioner body, then install the tensioner and tighten the mounting bolts to the torque setting specified at the beginning of the Chapter, all the time taking care not to release the plunger.

13 Release the plunger by removing the special tool or screwdriver. You should hear it click as it extends and takes up the slack in the chain.

14 Fit a new sealing washer onto the cap bolt. Install the cap bolt and tighten it to the specified torque setting.

K1 models onward

15 Ensure the tensioner and cylinder block surfaces are clean and dry.

16 If not already done, unscrew the cap bolt and withdraw the spring. Discard the sealing washer as a new one must be used. Release the ratchet mechanism and press the tensioner plunger all the way into the tensioner body **(see illustration 9.8)**.

17 Fit a new gasket onto the tensioner body, then fit the tensioner into the engine with the oil hole at the top **(see illustration)**. Tighten the bolts to the torque setting specified at the beginning of the Chapter.

10.2 The top guide is secured by two bolts

18 Install the spring and cap bolt with a new sealing washer and tighten the bolt to the specified torque setting **(see illustration)**. While you are installing the spring and tightening the bolt you should hear the plunger being forced out and clicking over the ratchet mechanism.

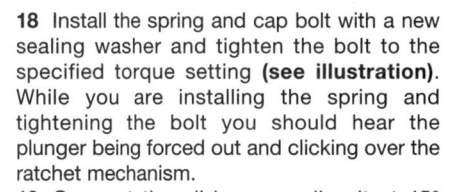

19 Connect the oil hose, angling it at 45° from the engine, and install the banjo bolt using a new sealing washer on each side of the union **(see illustration)**. Tighten the bolt to the specified torque setting.

On completion – all models

20 Check that the rear run of the cam chain is tensioned. If it is slack, the tensioner plunger did not release.

21 Check that all timing marks are correctly aligned (see Section 8, Steps 4, 26 and 29), then remove the cable ties securing the chain to the sprockets.

22 Rotate the engine clockwise through two full turns (720°).

23 Install the valve cover (see Section 7). Install the spark plugs (see Chapter 1).

24 Install the timing inspection cap using a new sealing washer if required, and the crankshaft end cap using a new O-ring if required – smear the O-ring and the cap threads with grease **(see illustration 8.37)**. Tighten the caps to the torque settings specified at the beginning of the Chapter.

10 Cam chain, tensioner blade and guide blades

Note: *The cam chain and blades can be removed with the engine in the frame.*

Cam chain guides and tensioner blade

Removal

1 Remove the valve cover (see Section 8).

2 To remove the top cam chain guide, unscrew the two bolts securing it to the cylinder head **(see illustration)**.

3 To remove the front cam chain guide, first remove the cylinder head (see Section 11). Lift the front cam chain guide out of the front of

2•18 Engine, clutch and transmission

10.3 Note how the front guide locates at the bottom and on the block (arrows)

10.4a Unscrew the pivot bolt . . .

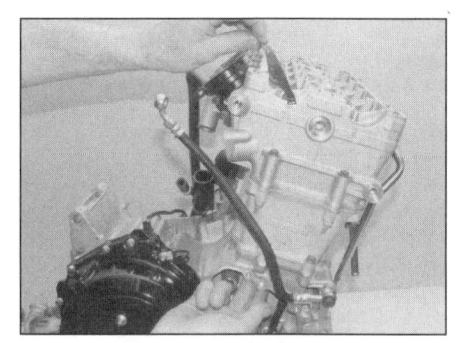

10.4b . . . then push the blade up and lift it out of the tunnel

the cam chain tunnel, noting which way round it fits and how it locates **(see illustration)**.

4 To remove the tensioner blade, first remove the intake camshaft (see Section 8) and the starter clutch (see Section 22). Unscrew the cam chain stopper bolt **(see illustration 10.11)**. Discard the seal as a new one must be fitted. Unscrew the tensioner blade pivot bolt, noting the wave washer where fitted **(see illustration)**. Push the blade up from the bottom and lift it out of the back of the cam chain tunnel, noting which way round it fits **(see illustration)**.

Inspection

5 Examine the sliding surface of the guides and blade for signs of wear or damage, and renew them if necessary. Check carefully for cracks in the blades and along the edges. Install new blades if necessary.

Installation

6 Fit the tensioner blade into the back of the cam chain tunnel, making sure it is the correct way round **(see illustration 10.4b)**. Apply a suitable non-permanent thread locking compound to the pivot bolt threads, making sure none gets on the pivot section, then install the bolt, not forgetting the wave washer where fitted, and tighten it to the torque setting specified at the beginning of the Chapter **(see illustration 10.4a)**. Fit a new seal smeared with clean oil onto the cam chain stopper bolt, making sure its metal side faces the bolt head. Install the bolt, making

sure the shaft sits between the two runs of chain, and tighten it to the torque setting specified at the beginning of the Chapter **(see illustration 10.11)**. Install the starter clutch (see Section 22) and the intake camshaft (see Section 8).

7 Fit the front guide blade into the front of the cam chain tunnel, making sure it locates correctly onto its seat and its lugs locate in their cut-outs **(see illustration 10.3)**. Install the cylinder head (see Section 11).

8 Fit the top guide onto the cylinder head and tighten the mounting bolts to the torque setting specified at the beginning of the Chapter **(see illustration 10.2)**.

9 Install the valve cover (see Section 8).

Cam chain

Removal

10 If the tensioner blade and front guide blade are also being removed, do that first (see above). If not, remove the camshafts (see Section 8) and the starter clutch (see Section 22).

11 Unscrew and remove the cam chain stopper bolt **(see illustration)**. Discard the seal as a new one must be fitted.

12 Slip the cam chain down the tunnel, then, if the blades are in situ, draw the drive sprocket along the shaft until it is clear of the blades and you can slip the chain off it **(see illustration)**. If you remove the sprocket from the shaft, note the alignment marks **(see illustration)**.

Inspection

13 Check the chain for binding, kinks and any obvious damage and replace it with a new one if necessary. Check the cam chain tensioner and guide blades for wear and damage.

14 Check the sprocket teeth for wear and damage, including those on the driven sprockets on the camshafts. If the drive sprocket is worn or damaged replace it with a new one, and fit a new chain as a matter of course. If the driven sprocket teeth are worn or damaged new camshafts must be installed.

Installation

15 If removed, slide the cam chain sprocket/timing rotor onto the end of the crankshaft, aligning the punch mark on the sprocket with that in the end of the shaft **(see illustration 10.12b)**. Using a piece of wire hooked over at the end, draw the cam chain up the tunnel and slip the bottom onto the sprocket, making sure it is properly engaged **(see illustration 10.12a)**. Wire the chain to another component to prevent it slipping back down the tunnel. Slide the sprocket fully onto the shaft.

16 Fit a new seal onto the cam chain stopper bolt, making sure its metal side faces the bolt head, and smear it with clean oil. Install the bolt, making sure the shaft sits between the two runs of chain, and tighten it to the torque setting specified at the beginning of the Chapter **(see illustration 10.11)**.

17 Install the camshafts (see Section 8) and the starter clutch (see Section 22).

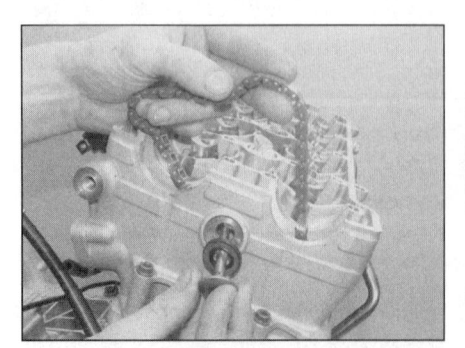

10.11 Unscrew the stopper bolt, noting the sealing washer

10.12a Slide the sprocket along and slip the chain off

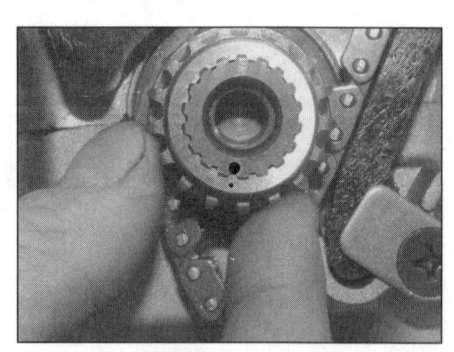

10.12b Note the alignment marks between the shaft and sprocket

Engine, clutch and transmission 2•19

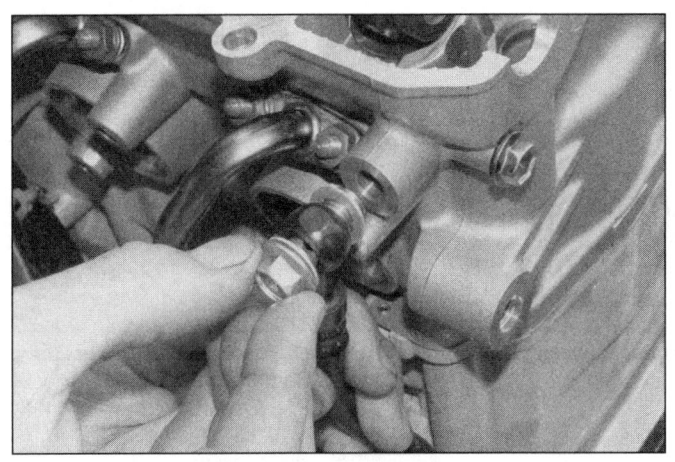

11.4 Unscrew the bolt and detach the hose

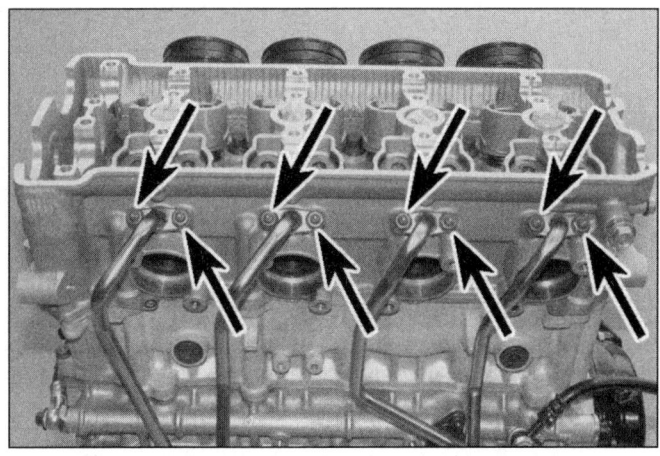

11.6 Unscrew the nuts (arrowed) and remove the pipes

11.7a Unscrew the bolts (arrowed)

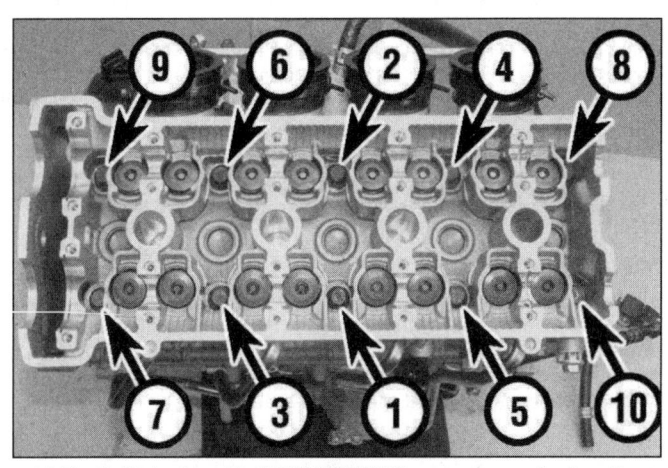

11.7b Cylinder head bolt TIGHTENING sequence – slacken the bolts in reverse order

11 Cylinder head removal and installation

Caution: The engine must be completely cool before beginning this procedure or the cylinder head may become warped.

Note: To remove the cylinder head the engine must be removed from the frame (see Section 4).

Removal

1 Remove the engine from the frame (see Section 4).

2 Remove the camshafts (see Section 8). If you are planning to overhaul the head, also remove the followers and shims.

3 Secure the cam chain with a piece of wire – do not let it fall into the tunnel. Unscrew and remove the cam chain stopper bolt **(see illustration 10.11)**. Discard the seal as a new one must be fitted.

4 Unscrew the oil hose banjo bolt and detach the hose from the cylinder head **(see illustration)**. Discard the sealing washers as new ones must be used.

5 Release the clamp securing the coolant bypass hose to its union on the cylinder head and detach the hose.

6 If required, mark each PAIR system pipe according to its location, then unscrew the nuts and detach the pipes **(see illustration)**. Remove the gaskets and discard them as new ones must be used.

7 The cylinder head is secured by three 6 mm bolts and ten 10 mm bolts. First unscrew and remove the 6 mm bolts **(see illustration)**, then slacken the two cylinder block nuts **(see illustration 13.4)**. Now slacken the 10 mm bolts evenly and a little at a time in a **reverse** of the numerical sequence shown, then remove the bolts and their washers **(see illustration)**.

8 Lift the head off the block, passing the cam chain down through the tunnel as you do **(see illustration)**. If the head is stuck, tap around the joint faces with a soft-faced mallet to free it. Do not attempt to free the head by inserting a screwdriver between it and the block – you'll damage the sealing surfaces.

9 Do not let the cam chain fall into the tunnel – secure it with a piece of wire or metal bar to prevent it from doing so. Remove the old cylinder head gasket and discard it.

10 If they are loose, remove the dowel from each end of the back of the cylinder block **(see illustration 11.14)**. If either appears to be missing it is probably stuck in the underside of the cylinder head.

11 Check the cylinder head gasket and the mating surfaces on the cylinder head and

11.8 Carefully lift the head up off the block

2•20 Engine, clutch and transmission

11.14 Fit the dowels (arrowed) into the head, then lay the gasket over them

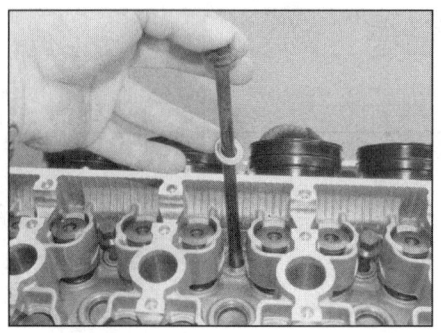

11.16a Lubricate the threads and washers with clean oil . . .

11.16b . . . then tighten the bolts as described to the specified torque

block for signs of leakage, which could indicate warpage. Refer to Section 12 and check the flatness of the cylinder head.

12 Clean all traces of old gasket material from the cylinder head and block. If a scraper is used, take care not to scratch or gouge the soft aluminium. Be careful not to let any of the gasket material fall into the cam chain tunnel, cylinder bores or oil passages.

> **HAYNES HiNT** *Refer to Tools and Workshop Tips for details of gasket removal methods.*

Installation

13 If removed, fit the two dowels into the cylinder block **(see illustration 11.14)**. Lubricate the cylinder bores with engine oil.

14 Ensure both cylinder head and block mating surfaces are clean, then lay the new head gasket in place on the cylinder block, making sure it locates over the dowels and all the holes are correctly aligned **(see illustration)**. Never re-use the old gasket.

15 Carefully lower the cylinder head onto the block. It is helpful to have an assistant to pass the cam chain up through the tunnel and slip a piece of wire through it to prevent it falling back into the engine. Keep the chain taut to prevent it becoming disengaged from the drive sprocket on the crankshaft.

16 Apply clean engine oil to the cylinder head 10 mm bolt washers and threads. Fit the washers onto the bolts with their rounded lips facing the bolt head. Install the bolts and tighten them finger-tight **(see illustration)**. Now tighten them in their correct numerical sequence **(see illustration 11.7b)** first to the initial torque setting specified at the beginning of the Chapter, then in the same sequence to the final torque setting specified **(see illustration)**.

17 When the bolts are correctly torqued, install the 6 mm bolts and tighten them to the specified torque setting **(see illustration 11.7a)**. Now tighten the cylinder block nuts to the specified torque.

18 Fit a new seal onto the cam chain stopper bolt, making sure its metal side faces the bolt head, and smear it with clean oil **(see illustration 10.11)**. Install the bolt, making sure the shaft sits between the two runs of chain, and tighten it to the specified torque setting.

19 If removed, fit a new gasket, with the seal side facing out, onto each PAIR system pipe union, then fit the pipes and tighten the nuts to the specified torque setting **(see illustration 11.6)**.

20 Install the oil hose using a new sealing washer on each side of the union and tighten the banjo bolt to the specified torque setting – butt the metal section below the union against the outside of the lug on the head **(see illustration 11.4)**.

21 Fit the coolant by-pass hose onto its union on the cylinder head and secure it with the clamp.

22 Install the camshafts (see Section 8).

23 Install the engine (see Section 4).

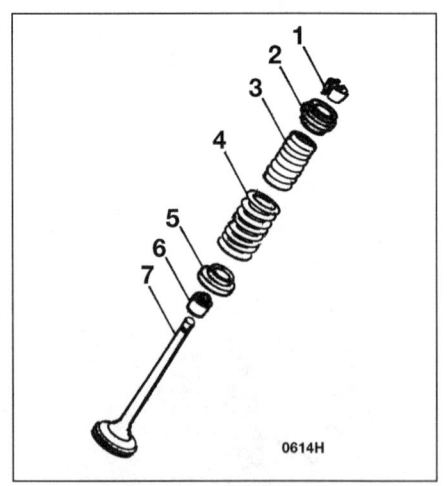

12 Cylinder head and valve overhaul

1 Because of the complex nature of this job and the special tools and equipment required, most owners leave servicing of the valves, valve seats and valve guides to a professional.

> **HAYNES HiNT** *You can make an initial assessment of whether the valves are seating correctly, and therefore sealing, by pouring a small amount of solvent into each of the valve ports. If the solvent leaks past any valve into the combustion chamber area the valve is not seating correctly and sealing.*

2 With the correct tools (a valve spring compressor is essential – make sure it is suitable for motorcycle work), you can also remove the valves and associated components from the cylinder head, clean them and check them for wear to assess the extent of the work needed, and, unless seat cutting or guide replacement is required, grind in the valves and reassemble them in the head.

3 A dealer service department or specialist can replace the guides and re-cut the valve seats.

4 After the valve service has been performed, be sure to clean it very thoroughly before installation on the engine to remove any metal particles or abrasive grit that may still be present from the valve service operations. Use compressed air, if available, to blow out all the holes and passages.

Disassembly

5 Before proceeding, arrange to label and store the valves along with their related components in such a way that they can be returned to their original locations without getting mixed up **(see illustration)**. A good way to do this is to use the same containers as the followers and shims are stored in (see Section 8), or to obtain a separate container and label each compartment with the location of a valve, i.e. cylinder number, intake or exhaust camshaft, left or right valve. If a container is not available, use labelled plastic bags (egg cartons also do very well!).

6 Clean all traces of old gasket material from the cylinder head. If a scraper is used, take care not to scratch or gouge the soft aluminium; refer to Tools and Workshop Tips for details of gasket removal methods.

12.5 Valve components

1 Collets
2 Spring retainer
3 Inner valve spring
4 Outer valve spring
5 Spring seat
6 Valve stem oil seal
7 Valve

Engine, clutch and transmission 2•21

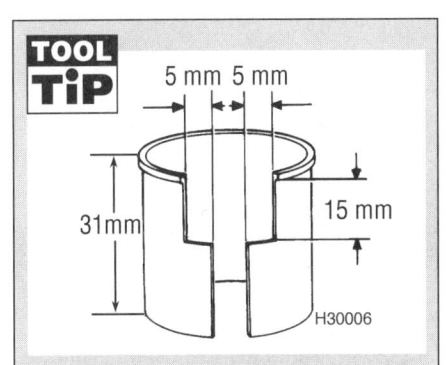

TOOL TiP

Protect the follower bore in the cylinder head from scratches by the valve spring compressor using a shield made from a 35 mm film canister. Cut the canister to the dimensions shown.

12.7a Fit the valve spring compressor...

12.7b ...making sure it locates correctly on the spring retainer...

12.7c ...and on the valve

7 First locate the valve spring compressor on each end of the valve assembly, making sure it is the correct size **(see illustration)**. On the underside of the head make sure the plate on the compressor only contacts the valve and not the soft aluminium of the head – if the plate is too big for the valve, use a spacer between them **(see illustration)**. On the top of the valve the adaptor needs to be about the same size as the spring retainer – if it is too big it will contact the follower bore and mark it, and if it is too small it will be difficult to remove and install the collets **(see illustration)**. If your adaptor is too big or small, change it for one that is a good fit.

8 Compress the springs on the first valve – do not compress them any more than is necessary to free the collets. Remove the collets, using either needle-nose pliers, tweezers, a mechanic's telescopic magnet, or a screwdriver with a dab of grease on it **(see illustration)**. Carefully release the valve spring compressor and remove it. Remove the spring retainer, noting which way up it fits **(see illustration 12.33c)**. Remove the springs, noting that the closer wound coils are at the bottom **(see illustrations 12.33b and a)**. Press down on the top of the valve stem and draw the valve out from the underside of the head **(see illustration 12.31)**. If the valve binds in the guide (won't pull through), push it back into the head and deburr the area around the collet groove with a very fine file or whetstone **(see illustration)**.

9 Once the valve has been removed pull the valve stem seal off the top of the valve guide with pliers and discard it – never reuse the old seals **(see illustration)**. Remove the spring seat using a mechanic's telescopic magnet or thin-nosed pliers, or turn the head upside down and tip it out, taking care not to lose it **(see illustration 12.30)**.

10 Repeat the procedure for the remaining valves. Remember to keep the parts for each valve together and in order so they can be reinstalled in the same location.

11 Next, clean the cylinder head with solvent and dry it thoroughly. Compressed air will speed the drying process and ensure that all holes and recessed areas are reached.

12 Clean all of the valve springs, collets, retainers and spring seats with solvent and dry them thoroughly. Do the parts from one valve at a time so they don't get mixed up.

13 Scrape off any deposits that may have formed on the valve, then use a motorised wire brush to remove deposits from the valve heads and stems. Again, make sure the valves do not get mixed up.

Inspection

14 Inspect the head very carefully for cracks and other damage. If cracks are found, a new head will be required. Check the camshaft bearing surfaces for wear and evidence of seizure. Check the camshafts and holders for wear as well (see Section 8).

15 Inspect the outer surfaces of the cam followers for evidence of scoring or other damage. If a follower is in poor condition, it is probable that the bore in which it works is also damaged. Check for clearance between the followers and their bores. Whilst no specifications are given, if slack is excessive, replace the followers with new ones. If the bores are seriously out-of-round or tapered, a new cylinder head is needed.

16 Using a precision straight-edge and a feeler gauge set to the warpage limit listed in the specifications at the beginning of the Chapter, check the head gasket mating surface for warpage. Refer to *Tools and Workshop Tips* in the Reference section for details of how to use the straight-edge.

17 Examine the valve seats in the combustion chamber. If they are pitted, cracked or burned, the head will require work beyond the scope of the home mechanic. Measure the valve seat width and compare it

12.8a Remove the collets as described

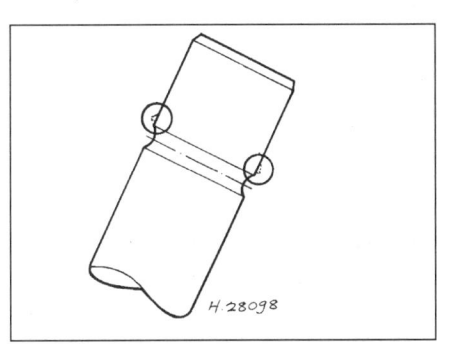

12.8b Remove any burrs (circled) if the valve stem won't pull through the guide

12.9 Pull the oil seal off the top of the guide

2•22 Engine, clutch and transmission

12.17 Measure the valve seat width (between the arrows)

12.18a Measure the amount of wobble as shown, relocating the gauge to measure in both directions

12.18b Measure the valve stem diameter with a micrometer . . .

to this Chapter's Specifications **(see illustration)**. If it exceeds the service limit, or if it varies around its circumference, overhaul is required.

18 Clean the valve guides to remove any carbon build-up, then install each valve in its guide in turn so that its face is 10 mm above the seat. Mount a dial gauge against the side of the valve face and measure the amount of stem deflection (wobble) between the valve stem and its guide – you need to measure in two perpendicular directions, so take the first measurement, then relocate the dial gauge and take a second measurement **(see illustration)**. If the deflection exceeds the limit specified, remove the valve and measure the valve stem diameter **(see illustration)**. Also measure the inside diameter of the guide with a small hole gauge and micrometer **(see illustration)**. Measure the guides at the ends and at the centre to determine if they are worn in a bell-mouth pattern (more wear at the ends). Subtract the stem diameter from the valve guide diameter to obtain the valve stem-to-guide clearance. If the stem-to-guide clearance is greater than listed in this Chapter's Specifications, replace whichever component is worn beyond its specifications with a new one. If the valve guide is within specifications, but is worn unevenly, replace it with a new one.

19 Carefully inspect each valve face, stem and collet groove area for cracks, pits and burned spots **(see illustration)**. Measure the thickness of the valve head and compare it to the specifications **(see illustration)**. If it is worn below the service limit replace it with a new one.

20 Rotate the valve and check for any obvious indication that it is bent, in which case it must be replaced with a new one. Using V-blocks and a dial gauge, measure the valve stem runout and the valve head runout and compare the results to the specifications **(see illustration)**. If either measurement exceeds the service limit specified, the valve must be replaced with a new one.

21 Check the end of the stem for pitting and excessive wear. The stem end can be ground down, provided that the amount of stem above the collet groove after grinding is sufficient.

22 Check the end of each valve spring for wear and pitting. Measure the spring free lengths and compare them to the specifications **(see illustration)**. If any spring is shorter than specified it has sagged and must be replaced with a new one. Also place the spring upright on a flat surface and check it for bend by placing a ruler against it, or alternatively lay it against a set square. If the bend in any spring is excessive, it must be replaced with a new one. Always replace the inner and outer springs as a set, never singly.

23 Check the spring seats, retainers and collets for obvious wear and cracks. Any questionable parts should not be reused, as extensive damage will occur in the event of failure during engine operation.

24 If the inspection indicates that no overhaul work is required, the valve components can be reinstalled in the head.

12.18c . . . then measure the guide bore using a small hole gauge, and measure the small hole gauge with a micrometer

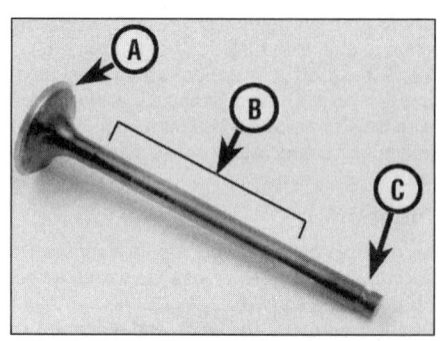

12.19a Check the valve face (A), stem (B) and collet groove (C) for signs of wear and damage

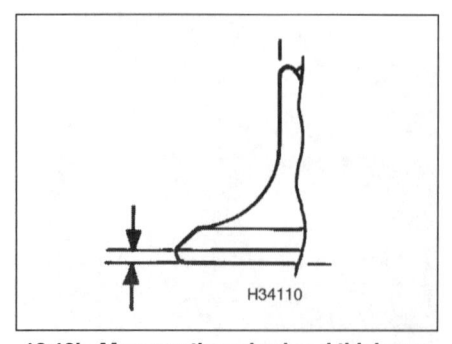

12.19b Measure the valve head thickness

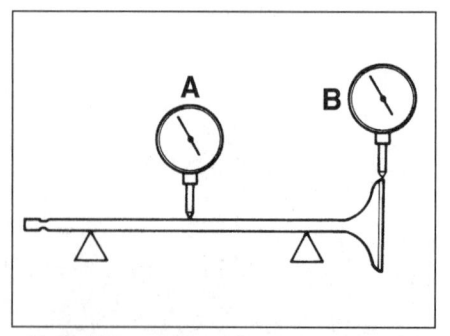

12.20 Measure the valve stem runout (A) and the valve head runout (B)

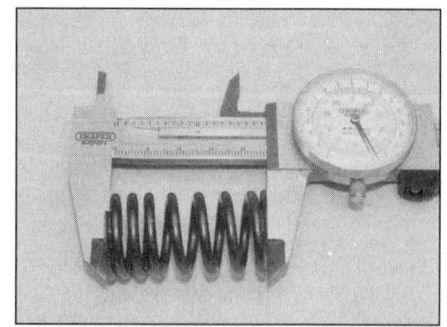

12.22 Measure the free length of the valve springs and check them for squareness

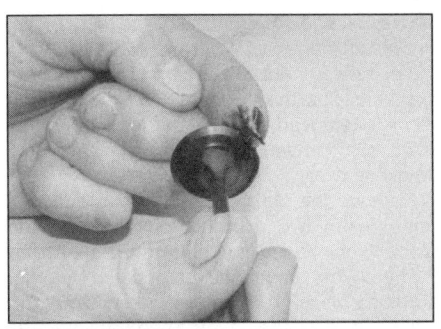

Engine, clutch and transmission 2•23

12.26 Apply the lapping compound sparingly, in small dabs, to the valve face only

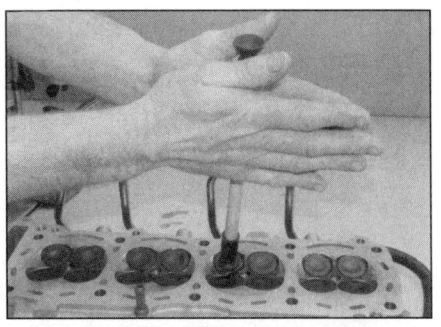

12.27 Rotate the valve grinding tool back and forth between the palms of your hands

12.30 Fit the spring seat, making sure it is the correct way up

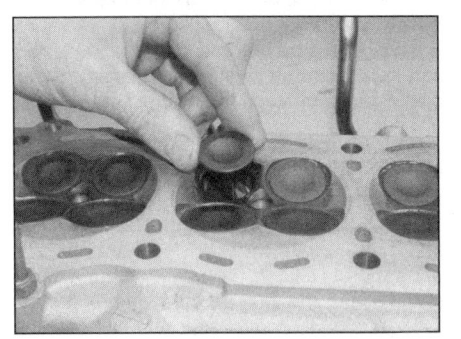

12.31 Lubricate the stem and insert the valve in its guide

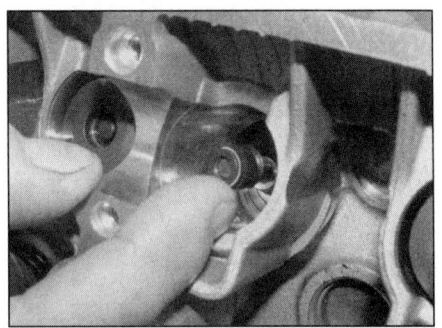

12.32a Fit a new seal onto the valve stem . . .

12.32b . . . using finger pressure to locate it onto the guide as described

Reassembly

25 Unless a valve service has been performed, before installing the valves in the head they should be ground in (lapped) to ensure a positive seal between the valves and seats. This procedure requires coarse and fine valve grinding compound and a valve grinding tool (either hand-held or drill driven – note that some drill-driven tools specify using only a fine grinding compound). If a grinding tool is not available, a piece of rubber or plastic hose can be slipped over the valve stem (after the valve has been installed in the guide) and used to turn the valve.

26 Apply a small amount of coarse grinding compound to the valve face (see illustration). Smear some molybdenum disulphide oil (a 50/50 mixture of molybdenum disulphide grease and engine oil) to the valve stem, then slip the valve into its guide (see illustration 12.31). Note: *Make sure each valve is installed in its correct guide and be careful not to get any grinding compound on the valve stem.* Attach the grinding tool to the valve.

27 If a hand tool is being used rotate the tool between the palms of your hands. Use a back-and-forth motion (as though rubbing your hands together) rather than a circular motion (i.e. so that the valve rotates alternately clockwise and anti-clockwise rather than in one direction only) (see illustration). Lift the valve off the seat and turn it at regular intervals to distribute the grinding compound properly. Continue the grinding procedure until the valve and seat contact area is of uniform width, and unbroken around the entire circumference.

28 Carefully remove the valve and wipe off all traces of grinding compound, making sure none gets in the guide. Use solvent to clean the valve and wipe the seat area thoroughly with a solvent soaked cloth.

29 Repeat the procedure with fine valve grinding compound, then use solvent to clean the valve and flush the guide, and wipe the seat area thoroughly with a solvent soaked cloth. Repeat the entire procedure for the remaining valves. On completion thoroughly clean the entire head again, then blow through all passages with compressed air. Make sure all traces of the grinding compound have been removed before assembling the head.

30 Working on one valve at a time, lay the spring seat in place in the cylinder head, making sure the shouldered side faces up (see illustration).

31 Coat the valve stem with molybdenum disulphide oil (a 50/50 mixture of molybdenum disulphide grease and engine oil), then slip the valve into its guide (see illustration). Check that the valve moves up and down freely in the guide.

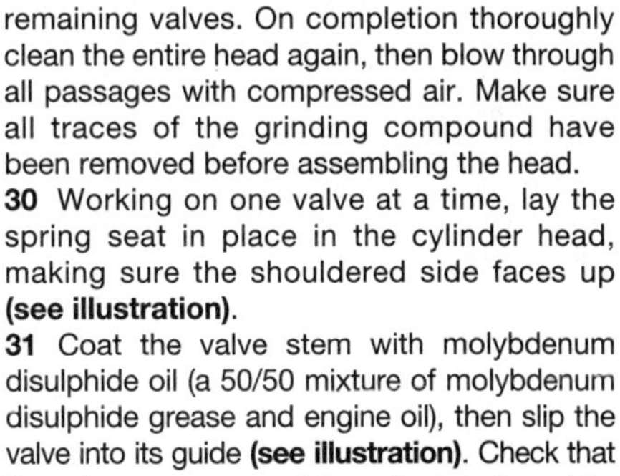

12.33a Fit the inner valve spring . . .

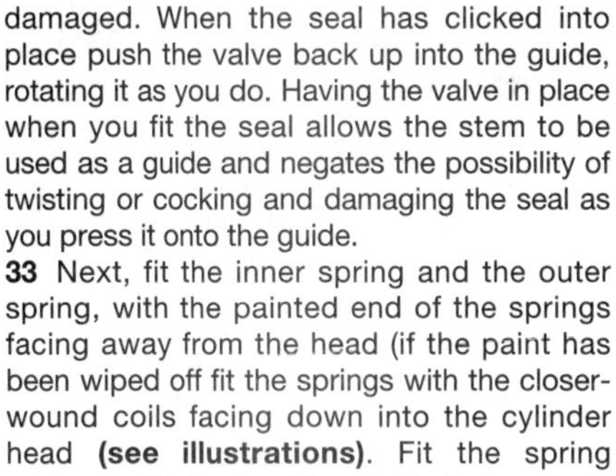

32 Hold the valve against the underside of the head to prevent it dropping out, then fit a new valve stem oil seal onto the top of the valve stem, rotating it slightly as you do, and leaving the top surface of both components flush (see illustration). Now slide the valve down in its guide and press the seal onto the top of the guide using finger pressure (see illustration). Don't remove the seal again or it will be damaged. When the seal has clicked into place push the valve back up into the guide, rotating it as you do. Having the valve in place when you fit the seal allows the stem to be used as a guide and negates the possibility of twisting or cocking and damaging the seal as you press it onto the guide.

33 Next, fit the inner spring and the outer spring, with the painted end of the springs facing away from the head (if the paint has been wiped off fit the springs with the closer-wound coils facing down into the cylinder head (see illustrations). Fit the spring retainer, with its shouldered side facing down

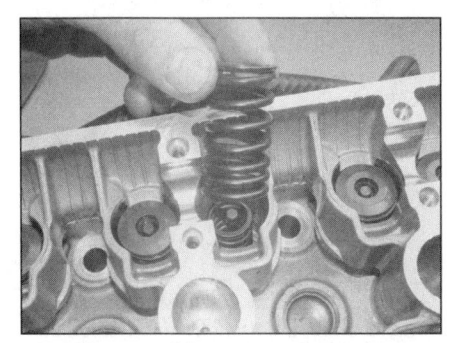

12.33b . . . and the outer valve spring . . .

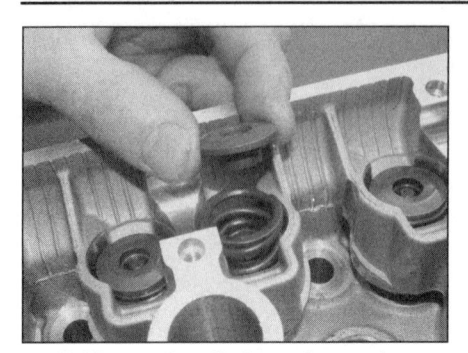

2•24 Engine, clutch and transmission

12.33c . . . then fit the spring retainer

12.35 Tap the valve stem end to make sure both collets are locked into the groove

so that it fits into the top of the springs **(see illustration)**.

34 Compress the valve springs with the spring compressor, making sure it is correctly located onto each end of the valve assembly (see Step 7) **(see illustrations 12.7a, b and c)**. Do not compress the springs any more than is necessary to slip the collets into place. The collets must be installed with the wider end at the top. Apply a small amount of grease to the collets to help hold them in place. Locate each collet in turn onto the valve stem, locating the ridge on its inside into the groove in the stem **(see illustration 12.8a)**, then carefully release the compressor, making sure the collets seat and lock as you do. Check that the collets are securely locked in the retaining groove.

35 Support the cylinder head on blocks so the valves can't contact the workbench top, then tap the top of the valve stem using a brass drift and hammer **(see illustration)**. This will help seat the collets in the groove. If you don't have a brass drift, use a soft-faced hammer and a piece of hard wood as an interface.

36 Repeat the procedure for the remaining valves. Remember to keep the parts for each valve together, and separate from the other valves, so they can be reinstalled in the same location. After the cylinder head and camshafts have been installed, check and adjust the valve clearances as required (see Chapter 1) – this is essential if the valves have been reground or if new valve components have been fitted.

13 Cylinder block

Note: *To remove the cylinder block the engine must be removed from the frame (see Section 4).*

Removal

1 Remove the cylinder head (see Section 11).
2 Lift the front cam chain guide out of the front of the cam chain tunnel, noting which way round it fits and how it locates **(see illustration 10.3)**.
3 Either slacken the clamp securing the coolant hose to the inlet union on the rear of the cylinder block and detach the hose, or unscrew the three bolts securing the union to the block and detach the union, or do both if required **(see illustration)**. If the union is detached, discard the O-ring as a new one must be used.
4 Unscrew the nuts which secure the right-hand side of the block to the crankcase, noting the hose clamp secured by the front nut **(see illustration)**.
5 Hold the cam chain up and lift the cylinder block up off the crankcase, then pass the cam chain down through the tunnel **(see illustration)**. Do not let the chain fall into the crankcase – secure it with a piece of wire or metal bar to prevent it from doing so. If the block is stuck, tap around the joint faces with a soft-faced mallet to free it. Don't attempt to free the block by inserting a screwdriver between it and the crankcase – you'll damage the sealing surfaces. When lifting the block off the pistons, try not to let them fall against the crankcase as they become free. When the block is removed, stuff clean rags around the pistons to prevent anything falling into the crankcase.
6 Remove the old gasket. If they are loose, remove the two dowels from the cylinder block or crankcase **(see illustration 13.16)**.
7 Check the base gasket and the mating surfaces on the cylinder head and block for signs of leakage, which could indicate warpage.
8 Clean all traces of old gasket material from the cylinder block and crankcase. If a scraper is used, take care not to scratch or gouge the soft aluminium. Be careful not to let any of the gasket material drop into the crankcase or the oil passages.

Inspection

9 The bores are electro-plated with Suzuki's SCEM (Suzuki Composite Electro-chemical Material), a highly wear resistant nickel-phosphorus silicon-carbide coating which should last the life of the engine. If any cylinder is badly scratched, scuffed or scored, the cylinder block must be renewed. The bore surface should not be honed.
10 Check the bore walls carefully for scratches and score marks (but do not confuse them with the fine cross-hatch lines which may still be present from the manufacturing process).
11 Using a precision straight-edge and a feeler gauge set to the warpage limit listed in the specifications at the beginning of the Chapter, check the top mating surface of the cylinder for warpage. Refer to *Tools and Workshop Tips* in the Reference section for details of how to use the straight-edge. If warpage is excessive the cylinder must be renewed.
12 Using a telescoping bore gauge and a micrometer (see *Tools and Workshop Tips*), check the dimensions of each cylinder bore to assess the amount of wear, taper and ovality. Measure near the top (but below the level of the top piston ring at TDC), centre and bottom (but above the level of the oil ring at BDC) of the bore, both parallel to and across the

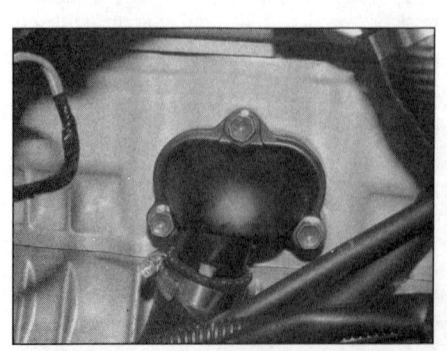

13.3 Detach the hose from the union or the union from the block as required

13.4 Unscrew and remove the nuts (arrowed)

13.5 Lift the cylinder block up off the crankcase and remove it

Engine, clutch and transmission 2•25

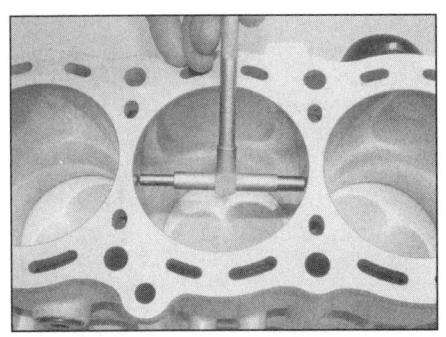

13.12a Use a bore gauge . . .

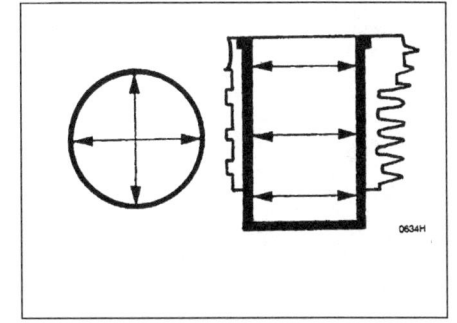

13.12b . . . and measure at the points shown

13.16 Fit the two dowels (arrowed) and locate the new gasket over them

crankshaft axis **(see illustrations)**. Compare the results to the specifications at the beginning of the Chapter. If the bores are worn beyond the service limit, or badly scratched, scuffed or scored, the cylinder block must be renewed.

13 If the precision measuring tools are not available, take the cylinder block to a Suzuki dealer or specialist motorcycle repair shop for assessment and advice.

Installation

14 Check that the mating surfaces of the cylinder and crankcase are free from oil or pieces of old gasket.
15 If removed, fit the dowels into the crankcase or into the block, and push them firmly home **(see illustration 13.16)**.
16 Remove the rags from around the piston, taking care not to let the connecting rod fall against the rim of the crankcase. Lay the new base gasket in place, locating it over the dowels (if they are in the crankcase), and making sure all holes align **(see illustration)**. The gasket can only fit one way, so if all the holes do not line up properly it is either the wrong way round or is not the correct gasket. Never re-use the old gasket.
17 Ensure the piston ring end gaps are positioned correctly before fitting the cylinder block (see Section 15). If required, fit piston ring compressors onto the pistons to ease their entry into the bore as the cylinder block is lowered. This is not essential as there is a good lead-in, enabling the piston rings to be hand-fed into the bore. If possible,

have an assistant support the block while this is done.
18 Rotate the crankshaft so that the middle pistons are at their highest point (top dead centre). It is useful to place a support under the pistons so that they remain at TDC while the block is fitted, otherwise the downward pressure will turn the crankshaft and the pistons will drop. Lubricate the cylinder bore, piston and piston rings with clean engine oil.
19 Carefully fit the block onto the middle pistons so the crowns fit into the bores **(see illustration)**. Gently push the block down, holding the underside of the pistons if you are not using a support to prevent them dropping, and making sure they enter the bores squarely and do not get cocked sideways. If you are doing this without piston ring compressors, carefully compress and feed each ring into the bores as the block is lowered **(see illustration)**. Do not use force if the block appears to be stuck as the pistons and/or rings will be damaged. If compressors were used, remove them once the rings are in the bore.
20 After locating the middle pistons in their bores feed or hook the cam chain up the tunnel and slip a piece of wire through it to prevent it falling back down. Try to keep the chain taut to prevent it becoming disengaged from the drive sprocket.
21 Remove the supports from the middle pistons if used then press the block down onto the outer pistons – they will raise as the middle pistons drop with the block. Feed the

outer piston rings into their bores as above. When they are correctly located press the block onto the base gasket, making sure the dowels locate.
22 Fit the cylinder block nuts, not forgetting the wiring clamp with the front nut fitted, and tighten them finger-tight only at this stage **(see illustration 13.4)**. Press down on the block and turn the crankshaft to check that all pistons move up and down smoothly in their bores. If they don't, or if there are any nasty scraping noises, remove the block and check the rings.
23 If removed, fit a new O-ring into the groove in the coolant union and smear it with grease, then attach the union and tighten the bolts to the specified torque setting **(see illustration 13.3)**. If detached, connect the hose to the union and secure it with the clamp.
24 Fit the front guide blade into the front of the cam chain tunnel, making sure it locates correctly onto its seat and its lugs locate in their cut-outs **(see illustration 10.3)**.
25 Install the cylinder head (see Section 11).

14 Pistons

Note: *To remove the pistons the engine must be removed from the frame (see Section 4).*

Removal

1 Remove the cylinder block (see Section 13).
2 Before removing the pistons from the connecting rods, use a sharp scriber or felt marker pen to write the cylinder identity on the crown of each piston (or on the inside of the skirt if the piston is dirty and going to be cleaned). Each piston crown should already have a circular indent on the crown that faces the exhaust side of the cylinder, though the mark may not be visible until the piston is cleaned. Stuff clean rag around each connecting rod to prevent a dropped circlip falling into the crankcase.
3 Carefully prise out the circlip on one side of the piston using needle-nose pliers or a small flat-bladed screwdriver inserted into the notch

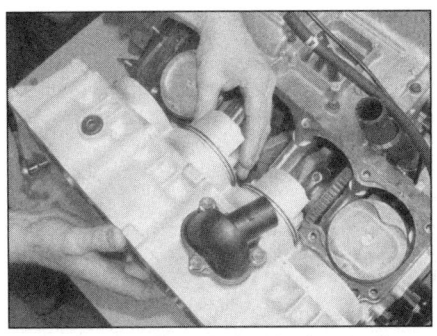

13.19a Carefully fit the block onto the pistons . . .

13.19b . . . and feed the rings into the bore

2•26 Engine, clutch and transmission

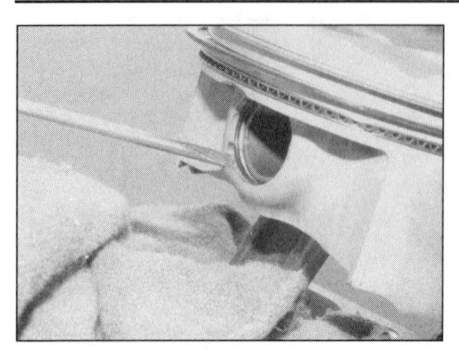

14.3a Prise the circlip out from one side of the piston

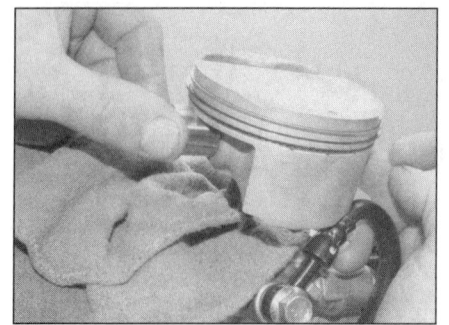

14.3b Push the piston pin out from the other side then withdraw it and remove the piston

14.10 Fit the ring into the groove and measure clearance with a feeler gauge

(see illustration). Push the piston pin out from the other side to free the piston from the connecting rod (see illustration). Remove the other circlip and discard them both as new ones must be used. When the piston has been removed, slide its pin back into its bore so that related parts do not get mixed up.

> **HAYNES HiNT** *To prevent the circlip from pinging away or from dropping into the crankcase, pass a rod or screwdriver, whose diameter is greater than the gap between the circlip ends, through the piston pin. This will catch the circlip if it springs out.*

> **HAYNES HiNT** *If a piston pin is a tight fit in the piston bosses, soak a rag in boiling water then wring it out and wrap it around the piston – this will expand the alloy piston sufficiently to release its grip on the pin. If the piston pin is particularly stubborn, extract it using a drawbolt tool, but be careful to protect the piston's working surfaces.*

Inspection

4 Using your thumbs or a piston ring removal and installation tool, carefully remove the rings from the pistons **(see illustrations 15.12, 11c, and 9c, b and a)**. Do not nick or gouge the pistons in the process. Carefully note which way up each ring fits and in which groove as they must be installed in their original positions if being re-used. The top rings should be marked with the letter R near one **(see illustration 15.11a)**. The second (middle) rings should be marked with the letters RN at one end **(see illustration 15.11b)**. The top and middle rings can also be identified by their different profiles and thickness.

5 Scrape all traces of carbon from the tops of the pistons. A hand-held wire brush or a piece of fine emery cloth can be used once most of the deposits have been scraped away. Do not, under any circumstances, use a wire brush mounted in a drill motor to remove deposits from the pistons; the piston material is soft and will be eroded away by the wire brush.

6 Use a piston ring groove cleaning tool to remove any carbon deposits from the ring grooves. If a tool is not available, a piece broken off an old ring will do the job. Be very careful to remove only the carbon deposits. Do not remove any metal and do not nick or gouge the sides of the ring grooves.

7 Once the deposits have been removed, clean the pistons with solvent and dry them thoroughly. If the identification previously marked on the piston is cleaned off, be sure to re-mark it with the correct identity. Make sure the oil return holes below the oil ring groove are clear.

8 Carefully inspect each piston for cracks around the skirt, at the pin bosses and at the ring lands. Normal piston wear appears as even, vertical wear on the thrust surfaces of the piston and slight looseness of the top ring in its groove. If the skirt is scored or scuffed, the engine may have been suffering from overheating and/or abnormal combustion, which caused excessively high operating temperatures. Check that the circlip grooves are not damaged.

9 A hole in the piston crown, an extreme to be sure, is an indication that abnormal combustion (pre-ignition) was occurring. Burned areas at the edge of the piston crown are usually evidence of spark knock (detonation). If any of the above problems exist, the causes must be corrected or the damage will occur again.

10 Measure the piston ring-to-groove clearance by laying each piston ring in its groove and slipping a feeler gauge in underneath it **(see illustration)**. Make sure you have the correct ring for the groove (see Step 4). Check the clearance at three or four locations around the groove. If new rings are being used, measure the clearance using the new rings. If the clearance is greater than specified with the old rings, measure the thickness of the rings and replace them with new ones if worn below the specified limit, then check the clearance again. If the clearance is greater than that specified with new rings, or if the old rings are not worn, the piston is worn and must be replaced with a new one. If you are fitting new pistons, fit new rings with them rather than using the old ones.

11 Check the piston-to-bore clearance by measuring the bore (see Section 13) and the piston diameter. Make sure each piston is matched to its correct cylinder. Measure the piston 15 mm up from the bottom of the skirt and at 90° to the piston pin axis **(see illustration)**. Subtract the piston diameter from the bore diameter to obtain the clearance. If it is greater than the specified figure, and if not already done, check the cylinder for wear (see Section 13). If the cylinder is good but the piston is worn, replace the piston with a new one.

12 Apply clean engine oil to the piston pin, insert it into the piston and check for any freeplay between the two **(see illustration)**.

14.11 Measure the piston diameter as shown

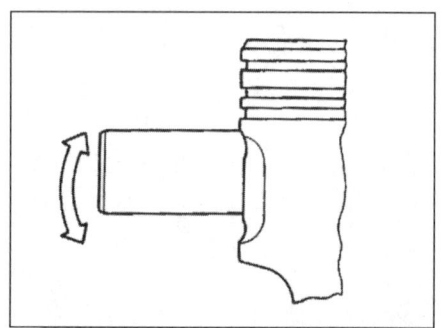

14.12a Slip the pin into the piston and check for freeplay between them

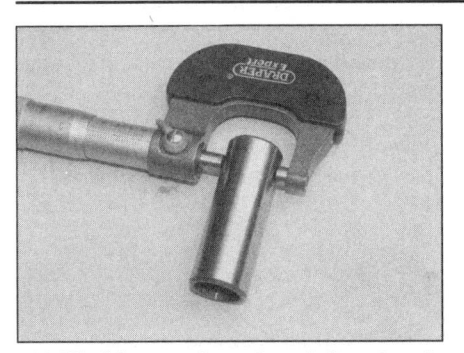

Engine, clutch and transmission 2•27

14.12b Measure the external diameter of the pin . . .

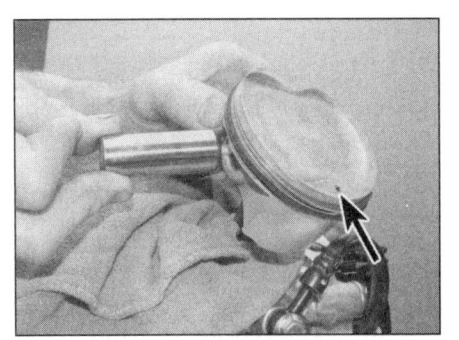

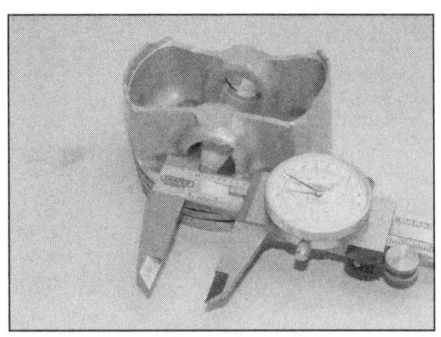

14.12c . . . and the internal diameter of the bore in the piston

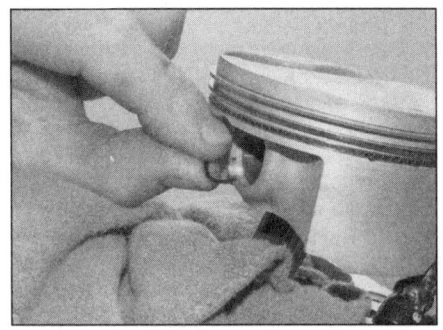

14.16a With the mark (arrowed) facing the front of the engine slide the pin through the piston and connecting rod . . .

14.16b . . . and secure it with the circlip, locating the open end away from the notch in the piston

Measure the pin external diameter at each end and the pin bore in the piston **(see illustrations)**. Calculate the difference to obtain the piston pin-to-piston pin bore clearance. Compare the result to the specifications at the beginning of the Chapter. If the clearance is greater than specified, replace the components that are worn beyond their specified limits with new ones. If not already done, repeat the measurements between the pin and the connecting rod small-end (see Section 29).

Installation

13 Inspect and install the piston rings (see Section 15).
14 Lubricate the piston pin, the piston pin bore and the connecting rod small-end bore with molybdenum disulphide oil (a 50/50 mixture of molybdenum disulphide grease and clean engine oil).

15 When installing the pistons onto the connecting rods, make sure you have the correct piston for the cylinder being worked on. Note that the small circular indent on the piston crown faces the exhaust side of the cylinder **(see illustration 14.16a)**.
16 Stuff clean rag around the connecting rod to prevent a dropped circlip falling into the crankcase. Install a *new* circlip in one side of the piston (do not re-use old circlips). Line up the piston on its correct connecting rod, and insert the piston pin from the other side **(see illustration)**. Secure the pin with the other *new* circlip **(see illustration)**. When installing the circlips, compress them only just enough to fit them in the piston, and make sure they are properly seated in their grooves with the open end away from the removal notch. Remove the rag from the crankcase.
17 Install the cylinder block (see Section 13).

15 Piston rings

1 It is good practice to fit new piston rings when an engine is overhauled. Before installing the rings (new or old), check the free end gap and installed end gap of the top and second (middle) rings as follows.
2 If new rings are being used, lay out each piston with a new ring set and keep them together so the rings will be matched with the same piston and bore during the end gap measurement procedure and engine assembly. If the old rings are being reused, make sure they are matched with their original piston and cylinder.
3 With the ring flat on the work surface, measure its end gap using a Vernier caliper **(see illustration)**. To measure the installed ring end gap, insert the ring into the top of the bore and square it up with the bore walls by pushing it in with the top of the piston **(see illustration)**. The ring should be about 20 mm below the top edge of the bore. Slip a feeler gauge between the ends of the ring and measure the gap **(see illustration)**. Compare the measurements to the specifications at the beginning of the Chapter.
4 If the gap is larger or smaller than specified, double check to make sure that you have the correct rings before proceeding.
5 If the gap is too small, the ring ends may come in contact with each other during engine operation, which can cause serious damage.
6 Excess end gap is not critical unless it exceeds the service limit. Again, double-check to make sure you have the correct rings for your engine and check that the bore is not worn (see Section 13).
7 Repeat the procedure for the other rings. Remember to keep the rings, pistons and bores matched up.
8 Once the ring end gaps have been checked, the rings can be installed on the pistons.
9 Install the oil control ring (lowest on the piston) first. It is composed of three separate components, namely the expander and the upper and lower side rails. Slip the expander into the groove, making sure the ends don't

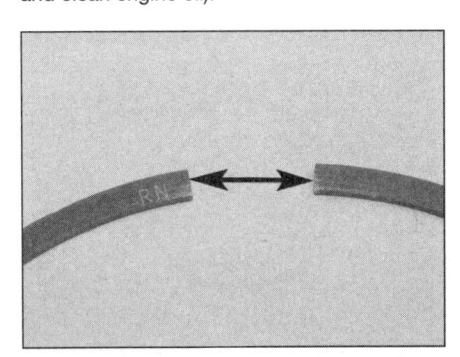

15.3a Measure the free end gap of the piston ring . . .

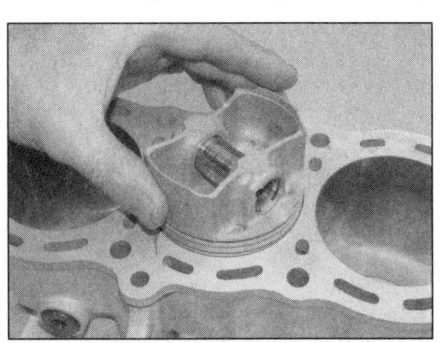

15.3b . . . then fit the ring into the bore and square it up as shown . . .

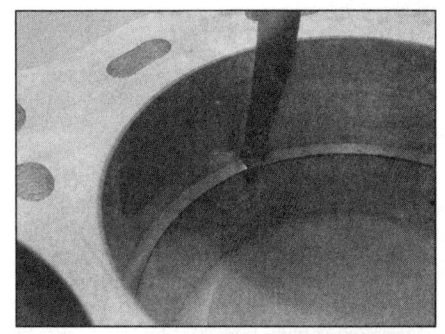

15.3c . . . and measure the installed end gap

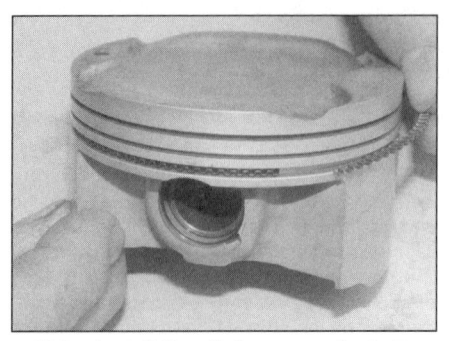

2•28 Engine, clutch and transmission

15.9a Install the oil ring expander in its groove . . .

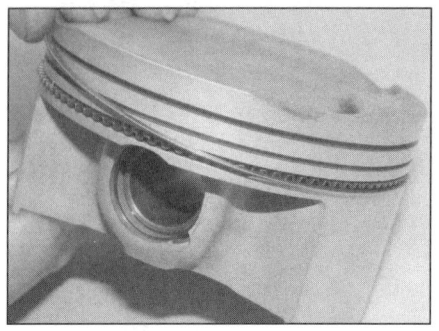

15.9b . . . then fit the lower side rail . . .

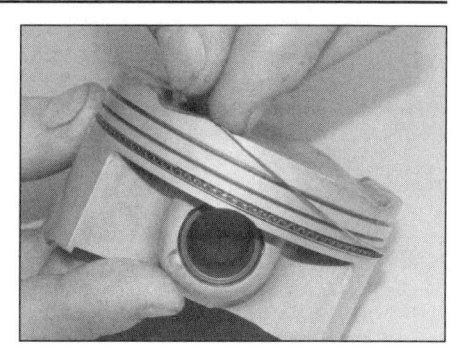

15.9c . . . and the upper side rail

overlap, then install the lower side rail **(see illustrations)**. Do not use a piston ring installation tool on the side rails as they may be damaged. Instead, place one end of the side rail into the groove between the expander and the ring land. Hold it firmly in place and slide a finger around the piston while pushing the rail into the groove. Next, install the upper side rail in the same manner **(see illustration)**. Check that the ends of the expander have not overlapped.

10 After the three oil ring components have been installed, check to make sure that both the upper and lower side rails can be turned smoothly in the ring groove.

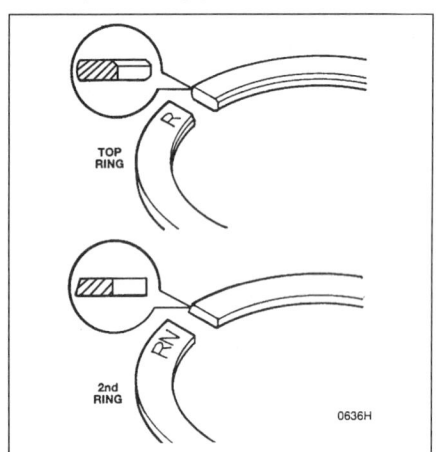

11 The top and middle rings can be identified by their different profiles and thicknesses **(see illustration)** – refer to the Specifications. The top rings should be marked with the letter R near one end. The second (middle) rings should be marked with the letters RN at one end **(see illustration)**. Install the second (middle) ring next. Make sure that the identification letters near the end gap are facing up. Fit the 2nd ring into the middle groove in the piston **(see illustration)**. Do not expand the ring any more than is necessary to slide it into place. To avoid breaking the ring, use a piston ring installation tool, or alternatively pieces of old feeler gauge blades can be used as shown **(see illustration)**.

12 Finally, install the top ring in the same manner into the top groove in the piston **(see illustration)**. Make sure the ring is the correct way up.

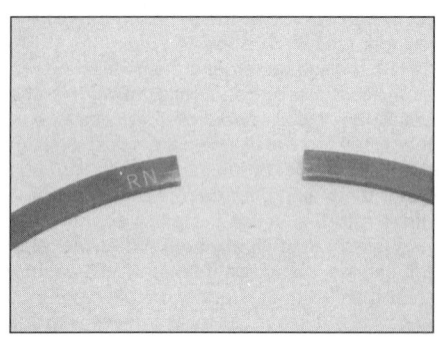

13 Once the rings are correctly installed, check they move freely without snagging and stagger their end gaps as shown **(see illustration)**.

16 Clutch

Note: *The clutch can be removed with the engine in the frame. If the engine has already been removed, ignore the steps which don't apply.*

Removal

1 Drain the engine oil (see Chapter 1). Remove the right-hand fairing side panel (see Chapter 8).

2 Working in a criss-cross pattern, evenly

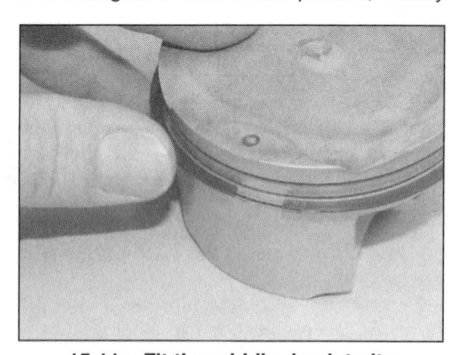

15.11a The rings are distinguishable by their profiles and letters on the top surface . . .

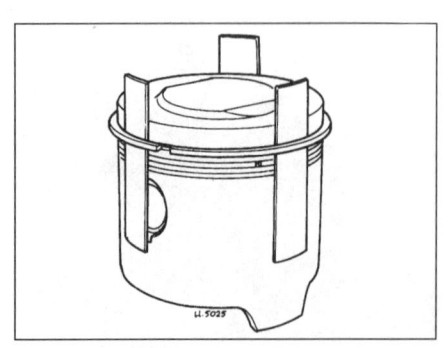

15.11b . . . the letters on the middle ring are larger and easier to see than on the top ring

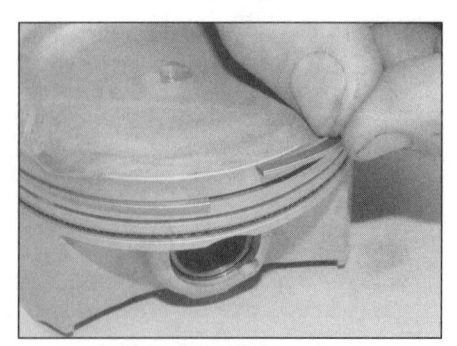

15.11c Fit the middle ring into its groove . . .

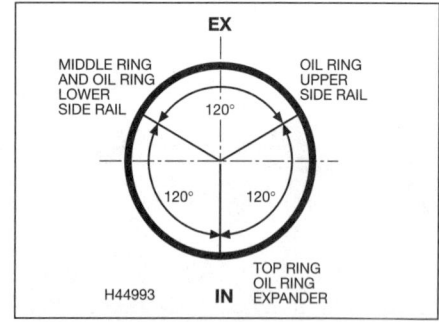

15.11d . . . using pieces of blade as shown to guide the rings on if required . . .

15.12 . . . then fit the top ring

15.13 Arrange the ring end gaps as shown

Engine, clutch and transmission 2•29

slacken the clutch cover bolts **(see illustration)**. If the engine is in the frame release the oxygen sensor (K2 models onward) and oil pressure switch wiring from its clamps to access the front bolts. Note which bolts secure wiring clamps. Lift the cover away from the engine, being prepared to catch any residual oil. Note that there is a leverage point on the front edge of the cover at the bottom if it is difficult to displace. Never lever between the cover and crankcase mating surfaces as you could gouge them and cause a leak.

3 Remove the gasket and discard it. Note the positions of the two locating dowels and remove them for safe-keeping if they are loose – they could be in either the crankcase or the cover.

4 Working in a criss-cross pattern, and holding the clutch housing to prevent it turning, gradually slacken the clutch pressure plate bolts until spring pressure is released, then remove the bolts and springs, and the pressure plate **(see illustrations)**.

5 Remove the thrust washer, bearing and pressure plate lifter **(see illustration)**. If the front sprocket cover has been displaced from the left-hand side of the engine, push the exposed short pushrod into the input shaft and withdraw the long pushrod from the right-hand end **(see illustration)**. Do not attempt to withdraw the long pushrod from the left-hand side as it has a knurled section on each end which could easily damage the oil seal (and you have to separate the crankcase halves to replace the oil seal). If the release mechanism is in place, pull the clutch lever in to push the rods as far into the shaft as possible and remove the long one from the right-hand end of the shaft, using a hooked piece of wire to draw it out.

6 Remove the clutch friction and plain plates one by one, keeping them in order, and using a bent piece of wire to hook them out where necessary **(see illustration)**. Keep the plates assembled in their original order, even if you are replacing them with new ones, as there are different types – the old ones can be used as a guide to installing the new ones. On K2 models onward also remove the anti-judder spring and spring seat **(see illustrations 16.29b and a)**.

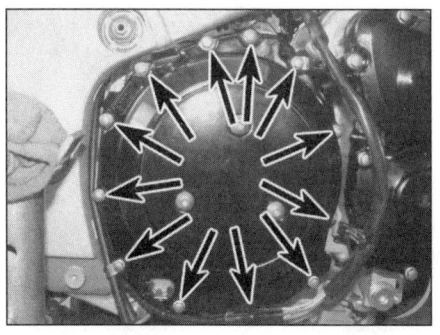

16.2 Clutch cover bolts (arrowed)

16.4a Unscrew the bolts . . .

16.4b . . . and remove the springs . . .

16.4c . . . and the pressure plate

16.5a Remove the thrust washer bearing and pressure plate lifter . . .

16.5b . . . and if required the pushrod

7 Using a suitable drift and hammer unstake the rim of the clutch nut from the indent in the shaft **(see illustration)**. To remove the clutch nut the transmission input shaft must be locked. This can be done in several ways. If the engine is in the frame, engage 5th gear and have an assistant hold the rear brake on hard with the rear tyre in firm contact with the ground. Alternatively, the Suzuki service tool (Pt. No. 09920-53740) or a commercially available (and inexpensive) equivalent (which combines as a starter clutch holding tool) can be used to stop the clutch centre from turning whilst the nut is slackened **(see illustration)**. Locate the shaped ends of the tool arms into opposed grooves in the clutch centre. With

16.6 Remove the clutch plates as described

16.7a Unstake the clutch nut . . .

16.7b . . . then unscrew it as described – here a commercially available holding tool is being used

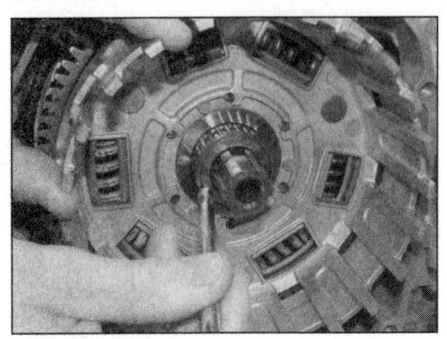

2•30 Engine, clutch and transmission

16.10 Draw the spacer and bearing out from the centre of the housing

16.11 Slide the thrust washer off

16.12 Measure the thickness of the friction plates . . .

the clutch centre held, unscrew the clutch nut, then remove the shaped washer. If the rim of the nut is badly distorted replace it with a new one, otherwise it can reused.
8 Slide the clutch centre off the shaft **(see illustration 16.27)**. Remove the back-torque limiter drive and driven cams from the clutch centre, noting how they fit **(see illustration 16.26a)**.
9 Slide the thrust washer off the shaft **(see illustration 16.25)**.
10 Draw the bearing and spacer from the centre of the clutch housing using a magnet and by sliding the housing down the shaft as far as possible, then sliding it back while attracting the spacer with the magnet **(see illustration)**. After removing the spacer and bearing remove the clutch housing, noting how it engages with the primary drive gear on the crankshaft and the oil pump driven gear **(see illustration 16.24a)**. Note the oil pump drive gear on the back of the clutch housing

and remove it if required, noting which way up it fits.
11 Slide the thrust washer off the shaft **(see illustration)**.

Inspection

Note: *Refer to illustrations 18.30a and 18.30b for clutch plate identification.*
12 After an extended period of service the clutch friction plates will wear and promote clutch slip. Measure the thickness of each friction plate using a Vernier caliper **(see illustration)**. If any plate has worn to or beyond the service limit given in the Specifications at the beginning of the Chapter, the friction plates must be replaced with new ones as a set. Also, if any of the plates smell burnt or are glazed, they must be replaced as a set. Note that there are different types of friction plate with different thicknesses – ensure the correct dimensions for your model are referred to in the Specifications.

13 Also measure the width of the friction plate tabs and replace any plates that are worn beyond the service limit specified with new ones – again note that the different plates have slightly different tab width specifications **(see illustration)**.
14 The plain plates should not show any signs of excess heating (bluing). Check for warpage using a flat surface and feeler gauges **(see illustration)**. If any plate exceeds the maximum amount of warpage, or shows signs of bluing, all plain plates must be renewed as a set. Note that there are two thicknesses of plain plate, and that from K2 models onward the number of each installed by the factory is not set (see Specifications) – however if they are being replaced with new ones Suzuki specify to install the standard number as listed (i.e. seven of one type and two of the other), irrespective of the number of each originally fitted.
15 Measure the free length of each clutch spring using a Vernier caliper **(see illustration)**. If any spring is below the service limit specified, replace all the springs with new ones as a set. Also place the spring upright on a flat surface and check it for bend by placing a ruler against it, or alternatively lay it against a set square **(see illustration)**. If the bend in any spring is excessive, all springs must be replaced with new ones.
16 Inspect the edges of the tabs on the friction plates and the corresponding slots in the clutch housing for burrs and indentations **(see illustration)**. Similarly check for wear between the inner teeth of the plain plates and the slots in the clutch centre **(see**

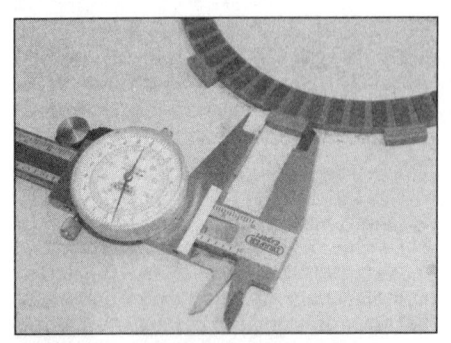

16.13 . . . and the width of the tabs

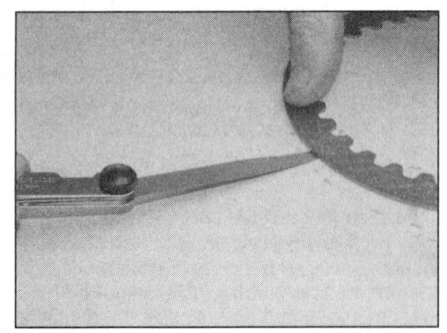

16.14 Check the plain plates for warpage

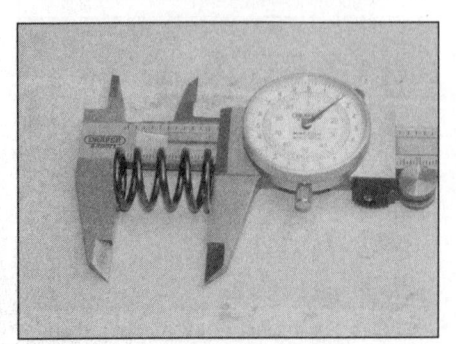

16.15a Measure the free length of the clutch springs . . .

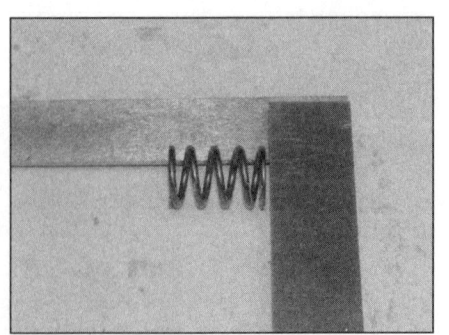

16.15b . . . and check that they are square

16.16a Check the friction plate tabs and clutch housing slots as described

Engine, clutch and transmission 2•31

16.16b Check the plain plate tongues and the clutch centre slots as described

16.17 Check the spacer, bearing and clutch housing as described

16.18a Check the lifter, its bearing and the other components as described

illustration). Wear of this nature will cause clutch drag and slow disengagement during gear changes as the plates will snag when the pressure plate is lifted. With care a small amount of wear can be corrected by dressing with a fine file, but if wear is excessive new components should be installed.

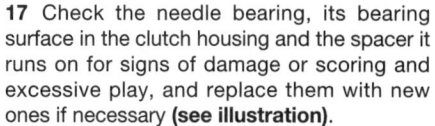

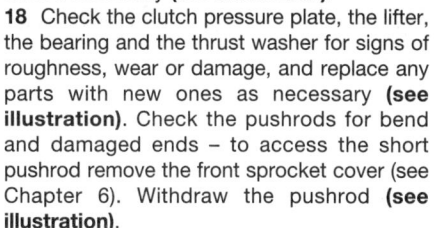

17 Check the needle bearing, its bearing surface in the clutch housing and the spacer it runs on for signs of damage or scoring and excessive play, and replace them with new ones if necessary **(see illustration)**.

18 Check the clutch pressure plate, the lifter, the bearing and the thrust washer for signs of roughness, wear or damage, and replace any parts with new ones as necessary **(see illustration)**. Check the pushrods for bend and damaged ends – to access the short pushrod remove the front sprocket cover (see Chapter 6). Withdraw the pushrod **(see illustration)**.

19 Check the pushrod oil seal on the left-hand side of the engine for signs of oil leakage and replace it with a new one it if necessary. To do this you have to separate the crankcase halves as the seal sits in a lipped rim in the crankcases – refer to Section 25.

20 Check the back-torque limiter drive and driven cams for wear of the engagement dogs and their slots, and replace them with a new set if necessary **(see illustration)**. Also check that the clutch spring bolt holders are tight in the driven cam – if any are loose, unscrew them all, then clean their threads, apply a suitable non-permanent thread-locking compound to them and tighten them to the torque setting specified at the beginning of the Chapter.

21 Check the teeth of the primary driven gear on the back of the clutch housing and the corresponding teeth of the primary drive gear on the crankshaft. Replace the clutch housing and/or crankshaft with new ones if worn or chipped teeth are discovered (refer to Section 28 for the crankshaft). Similarly check the oil pump drive gear on the back of the housing and its driven gear on the pump shaft – the drive gear is not listed as being available as a separate component from the clutch housing, but check with a Suzuki dealer before buying a whole new housing **(see illustration)**.

16.18b Withdraw the short pushrod and check it as described

16.20 Check the dogs and slots for wear and damage, and make sure the bolt holders are tight

Installation

22 Remove all traces of old gasket from the crankcase and clutch cover surfaces.

23 Slide the thrust washer onto the shaft with its chamfered side facing in **(see illustration)**. If removed, fit the oil pump drive gear onto the back of the clutch housing with the recessed side facing the housing **(see illustration)**.

24 Smear the spacer (inside and out) and the needle bearing with molybdenum disulphide oil (50% molybdenum grease and 50% engine oil). Slide the clutch housing onto the input shaft, angling it as required to clear the crankcase, and engaging the teeth on the oil pump drive gear with those on the driven gear, and the teeth on the primary driven gear with those on the primary drive gear **(see**

16.21 Check the teeth on the various related gears for wear and damage

16.23a Slide the thrust washer onto the shaft, making sure it is the correct way round

16.23b Fit the gear onto the housing, making sure it is the correct way round

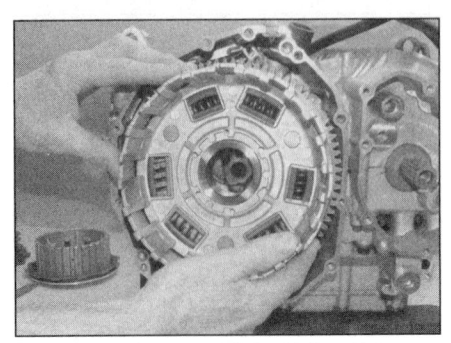

2•32 Engine, clutch and transmission

16.24a Locate the clutch housing, engaging the gear teeth . . .

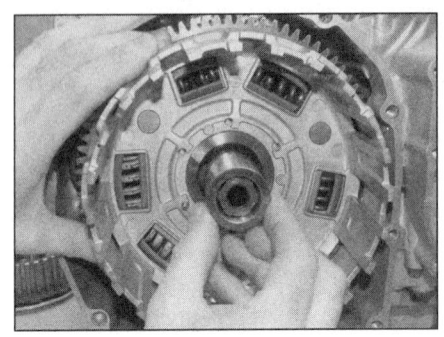

16.24b . . . then slide the spacer onto the shaft and into the housing . . .

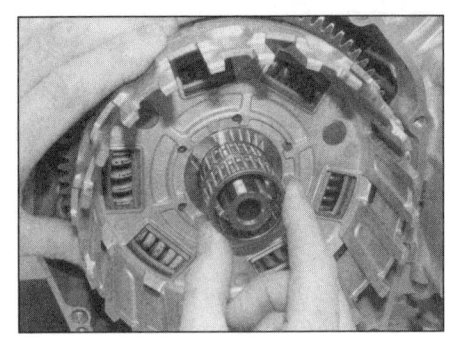

16.24c . . . and slide the needle bearing between them

16.24d Check that the gear teeth have engaged correctly

16.25 Slide the thrust washer onto the shaft

16.26a Fit the driven cam into the clutch centre . . .

16.26b . . . then fit the drive cam into the driven cam, aligning the punch marks

16.27 Slide the clutch centre onto the shaft

16.28a Fit the shaped washer . . .

16.28b . . . then fit the clutch nut . . .

16.28c . . . and tighten it to the specified torque

illustration). Hold the housing engaged with the gears and clear of the shaft and slide the spacer and bearing onto the shaft and into the centre of the housing (see illustrations). Try to turn the oil pump driven gear by hand to check that it has engaged correctly with the drive gear (see illustration).

25 Slide the thrust washer onto the shaft (see illustration).

26 Fit the back-torque limiter driven cam into the clutch centre, locating the cut-outs on its inner side over the raised sections in the centre (see illustration). Now fit the drive cam into the driven cam, locating the dogs in the slots and aligning the punch mark on the drive cam with that on the driven cam (see illustration).

27 Slide the clutch centre onto the shaft, engaging the splines in the centre of the drive cam with those on the shaft (see illustration).

28 Slide the shaped washer onto the shaft so that its inner rim is raised away from the engine (see illustration). Fit the clutch nut with its thin rim facing out, and using the method employed on removal to lock the input shaft (see Step 7), tighten the nut to the torque setting specified at the beginning of the Chapter (see illustrations). **Note:** *Check that the clutch centre rotates freely after tightening the clutch nut.* Stake the rim of the

Engine, clutch and transmission 2•33

16.28d Stake the rim of the clutch nut against the shaft indent

16.29a Fit the spring seat . . .

16.29b . . . and the spring . . .

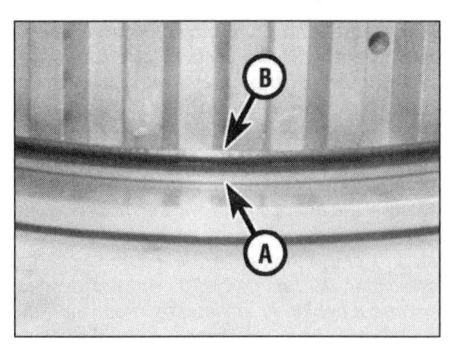

16.29c . . . as shown – spring seat (A), spring (B)

nut into one of the indents on the shaft **(see illustration)**.

29 On K2 models onward fit the anti-judder spring seat over the clutch centre, then fit the spring so that its outer rim is raised off the spring seat **(see illustrations)**.

30 Build up the clutch friction and plain plates in the housing according to the order for your model **(see illustrations)**. Coat each

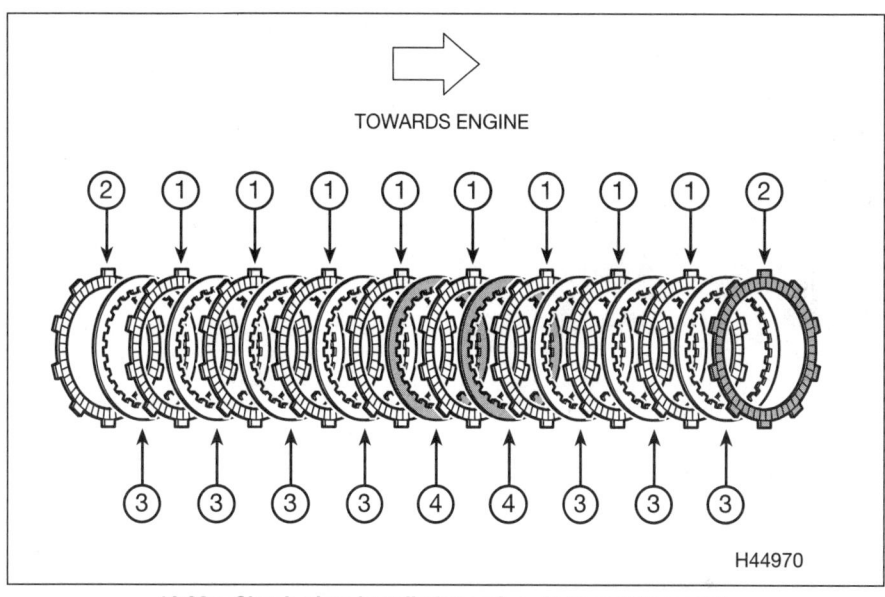

16.30a Clutch plate installation order – X, Y and K1 models

1 Type A friction plate – 3.0 mm thick (8 off)
2 Type B friction plate – 3.8 mm thick (2 off)
3 Type A plain plate – 2.0 mm thick (7 off)
4 Type B plain plate – 2.3 mm thick (2 off)

16.30b Clutch plate installation order – K2 models onwards

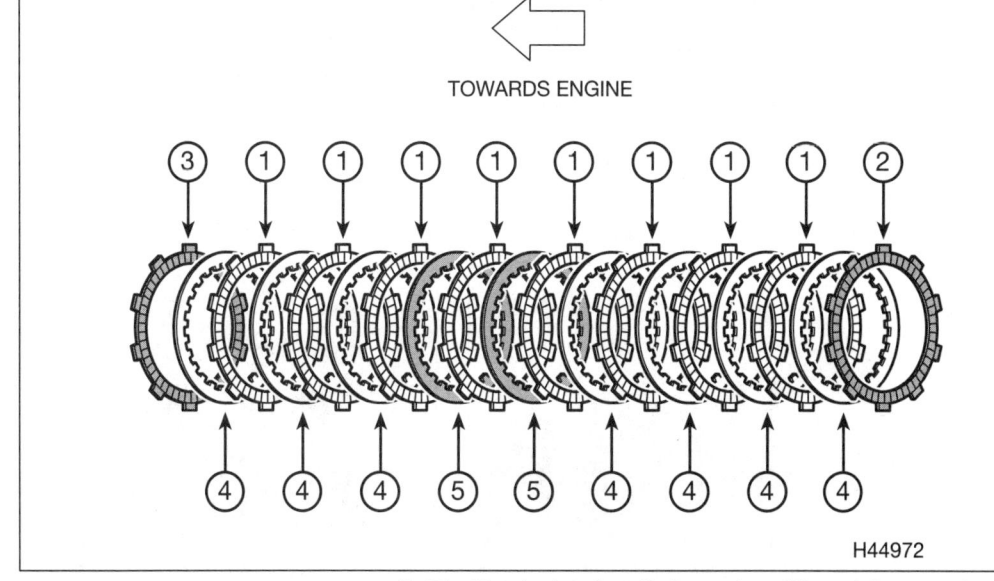

1 Type A friction plate – 3.0 mm thick (8 off)
2 Type B friction plate – 3.8 mm thick and 127 mm inside diameter (1 off)
3 Type C friction plate – 3.8 mm thick and 135 mm inside diameter (1 off)
3 Type A plain plate – 2.0 mm thick (7 off)
4 Type B plain plate – 2.3 mm thick (2 off)

2•34 Engine, clutch and transmission

16.30c Fit the innermost friction plate, which on K2-on models fits around the anti-judder spring and seat, . . .

16.30d . . . then alternate between plain plates . . .

16.30e . . . and friction plates in the specified order for your model . . .

16.30f . . . fitting the tabs on the outermost plate in the shallow slots (arrowed)

clutch plate with engine oil before installing it **(see illustrations)**. On all models locate the tabs on the outermost friction plate in the shallow slots in the housing so they are offset from the others **(see illustration)**.

31 If removed, smear molybdenum grease onto each end of the pushrod and slide it into the input shaft **(see illustration 16.5b)**. Lubricate the pressure plate lifter, the bearing and thrust washer with clean oil, then fit the bearing and the washer onto the lifter and slide the assembly into the shaft **(see illustration 16.5a)**.

32 Fit the pressure plate into the clutch centre, making sure the plate seats correctly with its inner rim castellations locating in the slots in the centre – if there is any clearance between the clutch plates as you push on the pressure plate then it has not located properly **(see illustration)**. Fit the clutch springs and bolts and tighten the bolts evenly in a criss-cross sequence to the specified torque setting **(see illustrations 16.4b and a)**.

33 Apply a smear of sealant (Suzuki Bond 1207B or equivalent) to the area around the crankcase joints as shown **(see illustration)**. If removed, insert the clutch cover dowels into the crankcase, then place a new gasket onto the crankcase, making sure it locates correctly over the dowels.

34 Install the clutch cover and tighten its bolts evenly in a criss-cross sequence, not forgetting to fit the wiring clamps **(see illustration and 16.2)**.

35 Refill the engine with the correct quantity of oil (see Chapter 1).

36 Check the action of the clutch. Install the fairing side panel (see Chapter 8).

17 Clutch master cylinder

⚠ *Warning: Do not, under any circumstances, use petroleum-based solvents to clean the clutch release mechanism parts. Use clean brake/clutch fluid or denatured alcohol only. Use care when working with brake/clutch fluid as it can injure your eyes and it will damage painted surfaces and plastic parts – cover surrounding components with rag, wipe up any spills immediately and wash the area with soap and water. Disassembly, overhaul and reassembly of the clutch master cylinder must be done in a spotlessly clean work area to avoid contamination and possible failure of the hydraulic release mechanism components.*

Note: *If the entire clutch release mechanism is being overhauled (i.e. release cylinder as well as master cylinder), or if you intend to change the clutch fluid as part of the master cylinder overhaul (which is advisable), drain the fluid completely from the system (after displacing the piston from the release cylinder if applicable) (see Section 19), as opposed to retaining the old fluid within it by blocking the hose as described (Step 6).*

1 If the master cylinder is leaking fluid, or if the clutch does not work properly when the lever is applied, and bleeding the system does not help (see Section 19), and the hydraulic hose is in good condition, then master cylinder overhaul is recommended.

2 Before disassembling the master cylinder, read through the entire procedure and make sure that you have the correct rebuild kit. Also, you will need some new DOT 4 hydraulic brake and clutch fluid, some clean rags and internal circlip pliers.

Removal

Note: *If the master cylinder is being displaced from the handlebar and not being removed completely or overhauled, follow Steps 4 and 7 only.*

3 Slacken the reservoir cover screws, then

16.32 Fit the pressure plate and make sure the castellations locate in the slots

16.33 Apply the sealant around the joints then fit the gasket . . .

16.34 . . . and install the cover, locating it on the dowels

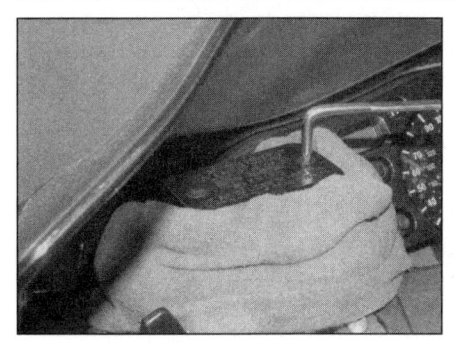

Engine, clutch and transmission 2•35

17.3 Slacken the screws

17.4 Disconnect the wiring connectors (arrowed)

17.6 Clutch hose banjo bolt (arrowed)

lightly tighten them again **(see illustration)** – turn the handlebars as required so that the top of the reservoir is level, supporting the motorcycle upright using an auxiliary stand if required. If you don't have a short or angled screwdriver that can fit between the reservoir and the windshield, slacken the screws with the reservoir clear of the windshield, keeping finger pressure on the cover until the reservoir is level again.

4 Disconnect the clutch switch wiring connectors **(see illustration)**. If required, remove the clutch switch (see Chapter 9).

5 If the master cylinder is being overhauled, remove the clutch lever (see Chapter 6). If it is just being displaced it can remain in situ.

6 If the master cylinder is being completely removed or overhauled, unscrew the clutch hose banjo bolt and separate the hose from the cylinder, noting its alignment **(see illustration)**. Discard the sealing washers as they must be replaced with new ones. Either clamp the hose using a hose clamp, block it using another suitable short piece of hose fitted through the eye of the banjo union (it needs to be a fairly tight fit to seal it properly), or using a suitable bolt with sealing washers and a capped (domed) nut, or wrap some plastic foodwrap tightly around (a finger cut off a latex glove also works well), the object being to minimise fluid loss and prevent dirt entering the system. Whatever you do, also cover the end of the hose in rag, just in case. If the master cylinder is just being displaced and not completely removed, do not disconnect the hose.

7 Unscrew the master cylinder clamp bolts,

17.7 Master cylinder clamp bolts (arrowed)

then lift the master cylinder and reservoir away from the handlebar **(see illustration)**.

Caution: Do not tip the master cylinder or brake fluid will run out.

8 Remove the reservoir cover, diaphragm plate and rubber diaphragm **(see illustration 17.24)**. If the system hasn't been drained, tip the brake fluid from the reservoir into a suitable container. Wipe any remaining fluid out of the reservoir with a clean rag.

Overhaul

9 Draw the pushrod out of the master cylinder, noting how it locates in the rubber boot – the boot may come away with the pushrod **(see illustration)**.

10 If it didn't come with the pushrod, remove the rubber boot from the end of the cylinder.

11 Push the piston in and, using circlip pliers, remove the circlip, then slide out the washer, piston and seal, primary cup, and spring, noting how they fit. Lay the parts out in the proper order and way round to prevent confusion during reassembly.

12 Clean all parts with clean brake/clutch fluid. Do not dry or wipe the components with a rag.

Caution: Do not, under any circumstances, use a petroleum-based solvent to clean the parts.

13 Check the master cylinder bore for corrosion, scratches, nicks and score marks. If the necessary measuring equipment is available, compare the diameters of the cylinder and piston to those given in the Specifications Section of this Chapter. If damage or wear is evident, the master cylinder must be replaced with a new one. If the master cylinder is in poor condition, then the release cylinder should be checked as well. Check that the fluid inlet and outlet ports in the master cylinder are clear.

14 The dust boot, circlip, washer, seal, piston, primary cup and spring are all included in the rebuild kit. Use all of the new parts, regardless of the apparent condition of the old ones. Fit all components according to the layout of the old one. Lubricate the bore, seal, piston, primary cup and spring with clean brake/clutch fluid.

15 Fit the primary cup into the narrow end of the spring. Fit the spring into the master cylinder, wide end first, making sure the cup lips do not turn inside.

16 If not already done, fit the seal onto the piston. Fit the piston into the master cylinder, making sure it is the correct way round and the seal lips do not turn inside out. Slide the washer into the cylinder. Depress the piston and install the new circlip, making sure that it locates in the groove.

17 Apply some silicone grease to the inside

1 Bush
2 Pushrod
3 Rubber boot
4 Circlip
5 Washer
6 Piston and seal
7 Primary cup
8 Spring

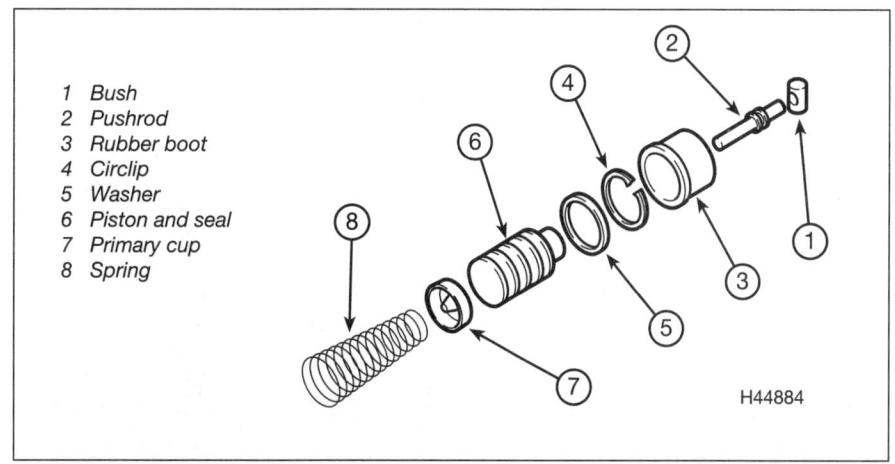

17.9 Clutch master cylinder components

17.19 Align the clamp mating surfaces with the punch mark (arrowed) in the handlebar

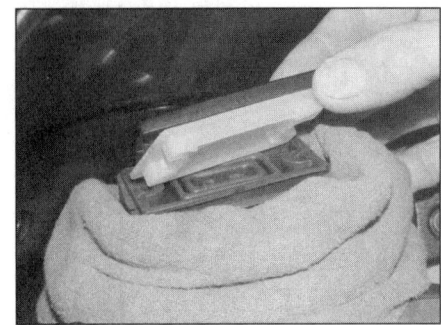

17.24 Make sure the diaphragm is properly seated in the reservoir

of the rubber boot and to the pushrod ends. Fit the boot, making sure the wide rim locates correctly in the groove in the end of the master cylinder. Fit the pushrod into the boot, locating its end against the piston, and locating the narrow rim of the boot into the groove.

18 Inspect the reservoir rubber diaphragm and replace it with a new one it if it is damaged or deteriorated.

Installation

19 Locate the master cylinder on the handlebar and fit the clamp with its UP mark facing up **(see illustration 17.7)**, aligning the clamp mating surfaces with the punch mark on the top of the handlebar **(see illustration)**. Tighten the upper bolt first, then the lower bolt, to the torque setting specified at the beginning of the Chapter.

20 If detached, connect the clutch hose to the master cylinder, using new sealing washers on each side of the union, and aligning the hose as noted on removal **(see illustration 17.6)**. Tighten the banjo bolt to the specified torque setting.

21 If removed, install the clutch switch (see Chapter 9). Otherwise, connect the clutch switch wiring connectors **(see illustration 17.4)**.

22 If removed, install the clutch lever (see Chapter 6).

23 Fill the fluid reservoir with new DOT 4 brake/clutch fluid as described in *Daily (pre-ride) checks*. Bleed the air from the system (see Section 19).

24 Fit the rubber diaphragm onto the master cylinder reservoir, making sure it is correctly seated, and the diaphragm plate **(see illustration)**. Fit the cover and tighten its screws (do not overtighten) **(see illustration 17.3)**.

25 Check the operation of the clutch before riding the motorcycle.

18 Clutch release cylinder

⚠️ **Warning: Do not, under any circumstances, use petroleum-based solvents to clean the clutch release mechanism parts. Use clean brake/clutch fluid or denatured alcohol only. Use care when working with brake/clutch fluid as it can injure your eyes and it will damage painted surfaces and plastic parts – cover surrounding components with rag, wipe up any spills immediately and wash the area with soap and water. Disassembly, overhaul and reassembly of the clutch release cylinder must be done in a spotlessly clean work area to avoid contamination and possible failure of the hydraulic release mechanism components.**

Note: *If the entire clutch release mechanism is being overhauled (i.e. master cylinder as well as release cylinder), or if you intend to change the clutch fluid as part of the release cylinder overhaul (which is advisable), drain the fluid completely from the system after displacing the piston (see Section 19), as opposed to retaining the old fluid within it by blocking the hose as described (Step 4).*

Removal

1 If the release cylinder is leaking fluid, or if the clutch does not work properly when the lever is applied, and bleeding the system does not help (see Section 19), and the hydraulic hose and master cylinder are in good condition, then release cylinder overhaul is recommended.

2 Before disassembling the release cylinder, read through the entire procedure and make sure that you have a new seal. Also, you will need some new DOT 4 hydraulic brake and clutch fluid, and some clean rags.

Removal

3 Remove the left-hand fairing side panel (see Chapter 8). To allow access to the release cylinder, undo the screws securing the coolant reservoir and displace it from the frame – support or tie it so that it remains upright but is clear of the release cylinder **(see illustration)**. If necessary drain and remove the reservoir completely (see Chapters 1 and 3 if required).

4 If the release cylinder is being overhauled, slacken the clutch hose banjo bolt then retighten it lightly, enough to prevent fluid leakage. The clutch hydraulic system can then be used to force the piston out of the cylinder. If the cylinder is being completely removed but not overhauled, unscrew the clutch hose banjo bolt and detach the hose, noting its alignment **(see illustration)**. Discard the sealing washers as new ones must be used on installation. Either clamp the hose, plug it using another suitable short piece of hose fitted through the eye of the banjo union (a tight fit is necessary for a good seal), block it using a suitable bolt with sealing washers and a capped (domed) nut, or wrap some plastic foodwrap tightly around (a finger cut off a latex glove also works well), the object being to minimise fluid loss and prevent dirt entering the system. Whatever you do, also cover the end of the hose in rag, just in case.

5 Slacken the two release cylinder bolts **(see illustration)**. Displace the front sprocket

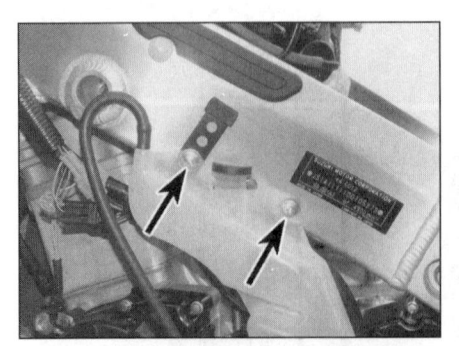

18.3 Undo the screws (arrowed) and displace the coolant reservoir

18.4 Clutch hose banjo bolt (arrowed)

18.5a Release cylinder bolts (arrowed)

Engine, clutch and transmission 2•37

18.5b Note the rubber diaphragm and remove it if required

cover (see Chapter 6). Where fitted, note the rubber diaphragm in the end of the release cylinder and remove it for safekeeping if it is loose **(see illustration)**. Unscrew the release cylinder bolts and withdraw it from the cover. Do not operate the clutch lever with the release cylinder removed.

> **HAYNES HiNT**
> *If the release cylinder is not being disassembled, wrap some cable ties around the piston and through the mounting bolt holes to prevent the piston creeping out, or from being displaced should the lever be accidentally pulled in.*

6 If required, withdraw the short pushrod from the engine **(see illustration 16.18b)**.

Overhaul

7 Have a supply of clean rags on hand, then displace the piston by pumping the clutch lever **(see illustration)**. Remove the piston – you should be able to pick it out by hand, but if necessary use a suitably sized piece of wooden dowel or a socket and/or extension bar inserted in the piston to jiggle it while simultaneously pulling it out with your hands. Grips can be used if their jaws are sufficiently covered in tape so that there is no possibility of scoring the piston. If you find that the piston is seized, and the hydraulic system is not sufficient to displace it, use compressed air directed into the fluid inlet once the hose has been detached. Take care to apply the compressed air gradually and progressively, starting with a fairly low pressure, until the piston is displaced, and hold the piston against the work surface so that the compressed air lifts the cylinder off it.

> ⚠ **Warning: Use only low air pressure, otherwise the piston may be forcibly expelled and cause damage or injury. Never place your fingers in front of the piston in an attempt to catch or protect it when applying compressed air, as serious injury could result.**

Caution: Do not try to remove the piston by levering it out.

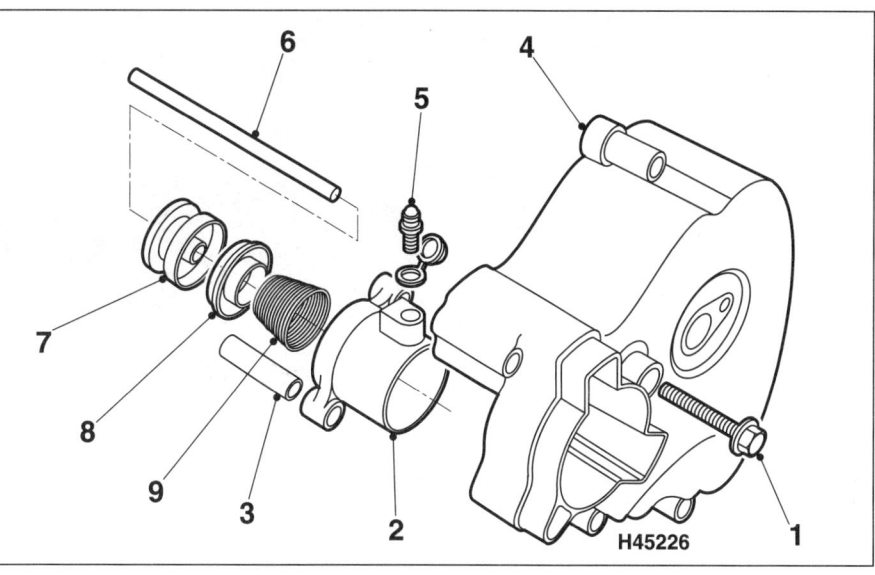

18.7 Clutch release cylinder components

1 Bolts	4 Sprocket cover	7 Piston
2 Release cylinder	5 Bleed valve	8 Piston seal
3 Dowel	6 Pushrod	9 Spring

8 Refer to Step 4 and detach the hydraulic hose from the cylinder, blocking or plugging it as described.

9 Separate the spring from the piston, noting how it fits, or withdraw it from the cylinder if it is still in there. Remove the piston seal from the groove in the piston, noting which way round it fits, and taking care not to mark the piston if using a metal tool. Discard it as a new one must be used.

10 Clean the piston and release cylinder bore with clean hydraulic fluid.

Caution: Do not, under any circumstances, use a petroleum-based solvent to clean hydraulic parts.

11 Inspect the piston and bore for signs of corrosion, nicks and burrs and loss of plating. If the necessary measuring equipment is available, compare the diameters of the bore and piston to those given in the Specifications Section of this Chapter. If surface defects are found, or if wear is evident, the piston and cylinder should be replaced with new ones (they are not available individually). If the release cylinder is in poor condition the master cylinder should also be overhauled (see Section 17).

12 Check that the pushrod is straight by rolling it on a flat surface – if it is bent, replace it with a new one. Clean off any corrosion from the outer end of the rod. Check the pushrod oil seal on the left-hand side of the engine for signs of leakage and replace it with a new one if necessary. To do this you have to separate the crankcase halves as the seal sits in a lipped rim in the crankcases – refer to Section 25.

13 Lubricate the new piston seal with clean hydraulic fluid and fit it into the groove in the piston with the wider side facing its inner end, i.e. towards the spring. Fit the narrow end of the spring over the lug on the inner end of the piston. Lubricate the cylinder bore, piston and seal with clean hydraulic fluid and insert the assembly into the cylinder, making sure the spring stays in place on the piston and the rim of the seal does not turn inside out. Use your thumbs to press it fully in.

Installation

14 Lubricate the pushrod with molybdenum disulphide oil (a 50/50 mixture of molybdenum disulphide grease and engine oil) then slide it through the seal and into the engine **(see illustration 16.18b)**. Wipe the outer end of the pushrod clean and smear some silicon grease onto it.

15 Fit the release cylinder into the sprocket cover and secure its bolts finger-tight **(see illustration 18.5a)**. Where fitted and if removed, press the rubber diaphragm into the end of the piston **(see illustration 18.5b)**. Install the front sprocket cover (see Chapter 6). Now fully tighten the release cylinder bolts.

16 If detached, connect the clutch hose to the release cylinder, using new sealing washers on each side of the union, and aligning the hose as noted on removal **(see illustration 18.4)**. Tighten the banjo bolt to the specified torque setting.

17 Refer to *Daily (pre-ride) checks* and fill the reservoir with new hydraulic fluid, then bleed the system (see Section 19). Check for fluid leaks.

18 The remainder of the installation procedure is the reverse of removal. Do not forget to fill the coolant reservoir if you drained it (see *Daily (pre-ride) checks*).

19 Check the operation of the clutch before riding the motorcycle.

2•38 Engine, clutch and transmission

19 Clutch release mechanism bleeding

Warning: *Use care when working with brake fluid as it can injure your eyes and it will damage painted surfaces and plastic parts.*

Note: *If required use a commercially available vacuum-type brake bleeding tool. If bleeding the system using the conventional method does not work sufficiently well, it is advisable to obtain a bleeder and repeat the procedure detailed below, following the manufacturers instructions for using the tool.*

Bleeding

1 Bleeding the clutch is simply the process of removing all the air bubbles from the fluid reservoir, the hoses and the release cylinder. Bleeding is necessary whenever an hydraulic connection is loosened, when a component or hose is replaced, or when the master cylinder or release cylinder is overhauled. Leaks in the system may also allow air to enter, but leaking clutch fluid will reveal their presence and warn you of the need for repair.

2 To bleed the clutch, you will need some new DOT 4 brake/clutch fluid, a length of clear vinyl or plastic tubing, a small container partially filled with clean brake/clutch fluid, some rags and a ring spanner to fit the release cylinder bleed valve.

3 Remove the left-hand fairing side panel (see Chapter 8). Cover the areas surrounding the master and release cylinders with rag to prevent damage in the event that brake fluid is spilled.

4 Undo the reservoir cover screws and remove the cover, diaphragm plate and diaphragm **(see illustration 17.3)** – turn the handlebars as required so that the top of the reservoir is level, supporting the motorcycle upright using an auxiliary stand if required. If you don't have a short or angled screwdriver that can fit between the reservoir and the windshield, slacken the screws with the reservoir clear of the windshield, keeping finger pressure on the cover until the reservoir is level again. Slowly pump the clutch lever a few times until no air bubbles can be seen floating up from the holes in the bottom of the reservoir. Doing this bleeds the air from the master cylinder end of the line. Loosely refit the reservoir cover.

5 Remove the rubber cap from the top of the bleed valve **(see illustration)**. If using a ring spanner (which is preferable as you can leave it fitted over the bleed valve throughout the procedure), fit it over the bleed valve now. Attach one end of the clear vinyl or plastic tubing to the bleed valve and submerge the other end in the brake fluid in the container **(see illustrations)**.

6 Check the fluid level in the reservoir – do not allow it to drop below the lower mark during the bleeding process.

19.5a Clutch release cylinder bleed valve

7 Carefully pump the clutch lever three or four times and hold it in while opening the release cylinder bleed valve. When the valve is opened, clutch fluid will flow into the clear tubing and the lever will move toward the handlebar.

8 Retighten the bleed valve, then release the clutch lever gradually. Repeat the process until no air bubbles are visible in the fluid leaving the release cylinder. On completion, disconnect the bleeding equipment, then tighten the bleed valve to the torque setting specified at the beginning of the chapter. Fit the rubber cap onto the top of the bleed valve.

> **HAYNES HiNT** *Old brake/clutch fluid is invariably darker in colour than new fluid, making it easy to see when all old fluid has been expelled from the system.*

9 Fit the rubber diaphragm onto the master cylinder reservoir, making sure it is correctly seated, and the diaphragm plate. Fit the cover and tighten its screws (do not overtighten) **(see illustration 17.24)**. Wipe up any spilled brake fluid and check the entire system for leaks. Install the left-hand fairing side panel (see Chapter 8).

> **HAYNES HiNT** *If it's not possible to produce a firm feel to the lever the fluid my be aerated. Let the fluid in the system stabilise for a few hours and then repeat the procedure when the tiny bubbles in the system have settled out. Also check to make sure that there are no 'high-spots' in the clutch hose in which an air bubble can become trapped – this will occur most often in an incorrectly mounted hose union or badly routed hose. Displacing and moving the offending component around will normally dislodge any trapped air.*

Changing the fluid

10 Changing the clutch fluid is a similar process to bleeding the clutch and requires the same materials, plus a suitable tool for siphoning the fluid out of the master cylinder

19.5b Bleeding the clutch

reservoir (such as a syringe, though if one isn't available it is no problem to displace the reservoir and tip the fluid out as described in Section 17). Ensure that your container is large enough to take all the old fluid when it is flushed out of the system.

11 Follow Steps 3, 4 and 5, but after removing the reservoir cover, diaphragm plate and diaphragm, siphon or tip the old fluid out of the reservoir (if you want to tip the contents out displace it from the handlebars). Fill the reservoir with new brake fluid, then follow Step 7.

12 Retighten the bleed valve, then release the lever gradually. Keep the reservoir topped-up with new fluid to above the LOWER level at all times or air may enter the system and greatly increase the length of the task. Repeat the process until new fluid can be seen emerging from the bleed valve.

13 Disconnect the hose, then tighten the bleed valve to the specified torque setting and fit the rubber cap.

14 Top-up the reservoir then install the diaphragm, plate and cover. Wipe up any spilled fluid and check the entire system for leaks.

15 Check the operation of the clutch before riding the motorcycle.

Draining the system for overhaul

16 Draining the clutch fluid is again a similar process to bleeding the clutch. The quickest and easiest way is to use a commercially available vacuum-type bleeding tool (see **Note** above) – follow the manufacturer's instructions. Otherwise follow the procedure described above for changing the fluid, but quite simply do not put any new fluid into the reservoir – the system fills itself with air instead.

20 Oil pump

Note: *The oil pump can be removed with the engine in the frame. If the engine has already been removed, ignore the steps which do not apply.*

Pressure check

1 Perform an oil pressure check (see Chapter 1). If the pressure is as specified at the beginning of the Chapter then the pump is good.

Engine, clutch and transmission 2•39

20.5a Remove the circlip . . .

20.5b . . . the driven gear . . .

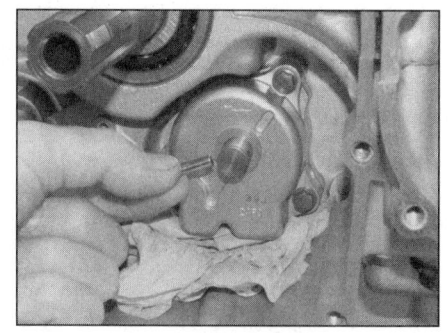

20.5c . . . its drive pin . . .

2 If the pressure is lower than it should be, and all other possible causes (as listed in Chapter 1) have been eliminated, then the pump is worn or faulty and must be replaced with a new one. No specifications are provided for clearance checks between the rotors, and no individual components are available. Suzuki specify that the pump should not be disassembled. If the engine is being fully overhauled due to wear it is advisable to fit a new oil pump as a matter of course.

Removal

3 Remove the clutch (see Section 16).
4 Stuff some rag into the opening to the sump in the bottom of the clutch housing. Turn the oil pump drive gear so that its drive pin is horizontal (this will prevent it from dropping out).
5 Remove the circlip from the end of the pump drive shaft, then remove the oil pump driven gear, noting how it locates over the drive pin (see illustrations). Remove the drive pin from the shaft, then remove the washer (see illustrations).
6 Unscrew the three bolts securing the pump to the crankcase, then remove the pump (see illustration). Remove the O-ring and discard it as a new one must be used.

Inspection

7 Inspect the pump body for any obvious damage such as cracks or distortion, and check that the shaft rotates smoothly and

20.5d . . . and the washer

freely and without any side-to-side play or excessive end-float.
8 Visually inspect the condition of the rotors and housing via the oil ports in the inner face of the pump, looking for evidence of wear and score marks (see illustration).
9 Check the pump driven gear teeth for wear and damage and replace it with a new one if necessary. Similarly check the drive gear on the back of the clutch housing (see illustration 16.21) – the drive gear is not available as a separate component.

Installation

10 Fit a new O-ring smeared with grease onto the oil pump, making sure it locates correctly in its groove (see illustration). Align the tabbed end of the pump drive shaft so that it will fit easily into the slot in the water

20.6 Unscrew the bolts (arrowed) and remove the pump

pump shaft on installation. Install the pump, wiggling the shaft if necessary to make it engage with the water pump shaft (see illustration). Apply a suitable non-permanent thread locking compound to the threads of the pump bolts and tighten them to the torque setting specified at the beginning of the Chapter (see illustration 20.6).
11 Turn the shaft so the drive pin hole is horizontal. Slide the washer onto the oil pump drive shaft, then fit the drive pin into its hole, making sure it is central (see illustrations 20.5d and c). Slide the driven gear onto the shaft and locate its slot over the drive pin (see illustration 20.5b). Secure the assembly with the circlip, making sure it is properly seated in its groove (see illustration 20.5a).
12 Remove the rag from the opening to the sump, then install the clutch (see Section 16).

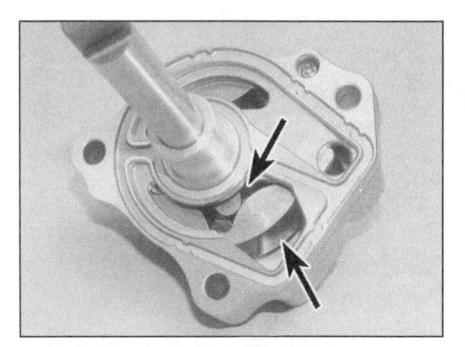

20.8 Check the condition of the rotors (arrowed)

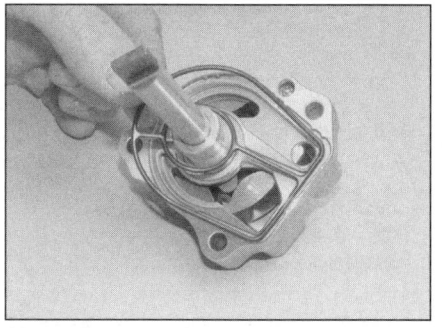

20.10a Fit a new O-ring into the groove . . .

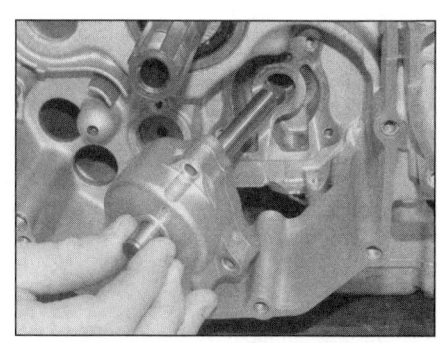

20.10b . . . then install the pump

2•40 Engine, clutch and transmission

21.4 Remove the sleeve, noting which way round it fits. Gearchange mechanism cover bolts (arrowed)

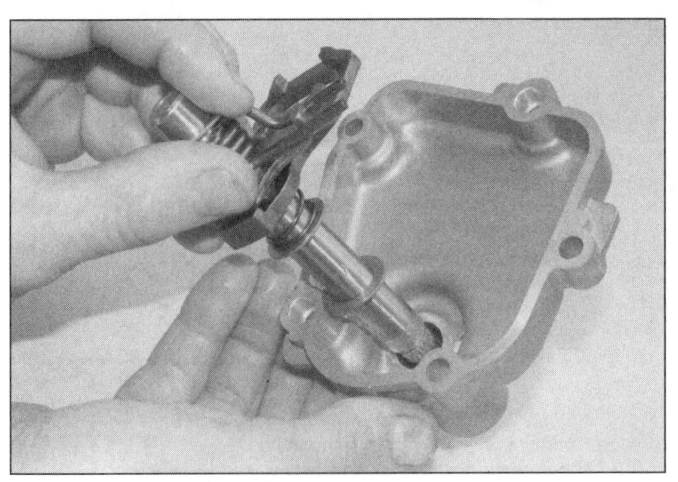

21.5 Withdraw the mechanism from the cover

21 Gearchange mechanism

Note: *The gearchange mechanism can be removed with the engine in the frame. If the engine has already been removed, ignore the steps which do not apply.*

Removal

1 Remove the left-hand fairing side panel (see Chapter 8).
2 Drain the engine oil and the coolant (see Chapter 1).
3 Remove the water pump (see Chapter 3).
4 Remove the front sprocket (see Chapter 6). Remove the protective sleeve on the sprocket cover bottom bolt boss if not already done **(see illustration)**.
5 Unscrew the gearchange mechanism cover bolts and remove the cover **(see illustration 21.4)** – on the model photographed the gearchange mechanism came away with the cover, in which case withdraw it **(see illustration)**. Remove the gasket and discard it – a new one must be used. Remove the dowels from the cover or crankcase if loose.
6 If the gearchange mechanism stayed on the engine, note how the selector arm locates over the pins in the selector drum cam plate, and how the shaft centralising spring ends locate over the pin in the crankcase **(see illustration 21.17b)**. Remove the mechanism from the engine **(see illustration 21.17a)**. Note the washer on each end of the shaft and remove them for safekeeping.
7 Note how the stopper arm spring ends locate and how the roller on the arm locates in the neutral detent on the selector drum cam, then unscrew the stopper arm bolt and remove the arm, the washer, and the spring, noting how they fit **(see illustration)**.

Inspection

8 Inspect the shaft centralising spring and thrust spring **(see illustrations)**. If they are fatigued, worn or damaged they must be replaced with new ones – the springs are each retained by a circlip, and the thrust spring has a washer that locates between them. Note how the centralising spring arms locate on each side of the lug. Also check the stopper arm return spring.
9 Check that the centralising spring locating

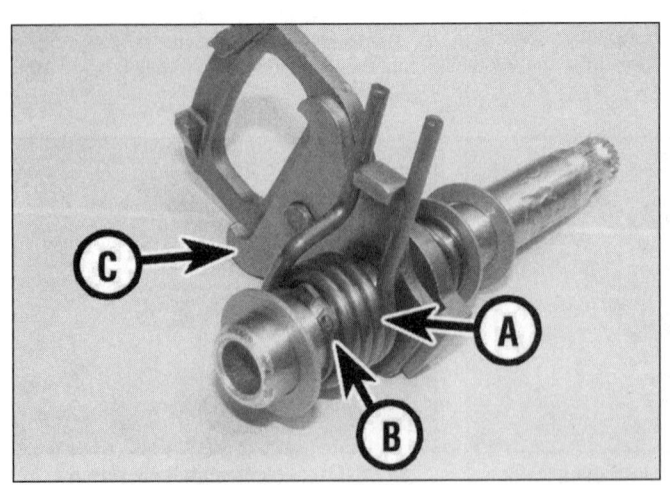

21.7 Unscrew the bolt (arrowed) and remove the stopper arm

21.8a Shaft centralising spring (A), circlip (B), lower pawl plate (C)

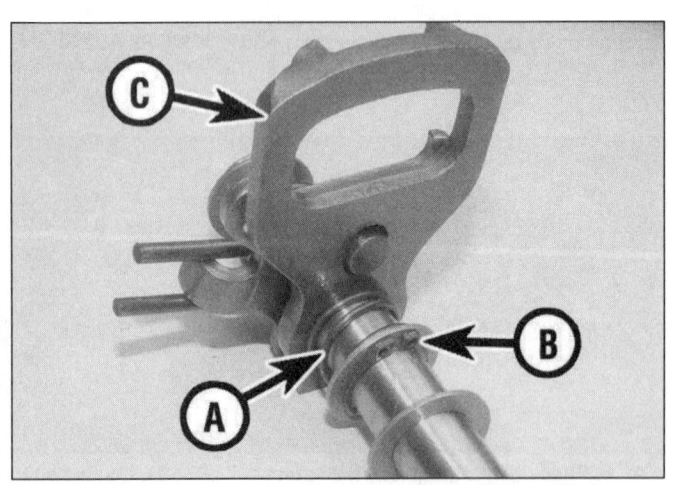

21.8b Thrust spring (A), circlip (B), upper pawl plate (C)

Engine, clutch and transmission 2•41

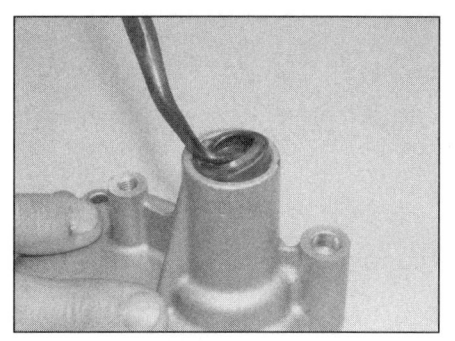

21.13 Lever out the old seal

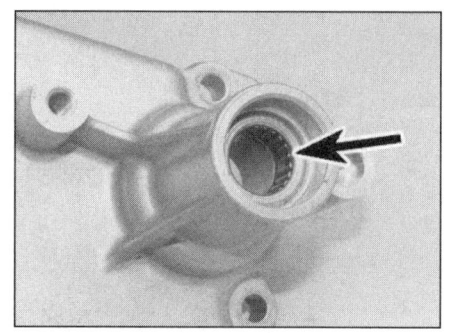

21.14a Check the bearing (arrowed) while the seal is out

21.14b Gearchange shaft bearing (A), centralising spring locating pin (B)

pin in the crankcase is tight **(see illustration 21.14b)**. If it is loose, remove it and apply a non-permanent thread locking compound to its threads, then tighten it to the torque setting specified at the beginning of the Chapter.

10 Inspect the selector arm pawls and the pins on the cam plate on the end of the selector drum for wear. The selector arm upper pawl plate can be separated from the lower (which is integral with the shaft) after removing the circlip, washer and thrust spring – note how the hole in the upper plate locates over the pin on the lower one.

11 Check the stopper arm roller and the selector drum cam plate detents **(see illustration 21.16b)**. Check that the roller spins freely.

12 Check the gearchange shaft for distortion and damage to the splines. If the shaft is bent you can attempt to straighten it, but if the splines are damaged the shaft must be replaced with a new one.

13 Check the condition of the shaft oil seal in the cover. If it is damaged, deteriorated or shows signs of leakage a new one must be fitted, but note that it is advisable to fit a new one as a matter of course if the shaft has been withdrawn. Lever out the old seal with a seal hook or screwdriver **(see illustration)**.

14 Check the condition of the shaft bearings in the cover and crankcase **(see illustrations)**. Check for play between each end of the shaft and its bearing, and check for signs of roughness when turning the shaft. If the bearings are worn or do not run smoothly replace them with new ones – refer to Section 5 of Tools and Workshop Tips in the Reference Section at the end of the book for more details on bearing checks and removal and installation methods. Note that once removed needle bearings cannot be reused.

15 Press or drive the new seal squarely into place, with its marked side facing out, using a seal driver or suitable socket **(see illustration)**. Smear the seal lips with grease.

Installation

16 Fit the stopper arm bolt through the stopper arm, then fit the washer and return spring **(see illustration)**. Apply a threadlock to the threads of the bolt. Install the assembly onto the crankcase, making sure the spring ends locate correctly over the stopper arm and against the crankcase, and locating the roller into the neutral detent on the cam plate **(see illustration)**. Tighten the bolt to the torque setting specified at the beginning of the Chapter. Make sure the stopper arm is free to move and is returned by the pressure of the spring.

17 Make sure the washers are on each end of the gearchange shaft and the centralising spring ends are correctly located on each side of the tab on the lower pawl plate **(see illustrations 21.8a and b)**. Slide the shaft into its bearing in the crankcase, making sure the centralising spring ends locate correctly each side of the locating pin in the crankcase **(see illustrations)**.

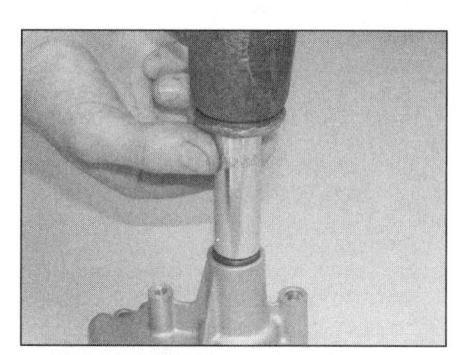

21.15 Fit the new seal into the cover

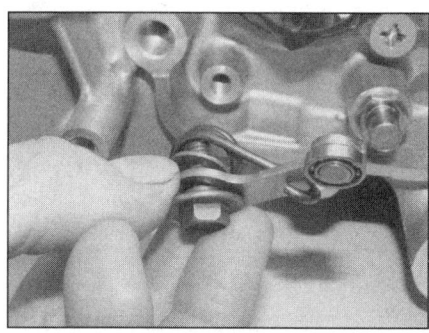

21.16a Assemble the stopper arm components . . .

21.16b . . . and install them as shown

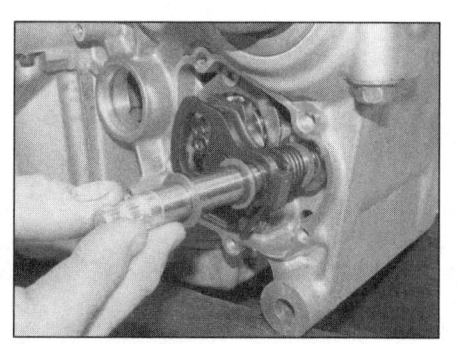

21.17a Install the mechanism . . .

21.17b . . . making sure it locates as shown

2•42 Engine, clutch and transmission

21.18a Locate the gasket onto the dowels (arrowed) . . .

21.18b . . . then install the cover

18 Fit the dowels into the crankcase if removed. Fit a new gasket over the dowels **(see illustration)**. Smear some grease onto the lips of the oil seal. Fit the cover, making sure it locates onto the dowels **(see illustration)**. Install and tighten the bolts to the specified torque setting **(see illustration 21.4)**. Fit the protective sleeve.

19 Install the remaining components in a reverse of the removal procedure (Steps 4 to 1).

22 Starter clutch

Note: *The starter clutch can be removed with the engine in the frame. If the engine has been removed, ignore the steps which do not apply.*

Check

1 The operation of the starter clutch can be checked while it is in situ. Remove the starter motor (see Chapter 9). Check that the No. 1 idle/reduction gear (X, Y, K1 and K2 models) or starter torque limiter gear (K3 models onward) is able to rotate freely clockwise as you look at it via the starter motor aperture, but locks when rotated anti-clockwise **(see illustration)**. If not, the starter clutch is faulty and should be removed for inspection.

Removal

2 Remove the right-hand fairing side panel (see Chapter 8).

3 Unscrew the bolts securing the idle/reduction or torque limiter gear cover to the starter clutch cover, noting which bolt fits where, and remove the cover **(see illustration)**. Remove the gasket and discard it. Note the position of the locating dowels and remove them for safe-keeping if loose.

4 On X, Y, K1 and K2 models remove the wave washer and outer thrust washer from the starter No. 1 idle/reduction gear shaft, then remove the gear with its bearing, noting which way round the gear fits, the inner thrust washer and the shaft. Separate the gear, shaft and bearing.

5 On all other models grasp the end of the torque limiter gear shaft and remove the shaft and gear together **(see illustration 22.21)**. Withdraw the shaft from the gear.

6 Now unscrew the bolts securing the starter clutch cover, noting the wiring clamp, and the sealing washer fitted with the upper front bolt **(see illustration)**. Remove the cover, being prepared to catch any residual oil. Remove the gasket and discard it. Note the position of the dowels and remove them for safe-keeping if loose.

7 Note the wave washer on the starter No. 2

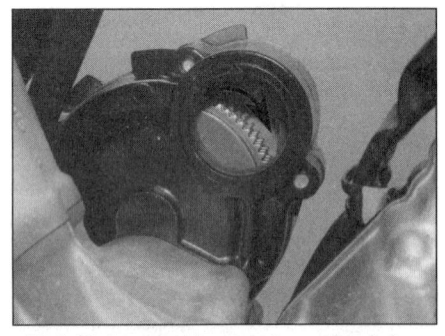

22.1 Make sure the gear turns freely in a clockwise direction as shown

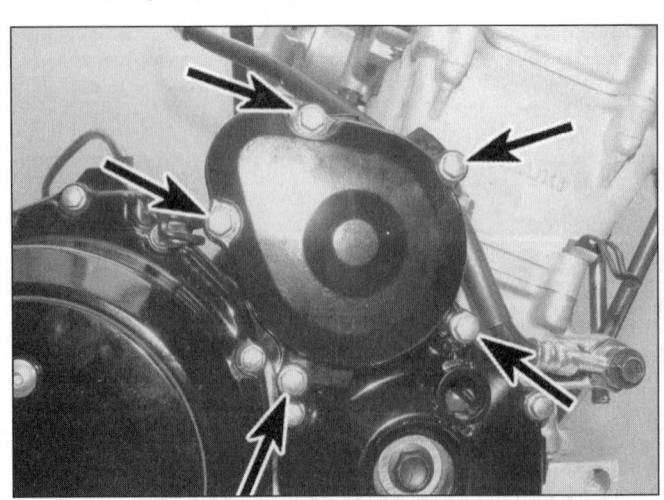

22.3 Unscrew the bolts (arrowed) and remove the cover

22.6 Unscrew the bolts (arrowed) and remove the cover

idle/reduction gear shaft, then remove the shaft and the gear, noting which way round it fits **(see illustration)**.

8 To remove the starter clutch bolt it is necessary to stop the starter clutch from turning. The Suzuki service tool (Pt. No. 09920-34830) or a commercially available (and inexpensive) equivalent (which also combines as a clutch holding tool) can be used to stop the starter clutch from turning whilst the bolt is slackened. Locate the pins on the tool into the holes in the starter clutch face. With the starter clutch held, unscrew the bolt **(see illustration)**. Slide the starter clutch and its thrust washer off the end of the crankshaft.

9 Clean all old gasket and sealant from the cover and crankcase.

Inspection

10 If separated fit the starter driven gear into the back of the starter clutch, turning it clockwise as you do to spread the clutch sprags and allow it to enter. With the starter clutch housing face down, check that the starter driven gear rotates freely in a clockwise direction and locks against the rotor in an anti-clockwise direction **(see illustration)**. If it doesn't, remove the needle bearing from between the driven gear hub and the starter clutch hub, then check again **(see illustration)**. If the driven gear now turns freely, replace the needle bearing with a new one. If it doesn't, replace the starter clutch with a new one. The starter clutch components (sprag assembly, housing and starter driven gear) come as an assembly and are not available individually.

11 Withdraw the starter driven gear from the starter clutch. If the gear appears stuck, rotate it clockwise as you withdraw it to free it from the sprags.

12 Check the condition of the sprags inside the clutch housing and the corresponding surface on the outside of the driven gear hub **(see illustration)**. If they are damaged,

22.7 Remove the shaft and gear assembly, noting the wave washer (arrowed)

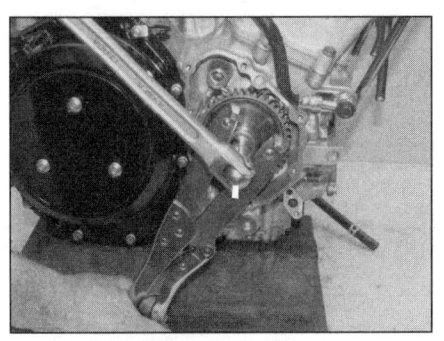

22.8 Counter-hold the starter clutch as described and unscrew the bolt

22.10a Make sure the driven gear turns freely in a clockwise direction as shown

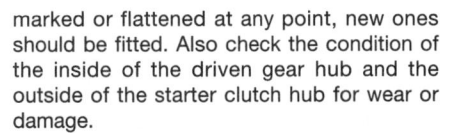

22.10b Remove the bearing from between the hubs

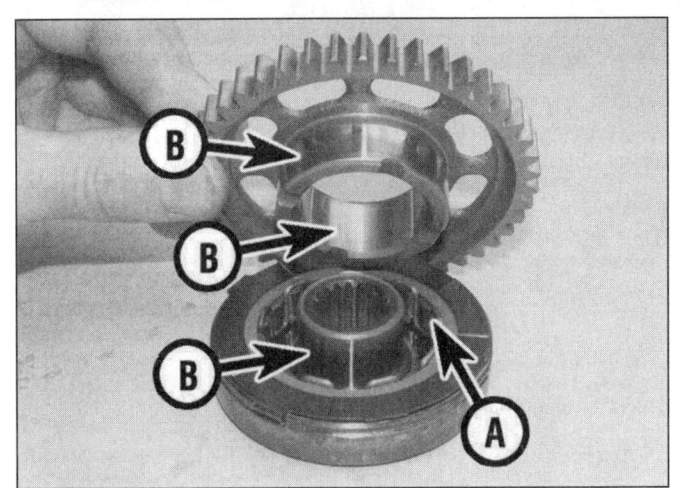

marked or flattened at any point, new ones should be fitted. Also check the condition of the inside of the driven gear hub and the outside of the starter clutch hub for wear or damage.

13 Check the splines in the centre of the starter clutch hub and the corresponding splines on the end of the crankshaft. If they are worn or damaged the starter clutch and/or crankshaft must be replaced with new ones (though in the case of the crankshaft it may be worth investigating the possibility of having them re-cut due to the cost of a new one).

14 Check the teeth of the starter motor drive shaft and all the gears in the train from that to the starter driven gear **(see illustration)**. If worn or chipped teeth are discovered on related gears replace the relevant components with new ones. Check the No. 2 idle gear shaft for damage, and check that the gear is not a loose fit on it. On X, Y, K1 and K2 models check the No. 1 idle/reduction gear needle bearing and replace it with a new one if worn or damaged – check for play and wear between the bearing, its shaft and the No. 1 idle/reduction gear. On all other models check the torque limiter gear shaft for damage, and check that the gear is not a loose fit on it. Check the shaft bores in the covers and crankcase for wear.

22.12 Check the sprags (A) and the surfaces of the hubs (B)

22.14 Check the various gears in the train for wear and damage – torque limiter gear assembly shown (K3 models on)

2•44 Engine, clutch and transmission

22.17a Slide the thrust washer onto the shaft . . .

22.17b . . . followed by the starter clutch, making sure the line and punch mark align

22.17c Fit the bolt with its washer . . .

22.17d . . . and tighten the bolt to the specified torque

15 On K3 models onward the torque limiter is set to slip within a certain torque range and can be checked with the use of a special service tool. Refer to a Suzuki dealer for details.

Installation

16 Lubricate the needle bearing and the hubs of the starter clutch and driven gear with clean engine oil, then install the bearing and the gear into the clutch, rotating the gear clockwise as you do so to spread the sprags and allow the hub of the gear to enter **(see illustrations 22.10b and 12)**.

17 Slide the thrust washer and the starter clutch assembly onto the end of the crankshaft, aligning the scribe line on the clutch with the punch mark on the crankshaft end – note that this alignment is crucial to the valve timing set-up **(see illustrations)**. Install the starter clutch bolt and its washer **(see illustration)**. Using the method employed on removal to stop the clutch from turning, tighten the bolt to the torque setting specified at the beginning of the Chapter **(see illustration)**.

18 Lubricate the No. 2 idle/reduction gear shaft with clean engine oil and slide it through the gear. Install the idle/reduction gear, making sure the smaller (14T) pinion faces inwards and meshes correctly with the teeth of the starter driven gear, and fit the wave washer onto the end of the shaft **(see illustration 22.7)**.

19 Apply a smear of sealant (Suzuki Bond 1207B or equivalent) to the area around the crankcase joints. If removed, insert the starter clutch cover dowels in the crankcase, then install the cover using a new gasket, making sure it locates correctly onto the dowels **(see illustrations)**. Tighten the cover bolts evenly in a criss-cross sequence to the specified torque setting, not forgetting the wiring clamp and making sure the sealing washer is installed on the upper front bolt **(see illustration 22.6)**.

20 On X, Y, K1 and K2 models lubricate the No. 1 idle/reduction gear shaft with clean engine oil and fit it into its bore in the crankcase, then slide on the inner thrust washer. Lubricate the needle bearing and slide it into the gear, then slide the gear onto the shaft, making sure the smaller (14T) pinion faces inwards and meshes correctly with the teeth of the No. 2 gear outer pinion, and the larger pinion meshes with the starter motor drive shaft (if installed). Fit the outer thrust washer followed by the wave washer onto the end of the shaft.

21 On all other models lubricate the torque limiter gear shaft with oil and slide it into the torque limiter. Install the assembly with the smaller pinion facing inwards, making sure the teeth mesh with the teeth of the No. 2 gear outer pinion, and the torque limiter pinions mesh with the starter motor drive shaft (if installed) **(see illustration)**.

22 If removed, insert the idle/reduction or torque limiter gear cover dowels in the crankcase, then install the cover using a new gasket, making sure it locates correctly onto the dowels **(see illustrations)**. Tighten the cover bolts evenly in a criss-cross sequence to the specified torque setting **(see illustration 22.3)**.

23 Check the engine/transmission oil level and top up if necessary (see *Daily (pre-ride) checks*).

22.19a Locate the gasket over the dowels (arrowed) . . .

22.19b . . . then install the cover

22.21 Locate the torque limiter shaft in its bore

22.22a Locate the gasket over the dowels (arrowed) . . .

Engine, clutch and transmission 2•45

22.22b ... then install the cover

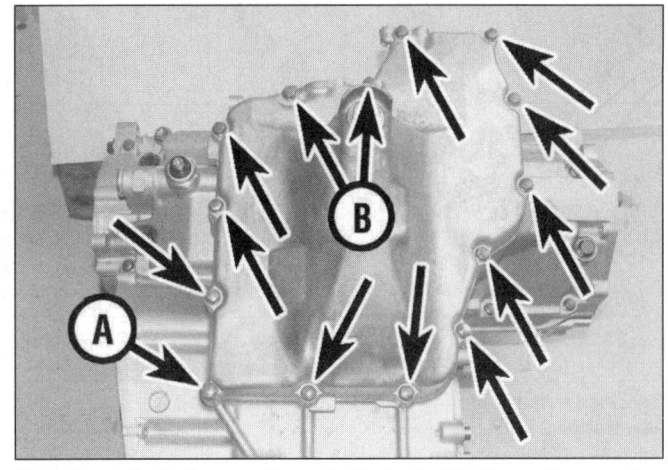

23.3 Sump bolts (arrowed) – note the bolt with the sealing washer (A), and the positions of the longer bolts (B)

24 Install the right-hand fairing side panel (see Chapter 8).

23 Oil sump, strainer and pressure regulator

Note: *The oil sump, strainer and pressure regulator can be removed with the engine in the frame. If work is being carried out with the engine removed ignore the preliminary steps.*

Removal

1 Drain the engine oil and the coolant (see Chapter 1).
2 Remove the exhaust system (see Chapter 4) – when removing the oil cooler detach the oil cooler hoses from the engine rather than the cooler itself, and remove the cooler bracket as it bolts to the sump **(see illustration 4.11)**.
3 Unscrew the sump bolts, slackening them evenly in a criss-cross sequence to prevent distortion, and remove the sump **(see illustration)**. Note the positions of the longer bolts and the bolt with the sealing washer. Discard the gasket as a new one must be used.
4 Unscrew the two bolts securing the strainer to the underside of the crankcase **(see illustration)**. Remove the O-ring and discard it as a new one must be used.
5 Unscrew the bolt securing the breather tube and remove it **(see illustration)**.
6 Pull the oil pressure regulator from its bore **(see illustration)**. Remove the O-ring and discard it as a new one must be used.
7 Remove all traces of gasket from the sump and crankcase mating surfaces.

Inspection

8 Clean the sump, making sure all the oil passages are free of any debris.
9 Make sure the oil strainer is clean and remove any debris caught in the mesh, using compressed air if available. Inspect the strainer for any signs of wear or damage and replace it with a new one it if necessary.
10 Clean the pressure regulator. Press down on the plunger and check that it moves freely in the body and returns under spring pressure **(see illustration)**. Replace the regulator with a new one it if the plunger does not move smoothly – it cannot be disassembled and no individual components are available.

Installation

11 Install the oil pressure regulator using a new O-ring smeared with grease **(see illustration 23.6)**.
12 Apply a suitable non-permanent thread-locking compound to the breather tube bolt, then fit the tube and tighten the bolt to the torque setting specified at the beginning of the Chapter **(see illustration 23.5)**.
13 Fit a new strainer O-ring smeared with grease **(see illustration)**. Apply a suitable non-permanent thread-locking compound to the strainer bolts, then fit the strainer and tighten the bolts to the torque setting

23.4 Unscrew the bolts and remove the strainer

23.5 Unscrew the bolt and remove the tube

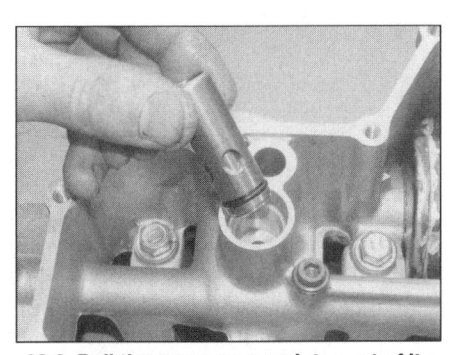

23.6 Pull the pressure regulator out of its bore

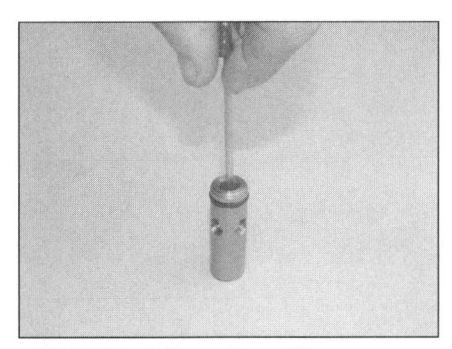

23.10 Check the action of the pressure regulator plunger

2•46 Engine, clutch and transmission

23.13 Fit the strainer O-ring onto the crankcase

23.14 Fit a new gasket . . .

23.15 . . . then install the sump

specified at the beginning of the Chapter **(see illustration 23.4)**.

14 Lay a new gasket onto the sump or crankcase (according to whether the engine is in the frame or upside down on the bench), making sure it fits over the pressure regulator and the holes in the gasket align correctly with the bolt holes **(see illustration)**.

15 Position the sump on the crankcase and install the bolts, using a new sealing washer on the right-hand rear corner bolt **(see illustration and 23.3)**. The two longer bolts fit either side of the oil cooler hose union on the front. Tighten the bolts evenly in a criss-cross pattern to the specified torque setting.

16 Install the oil cooler bracket, positioning it so that the ledge along the bolt hole section is at the bottom **(see illustration 4.11)**.

17 Install the exhaust system (see Chapter 4), but do not yet fit the fairing side panels.

18 Fill the engine with the correct type and quantity of oil as described in Chapter 1. Start the engine and check for leaks around the sump, then install the fairing side panels (see Chapter 8).

24 Balancer shaft assembly

Note: The balancer shaft can be removed with the engine in the frame. If the engine has been removed or partially disassembled, ignore the steps which don't apply.

Removal

1 Remove the sump (see Section 23). Unscrew the balancer shaft cover bolt and remove the cover **(see illustration)**.
2 Remove the spark plugs to allow the engine to be turned over easier (see Chapter 1).

3 Unscrew the crankshaft end cap and the timing mark inspection cap from the starter clutch cover **(see illustration 8.3)**. Check the condition of the cap O-ring and sealing washer and discard them if they are damaged, deformed or deteriorated, but note that new ones should be used as a matter of course.
4 Turn the engine using a socket or offset ring spanner on the starter clutch bolt, turning it in a clockwise direction only, until the scribe line on the starter clutch aligns with the notch in the timing mark inspection hole **(see illustrations 8.4a and b)**. *Note: Turn the engine in the normal direction of rotation (clockwise) only, viewed from the right-hand end of the engine.* Now note the alignment of the punch mark and scribe line on the balancer shaft with the triangular mark on the crankcase – this is how the crankshaft and balancer shaft must be positioned for installation later **(see illustration)**.
5 Make an alignment mark between the shaft holder and the slot in the end of the shaft – this will give a good indication as to the starting point for the backlash setting when the shaft is installed (the shaft provides an eccentric adjustment to allow the backlash between the balancer gear and its drive gear on the crankshaft to be optimised to reduce noise) **(see illustration)**.
6 Unscrew the holder mounting bolt, then hold the balancer gear/weight assembly in the crankcase and slide the holder and shaft out **(see illustrations)**. Remove the balancer gear/weight assembly, noting the washer on each end. Leave the holder on the shaft if

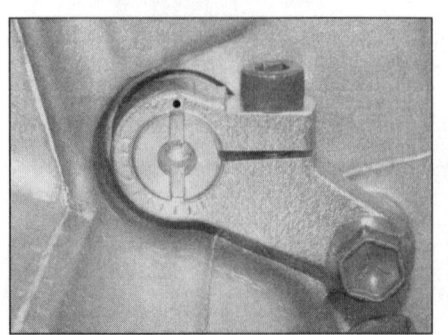

24.1 Unscrew the bolt (arrowed) and remove the cover

24.4 Note the balancer shaft alignment marks

24.5 Make an alignment mark between the holder and the slot in the end of the shaft

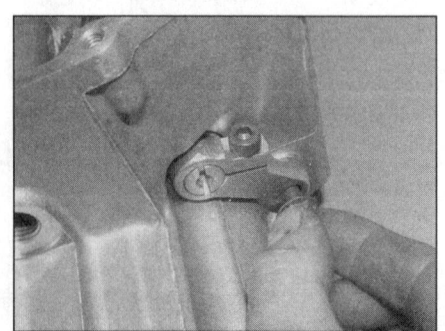

24.6a Unscrew the holder bolt . . .

24.6b . . . then withdraw the shaft and remove the balancer

Engine, clutch and transmission 2•47

24.7a Remove the washer from each end and check the shaft bearings as described

24.7b Separate the weight and gear, noting the alignment of the scribe line with the punch mark

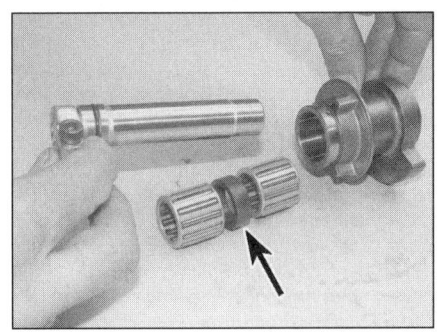

24.7c The bearings are separated by a spacer (arrowed)

possible then there is no chance of upsetting the existing backlash setting. Discard the shaft O-ring as a new one must be used.

Inspection

7 Remove the washer from each end of the gear/weight assembly **(see illustration)**. Separate the weight from the gear, noting their alignment **(see illustration)**. Slide the shaft back into the weight and check that it runs freely and smoothly in the bearings, and that the shaft is a good fit. Replace the bearings with new ones if necessary – they are a sliding fit with a spacer between them **(see illustration)**. If there is any evidence of wear on the shaft, or if it is still a sloppy fit in the new bearings, replace the shaft with a new one – slacken the holder pinch bolt and slide the holder off it, but do not fit the holder onto the new shaft until later. Check for wear on the faces of each washer and replace them with new ones if necessary.

8 Inspect the teeth on the gear for signs of wear or damage, and replace it with a new one if necessary. If damage is found, check the teeth on the drive gear on the crankshaft.

9 Check the condition of the rubber damper assembly in the gear for damage, deformation and deterioration, and replace them with new ones if necessary **(see illustration)**.

10 On reassembly of the shaft/weight assembly, lubricate each part with molybdenum disulphide oil (a 50/50 mixture of molybdenum disulphide grease and clean engine oil). Fit the rubber dampers into the gear, butting each one against a lug **(see illustration 24.9)**. Fit the balancer weight into the gear, slotting the tabs into the gaps between the dampers, and making sure the scribe line on the weight aligns with the punch mark on the gear **(see illustration 24.7b)**. Do not forget to fit the spacer between the needle bearings **(see illustration 24.7c)**.

Installation

11 Fit a new O-ring onto the balancer shaft and smear the shaft with molybdenum disulphide oil (a 50/50 mixture of molybdenum disulphide grease and clean engine oil). Check that the crankshaft is still positioned so that the scribe line on the starter clutch aligns with the notch in the timing mark inspection hole, and realign it if necessary (see Step 4) – if the engine has been disassembled you will need to temporarily install the cam chain drive sprocket, starter clutch and starter clutch cover (with its dowels) in order to align the crankshaft correctly.

12 Make sure the washers are correctly fitted on each end of the balancer gear/weight. Position the gear/weight assembly in the crankcase so that the punch mark and scribe line align with the triangular mark on the crankcase **(see illustration 24.4)**, then slide in the shaft, aligning the holder with its bolt hole if fitted **(see illustration 24.6b)**. If not already fitted, slide the holder onto the end of the shaft. In all cases apply a suitable non-permanent thread locking compound to the holder bolt and tighten it to the torque setting specified at the beginning of the Chapter **(see illustration 24.6a)**. If the shaft is difficult to install (because the gears are meshed too tight) turn it until it becomes easier.

13 If the holder was removed from the original shaft and no new components have been installed, turn the shaft using a screwdriver until the previously made mark between the shaft holder and the slot in the end of the shaft align **(see illustration)**. Temporarily tighten the shaft pinch bolt.

14 In all cases carry out the static backlash adjustment procedure (see below).

15 Turn the engine clockwise through 360° (one full turn) and check that the crankshaft and balancer marks still align (see Step 4).

16 Apply a suitable non-permanent thread locking compound to the balancer shaft cover bolt, then fit the cover and tighten the bolt to the specified torque setting. Install the sump (see Section 23).

17 Install the timing inspection cap using a new sealing washer if required, and the crankshaft end cap using a new O-ring if required – smear the O-ring and the cap threads with grease **(see illustration 8.37)**. Tighten the caps to the torque settings specified at the beginning of the Chapter.

18 Install the spark plugs (see Chapter 1).

19 When the engine is first run after this procedure carry out the dynamic backlash adjustment procedure (see below).

Backlash adjustment

Note: *A backlash adjustment is provided so that the balancer shaft drive and driven gears*

24.9 Check the damper segments in the gear

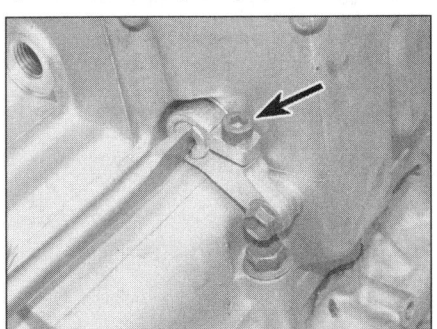

24.13 Use a screwdriver to turn the shaft for alignment or adjustment. Holder pinch bolt (arrowed)

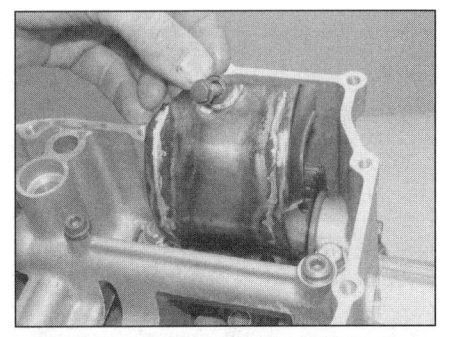

24.16 Locate the cover and tighten the bolt as described

2•48 Engine, clutch and transmission

mesh at their optimum point for quiet running with minimal wear. If the amount of backlash is too great, the shafts will clatter. If the shafts are running tight, they will whine, and wear very quickly. At the optimum point the gears will run very quietly – it is easy to tell the difference with the engine running. Adjustment is possible due to the offset on the shaft which allows eccentric movement of the balancer gear in relation to its drive gear when the shaft is turned. The static adjustment procedure allows the backlash to be set up in roughly the optimum position, but the dynamic procedure should always be carried out as well to fine tune the setting. The static procedure need only be carried out if the shaft has been removed and reinstalled. If the shaft has not been removed, the dynamic procedure can be carried out on its own. If, having carried out the backlash adjustment, there is still noise from the engine, remove the assembly and check for wear and damage on all components as described above.

Static adjustment

Note: *This procedure must be carried out when the engine is cold.*

20 Slacken the balancer shaft holder pinch bolt **(see illustration 24.13)**.
21 Turn the shaft slightly anti-clockwise, then turn it clockwise until resistance is felt – at this point backlash between the gears has been eliminated **(see illustration 24.13)**. Now turn the shaft anti-clockwise 1 1/2 to 2 graduations as marked on the holder, then temporarily tighten the pinch bolt.
22 Now carry out the dynamic adjustment procedure (see below).

Dynamic adjustment

Note: *This procedure must be carried out when the engine is warm.*

23 Remove the left-hand fairing side panel (see Chapter 8). Start the engine and allow it to warm up, then let it idle.
24 Slacken the balancer shaft holder pinch bolt **(see illustration 24.13)**.
25 Turn the shaft clockwise until the gears begin to whine, then turn it slowly anti-clockwise until the whine disappears, but not so much that the whine is replaced by a clatter – the optimum point is when the gears run at their quietest, and Suzuki specify that this should not be more than 1 graduation from the dynamic setting, but use your own judgement as well. Rev the engine and check that there is no unwanted noise at varying speeds.
26 On completion, tighten the pinch bolt. Install the left-hand fairing side panel (see Chapter 8).

25 Crankcase separation and reassembly

Separation

1 To access the crankshaft and connecting rods, transmission components, and bearings, the crankcase must be split into two parts, and to do this the engine must be removed from the frame (see Section 4). Refer to the relevant Sections for the above components to determine what needs to be removed before separating the crankcases.
2 If the crankcases are being separated as part of a complete engine strip and overhaul, remove all the components and assemblies in the Sections preceding this one, then refer to Chapter 9 and remove the oil pressure switch, gear position switch, starter motor and alternator.
3 Before the crankcases can be separated the following components must be removed:
 Cylinder head (Section 11).
 Starter clutch (Section 22).
 Cam chain tensioner blade and front guide blade (Section 10).
 Clutch (Section 16).
 Alternator cover (see Chapter 9).
 Oil sump and strainer (Section 23).
 Balancer shaft (Section 24).

Note: *It is possible to separate the crankcases leaving the cylinder head, starter clutch and tensioner and guide blades in place, but the front guide blade locates in a seat in the lower crankcase half, and without removing it, it could be tricky to locate this, especially with the starter clutch in situ, as well as making sure the selector forks engage correctly with the transmission shafts. Having an assistant available will help, but the success of the job will depend on your strength and mechanical ability.*

4 Remove the PAIR system control valve along with its front bracket (see Chapter 4).
5 Unscrew the banjo bolt and union bolts securing the crankcase oil pipe between the lower half on the left-hand side and the upper half on the front, noting how the rubber cushion block locates **(see illustrations)**. Discard the sealing rings and O-ring as new ones must be used.
6 If the gear position switch has not been removed, slacken or unscrew the bolts securing its upper wiring guides and free the wiring, then pull the grommet from its cut-out in the upper crankcase **(see illustration)**.
7 Slacken the clamps on any remaining coolant hoses between the pump and the cylinder block and head (if they are still in situ) and detach them from their unions.
8 Unscrew the seven upper crankcase bolts, noting the three fitted with sealing washers **(see illustration)**. Unscrew the bolts evenly, a little at a time and in a criss-cross sequence until they are finger-tight, then remove them. Note that new sealing washers should be used on assembly, though it is wise to keep the old ones with the bolts for the time being as a pattern for the new ones.

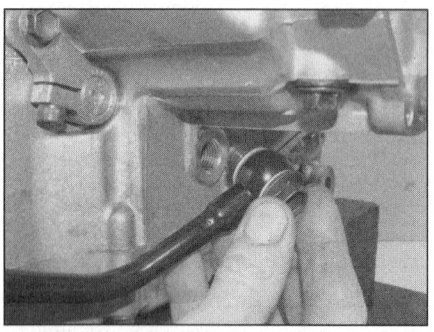

25.5a Unscrew the banjo bolt . . .

25.5b . . . and the union bolts, noting the position of the rubber block (arrowed)

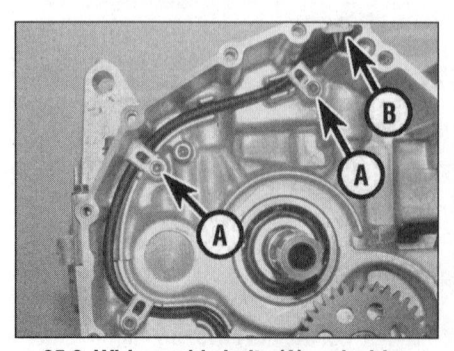

25.6 Wiring guide bolts (A) and wiring grommet (B)

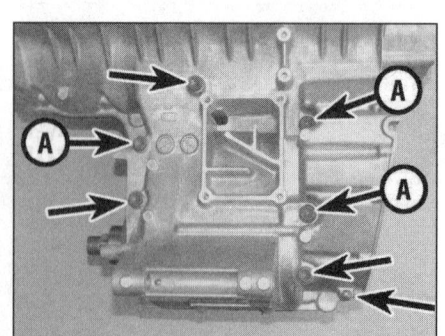

25.8 Upper crankcase bolts (arrowed, ones with sealing washers marked A)

HAYNES HiNT *As each bolt is removed, store it in its relative position in a cardboard template of the crankcase halves along with any washer or wiring clamp that goes with the bolt. This will ensure all bolts are installed in the correct location on reassembly.*

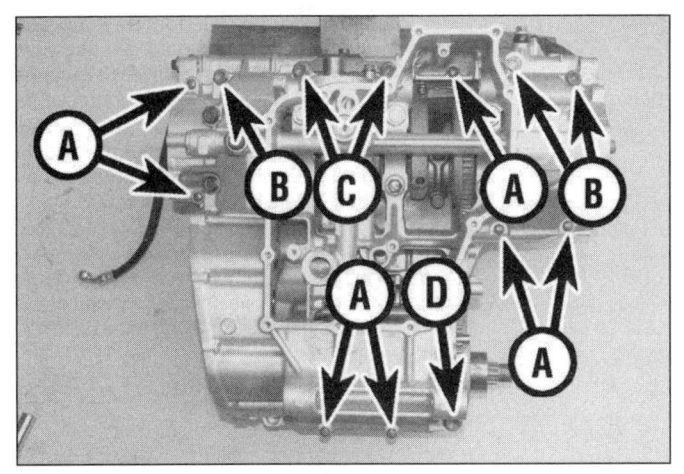

Engine, clutch and transmission 2•49

25.10a Lower crankcase 6 mm bolts (A), 8 mm bolts (B), 8 mm bolts with PAIR valve bracket (C), and 10 mm bolt (D)

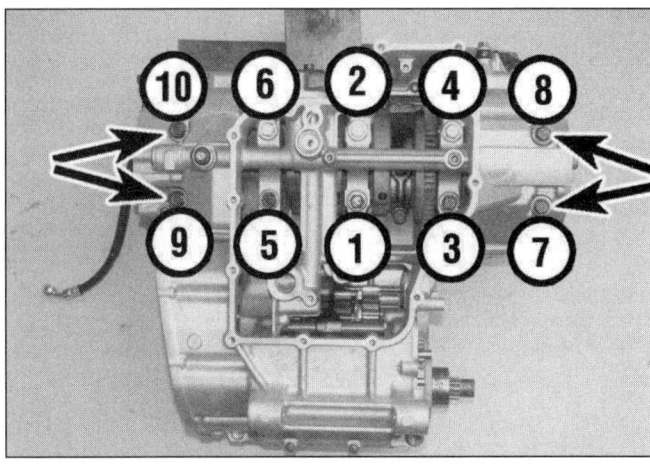

25.10b Lower crankcase 9 mm crankshaft journal bolt TIGHTENING sequence – slacken the bolts in reverse order. The arrowed bolts have sealing washers

9 Turn the engine upside down and support it on blocks of wood to keep any component that has not been removed (such as pistons, connecting rods, cam chain tensioner and guide blades) from taking the weight of the engine.

10 Unscrew the 6 mm, 8 mm and 10 mm lower crankcase bolts (i.e. all except the crankshaft journal bolts), noting the PAIR system control valve lower bracket secured by two of the 8 mm bolts **(see illustration)**. Now unscrew the ten 9 mm crankshaft journal bolts evenly, a little at a time and in a **reverse** of the tightening sequence, i.e. starting from the outside and working to the centre, until they are finger-tight, then remove them, noting the copper washers with the end bolts **(see illustration)**.

11 Carefully lift the lower crankcase half off the upper half, using a screwdriver in the leverage point on each front corner and a soft-faced hammer to tap around the joint to initially separate the halves if necessary **(see illustrations)**. **Note:** *If the halves do not separate easily, make sure all fasteners have been removed. Do not try and separate the halves by levering against the crankcase mating surfaces as they are easily scored and will leak oil in the future if damaged.* The lower crankcase half will come away with the oil pump, water pump and gearchange mechanism (if not already removed), and the selector drum and forks, leaving the crankshaft and transmission shafts in the upper crankcase half.

12 Remove the four locating dowels from the crankcase if they are loose (they could be in either crankcase half) **(see illustration 25.19)**.

13 Remove the clutch pushrod oil seal and the transmission output shaft oil seal and discard them as new ones must be used **(see illustration)** – if you are going to remove the transmission shafts you can remove the output shaft seal after lifting the shaft out – see Section 30.

14 Refer to Sections 26 to 32 for the removal, inspection and installation of the components housed within the crankcases.

Reassembly

15 Remove all traces of sealant from the crankcase mating surfaces.

16 Unless already done (see Section 30), fit a new oil seal, with grease smeared on its lips, onto the left-hand end of the transmission output shaft. Fit a new clutch pushrod oil seal also smeared with grease into its cut-out in the upper crankcase half **(see illustration 25.13)**.

17 Ensure that all components and their bearings are in place in the upper and lower crankcase halves.

18 Generously lubricate the crankshaft and transmission shafts, particularly around the bearings, with clean engine oil, then use a rag soaked in high flash-point solvent to wipe over the mating surfaces of both crankcase halves to remove all traces of oil.

19 If removed, fit the four locating dowels into the upper crankcase half **(see illustration)**.

20 Apply a small amount of suitable sealant (Suzuki-Bond 1207B or equivalent RTV sealant – ask your dealer) to the mating

25.11a Use a screwdriver on the leverage points if required . . .

25.11b . . . to separate the crankcase halves

25.13 Remove the clutch pushrod oil seal and the output shaft oil seal (arrowed)

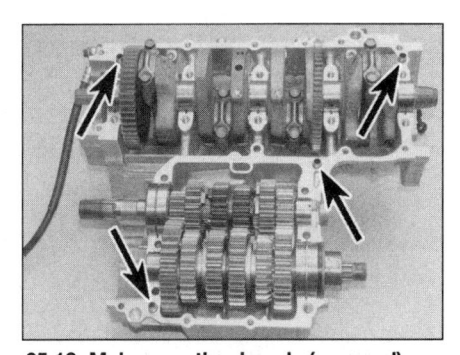

25.19 Make sure the dowels (arrowed) are installed

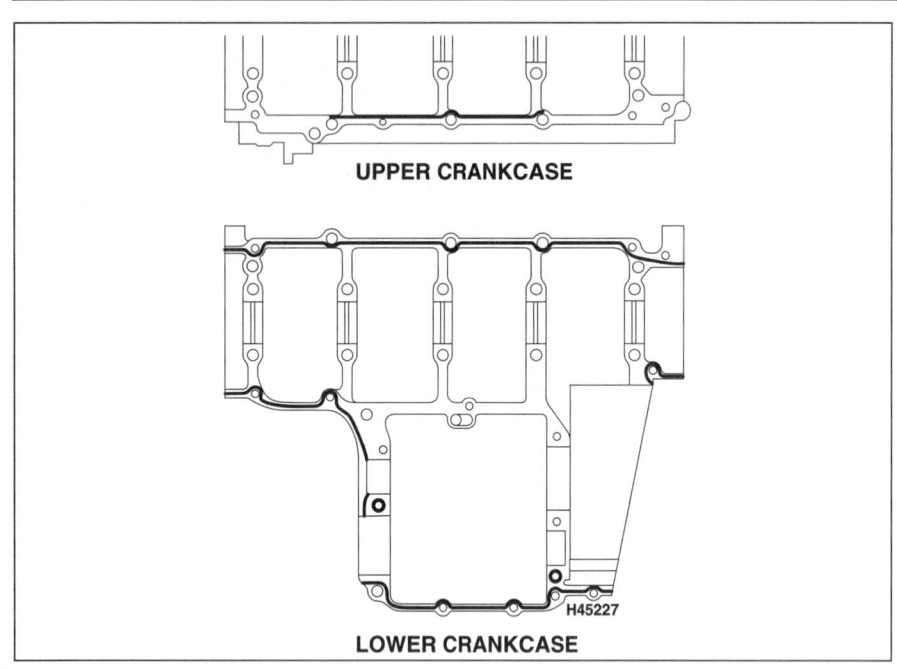

2•50 Engine, clutch and transmission

25.20 Apply sealant to the shaded areas shown

surfaces of the crankcase halves as shown **(see illustration)**. Note that the sealant starts to go off immediately, and will have gone off after a few minutes, and so no time should be wasted in assembling the crankcases.

Caution: Apply the sealant only to the shaded areas shown. Do not apply an excessive amount as it will ooze out when the case halves are assembled and may obstruct oil passages. Do not apply the sealant close to any of the bearing shells or surfaces, or oil passages.

21 Check again that all components are in position, particularly that the bearing shells are still correctly located in the lower crankcase half. Carefully fit the lower crankcase half down onto the upper crankcase half **(see illustration 25.11b)**, making sure the dowels all locate correctly, that each selector fork locates correctly in the groove in its pinion, and that if not removed the cam chain front guide blade locates correctly in its seat **(see illustration)**.
22 Check that the lower crankcase half is correctly seated, and the oil seals have not become cocked or dislodged.

Caution: The crankcase halves should fit together without being forced. If the casings are not correctly seated, remove the lower crankcase half and investigate the problem. Do not attempt to pull them together using the crankcase bolts as the casing will crack and be ruined. If you have to do this, clean off the sealant and apply fresh.

23 Clean the threads of the ten 9 mm crankshaft journal bolts. Insert them in their original locations, using new copper sealing washers with the end bolts as indicated, and noting that the three longer (silver) bolts fit in the front centre holes **(see illustration 25.10b)**. Secure all bolts finger-tight at first, then tighten them evenly and a little at a time in the numerical sequence shown first to the initial torque setting specified at the beginning of the Chapter, and then to the final torque setting. When the bolts are tightened, check that the crankshaft rotates smoothly and easily.

25.21 Make sure the selector forks locate in their grooves

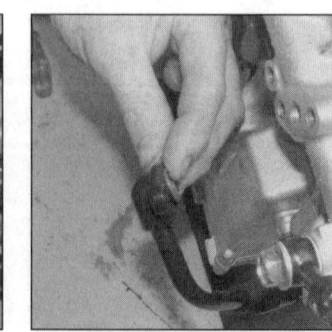

25.27 Fit a new O-ring smeared with grease onto the upper union

24 Clean the threads of the 6 mm, 8 mm and 10 mm lower crankcase bolts and insert them in their original locations, applying a suitable non-permanent thread locking compound to all the bolts along the front, and not forgetting to secure the PAIR system lower bracket with the front centre bolts indicated **(see illustration 25.10a)**. Secure all bolts finger-tight at first, then tighten them evenly and a little at a time in a criss-cross sequence, starting in the centre and working outwards, first to the initial torque setting specified at the beginning of the Chapter, and then to the final torque setting.
25 Turn the engine over. Clean the threads of the seven upper crankcase bolts and insert them in their original locations, not forgetting to fit new copper sealing washers with the bolts indicated **(see illustration 25.8)**. Secure all bolts finger-tight at first, then tighten them evenly and a little at a time in a criss-cross sequence, starting in the middle and working outwards, first to the initial torque setting specified at the beginning of the Chapter, and then to the final torque setting.
26 With all crankcase bolts tightened, check that the crankshaft and transmission shafts rotate smoothly and easily. Check that the transmission shafts rotate independently in neutral, then rotate the selector drum and select each gear in turn whilst turning the input shaft. Check that all gears can be selected and that the shafts rotate freely in every gear. If there are any signs of undue stiffness, tight or rough spots, or of any other problem, the fault must be rectified before proceeding further.
27 Install all other removed components and assemblies in a reverse of the sequence given in Steps 7 to 2, noting the following:
● When fitting the crankcase oil pipe, fit a new O-ring smeared with grease to the union at the upper crankcase **(see illustration)**. Locate the oil pipe cushion correctly, and apply a suitable non-permanent thread locking compound to the union bolts and tighten them to the specified torque **(see illustration 25.5b)**. Use new sealing washers on each side of the union to the lower crankcase and tighten the banjo bolt to the specified torque setting **(see illustration 25.5a)**.
● Apply a suitable non-permanent thread locking compound to the gear position switch wiring guide bolts and locate each one with its flat side facing in and butted against its adjacent lug **(see illustration 25.6)**. Apply some sealant to the wiring grommet before fitting it into its cut-out.

26 Crankcase inspection and servicing

1 After the crankcases have been separated, remove all the components housed within them (if not already done), referring to the relevant Sections of this Chapter and to Chapter 9 for the oil pressure and gear position switches.

2 Unscrew the transmission oil jets from the upper and lower crankcases **(see illustrations)**. Unscrew the alternator oil jet from the upper crankcase **(see illustration)**. Unscrew the bolts securing the piston oil jets in the upper crankcase and remove the jets, noting how they fit – there are four of them **(see illustration)**. Remove the O-rings and discard them as new ones should be used.

3 Unscrew the cylinder head oil hose banjo bolt and detach the hose from the crankcase **(see illustration)**. Discard the sealing washers as new ones must be used. On K1 models onward also unscrew the cam chain tensioner oil hose banjo bolt and detach the hose from the crankcase. Discard the sealing washers as new ones must be used.

4 Unscrew the breather housing bolts and remove the housing **(see illustration)**. Discard the gasket as a new one must be used.

5 Clean the crankcases thoroughly with new solvent and dry them with compressed air. Blow out all oil passages and oil jets with compressed air.

6 Remove all traces of old sealant from the mating surfaces. Carefully remove any raised edges on the surfaces with a fine sharpening stone or grindstone.

Caution: Be very careful not to nick or gouge the crankcase mating surfaces or oil leaks will result. Check the crankcases very carefully for cracks and other damage.

7 Small cracks or holes in aluminium castings may be repaired with an epoxy resin adhesive as a temporary measure. Permanent repairs can only be effected by argon-arc welding, and only a specialist in this process is in a position to advise on the economy or practical aspect of such a repair. If any damage is found that can't be repaired, replace the crankcase halves as a set.

8 Damaged threads can be economically reclaimed by installing a thread insert, which is easily fitted after drilling and re-tapping the affected thread.

9 Studs or bolts that have sheared on or below their bore line can usually be removed with extractors, which consist of a tapered, left-hand thread screw of very hard steel.

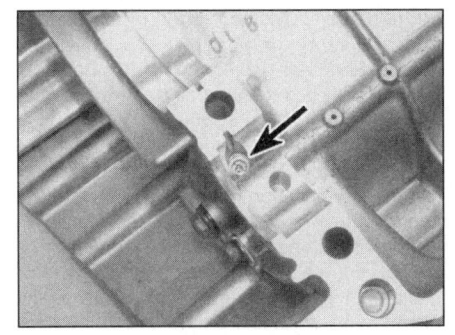

26.2a Unscrew the jets (arrowed) from the upper crankcase half . . .

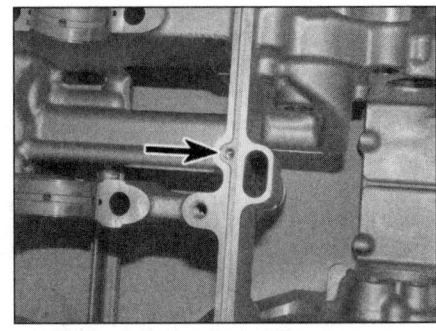

26.2b . . . and from the lower half

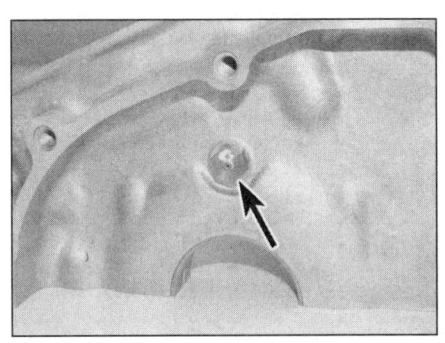

26.2c Also unscrew the alternator oil jet (arrowed) . . .

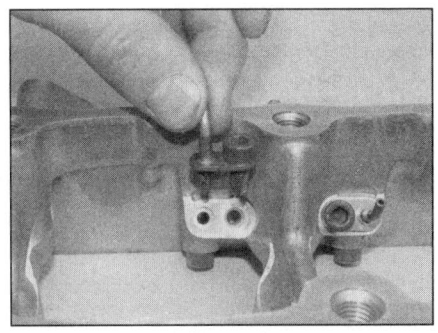

26.2d . . . and remove the piston oil jets

These are inserted into a pre-drilled hole in the stud or bolt, and usually succeed in dislodging the stud or bolt. If a stud or bolt has sheared above its bore line, use a conventional stud extractor which avoids the need for drilling.

> **HAYNES HINT** *Refer to Tools and Workshop Tips for details of installing a thread insert and using screw extractors.*

10 Install the cylinder head oil hose using a new sealing washer on each side of the union and tighten the banjo bolt to the specified torque setting – butt the metal section to the side of the union against the lug **(see illustration 26.3)**. On K1 models onward install the cam chain tensioner oil hose using a new sealing washer on each side of the union and tighten the banjo bolt to the specified torque setting – align the pipe section of the union so that it is horizontal and facing back.

11 Fit a new O-ring onto the base of each piston oil jet and smear it with clean engine oil **(see illustration)**. Push each jet into its bore in the upper crankcase, making sure the oil nozzle points up **(see illustration 26.2d)**. Apply a suitable non-permanent thread locking compound to the jet bolts and tighten them to the torque setting specified at the beginning of the Chapter. Fit the alternator oil jet in the upper crankcase and tighten it to the torque setting specified at the beginning of the Chapter **(see illustration 26.2c)**. Screw the transmission oil jets into the upper and lower crankcases **(see illustrations 26.2a and b)**.

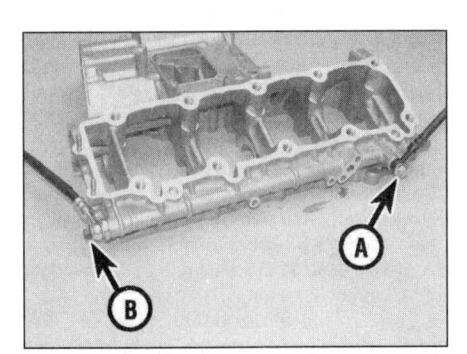

26.3 Detach the cylinder head oil hose (A), and where fitted the tensioner oil hose (B)

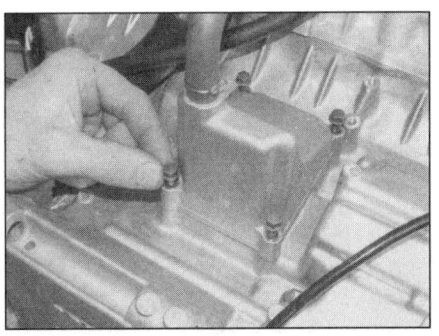

26.4 Unscrew the bolts and remove the breather housing

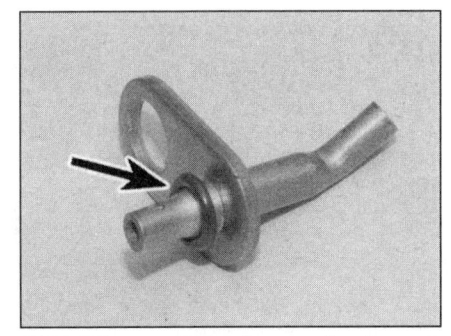

26.11 Fit a new O-ring (arrowed) onto each piston jet

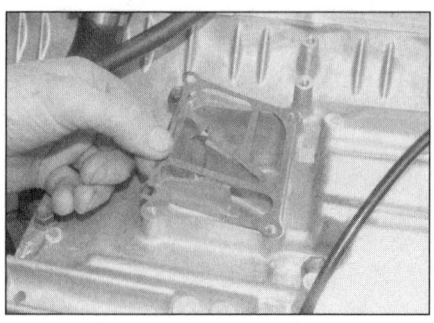

2•52 Engine, clutch and transmission

26.12 Fit a new gasket to the breather housing

12 Install the breather housing using a new gasket **(see illustration)**.
13 Install all other components and assemblies, referring to the relevant Sections of this Chapter and to Chapter 9, before reassembling the crankcase halves.

27 Main and connecting rod bearing information

1 Even though main and connecting rod bearings are generally replaced with new ones during the engine overhaul, the old bearings should be retained for close examination as they may reveal valuable information about the condition of the engine.
2 Bearing failure occurs mainly because of lack of lubrication, the presence of dirt or other foreign particles, overloading the engine and/or corrosion. Regardless of the cause of bearing failure, it must be corrected before the engine is reassembled to prevent it from happening again.
3 Dirt and other foreign particles get into the engine in a variety of ways. It may be left in the engine during assembly or it may pass through filters or breathers. It may get into the oil and from there into the bearings. Metal chips from machining operations and normal engine wear are often present. Abrasives are sometimes left in engine components after reconditioning operations, especially when parts are not thoroughly cleaned using the proper cleaning methods. Whatever the source, these foreign objects often end up imbedded in the soft bearing material and are easily recognised.

Large particles will not imbed in the bearing and will score or gouge the bearing and journal. The best prevention for this cause of bearing failure is to clean all parts thoroughly and keep everything spotlessly clean during engine reassembly. Frequent and regular oil and filter changes are also recommended.
4 Lack of lubrication or lubrication breakdown has a number of interrelated causes. Excessive heat (which thins the oil), overloading (which squeezes the oil from the bearing face) and oil leakage or throw off (from excessive bearing clearances, worn oil pump or high engine speeds) all contribute to lubrication breakdown. Blocked oil passages will also starve a bearing and destroy it. When lack of lubrication is the cause of bearing failure, the bearing material is wiped or extruded from the steel backing of the bearing. Temperatures may increase to the point where the steel backing and the journal turn blue from overheating.
5 Riding habits can have a definite effect on

> **HAYNES HINT** *Refer to Tools and Workshop Tips for bearing fault finding.*

bearing life. Full throttle low speed operation, or labouring the engine, puts very high loads on bearings, which tend to squeeze out the oil film. These loads cause the bearings to flex, which produces fine cracks in the bearing face (fatigue failure). Eventually the bearing material will loosen in pieces and tear away from the steel backing. Short trip riding leads to corrosion of bearings, as insufficient engine heat is produced to drive off the condensed water and corrosive gases produced. These products collect in the engine oil, forming acid and sludge. As the oil is carried to the engine bearings, the acid attacks and corrodes the bearing material.
6 Incorrect bearing installation during engine assembly will lead to bearing failure as well. Tight fitting bearings that leave insufficient bearing oil clearances result in oil starvation. Dirt or foreign particles trapped behind a bearing insert result in high spots on the bearing that lead to failure.
7 To avoid bearing problems, clean all parts thoroughly before reassembly, double check all bearing clearance measurements and lubricate the new bearings with clean engine oil or preferably molybdenum disulphide oil (a mixture of 50% molybdenum disulphide grease and 50% engine oil) during installation.

28 Crankshaft and main bearings

Note 1: *To remove the crankshaft the engine must be removed from the frame and the crankcases separated.*
Note 2: *References to the right and left-hand ends or sides are made as though the engine is the correct way up, even though throughout this procedure it is upside down. Therefore the right-hand side will actually be on your left as you look down onto the underside of the upper crankcase assembly.*

Removal

1 Remove the cylinder head, cylinder block and pistons, referring to the relevant Sections. Note that while it is possible to remove the crankshaft without removing the head, block and pistons (by first removing the camshafts and later separating the connecting rods from the crankshaft), it is advisable not to do so as it is easy for the crankshaft to unseat from the crankcase when you are loosening and tightening the connecting rod bolts, in which case you will probably damage the bearing shells and possibly the crankcase – having an assistant on hand to counter-hold the crankshaft is advised. If you just want to inspect the crankshaft or to perform an oil clearance check on the main bearings, the cylinder head, block and pistons can remain in place. If you do leave the head in place (and therefore the front cam chain guide blade), bear in mind the information given in the **Note** in Step 3 of Section 25 regarding the separation of the crankcase halves.
2 Separate the crankcase halves (see Section 25).
3 If you haven't removed the pistons and want to remove the crankshaft, separate the connecting rods from it and gently push them towards the top of the bores (see Section 29). If you have removed the pistons, leave the rods on the crankshaft and detach them after removing it (see Step 1).
4 Before removing the crankshaft check its end-float. The thrust bearings are located between the crank webs and the centre main bearing housing between cylinder Nos. 2 and 3. Push the crankshaft as far as it will go toward the left-hand (alternator) end (this eliminates play in the right-hand bearing). Insert a feeler gauge between the crankshaft and the left-hand thrust bearing and record the clearance **(see illustration)**. Compare the measurement with this Chapter's Specifications. If the end-float is excessive, refer to Steps 24 and 25 for selection of replacement bearings.
5 Remove the thrust bearings, noting how and where they fit – do not get the left- and right-hand bearings mixed up (note their different coloured ends) **(see illustration)**.

28.4 Check crankshaft end-float using a feeler gauge

28.5 Manoeuvre the thrust bearing to expose its end (arrowed) then remove it

Engine, clutch and transmission 2•53

28.6 Carefully lift the crankshaft out

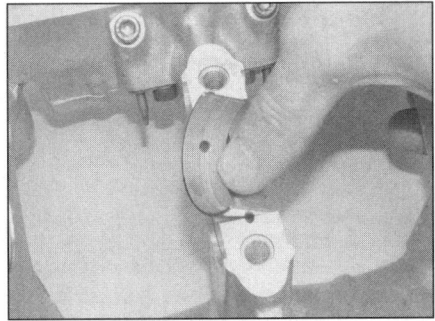

28.7 Remove the main bearing shells if required

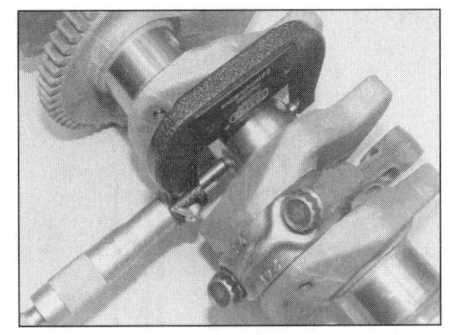

28.23 Measure the diameter of each journal

6 Lift the crankshaft, together with the cam chain and connecting rods if they haven't been separated, out of the upper crankcase **(see illustration)**. If the crankshaft appears stuck, tap it gently on each end using a soft-faced mallet.

7 If required remove the main bearing shells by pushing their centres to the side, then lifting them out **(see illustration)**. Make sure you keep the shells in order as they must be returned to their original location if they are being re-used.

8 If required and not already done, separate the connecting rods from the crankshaft (see Section 29).

Inspection

9 Clean the crankshaft with solvent, using a rifle-cleaning brush to scrub out the oil passages. If available, blow the crank dry with compressed air, and also blow through the oil passages. Check the primary drive gear and balancer drive gear. If any of the gear teeth are excessively worn, chipped or broken, the crankshaft must be replaced with a new one. Similarly check the driven gears on the back of the clutch housing and the balancer shaft if not already done.

10 Refer to Section 27 and examine the main bearing shells. If they are scored, badly scuffed or appear to have been seized, new bearings must be installed. Always replace the main bearings as a set. If they are badly damaged, check the corresponding crankshaft journals. Evidence of extreme heat, such as discoloration, indicates that lubrication failure has occurred. Be sure to thoroughly check the oil pump and pressure regulator as well as all oil holes and passages before reassembling the engine.

11 Give the crankshaft journals a close visual examination, paying particular attention where damaged bearings have been discovered. If the journals are scored or pitted in any way a new crankshaft will be required. Note that undersizes are not available, precluding the option of re-grinding the crankshaft.

12 Place the crankshaft on V-blocks and check the runout at the main bearing journals using a dial gauge. Compare the reading to

the maximum specified at the beginning of the Chapter. If the runout exceeds the limit, a new crankshaft must be installed.

Oil clearance check

13 Whether new bearing shells are being fitted or the original ones are being re-used, check the main bearing oil clearance before the engine is reassembled. Main bearing oil clearance is measured with a product known as Plastigauge.

14 Clean the backs of the bearing shells and the bearing housings in both crankcase halves.

15 Press the bearing shells into their cut-outs, ensuring that the tab on each shell engages in the notch in the crankcase **(see illustration 28.30)**. Make sure the bearings are fitted in the correct locations.

16 Ensure the shells and crankshaft are clean and dry. Lay the crankshaft in position in the upper crankcase **(see illustration 28.6)**. Install the four crankcase dowels if removed **(see illustration 25.19)**.

17 Cut five lengths of the appropriate size Plastigauge (they should be slightly shorter than the width of the crankshaft journals). Place a strand of Plastigauge on each (cleaned) journal, avoiding the oil hole. Make sure the crankshaft is not rotated.

18 Carefully fit the lower crankcase half down onto the upper crankcase half, making sure the dowels all locate correctly, that each selector fork locates correctly in the groove in its pinion and the cam chain front guide blade locates correctly in its seat **(see illustrations 25.11b and 21)**. **Note:** *Do not tighten the crankcase bolts if the casing is not correctly seated.* Clean the threads of the ten 9 mm crankshaft journal bolts. Insert them in their original locations, using the original copper sealing washers with the end bolts as indicated, and noting that the three longer (silver) bolts fit in the front centre holes **(see illustration 25.10b)**. Secure all bolts finger-tight at first, then tighten them evenly and a little at a time in the numerical sequence shown first to the initial torque setting specified at the beginning of the Chapter, and then to the final torque setting. Make sure that the crankshaft is not rotated as the bolts are tightened.

19 Now slacken each bolt evenly and a little at a time in a **reverse** of the tightening sequence, i.e. starting from the outside and working to the centre, until they are all finger-tight, then remove the bolts. Carefully lift off the lower crankcase half, making sure the Plastigauge is not disturbed.

20 Compare the width of the crushed Plastigauge on each crankshaft journal to the scale printed on the Plastigauge envelope to obtain the main bearing oil clearance. Compare the reading to the specifications at the beginning of the Chapter.

21 On completion carefully scrape away all traces of the Plastigauge material from the crankshaft journal and bearing shells; use a fingernail or other object which is unlikely to score them.

22 If the oil clearance falls into the specified range, no bearing shell replacement is required (provided they are in good condition). If the clearance is beyond the service limit, refer to the marks on the case and the marks on the crankshaft and select new bearing shells (see Steps 26 and 27). Install the new shells and check the oil clearance once again (the new shells may bring the bearing clearance within the specified range). Always renew all of the shells at the same time.

23 If the clearance is still greater than the service limit listed in this Chapter's Specifications (even with replacement shells), the crankshaft journals are worn and the crankshaft should be replaced with a new one. Measure the diameter of each journal and compare the measurements to the specifications to confirm **(see illustration)**. By measuring the diameter at a number of points around each journal's circumference, you'll be able to determine whether or not the journal is out-of-round. Also take a measurement at each end of the journal, near the crank throws, as well as in the middle, to determine if the journal is tapered.

Thrust bearing selection

24 If end-float was excessive (see Step 4), measure the thickness of the right-hand thrust bearing, and compare the result to the specifications at the beginning of the Chapter

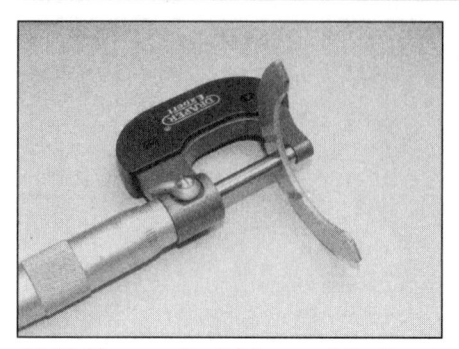

2•54 Engine, clutch and transmission

28.24 Measure the thickness of the thrust bearing using a micrometer

28.26a Main bearing journal size letters (A), crankpin journal size numbers (B)

28.26b Main bearing housing size letters

(see illustration). If the thickness measured is below the service limit specified, the right-hand thrust bearing must be replaced with a new one. There is only one size of replacement bearing. Install the replacement and check the clearance again. If the clearance is still excessive, or if the bearing was within specifications, select a replacement left-hand bearing as follows:

25 Remove the left-hand thrust bearing. Install the right-hand bearing and push the crankshaft as far as it will go toward the left-hand (alternator) end to eliminate any clearance. Insert feeler gauges between the crankshaft and the main bearing housing where the left-hand bearing fits, and record the clearance. Using the table below, select a replacement left-hand thrust bearing according to the clearance measured. For example, if the clearance recorded was 2.475 mm, the bearing colour-code required is black. Re-check the clearance with the new bearings (see Step 4).

Left-hand bearing clearance (bearing removed)	Bearing colour-code required
2.430 to 2.460 mm	Red
2.460 to 2.485 mm	Black
2.485 to 2.510 mm	Blue
2.510 to 2.535 mm	Green
2.535 to 2.560 mm	Yellow
2.560 to 2.585 mm	White

Main bearing shell selection

26 Replacement bearing shells for the main bearings are supplied on a selected fit basis. Code numbers stamped on the crankshaft and crankcase are used to identify the correct replacement bearings. The crankshaft main bearing journal size letters, one for each journal (either A, B or C), are stamped on the outer left-hand web **(see illustration)**. The corresponding main bearing housing size letters (either A or B), are stamped into the rear of the upper crankcase **(see illustration)**. The first letter of each set of five is for the outer left-hand journal, the second for the inner left-hand, the third for the middle, the fourth for the inner right-hand, and the fifth for the outer right-hand journal. **Note:** *Referrals to left- and right-hand are made as though the engine is the correct way up. Do not confuse the two as the engine is upside down.*

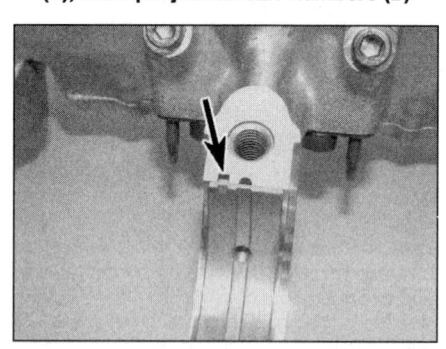

27 A range of bearing shells is available. To select the correct bearing for a particular journal, use the table below to cross-refer the main bearing journal size letter (stamped on the crank web) with the main bearing housing size letter (stamped on the crankcase) to determine the colour code of the bearing required. For example, if the journal code is C, and the housing code is B, then the bearing required is Yellow. The colour is marked on the side of the shell.

Crankcase housing code	Crankshaft journal code		
	A	B	C
A	Green	Black	Brown
B	Black	Brown	Yellow

Installation

28 If removed with the crankshaft and separated from it, fit the connecting rods onto the crankshaft (see Section 29), as well as the cam chain.

29 Clean the backs of the bearing shells and the bearing cut-outs in the upper and middle crankcases. If new shells are being fitted, ensure that all traces of the protective grease are cleaned off using paraffin (kerosene). Wipe the shells and crankcases dry with a lint-free cloth. Make sure all the oil passages and holes are clear, and blow them through with compressed air if it is available.

30 Press the bearing shells into their locations. Make sure the tab on each shell engages in the notch in the casing **(see illustration)**. Make sure the bearings are fitted

28.30 Fit the shell into its housing making sure the tab locates in the notch (arrowed)

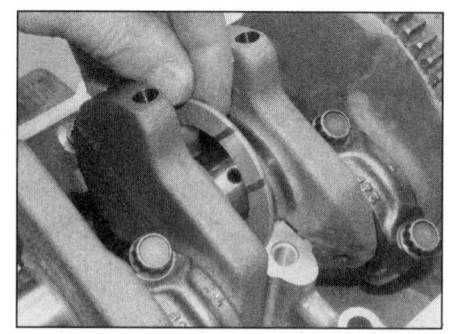

28.32 Fit each thrust bearing with its oil grooves facing the web

in the correct locations. Lubricate the bearing surface of each shell, preferably with molybdenum paste, molybdenum disulphide oil (a 50/50 mixture of molybdenum disulphide paste or grease and clean engine oil), or if not available then with clean engine oil.

31 Lower the crankshaft into position in the upper crankcase **(see illustration 28.6)**.

32 Install the thrust bearings into their correct locations (do not mix up the two – the right-hand bearing is colour-coded green) between the crank webs and the centre main bearing housing between cylinder Nos. 2 and 3, making sure that the oil grooves face towards the crankshaft web **(see illustration)**. Push them round so their ends are flush with the crankcase surfaces.

33 If the crankshaft only was removed and the piston/connecting rod assemblies are in the engine, draw each connecting rod/piston down its bore and fit them onto the crankshaft (see Section 29).

34 Reassemble the crankcases (see Section 25), and the engine as required according to your disassembly method.

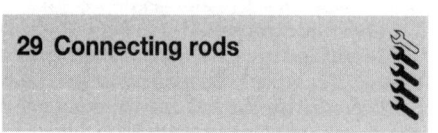

29 Connecting rods

Removal

1 Remove the crankshaft (see Section 28).
2 Before removing the rods from the crankshaft, measure the big-end bearing side clearance between the rods and the crank

Engine, clutch and transmission 2•55

29.2 Measure the connecting rod side clearance

29.4a Unscrew the connecting rod big-end cap bolts (arrowed) and detach the rod from the shaft

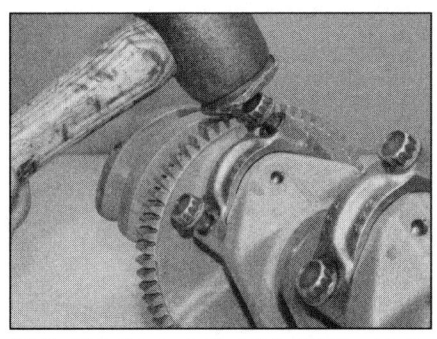

29.4b Tap the end of each bolt to separate the rod and cap if necessary

web with a feeler gauge **(see illustration)**. If the clearance is greater than the service limit listed in this Chapter's Specifications, refer to Step 6.

3 Using paint or a felt marker pen, mark the relevant cylinder identity on each connecting rod (i.e. 1 to 4). Mark across the cap-to-connecting rod join to ensure that the cap is fitted the correct way around on reassembly. Do not obscure the existing marking on the intake (rear) side of each connecting rod (mark the cylinder ID on the exhaust (front) side). The number already marked is the connecting rod big-end size code **(see illustration 29.17)**.

4 Unscrew the big-end cap bolts using a standard bi-hex socket (the bolts are 12-point, not Torx) and separate the connecting rod and cap from the crankpin – the bearing shells will stay on the rod and cap **(see illustration)**. When the bolts are partially unscrewed tap their heads with a soft-faced hammer to separate the rod and cap if required **(see illustration)**. Keep the rod, cap, bolts and (if they are to be re-used) the bearing shells together in their correct positions to ensure correct installation.

Inspection

5 Check the connecting rods for cracks and other obvious damage.

6 If the side clearance measured in Step 1 on any rod exceeds the service limit, measure the width of that rod's big-end and the width of its crankpin **(see illustrations)**. If the big-end is narrower than specified, replace the rod with a new one. If the width of the crankpin is greater than specified replace the crankshaft with a new one.

7 Apply clean engine oil to the piston pin, insert it into the connecting rod small-end and check for any freeplay between the two. Measure the external diameter of the middle of the pin and the diameter of the small-end bore and compare the measurements to the specifications at the beginning of the Chapter **(see illustrations)**. Calculate the difference between the measurements taken to obtain the piston pin-to-small end clearance and compare the result to the specifications. Replace components that are worn beyond the specified limits with new ones.

8 Refer to Section 27 and examine the connecting rod bearing shells. If they are scored, badly scuffed or appear to have seized, new shells must be installed. Always renew the shells in the connecting rods as a set. If they are badly damaged, check the corresponding crankpin. Evidence of extreme heat, such as discoloration, indicates that lubrication failure has occurred. Be sure to thoroughly check the oil pump and pressure regulator as well as all oil holes and passages before reassembling the engine.

9 Have the rods checked for twist and bend by a Suzuki dealer if you are in doubt about their straightness.

Oil clearance check

10 Whether new bearing shells are being fitted or the original ones are being re-used, check the connecting rod bearing oil clearance prior to reassembly. If possible position or clamp the crankshaft and/or rod to eliminate the possibility of either moving and disturbing the Plastigauge.

11 Check one rod at a time. Remove the bearing shells from the connecting rod and cap **(see illustration)**. Clean the backs of the shells and their housing in the rod and cap, and the corresponding crankpin.

29.6a Measure the width of the rod's big-end ...

29.6b ... and the width of the crankpin

29.7a Measure the piston pin diameter ...

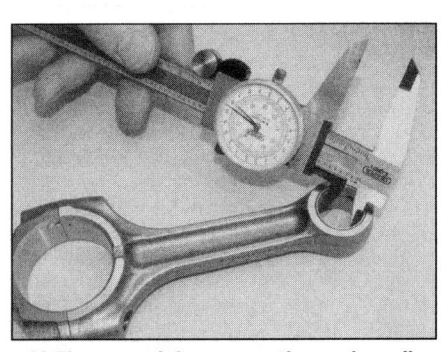

29.7b ... and the connecting rod small-end internal diameter

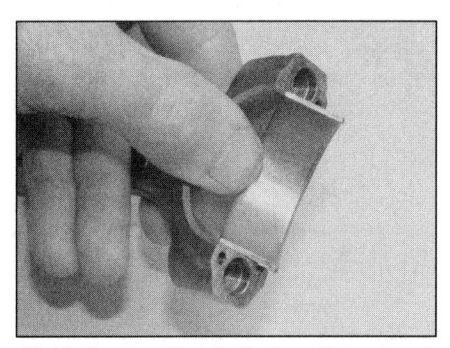

29.11 Remove the shells from the rod and cap

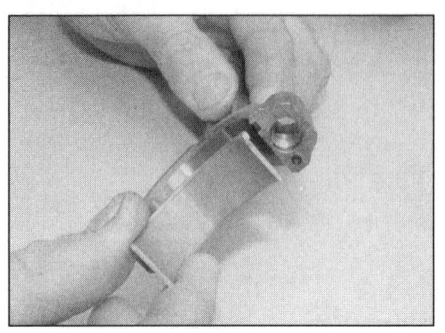

2•56 Engine, clutch and transmission

29.12 Fit the shell into its housing making sure the tab locates in the notch

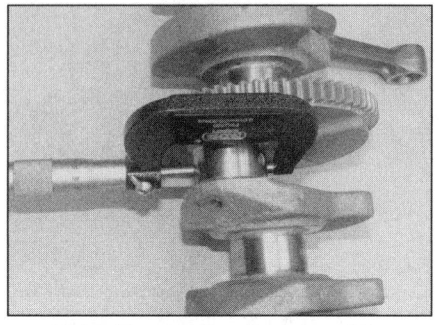

29.15 Measure the diameter of the crankpin to see if it is worn

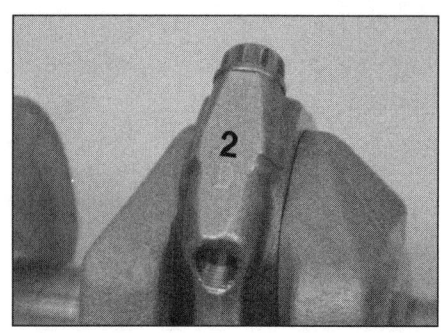

29.17 Connecting rod size code number

12 Press the shells into place, making sure they are in their original position if checking the original shells, and ensuring that the tab on each shell engages the notch in the rod or cap **(see illustration)**.

13 Cut a length of the Plastigauge (it should be slightly shorter than the width of the crankpin) and place it on the crankpin journal away from the oil holes. Lubricate the connecting rod bolts with clean engine oil. Fit the connecting rod assembly onto the crankpin **(see illustrations 29.20 and 21a)**. Make sure the rod and cap are fitted the correct way around so the previously made markings align (see Step 3), and tighten the bearing cap bolts in two stages, first to the initial torque setting specified at the beginning of the Chapter and then to the final torque setting, whilst ensuring that the connecting rod does not rotate **(see illustrations 29.21b)**. Now slacken the cap bolts and remove the connecting rod, again taking great care not to rotate it.

14 Compare the width of the crushed Plastigauge at its widest point to the scale printed on the Plastigauge envelope to obtain the connecting rod bearing oil clearance.

15 If the clearance is not within the specified limits, the bearing shells may be the wrong grade (or excessively worn if the original shells are being re-used). Before deciding that different grade shells are needed, make sure that no dirt or oil was trapped between the bearing shells and the connecting rod or cap when the clearance was measured, and be certain the rod did not turn on the crankpin and distort the strand of Plastigauge. If the clearance is excessive, even with new shells (of the correct size), measure the diameter of the crankpin and compare it to the specifications **(see illustration)**. If it is worn beyond the specified range, replace the crankshaft with a new one.

16 On completion carefully clean off all traces of the Plastigauge material from the crankpin and bearing shells.

Bearing shell selection

17 New bearing shells for the big-end bearings are supplied on a selected fit basis. Codes stamped on the crankshaft and rods are used to identify the correct replacement bearings. The crankpin journal size numbers, one number for each journal (either a 1, 2 or 3), are stamped on the inner left-hand crankshaft web **(see illustration 28.26a)**. The left-hand number with the L before it corresponds to the left-hand (alternator end) of the crankshaft which holds the No. 1 cylinder rod, and so on. The connecting rod size code is marked on the flat face of the connecting rod and cap and will be either 1 or a 2 **(see illustration)**.

18 A range of bearing shells is available. Select the correct bearing shells for each connecting rod in accordance with the table below. The bearings themselves are identified by colour (see table). The colour code is marked on the side of each shell. The dimensions relating to the particular codes are given in the table.

Installation

19 Work on one rod at a time, and make sure it is installed the correct way round (see Step 3). Clean the backs of the shells and their housing in the rod and cap. If new shells are being fitted, ensure that all traces of any protective grease are cleaned off using paraffin (kerosene). Wipe the shells, cap and rod dry with a clean lint free cloth. Fit the bearing shells in the connecting rod and cap, making sure the tab on each shell engages the notch **(see illustration 29.12)**.

20 Lubricate each shell's bearing surface with molybdenum disulphide oil (a 50/50 mixture of molybdenum disulphide grease and clean engine oil). Fit the connecting rod onto the crankpin and fit the cap onto the rod **(see illustration)**. Make sure the cap is fitted the correct way around so the previously made markings align (see Step 3). Check to make sure that all components have been returned to their original locations using the marks made on disassembly.

21 Apply engine oil to the threads and under the heads of the connecting rod bolts. Fit the bolts and tighten them in two stages, first to the initial torque setting specified at the beginning of the Chapter and then to the final torque setting **(see illustrations)**.

22 Check that each rod rotates smoothly and

	Connecting rod code	
Crankpin journal code	1 – (41.000 to 41.008 mm)	2 – (41.0081 to 41.016 mm)
1 – (37.9921 to 38.000 mm)	Green – (1.480 to 1.484 mm)	Black – (1.484 to 1.488 mm)
2 – (37.9841 to 37.992 mm)	Black – (1.484 to 1.488 mm)	Brown – (1.488 to 1.492 mm)
3 – (37.976 to 37.984 mm)	Brown – (1.488 to 1.492 mm)	Yellow – (1.492 to 1.496 mm)

29.20 Fit the rod and its cap onto the crankpin . . .

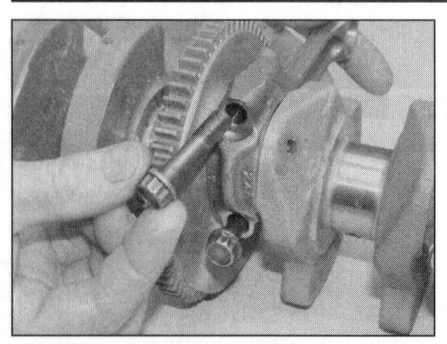

29.21a . . . then install the bolts . . .

29.21b . . . and tighten them as described

Engine, clutch and transmission 2•57

30.2a Remove the output shaft . . .

30.2b . . . and the input shaft

30.2c Remove the retainer . . .

freely on its crankpin. If there are any signs of roughness or tightness, remove the rod and re-check the oil clearance.
23 Install the crankshaft (see Section 28).

30 Transmission shaft removal and installation

Removal

1 Remove the engine from the frame (see Section 4) and separate the crankcase halves (see Section 25).
2 Lift the output shaft and input shaft out of the casing, noting their relative positions, how they fit together, and how the hole in each needle bearing housing locates onto the dowel **(see illustrations)**. If the shafts are stuck, use a soft-faced hammer and gently tap on the ends of the shafts to free them. Remove the input shaft ball bearing half-ring retainer from either the crankcase or the bearing **(see illustration)**. Also remove the needle bearing dowels – if they are not in their holes in the crankcase, remove them from the bearings on the shafts **(see illustration)**. If necessary, the input shaft and output shaft can be disassembled and inspected for wear or damage (see Section 31).
3 If not already done remove the transmission output shaft oil seal and discard it as a new one must be used **(see illustration)**.
4 Referring to *Tools and Workshop Tips* (Section 5) in the Reference Section, check the bearings on the transmission shafts.

30.2d . . . and the bearing dowels

Replace the bearings with new ones if necessary.

Installation

5 Fit the needle bearing dowels into their holes in the crankcase, and the half-ring retainer for the input shaft ball bearing into its slot **(see illustrations 30.2d and c)**.
6 Fit a new oil seal, with grease smeared on its lips, onto the left-hand end of the transmission output shaft **(see illustration 30.3)**.
7 Lower the input shaft into position in the upper crankcase **(see illustration 30.2b)**, making sure the hole in the needle bearing engages correctly with the dowel, the bearing retainer locates in its groove, and the bearing pin faces forwards and locates in its cut-out **(see illustration)**.
8 Lower the output shaft into position in the upper crankcase **(see illustration 30.2a)**,

30.3 Remove the oil seal from the end of the output shaft

making sure the hole in the needle bearing engages correctly with the dowel, the ring on the ball bearing locates correctly in its groove, and the pin faces forwards and locates in its cut-out **(see illustration)**.
Caution: If the ring retainer or dowel do not locate correctly, the crankcase halves will not seat properly.
9 Make sure both transmission shafts are correctly seated and their related pinions are correctly engaged.
10 Position the gears in the neutral position and check the shafts are free to rotate easily and independently (i.e. the input shaft can turn whilst the output shaft is held stationary) before proceeding further.
11 Reassemble the crankcase halves (see Section 25).

31 Transmission shaft overhaul

Note: *References to the right- and left-hand ends of the transmission shafts are made as though they are installed in the engine and the engine is the correct way up.*

HAYNES HiNT *When disassembling the transmission shafts, place the parts on a long rod or thread a wire through them to keep them in order and facing the proper direction.*

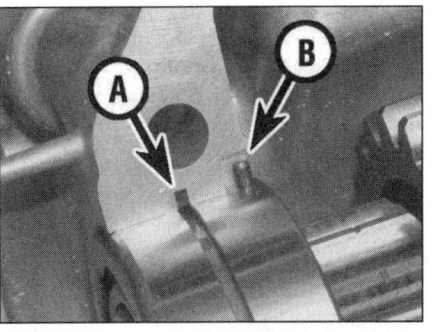

30.7 Make sure the retainer locates in the groove (A), and the pin sits in its cutout (B)

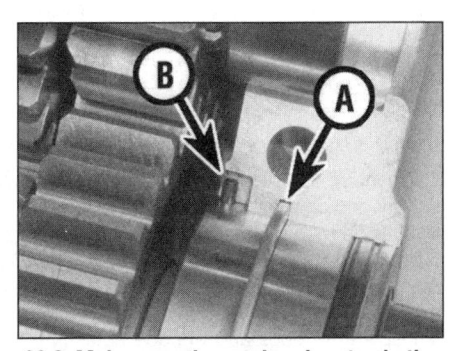

30.8 Make sure the retainer locates in the groove (A), and the pin sits in its cutout (B)

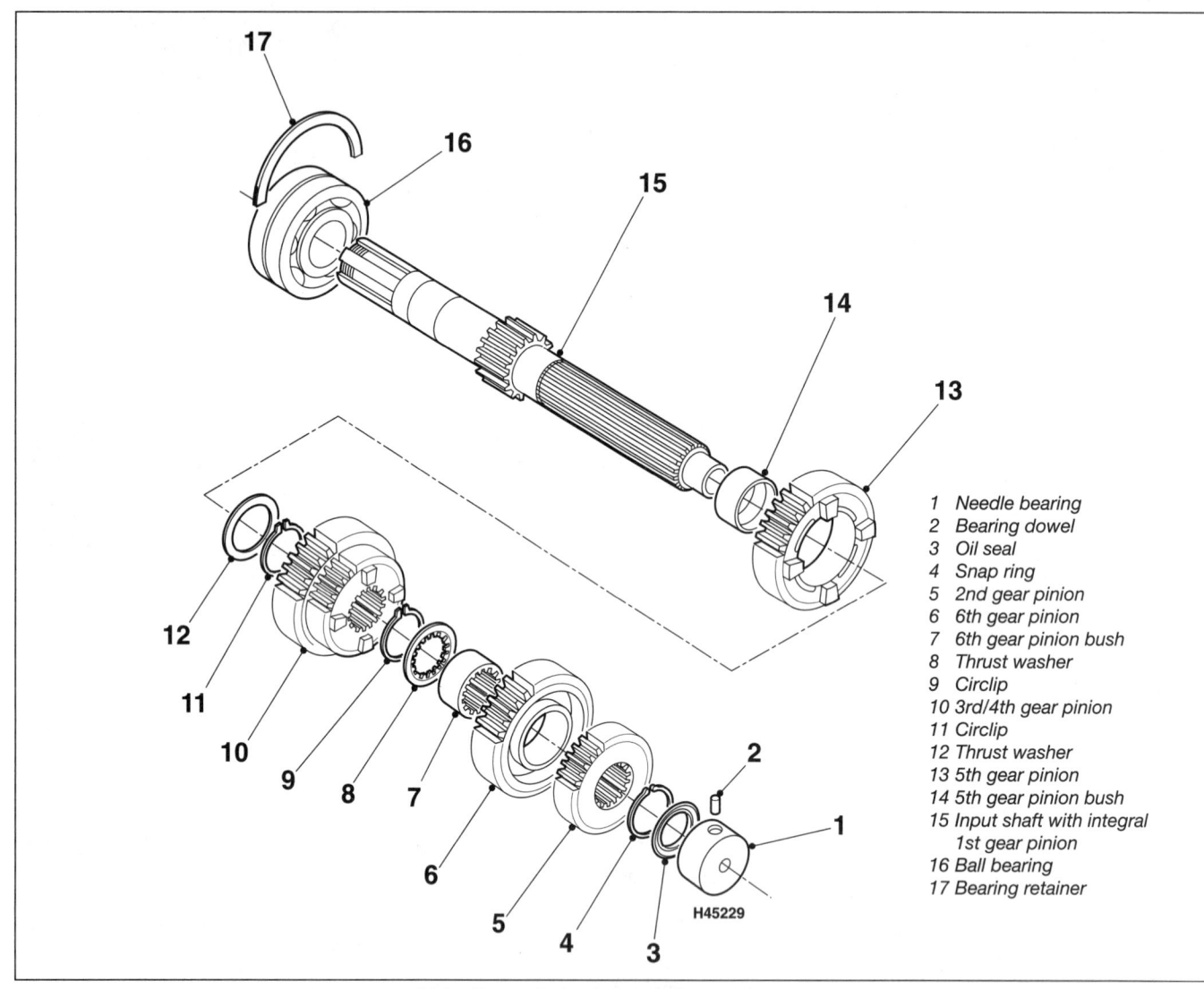

2•58 Engine, clutch and transmission

1 Needle bearing
2 Bearing dowel
3 Oil seal
4 Snap ring
5 2nd gear pinion
6 6th gear pinion
7 6th gear pinion bush
8 Thrust washer
9 Circlip
10 3rd/4th gear pinion
11 Circlip
12 Thrust washer
13 5th gear pinion
14 5th gear pinion bush
15 Input shaft with integral 1st gear pinion
16 Ball bearing
17 Bearing retainer

31.1a Transmission input shaft components

1 Remove the transmission shafts from the crankcase (see Section 30). Always disassemble the transmission shafts separately to avoid mixing up the components **(see illustrations)**.

Input shaft disassembly

2 Remove the needle bearing and oil seal from the left-hand end of the shaft **(see illustrations 31.20b and a)**.

3 Reach behind the 6th gear pinion with circlip pliers, spread the circlip and slide it toward the 3rd/4th gear pinion – pushing it back with the 6th gear pinion makes it easier **(see illustrations)**. Slide the 6th and 2nd gear pinions back to expose the snap-ring on the end of the shaft, then remove the snap-ring **(see illustrations)**. Slide the 2nd gear pinion off the shaft, noting which way round it fits, followed by the 6th gear pinion, its bush and the thrust washer **(see illustrations 31.19a, and 31.18c, b and a)**.

4 Remove the circlip securing the combined 3rd/4th gear pinion **(see illustration)**. Slide the combined 3rd/4th gear pinion off the shaft **(see illustration 31.17a)**.

5 Remove the circlip securing the 5th gear pinion, then slide the thrust washer, the 5th gear pinion and its bush off the shaft **(see illustrations 31.16d, c, b and a)**.

6 The 1st gear pinion is integral with the shaft **(see illustration)**.

Input shaft inspection

7 Wash all of the components in clean solvent and dry them off.

8 Check the gear teeth for cracking chipping, pitting and other obvious wear or damage. Any pinion that is damaged as such must be replaced with a new one.

9 Inspect the dogs and the dog holes in the gears for cracks, chips, and excessive wear especially in the form of rounded edges. Make sure mating gears engage properly. Replace paired gears as a set if necessary.

10 Check for signs of scoring or bluing on the pinions, bushes and shaft. This could be caused by overheating due to inadequate lubrication. Check that all the oil holes and passages are clear. Replace any damaged pinions or bushes with new ones.

11 Check that each pinion moves freely on the shaft or its bush but without undue freeplay. Check that each bush moves freely on the shaft but without undue freeplay.

12 The shaft is unlikely to sustain damage unless the engine has seized, placing an unusually high loading on the transmission, or the machine has covered a very high mileage. Check the surface of the shaft, especially where a pinion turns on it, and replace it with a new one if it has scored or picked up, or if there are any cracks.

13 Check the bearings for play or roughness. Replace them with new ones if necessary,

Engine, clutch and transmission 2•59

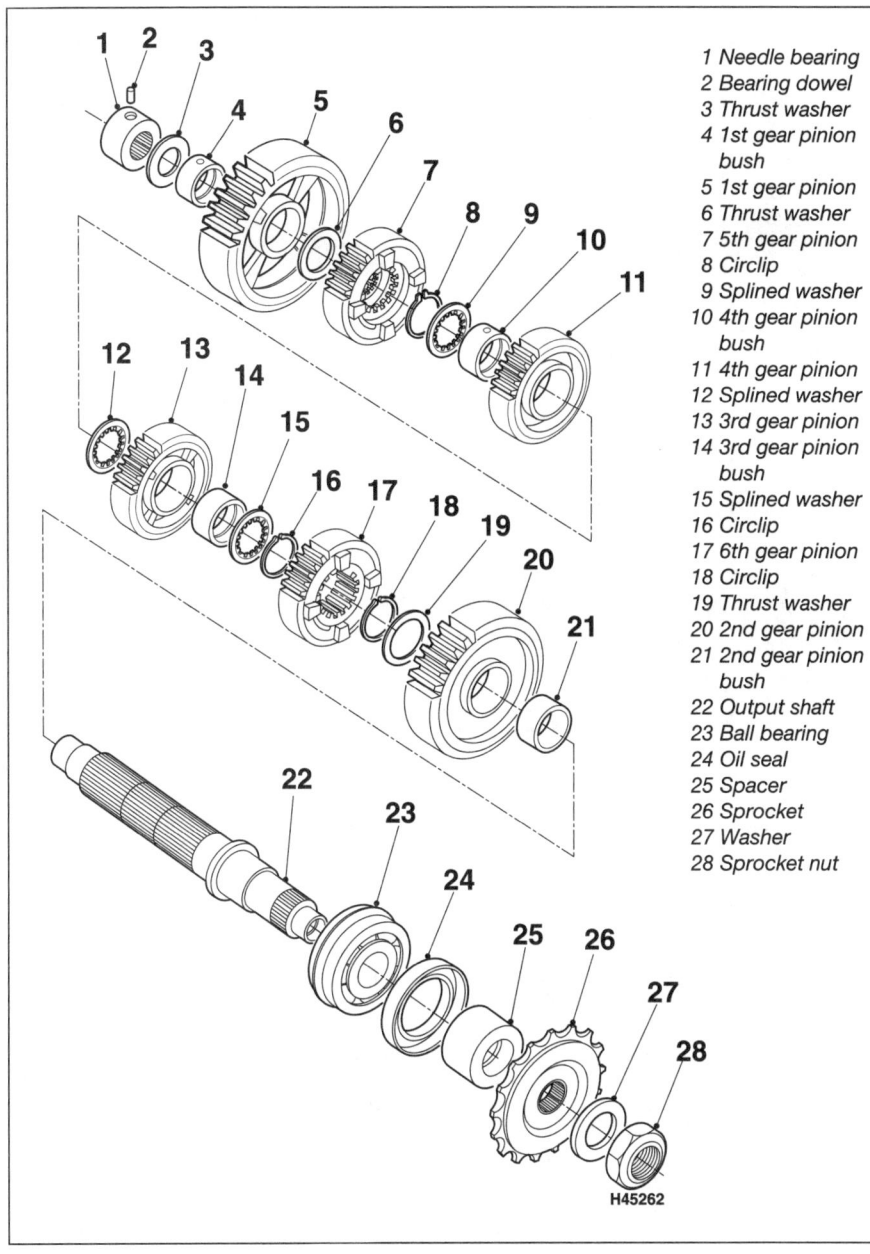

1 Needle bearing
2 Bearing dowel
3 Thrust washer
4 1st gear pinion bush
5 1st gear pinion
6 Thrust washer
7 5th gear pinion
8 Circlip
9 Splined washer
10 4th gear pinion bush
11 4th gear pinion
12 Splined washer
13 3rd gear pinion
14 3rd gear pinion bush
15 Splined washer
16 Circlip
17 6th gear pinion
18 Circlip
19 Thrust washer
20 2nd gear pinion
21 2nd gear pinion bush
22 Output shaft
23 Ball bearing
24 Oil seal
25 Spacer
26 Sprocket
27 Washer
28 Sprocket nut

31.1b Transmission output shaft components

31.3a Release the circlip from its groove . . .

31.3b . . . then push it back using the 6th gear pinion

31.3c Slide the 2nd gear pinion back to expose the snap ring . . .

31.3d . . . and remove it

31.4 Release the circlip and slide it off the shaft

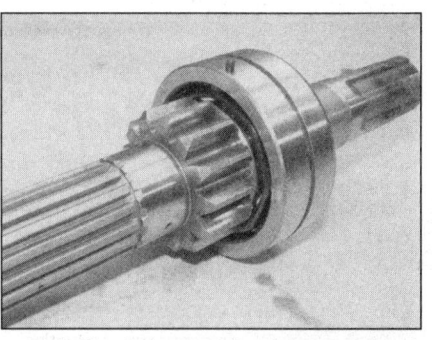

31.6 The 1st gear pinion is part of the shaft

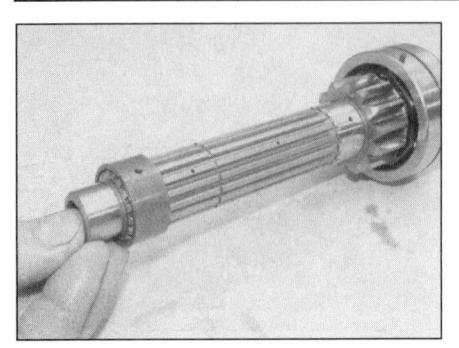

2•60 Engine, clutch and transmission

31.16a Slide the 5th gear pinion bush onto the shaft . . .

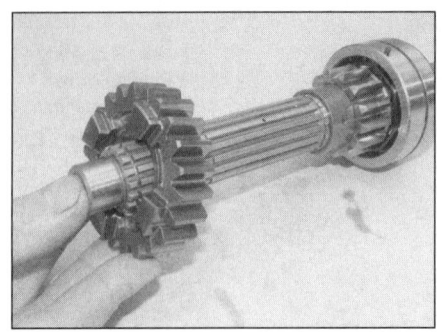

31.16b . . . then slide the pinion onto the bush

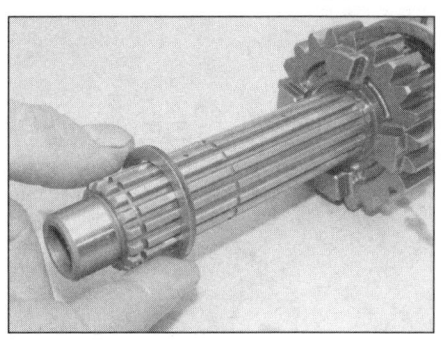

31.16c Slide the thrust washer against the pinion . . .

35.16d . . . then fit the circlip . . .

31.16e . . . locating it in its groove

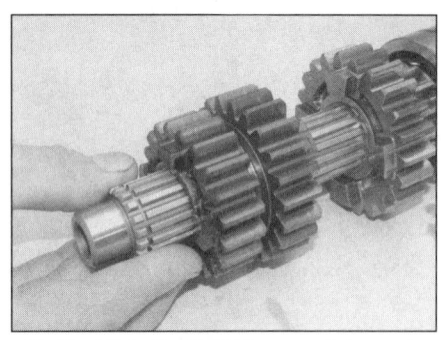

31.17a Slide the 3rd/4th gear pinion onto the shaft . . .

referring to Section 5 of *Tools and Workshop Tips* in the Reference Section for more information on bearing checks and removal and installation methods.

31.17b . . . then slide the circlip past its groove (arrowed) towards the pinion

14 Check the needle bearing oil seal and replace it with a new one it if it is damaged or deteriorated. Discard all the circlips and the snap-ring as new ones must be used.

Input shaft reassembly

15 During reassembly, apply molybdenum disulphide oil (a 50/50 mixture of molybdenum disulphide paste or grease and clean engine oil) to the mating surfaces of the shaft, pinions and bushes **(see illustration 31.1a)**. When installing the circlips, do not expand the ends any further than is necessary. Install the stamped circlips so that their chamfered side faces the pinion it secures, i.e. so that its sharp edge faces the direction of thrust load (see *correct fitting of a stamped circlip* illustration in Tools and Workshop Tips of the Reference section).
16 Slide the 5th gear bush onto the shaft

(see illustration). Slide the 5th gear pinion, with its dogs facing away from the integral 1st gear, onto its bush, then slide the thrust washer on **(see illustrations)**. Install the circlip, making sure that it locates correctly in the groove in the shaft **(see illustrations)**.
17 Slide the combined 3rd/4th gear pinion onto the shaft, so that the larger (4th gear) pinion faces the 5th gear pinion dogs **(see illustration)**. Fit the circlip onto the shaft but do not locate it in its groove – slide it past the groove and as far towards the 3rd/4th gear pinion as possible **(see illustration)**.
18 Slide the thrust washer onto the shaft, followed by the 6th gear pinion splined bush, aligning the oil hole in the bush with that in the shaft **(see illustrations)**. Slide the 6th gear pinion onto the bush, with its dogs facing the dogs on the 3rd gear pinion **(see illustration)**.

31.18a Slide the thrust washer up to the circlip . . .

31.18b . . . followed by the 6th gear pinion bush . . .

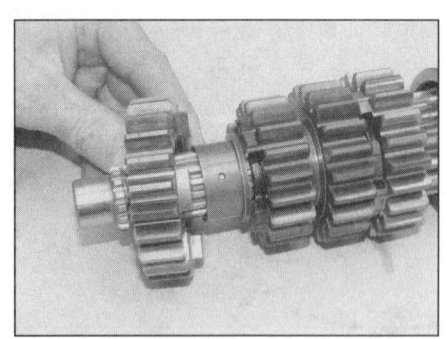

31.18c . . . then slide the 6th gear pinion onto the bush

Engine, clutch and transmission 2•61

31.19a Slide the 2nd gear pinion onto the shaft . . .

31.19b . . . then fit the snap-ring into the groove

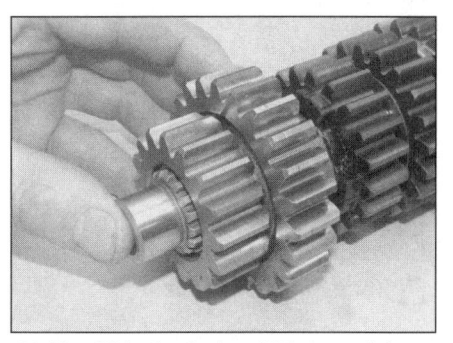

31.19c Slide the 2nd and 6th gear pinions up against the snap-ring . . .

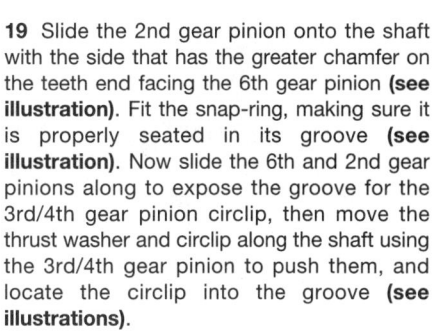

31.19d . . . then use the 3rd/4th gear pinion to push the thrust washer and circlip up the shaft . . .

31.19e . . . and locate the circlip it in its groove

19 Slide the 2nd gear pinion onto the shaft with the side that has the greater chamfer on the teeth end facing the 6th gear pinion (see illustration). Fit the snap-ring, making sure it is properly seated in its groove (see illustration). Now slide the 6th and 2nd gear pinions along to expose the groove for the 3rd/4th gear pinion circlip, then move the thrust washer and circlip along the shaft using the 3rd/4th gear pinion to push them, and locate the circlip into the groove (see illustrations).

20 Apply some grease to the needle bearing oil seal. Slide the oil seal and the needle bearing onto the shaft end (see illustrations). Check that all components have been correctly installed (see illustration).

Output shaft disassembly

21 Remove the needle bearing and the thrust washer from the right-hand end of the shaft (see illustrations 31.34b and a).
22 Slide the 1st gear pinion and its bush off the shaft, followed by the thrust washer and the 5th gear pinion (see illustrations 31.33b and a and 31.32b and a).
23 Remove the circlip securing the 4th gear pinion, then slide the splined washer, the pinion and its bush off the shaft, followed by the splined washer, the 3rd gear pinion, its bush and the splined washer (see illustrations 31.31e, d, c, b and a, and 31.30c, b and a).
24 Remove the circlip securing the 6th gear pinion, then slide the pinion off the shaft (see illustrations 31.29b and a).

25 Remove the circlip securing the 2nd gear pinion, then slide the thrust washer, the 2nd gear pinion and its bush off the shaft (see illustrations 31.28d, c, b and a).

Output shaft inspection

26 Refer to Steps 7 to 14 above.

Output shaft reassembly

27 During reassembly, apply molybdenum disulphide oil (a 50/50 mixture of molybdenum disulphide paste or grease and clean engine oil) to the mating surfaces of the shaft, pinions and bushes (see illustration 31.1b). When installing the circlips, do not expand the ends any further than is necessary. Install the stamped circlips so that their chamfered side faces the pinion it secures, i.e. so that its sharp edge faces the

31.20a Fit the oil seal . . .

31.20b . . . and the needle bearing

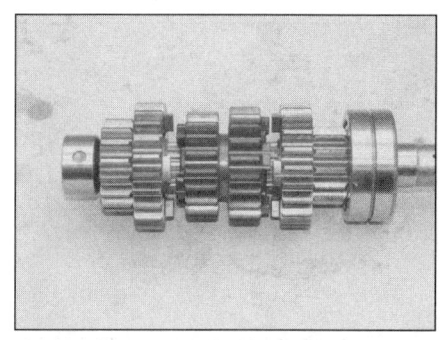

31.20c The assembled input shaft should look like this

2•62 Engine, clutch and transmission

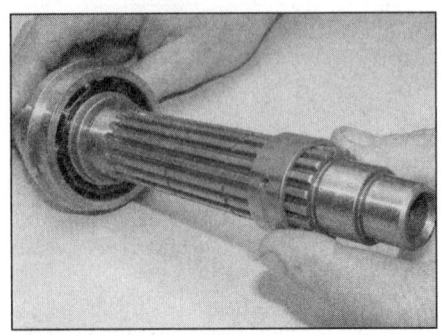

31.28a Slide the 2nd gear pinion bush onto the shaft . . .

31.28b . . . then slide the pinion onto the bush

31.28c Slide the thrust washer against the pinion . . .

31.28d . . . then fit the circlip . . .

31.28e . . . locating it in its groove

31.29a Slide the 6th gear pinion onto the shaft . . .

31.29b . . . then fit the circlip . . .

31.29c . . . locating it in its groove

31.30a Slide the splined washer . . .

direction of thrust load (see *correct fitting of a stamped circlip* illustration in Tools and Workshop Tips of the Reference section).
28 Slide the 2nd gear pinion bush onto the shaft, then fit the pinion onto the bush **(see illustrations)**. Slide on the thrust washer, and

secure them in place with the circlip, making sure it is properly seated in its groove **(see illustrations)**.
29 Slide the 6th gear pinion onto the shaft with its selector fork groove facing away from the 2nd gear pinion, and secure it in

place with the circlip, making sure it is properly seated in its groove **(see illustrations)**.
30 Slide the splined washer onto the shaft, followed by the 3rd gear pinion bush, then slide the 3rd gear pinion onto the bush **(see illustrations)**.

31.30b . . . and the 3rd gear pinion bush onto the shaft . . .

31.30c . . . then fit the 3rd gear pinion onto its bush

31.31a Slide the splined washer onto the shaft . . .

Engine, clutch and transmission 2•63

31.31b ... followed by the 4th gear pinion bush ...

31.31c ... then slide the 4th gear pinion onto the bush

31.31d Slide the splined washer against them ...

31.31e ... then fit the circlip ...

31.31f ... locating it in its groove

31.32a Slide the 5th gear pinion onto the shaft ...

31.32b ... followed by the thrust washer ...

31.33a ... the 1st gear pinion bush ...

31.33b ... the 1st gear pinion ...

31 Slide the splined washer and the 4th gear pinion bush onto the shaft, then fit the 4th gear pinion onto the bush **(see illustrations)**. Slide the splined washer onto the shaft then fit the circlip, making sure it is properly seated in its groove **(see illustrations)**.

32 Slide the 5th gear pinion onto the shaft with its selector fork groove facing the 4th gear pinion, followed by the thrust washer **(see illustrations)**.

33 Slide the 1st gear pinion bush onto the shaft, then fit the pinion onto its bush so that its open side faces the 5th gear pinion **(see illustrations)**.

34 Slide the thrust washer onto the shaft, then fit the needle bearing onto the end **(see illustrations)**.

35 Check that all components have been correctly installed **(see illustration)**.

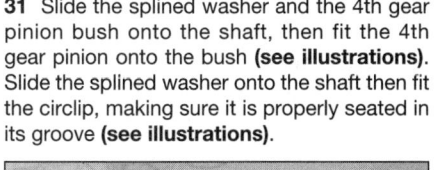

31.34a ... the thrust washer ...

31.34b ... and the needle bearing

31.35 The assembled output shaft should look like this

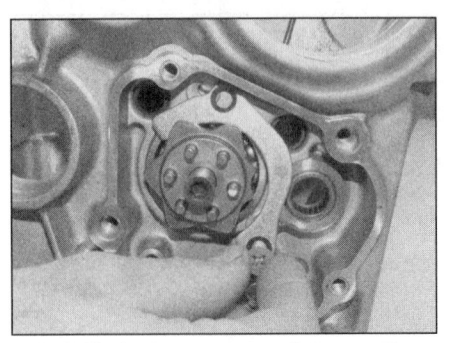

2•64 Engine, clutch and transmission

32.3 Undo the screws and remove the plate

32.4a Withdraw the shaft and remove the input shaft fork

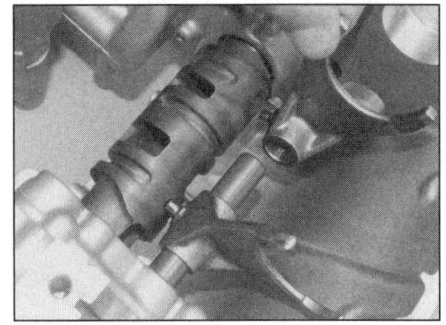

32.4b Withdraw the shaft and remove the output shaft forks

32 Selector drum and forks

Note: *To access the selector drum and forks the engine must be removed from the frame and the crankcases separated.*

Removal

1 Separate the crankcase halves (Section 25). Remove the gearchange mechanism (see Section 21)

2 The selector forks and their shafts are not marked for identification, so before removal mark them yourself using a felt pen according to where they fit and which way round.

3 Undo the screws securing the selector drum and fork retainer plate and remove the plate, noting how it fits **(see illustration)**.

4 Withdraw the input selector fork shaft, then remove the fork, noting how the guide pin locates in its track in the selector drum **(see illustration)**. Now withdraw the output selector fork shaft and remove the forks **(see illustration)**. Once removed, slide the forks back onto the shafts in their correct order and way round.

5 Withdraw the selector drum from the crankcase **(see illustration)**.

Inspection

6 Inspect the selector forks for any signs of wear or damage, especially around the fork ends where they engage with the groove in the gear pinion. Check closely to see if the forks are bent. If the forks are in any way damaged they must be replaced with new ones.

7 Slip each fork in turn into the groove in its gear pinion on the transmission shaft and measure the fork-to-groove clearance using a feeler gauge **(see illustration)**. Compare the results to the specifications at the beginning of the Chapter. If the clearance exceeds the service limit specified, measure the thickness of the fork ends and the width of the groove and compare the readings to the specifications **(see illustrations)**. Replace whichever components that are worn beyond their specifications with new ones.

8 Check that the forks fit correctly on their shaft **(see illustration)**. They should move freely with a light fit but no appreciable freeplay. Replace the forks and/or shafts with new ones if they are worn. Check that the fork shaft holes in the casing are neither worn nor damaged.

9 Check the selector fork shafts for trueness by rolling them along a flat surface. A bent shaft will cause difficulty in selecting gears and make the gearchange action heavy. Replace the shafts with new ones if they are bent.

10 Inspect the selector drum grooves and selector fork guide pins for signs of wear or

32.5 Withdraw the drum from the crankcase, noting the needle bearing (arrowed)

32.7a Measure the fork-to-groove side clearance using a feeler gauge

32.7b Measure the thickness of the fork ends . . .

32.7c . . . and the width of its pinion groove

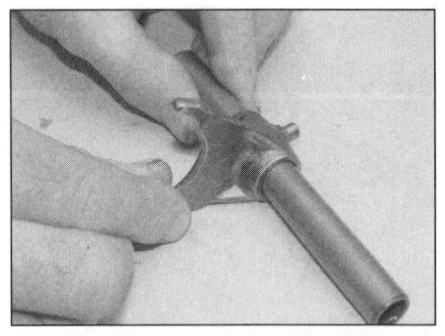

32.8 Check the fit of each fork on its shaft as described

Engine, clutch and transmission 2•65

damage and replace them with new ones if necessary **(see illustration)**.

11 Check the needle bearing in the crankcase **(see illustration 32.5)** and the roller bearing on the drum for wear **(see illustration 32.12)** and damage, and fit new ones if necessary, referring to Section 5 of *Tools and Workshop Tips* in the Reference Section for information on checks and removal and installation methods. If the roller bearing needs to be removed, first remove the cam plate (see Step 12), then slide the bearing off the drum.

12 Check the cam plate on the end of the drum for wear and damage **(see illustration)**. If required unscrew the bolt securing it to the drum and remove it – insert a bar through the drum to counter-hold it while unscrewing the bolt. Note the locating pin that fits between the cam plate and the drum and remove it for safekeeping if it is loose.

13 If removed, fit the locating pin into the end of the selector drum. Make sure the roller bearing is on the drum **(see illustration 32.12)**. Install the cam plate, making sure the offset hole in the back locates correctly on the pin. Apply a suitable thread locking compound to the threads of the cam bolt and tighten it to the specified torque setting, counter-holding the drum using a bar as on removal.

Installation

14 Slide the drum into position in the crankcase **(see illustration 32.5)**, aligning it so that the neutral detent in the cam plate is at the 5 o'clock position – this locates it in the neutral position **(see illustration 21.16b)**.
15 Apply molybdenum disulphide oil (a 50/50 mixture of molybdenum disulphide grease and clean engine oil) to the selector fork shafts and fork ends and guide pins. Slide the output fork shaft into its bore, locating the forks onto the shaft as you do, making sure they are the correct way round, and locating the guide pins into their grooves in the selector drum **(see illustration 32.4b)**. Now slide in the input shaft and similarly locate its fork **(see illustration 32.4a)**.
16 Apply a suitable non-permanent thread locking compound to the drum and fork retainer plate screws, then locate the plate

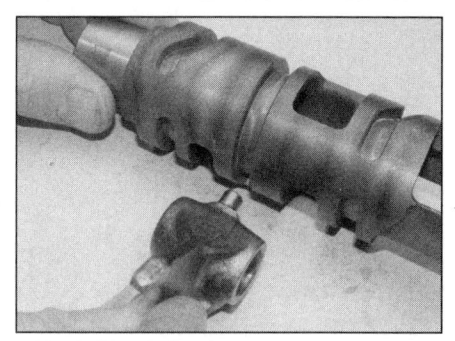

32.10 Check the drum grooves and fork guide pins

and tighten the screws to the specified torque setting **(see illustration 32.3)**.
17 Reassemble the crankcase halves (see Section 25).

33 Running-in procedure

1 Make sure the engine oil and coolant levels are correct (see *Daily (pre-ride) checks*). Make sure there is fuel in the tank.
2 Turn the ignition ON. If necessary turn the engine kill switch to the ON position and place the transmission in neutral. Set the fast idle lever enough to encourage the bike to start, but not so much as to allow it to race.
3 Pull in the clutch lever and start the engine in the normal way, allowing it to run at a moderately fast idle until it reaches operating temperature.

⚠ *Warning: If the oil pressure warning light doesn't go off, or it comes on while the engine is running, stop the engine immediately.*

4 Check carefully that there are no oil or coolant leaks and make sure the transmission

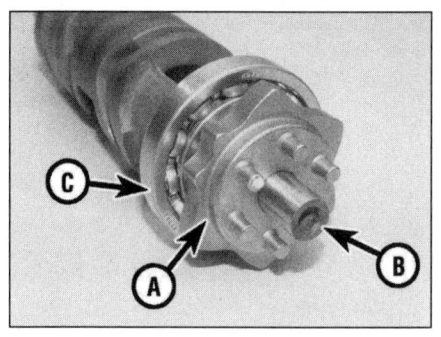

32.12 Cam plate (A), cam plate bolt (B), roller bearing (C)

and controls, especially the brakes, function properly before road testing the machine.
5 If a lubrication failure is suspected, stop the engine immediately and try to find the cause. If an engine is run without oil, even for a short period of time, severe damage will occur.
6 Treat the machine gently for the first few miles to make sure oil has circulated throughout the engine and any new parts installed have started to seat.
7 Even greater care is necessary if new rings, pistons, cylinder block or a new crankshaft has been fitted. The engine will have to be run in as when new. This means greater use of the transmission and a restraining hand on the throttle until at least 500 miles (800 km) have been covered. There's no point in keeping to any set speed limit – the main idea is to keep from labouring the engine and to gradually increase performance up to the 500 mile (800 km) mark. Experience is the best guide, since it's easy to tell when an engine is running freely. The following maximum engine speed limitations, which Suzuki provide for new motorcycles, can be used as a guide.
8 Upon completion of the road test, and after the engine has cooled down completely, recheck the valve clearances (see Chapter 1) and check the engine oil and coolant levels (see *Daily (pre-ride) checks*).

Up to 500 miles (800 km)	5500 rpm max	Vary throttle position/speed
500 to 1000 miles (800 to 1600 km)	8000 rpm max	Vary throttle position/speed. Use full throttle for short bursts
Over 1000 miles (1600 km)	11,000 rpm max	Do not exceed tachometer red line

Notes

Chapter 3
Cooling system

Contents

Coolant hoses and unions	8	General information	1
Coolant level check	see Daily (pre-ride) checks	Radiator	6
Cooling fan, fan switch and relay	3	Radiator pressure cap	2
Cooling system checks	see Chapter 1	Thermostat	5
Cooling system draining, flushing and refilling	see Chapter 1	Water pump	7
Engine coolant temperature (ECT) sensor	4		

Degrees of difficulty

Easy, suitable for novice with little experience	**Fairly easy,** suitable for beginner with some experience	**Fairly difficult,** suitable for competent DIY mechanic	**Difficult,** suitable for experienced DIY mechanic	**Very difficult,** suitable for expert DIY or professional

Specifications

Coolant
Mixture type and capacity .... see Chapter 1

Cooling fan switch
Switch closes (fan ON) .... approx. 105°C
Switch opens (fan OFF) .... approx. 100°C

Engine coolant temperature (ECT) sensor
Resistance @ 20°C .... approx. 2.45 K-ohms
Resistance @ 50°C .... approx. 811 ohms
Resistance @ 80°C .... approx. 318 ohms
Resistance @ 110°C .... approx. 142 ohms
Resistance @ 130°C .... approx. 88 ohms

Thermostat
Opening temperature .... 80.5 to 83.5°C
Fully open .... 95°C
Valve lift .... 8 mm (min)

Radiator
Cap valve opening pressure .... 13.5 to 17.8 psi (0.95 to 1.25 Bar)

Torque settings
Coolant inlet union bolts .... 10 Nm
Engine coolant temperature (ECT) sensor .... 18 Nm
Fan switch .... 17 Nm
Thermostat cover bolts .... 10 Nm
Water pump cover screws .... 6 Nm
Water pump impeller bolt .... 8 Nm
Water pump mounting bolts .... 10 Nm

3•2 Cooling system

1 General information

The cooling system uses a water/antifreeze coolant to carry away excess heat from the engine and maintain as constant a temperature as possible. The cylinders are surrounded by a water jacket from which the heated coolant is circulated by thermosyphonic action in conjunction with a water pump, which is driven by shaft off the oil pump. The hot coolant passes over the thermostat and into the radiator, then onto the water pump and back to the engine where the cycle is repeated.

A thermostat is fitted in the system to prevent the coolant flowing through the radiator when the engine is cold, therefore accelerating the speed at which the engine reaches normal operating temperature. A coolant temperature sensor, mounted in the back of the cylinder head on the left-hand end, transmits information to the engine management system which in turn feeds the temperature gauge and high temperature warning light in the instrument panel. A cooling fan fitted to the back of the radiator aids cooling in extreme conditions by drawing extra air through. The fan motor is controlled by a thermostatic switch fitted in the radiator.

The complete cooling system is partially sealed and pressurised, the pressure being controlled by a valve contained in the spring-loaded radiator cap. By pressurising the coolant the boiling point is raised, preventing premature boiling in adverse conditions. The overflow pipe from the system is connected to a reservoir into which excess coolant is expelled under pressure. The discharged coolant automatically returns to the radiator by the vacuum created when the engine cools.

Warning: Do not remove the pressure cap from the filler neck when the engine is hot. Scalding hot coolant and steam may be blown out under pressure, which could cause serious injury. When the engine has cooled, place a thick rag, like a towel, over the pressure cap; slowly rotate the cap anti-clockwise to the first stop. This procedure allows any residual pressure to escape. When the steam has stopped escaping, press down on the cap while turning it anti-clockwise and remove it.

Caution: Do not allow antifreeze to come in contact with your skin or painted surfaces of the motorcycle. Rinse off any spills immediately with plenty of water. Antifreeze is highly toxic if ingested. Never leave antifreeze lying around in an open container or in puddles on the floor; children and pets are attracted by its sweet smell and may drink it. Check with the local authorities about disposing of used antifreeze. Many communities will have collection centres which will see that antifreeze is disposed of safely.

Caution: At all times use the specified type of antifreeze, and always mix it with distilled water in the correct proportion. The antifreeze contains corrosion inhibitors which are essential to avoid damage to the cooling system. A lack of these inhibitors could lead to a build-up of corrosion which would block the coolant passages, resulting in overheating and severe engine damage. Distilled water must be used as opposed to tap water to avoid a build-up of scale which would also block the passages.

2 Radiator pressure cap check

1 If problems such as overheating or loss of coolant occur, check the entire system as described in Chapter 1. The radiator cap opening pressure should be checked by a Suzuki dealer with the special tester required to do the job. If the cap is defective, replace it with a new one.

3 Cooling fan, fan switch and relay

1 If the engine is overheating and the cooling fan isn't coming on, first check the cooling fan and ignition circuit fuses (see Chapter 9). If either fuse is blown, check the fan circuit for a short to earth (see the wiring diagrams at the end of Chapter 9). If the fuses are good, check the fan switch and then the relay as described below.

Cooling fan

Check

2 To access the wiring connector, remove the left-hand fairing side panel (see Chapter 8). Disconnect the wiring connector **(see illustration)**.

3 Using a 12 volt battery and two jumper wires with suitable connectors, connect the battery positive (+) lead to the blue wire terminal on the fan side of the wiring connector, and the battery negative (–) lead to the black wire terminal. Once connected the fan should operate. If it doesn't, and the wiring is all good, then the fan motor is faulty – replace the fan with a new one.

4 If it does come on, then check for battery voltage at the orange/red terminal on the loom side of the fan wiring connector with the ignition on. If there is no voltage check the wiring between the fan connector and the ignition switch via the fusebox for continuity, referring to the wiring diagram for your model at the end of Chapter 9. If there is voltage check the black/red wire between the connector and the relay for continuity.

Replacement

Warning: The engine must be completely cool before carrying out this procedure.

5 Remove the radiator (see Section 6).
6 Unscrew the bolts securing the fan to the radiator and remove it **(see illustration)**.
7 Installation is the reverse of removal.

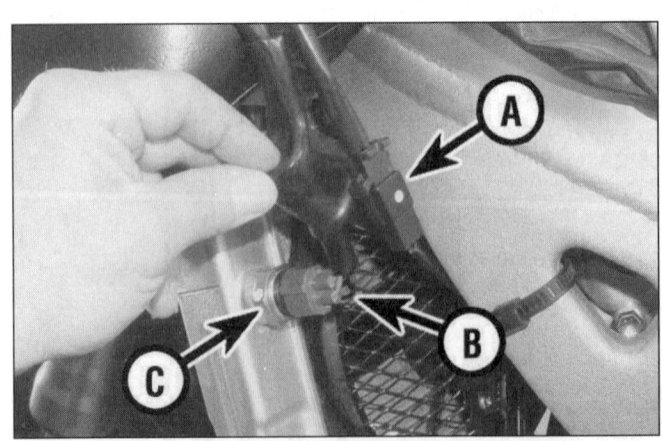

3.2 Fan motor wiring connector (A), fan switch wiring connector (B), fan switch (C)

3.6 Fan motor bolts (arrowed)

Cooling system 3•3

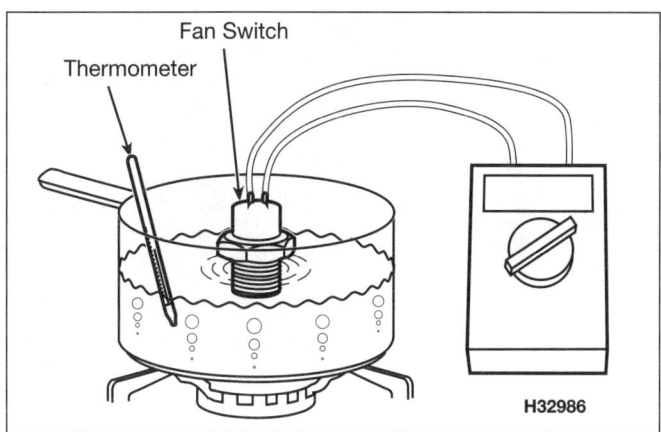

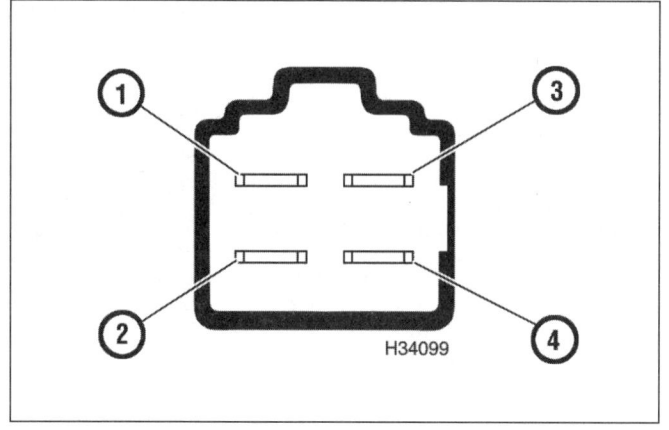

3.12 Cooling fan switch test set-up

3.18 Cooling fan relay terminal identification

Fan switch

Check

8 Remove the left-hand fairing side panel (see Chapter 8). Disconnect the wiring connector from the fan switch **(see illustration 3.2)**. Check that there is battery voltage at the orange/yellow wire terminal on the loom side of the connector with the ignition on. If not, check the wiring for continuity and the connections as described in Chapter 9, following the relevant Wiring Diagram. Turn the ignition off.

9 If the voltage is good, connect the across the fan switch wiring connector terminals using a jumper wire. Turn the ignition switch on. The fan should come on. If it does, the fan switch is defective and must be replaced with a new one. If it does not come on, test the fan motor itself (see above). If the fan is good, check for continuity in the orange/red wire from the fan switch connector to the fan relay.

10 If the fan is on the whole time, disconnect the switch wiring connector **(see illustration 3.2)**. The fan should stop. If it does, the switch is defective and must be replaced with a new one.

11 If the fan works but is suspected of cutting in at the wrong temperature, a more comprehensive test of the switch can be made as follows.

12 Remove the switch (see Step 15). Fill a small heatproof container with oil and place it on a stove. Connect the positive (+) probe of an ohmmeter or continuity tester to one terminal on the switch and the negative (–) probe to the other terminal, and using some wire or other support suspend the switch in the oil so that just the sensing portion and the threads are submerged **(see illustration)**. Also place a thermometer capable of reading temperatures up to 120°C in the oil so that its bulb is close to the switch. **Note:** *None of the components should be allowed to directly touch the container.*

13 Initially the meter reading should be very high or show no continuity indicating that the switch is open (OFF). Heat the oil, stirring it gently.

⚠ **Warning: This must be done very carefully to avoid the risk of personal injury.**

When the temperature reaches around 105°C the meter reading should drop to around zero ohms or show continuity, indicating that the switch has closed (ON). Now turn the heat off. As the temperature falls to around 100°C the meter reading should again show infinite (very high) resistance or no continuity, indicating that the switch has opened (OFF). If the meter readings obtained are different, or they are obtained at different temperatures, then the switch is faulty and must be replaced with a new one. On completion, fit the switch as described in Steps 16 and 17.

Replacement

⚠ **Warning: The engine must be completely cool before carrying out this procedure.**

14 Drain the cooling system (see Chapter 1) – note that as the switch is located quite high up in the radiator it is not necessary to completely drain the system, only enough to ensure that the coolant is below the level of the switch bore.

15 Disconnect the wiring connector from the switch **(see illustration 3.2)**. Unscrew the switch and withdraw it from the filler neck. Discard the O-ring as a new one must be used.

16 Install the switch using a new O-ring and tighten it to the torque setting specified at the beginning of the Chapter.

17 Reconnect the switch wiring and refill the cooling system (see Chapter 1).

Fan relay

Check

18 Remove the relay (see below). Using an ohmmeter or continuity tester, check for continuity between Nos. 1 and 2 terminals on the relay as shown **(see illustration)**. There should be no continuity (infinite resistance). Leaving the meter connected, now connect a fully charged 12 volt battery to the relay Nos. 3 and 4 terminals, positive (+) side to the No. 3 terminal and negative (–) to the No. 4 terminal. There should now be continuity (zero resistance) on the meter or tester. If this is the case the relay is good. Otherwise replace the relay with a new one.

19 If the relay is good, check each of the black/white wires from the connector for continuity to earth. If there is no continuity locate and repair the fault.

Replacement

20 Remove the left-hand cockpit trim panel (see Chapter 8).

21 Displace the relay from its mount and disconnect the wiring connector **(see illustration)**.

22 Connect the wiring connector to the new relay, then fit the relay on its mount.

4 Engine coolant temperature (ECT) sensor

Check

1 The engine coolant temperature (ECT) sensor is mounted in the back of the cylinder head on the left-hand end. If a sensor fault is indicated by the fuel injection system diagnostic process (see Chapter 4), carry out the preliminary checks as described in Chapter 4, Section 11.

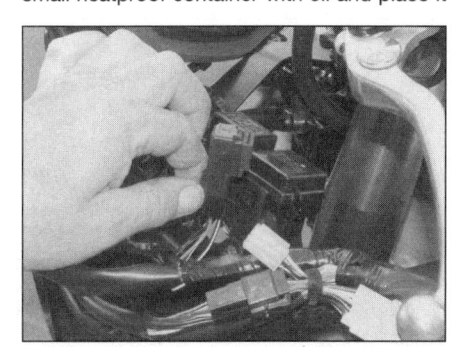

3.21 Lift the fan relay off its mount and disconnect it

3•4 Cooling system

2 To check the sensor resistance remove it from the cylinder head (see Steps 5 to 9).
3 Fill a small heatproof container with oil and place it on a stove. Using an ohmmeter set initially to the K-ohms scale, connect the meter probes to the sensor terminals, and using some wire or other support, suspend the sensor in the oil so that just the sensing portion and the threads are submerged **(see illustration 3.12)**. Also place a thermometer capable of reading temperatures up to 140°C in the oil so that its bulb is close to the switch. **Note:** *None of the components should be allowed to touch the container directly.*
4 Check the meter reading and compare the result with the specifications at the beginning of this Chapter, then heat the oil slowly, stirring it gently.

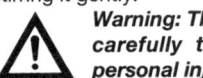

⚠️ *Warning: This must be done very carefully to avoid the risk of personal injury.*

As the temperature of the oil rises, the sensor resistance should fall (depending on your meter you may need to change scale to get an accurate reading). Check that the specified resistance is obtained at the correct temperature (see Specifications at the beginning of this Chapter). If the readings obtained are different, or are obtained at different temperatures, the sensor is faulty and must be replaced with a new one. If the readings are as specified, the fault could lie in the coolant temperature display circuit in the instrument cluster (see Chapter 9).

Removal and installation

⚠️ *Warning: The engine must be completely cool before carrying out this procedure.*
Caution: *Handle the sensor with care as it could be damaged if dropped.*

5 The engine coolant temperature (ECT) sensor is mounted in the back of the cylinder head on the left-hand end **(see illustration)**.
6 Drain the cooling system (see Chapter 1) – note that as the sensor is located quite high up in the system it is not necessary to completely drain it, only enough to ensure that the coolant is below the level of the sensor bore.
7 Remove the fuel tank (see Chapter 4). Depending on the tools available, it may also be necessary to remove the air filter housing and displace the throttle bodies, though it may be enough to displace the IAP sensor vacuum damper with its bracket from the frame **(see illustration)**.
8 Disconnect the sensor wiring connector.
9 Place a rag underneath the sensor and unscrew it. Discard the sealing washer as a new one must be fitted on installation.
10 Installation is the reverse of removal, noting the following:
● Fit a new sealing washer onto the sensor.
● Tighten the sensor to the torque setting specified at the beginning of this Chapter. Reconnect the wiring connector.
● Refill the cooling system (see Chapter 1).

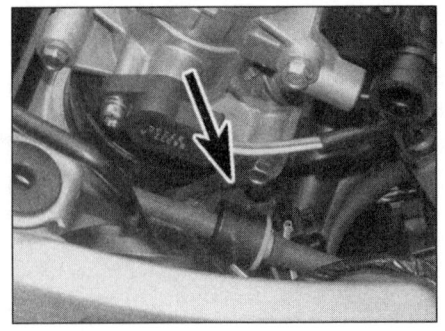

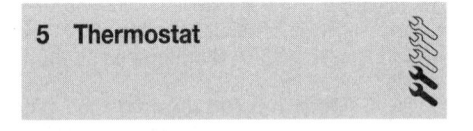

5 Thermostat

Removal

⚠️ *Warning: The engine must be completely cool before carrying out this procedure.*

1 The thermostat is automatic in operation and should give many years service without requiring attention. In the event of a failure, the valve will probably jam open, in which case the engine will take much longer than normal to warm up. Conversely, if the valve jams shut, the coolant will be unable to circulate and the engine will overheat. Neither condition is acceptable, and the fault must be investigated promptly.

4.5 Coolant temperature sensor (arrowed)

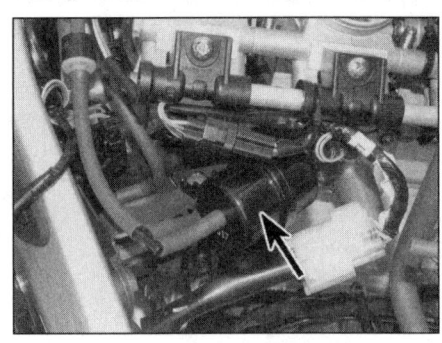

4.7 Displace the vacuum damper (arrowed) with its bracket to access the sensor

2 The thermostat housing is on the back of the cylinder head in the middle. Drain the cooling system (see Chapter 1) – note that as the thermostat is located quite high up in the system it is not necessary to completely drain it, only enough to ensure that the coolant is below the level of the thermostat housing.
3 Remove the fuel tank (see Chapter 4).
4 Unscrew the two bolts securing the cover and detach it from the housing – there should be no need to detach the hoses from the cover unless you want to **(see illustration)**. Remove the thermostat, noting how it fits – it may come away with the cover **(see illustration)**.

Check

5 Examine the thermostat visually before carrying out the test. If it remains in the open position at room temperature, it should be replaced with a new one. Check the condition of the rubber seal around the thermostat and replace it with a new one if it is damaged, deformed or deteriorated, but note that it is not listed as being available separately, though it is worth checking with a Suzuki dealer.
6 Suspend the thermostat by a piece of wire in a container of cold water. Place a thermometer capable of reading temperatures up to 110°C in the water so that the bulb is close to the thermostat **(see illustration)**. Heat the water, noting the temperature when the thermostat opens, and compare the result with the specifications given at the beginning of the Chapter. Also check the amount the valve opens (valve lift) after it has been heated

5.4a Unscrew the two bolts (arrowed) and detach the cover . . .

5.4b . . . and remove the thermostat

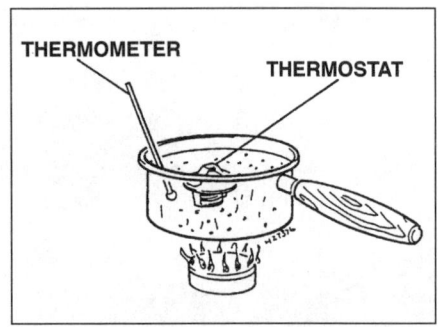

5.6 Thermostat testing set-up

Cooling system 3•5

for a few minutes and compare the measurement to the specifications. If the readings obtained differ from those given, the thermostat is faulty and must be replaced with a new one.

7 In the event of thermostat failure, as an emergency measure only, it can be removed and the machine used without it (this is better than leaving a permanently closed thermostat in, but if it is permanently open, you might as well leave it in). **Note:** *Take care when starting the engine from cold as it will take much longer than usual to warm up. Ensure that a new unit is installed as soon as possible.*

Installation

8 Make sure the seal fitted around the thermostat is in good condition, otherwise use a new one if available. Smear some clean coolant over the seal. Install the thermostat with the jiggle pin at the top and make sure it locates correctly **(see illustration)**. Fit the cover onto the housing, then install the bolts and tighten them to the torque setting specified at the beginning of the Chapter **(see illustration 5.4a)**.

9 Attach the hoses to the cover if removed and tighten/locate the clamps.

10 Install the fuel tank (see Chapter 4). Refill the cooling system (see Chapter 1).

6 Radiator

Removal

⚠️ **Warning:** *The engine and exhaust must be completely cool before carrying out this procedure.*

Note: *If the radiator is being removed as part of the engine removal procedure, detach the hoses from their unions on the engine rather than on the radiator and remove the radiator with the hoses attached to it. Note the routing of the hoses.*

1 Remove the fairing side panels (see Chapter 8). Drain the cooling system (see Chapter 1).

2 Displace the oil cooler (see Chapter 2) – there is no need to detach the oil hoses.

3 If required remove the horn (see Chapter 9) – if you leave it in place make sure you don't knock the radiator against it as you are likely to damage the fins.

4 Disconnect the cooling fan and fan switch wiring connectors **(see illustration 3.2)**.

5 Slacken the clamps securing the hoses to the radiator and detach them, noting which fits where **(see illustrations)**. Tie the overflow hose to the reservoir above the level of the reservoir or it will drain itself.

6 Unscrew the radiator mounting bolts and carefully manoeuvre the radiator out **(see illustration)**.

7 If necessary, remove the cooling fan from the radiator (see Section 3). Check the radiator for signs of damage and clear any dirt or debris that might obstruct air flow and inhibit cooling. If the radiator fins are badly

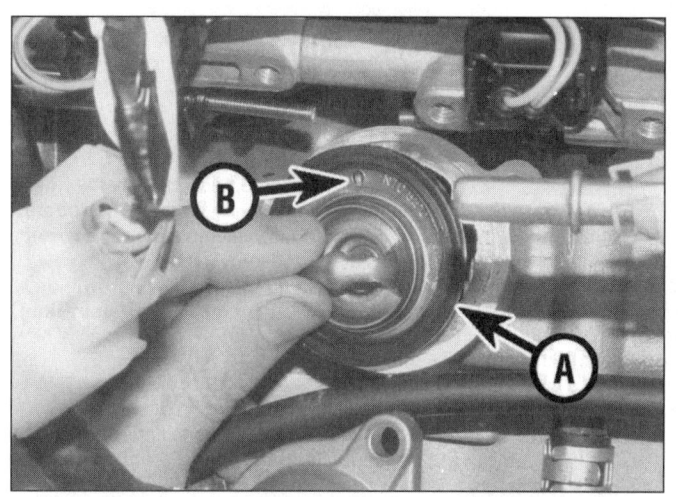

5.8 Make sure the seal (A) is in good condition, and fit the thermostat with the jiggle pin (B) at the top

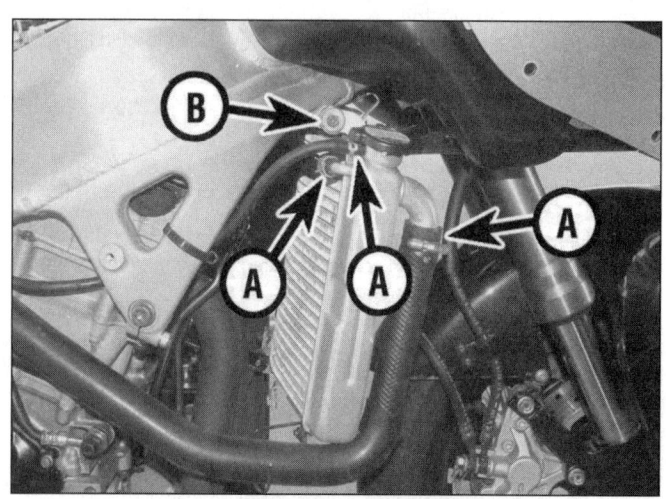

6.5a Radiator hoses (A) and mounting bolt (B) – right-hand side

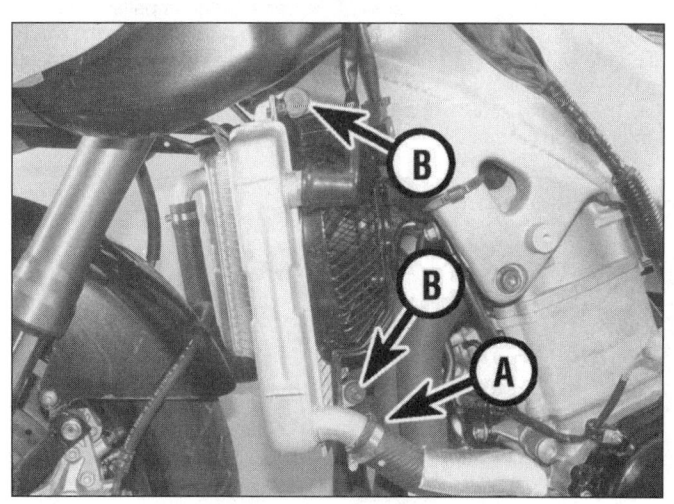

6.5b Radiator hose (A) and mounting bolts (B) – left-hand side

6.6 Carefully remove the radiator

3•6 Cooling system

7.2 Check the drain hole (arrowed) for signs of leakage

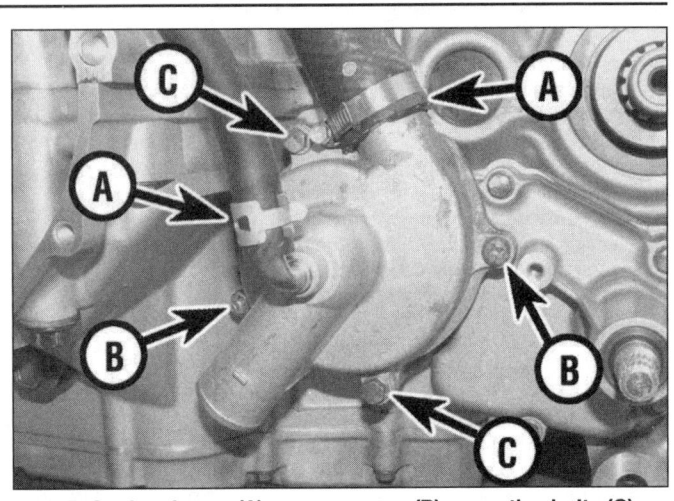

7.5 Coolant hoses (A), cover screws (B), mounting bolts (C)

damaged or broken the radiator must be replaced with a new one. Also check the rubber mounting grommets, and replace them with new ones if they are damaged deformed or deteriorated, noting the spacers that fit inside them.

Installation

8 Installation is the reverse of removal, noting the following.
- Make sure the rubber grommets are correctly located in their mounts.
- Make sure that the spacers are fitted in the grommets.
- Make sure that the wiring is correctly routed and connected.

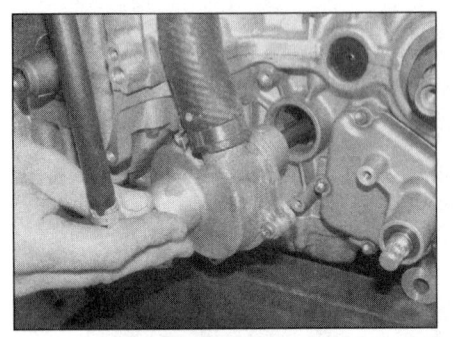

7.7 Withdraw the pump from the engine

- Ensure the coolant hoses are in good condition (see Chapter 1), and are securely retained by their clamps, using new ones if necessary.
- On completion refill the cooling system as described in Chapter 1.

7 Water pump

Check

1 The water pump is located on the lower left-hand side of the engine below the front sprocket. Visually check the area below the pump for signs of leakage.

2 To prevent leakage of coolant from the cooling system to the lubrication system and vice versa, two seals are fitted on the pump shaft. There is a drain hole in the pump body, which is just visible if you look up at the underside of the pump at the point just before it enters the crankcase **(see illustration)**. If either seal fails, the drain allows the coolant or oil to escape and prevents them mixing. If both seals fail the oil and coolant mix to form a white emulsion. The seal on the water pump side is of the mechanical type which bears on the rear face of the impeller. The second seal, which is mounted behind the mechanical seal

is of the normal feathered lip type. Both seals are available separately. If on inspection there is evidence of leakage from the drain hole, remove the water pump and replace both seals with new ones (see below).

Removal

3 Drain the coolant and the engine oil (see Chapter 1).
4 Displace the front sprocket cover (see Chapter 6).
5 Release the clamps and detach the hoses from the water pump cover **(see illustration)**.
6 If you want to disassemble the water pump, slacken the cover screws now.
7 Unscrew the mounting bolts and withdraw the pump from the engine **(see illustration)**. Remove the O-ring and discard it as a new one must be used.

Inspection and disassembly

8 Undo the cover screws and detach the cover **(see illustration)**. Discard the O-ring as a new one must be used.
9 Check for corrosion or a build-up of scale in the pump cover and around the impeller and clean it off. To remove the impeller, counter-hold the shaft using a screwdriver in the slot in the end and unscrew the impeller bolt, noting the washers **(see illustration)**. Draw the impeller off the shaft, noting how it locates **(see illustration)**.

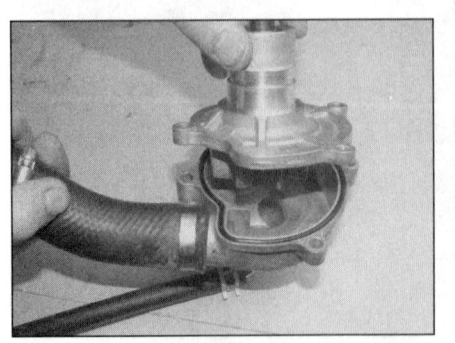

7.8 Detach the cover from the housing

7.9a Unscrew the bolt and remove the washers . . .

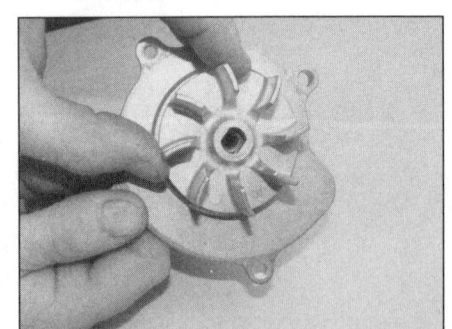

7.9b . . . then remove the impeller

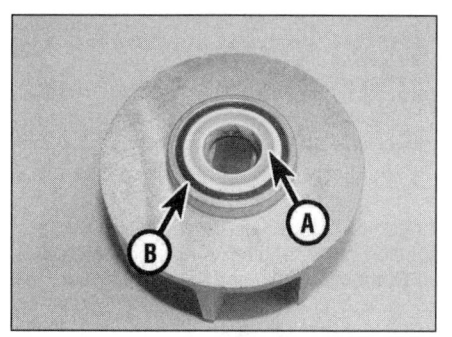

Cooling system 3•7

7.10 Check the seal seat (A) and damper (B)

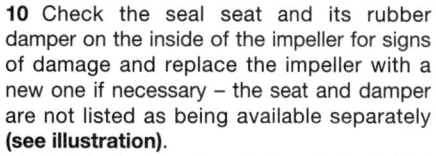

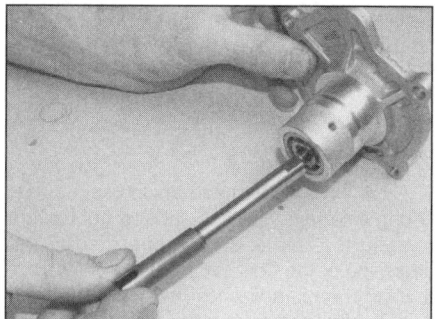

7.11a Withdraw the shaft

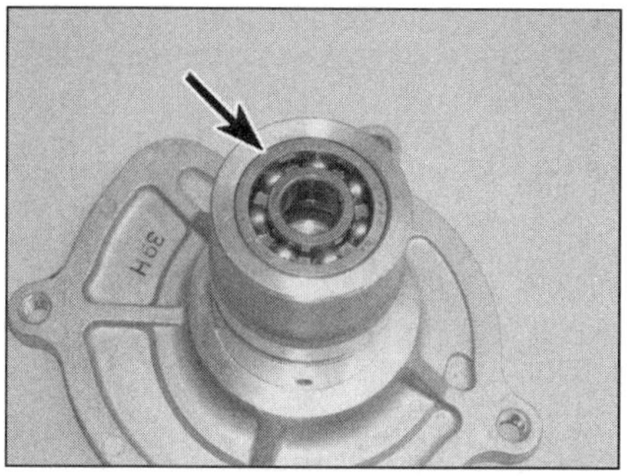

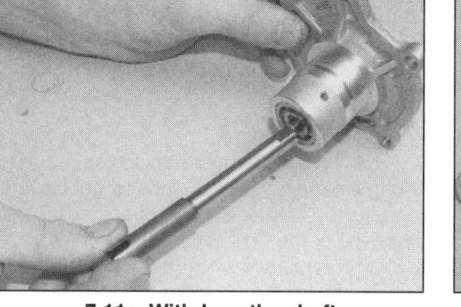

7.11b Use a puller to remove the bearing (arrowed)

10 Check the seal seat and its rubber damper on the inside of the impeller for signs of damage and replace the impeller with a new one if necessary – the seat and damper are not listed as being available separately **(see illustration)**.

11 Rotate the impeller shaft and check that the bearing turns smoothly and that there is no play. Withdraw the shaft and replace the bearing with a new one if necessary - refer to Section 5 in Tools and Workshop Tips in the Reference Section for information on bearing checks and removal and installation methods – a knife-edge puller is required to remove this bearing **(see illustrations)**. With the bearing removed check the condition of the shaft bush in the pump body and replace the pump with a new one if wear or damage is found.

12 On reassembly apply grease to the impeller shaft. Check the condition of the impeller bolt inner washer and replace it with a new one if necessary – the metal side faces the bolt head, as does the raised inner rim of the lock washer. Apply a suitable non-permanent thread locking compound to the bolt threads and tighten it to the torque setting specified at the beginning of the Chapter.

Seal renewal

13 Remove the cover and the impeller (see Steps 8 and 9). Withdraw the shaft from the pump **(see illustration 7.11a)**.

14 Remove the mechanical seal from the pump using a knife-edge puller (see Tools and Workshop Tips in the Reference Section) **(see illustration)**. Discard it as a new one must be used.

15 Lever the oil seal out using a seal hook or screwdriver. Discard it as a new one must be used.

16 Drive the oil seal in using a suitable socket, making sure its marked side will face the mechanical seal. Smear some grease onto its lips.

17 The new mechanical seal comes with sealant already applied round its inner rim. Drive the seal in using a suitable socket or tube that bears only on the outer rim of the seal body, until the rim seats on the hub.

Installation

18 Smear a new water pump body O-ring with grease and fit it into its groove **(see illustration)**.

19 Fit the pump into the engine, aligning the slot in the shaft end with the tab on the oil pump shaft – if the cover has been removed alignment is made easier by the fact you can turn the impeller as you fit the pump **(see illustration 7.7)**. Tighten the pump mounting bolts to the torque setting specified at the beginning of the Chapter **(see illustration 7.5)**.

20 If removed, fit a new O-ring smeared with coolant into the rim of the cover, then fit the cover and tighten its screws to the specified torque **(see illustration)**.

21 Fit the hoses back onto the pump cover and secure them with the clamps **(see illustration 7.5)**.

22 Install the front sprocket cover (see Chapter 6).

23 Refill the cooling system and replenish the engine oil (see Chapter 1).

8 Coolant hoses and unions

Removal

1 Before removing a hose, drain the coolant (see Chapter 1). To access the hoses and unions on the engine raise, or for best access remove, the fuel tank (see Chapter 4).

2 Use a screwdriver to slacken the larger-bore hose clamps, then slide them back along the hose and clear of the union spigot. The smaller-bore hoses are secured by spring clamps which can be expanded by squeezing their ears together with pliers. Note the orientation of the hose and clamp before removal – some have alignment marks which correspond to a mark on their union, and these ensure clamps are easy to access and shaped hoses do not become twisted.

Caution: The radiator unions are fragile. Do not use excessive force when attempting to remove the hoses.

3 If a hose proves stubborn, release it by rotating it on its union before working it off. If all else fails, cut the hose with a sharp knife.

7.14 Mechanical seal (arrowed)

7.18 Install the pump using a new O-ring on the body

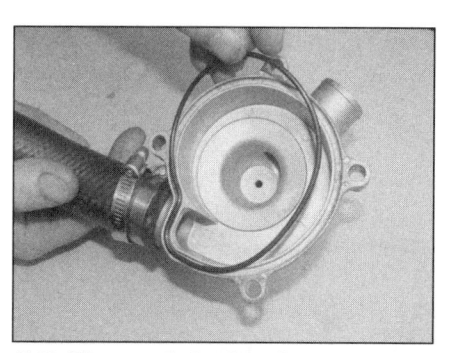

7.20 Fit a new O-ring into the groove then install the cover

8.4 Coolant inlet union bolts (arrowed)

Whilst this means replacing the hose, it is preferable to buying a new radiator.

4 To remove the inlet union on the cylinder block unscrew its bolts **(see illustration)**. Discard the O-ring as a new one must be used.

Installation

5 Install the cylinder head union using a new O-ring smeared with coolant and tighten the bolts to the torque setting specified at the beginning of the Chapter.

6 Slide the clamps onto the hose and then work the hose on to its union.

> **HAYNES HiNT** *If the hose is difficult to push on its union, soften it by soaking it in very hot water, or alternatively a little soapy water on the union can be used as a lubricant.*

7 Rotate the hose on its union to settle it in position before sliding the clamps into place and tightening them securely – make sure the hoses and clamps are aligned as noted on removal, where relevant.

Chapter 4
Fuel, engine management and exhaust systems

Contents

Air filter check, cleaning and renewal	see Chapter 1	Fuel pump, filter and strainer	5
Air filter housing	8	Fuel pump relay	4
Catalytic converter	20	Fuel rail and injectors	14
Electronic control module (ECM)	see Chapter 5	Fuel system check	see Chapter 1
EVAP system (California models)	19	Fuel tank	2
Exhaust system	17	General information and precautions	1
Fast idle system	16	Idle speed check and adjustment	see Chapter 1
Fuel hose renewal	see Chapter 1	Intake air control valve system	9
Fuel injection system description	10	PAIR system	18
Fuel injection system fault finding	11	Throttle bodies	13
Fuel injection system components	12	Throttle and fast idle cable check and adjustment	see Chapter 1
Fuel level sensor	6	Throttle cables	15
Fuel pressure regulator	7	Throttle body synchronisation	see Chapter 1
Fuel pressure check	3		

Degrees of difficulty

Easy, suitable for novice with little experience	Fairly easy, suitable for beginner with some experience	Fairly difficult, suitable for competent DIY mechanic	Difficult, suitable for experienced DIY mechanic	Very difficult, suitable for expert DIY or professional

Specifications

Fuel
Grade
  European models .... Unleaded, minimum 91 RON (Research Octane Number)
  US models and Canada .... Unleaded, minimum 87 ((R+M) /2 method)
Fuel tank capacity including reserve
  X and Y models
    California models .... 20 litres
    All other models .... 22 litres
  K1 models onward
    California models .... 19 litres
    All other models .... 21 litres

Fuel supply system
Operating pressure .... 43 psi (3.0 Bar)
Pump flow rate
  X and Y models .... 1.08 litres per min at operating pressure
  K1 models onward .... 2.40 litres per min at operating pressure

Fuel level sensor
Resistance
  Full position .... 11 to 13 ohms
  Half position .... 70 to 77 ohms
  Empty position .... 130 to 135 ohms

Intake air control valve system

Opening rpm	above 2500 rpm
Closing rpm	below 2200 rpm
VCSV resistance	36 to 44 ohms

Component test data

Air pressure (AP) sensor
    Input voltage .... 4.5 to 5.5 V
    Output voltage .... approx. 3.6 V @ 760 mmHg
Camshaft position (CMP) sensor
    Resistance .... 0.9 to 1.3 K-ohms
    Peak voltage .... above 0.7 V
Crankshaft position (CKP) sensor
    Resistance .... 180 to 280 ohms
    Peak voltage .... above 3.0 V
Engine coolant temperature (ECT) sensor
    Input voltage .... 4.5 to 5.5 V
    Resistance .... 2.3 to 2.6 K-ohms @ 20°C
Gear position (GP) sensor voltage .... above 0.6 V
Injector voltage .... Battery voltage (12 V approx)
Injector resistance .... 11 to 16 ohms @ 20°C
Intake air pressure (IAP) sensor
    Input voltage .... 4.5 to 5.5 V
    Output voltage .... approx 2.5 V at idle speed
Intake air temperature (IAT) sensor
    Input voltage .... 4.5 to 5.5 V
    Resistance .... 2.2 to 2.7 K-ohms @ 20°C
Oxygen sensor – K2 models onward
    Output voltage (engine warm)
        At idle .... less than 0.4 volt
        At 3000 to 4000 rpm .... more than 0.6 volt
    Resistance .... 4 to 5 ohms @ 23°C
Throttle position (TP) sensor
    Input voltage .... 4.5 to 5.5 V
    Output voltage
        Closed .... approx 1.1 V
        Open .... approx 4.5 V
    Resistance
        Closed .... approx 1.3 K-ohms
        Open .... approx 4.5 K-ohms
Tip over (TO) sensor
    Resistance .... 60 to 64 K-ohms
    Voltage .... approx 2.5 V

Throttle body

Cylinder identification	1–2–3–4, from left to right
Idle speed	see Chapter 1
Fast idle speed	3500 rpm (when warm)

PAIR system

Control valve resistance – K2 models onward .... 16 to 24 ohms @ 20°C

Torque settings

Camshaft position (CMP) sensor mounting bolts .... 8 Nm
Exhaust system – all mountings .... 23 Nm
Fuel pump assembly – X and Y models
    Filter housing screws .... 3 Nm
    Pressure check bolt .... 10 Nm
    Pressure regulator screws .... 3 Nm
    Pump mounting screws .... 5 Nm
Fuel pump mounting bolts – K1 models onward .... 10 Nm
Injector holder/fuel rail screws .... 5 Nm
Intake air temperature (IAT) sensor .... 18 Nm
Oxygen sensor – K2 models onward .... 47.5 Nm
PAIR system pipe nuts .... 10 Nm

Fuel, engine management and exhaust systems 4•3

1 General information and precautions

General information

The fuel system consists of the fuel tank, the fuel pump and filter, the fuel supply hose to the fuel rail on the throttle bodies, on X and Y models the fuel return hose to the tank, and the injectors that are located in the throttle bodies. All models have single valve throttle bodies with one injector per body.

On X and Y models the fuel pump (incorporating the filter and pressure regulator) is mounted on the back of the throttle bodies, and there is a fuel level sensor housed inside the tank. On all other models the fuel pump (incorporating the filter, pressure regulator and level sensor) is housed inside the fuel tank, negating the need for a fuel return hose.

The fuel pump is activated initially by the ignition switch and continues to deliver fuel so long as the engine is running. Fuel pressure is controlled within the pump by a pressure regulator. In the event of the machine falling over, a tip-over sensor cuts power to the fuel pump, injectors and ignition coils.

The entire fuel injection system is controlled by the engine control module (ECM) which monitors data sent from the various system sensors and adjusts fuel delivery to the engine accordingly. If a fault develops in the injection system, the FI warning LED illuminates on the instrument cluster and an LCD code is displayed. In the case of a minor fault the engine will continue to run enabling the machine to be ridden, although performance will be significantly reduced. For comprehensive fault diagnosis and certain service procedures, a Suzuki mode select switch (Pt. No. 09930-82710) is useful (and inexpensive), though not essential as its function can be copied using a simple jumper wire (see Section 11).

For running the engine from cold, a fast idle lever is incorporated in the left-handlebar switch housing and is connected to the throttle body assembly by a cable.

The exhaust system is a four-into-two design. On K2 models onward the system incorporates an oxygen sensor.

All models feature a PAIR system which introduces filtered air into the exhaust ports to promote the burning of excess fuel in the exhaust gases. On X, Y and K1 models the system is controlled by vacuum sourced from the throttle bodies, while on all other models it is electronically controlled by a solenoid valve which receives a signal from the ECM. California models feature an EVAP emission control system that prevents fuel vapour escaping into the atmosphere from the fuel tank.

Precautions

Warning: Petrol (gasoline) is extremely flammable, so take extra precautions when you work on any part of the fuel system. Don't smoke or allow open flames or bare light bulbs near the work area, and don't work in a garage where a natural gas-type appliance is present. If you spill any fuel on your skin, rinse it off immediately with soap and water. When you perform any kind of work on the fuel system, wear safety glasses and have a fire extinguisher suitable for a class B type fire (flammable liquids) on hand.

Always perform service procedures in a well ventilated area to prevent a build-up of fumes.

Never work in a building containing a gas appliance with a pilot light, or any other form of naked flame. Ensure that there are no naked light bulbs or any sources of flame or sparks nearby.

Do not smoke (or allow anyone else to smoke) while in the vicinity of petrol (gasoline) or of components containing it. Remember the possible presence of vapour from these sources and move well clear before smoking.

Check all electrical equipment belonging to the house, garage or workshop where being undertaken (see the Safety first! section of this manual). Remember that certain electrical appliances such as drills, cutters etc. create sparks in the normal course of operation and must not be used near petrol (gasoline) or any component containing it. Again, remember the possible presence of fumes before using electrical equipment.

Always mop up any spilt fuel and safely dispose of the rag used.

Any stored fuel that is drained off during servicing work must be kept in sealed containers that are suitable for holding petrol (gasoline), and clearly marked as such; the containers themselves should be kept in a safe place. Note that this last point applies equally to the fuel tank if it is removed from the machine; also remember to keep its filler cap closed at all times.

Read the Safety first! section of this manual carefully before starting work.

Owners of machines used in the US, particularly California, should note that their machines must comply at all times with Federal or State legislation governing the permissible levels of noise and of pollutants such as unburnt hydrocarbons, carbon monoxide etc. that can be emitted by those machines. All vehicles offered for sale must comply with legislation in force at the date of manufacture and must not subsequently be altered in any way which will affect their emission of noise or of pollutants.

In practice, this means that adjustments may not be made to any part of the fuel, ignition or exhaust systems by anyone who is not authorised or mechanically qualified to do so, or who does not have the tools, equipment and data necessary to properly carry out the task. Also if any part of these systems is to be renewed it must be renewed with only genuine Suzuki components or by components which are approved under the relevant legislation. The machine must never be used with any part of these systems removed, modified or damaged.

2 Fuel tank

Warning: Refer to the precautions given in Section 1 before starting work.

Raise

1 Make sure the fuel cap is secure. Remove the seats (see Chapter 8). Remove the fuel tank prop from the storage space underneath the seat.

2 Unscrew the mounting bolts at the front of the tank, then raise the front and support it with the prop, locating it between the hole in the steering stem nut and one of the fuel tank mounting bolt holes **(see illustrations)** – note the spacer in the bottom of each mounting rubber and take care not to lose them.

Removal

X and Y models

3 Ensure the ignition switch is OFF. Raise the tank (see above).

4 Disconnect the fuel level sensor and tip over (TO) sensor wiring connectors **(see illustrations 2.10a and b)**.

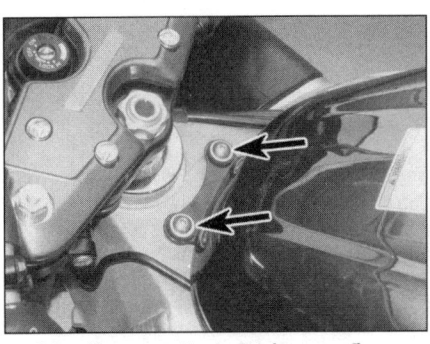

2.2a Unscrew the bolts (arrowed) ...

2.2b ... then raise the front of the tank and support it with the prop as shown

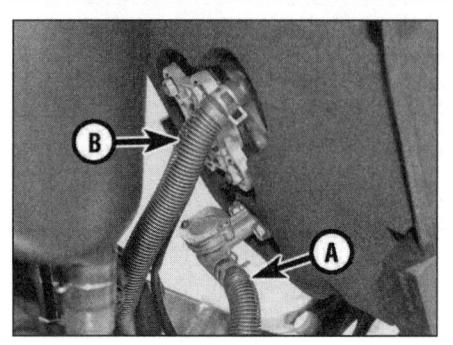

4•4 Fuel, engine management and exhaust systems

2.5 Fuel supply hose (A) and return hose (B)

2.10a Disconnect the fuel pump wiring connector . . .

2.10b . . . and the TO sensor wiring connector

5 Have to hand the rubber caps for blocking the fuel supply and return hose unions, which are fitted onto pegs under the passenger seat. If they are missing, obtain new ones. Also have to hand two hose clamps to fit on the supply and return hoses to prevent the residual fuel in the pump and fuel rail from draining **(see illustration)**. Place some rag underneath the fuel return hose union on the bottom of the tank, then release the clamp on the hose and detach it from the union, and immediately fit the rubber cap onto it to prevent fuel loss. Now do exactly the same for the fuel supply hose.

6 Pull the overflow and breather hoses off their unions on the underside of the tank **(see illustration 2.12)**.

7 Unscrew the bolts securing the rear tank bracket to the frame, then remove the prop and lift the tank away **(see illustrations 2.13a and b)**.

8 Inspect the mounting rubbers for signs of damage or deterioration and replace them with new ones if necessary.

K1 models onward

9 Ensure the ignition switch is OFF. Have ready some wooden blocks on which to rest the tank so that the fuel hose coupling takes no weight. Raise the tank (see above).

10 Disconnect the fuel pump and tip over (TO) sensor wiring connectors **(see illustrations)**.

11 Place some rag underneath the fuel supply hose union on the fuel rail to catch any residual fuel, then release the clips on the hose coupling and pull it off its union **(see illustrations)**.

12 Pull the overflow and breather hoses off their unions on the underside of the tank **(see illustration)**.

13 Unscrew the bolts securing the rear tank bracket to the frame, then remove the prop and lift the tank away, placing it on the wooden blocks, and making sure the fuel hose coupling takes no weight **(see illustrations)**.

14 Inspect the mounting rubbers for signs of damage or deterioration and replace them with new ones if necessary.

Installation

15 Installation is the reverse of removal, noting the following:
- Check that the tank mounting rubbers are fitted.
- Refer to Chapter 1 and check the condition of the fuel system hoses before installing the tank.
- On X and Y models make sure the supply and return hoses are correctly routed (see Chapter 1, Section 28), are pushed fully onto their unions and secured by their clamps. Also make sure the overflow and breather hoses are pushed fully onto their unions **(see illustration 2.12)**. Fit the hose union blanking caps back onto their pegs.
- On K1 models onward, align the fuel supply hose connector with its union on the fuel rail and push it on fully so that the clips engage **(see illustration 2.11b)**. Make sure the overflow and breather hoses are pushed fully onto their unions **(see illustration 2.12)**.

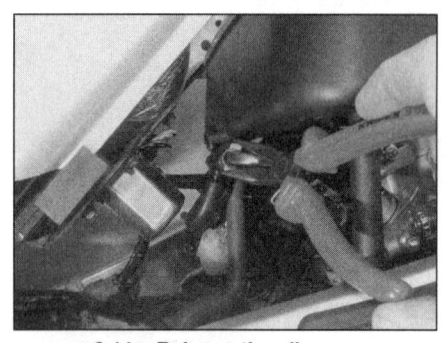

2.11a Release the clips . . .

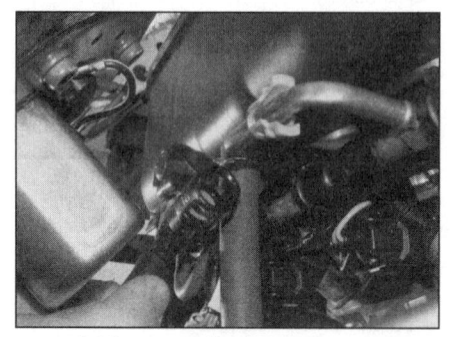

2.11b . . . and pull the hose off its union

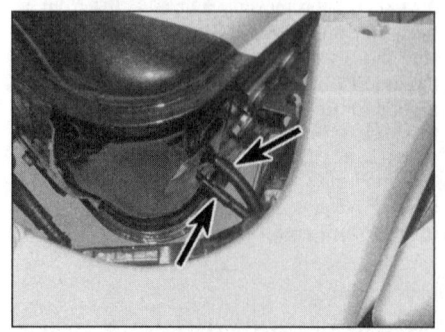

2.12 Pull the overflow and breather hoses (arrowed) off their unions

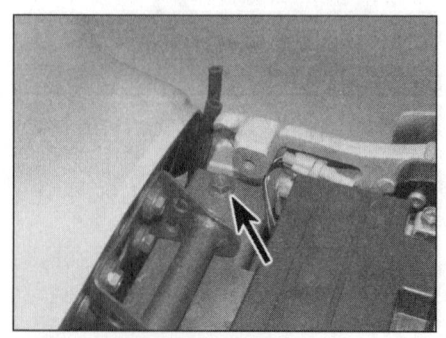

2.13a Unscrew the bolt (arrowed) on each end of the bracket . . .

2.13b . . . and remove the tank

… On X and Y models make sure the fuel supply and return hoses do not become pinched when lowering the tank.
● Start the engine and check that there is no sign of fuel leakage.

Cleaning and repair

16 All repairs to the fuel tank should be carried out by a professional who has experience in this critical and potentially dangerous work. Even after cleaning and flushing the fuel system, explosive fumes can remain and ignite during repair of the tank.
17 If the fuel tank is removed from the bike, it should not be placed in an area where sparks or open flames could ignite the fumes coming out of the tank. Be especially careful inside garages where a natural gas-type appliance is located, because the pilot light could cause an explosion.

3 Fuel pressure check

Warning: Refer to the precautions given in Section 1 before starting work.

X and Y models

1 The fuel pump is mounted on the back of the throttle bodies. If the pump is working but is suspected of not delivering enough fuel, check the pressure.
2 To check the fuel pressure, a suitable gauge, gauge hose and adapters are needed. Suzuki provides service tools (Pt. Nos. 09915-77330, 09915-74520 and 09940-40210) for this purpose.
3 Raise the fuel tank (see Section 2).
4 On X and Y models, place some rag and a suitable container underneath the fuel pressure check bolt **(see illustration)**. Carefully undo the bolt and catch any residual fuel in the container. Discard the bolt washer as a new one must be fitted on reassembly. Connect the gauge and hose in place of the check bolt.
5 Turn the ignition switch ON and check the pressure reading on the gauge. The pressure should be as specified at the beginning of this Chapter.
6 Turn the ignition OFF and disconnect the gauge and adapters. Use a rag to catch any

3.4 Fuel pressure check bolt (arrowed)

residual fuel as before. On X and Y models fit a new sealing washer onto the pressure check bolt and tighten the bolt to the torque setting specified at the beginning of this Chapter.
7 If the pressure is too low, check for a leak in the fuel supply system, a blocked fuel filter (see Section 5), a faulty pressure regulator (see Section 7) or a faulty fuel pump.
8 If the pressure is too high, either the pressure regulator or the fuel pump check valve is faulty or the return hose may be pinched.
9 On completion run the engine and check that there are no leaks from the fuel hoses.

K1 models onward

10 The pump is located inside the fuel tank. If the pump is working but is suspected of not delivering enough fuel, check the pressure.
11 To check the fuel pressure, a suitable gauge, gauge hose and adapters are needed. Suzuki provides service tools (Pt. Nos. 09915-77330, 09915-74520, 09940-40211 and 09940-40220) for this purpose.
12 Raise the fuel tank (see Section 2).
13 Place some rag underneath the fuel supply hose union on the fuel rail to catch any residual fuel, then release the clips on the hose coupling and pull it off its union **(see illustrations 2.11a and b)**. Connect the gauge assembly between the fuel rail and the fuel supply hose as shown **(see illustration)**.
14 Turn the ignition switch ON and check the pressure reading on the gauge. The pressure should be as specified at the beginning of this Chapter.
15 Turn the ignition OFF and disconnect the gauge and adapters. Use a rag to catch any residual fuel as before. Align the fuel supply hose connector with its union on the fuel rail

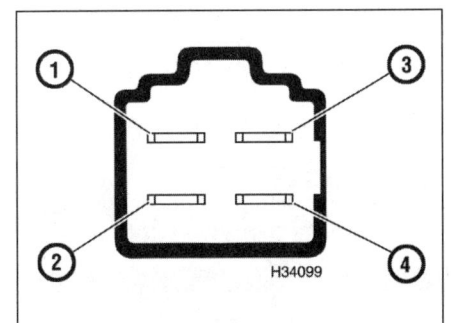

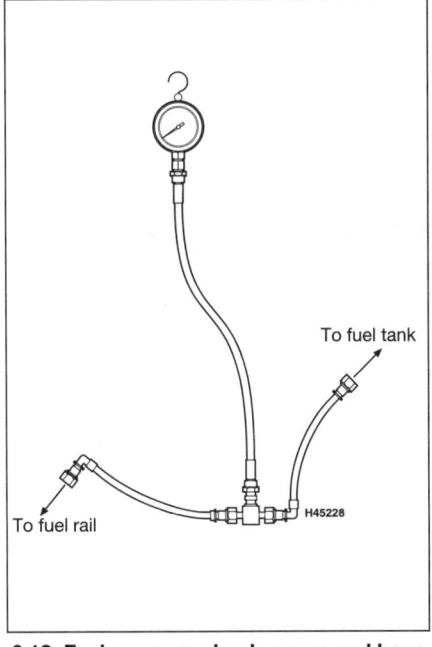

3.13 Fuel pressure check gauge and hose set-up for K1 models onwards

and push it on fully so that the clips engage **(see illustration 2.11b)**.
16 If the pressure is too low, check for a leak in the fuel supply system, a blocked fuel filter (see Section 5), a faulty pressure regulator (see Section 7) or a faulty fuel pump.
17 If the pressure is too high, either the pressure regulator or the fuel pump check valve is faulty.
18 On completion run the engine and check that there are no leaks from the fuel hoses.

4 Fuel pump relay

1 The relay is mounted behind the seat cowling on the left-hand side **(see illustration)** – remove the cowling to access it (see Chapter 8).
2 Pull the relay off its mounting and disconnect the wiring connector. Using a multimeter or test light, check for continuity between terminals 1 and 2 on the relay **(see illustration)**. There should be no continuity. Now use jumper wires to connect the positive (+) terminal of a fully charged 12 volt battery to terminal 3 on the relay and the negative (–) battery terminal to relay terminal 4. There should now be continuity shown across terminals 1 and 2. If the relay fails either of the checks, replace it with a new one.
3 If the relay is good, check that there is battery voltage at the red/blue wire terminal on the loom side of the connector with the ignition on. If not, check the wiring for continuity and the connections as described in Chapter 9, following the relevant Wiring Diagram. Turn the ignition off. If there is voltage, check the wiring and connectors between the relay and the ECM for continuity

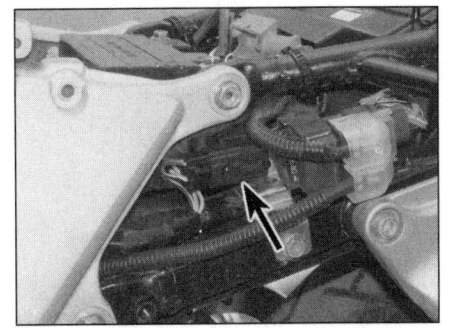

4.1 Fuel pump relay (arrowed)

4.2 Fuel pump relay terminal identification

4•6 Fuel, engine management and exhaust systems

5 Fuel pump, filter and strainer

Warning: Refer to the precautions given in Section 1 before starting work.

Check

1 On X and Y models the fuel pump assembly, incorporating the filter, strainer and pressure regulator, is mounted on the back of the throttle bodies. On all later models the pump assembly, incorporating the filter, strainer, pressure regulator and level sensor, is located inside the fuel tank. When the ignition is switched ON, it should be possible to hear the pump run for a few seconds until the system is up to pressure. If you can't hear anything, first check the fuse (see Chapter 9), then check the relay (see Section 4), and the tip-over (TO) sensor (see Section 12). If they are good, check the wiring and terminals for physical damage or loose or corroded connections and rectify as necessary (see the *Wiring Diagrams* at the end of Chapter 9). If the pump still will not run, it is possible the ECM is faulty – take it to a Suzuki dealer for assessment (see Chapter 5). If that is good the pump is faulty – on X and Y models the pump itself is available as an individual component, along with all other components in the assembly. On K1 models onward all components in the assembly except the pump itself are available, which means that if the pump is faulty a whole new assembly must be fitted, irrespective of the condition of the other components.

X and Y models

Removal

2 The fuel pump is mounted on the back of the throttle bodies. Raise the fuel tank, or for best access remove it (see Section 2). If you only raise it, refer to Step 5 in Section 2 and detach the fuel supply and return hoses from the tank.
3 Remove the cover from the pump assembly.
4 Place some rag and a suitable container underneath the fuel pressure check bolt **(see illustration 3.4)**. Carefully undo the bolt and catch any residual fuel in the container. Discard the bolt washer as a new one must be fitted on reassembly.
5 Disconnect the fuel pump wiring connector **(see illustration)**. Detach the vacuum hose from its union on the pressure regulator. Release the injector wiring from the clamp on the pressure regulator screw, where fitted. Release the clamp securing the fuel hose to the fuel rail and detach the hose – if there is not enough flex, detach it as you remove the pump (Step 6).
6 Undo the screws on the fuel pump bracket and remove the pump assembly. Place the end of each fuel hose into a suitable container, then release the clamp on each hose and allow any residual fuel to drain.

Disassembly

7 To remove the filter, undo the screws securing the filter housing and detach it from the pump housing. Discard the O-ring in the groove in the pump housing flange as a new one must be used. Remove the filter retainer plate from the filter housing. Discard the retainer and fuel passage O-rings – if the passage O-ring is not in the filter retainer it will be on the pump union. Remove the spring from the filter, then remove the filter, noting which way round it fits. Refer to Section 7 for the fuel pressure regulator, which is mounted on the filter housing.
8 To remove the pump itself, first separate the filter housing from the pump housing (see Step 7 – there is no need to remove the filter retainer and filter from its housing). Disconnect the pump wiring connectors, noting which fits where, and remove the retainer. Withdraw the pump from its housing, then separate the strainer from it. Discard the O-ring as new ones must be installed.
9 Check the condition of the strainer and clean any sediment off with a soft brush or low pressure compressed air. If the strainer is damaged, or if there is sediment inside it, replace it with a new one, and also replace the filter with a new one (see Step 7).
10 Note that there is also a strainer inside the fuel tank, integrated with the fuel cock. Remove the tank (see Section 2). Make sure the fuel cap is secure. Turn the tank upside down and rest it on some clean rag to protect the paintwork and soak up any fuel that may leak from the cap. Undo the bolts securing the fuel cock to the underside of the tank and withdraw the strainer. Discard the O-ring as a new one must be fitted on reassembly. Check and clean the strainer as in Step 9, replacing the cock/strainer assembly with a new one if necessary. Use a new O-ring smeared with grease on installation.

Reassembly and installation

11 Reassemble the pump in the reverse order, noting the following:
- Use new O-rings smeared sparingly with oil around the filter retainer, in the fuel passage in the filter retainer, and on the pump housing flange.
- Make sure the open end of the fuel filter is fitted facing into the filter housing.
- Locate the tab on the filter retainer in the cut-out in the filter housing.
- Fit the pump into the housing so that, with the wires coming out of the bottom of the housing, the wire terminals on the pump are at the top of the housing. As you look at the assembly, connect the left-hand wire to the left-hand terminal.
- Tighten the filter housing screws to the torque setting specified at the beginning of the Chapter.
- Fit a new sealing washer onto the pressure check bolt and tighten the bolt to the torque setting specified at the beginning of this Chapter.
- Tighten the pump mounting screws to the specified torque.
- Check that there are no fuel leaks when the pump is running.

K1 models onward

Removal

12 The fuel pump is located inside the fuel tank. Remove the tank (see Section 2). Make sure the fuel cap is secure.
13 Turn the tank upside down and rest it on some clean rag to protect the paintwork and soak up any fuel that may leak from the cap. Undo the bolts securing the pump base to the underside of the tank and carefully lift out the pump, taking care not to snag the level sensor arm **(see illustrations)**. Discard the O-ring as

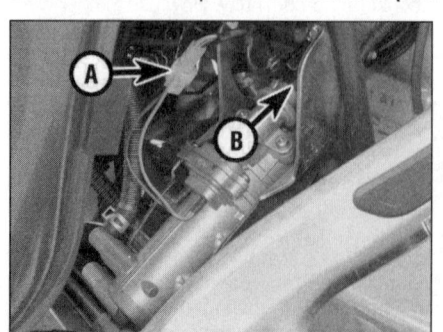

5.5 Fuel pump wiring connector (A), pressure regulator vacuum hose (B)

5.13a Unscrew the bolts (arrowed)...

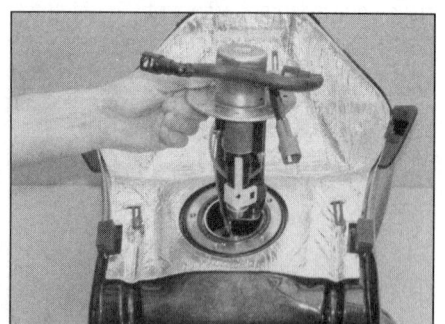

5.13b ...and withdraw the pump from the tank

Fuel, engine management and exhaust systems 4•7

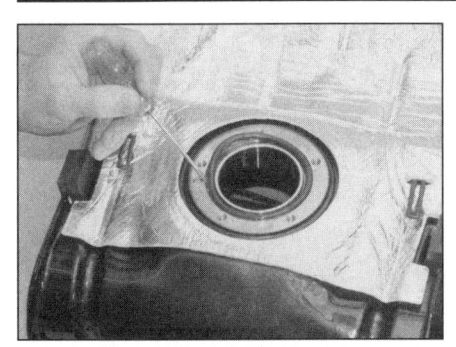

5.13c Remove the O-ring and discard it

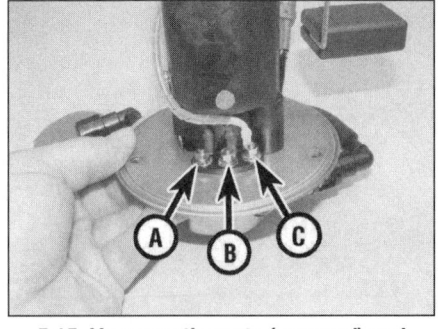

5.15 Unscrew the nuts (arrowed) and detach the wires. Fuel level sensor red/black wire (A), level sensor black/light green wire (B), fuel pump wire (C)

5.16 Fuel level sensor bracket screws (arrowed)

a new one must be fitted on reassembly **(see illustration)**.

Disassembly

14 Refer to Section 6 for the fuel level sensor. Refer to Section 7 for the fuel pressure regulator.

15 Undo the nuts securing the pump and level sensor wiring terminals and detach the wires, making a note of which fits where, and noting the washers **(see illustration)**.

16 Undo the screws securing the level sensor bracket to the pump housing and remove the sensor assembly **(see illustration)**.

17 Undo the screws securing the pump assembly to the pump base, noting the threaded clips and the wiring terminal secured by the upper screw **(see illustration)**.

18 Pull the pump assembly off the base **(see illustration)**. Discard the O-ring on the base fuel union as a new one must be fitted on reassembly.

19 Clean any sediment out of the pump base **(see illustration)**. Slide the shield off the strainer and clean any sediment off the strainer with a soft brush or low pressure compressed air **(see illustration)**. If the strainer is damaged, or if there is sediment inside it, unclip and remove the pump seat, then remove the pump cover and detach the strainer **(see illustrations)**. Replace it with a new one.

20 If there was sediment on the strainer, the filter cartridge could be clogged. Remove the strainer (Step 19) if not already done, then

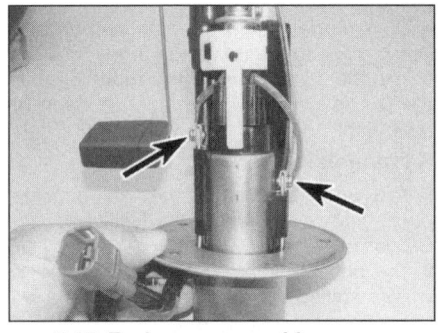

5.17 Fuel pump assembly screws (arrowed)

5.18 Pull the pump assembly off and discard the O-ring (arrowed)

5.19a Clean any sediment out of the base

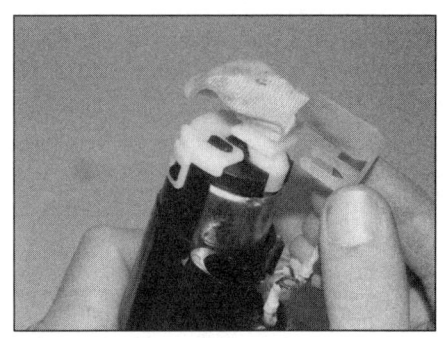

5.19b Slide the shield off and clean the strainer

5.19c Detach the clip . . .

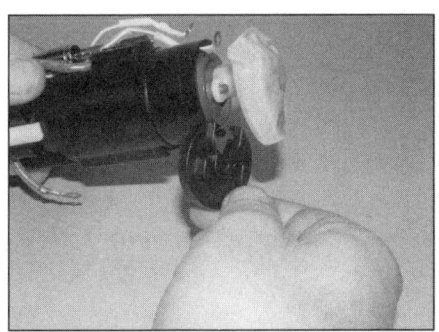

5.19d . . . then pull off the cover . . .

5.19e . . . and remove the strainer

4

4•8 Fuel, engine management and exhaust systems

draw the pump out of the holder, which incorporates the filter cartridge.

Reassembly and installation

21 Reassemble the pump in the reverse order, noting the following:
● Use new O-rings smeared sparingly with oil on the pressure regulator and the base fuel union **(see illustration 5.18)**.
● Make sure the threaded clips for the pump screws are in place on the base brackets, and do not forget to secure the wiring terminal with the upper screw **(see illustration 5.17)**.
● Check that the wiring terminals are correctly connected as shown, and the nuts are tight **(see illustration 5.15)**.
● Fit a new O-ring smeared with grease into the recess around the aperture on the underside of the fuel tank **(see illustration)**.
● Clean the threads of the bolts, then apply a suitable thread locking compound and install them finger-tight **(see illustration 5.13a)**. Now tighten them gradually in a criss-cross pattern to the torque setting specified at the beginning of this Chapter.
● Make sure there are no signs of fuel leakage around the pump base.

6 Fuel level sensor

Warning: Refer to the precautions given in Section 1 before starting work.

Note: *When the ignition is switched ON the low fuel warning LED will come on, then either extinguish or remain on according to the level of fuel in the tank. The low fuel warning LED stays on, or comes on during use, when the volume of fuel in the tank drops below 3.5 litres. Refer to Chapter 9 to check the instrument function of the low fuel warning circuit.*

Removal

X and Y models

1 The level sensor is located inside the fuel tank. Remove the tank (see Section 2). Make sure the fuel cap is secure.
2 Turn the tank upside down and rest it on some clean rag to protect the paintwork and soak up any fuel that may leak from the cap.

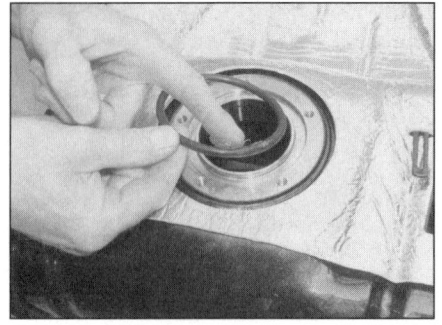

5.21 Smear the O-ring with grease before fitting it into the groove

3 On X models undo the bolts securing the sensor base to the underside of the tank and lift out the sensor. Discard the gasket as a new one must be used on reassembly.
4 On Y models undo the nuts securing the sensor base to the underside of the tank and lift out the sensor **(see illustration)**. Discard the O-ring as a new one must be used on reassembly.

K1 models onward

5 The level sensor is part of the fuel pump assembly. Remove the fuel pump (see Section 5).
6 The function of the sensor can be checked while installed on the pump assembly – see Steps 9 and 10.
7 To remove the sensor, trace the wires from it to their terminals on the pump base, then undo the nuts and detach the wires, noting which fits where, and noting the washers **(see illustration 5.15)**.
8 Undo the screws securing the sensor bracket to the pump housing and remove the sensor assembly, noting how it fits **(see illustration 5.16)**. If required undo the screw and separate the sensor from its bracket.

Inspection

9 Connect an ohmmeter between the terminals of the fuel pump wiring connector, on K1 models onward connecting between the terminals as shown **(see illustration)**.
10 With the sensor float in its lowest (empty) position the meter should show a resistance of between 11 and 13 ohms **(see illustration)**. Carefully raise the float to its highest (full)

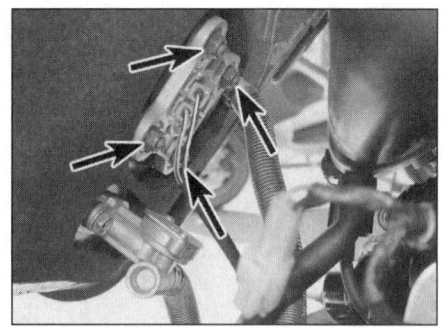

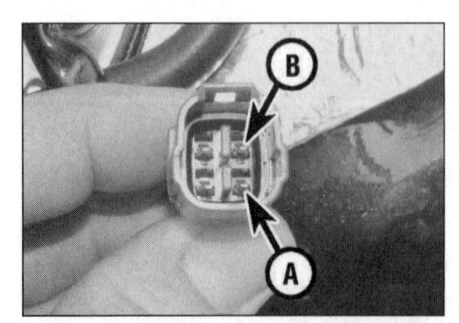

6.9 Connect the positive (+) probe of the meter to terminal A on the connector, and the negative (–) probe to terminal B

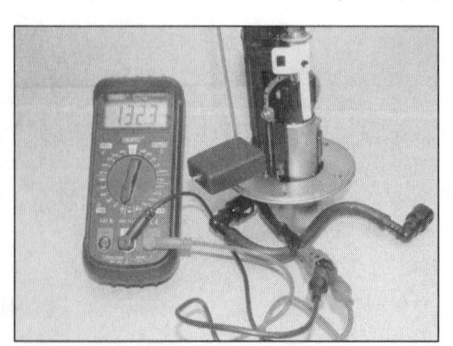

6.10a Check the resistance reading in the empty position . . .

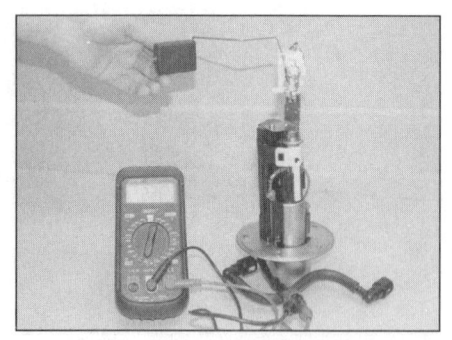

6.4 Fuel level sensor nuts (arrowed) – Y models

position – the meter should now show a resistance of between 130 and 135 ohms **(see illustration)**.
11 If no readings are obtained, or if they differ greatly from those specified, replace the sensor with a new one.
12 If the tests show the sensor to be good, check for voltage at the yellow/black (X and Y models) or black/light green (K1 models onward) wire terminal on the loom side of the sensor wiring connector with the ignition on. If there is voltage, check for continuity to earth in the black/white wire. If there is no voltage, check the wiring between the sensor and the instrument cluster and the cluster itself (see Chapter 9).

Installation

13 Installation is the reverse of removal, noting the following:
● On X models install the sensor using a new gasket, and tighten the bolts evenly and a little at a time in a criss-cross pattern to the torque setting specified at the beginning of the Chapter. Do not over tighten them.
● On Y models fit a new O-ring smeared sparingly with oil onto the sensor base. Fit the sensor with the wiring facing the right-hand side of the tank and tighten the nuts, not forgetting the washers, in a criss-cross pattern to the torque setting specified art the beginning of the Chapter. Do not over tighten them
● On K1 models onward check that the wiring terminals are correctly connected as shown, and the nuts are tight **(see illustration 5.15)**.
● Make sure there are no signs of fuel leakage around the sensor or pump base.

6.10b . . . then the full position

Fuel, engine management and exhaust systems

7.8 Fuel pressure regulator screws (arrowed)

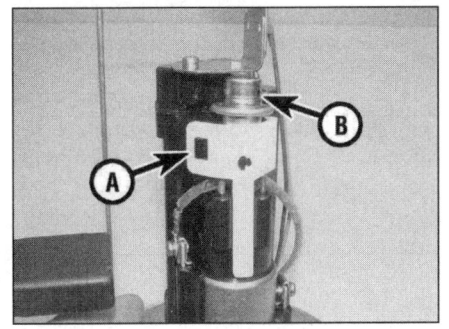

7.11 Release the clip on the holder (A) and remove the pressure regulator (B)

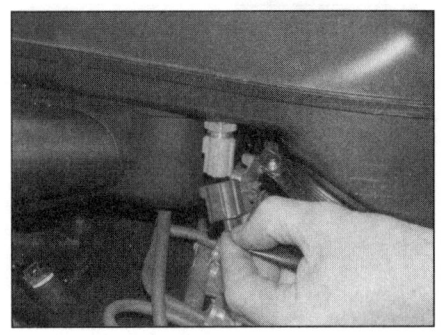

8.2 Disconnect the IAT sensor wiring connector . . .

7 Fuel pressure regulator

⚠️ *Warning: Refer to the precautions given in Section 1 before starting work.*

Check

1 To check the regulator, remove it as described below.
2 Suzuki provides no test procedure for the pressure regulator. However, if it is stuck open, it will be possible to blow through it with a low pressure air source. If it is stuck closed, then a high pressure air source with a gauge can be used to check the pressure at which it does open, if at all. On X and Y models bear in mind that during normal operation a vacuum is acting on the diaphragm, so a static test will require a slightly higher pressure than specified to open the valve (no figures are available for the level of vacuum applied during operation). Make sure the vacuum hose from the throttle bodies to the T-piece, and the hoses from the T-piece to the regulator and intake air pressure (IAP) sensor are all in good condition and securely connected.
3 The definitive test is to substitute the suspect regulator with a known good one, repeat the fuel pressure check and assess any difference.

Removal and installation

X and Y models

4 The fuel pump is mounted on the back of the throttle bodies. Raise the fuel tank, or for best access remove it (see Section 2).
5 Remove the cover from the pump assembly.
6 Place some rag and a suitable container underneath the fuel pressure check bolt **(see illustration 3.4)**. Carefully undo the bolt and catch any residual fuel in the container. Discard the bolt washer as a new one must be fitted on reassembly.
7 Detach the vacuum hose from its union on the top of the regulator **(see illustration 5.5.)**.
8 Undo the two screws securing the regulator to the filter housing, noting the wiring clamp where fitted, and pull the regulator out of its socket **(see illustration)**. Discard the O-rings as new ones must be used.
9 Fit new O-rings smeared lightly with oil, then press the regulator into its socket and onto the filter housing. Tighten the screws to the torque setting specified at the beginning of the Chapter, not forgetting the wiring clamp where fitted. Fit the vacuum hose back onto its union. Fit a new sealing washer onto the pressure check bolt and tighten the bolt to the torque setting specified at the beginning of this Chapter.

K1 models onward

10 Remove the fuel pump assembly (see Section 5).
11 Release the clip securing the fuel pressure regulator holder to the pump assembly then pull the regulator out of its socket **(see illustration)**. Discard the O-ring as a new one must be used. Note that if the regulator is faulty a new filter cartridge/regulator assembly must be installed as the regulator is not available as a separate component.
12 Fit a new O-ring and smear it lightly with oil, then press the regulator into place and secure it with the holder.

8 Air filter housing

Removal

1 Raise the fuel tank and support it with the prop, or remove it if better access is required (see Section 2).
2 Disconnect the wiring connector from the intake air temperature (IAT) sensor on the left-hand side of the housing **(see illustration)**.
3 Disconnect the wiring connector and the vacuum hose from the intake air pressure (IAP) sensor **(see illustration)**.
4 Release the clips securing the crankcase breather hose and PAIR system hose and detach them from their unions **(see illustration)**.
5 Slacken the clamp screws, one on each side, securing the housing to the throttle bodies **(see illustration)**. Undo the bolt

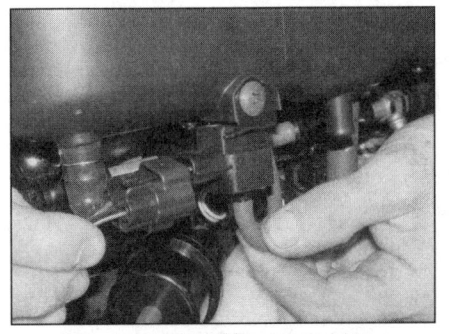

8.3 . . . and the IAP sensor wiring connector and vacuum hose

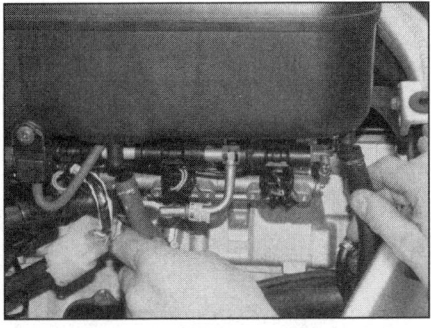

8.4 Release the clamps and detach the hoses

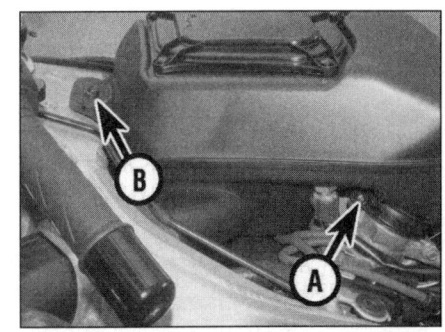

8.5a Slacken the clamp screw (A) on each side and unscrew the bolt (B) . . .

4•10 Fuel, engine management and exhaust systems

8.5b ... then displace the housing and detach the vacuum hose (arrowed)

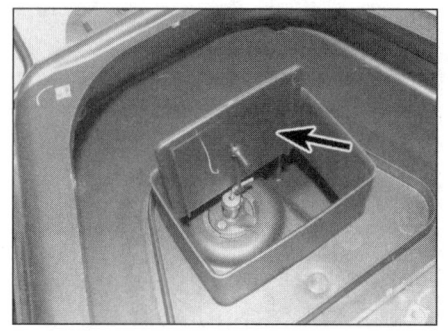

9.2 Remove the air filter to see the valve (arrowed)

9.4 VCSV (arrowed)

securing the front of the housing to the frame. Lift the housing off the throttle bodies, moving the throttle and choke cables aside as necessary, and disconnect the vacuum hose from the vacuum control solenoid valve (VCSV) on the underside **(see illustration)**.

Installation

6 Installation is the reverse of removal.
● Make sure the housing rubbers locate correctly over the throttle bodies and the clamps are secure.
● Make sure all hoses are in good condition and are securely connected.
● Make sure all wiring connectors are securely connected.

9 Intake air control valve system

1 The system operates a single air control valve (basically a flap in the air passage) in the air filter housing which regulates the air flow into it according to engine speed (see Specifications). At low engine speeds, the valve is closed. At the pre-set engine speed the valve opens. The valve is opened and closed by a rod connected to a diaphragm unit on the air filter housing, which itself is activated by a vacuum taken from the throttle bodies. The vacuum to the diaphragm is controlled firstly by the vacuum transmitting valve (VTV), which allows air-flow in one direction only, and secondly by the vacuum control solenoid valve (VCSV), which is controlled by the ECM. At low engine speeds the solenoid valve is open so the vacuum passes through it and acts on the diaphragm which closes the valve. At the pre-set engine speed the solenoid valve closes so the vacuum is cut off and the control valve opens. A damper is incorporated in the vacuum hose between the throttle body and the solenoid valve to stabilise fluctuation.

2 To check that the system is operating correctly, remove the air filter so you can see the valve (see Chapter 1) **(see illustration)**. Start the engine and slowly open the throttle while looking inside the filter housing. At idle speed the valve should be closed. Slowly open the throttle – the valve should open at the specified engine speed and stay open at engine speeds above that. Slowly close the throttle – the valve should close at the specified engine speed and remain closed at engine speeds below that. If the system does not operate as described, check the components as described below.

3 First check that all the hoses are securely connected, that they are in good condition without any signs of cracks or splits, and are not kinked or trapped. It will be necessary to displace the air filter housing to check all the hoses in the system (see Section 8).

4 To check the VCSV, located on the inside of the frame on the left-hand side, first disconnect the wiring connector from it **(see illustration)**. Using an ohmmeter or multimeter set to the ohms x 10 scale, measure the resistance between the terminals on the solenoid and compare the reading to that specified at the beginning of the Chapter. If the reading obtained is not within the specified range, a new VCSV must be installed.

5 To check the VTV, which is fitted in the vacuum hose close to the VCSV, disconnect the hoses from it **(see illustration)**. Blow through the valve from the orange side – the valve should be open and allow air to pass through. Now reverse the valve and blow through from the other side – the valve should be closed and not allow air to pass through. If either of the conditions are not as described, the valve is faulty and a new one must be installed. Make sure it is fitted with the orange side facing towards the solenoid valve.

6 Visually check the damper for cracks, dents or any other damage and replace it with a new one if any are found **(see illustration)**.

7 To check the diaphragm unit, remove the air filter (see Chapter 1). First check that the connecting rod between the diaphragm unit and the valve has not come away **(see illustration 9.2)**. Displace the air filter housing – do not disconnect the vacuum hose from the diaphragm (see Section 8). Now trace the vacuum hose from the diaphragm and disconnect it from the VCSV. Using a hand-operated vacuum pump, apply a vacuum through the hose and check whether the valve closes when the vacuum is applied and opens when it is released. Do not apply more than - 180 mmHg of vacuum (negative pressure) to avoid damaging the diaphragm. If the valve does not open and close, a new diaphragm unit must be installed – twist it anti-clockwise to release it from the air filter housing, then detach the connecting rod from the flap **(see illustration)**.

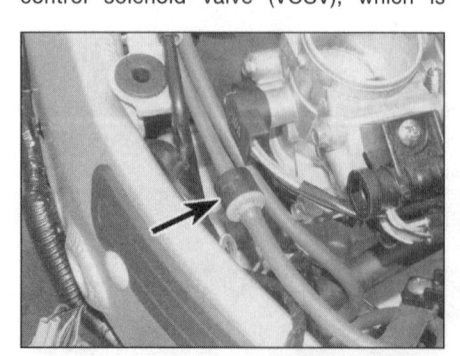

9.5 Disconnect the hoses from the VTV (arrowed) and test it as described

9.6 Vacuum damper unit (arrowed)

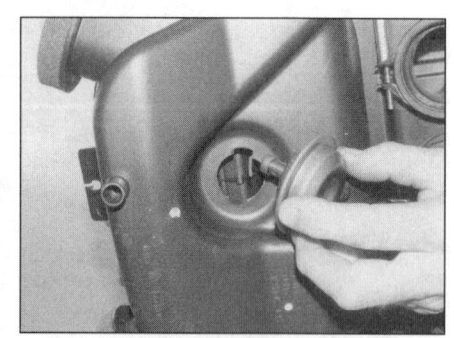

9.7 Twist the diaphragm unit anti-clockwise to release it and detach the rod

Fuel, engine management and exhaust systems 4•11

10 Fuel injection system description

1 The fuel injection system consists of two main component groups, the fuel supply circuit and the electronic control circuit.
2 The fuel supply circuit consists of the tank, pump, filter, pressure regulator and injectors. Fuel is pumped under pressure to the fuel rail, from which the individual injectors are fed. Operating pressure is maintained initially by the pump check valve (a one-way valve that maintains pressure in the system even when the pump has stopped), and, once the engine is running, by the pressure regulator. The pump also incorporates a pressure relief valve, which releases fuel back into the tank should the system become over-pressurised. The injectors spray pressurised fuel into the throttle body where it mixes with air and vaporises, before entering the cylinder where it is compressed and ignited.
3 The electronic control circuit consists of the engine control module (ECM), which operates and co-ordinates both the fuel injection and ignition systems, and the various sensors which provide the ECM with information on engine operating conditions.
4 The ECM monitors signals from the following sensors:
- Intake air temperature (IAT) sensor
- Intake air pressure (IAP) sensor
- Throttle position (TP) sensor
- Camshaft position (CMP) sensor
- Crankshaft position (CKP) sensor
- Engine coolant temperature (ECT) sensor
- Atmospheric pressure (AP) sensor
- Gear position (GP) sensor
- Tip-over (TO) sensor
- Oxygen sensor – K2 models onward

5 Based on the information it receives, the ECM calculates the appropriate ignition and fuel requirements for the engine. By varying the length of the electronic pulse it sends to each injector, the ECM controls the length of time the injectors are held open and thereby the amount of fuel that is supplied to the engine. Fuel supply varies according to the engine's needs for starting, warming-up, idling, cruising and acceleration.
6 In the event of an abnormality in any of the sensor signals, the ECM will determine whether the engine can still be run safely. If it can, a back-up mode replaces the sensor signal with a fixed signal, restricting performance but allowing the bike to be ridden home or to a dealer. When this occurs, the LCD clock display in the instrument cluster will indicate the letters FI every two seconds (alternating with the clock display), and the fuel injection system warning LED will come on. If the unit decides that the fault is too serious, the appropriate system will be shut down and the engine will not run. When this occurs, the LCD clock display in the instrument cluster will indicate the letters FI continuously, and the warning LED will flash. See Section 11 for fault finding.
7 In the event of no signal being received from the ECM within 5 seconds of the ignition being switched ON the LCD panel will display the letters CHEC. This is not a fault code in itself, but will occur if the ignition is ON for the stated time but if the kill switch is in the OFF position, or if the starter interlock circuit has a fault (see Chapter 9), or if the ignition fuse has blown (see Chapter 9). It will also occur if a wiring connector between the ECM and instrument cluster has become disconnected.
8 The system incorporates two safety circuits. When the ignition is switched ON, the fuel pump runs for three seconds and pressurises the system. Thereafter the pump automatically switches off until the engine is started. The second circuit incorporates a tip-over sensor, which automatically switches off the fuel pump and cuts the ignition and injection circuits if the motorcycle falls over.

11 Fuel injection system fault finding

1 The system incorporates a self-diagnostic function whereby any faults are stored in the ECM memory. To access the appropriate fault code, and to perform certain tests, the Suzuki mode select switch (Pt. No. 09930-82710) is very useful **(see illustration)**, though its function can easily be replicated using a short

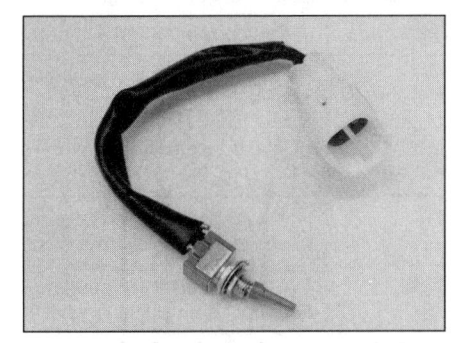

11.1 The Suzuki mode select switch

piece of auxiliary wire, either bared at the ends or with suitable terminals that will fit into the terminals on the connector, to jump between the two terminals in the connector that the switch plugs into. The mode select switch is not expensive.
2 Remove the passenger seat (and if necessary the seat cowling, depending on access) (see Chapter 8) and locate the mode select switch wiring connector (it has white/red and black/white wires going to it). Remove the connector cover, ensure the ignition and the select switch are OFF, then connect the select switch. If a piece of auxiliary wire is being used in place of the switch, connect one end of the wire to one of the wire terminals in the connector, but leave the other end free for the moment.
3 Start the engine and run it for at least 4 seconds, or if it will not start, crank the engine on the electric starter for at least 4 seconds. Turn the mode select switch ON or connect the free end of the wire to the other terminal. The fault code(s) will be displayed on the LCD panel on the instrument cluster, in ascending order if there are more than one. Note the codes and identify the faults from the following table. **Note:** *Do not disconnect the ECM wiring connectors, battery leads or main fuse before recording the fault codes. The ECM memory is erased when the connectors are disconnected.* If no fault codes are displayed, turn the mode select switch OFF or remove the jumper wire, then turn the ignition switch OFF and disconnect the mode select switch. Refit the wiring connector cover and install the seat (see Chapter 8).

Fault code	Faulty component – symptoms	Possible causes
CHEC	No ECM signal – engine will not run	Kill switch OFF Faulty wiring or wiring connector Faulty ignition safety interlock system (clutch switch, sidestand switch, diode or gear position switch) Damaged ignition fuse
C00	No fault. Note that the line in front of the C should be in the middle – if it is above or below the middle, the TP sensor needs adjusting (see Section 12)	System clear
C11	Camshaft position sensor – engine will continue to run but will not restart once turned OFF	Faulty wiring or wiring connector Damaged sensor or intake cam pin

4•12 Fuel, engine management and exhaust systems

Fault code	Faulty component – symptoms	Possible causes
C12	Crankshaft position sensor – engine will not run	Faulty wiring or wiring connector Damaged sensor or timing rotor
C13	Intake air pressure sensor – engine will run, air pressure signal fixed at 760 mmHg	Faulty wiring or wiring connector Damaged sensor
C14	Throttle position sensor – engine will run, throttle position signal and ignition timing fixed	Faulty wiring or wiring connector Damaged sensor
C15	Engine coolant temperature sensor – engine will run, coolant temperature signal fixed at 80°C	Faulty wiring or wiring connector Damaged sensor
C21	Intake air temperature sensor – engine will run, air temperature signal fixed at 40°C	Faulty wiring or wiring connector Damaged sensor
C22	Atmospheric pressure sensor – engine will run, atmospheric pressure signal fixed at 760 mmHg	Faulty wiring or wiring connector Damaged sensor
C23	Tip-over sensor – engine will not run	Faulty wiring or wiring connector Damaged sensor
C24*	No. 1 cylinder ignition coil – engine will run on other cylinders, ignition signal to No. 1 cylinder cut	Faulty wiring or wiring connector Damaged ignition coil Faulty power supply for the ignition system *(see Chapter 5 for details)*
C25*	No. 2 cylinder ignition coil – engine will run on other cylinders, ignition signal to No. 2 cylinder cut	Faulty wiring or wiring connector Damaged ignition coil Faulty power supply for the ignition system *(see Chapter 5 for details)*
C26*	No. 3 cylinder ignition coil – engine will run on other cylinders, ignition signal to No. 3 cylinder cut	Faulty wiring or wiring connector Damaged ignition coil Faulty power supply for the ignition system *(see Chapter 5 for details)*
C27*	No. 4 cylinder ignition coil – engine will run on other cylinders, ignition signal to No. 4 cylinder cut	Faulty wiring or wiring connector Damaged ignition coil Faulty power supply for the ignition system *(see Chapter 5 for details)*
C31	Gear position sensor – engine will run, signal fixed to 6th gear	Faulty wiring or wiring connector Damaged sensor Faulty gearchange mechanism
C32*	No. 1 cylinder fuel injector – engine will run on other cylinders	Faulty wiring or wiring connector Damaged fuel injector
C33*	No. 2 cylinder fuel injector – engine will run on other cylinders	Faulty wiring or wiring connector Damaged fuel injector
C34*	No. 3 cylinder fuel injector – engine will run on other cylinders	Faulty wiring or wiring connector Damaged fuel injector
C35*	No. 4 cylinder fuel injector – engine will run on other cylinders	Faulty wiring or wiring connector Damaged fuel injector
C41	Fuel pump control system – engine will not run	Faulty wiring or wiring connector to pump and/or pump relay Faulty pump relay *(see Section 4)* Damaged fuel pump *(see Section 5)*
C42	Ignition switch – engine will not run	Faulty wiring or wiring connector Damaged switch *(see Chapter 9 for details)*
C44 – K2 models on	Oxygen sensor – engine will run, fuel/air compensation ration fixed to normal condition	Faulty wiring or wiring connector Faulty sensor
C92	Fuel level sensor – engine will run, fuel/air compensation ration fixed to normal condition	Faulty wiring or wiring connector Faulty sensor

*The engine will not run when two or more ignition coils or fuel injectors fail

Fuel, engine management and exhaust systems 4•13

4 To check the fuel injection system components see Section 12.
5 Once the fault has been corrected, turn the ignition switch ON. If the fault has been cleared, the instrument display with indicate the code C00. Turn the mode select switch OFF or remove the jumper wire, then turn the ignition switch OFF and disconnect the mode select switch. Refit the wiring connector cover and install the seat (see Chapter 8).

12 Fuel injection system components

1 If a fault is indicated on any of the system components, first check the wiring and connectors between the appropriate component and the engine control module (ECM); see *Wiring Diagrams* at the end of Chapter 9. A continuity test of all wires will locate a break or short in any circuit. Inspect the terminals inside the wiring connectors and ensure they are not loose or corroded. Spray the inside of the connectors with an electrical terminal cleaner before reconnection.
2 It is possible to undertake some checks on system components using a multimeter and comparing the results with the specifications at the beginning of this Chapter. **Note:** *Different meters may give slightly different results to those specified even though the component being tested is not faulty – do not consign a component to the bin before having it double-checked. However, some faults will only become evident when a component is tested with a peak voltage tester, in which case the checks should be undertaken by a Suzuki dealer.*
3 If after a thorough check the source of a fault has not been identified, it is possible that the ECM itself is faulty. Suzuki provides no test specifications for the ECM. In order to determine conclusively that the unit is defective, it should be substituted with a known good one. If the problem is then rectified, the original unit is faulty.

Camshaft position (CMP) sensor

4 Make sure the ignition is OFF. Raise the fuel tank (see Section 2). The CMP sensor is on the left-hand end of the valve cover **(see illustration)**. Disconnect the wiring connector. Before testing the sensor it is worth removing it (see Step 7) and cleaning the tip with a carburettor cleaner – a build-up of dirt and/or debris can affect the signal sent to the ECM.
5 Use an ohmmeter or multimeter set to the K-ohms scale and measure the resistance between the sensor terminals. If the result is as specified, check that there is no continuity between each terminal and earth (ground).
6 If the results are good, have the sensor peak voltage tested by a Suzuki dealer.
7 To remove the sensor undo its bolts and draw it out of the valve cover. Install the sensor using a new gasket and tighten its bolts to the torque setting specified at the beginning of the Chapter.
8 To inspect the sensor trigger on the intake camshaft, remove the valve cover (see Chapter 2) and check the trigger for damage **(see illustration)**.

Crankshaft position (CKP) sensor

9 Make sure the ignition is OFF. To access the CKP sensor wiring connector raise the fuel tank (see Section 2). The sensor itself is in the alternator cover and is actuated by a trigger on the alternator rotor. Before testing the sensor it is worth removing the alternator cover (see Chapter 9) and cleaning the sensor – a build-up of dirt and/or debris can affect the signal sent to the ECM. Also check the trigger on the rotor for damage.
10 Trace the wiring from the alternator cover and disconnect it at the wiring connector **(see illustration)**. Using an ohmmeter or multimeter set to the ohms scale, measure the resistance between the terminals on the sensor side of the connector. If the result is as specified, check that there is no continuity between each terminal and earth (ground).
11 If the results are good, have the sensor peak voltage tested by a Suzuki dealer.
12 To remove the sensor, see Chapter 9 – it is part of the alternator stator and is not available separately.

Intake air pressure (IAP) sensor

13 Make sure the ignition is OFF. Raise the fuel tank (see Section 2). The IAP sensor is on the back of the air filter housing **(see illustration 8.3)**. Check the condition of the vacuum hose between the sensor and the throttle bodies. If the hose is cracked or perished replace it with a new one. Ensure the hose is a tight fit on the sensor union, the hose joint pieces and the throttle bodies.
14 Disconnect the sensor wiring connector and turn the ignition ON. Connect the positive (+) probe of a voltmeter to the red wire terminal on the loom side of the wiring connector and the negative (–) probe first to earth (ground), then to the black/brown wire terminal to check the input voltage. Turn the ignition OFF. If the input voltage is not as specified in both cases, check the wiring to the ECM and the ECM connector terminals.
15 If the input voltage is good, reconnect the wiring to the sensor, then start the engine and allow it idle. Insert the positive (+) probe of a voltmeter into the green/black wire terminal in the connector and the negative (–) probe into the black/brown wire terminal to check the output voltage. If the result is as specified, take the sensor to a Suzuki dealer for vacuum testing. Note that the output voltage can vary between 2.4 and 3.6 volts depending on the altitude and atmospheric pressure at which the test is being carried out.
16 To remove the IAP sensor, first disconnect the vacuum hose and the wiring connector. Undo the screw securing the sensor to the air filter housing and withdraw the sensor. On installation, ensure the wiring connector terminals are clean and that the vacuum hose is a tight fit on the sensor union.

Throttle position (TP) sensor

Note: *The colour coding for the TP sensor wiring changes at both the sensor 3-pin wiring connector and the throttle body assembly sub-loom wiring connector (see Wiring Diagrams at end of Chapter 9).*
17 Make sure the ignition is OFF. Raise the fuel tank (see Section 2) – the TP sensor is

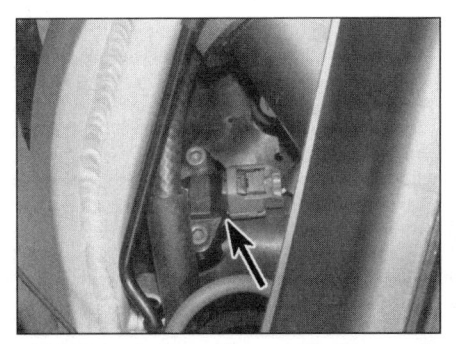

12.4 Camshaft position sensor (arrowed)

12.8 Camshaft position sensor trigger (arrowed)

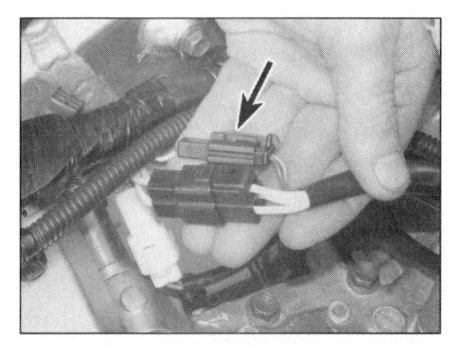

12.10 Crankshaft position sensor wiring connector (arrowed)

4•14 Fuel, engine management and exhaust systems

located on the left-hand end of the throttle bodies **(see illustration)**. Disconnect the sensor wiring connector. Turn the ignition ON and connect the positive (+) probe of a voltmeter to the blue wire terminal on the loom side of the wiring connector and the negative (–) probe first to earth (ground), and then to the black/brown wire terminal to check the input voltage. Turn the ignition OFF. If the input voltage is not as specified in both cases, check the wiring and the connectors and terminals between the TP sensor and the ECM.

18 If the input voltage is good, check for continuity between the yellow wire terminal on the sensor side of the connector and earth (ground). There should be no continuity.

19 Using an ohmmeter set to the K-ohms scale, measure the resistance between the yellow and black wire terminals on the sensor side of the connector, first with the throttle closed, then with the throttle fully open. If the results are as specified, reconnect the wiring connector and follow step 20. If the results are slightly out, reset the sensor position as described in Steps 23 and 24. If there are no readings replace the sensor with a new one.

20 Turn the ignition ON and insert the probes of a voltmeter between the yellow and black/brown wire terminals in the back of the loom side of the connector to check the output voltage, first with the throttle closed, then with the throttle fully open. Turn the ignition OFF. If the results are not as specified, the sensor is faulty.

21 To remove the TP sensor, first disconnect its wiring connector. Mark the position of the sensor to aid installation, then undo the Torx screws securing the sensor and remove it, on X, Y and K1 models noting the washers with the screws and the collar between the sensor and the shaft. Note how the end of the throttle shaft engages the slot in the sensor.

22 Installation is the reverse of removal. Apply some grease to the O-ring. Ensure that the throttle shaft engages correctly in the slot in the sensor and align any register marks before lightly tightening the Torx screws. Ensure the wiring connector terminals are clean. Check and adjust the sensor position as follows.

23 To check and adjust the position of the TP sensor, first check the engine idle speed and adjust it if necessary (see Chapter 1). Turn the engine OFF and connect the mode select switch to its wiring connector (see Section 10). Start the engine again.

24 Turn the select switch ON. A code C00 will be displayed on the LCD panel on the instrument cluster with a line in front of it. If the line is in the mid-way position i.e. -C00, the TP sensor is adjusted correctly. If the line is above or below the mid-way position (¯C00 or ¯C00), loosen the Torx screws and carefully rotate the sensor until the line is in the mid-way position, then tighten the Torx screws.

Engine coolant temperature (ECT) sensor

25 Make sure the ignition is OFF. The engine coolant temperature (ECT) sensor is mounted in the back of the cylinder head on the left-hand side **(see illustration)**.

26 Remove the fuel tank (see Chapter 4). Depending on the tools available, it may also be necessary to remove the air filter housing and displace the throttle bodies, though it may be enough to displace the IAP sensor vacuum damper with its bracket from the frame **(see illustration 9.6)**.

27 Disconnect the sensor wiring connector and turn the ignition ON. Connect the positive (+) probe of a voltmeter to the black/blue wire terminal on the loom side of the connector and the negative (–) probe first to earth (ground), then to the black/brown wire terminal to check the input voltage. Turn the ignition OFF. If the input voltage is not as specified in both cases, check the wiring to the ECM and the ECM connector terminals.

28 Using an ohmmeter or multimeter set to the K-ohms scale, measure the resistance between the terminals on the sensor itself with the engine cold. If the result is not as specified, the sensor is faulty.

29 If the sensor is working correctly, the resistance should drop as the engine warms up. A check for sensor performance is described in Chapter 3. Also refer to Chapter 3 for the removal and installation procedure.

Intake air temperature (IAT) sensor

30 Make sure the ignition is OFF. Raise the fuel tank (see Section 2). The IAT sensor is on the left-hand side of the air filter housing **(see illustration 8.2)**. Disconnect the sensor wiring connector and turn the ignition ON. Connect the positive (+) probe of a voltmeter to the dark green wire terminal on the loom side of the wiring connector and the negative (–) probe first to earth (ground), then to the black/brown wire terminal to check the input voltage. Turn the ignition OFF. If the input voltage is not as specified in both cases, check the wiring to the ECM and the ECM connector terminals.

31 Using an ohmmeter or multimeter set to the K-ohms scale, measure the resistance between the terminals on the sensor itself. If the result is not as specified, the sensor is faulty.

32 The sensor screws into an insert in the bottom of the air filter housing. To remove the sensor, first disconnect the wiring connector, then unscrew the sensor. Note the O-ring on the sensor body and replace it with a new one on installation if it is damaged. Tighten the sensor to the specified torque setting.

Atmospheric pressure (AP) sensor

33 Make sure the ignition is OFF. Raise the fuel tank (see Section 2) – the AP sensor is on the left-hand side of the frame **(see illustration)**.

34 Disconnect the sensor wiring connector and turn the ignition ON. Connect the positive (+) probe of a voltmeter to the red wire terminal on the loom side of the wiring connector and the negative (–) probe first to earth (ground), then to the black/brown wire terminal to check the input voltage. Turn the ignition OFF. If the input voltage is not as specified in both cases, check the wiring to the ECM and the ECM connector terminals.

35 If the input voltage is good, reconnect the wiring to the sensor, then turn the ignition ON. Insert the positive (+) probe of a voltmeter into the green/yellow wire terminal in the connector and the negative (–) probe into the black/brown wire terminal to check the output voltage. Turn the ignition OFF.

36 If the output voltage is not as specified, the AP sensor air passage may be clogged with dirt. Clean the outside of the sensor with a damp cloth and check the air passage for any obstruction, then retest the output voltage. Note that the output voltage can vary between 2.4 and 3.6 volts depending on the altitude and atmospheric pressure at which the test is being carried out.

12.17 Throttle position sensor (A) and its wiring connector (B)

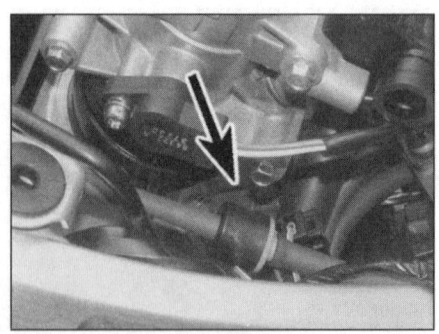

12.25 Engine coolant temperature sensor (arrowed)

12.33 Atmospheric pressure sensor (arrowed)

Fuel, engine management and exhaust systems 4•15

12.38 Tip-over sensor (arrowed) – tank removed for clarity

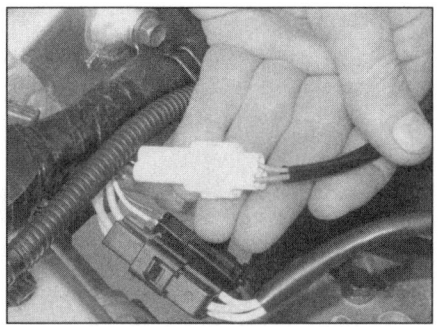

12.43 Gear position switch wiring connector

12.47a Free the wiring and unscrew the switch bolts (arrowed) . . .

37 If the output voltage is as specified, take the sensor to a Suzuki dealer for vacuum testing – it is secured by two screws.

Tip-over (TO) sensor

38 Make sure the ignition is OFF. Remove the rider's seat (see Chapter 8). The TO sensor is mounted on the underside of the tank bracket **(see illustration)**. Note the TO sensor holder is marked UPPER on the top edge.
39 Trace the wiring from the sensor and disconnect it at the connector **(see illustration 2.10b)**. Using an ohmmeter or multimeter set to the K-ohms scale, measure the resistance between the black and black/white wire terminals on the sensor side of the connector. Compare the result to that given in the Specifications at the beginning of this Chapter; if the result is good, reconnect the wiring connector.
40 With the connector reconnected, turn the ignition ON and insert the probes of a voltmeter into the black and black/brown wire terminals into the loom side of the wiring connector to check the voltage. If the result is good, raise the fuel tank (see Section), then release the sensor from its bracket – if you find it difficult to release, unscrew the tank bracket bolts and lift the right-hand side. Check the voltage reading when the sensor is leaned 43° to one side and then to the other – this simulates the cut-off point reached if the motorcycle falls over – at each point the voltage should drop to zero volts. If not the sensor is faulty.
41 To remove the sensor, first disconnect the wiring connector. Raise the fuel tank (see Section 2), then release the sensor from its bracket – if you find it difficult to release, unscrew the tank bracket bolts and lift the right-hand side. Remove the sensor from the holder, noting which way round it fits. Installation is the reverse of removal.

Gear position (GP) switch

Note: *Do not disconnect the pink wire from the gear position switch in the mistaken belief that this will lead to increased performance, as reported in certain circles. In the case of the GSX1300R this action will lead to rough running, hesitation and plug fouling.*
42 Support the bike on its centrestand or an auxiliary stand and raise the sidestand. Ensure the engine kill switch is in the RUN position. The GP switch is located in the engine behind the clutch, with its wiring exiting the top of the clutch cover.
43 Raise the fuel tank (see Section 2). Trace the wiring from the switch to the connector and disconnect it **(see illustration)**. Connect the probes of an ohmmeter or continuity tester between the blue and black/white wire terminals on the switch side of the connector. With the transmission in neutral there should be continuity. If not, remove the switch and check the contacts on its inside and the plungers in the end of the selector drum.
44 Reconnect the wiring connector. Turn the ignition switch ON and insert the positive (+) probe of a voltmeter into the pink wire terminal in the connector and connect the negative (–) probe to earth (ground) to check the output voltage. Select each gear in turn and check that the voltage is above the specified minimum in each gear. Turn the ignition OFF.
45 If the output voltage is not as specified, either the pink wire to the GP switch or the GP switch itself is faulty.
46 If the output voltage is as specified check the wiring from the switch connector to the ECM and check the ECM connector terminals.
47 To remove the GP switch first disconnect the wiring connector **(see illustration 12.43)**, then remove the clutch (see Chapter 2). Stuff some rag into the opening to the sump in the bottom of the clutch housing. Undo the screws securing the switch and the bolts securing the wiring guides **(see illustration)**. Free the wiring grommet from its cut-out and remove the switch **(see illustration)**. Remove the contact plungers and springs for safekeeping if required **(see illustration)**.
48 On installation make sure the plungers move freely in the bores. Apply a smear of sealant to the wiring grommet, and apply a suitable non-permanent thread locking compound to the switch screws and switch wiring guide bolts and locate each guide with its flat side facing in and butted against its adjacent lug. Do not forget to remove the rag before installing the clutch.

Fuel injectors

49 Make sure the ignition is OFF. Raise the fuel tank (see Section 2). Identify the faulty injector by the fault code and disconnect the wiring connector from it **(see illustration)**. Using an ohmmeter or multimeter set to the

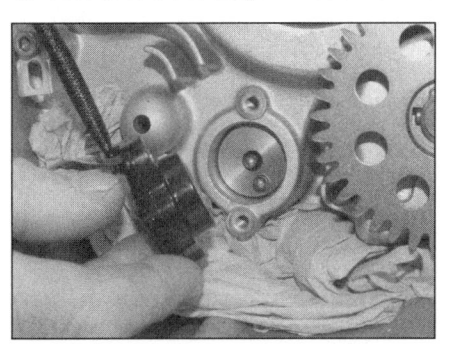

12.47b . . . then remove the switch . . .

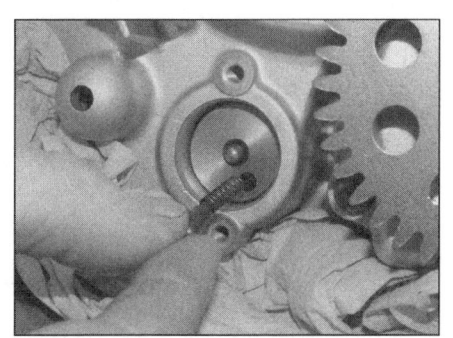

12.47c . . . and if required the plungers

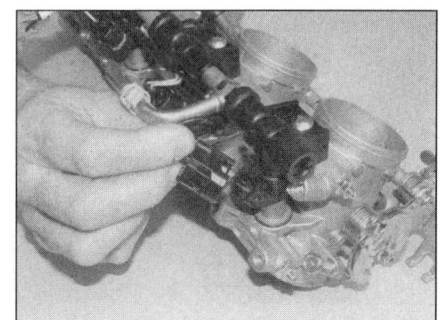

12.49 Disconnect the wiring connector from the injector

ohms scale, measure the resistance between the terminals on the injector. If the result is as specified, check that there is no continuity between each terminal and earth (ground). If there is, the injector is faulty and a new one must be installed (see Section 14).

50 Turn the ignition ON. Connect the positive (+) probe of a voltmeter to the yellow/red wire terminal on the loom side of the wiring connector and the negative (–) probe to earth (ground) to check the input voltage. **Note:** *Injector voltage can only be detected for 3 seconds after the ignition has been turned ON.* Turn the ignition OFF. If the input voltage is not as specified, refer to the Wiring Diagrams at the end of Chapter 9 and check for a fault in the yellow/red wire.

51 If the input voltage is as specified, refer to the Wiring Diagrams at the end of Chapter 9 and check for a fault in the other injector wire to the ECM.

Oxygen sensor – K2 models onward (not fitted in all markets)

52 Make sure the ignition is OFF. Remove the rider's seat and the right-hand fairing side panel (see Chapter 8).
53 Trace the wiring from the sensor in the exhaust system to the wiring connector and disconnect it **(see illustration)**. Check that there is no continuity between the white/green wire terminal on the loom side of the connector and earth (ground).
54 Reconnect the sensor wiring connector. Start the engine and warm it up to normal operating temperature.
55 With the engine idling insert the positive (+) probe of a voltmeter into the white/green

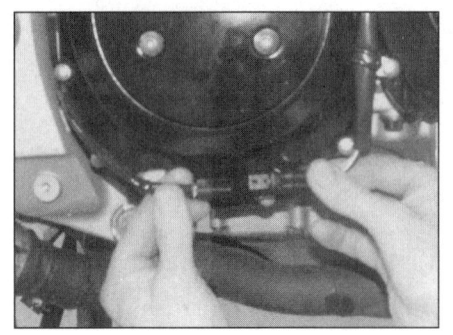

12.53 Oxygen sensor wiring connector

wire terminal in the connector and connect the negative (–) probe to the black/brown wire terminal and check the output voltage. Now increase engine speed to 4000 rpm and check the output voltage again. Turn the engine OFF. If the readings are not as specified replace the sensor with a new one.
56 Check for battery voltage at the white/black wire terminal in the connector with the ignition ON and the connector connected, bearing in mind that the voltage will only register for a few seconds – connect the meter probes between the terminal and ground before turning the ignition on. If there is no voltage check the wiring and connectors between the connector and the ECM. If the wiring is good, either the sensor or the ECM is faulty. Turn the ignition OFF.
57 Disconnect the sensor wiring connector. Measure the resistance between the two white wire terminals on the sensor side of the wiring connector. If it is not as specified sensor is faulty. Bear in mind that the

12.59 Oxygen sensor (arrowed)

resistance will vary with temperature, so try to take the reading at the temperature specified.
58 If the resistance is good, and all the wiring and connectors to the ECM are good, the ECM could be faulty and should be checked by a Suzuki dealer.
59 To remove the sensor, first make sure it is cold, then disconnect the wiring connector. Unscrew the sensor from the exhaust **(see illustration)**. On installation tighten the sensor to the specified torque setting.

13 Throttle bodies

⚠️ *Warning: Refer to the precautions given in Section 1 before starting work.*

Removal

1 Remove the air filter housing (see Section 8).
2 If the fuel tank has been raised and not removed, refer to Section 2, Step 5 or 11 (according to model), and disconnect the fuel hose(s).
3 Disconnect the fast idle cable (see Section 16).
4 Disconnect the throttle cables (see Section 15).
5 On X and Y models detach the idle speed adjuster from its holder. Disconnect the intake air control valve system vacuum hose from the outer union on the No. 1 throttle body **(see illustration 13.6)**, and disconnect the PAIR valve vacuum hose from the inner union on the No. 4 throttle body.
6 On K1 models onward, disconnect the intake air control valve system vacuum hose from the outer union on the No. 1 throttle body **(see illustration)**.
7 Disconnect the throttle body assembly wiring connector **(see illustration)**.
8 Remove the blanking cap from each throttle body clamp screw access hole in the frame **(see illustration)**. Slacken the clamp screws (each screw secures a pair of throttle bodies) securing the throttle bodies to the inlet stubs, then ease the bodies up off the stubs and remove them, on X and Y models bringing the fuel pump assembly with it **(see illustration)**.
9 On X and Y models place the end of each

13.6 Pull the vacuum hose off its union

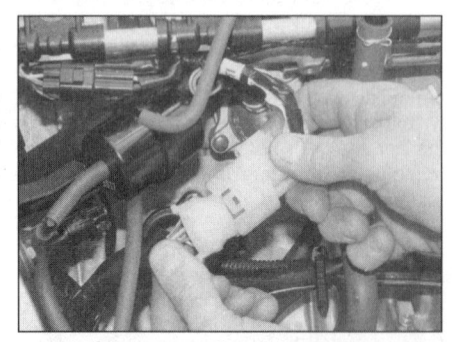

13.7 Disconnect the wiring connector

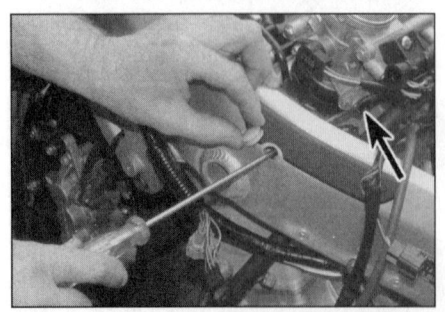

13.8a Remove the access hole blanking cap and undo the screw (arrowed) on each side . . .

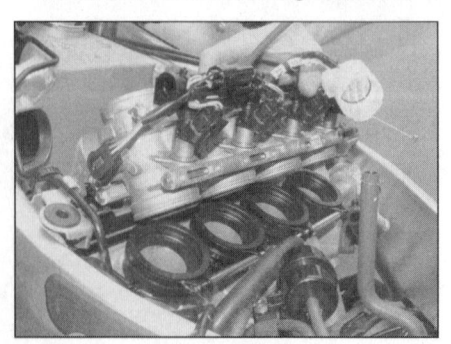

13.8b . . . and remove the throttle bodies

Fuel, engine management and exhaust systems 4•17

fuel hose into a suitable container, then release the clamp on each hose and allow the residual fuel to drain. If required separate the fuel pump assembly from the throttle bodies, referring to Section 5 and following the relevant Steps.

Cleaning

Caution: Use only a petroleum based solvent or dedicated injector cleaner for throttle body cleaning. Don't use caustic cleaners.

10 Use a dedicated carburettor/throttle body spray cleaner to spray through and clean out all passages. If it is necessary to use a dip-type cleaner, remove the fuel rail and injectors first, and ensure that only metal components are submerged in cleaning solvent. Always follow manufacturers recommendations as to the cleaning time and method.

11 After the cleaner has loosened and dissolved most of the varnish and other deposits, use a nylon-bristled brush to remove any stubborn deposits. Rinse the throttle bodies again, then dry them with compressed air. Do not poke any metal wire through the passages.

12 Use compressed air to blow out all of the fuel and air passages. If you remove the air jets (where possible) make sure you don't lose one as they are not listed as being available separately.

Caution: Never clean the jets or passages with a piece of wire or a drill bit, as they will be enlarged, causing the fuel and air metering rates to be upset.

Inspection

13 Check the throttle bodies for cracks or any other damage which may result in air getting in. Make sure the joining bolts, cable bracket screw and throttle position sensor screws are tight.

14 Check that the throttle valves and linkages move smoothly and freely in the bodies. Inspect the valve shafts and throttle bodies for wear. Check the condition of the valve shaft springs.

Disassembly and reassembly

15 Disassembly of the throttle bodies is not advised (apart from removing the fuel rail and injectors, and the throttle position sensor, in which case refer to the relevant Sections to do so). If a component on the throttle body assembly is worn or damaged and does need replacing, disassemble them as follows **(see illustration)**.

16 Remove the fuel rail and injectors (see Section 14).

17 Remove the throttle position sensor (see Section 12).

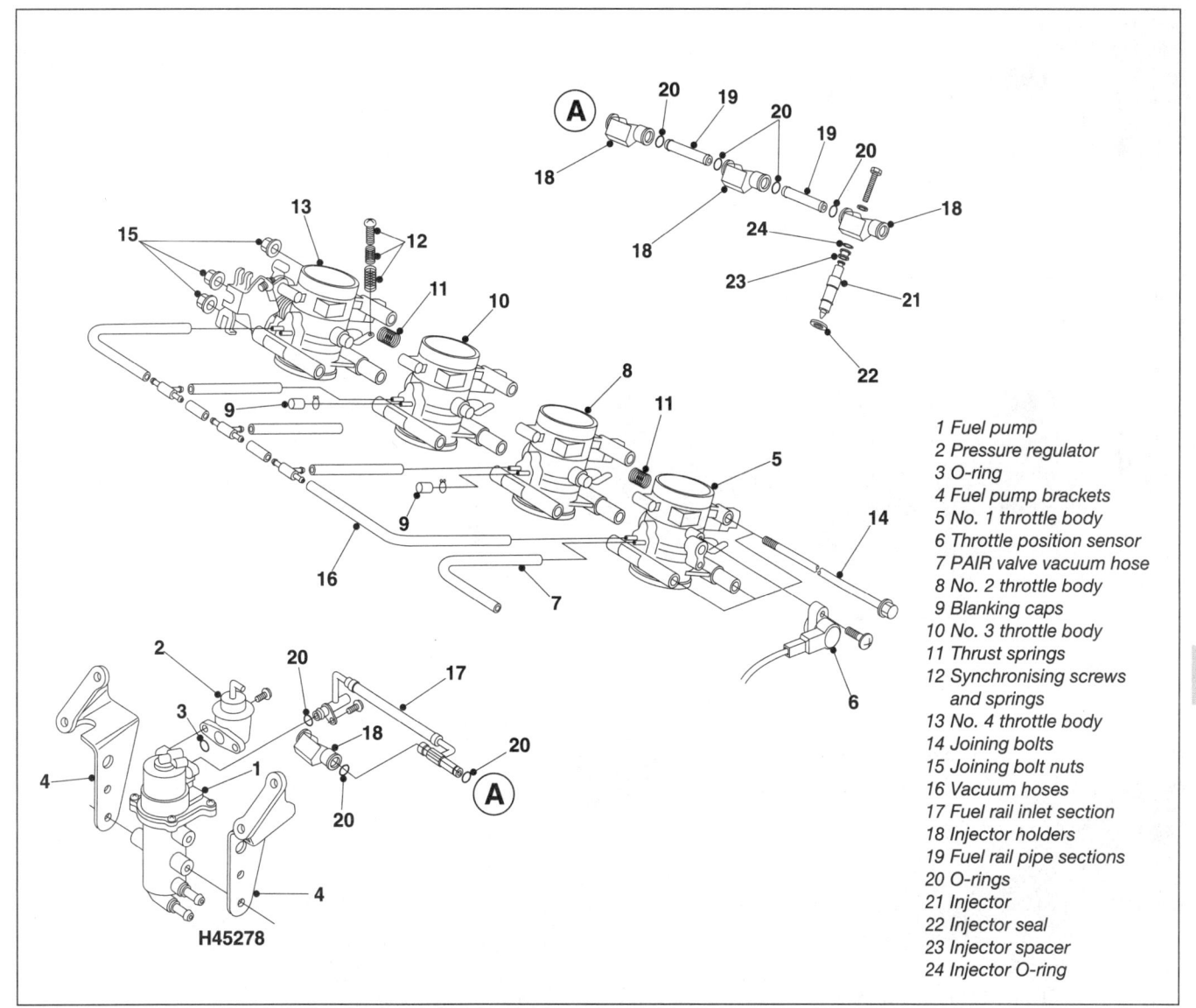

1 Fuel pump
2 Pressure regulator
3 O-ring
4 Fuel pump brackets
5 No. 1 throttle body
6 Throttle position sensor
7 PAIR valve vacuum hose
8 No. 2 throttle body
9 Blanking caps
10 No. 3 throttle body
11 Thrust springs
12 Synchronising screws and springs
13 No. 4 throttle body
14 Joining bolts
15 Joining bolt nuts
16 Vacuum hoses
17 Fuel rail inlet section
18 Injector holders
19 Fuel rail pipe sections
20 O-rings
21 Injector
22 Injector seal
23 Injector spacer
24 Injector O-ring

13.15 Throttle body assembly and fuel rail – X and Y models

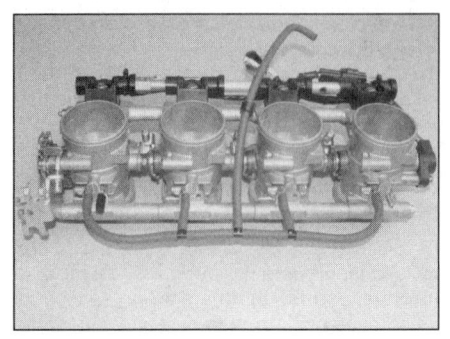

4•18 Fuel, engine management and exhaust systems

13.18 Note the vacuum hose set-up before detaching them – K1-on models shown

13.19a Note the arrangement of the various springs . . .

13.19b . . . before separating the bodies

13.19c Unscrew the nuts (arrowed) and withdraw the bolts

14.4 Release the wiring from any ties

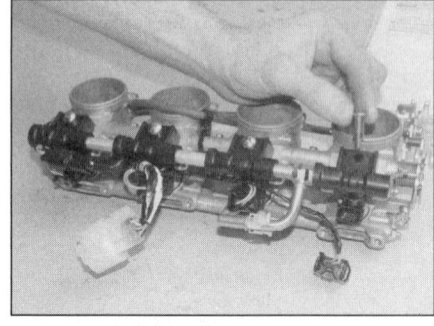

14.5a Undo the screws . . .

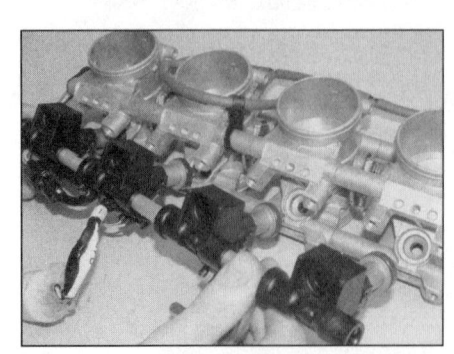

14.5b . . . and remove the fuel rail and injectors

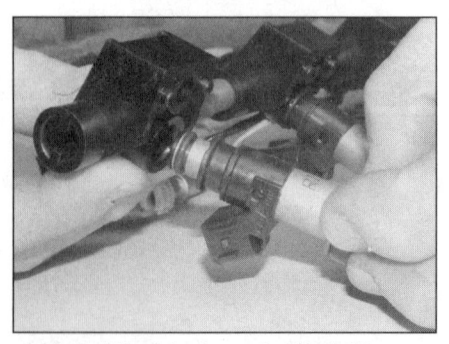

14.6 Pull the injector out of its holder . . .

18 Make a note or sketch of the vacuum hose routing, then detach each hose from its union on the throttle bodies **(see illustration)**. Also release the clamps and detach the blanking caps from their unions, noting where they fit.

19 Make a note or sketch of the synchronisation and thrust spring arrangement between each throttle body **(see illustrations)**. Unscrew the nut on the end of each joining bolt, then withdraw the bolts **(see illustration)**. Carefully separate the throttle bodies, taking care not to lose any of the springs, and noting how they interconnect.

20 Reassemble the throttle bodies in a reverse of the above procedure. When tightening the nuts on the joining bolts, place the throttle bodies on a surface plate to ensure they are all correctly aligned. Make sure all springs are correctly installed.

Installation

21 Installation is the reverse of removal, noting the following:
● Ensure the throttle bodies are fully engaged with the inlet stubs on the cylinder heads before tightening the clamps.
● Ensure the throttle body wiring connector is securely connected.
● Make sure all detached vacuum hoses are secured back on their correct unions. Make sure all hoses are in good condition, correctly routed and not pinched.
● Check the operation of the fast idle and throttle cables and adjust them as necessary (see Chapter 1).
● Check the engine idle speed and adjust as necessary (see Chapter 1).
● If the throttle bodies have been disassembled, synchronise them (see Chapter 1).
● If the throttle position sensor was removed, check and adjust its position (see Section 12).

14 Fuel rail and injectors

⚠ *Warning: Refer to the precautions given in Section 1 before proceeding.*

Removal

Note: *The fuel injectors can be removed with the throttle bodies in place. If the bodies have been removed, ignore the Steps which do not apply.*

1 Make sure the ignition is OFF. Remove the air filter housing (see Section 8).
2 If the fuel tank has been raised and not removed, refer to Section 2, Step 5 or 11 (according to model), and disconnect the fuel hose(s).
3 On X and Y models separate the fuel pump assembly from the throttle bodies, referring to Section 5 and following the relevant Steps.
4 Release any ties or clamps holding the fuel injector wiring **(see illustration)**. Mark each connector according to its location. Disconnect the individual injector wiring connectors **(see illustration 12.49)**.
5 Undo the screws securing the injector holders/fuel rail to the throttle bodies, on X and Y models noting the washers **(see illustration)**. Carefully lift the rail off – the injectors should come away with their holders in the rail, but if they don't carefully pull them out of the throttle bodies **(see illustration)**.
6 If they are still in their holders pull each injector out **(see illustration)**. Discard the

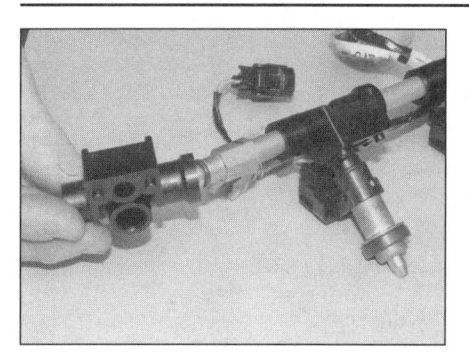

Fuel, engine management and exhaust systems 4•19

14.7 . . . and if required pull the holder off the fuel pipe

14.9 Fit a new O-ring onto each holder union

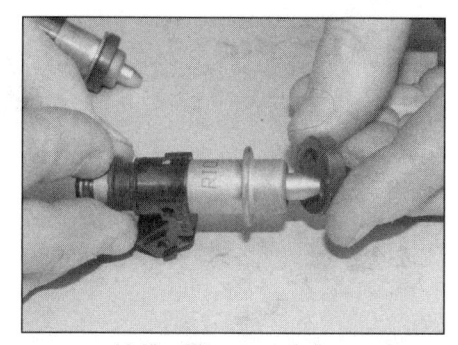

14.10a Fit a new seal . . .

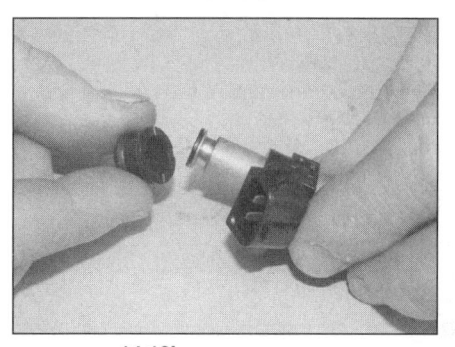

14.10b . . . spacer . . .

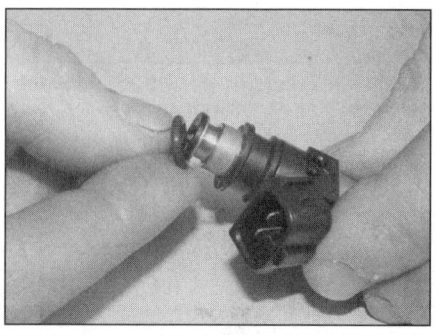

14.10c . . . and O-ring onto each injector

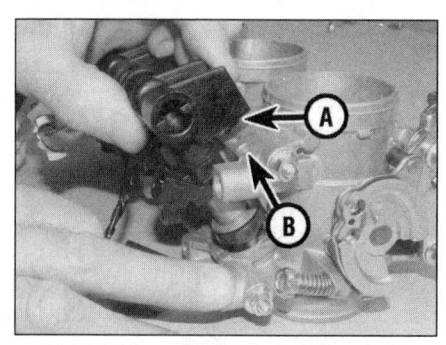

14.11 Make sure the pegs (A) on each holder locate in the holes (B)

injector O-ring, spacer and seal as new ones must be fitted on reassembly.

7 If required separate the four injector holders from the pipe sections **(see illustration)**. Discard the O-rings as new ones must be used. Note where and which way round the section with the fuel inlet union fits.

8 Modern fuels contain detergents which should keep the injectors clean and free of gum or varnish from fuel residue. If an injector is suspected of being blocked, clean it through with injector cleaner. If the injector is clean but its performance is suspect, check it as described in Section 12, then if necessary take it to a Suzuki dealer for further assessment.

Installation

Note: *Apply a smear of clean engine oil to all new seals and O-rings before reassembly.*

9 If the injector holders and fuel rail pipe sections were separated, fit new O-rings smeared with oil onto each end of each pipe section **(see illustration)**. Join the holders and pipes, making sure the holders with blanked ends are on each end, and that the section with the fuel inlet union locates between the two right-hand end holders, i.e. between the injectors for cylinders 3 and 4 **(see illustration 14.7)**.

10 Fit a new seal onto the bottom of each injector, and a new spacer and O-ring onto the top, and smear them with clean oil **(see illustrations)**. Carefully press the injectors into the holders, aligning them so the wiring connectors will face away from the throttle bodies **(see illustration 14.6)**. **Note:** *Avoid twisting the injectors as this may damage the seals.*

11 Fit the injectors and fuel rail onto the throttle bodies, locating the pegs on the holders in the as you do **(see illustration)**. Install the holder/fuel rail screws, on X and Y models not forgetting the washers, and tighten them to the specified torque setting **(see illustration 14.5a)**.

12 Connect the injector wiring connectors as follows: the connector with the grey/white wire is for the No. 1 (left-hand) injector; the connector with the grey/black wire is for the No. 2 (inner left) injector; the connector with the grey/yellow wire is for the No. 3 (inner right) injector; connector with the grey/red wire is for the No. 4 (right-hand) injector. Make sure they are securely connected. Secure the wiring in any clamps or with new cable ties according to removal.

13 On X and Y models fit the fuel pump assembly onto the throttle bodies, referring to Section 5 and following the relevant Steps.

14 Install the remaining components in the reverse order of removal. On completion, start the engine and check carefully that there are no fuel leaks.

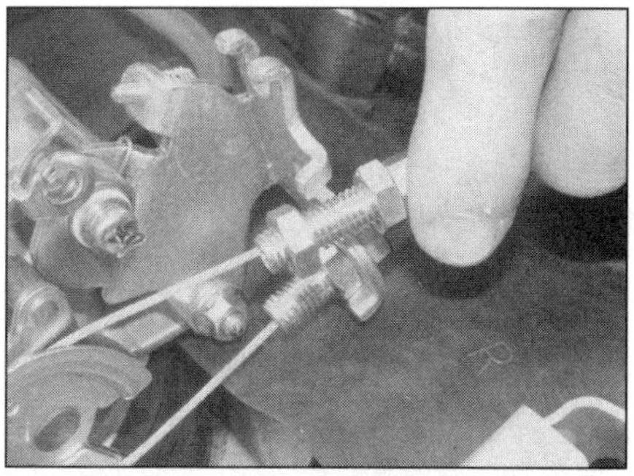

15 Throttle cables

Removal

1 Raise the fuel tank (see Section 2).

2 Fully loosen the locknuts securing the throttle cable adjusters in the bracket, then if necessary thread the adjusters out until the captive nuts can be freed **(see illustration)**. Slip the cables out of the bracket and detach the ends from the throttle pulley, noting how they fit – the lower cable is the throttle opening cable, the upper cable is the throttle closing cable **(see illustration)**.

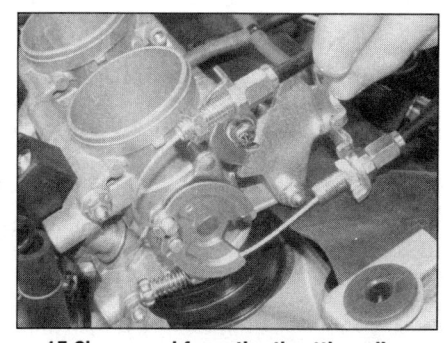

15.2a Slacken the adjuster locknuts and release the cables from the bracket . . .

15.2b . . . and from the throttle pulley

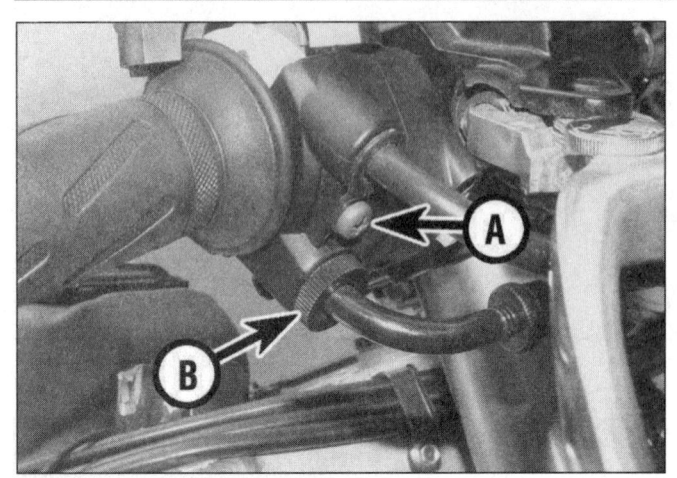

4•20 Fuel, engine management and exhaust systems

15.3a Undo the retaining plate screw (A) and unscrew the ring (B)

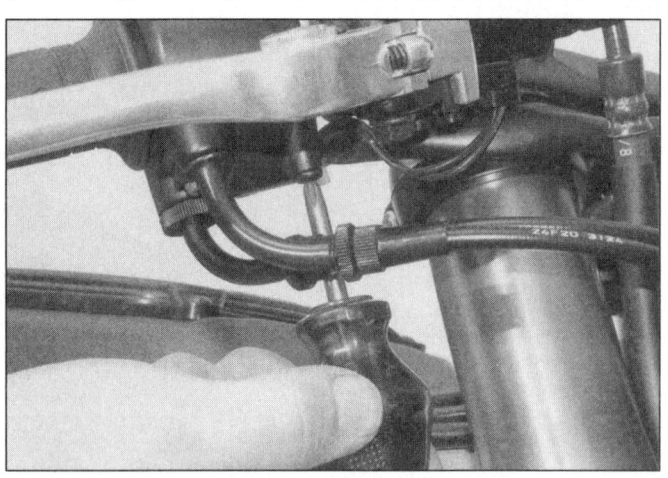

15.3b Undo the screws on the underside of the housing and separate the halves . . .

15.3c . . . then detach the cable ends (arrowed) from the pulley and draw them out of the housing

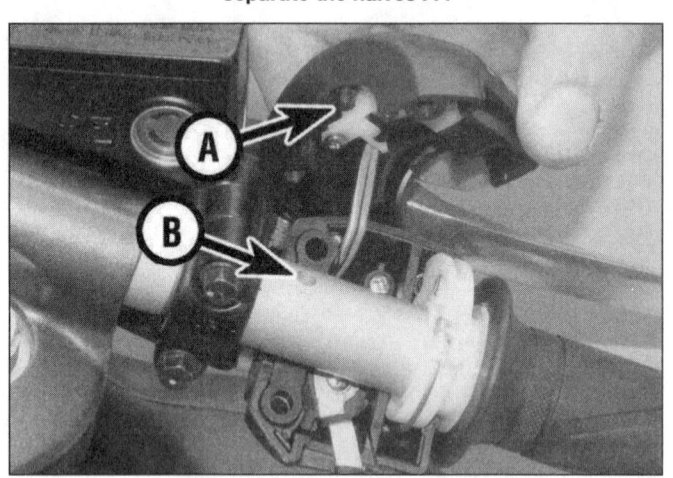

15.6 Locate the pin (A) in the hole (B)

3 Undo the screw securing the front (opening) cable retaining plate to the handlebar switch/throttle twistgrip housing, and unscrew the rear (closing) cable retaining ring **(see illustration)**. Remove the handlebar housing screws and separate the halves **(see illustration)**. Note how the pin on the upper half of the housing locates in the hole in the handlebar. Detach the cable ends from the twistgrip pulley, noting how they fit, then pull the cables out of the lower half of the housing **(see illustration)**.
4 Remove the cables from the machine, noting their correct routing, and how they pass through the guide on the frame – slacken the bolt if required to help removal, or unscrew the bolt and remove the guide altogether.

Installation

5 Thread the cables through to the throttle bodies and up to the handlebars, making sure they are correctly routed – they must not interfere with any other component and should not be kinked or bent sharply. Fit the guide and/or tighten the bolt as required.
6 Fit the opening cable elbow in the front socket in the lower half of the handlebar housing, then lubricate the cable end with multi-purpose grease and attach it to the pulley **(see illustration 15.3c)**. Similarly fit the closing end into the rear socket and attach it to the pulley. Ensure the cables are correctly aligned in the groove in the pulley, then fit the upper half of the housing, locating the pin in the hole in the top of the handlebar **(see illustration)**. Fit the lower half of the housing onto the twistgrip pulley then install the screws and tighten them **(see illustration 15.3b)**. Secure the opening cable elbow with the retaining plate and tighten the screw, and secure the closing cable elbow with the retaining ring **(see illustration 15.3a)**.
7 Check that the twistgrip pulley turns freely.
8 Fit the lower end of the opening cable into the bottom socket in the throttle pulley, then locate the cable adjuster in the bracket, ensuring the nuts are on each side **(see illustrations)**. Locate the bottom nut against

15.8a Fit the cable end into the pulley . . .

15.8b . . . and the adjuster into the bracket

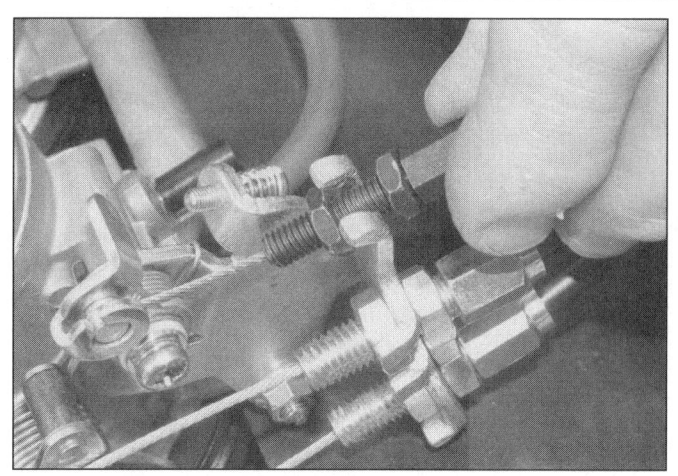

Fuel, engine management and exhaust systems 4•21

16.2a Slacken the adjuster locknut and release the cable from the bracket...

16.2b ...and from the fast idle cam

the lug so its is captive and thread the adjuster in far enough so the adjuster is held in the bracket, but not so it is tight. Repeat the procedure for the closing cable, locating its end in the top socket in the throttle pulley **(see illustrations 15.2b and a)**. Adjust the cables as described in Chapter 1.

9 Lower the fuel tank (see Section 2).
10 Start the engine and check the action of the throttle, and that the idle speed does not rise as the handlebars are turned. If it does, correct the problem before riding the motorcycle.

16 Fast idle system

Cable removal

1 Raise the fuel tank (see Section 2).
2 Fully loosen the locknut securing the cable adjuster in the bracket, then if necessary thread the adjuster out until the captive nut can be freed **(see illustration)**. Slip the adjuster out of its bracket and disconnect the cable from the fast idle cam, pushing the cam forwards if there is not enough slack in the cable **(see illustration)**.
3 Undo the two switch/lever housing screws, one of which secures the cable elbow retainer plate, and separate the halves **(see illustration)**. Note how the pin on the upper half of the housing locates in the hole in the handlebar. Pull the lever out of the lower half and detach the cable end from it, noting how it fits **(see illustration)**. Pull the cable elbow out of the housing **(see illustration)**.
4 Remove the cable from the machine, noting its routing, and how it passes through the guide on the frame – slacken the bolt if required to help removal, or unscrew the bolt and remove the guide altogether.

Cable installation

5 Thread the cable through to the throttle bodies and up to the handlebars, making sure it is correctly routed – it must not interfere with any other component and should not be kinked or bent sharply. Fit the guide and/or tighten the bolt as required.
6 Lubricate the end of the cable with multi-purpose grease. Fit the cable elbow into the lower half of the housing, then attach the cable end to the lever, and fit the lever into the lower half of the switch housing **(see illustrations 16.3c and b)**. Fit the two halves of the housing onto the handlebar, locating

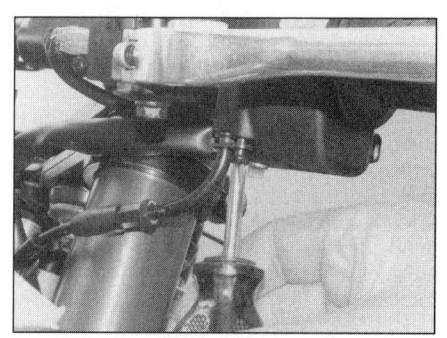

16.3a Undo the housing screws and separate the halves

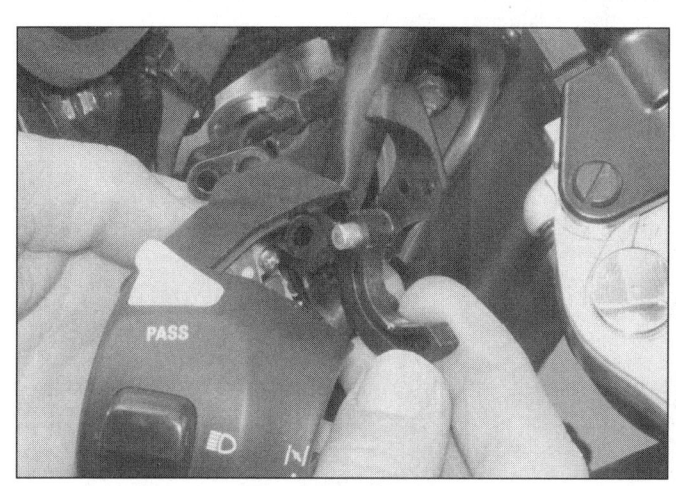

16.3b Free the lever, then detach the cable end...

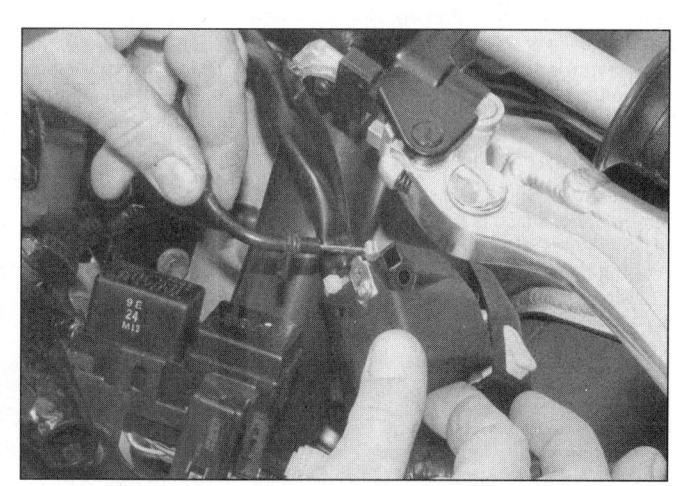

16.3c ...and draw the cable out of the housing

4•22 Fuel, engine management and exhaust systems

16.6 Locate the pin (A) in the hole (B)

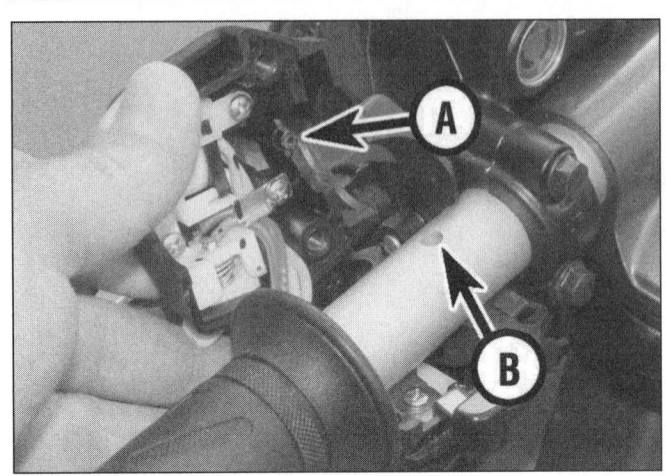

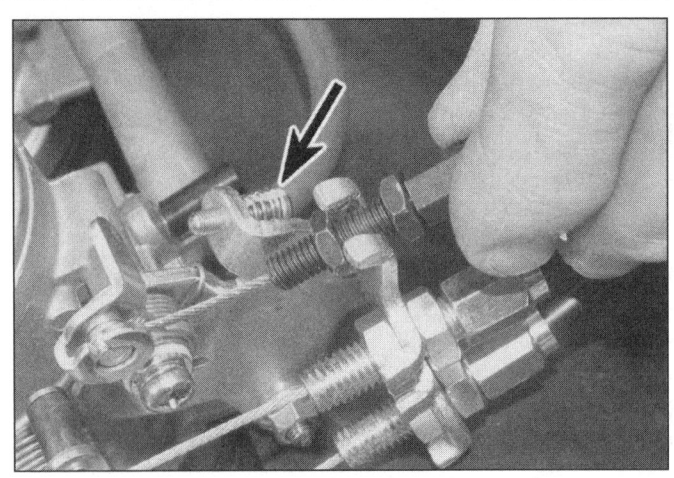

16.12 Fast idle adjuster screw (arrowed)

the pin in the upper half in the hole in the top of the handlebar **(see illustration)**. Install the retaining screws, securing the cable retainer with the front one **(see illustration 16.3a)**. Check that the lever turns freely.

7 Fit the lower end of the cable onto the fast idle cam, holding it forwards if necessary, and locate the cable adjuster in the bracket, ensuring the adjuster locknuts are located on each side **(see illustrations 16.2b and a)**. Locate the bottom nut against the lug so it is captive and thread the adjuster in far enough so the adjuster is held in the bracket, but not so it is tight. Check the action of the linkage – it is possible for the cam to stick on the roller. Smear some molybdenum grease over the roller to prevent this.

8 Make sure the fast idle handlebar lever is in the closed (forward) position, then turn the adjuster until there is a small amount of freeplay left in the cable, and tighten the locknut. Fine adjustment of cable freeplay can be made using the in-line adjuster at the cable elbow near the fast idle lever (see Chapter 1).
Note: *Suzuki gives no specifications for fast idle cable freeplay. Ensure that with the handlebar lever in the OFF position the fast idle cam does not engage the throttle valve mechanism.*

Fast idle speed check and adjustment

9 The engine should be at normal operating temperature, which is usually reached after 10 to 15 minutes of stop/start riding. Make sure that the idle speed is correctly adjusted (see Chapter 1). Raise the fuel tank (see Section 2).
10 Check the cable freeplay (see Chapter 1).
11 With the engine running, pull the handlebar lever back to the fully open position and check that the idle speed increases to the specified fast idle speed.
12 To adjust the fast idle speed, turn the adjuster screw as required until the specified speed is obtained **(see illustration)**.
13 Return the handlebar lever to the OFF position and check that the idle speed returns to normal. If necessary, adjust the idle speed (see Chapter 1) then lower the fuel tank (see Section 2).

17 Exhaust system

⚠ **Warning:** *If the engine has been running the exhaust system will be very hot. Allow the system to cool before carrying out any work.*

Silencers

Removal

1 Unscrew the nuts and remove the washers securing the silencer on the downpipe/silencer pipe flange.
2 Unscrew the nut from the bolt securing the silencer to the passenger footrest bracket and remove the washer **(see illustration)**. Support the silencer and withdraw the bolt, noting the washer. Draw the silencer off the downpipe/silencer pipe flange.
3 Note the spacer in the mounting bush. Discard the silencer gasket as a new one must be used. Remove the O-rings from the silencer studs and discard them as new ones must be used.
4 On X, Y and K1 models the left-hand silencer pipe can be separated from the downpipe assembly if required, either with the silencer attached or after removing the silencer (if the silencer is left attached you must still remove the mounting bolt as in Step 2). On all other models both silencer pipes can be removed in the same way. Remove the fairing bottom panel first (see Chapter 8). Slacken the clamp securing the pipe in the downpipe assembly and draw the pipe out **(see illustration)**.

Installation

5 Installation is the reverse of removal, noting the following:
● Where seized or corroded fasteners have been encountered, clean up their threads and apply a smear of copper grease before installing them.
● Use new gaskets and/or O-rings, according to removal method. Apply a smear of grease to the new silencer gasket to keep it in place if necessary.
● Apply a suitable exhaust gas sealant (such as Permatex 1312) to the sealing ring located between the silencer pipe(s) and downpipe assembly.

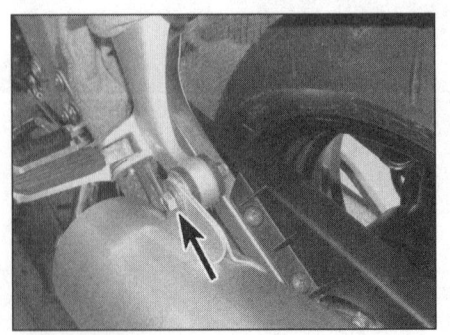

17.2 Silencer mounting bolt (arrowed)

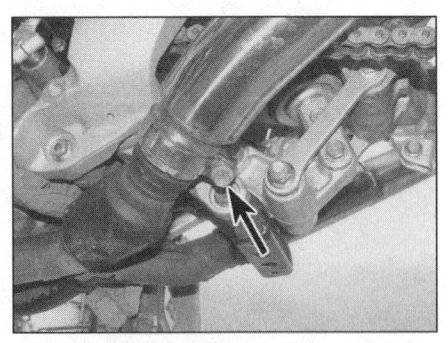

17.4 Slacken the clamp bolt (arrowed) to release the pipe

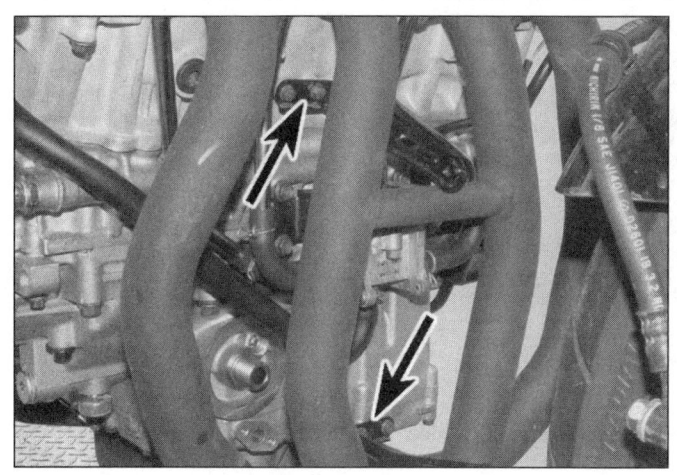

Fuel, engine management and exhaust systems 4•23

17.7 Unscrew the bolts (arrowed) and remove the brackets

17.10a Unscrew the bolt (arrowed) . . .

● Leave the fasteners finger-tight until all are installed, then tighten them to the torque settings specified at the beginning of the Chapter, tightening the silencer flange nuts first if undone.
● Run the engine and check that there are no exhaust gas leaks.

Complete system

Removal

6 Remove the fairing side panels and the bottom panel (see Chapter 8).
7 Drain the engine oil and coolant (see Chapter 1). Remove the oil cooler (see Chapter 2). Remove the radiator (see Chapter 3). Remove the oil cooler and radiator mounting brackets – each is secured by two bolts **(see illustration)**. Note which way round they fit.
8 Slacken the clamp bolt securing the left-hand silencer pipe in the downpipe assembly **(see illustration 17.4)**.
9 Unscrew the nut from the bolt securing the left-hand silencer to the passenger footrest bracket and remove the washer **(see illustration 17.2)**. Support the silencer and withdraw the bolt, noting the washer. Draw the silencer off the downpipe assembly. Note the spacer in the mounting bush.

10 Unscrew the downpipe assembly rear mounting bolt – it threads into a captive nut which is held by tabs, and if the nut is seized these tabs will distort before the nut comes undone, whereupon the nut will just spin **(see illustrations)**. If this happens first spray the nut and bolt end with a penetrating lubricant, then bend the tabs down and hold them against the nut with a pair of grips while undoing the bolt – having the help of an assistant makes this a lot easier.
11 On K2 models onward and where fitted, disconnect the oxygen sensor wiring connector **(see illustration 12.53)**.
12 Unscrew the nut from the bolt securing the right-hand silencer to the passenger footrest bracket and remove the washer.
13 Unscrew the downpipe flange bolts **(see illustration)**. Support the right-hand silencer and withdraw the bolt, noting the washer. Support the downpipe assembly, then withdraw the silencer bolt and remove the exhaust assembly **(see illustration)**. Note the spacer in the silencer and downpipe mounting bushes.
14 Remove the gasket from each exhaust port and discard them as new ones must be used **(see illustration)**.

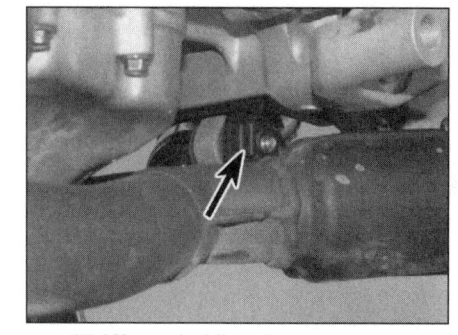

17.10b . . . holding the captive nut (arrowed) as described if required

Installation

15 Installation is the reverse of removal, noting the following:
● Where seized or corroded fasteners have been encountered, clean up their threads and apply a smear of copper grease before installing them.
● Use new gaskets for the exhaust ports, fitting them with their tabs innermost **(see illustration)**. Apply a smear of grease to them to keep them in place if necessary.
● Manoeuvre the downpipe assembly into position so that each pipe locates in the

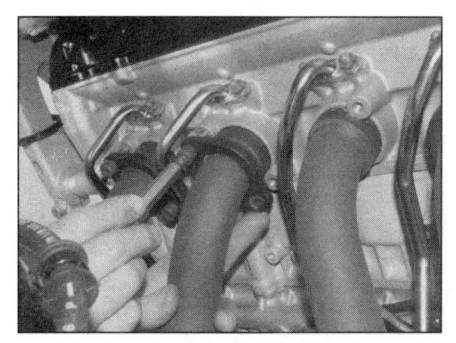

17.13a Unscrew the flange bolts . . .

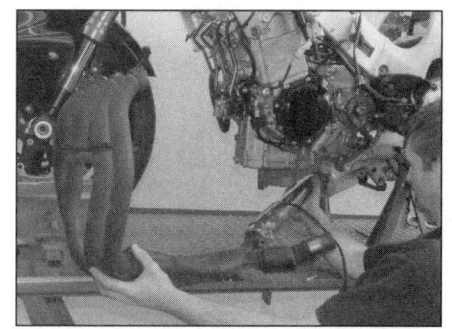

17.13b . . . and remove the exhaust assembly

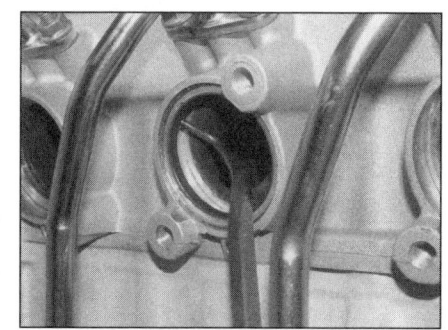

17.14 Hook the old gaskets out and discard them

4•24 Fuel, engine management and exhaust systems

cylinder head, then align the right-hand silencer mounting bracket with the footrest bracket and install the bolt with its washer **(see illustration)**.
● Leave the fasteners finger-tight until all are installed, then tighten them to the torque settings specified at the beginning of the Chapter, tightening the silencer flange nuts first if undone.
● Apply a suitable exhaust gas sealant (such as Permatex 1312) to the sealing ring located between the left-hand silencer pipe and downpipe assembly.
● On K2 models onward and where fitted, do not forget to reconnect the oxygen sensor wiring connector.
● Install radiator and oil cooler brackets with the ledge along the bolt hole section at the bottom – the longer bracket is for the oil cooler **(see illustration 17.7)**. Install the radiator (see Chapter 3). Install the oil cooler (see Chapter 2). Replenish the engine oil and coolant (see Chapter 1).
● Run the engine and check that there are no exhaust gas leaks.
● Install the fairing bottom panel and side panels (see Chapter 8).

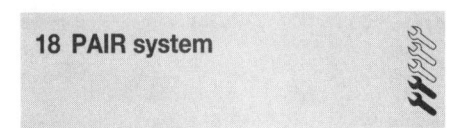

18 PAIR system

General information

1 To reduce the amount of unburned hydrocarbons released in the exhaust gases, a pulse secondary air (PAIR) system is fitted. The system consists of the control valve (mounted on the front of the engine), the reed valves (incorporated in the control valve) and the hoses. The control valve is actuated on X, Y and K1 models by a vacuum sourced from the throttle bodies, and on all other models electronically by the ECM.
2 Under certain operating conditions, the PAIR control valve allows filtered air to be drawn through it, the reed valves and into the exhaust ports. The air mixes with the exhaust gases, causing any unburned particles of fuel to be burnt in the exhaust port/pipes. This process changes a considerable amount of hydrocarbons and carbon monoxide into relatively harmless carbon dioxide and water. The reed valves are fitted to prevent the flow of exhaust gases back into the control valve and air filter housing.
3 The system is not adjustable and requires no maintenance, except to ensure that the hoses are in good condition and are securely connected at each end, and that there is no build-up of carbon on the reed valves. Replace any hoses that are cracked, split or generally deteriorated with new ones, noting their routing. The reed valves can be checked for any build-up of carbon by undoing the cover screws **(see illustration 18.9b)** – if any

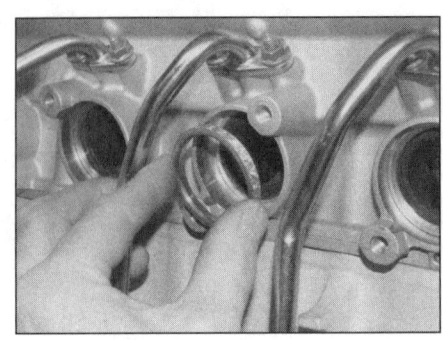

17.15a Fit a new gasket into each port

is found, clean up the valves and their housings (steps 8 and 9).

Testing

Control valve

4 Remove the valve from the motorcycle (see below).
5 Check the operation of the control valve by blowing through the air filter housing hose union; air should flow freely through the valve **(see illustration)**.
6 On X, Y and K1 models with a vacuum controlled valve, now apply a vacuum of 330 to 490 mmHg to the vacuum hose and repeat the check; no air should flow through the valve if it is functioning correctly.
7 On all other models with an electronically controlled valve, now connect battery voltage (12 volts) across the valve wiring connector terminals and repeat the check; no air should

18.5 Air should flow through the valve and out of the hoses

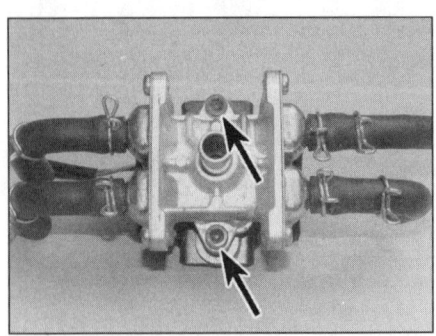

18.9a Control valve bolts

17.15b Start by fitting each downpipe into its port

flow through the valve if it is functioning correctly **(see illustration)**. If an ohmmeter is available, check the resistance of the control valve windings by connecting an ohmmeter between its wiring connector terminals and compare the reading obtained to that given in the Specifications. Replace the valve with a new one if faulty.

Reed valves

8 Remove the valve from the motorcycle (see below). Refer to the check in Step 5 – if you can blow through the valve the reeds are working correctly. Now try to blow back through the valve via each exit hose union in turn – you should not be able to do so.
9 If this is not the case, separate the control valve from its bracket by unscrewing the nuts, noting the washers, and removing the bolts **(see illustration)**. Undo the reed valve cover screws and check the reed valves for any build-up of carbon **(see illustration)** – if any is

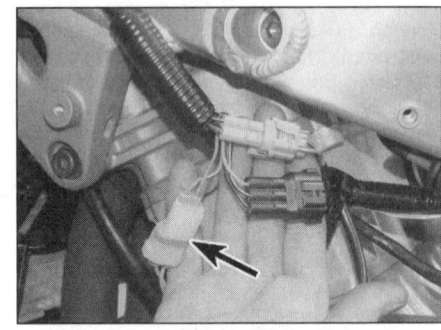

18.7 Control valve wiring connector (arrowed)

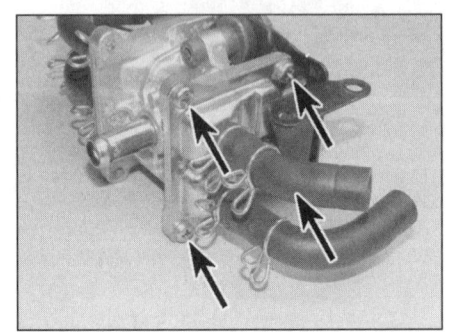

18.9b Reed valve cover screws (arrowed)

Fuel, engine management and exhaust systems 4•25

18.12a Unscrew the bolts (arrowed) . . .

18.12b . . . then displace the valve and detach the hoses

found, clean up the valves and their housings, then fit the covers and repeat Step 8. If there is still a problem replace the control valve with a new one.

Component renewal

Control valve

Note: *The reed valves are incorporated in the control valve and are not available separately.*

10 Remove the fairing side panels (see Chapter 8). Make sure the exhaust system is cold. Remove it for best access (see Section 17).

11 On X, Y and K1 models detach the vacuum hose from its union on the valve. On all other models disconnect the solenoid wiring connector **(see illustration 18.7)**.

12 Release the clamps securing the hoses to the air pipes on the engine. Unscrew the bolts securing the control valve bracket to the engine and remove the valve, drawing the hoses off the pipes as you do **(see illustrations)**. If required separate the control valve from its bracket by unscrewing the nuts, noting the washers, and removing the bolts **(see illustration 18.9a)**. Note the spacers in the rubber mounts, and check the mounts for cracks and hardening, replacing them with new ones if necessary.

13 Installation is the reverse of removal. Feed the hoses onto the pipes first, then install the bolts when the hole align. Use a suitable thread-locking compound on the bolts.

Hoses and pipes

14 To replace the hoses between the control valve and the air pipes to the cylinder head, first remove the fairing side panels (see Chapter 8). Make sure the exhaust system is cold. Remove it for best access (see Section 17). Release the clamps and detach the hoses from their unions, noting which fits where.

15 To replace the air supply hose from the air filter housing, remove the right-hand fairing side panel (see Chapter 8), and raise the fuel tank (see Section 2). Release the clamp securing each end of the hose and detach it from the unions. Release the hose from its clamp on the right-hand side of the engine. Remove the hose noting its routing.

16 On X, Y and K1 models, to replace the vacuum hose from the throttle bodies, remove the right-hand fairing side panel (see Chapter 8), and the air filter housing (see Section 8). Detach the hose from its unions. Release the hose from its clamp on the right-hand side of the engine. Remove the hose noting its routing.

17 To remove the pipes from the cylinder head, first remove the fairing side panels (see Chapter 8). Make sure the exhaust system is cold. Remove it for best access (see Section 17). Release the clamps and detach the hoses from their unions on the pipes, noting which fits where. Unscrew the two nuts securing each pipe, then unscrew the pipes, noting which fits where. Discard the gaskets as new ones must be used.

18 Installation is the reverse of removal. Make sure all hoses are correctly routed as noted on removal. Make sure each air pipe is returned to its correct location. Fit a new gasket, with the seal side facing out, onto each pipe union, then fit the pipes and tighten the nuts to the torque setting specified at the beginning of the Chapter.

19 EVAP system (California models)

General information

1 This system prevents the escape of fuel vapour into the atmosphere by storing it in a charcoal-filled canister.

2 When the engine is not running, excess fuel vapour from the tank passes into the canister via a control valve. When the engine is started, intake manifold depression draws the vapour from the canister into the throttle bodies to be burned during the normal combustion process.

3 The canister has a one way valve which allows air to be drawn into the system as the volume of fuel decreases in the tank. A shut-off valve also prevents any fuel escaping in the event of the bike falling over.

4 The system is not adjustable and can only be properly tested by a Suzuki dealer. However the owner can check that all the hoses are in good condition and are securely connected at each end. Renew any hoses that are cracked, split or generally deteriorated.

Removal and installation

5 To access the canister remove the seat cowling (see Chapter 8). The canister is mounted on the rear sub-frame on the right-hand side. Label and disconnect the hoses, then remove the clamp screw and take the canister out. Make sure the hoses are correctly reconnected on installation.

6 The control valve and shut-off valve are fitted in the hose between the fuel tank and the canister.

20 Catalytic converter

General information

1 A catalytic converter is incorporated in each silencer to minimise the level of exhaust pollutants released into the atmosphere.

2 The catalytic converter consists of a canister containing a fine mesh impregnated with a catalyst material, over which the hot exhaust gases pass. The catalyst speeds up the oxidation of harmful carbon monoxide, unburned hydrocarbons and soot, effectively reducing the quantity of harmful products released into the atmosphere via the exhaust gases.

3 The catalytic converter is of the closed-loop

type on K2 models onward, with exhaust gas oxygen content information being fed back to the ECM by the oxygen sensor. Earlier models have an open-loop design.

4 The oxygen sensor contains a heating element which is controlled by the ECM. When the engine is cold, the ECM switches on the heating element which warms the exhaust gases as they pass over the sensor. This brings the catalytic converter quickly up to its normal operating temperature and decreases the level of exhaust pollutants emitted whilst the engine warms up. Once the engine is sufficiently warmed up, the ECM switches off the heating element.

5 Refer to Section 17 for exhaust system removal and installation, and Section 12 for oxygen sensor removal and installation information.

Precautions

6 The catalytic converter is a reliable and simple device which needs no maintenance in itself, but there are some facts of which an owner should be aware if the converter is to function properly for its full service life.

- DO NOT use leaded or lead replacement petrol (gasoline) – the additives will coat the precious metals, reducing their converting efficiency and will eventually destroy the catalytic converter.
- Always keep the ignition and fuel systems well-maintained in accordance with the manufacturer's schedule – if the fuel/air mixture is suspected of being incorrect have it checked on an exhaust gas analyser.
- If the engine develops a misfire, do not ride the bike at all (or at least as little as possible) until the fault is cured.
- DO NOT use fuel or engine oil additives – these may contain substances harmful to the catalytic converter.
- DO NOT continue to use the bike if the engine burns oil to the extent of leaving a visible trail of blue smoke.
- Remember that the catalytic converter and oxygen sensor are FRAGILE – do not strike them with tools during servicing work.

Chapter 5
Ignition system

Contents

Clutch switch .... see Chapter 9
Crankshaft position sensor .... see Chapter 4
General information 1
Ignition (main) switch .... see Chapter 9
Engine control module (ECM) 4
Gear position switch check .... see Chapter 4
Gear position switch removal and installation .... see Chapter 9
Ignition HT coils 3
Ignition system check 2
Sidestand switch .... see Chapter 9
Spark plugs .... see Chapter 1

Degrees of difficulty

Easy, suitable for novice with little experience	**Fairly easy,** suitable for beginner with some experience	**Fairly difficult,** suitable for competent DIY mechanic	**Difficult,** suitable for experienced DIY mechanic	**Very difficult,** suitable for expert DIY or professional

Specifications

General information
Spark plugs .... see Chapter 1
Cylinder identification .... 1–2–3–4, from left to right
Firing order 1–2–4–3
Rev limiter cut-in speed .... 10,600 rpm

Ignition timing
At idle
  X models .... 4° BTDC
  Y models
    Cylinders 1 and 4 .... 11° BTDC
    Cylinders 2 and 3 .... 3° BTDC
  K1 models onward
    US and Canada models .... 4° BTDC
    All other markets
      Cylinders 1 and 4 .... 11° BTDC
      Cylinders 2 and 3 .... 3° BTDC

Ignition HT coils
Primary winding resistance
  X, Y and K1 models .... 0.8 to 1.2 ohms @ 20°C
  K2 models onward .... 1.0 to 1.6 ohms @ 20°C
Secondary winding resistance
  X, Y and K1 models .... 8.0 to 15.0 K-ohms @ 20°C
  K2 models onward .... 10.0 to 16.5 K-ohms @ 20°C
Minimum spark gap (see Section 2) .... 8 mm
Peak voltage .... 80 volts minimum when cranking

Torque settings
Timing mark inspection cap .... 23 Nm

5•2 Ignition system

1 General information

All models are fitted with a fully transistorised electronic ignition system, which due to its lack of mechanical parts is totally maintenance free. The system comprises a trigger, crankshaft position sensor, engine control module (ECM) and stick-type combined ignition HT coils/spark plug caps. Refer to the wiring diagrams at the end of Chapter 9 for details.

The ignition trigger, which is on the alternator rotor on the left-hand end of the crankshaft, magnetically operates the crankshaft position sensor as the crankshaft rotates. The sensor sends a signal to the ECM which then supplies the ignition HT coils with the power necessary to produce a spark at the plugs.

The ignition timing setting is determined by the ECM, which compares the signals it receives from the sensors to stored data in the form of ignition maps in its ROM. The ignition timing is non-adjustable.

The system also incorporates a safety interlock circuit which will cut the ignition if the sidestand is extended whilst the engine is running and in gear, or if a gear is selected whilst the engine is running and the sidestand is extended. It also prevents the engine from being started unless the clutch lever is pulled in, and if the engine is in gear while the sidestand is down. The engine can be started in gear as long as the sidestand is up and the clutch is pulled in.

Because of their nature, the individual ignition system components can be checked but not repaired. If ignition system troubles occur, and the faulty component can be isolated, the only cure for the problem is to replace the part with a new one. Keep in mind that most electrical parts, once purchased, cannot be returned. To avoid unnecessary expense, make very sure the faulty component has been positively identified before buying a replacement part.

Note that there is no provision for adjusting the ignition timing on these models.

2 Ignition system check

Warning: The energy levels in electronic systems can be very high. On no account should the ignition be switched on whilst the plugs or plug caps are being held. Shocks from the HT circuit can be most unpleasant. Secondly, it is vital that the engine is not turned over or run with any of the plug caps removed, and that the plugs are soundly earthed (grounded) when the system is checked for sparking. The ignition system components can be seriously damaged if the HT circuit becomes isolated.

1 As no means of adjustment is available, any failure of the system can be traced to failure of a system component or a simple wiring fault. Of the two possibilities, the latter is by far the most likely. In the event of failure, check the system in a logical fashion, as described below. Work on one cylinder at a time.

2 Remove the air filter housing (see Chapter 4).

3 Disconnect the wiring connector from the combined ignition coil/spark plug cap **(see illustration)**. Clean the area around the coil/cap seal on the valve cover before removing the coil/cap to prevent any dirt falling into the spark plug channel. Carefully pull the coil/cap off the spark plug **(see illustration)**.

4 Fit a spare spark plug that is known to be good into the coil/cap. Reconnect the wiring connector, then lay the plug against the cylinder head with the threads contacting it – do not lay the plug against the valve cover as it is made of magnesium and will be damaged by the spark. If necessary, hold the spark plug with an insulated tool.

Warning: Do not remove any of the spark plugs from the engine to perform this check – atomised fuel being pumped out of the open spark plug hole could ignite, causing severe injury! Make sure the plugs are securely held against the engine – if they are not earthed when the engine is turned over, the ECM could be damaged.

5 Check that the kill switch is in the 'RUN' position and the transmission is in neutral, then turn the ignition switch ON, pull in the clutch lever and turn the engine over on the starter motor. If the system is in good condition a regular, fat blue spark should be evident at the plug electrodes. If the spark appears thin or yellowish, or is non-existent, further investigation will be necessary. Turn the ignition off and repeat the test for the other spark plugs.

6 The ignition system must be able to produce a spark which is capable of jumping a particular size gap. Suzuki specify that a healthy system should produce a spark capable of jumping at least 8 mm. Simple ignition spark gap testing tools are commercially available – follow the manufacturer's instructions, and check each spark plug.

7 If the test results are good the entire ignition system can be considered good. If the spark appears thin or yellowish, or is non-existent, further investigation is necessary.

8 Ignition faults can be divided into two categories, namely those where the ignition system has failed completely, and those which are due to a partial failure. The likely faults are listed below, starting with the most probable source of failure. Work through the list systematically, referring to the subsequent sections for full details of the necessary checks and tests, and to the *Wiring Diagrams* at the end of Chapter 9. **Note:** *Before checking the following items ensure that the battery is fully charged and that all fuses are in good condition.*

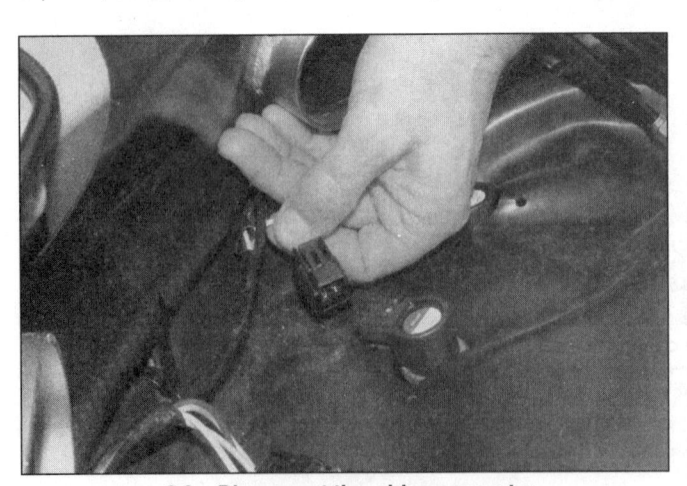

2.3a Disconnect the wiring connector...

2.3b ...then pull the coil/cap up off the spark plug

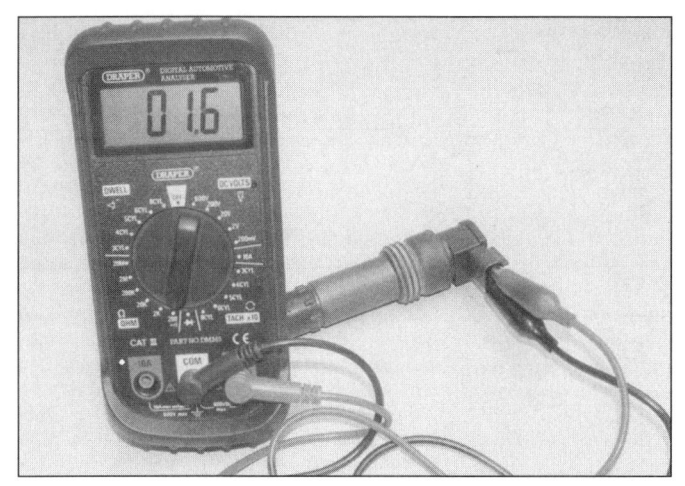

Ignition system 5•3

3.4 To test the coil primary resistance, connect the multimeter leads between the primary circuit connector terminals

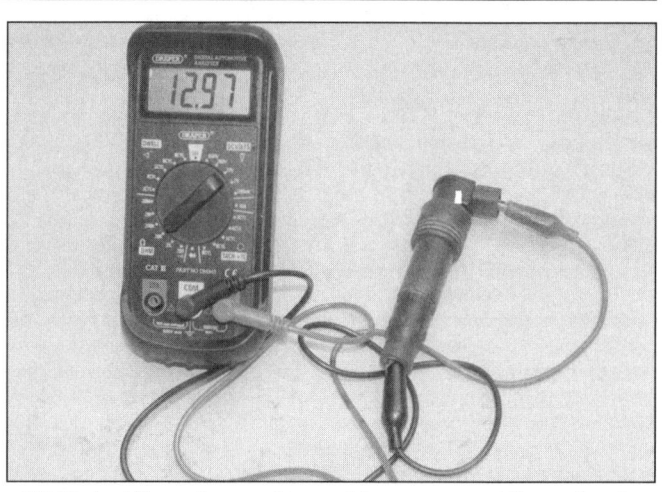

3.5 To test the coil secondary resistance, connect the probes to the spark plug cap socket and the specified connector terminal

- Loose, corroded or damaged wiring connections, broken or shorted wiring between any of the component parts of the ignition system (see Chapter 9).
- Faulty spark plug, dirty, worn or corroded plug electrodes, or incorrect gap between electrodes.
- Faulty ignition (main) switch or engine kill switch (see Chapter 9).
- Faulty gear position, clutch or sidestand switch, or diode unit (see Chapter 9).
- Faulty crankshaft position sensor or damaged trigger.
- Faulty ignition HT coil(s)/spark plug caps.
- Faulty ECM.

9 If the above checks don't reveal the cause of the problem, have the ignition system tested by a Suzuki dealer.

3 Ignition HT coils

Check

1 Make sure the ignition is switched OFF.
2 Remove the air filter housing (see Chapter 4).
3 Disconnect the wiring connector from the combined ignition coil/spark plug cap **(see illustration 2.3a)**. Clean the area around the coil/cap seal on the valve cover before removing the coil/cap to prevent any dirt falling into the spark plug channel. Carefully pull the coil/cap off the spark plug **(see illustration 2.3b)**.
4 Measure the primary circuit resistance with an ohmmeter or multimeter as follows: set the meter to the ohms x 1 scale and measure the resistance between the terminals on the coil **(see illustration)**. If the reading obtained is not within the range shown in the Specifications, it is likely that the coil is defective.
5 Measure the secondary circuit resistance with a multimeter as follows: set the meter to the K-ohm scale. Connect the positive (+) meter probe to the spark plug cap socket and the negative (–) probe to the left-hand (–) terminal on the coil **(see illustration)**. If the reading obtained is not within the range shown in the Specifications, it is possible that the coil is defective. To confirm this, it must be tested using a peak voltage adapter by a Suzuki dealer.
6 If a coil is confirmed to be faulty, it must be replaced with a new one: the coils are sealed units and cannot therefore be repaired.

Removal

7 Make sure the ignition is switched OFF.
8 Remove the air filter housing (see Chapter 4).

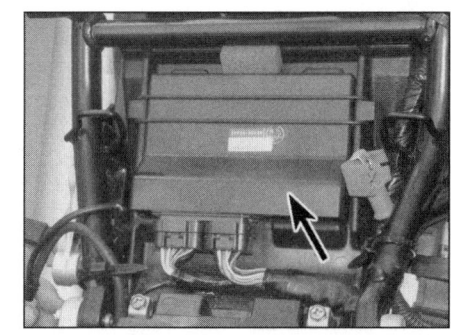

4.3 Engine control module (arrowed)

9 Disconnect the wiring connector from the combined ignition coil/spark plug cap **(see illustration 2.3a)**. Clean the area around the coil/cap seal on the valve cover before removing the coil/cap to prevent any dirt falling into the spark plug channel. Carefully pull the coil/cap off the spark plug **(see illustration 2.3b)**.

Installation

10 Installation is the reverse of removal. Make sure the wiring connectors are securely connected.

4 Engine control module (ECM)

Check

1 If the tests shown in the preceding or following Sections have failed to isolate the cause of an ignition fault, it is possible that the ECM is faulty. No test details are available with which the unit can be tested.

Removal

2 Remove the rider's seat (see Chapter 8). Make sure the ignition is OFF.
3 Release the strap holding the ECM **(see illustration)**. Lift it off its holder, then disconnect the wiring connectors and remove it.

Installation

4 Installation is the reverse of removal. Make sure the wiring connectors are correctly and securely connected.

Notes

# Chapter 6
Frame, suspension and final drive

Contents

Drive chain removal and installation 17
Drive chain and sprocket check, adjustment and
  lubrication .... see Chapter 1
Footrests, brake pedal and gearchange lever 3
Fork disassembly, inspection and reassembly 8
Fork oil change 7
Fork removal and installation 6
Frame 2
General information 1
Handlebars and levers 5
Handlebar switch check .... see Chapter 9
Handlebar switch removal and installation .... see Chapter 9
Rear sprocket coupling/rubber damper 19
Rear suspension linkage 12
Rear shock absorber 13
Sidestand and centrestand check and lubrication ..... see Chapter 1
Sidestand and centrestand removal and installation 4
Sidestand switch .... see Chapter 9
Sprocket cover and sprockets 18
Steering damper 11
Steering head bearing freeplay check and adjustment .. see Chapter 1
Steering head bearing inspection 10
Steering head bearing lubrication .... see Chapter 1
Steering stem and head bearings 9
Suspension adjustment 14
Suspension check .... see Chapter 1
Swingarm inspection, bearing check and renewal 16
Swingarm removal and installation 15
Swingarm and suspension linkage bearing lubrication .. see Chapter 1

Degrees of difficulty

Easy, suitable for novice with little experience	Fairly easy, suitable for beginner with some experience	Fairly difficult, suitable for competent DIY mechanic	Difficult, suitable for experienced DIY mechanic	Very difficult, suitable for expert DIY or professional

Specifications

Front forks

Fork oil type	Suzuki L01 fork oil
Fork oil capacity	480 cc
Fork oil level*	98 mm
Fork spring free length	
Standard	245.1 mm
Service limit (min)	240 mm
Fork inner tube runout limit	0.2 mm

*Oil level is measured from the top of the tube with the fork spring removed and the leg fully compressed.

Rear suspension

Swingarm pivot bolt runout (max)	0.3 mm
Spring unit – spring set length	183 mm

Final drive

Drive chain slack and lubricant	see Chapter 1
Drive chain stretch limit	see Chapter 1
Drive chain	
Type	RK GB50GSVZ3
Length	112 links
Distance between outside of joining link and side plate (unriveted)	21.85 to 22.15 mm (RK chain)
Joining link riveted ends diameter	5.45 to 5.85 mm (RK chain)
Sprocket sizes	
Front (engine) sprocket	17T
Rear (wheel) sprocket	40T

6•2 Frame, suspension and final drive

Torque settings

Axle nut clamp bolts	23 Nm
Brake hose banjo bolt	23 Nm
Brake torque arm nuts	
Front (swingarm) mount	28 Nm
Rear (caliper bracket) mount	35 Nm
Centrestand pivot bolt	73 Nm
Footrest bracket bolts	26 Nm
Fork clamp bolts – upper and lower	23 Nm
Fork damper rod bolt	40 Nm
Fork top bolt-to-damper rod locknut	29 Nm
Fork top bolt-to-fork tube	23 Nm
Front brake/clutch master cylinder clamp bolts	10 Nm
Front sprocket nut	145 Nm
Handlebar bridge bolts	35 Nm
Handlebar holder bolts	10 Nm
Rear shock absorber mounting bolt nuts	50 Nm
Rear sprocket nuts	60 Nm
Rear suspension linkage	
Linkage arm-to-frame bolt nut	78 Nm
Linkage rod-to-linkage arm bolt nut	78 Nm
Linkage rod-to-swingarm bolt nut	78 Nm
Rear shock absorber-to-linkage arm bolt nut	50 Nm
Sidestand bracket-to-frame bolts	95 Nm
Speed sensor bolt	4.5 Nm
Speed sensor rotor bolt	18 Nm
Steering damper mounting bolt and nut	23 Nm
Steering head bearing adjuster nut preload	45 Nm
Steering head bearing locknut	80 Nm
Steering stem nut	90 Nm
Swingarm pivot bolt	15 Nm
Swingarm pivot bolt nut	100 Nm
Swingarm pivot bolt locknut	90 Nm

1 General information

All models have an aluminium frame with the engine acting as a stressed member.

Front suspension is by a pair of oil-damped upside-down telescopic forks that are adjustable for spring pre-load and both rebound and compression damping.

At the rear, a box-section aluminium swingarm acts on a single shock absorber via a three-way linkage. The shock absorber is adjustable for spring pre-load and both rebound and compression damping.

Drive to the rear wheel is by chain and sprockets.

2 Frame

1 The frame should not require attention unless accident damage has occurred. In most cases, frame renewal is the only satisfactory remedy for such damage. A few frame specialists have the jigs and other equipment necessary for straightening the frame to the required standard of accuracy, but even then there is no simple way of assessing to what extent the frame may have been over stressed.

2 After the machine has accumulated a lot of miles the frame should be examined closely for signs of cracking or splitting at the welded joints. Loose engine mount bolts can cause ovaling or fracturing of the mounting tabs. Minor damage can often be repaired by welding, depending on the extent and nature of the damage.

3 Remember that a frame which is out of alignment will cause handling problems. If misalignment is suspected as the result of an accident, it will be necessary to strip the machine completely so the frame can be thoroughly checked.

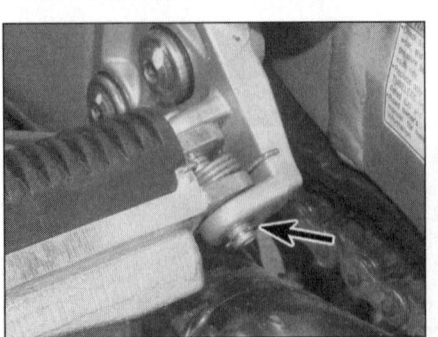

3 Footrests, brake pedal and gearchange lever

Footrests

1 To remove the rider's footrests, remove the E-clip from the bottom of the pivot pin, then withdraw the pin and remove the footrest, noting how the return spring ends locate (see illustration).

2 To remove the passenger's footrests, remove the E-clip from the bottom of the pivot pin, then withdraw the pin and remove the footrest, noting how the detent plate, ball and spring are fitted (see illustration). Take care not to let the spring and ball ping out.

3 The front footrest rubbers can be replaced

3.1 Remove the E-clip (arrowed) and withdraw the pivot pin

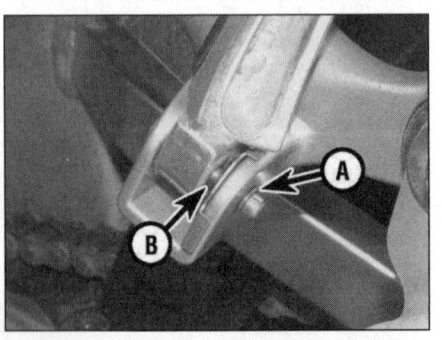

3.2 Remove the E-clip (A) and withdraw the pivot pin. Take care not to lose the ball (B) and spring

Frame, suspension and final drive 6•3

3.3 Footrest rubber screws (arrowed)

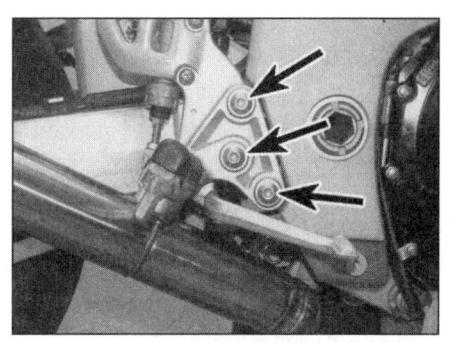

3.5 Footrest bracket bolts (arrowed)

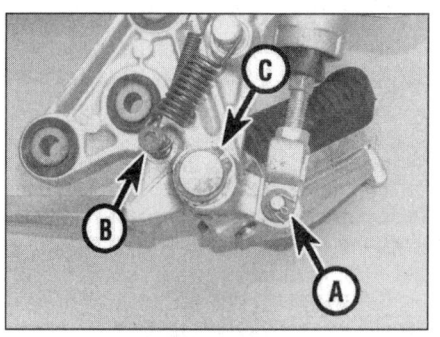

3.6 Remove the split pin (A) and withdraw the pivot pin. Unhook the spring ends (B). Brake pedal circlip (C)

3.10 Slacken the locknuts (arrowed) then unscrew the linkage rod

3.11 Remove the circlip (arrowed) to release the lever

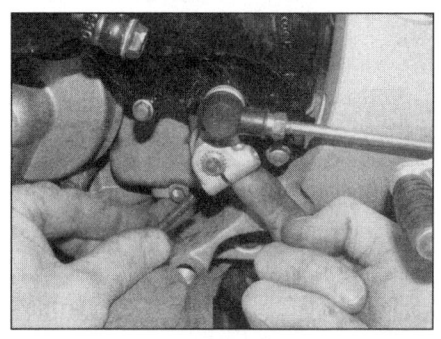

3.12 Unscrew the bolt and slide the arm off the shaft

with new ones by undoing the screws on the underside – note their different lengths, and the plate that fits between the screws and the footrest **(see illustration)**.
4 Installation is the reverse of removal. Apply some grease to the pivot pin and to the mating surfaces of the footrest and its bracket, and on the rear footrests to the detent plate and ball.

Brake pedal

Removal

5 Unscrew the footrest bracket bolts and displace the assembly from the frame **(see illustration)**.
6 Remove the split pin and washer from the clevis pin securing the brake pedal to the master cylinder pushrod **(see illustration)**. Withdraw the clevis pin and separate the pushrod from the pedal.
7 Unhook the brake pedal return spring and the brake light switch spring from the peg on the pedal, noting which fits where.
8 Release the circlip securing the pedal on its pivot on the inside of the bracket, then slide the pedal off, noting the washer.

Installation

9 Installation is the reverse of removal, noting the following:
● Apply grease to the pivot.
● Tighten the footrest bracket bolts to the specified torque setting.
● Use a new split pin on the clevis pin

securing the brake pedal to the master cylinder pushrod.
● Check the operation of the rear brake light switch (see Chapter 1).

Gearchange lever

Removal

10 Slacken the gearchange lever linkage rod locknuts, then unscrew the rod and separate it from the lever and the arm (the rod is reverse-threaded on one end and so will simultaneously unscrew from both lever and arm when turned in the one direction) **(see illustration)**. Note how far the rod is threaded into the lever and arm as this determines the height of the lever relative to the footrest.
11 Release the circlip securing the lever on its pivot, then remove the washer and slide the lever off **(see illustration)**.
12 To remove the linkage arm, make an alignment mark between the gearchange shaft end and the slit in the arm clamp, then unscrew the pinch bolt and slide the arm off the shaft **(see illustration)**.

Installation

13 Installation is the reverse of removal, noting the following:
● If the linkage arm was removed, align the slit in the clamp with the mark made on the end of the shaft.
● Apply grease to the gear lever pivot.
● Adjust the gear lever height by screwing the linkage rod in or out of the lever and arm, so

that the top of the lever end is 50 to 60 mm below the height of the top of the footrest as shown, or set it as required if preferred. Tighten the locknuts securely.

4 Sidestand and centrestand

Removal

1 The sidestand is attached to a bracket on the frame. Two springs ensure the stand is held in the retracted or extended position.
2 Support the bike on its centrestand (if fitted) or on an auxiliary stand. Unhook the stand springs **(see illustration)**.

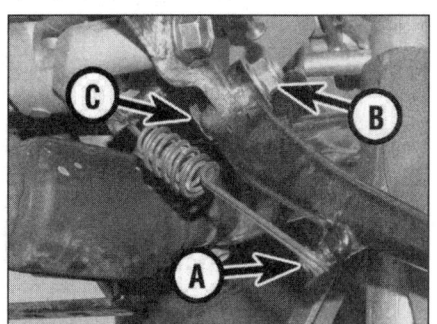

4.2 Unhook the springs (A), then unscrew the nut (B) followed by the pivot bolt (C)

6

6•4 Frame, suspension and final drive

3 Unscrew the nut from the pivot bolt, then unscrew the bolt and remove the stand.

4 A centrestand is available as an optional extra – it is secured to the frame by a pivot bolt. Support the bike on its sidestand. Unhook the stand springs, then remove the pivot bolt and the stand.

Installation

5 Apply grease to the pivot bolt shank and to the mating surfaces of the stand and its bracket. Install the bolt and tighten it, then fit the nut onto the bolt and tighten it.

6 Reconnect the springs and check that they hold the stand securely up when not in use – an accident is almost certain to occur if the stand extends while the machine is in motion.

5 Handlebars and levers

Handlebars

1 Remove the fairing side panels and/or the fairing (see Chapter 8) – although it is not essential, doing so improves access and negates the possibility of scratching anything should a tool slip.

Right handlebar removal

2 Free the throttle cable ends from the throttle pulley (see Chapter 4), creating slack in the cable as necessary using the adjusters (see Chapter 1) – this procedure incorporates detaching the handlebar switch housing.

3 Displace the front brake master cylinder (see Chapter 7). Keep it upright to prevent possible fluid leakage – wrap it in some rag just in case.

4 Unscrew the handlebar end-weight retaining screw, then remove the weight from the end of the handlebar. Slide the twistgrip off the handlebar.

5 Carefully remove the blanking cap from each handlebar holder bolt **(see illustration)**. Slacken the bolts then draw the handlebar out.

Left handlebar removal

6 Refer to Chapter 4 and detach the fast idle cable from the lever – this procedure incorporates detaching the handlebar switch housing.

7 Displace the clutch master cylinder assembly (see Chapter 2). Keep the master cylinder reservoir upright to prevent possible fluid leakage – wrap it in some rag just in case.

8 Unscrew the handlebar end-weight retaining screw, then remove the weight from the end of the handlebar and slide off the grip. If the grip has been glued on, you will probably have to slit it with a knife to remove it.

9 Carefully remove the blanking cap from each handlebar holder bolt **(see illustration 5.5)**. Slacken the bolts then draw the handlebar out.

Handlebar bridge removal

10 Either remove the handlebars or detach the assemblies from them, leaving the bars in the bridge (see above). Note that the whole handlebar assembly can be displaced from the top yoke without removing or disconnecting anything, for example for removal of the top yoke or ignition switch where the forks will not be removed (if the forks are in place the complete handlebar and top yoke assembly cannot be displaced as one because there is not enough flex in the clutch hose to lift the assembly up off the forks, though simply displacing the clutch master cylinder makes it possible). If you displace the assembly, it is best to remove the instrument cluster (see Chapter 9), as there is then more room to lay the assembly down, and negates the possibility of scratching or damaging the instruments.

11 Carefully remove the blanking cap from each handlebar bridge bolt **(see illustration)**. Counter-hold the bolts and unscrew the nuts on the underside of the top yoke, noting the washers **(see illustration)**. Withdraw the bolts and remove the bridge **(see illustration)**.

12 Note the damper and spacer arrangement in the top yoke and remove the components if required for safekeeping **(see illustration)**. Replace the dampers with new ones if they are damaged, deformed or deteriorated. Also note the spacer ring on the top of each fork and remove them if required **(see illustration)**.

Installation

13 Installation is the reverse of removal, noting the following.

● Make sure the handlebar bridge dampers and spacers are installed in the top yoke, and the spacer rings are located on the top of the forks **(see illustrations 5.12a and b)**.

5.5 Handlebar holder bolts (arrowed)

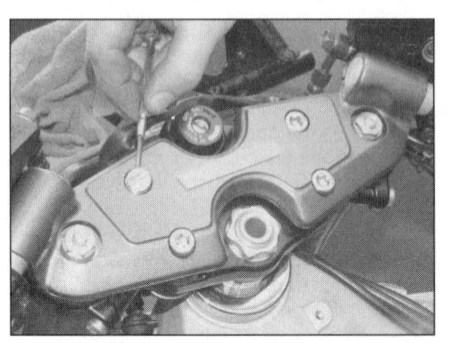

5.11a Remove the blanking caps . . .

5.11b . . . then unscrew the nuts and withdraw the bolts . . .

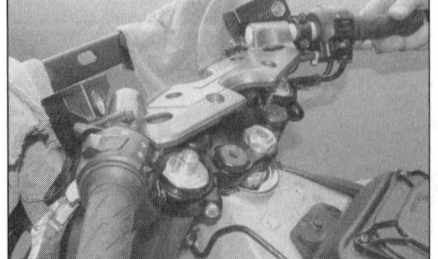

5.11c . . . and lift the bridge off the top yoke

5.12a Remove the dampers and spacers . . .

5.12b . . . and the spacer rings for the forks from the yoke if required

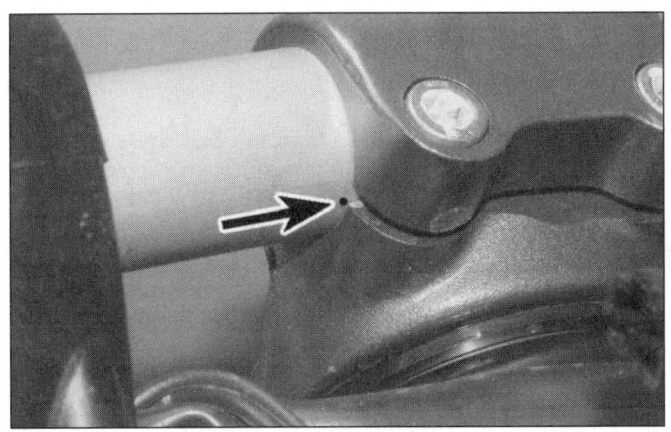

Frame, suspension and final drive 6•5

5.13 Where applicable align the punch mark (arrowed) on the bar with the slit in the holder

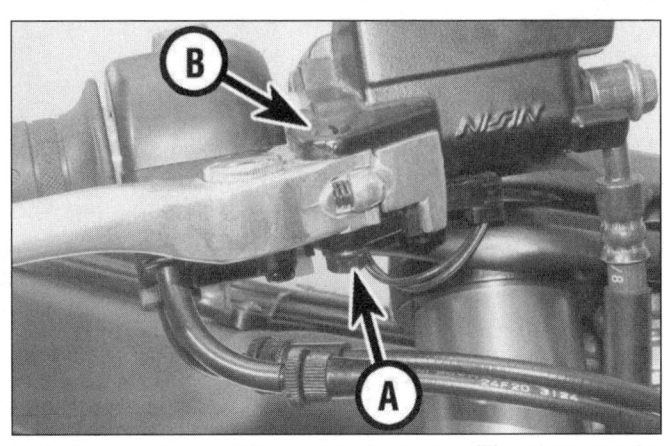

5.14 Unscrew the nut (A), then the pivot screw (B) and remove the lever

- Counter-hold the fork bridge nuts and tighten the bolts to the torque setting specified at the beginning of the Chapter. Ideally the bolts should be held while the nuts are tightened, but there is not enough room to get a torque wrench on the nuts.
- Align the bolt cut-out in each handlebar with the bolt hole in the holder, or the punch mark on each handlebar with the slit in the holder, according to model (see illustration). Tighten the handlebar holder bolts to the torque setting specified at the beginning of the Chapter. Fit the blanking caps.
- Apply some grease to the throttle twistgrip section of the right handlebar.
- Refer to Chapters 2, 4 and 7 for the installation of the master cylinders and cables/switch housings.
- Adjust the throttle and fast idle cable freeplay (see Chapter 1).

Handlebar levers

14 Unscrew the nut on the underside of the lever bracket (see illustration). Unscrew the pivot bolt and remove the lever. Note the bush for the master cylinder pushrod end in the clutch lever and take care not to lose it.

15 Installation of the levers is the reverse of removal. Apply grease to the pivot bolt shafts and the contact areas between the lever and its bracket. Apply silicone grease to the tip of the brake master cylinder pushrod, and to the bush for the clutch master cylinder pushrod end in the clutch lever.

6 Fork removal and installation

Removal

Caution: Although not strictly necessary, before removing the forks it is recommended that the fairing and fairing panels are removed (see Chapter 8). This will prevent accidental damage to the paintwork.

1 Remove the fairing side panels (see Chapter 8). Also remove the fairing if required to prevent the possibility of damage should a tool slip.

2 Remove the front wheel (see Chapter 7).

3 Remove the front mudguard (see Chapter 8). Tie the front brake calipers and hoses back so that they are out of the way.

4 For best access to the fork clamp bolts in the bottom yoke, remove the air ducts – each is secured by a single bolt (see illustration). Before removing the left-hand duct displace the cooling fan relay, then unscrew the bolts securing the relay/fusebox bracket and displace it (see illustrations). Also release the cable tie holding the wiring loom.

5 Working on one fork at a time, slacken the fork clamp bolt in the top yoke (see illustration).

6.4a On the right-hand side unscrew the bolt and remove the air duct

6.4b On the left, displace the relay and release the cable tie (arrowed) . . .

6.4c . . . then unscrew the bolts and displace the bracket . . .

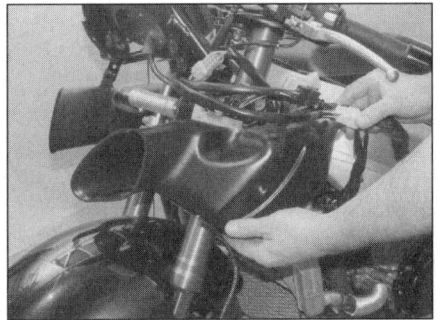

6.4d . . . before removing the air duct

6.5 Slacken the clamp bolt (arrowed) in the top yoke . . .

6•6 Frame, suspension and final drive

6.6a ... then the clamp bolts (arrowed) in the bottom yoke

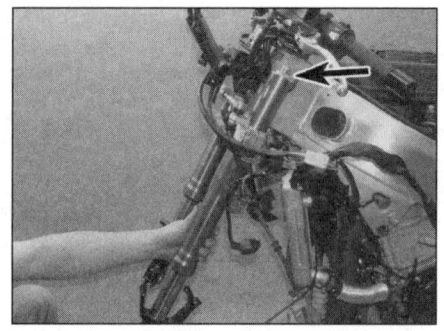

6.6b ... and remove the fork – slacken the top bolt (arrowed) with the fork in this position and held in the bottom yoke if required

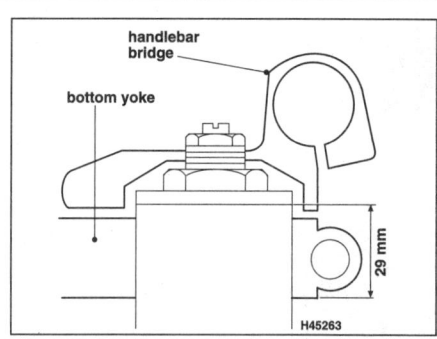

6.8 Make an alignment mark as shown

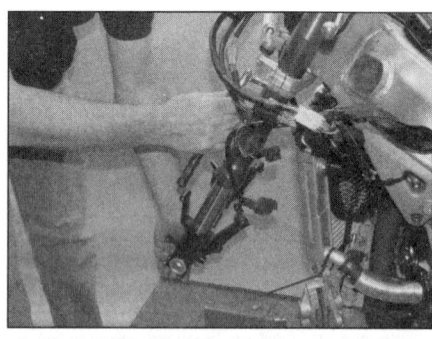

If the fork is to be disassembled, or if the fork oil is being changed, note the spring pre-load and rebound damping settings, then set them to their minimum amounts (see Section 14).

6 Slacken the fork clamp bolts in the bottom yoke, and remove each fork by twisting it and pulling it downwards – if the fork is to be disassembled, or if the fork oil is being changed, when the fork top bolt is clear of the top yoke but before you draw it down through the bottom yoke, tighten the bottom yoke clamp bolts again then slacken the fork top bolt **(see illustrations)**.

> **HAYNES HiNT** *If the fork legs are seized in the yokes, spray the area with penetrating oil and allow time for it to soak in before trying again. If necessary lever the clamp open by using a large flat-bladed screwdriver, taking care not to scratch anything.*

Installation

7 Remove all traces of corrosion from the fork tube and the yokes.
8 Before installing the fork, make an alignment mark 29 mm down from the top of the fork outer tube (not the top of the top bolt) as shown **(see illustration)**.

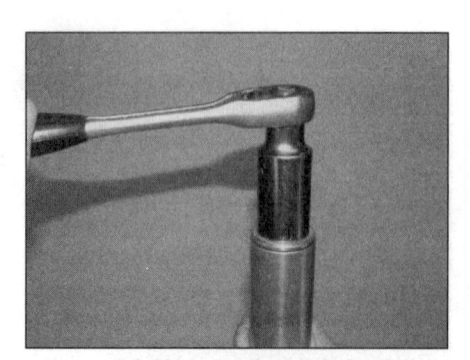

9 Slide the fork up through the bottom yoke – if the fork has been dismantled or if the fork oil was changed, before the fork reaches the top yoke, temporarily tighten the fork clamp bolts in the bottom yoke to hold the fork, then tighten the fork top bolt to the specified torque setting, then release the clamp bolts again **(see illustration 6.6b)**. Slide the fork into the top yoke, making sure all cables, hoses and wiring are routed on the correct side of the fork, and align the mark made earlier with the underside of the top yoke **(see illustration 6.8)**.
10 Keeping the fork held in position, tighten the clamp bolts in the bottom yoke to the torque setting specified at the beginning of the Chapter **(see illustration)**. Now tighten the clamp bolt in the top yoke to the specified torque **(see illustration 6.5)**.
11 Install the air ducts, making sure they locate correctly **(see illustration 6.4a)**. On the left-hand duct fit the relay/fusebox bracket and the cooling fan relay, and secure the wiring loom with the cable tie **(see illustrations 6.4c and b)**.
12 Set the spring pre-load and damping adjustment as required (see Section 14).
13 Install the front mudguard (see Chapter 8), and the front wheel (see Chapter 7). Install the fairing panels as required (see Chapter 8).
14 Check the operation of the front forks and brakes before taking the machine out on the road.

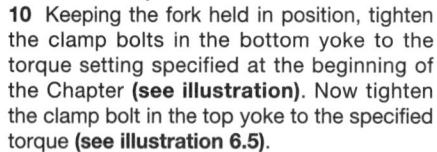

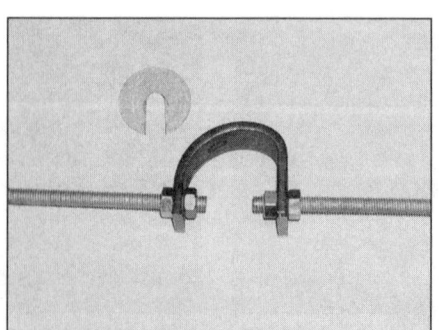

6.10 Hold the fork in position and tighten the bottom yoke clamp bolts

7 Fork oil change

1 Remove the forks (see Section 6). Always work on the fork legs separately to avoid interchanging parts and thus causing an accelerated rate of wear.
2 If the fork top bolt was not slackened with the fork in situ, re-locate it in the bottom yoke and tighten the clamp bolts, then slacken the top bolt **(see illustration 6.6b)**.
3 Unscrew the top bolt from the top of the fork **(see illustration)**. The bolt will remain threaded on the damper cartridge rod.
4 Obtain either the Suzuki service tools (Pt. Nos. 09940-94930 and 09940-94922, a holding tool and retaining plate respectively), or construct home-made equivalents from a piece of steel strap bent into a U-shape and some threaded rod and nuts (for the holding tool) and a suitably sized washer with a slot cut into it (the retaining plate) **(see illustration)**. Either place the fork upright on the floor or carefully clamp the brake caliper lugs between the padded jaws of a vice. Slide the outer tube fully down onto the inner tube (wrap a rag around the top of the outer tube to minimise oil spillage) while, with the aid of an assistant if necessary, keeping the damper rod fully extended. Fit the holding tool onto the spacer, locating it into the holes **(see**

7.3 Unscrew the top bolt

7.4a Home-made holding tool

Frame, suspension and final drive 6•7

7.4b Locate the holding tool into the holes in the spacer...

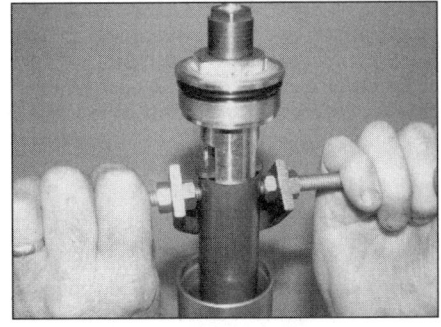

7.4c ...then grasp the handles of the tool and pull the spacer down to compress the spring...

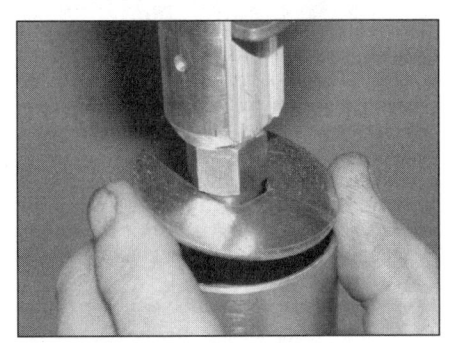

7.4d ...and locate the retaining plate between the spacer and the nut

illustration). Push down on the spacer using the tool and have an assistant insert the retaining plate between the top of the spacer and the base of the locknut on the damper cartridge **(see illustrations)**. This will keep the spacer and spring compressed while removing the top bolt assembly.

5 Using two spanners, one on the locknut and one on the fork top bolt, counter-hold the locknut and thread the top bolt assembly off the damper rod **(see illustration)**.

6 Push down on the spacer using the holding tool and have an assistant remove the retaining plate **(see illustration 7.4c and d)**, then slowly release the spring pressure. Remove the spacer (you can leave the holding tool attached) **(see illustration)**. Using a piece of wire bent over at the end, remove the spring from the tube, noting which way up fits **(see illustration)**. Withdraw the adjuster rod from inside the damper rod – if the damper rod has sunk into the cartridge, draw it out using a pair of thin-nosed pliers **(see illustration)**.

7 Invert the fork over a suitable container and pump the tubes and damper rod vigorously to expel as much oil as possible, but take care not to over-extend the tubes as they will slide apart and the seal could be damaged **(see illustration)**. Support the fork upside down in the container for a while to allow as much oil as possible to drain, and pump the fork and damper rod again.

8 Slowly pour in the specified quantity of the specified grade of fork oil and pump the damper rod at least ten times to distribute it evenly **(see illustration)**. To allow the full stroke of the rod to be used attach a suitable internally threaded rod to the top of the damper rod (a special tool, Pt. No. 09940-50120 is available from Suzuki), or use a pair of long-nosed pliers. Also pump the fork tubes. Allow the fork to stand upright for at least five minutes, then pump the damper rod and tubes some more and watch for any air bubbles in the oil. Do this until no bubbles can be seen – it is important that all air is expelled from the damper cartridge. Slide the outer tube fully down onto the inner tube. Measure the oil level, and make any adjustment by adding more or tipping some out until the oil is

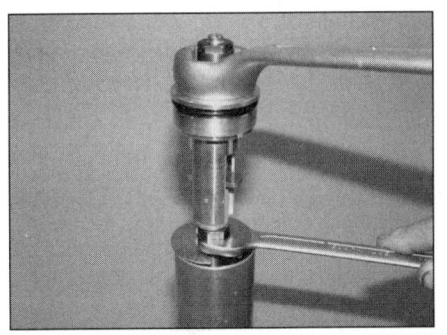

7.5 Counter-hold the locknut and unscrew the top bolt

7.6a Remove the spacer...

7.6b ...the spring...

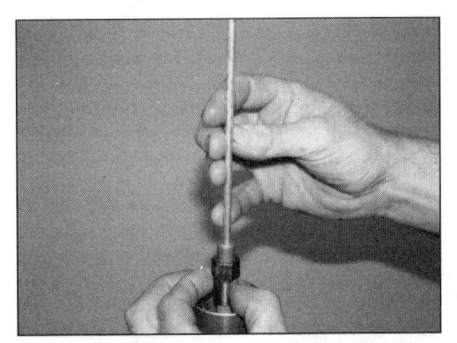

7.6c ...and the damping adjuster rod

7.7 Invert the fork over a container and pump the fork as described to expel the oil

7.8a Pour the oil into the top of the tube

6•8 Frame, suspension and final drive

at the level specified at the beginning of the Chapter (see illustration). Do not rely on the quantity of oil put in as an accurate gauge as it is impossible to tell how much old oil was left in the forks after draining – always measure the oil level as well.

9 Measure the amount of exposed thread above the locknut on the top of the damper rod and adjust it by turning the locknut as required (see illustration) – there should be 11 mm of thread exposed.

10 Fit the adjuster rod into the damper rod (see illustration 7.6c). Install the spring with its tapered end upwards (see illustration 7.6b). Withdraw the damper rod fully from the fork, using a pair of thin-nosed pliers to grab it if necessary. As the damper rod will have to be kept extended out of the cartridge, tie a piece of wire around the threads on the top of the rod to use as a holder. Install the spacer, sliding it over the wire, and making sure the lip on the bottom fits into the top of the spring (see illustration). If the holding tool used on disassembly was removed from the spacer, fit it back on (see illustration). Keeping the damper rod fully extended (an assistant is useful) push down on the spacer using the holding tool and insert the retaining plate between the top of the spacer and the base of the locknut (see illustration). This will keep the spacer and spring compressed while installing the top bolt assembly. You can now remove the piece of wire.

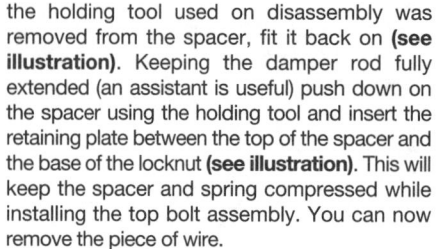

11 If required fit a new O-ring onto the top bolt. Thread the top bolt onto the damper rod until it seats against the locknut, holding the rod to prevent it from turning. Counter-hold the locknut and tighten the top bolt against it, to the specified torque setting (see illustration 7.5).

12 Push down on the spacer using the holding tool and have an assistant remove the retaining plate, then slowly release the spring pressure and allow the spacer to settle against the pre-load adjuster arms (see illustrations 7.4d and c). Remove the holding tool from the spacer.

13 Apply a smear of the specified clean oil to the top bolt O-ring. Fully extend the outer tube and carefully screw the top bolt into the tube making sure it is not cross-threaded (see illustration). Note: *The top bolt can be tightened to the specified torque setting at this stage if the tube is held between the padded jaws of a vice, but do not risk distorting the tube by doing so. A better method is to tighten the top bolt when the fork leg has been installed and is securely held in the bottom yoke.*

> **TOOL TIP** *Use a ratchet-type tool when installing the fork top bolt. This makes it unnecessary to remove the tool from the bolt whilst threading it in.*

14 Install the forks (see Section 6).

8 Fork disassembly, inspection and reassembly

Disassembly

1 Remove the forks (see Section 6). Always dismantle the fork legs separately to avoid interchanging parts and thus causing an accelerated rate of wear. Store all components in separate, clearly marked containers (see illustrations).

2 Before dismantling the fork, slacken the damper cartridge bolt now as there is less chance of the cartridge rotating with it (due to the pressure of the spring). When working on the left-hand fork, first slacken the axle nut clamp bolts and remove the nut (see illustration). Compress the fork so that the spring exerts maximum pressure on the damper cartridge, then have an assistant slacken the bolt in the base of the fork (see illustration). If the bolt does not unscrew, but merely rotates the damper cartridge inside the fork, use an air-wrench, or hold the damper cartridge as described in Step 4.

3 Refer to Section 7, Steps 2 to 7, and drain the oil from the fork.

4 Remove the previously slackened damper cartridge bolt and its copper sealing washer (see illustration 8.2b). Discard the sealing washer as a new one must be used on reassembly. Invert the fork and tip the damper cartridge out of the top (see illustration). Note: *If the damper cartridge bolt couldn't be successfully slackened earlier, the head of the cartridge can be held by passing a holding tool down through the top of the fork – Suzuki produce a service tool (Pt. No. 09940-30221) for this purpose.*

5 Draw the outer tube fully off the inner tube (see illustration).

6 Carefully prise out the dust seal from the bottom of the outer tube to gain access to the oil seal retaining clip (see illustration). Remove the retaining clip (see illustration).

7.8b Measure the oil level and adjust if necessary

7.9 Measure the amount of exposed thread and set it as specified

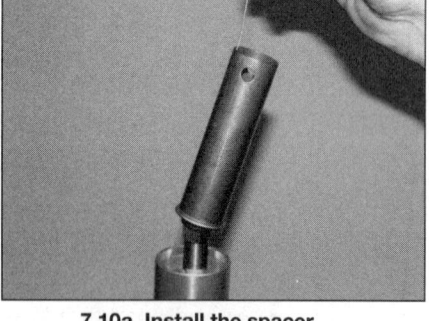

7.10a Install the spacer . . .

7.10b . . . then fit the tool if it was removed . . .

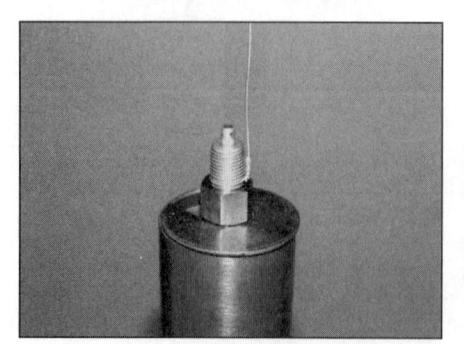

7.10c . . . then compress the spring and fit the retaining plate as shown

7.13 Smear the O-ring with oil then thread the top bolt into the fork tube

Frame, suspension and final drive 6•9

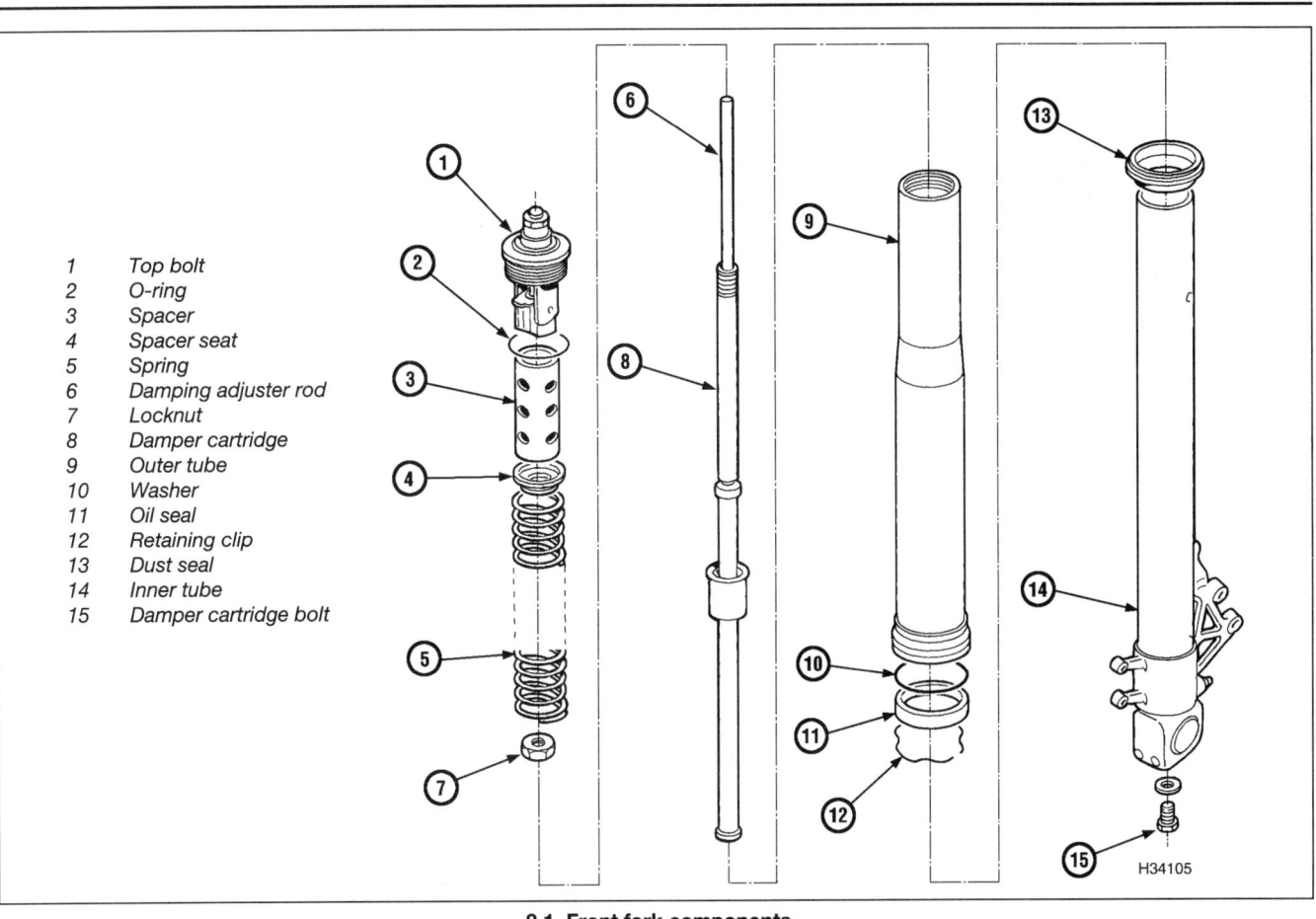

1 Top bolt
2 O-ring
3 Spacer
4 Spacer seat
5 Spring
6 Damping adjuster rod
7 Locknut
8 Damper cartridge
9 Outer tube
10 Washer
11 Oil seal
12 Retaining clip
13 Dust seal
14 Inner tube
15 Damper cartridge bolt

8.1 Front fork components

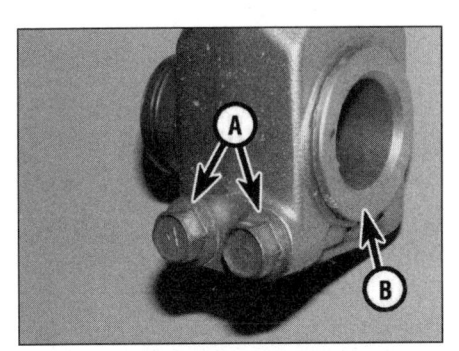

8.2a Slacken the clamp bolts (A) and remove the axle nut (B)

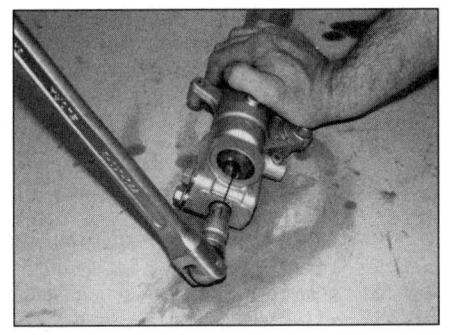

8.2b Slacken the damper cartridge bolt

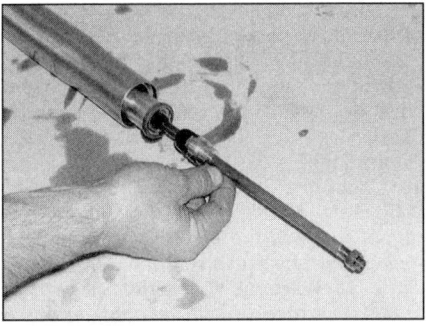

8.4 Withdraw the damper cartridge from the fork

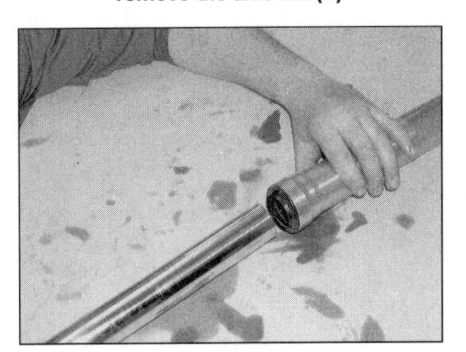

8.5 Draw the inner tube out of the outer tube

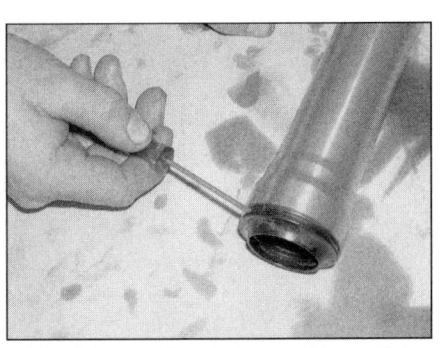

8.6a Prise out the dust seal using a flat-bladed screwdriver . . .

8.6b . . . then remove the retaining clip

6•10 Frame, suspension and final drive

8.7a Prise out the oil seal ...

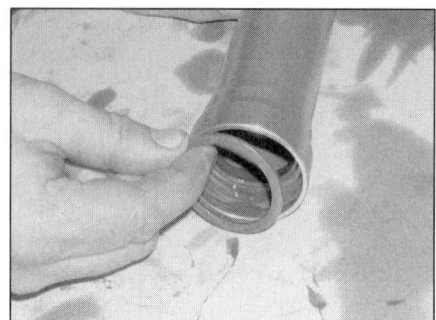

8.7b ... and remove the washer

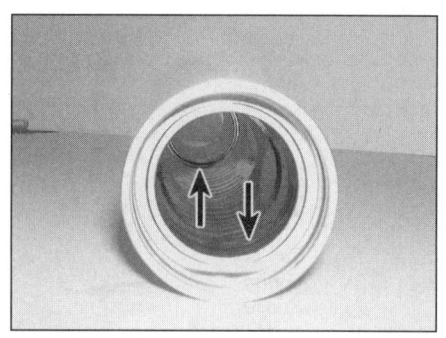

8.9 Check the bushes (arrowed) for wear

7 Carefully prise out the oil seal using a seal hook, then remove the oil seal washer **(see illustrations)**. Take care not to damage the rim of the tube, especially if a hook is not available and a screwdriver is being used. Discard the oil seal and dust seal as new ones must be used.

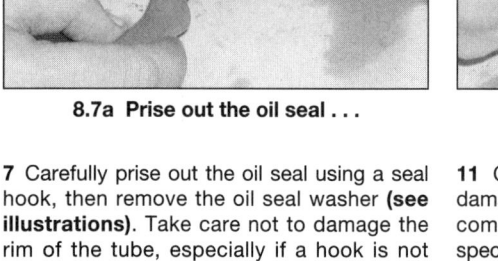

Inspection

8 Clean all parts in solvent and blow them dry with compressed air, if available. Check the outer surface of the inner tube and the inner surface of the outer tube for score marks, dents, scratches, pitting or flaking of the finish, and excessive or abnormal wear. Check the fork seal seat in the outer tube for nicks, gouges and scratches. If damage is evident, leaks will occur. Also check the oil seal washer for damage or distortion and renew it if necessary.

9 Examine the working surfaces of the two bushes in the outer tube; if worn or scuffed the tube must be replaced with a new one (the bushes are not available separately) – they are worn if the grey Teflon coating on the sliding surface has rubbed off to reveal the copper surface (in which case you may find traces of copper in the drained fork oil) **(see illustration)**.

10 Check the inner tube for runout using V-blocks and a dial gauge. If the amount of runout exceeds the service limit specified, replace the tube with a new one.

⚠ *Warning: If the tube is bent or exceeds the runout limit, it should not be straightened; renew it.*

11 Check the spring for cracks and other damage. Measure the spring free length and compare the measurement to the specifications at the beginning of the Chapter **(see illustration)**. If it is defective or sagged below the service limit, replace the springs in both forks with new ones – never replace only one spring.

12 Check the damper cartridge for damage and wear. Holding the damper cartridge over your oil tray, pump the rod in and out. If the rod does not move smoothly in the cartridge the damper must be replaced with a new one.

Reassembly

13 Apply some new fork oil to the bushes in the outer tube. Apply a smear of grease to the inner lips of the new oil seal.

14 Fit the oil seal washer into the outer tube **(see illustration 8.7b)**. Press the new oil seal, with its marked side facing out, into the outer tube. Using a suitable socket drive the seal in until the retaining clip groove is visible – make sure the socket locates on the outer rim of the seal but does not contact the wall of the tube.

15 Once the oil seal is correctly seated, fit the retaining clip, making sure it is correctly located in its groove **(see illustration 8.6b)**. Apply a smear of grease to the inner lips of the new dust seal, then press the seal into place.

16 Carefully slide the outer tube onto the inner tube, making sure they remain parallel and that the inner tube rim does not catch the lips of the seals, twisting the inner tube slightly to ease its entry will help **(see illustration 8.5)**.

17 Lay the fork flat and push the inner tube fully into the outer tube. Insert the damper cartridge in the top of the fork until it seats on the bottom of the inner tube **(see illustration 8.4)**. Fit a new sealing washer onto the damper cartridge bolt and apply a few drops of a suitable non-permanent thread locking compound, then install the bolt into the bottom of the inner tube and tighten it to the torque setting specified at the beginning of the Chapter **(see illustration)**. If the damper cartridge rotates inside the tube, either wait until the fork is fully reassembled before tightening the bolt, or fit the spring and spacer, then turn the fork upside down and press it down on the spacer to compress the spring (which then holds the cartridge) as you tighten the bolt **(see illustration)**. Remove the spacer and spring after the bolt is tightened.

18 When working on the left-hand fork, fit the axle nut into the bottom of the fork, pushing the shouldered end up against the outside of the fork, and tighten the clamp bolts to the specified torque setting **(see illustration 8.2a)**.

19 Refer to Section 7, Steps 8 to 14 to add the fork oil and finish rebuilding the fork.

9 Steering stem and head bearings

Removal

1 Remove the fairing side panels and the fairing (See Chapter 8).

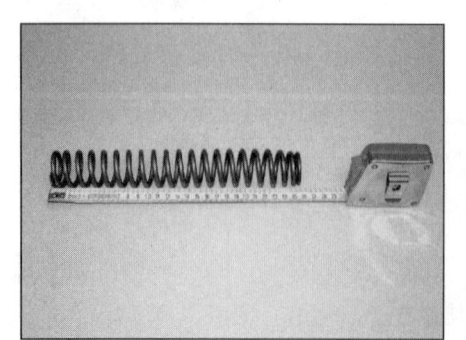

8.11 Check the spring free length

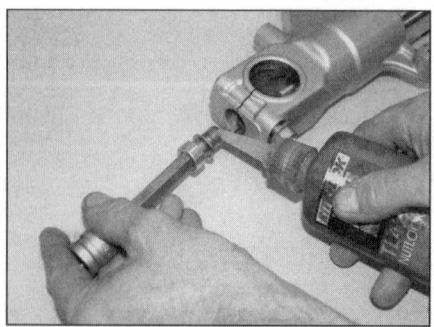

8.17a Apply threadlock to the bolt and use a new sealing washer ...

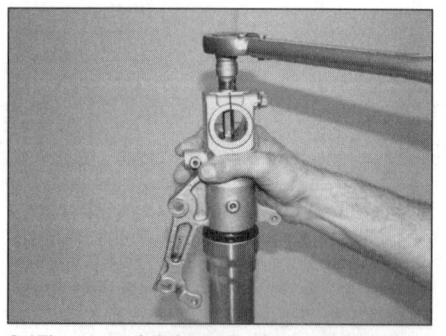

8.17b ... and tighten the bolt as described to the specified torque setting

Frame, suspension and final drive 6•11

9.5 Unscrew the bolt (arrowed) to release the brake hose

9.6 Ignition switch wiring connector (arrowed)

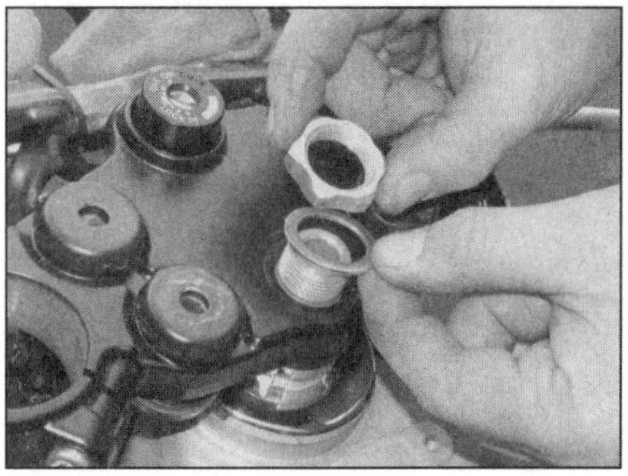

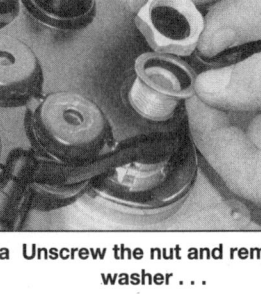

9.7a Unscrew the nut and remove the washer . . .

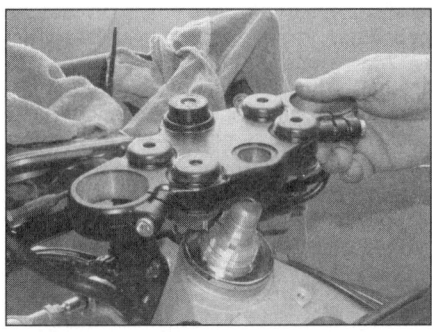

9.7b . . . then lift the yoke off the stem

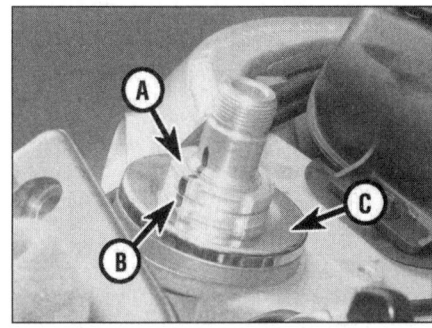

9.8 Unscrew the locknut (A) then remove the lockwasher and unscrew the adjuster nut (B). Bearing cover (C)

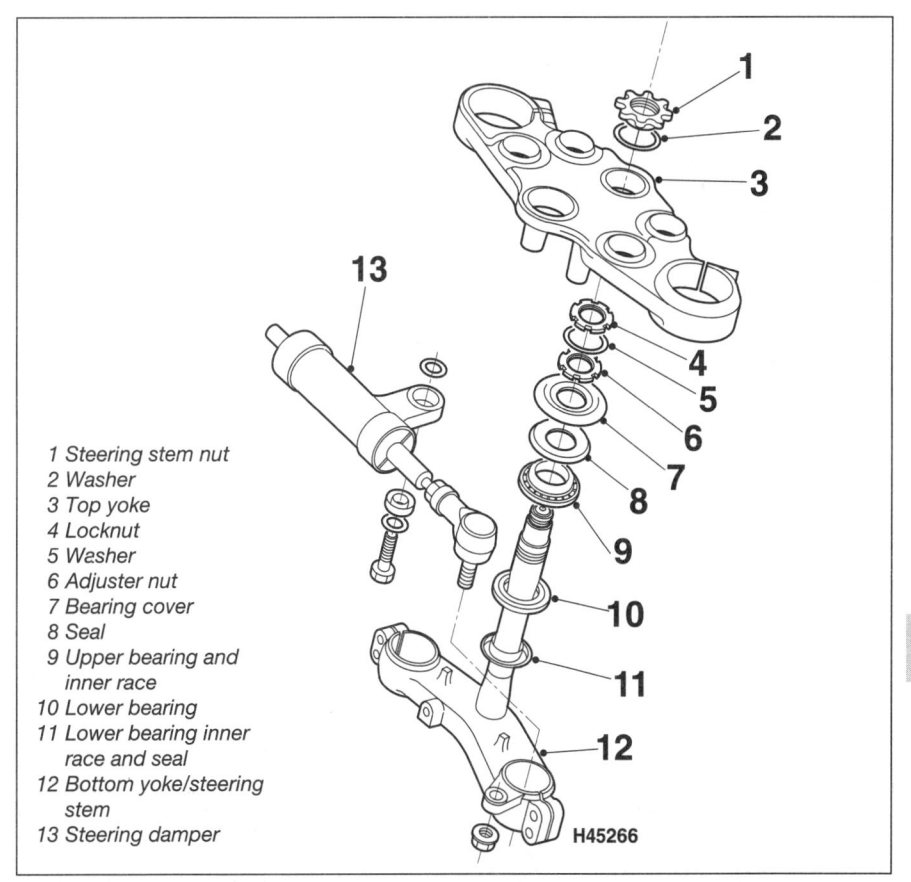

2 Remove the fuel tank (see Chapter 4) – this will prevent the possibility of damage should a tool slip.
3 Remove the front forks (see Section 6).
4 Remove the steering damper (see Section 11).
5 Unscrew the bolt securing the front brake hose holder and guide to the bottom yoke **(see illustration)**.
6 If preferred, remove the top yoke from the bike rather than laying it aside, displace the handlebars and/or bridge as required (see Section 5) – there is no need to disconnect the cables or remove the switchgear, end-weights and grips, although you will need to displace the master cylinders to get to the holder bolts (see Chapters 2 and 7). Also free the handlebar switch wiring from its guide on the top yoke (this can appear to be a bit of a Chinese puzzle at first, but once mastered is obvious), and disconnect the ignition switch wiring connector **(see illustration)**. If you prefer to leave the handlebars intact with the bridge and top yoke assembly, it is best to remove the instrument cluster (see Chapter 9), as there is then more room to lay the handlebar/bridge/yoke down, and negates the possibility of scratching or damaging the instruments.
7 Unscrew the steering stem nut using a 32 mm bi-hex socket, and remove the washer **(see illustration)**. Ease the top yoke/handlebar bridge up and off the steering stem and either remove it or position it clear, tying it to the fairing bracket and using a rag to protect other components **(see illustration)**.
8 Unscrew the steering head bearing adjuster locknut using either a C-spanner, a peg-spanner (Suzuki Pt. No. 09940-14960), or a drift located in one of the notches **(see illustration)**. Remove the washer. Support the bottom yoke, then unscrew the adjuster nut in the same way as the locknut.
9 Gently lower the bottom yoke and steering stem out of the frame **(see illustration)**.
10 Remove the bearing cover and seal, inner race and bearing from the top of the steering head. Remove the bearing from the base of the steering stem **(see illustration)**. Remove all traces of old grease from the bearings and races and check them for wear or damage as

1 Steering stem nut
2 Washer
3 Top yoke
4 Locknut
5 Wesher
6 Adjuster nut
7 Bearing cover
8 Seal
9 Upper bearing and inner race
10 Lower bearing
11 Lower bearing inner race and seal
12 Bottom yoke/steering stem
13 Steering damper

9.9 Steering stem and head bearing components

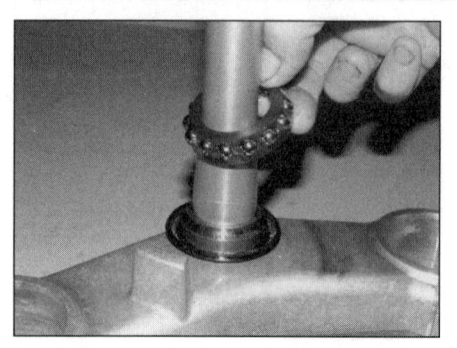

6•12 Frame, suspension and final drive

9.10 Remove the lower bearing from the steering stem

described in Section 10. **Note:** *Do not attempt to remove the outer races from the steering head or the inner race from the steering stem unless they are to be replaced with new ones.*

Installation

11 Smear a liberal quantity of multi-purpose grease onto the bearing races, and work some grease well into both the upper and lower bearings. Also smear the grease seal. Fit the lower bearing onto the steering stem **(see illustration 9.10)**.

12 Carefully lift the steering stem/bottom yoke up through the steering head **(see illustration 9.9)**. Fit the upper bearing and its inner race into the top of the steering head. Fit the grease seal and the bearing cover **(see illustration 9.8)**. Thread the adjuster nut onto the steering stem and tighten it finger-tight.

13 If the Suzuki peg spanner is available (see Step 8), tighten the adjuster nut to the preload torque setting specified at the beginning of the Chapter, then turn the steering stem through its full lock at least five times. Now slacken the adjuster nut by 1/4 to 1/2 a turn – the actual amount required will vary from bike to bike, but start with a 1/4 turn, then go to Step 16.

14 If the Suzuki tool is not available, tighten the nut fairly tight using a C-spanner or drift to pre-load the bearings, then slacken it off slightly, but not so much that freeplay can be felt.

15 Fit the washer onto the steering stem, locating the tab on its inner rim in the slot in the stem. Fit the locknut and tighten it against the adjuster nut, but not too tight at this stage **(see illustration 9.8)**. Fit the top yoke/handlebar bridge (according to removal), aligning it with the bottom yoke by temporarily inserting one of the forks, then fit the washer and the steering stem nut and tighten the nut to the torque setting specified at the beginning of the Chapter **(see illustrations 9.7b and a)**. Now install all remaining components (except the fuel tank and fairing panels) as their leverage and inertia needs to be taken into account. Now check and finely adjust the amount of freeplay as described in Chapter 1.

Caution: Take great care not to overtighten the bearings as this will cause premature failure.

16 When the bearings are correctly adjusted, tighten the fork clamp bolts in the bottom yoke to the specified torque setting, then slacken the top yoke clamp bolts, unscrew the steering stem nut and remove the top yoke/handlebar bridge again – if the handlebar assembly is fully intact you will need to displace the clutch master cylinder as there is not enough flex in the hose (see Chapter 2). Tighten the adjuster locknut to the specified torque setting if the Suzuki tool is available, or very tight if not, making sure the adjuster nut does not turn as you do. Install the top yoke/handlebar bridge and washer and tighten the steering stem nut and the fork clamp bolts in the top yoke to the torque settings specified at the beginning of the Chapter.

17 Install the remaining components in a reverse of the removal procedure.

18 Carry out a final check of the steering head bearing freeplay as described in Chapter 1, and if necessary re-adjust.

10 Steering head bearing inspection

Inspection

1 Remove the steering stem (see Section 9).
2 Remove all traces of old grease from the bearings and races and check them for wear or damage.

3 The outer races should be polished and free from indentations. Inspect the bearing balls for signs of wear, damage or discoloration, and examine the ball retainer cage for signs of cracks or splits. If there are any signs of wear on any of the above components both upper and lower bearing assemblies must be replaced with new ones as a set. Only remove the outer races in the steering head and the lower bearing inner race on the steering stem if new ones are needed – do not re-use them once they have been removed.

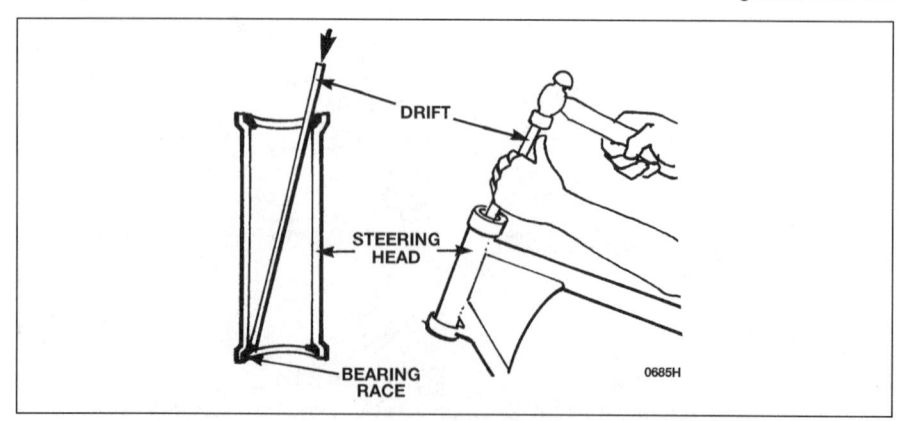

Removal and installation

4 The outer races are an interference fit in the steering head and can be tapped from position with a suitable drift **(see illustration)**. Tap firmly and evenly around each race to ensure that it is driven out squarely. It may prove advantageous to curve the end of the drift slightly to improve access.

5 Alternatively, the races can be removed using a slide-hammer type bearing extractor; these can often be hired from tool shops.

6 The new outer races can be pressed into the head using a drawbolt arrangement **(see illustration)**, or by using a large diameter tubular drift. Ensure that the drawbolt washer or drift (as applicable) bears only on the outer edge of the race and does not contact the working surface. Alternatively, have the races installed by a Suzuki dealer equipped with the bearing race installation tools.

> **HAYNES HINT** *Installation of new bearing outer races is made much easier if the races are left overnight in the freezer. This causes them to contract slightly making them a looser fit. Alternatively, use a freeze spray.*

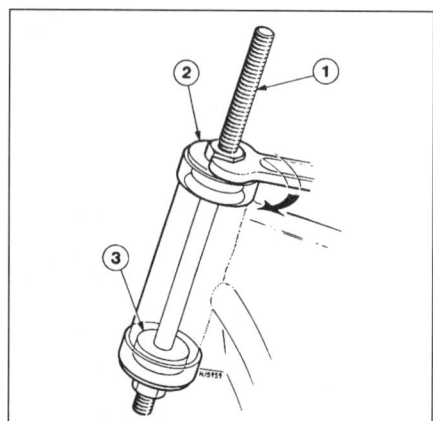

10.4 Drive the bearing races out with a brass drift locating it as shown

10.6 Drawbolt arrangement for fitting steering stem bearing races

1 Long bolt or threaded bar
2 Thick washer
3 Guide for lower race

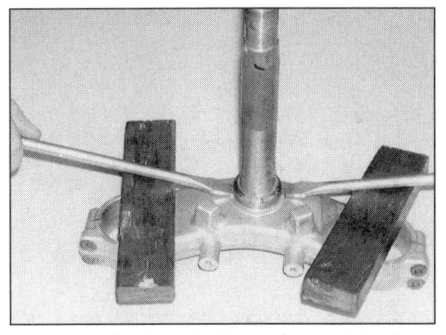

Frame, suspension and final drive 6•13

10.7a Remove the lower bearing inner race as shown . . .

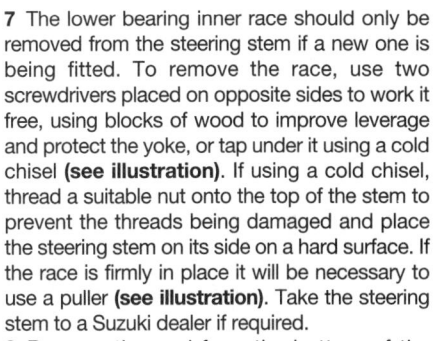

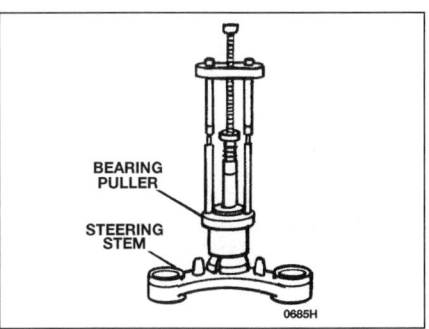

10.7b . . . or using a puller if necessary

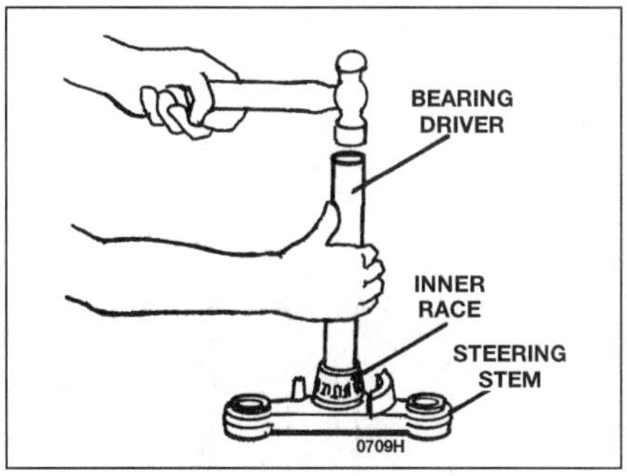

10.9 Drive the new race on using a suitable driver or a length of pipe

7 The lower bearing inner race should only be removed from the steering stem if a new one is being fitted. To remove the race, use two screwdrivers placed on opposite sides to work it free, using blocks of wood to improve leverage and protect the yoke, or tap under it using a cold chisel **(see illustration)**. If using a cold chisel, thread a suitable nut onto the top of the stem to prevent the threads being damaged and place the steering stem on its side on a hard surface. If the race is firmly in place it will be necessary to use a puller **(see illustration)**. Take the steering stem to a Suzuki dealer if required.

8 Remove the seal from the bottom of the stem and replace it with a new one. Smear the new one with grease.

9 Fit the new lower race onto the steering stem. A length of tubing with an internal diameter slightly larger than the steering stem will be needed to tap the new race into position – make sure the drift contacts the inner rim of the race only and not the bearing sliding surface **(see illustration)**.

10 Install the steering stem (see Section 9).

11 Steering damper

Removal

1 For best access and to negate the possibility of damage, remove the fairing (see Chapter 8). Alternatively release the trim clips securing the access panel to the underside of the fairing and remove the panel (see Chapter 8).

2 Counter-hold the hex on the rod end above the steering damper lug on the bottom yoke and unscrew the nut **(see illustration)**.

3 Unscrew the bolt securing the damper to the steering head and remove the damper, making sure the seals do not drop off the body mount.

Inspection

4 Inspect the damper for obvious physical damage. Check that the rod moves smoothly in and out of the body.

5 Inspect the damper rod for signs of bending, pitting and oil leakage.

6 Inspect the pivot hardware for wear or damage. Remove the seals and check the bearing in the body mount for damage and play.

7 The damper comes as a unit and no individual components are available, with the exception of the mounting hardware, seals and the bearing in the body mount. If any wear or damage is found replace the necessary component(s) with new.

Installation

8 Installation is the reverse of removal, noting the following points.
● Apply multi-purpose grease to the bearing, seals, mounting hardware and pivot points – remove the seals and washers and clean off all old grease first.
● Tighten the mounting bolt and nut to the torque setting specified at the beginning of the Chapter, counter-holding the hex on the rod end as before when tightening the nut **(see illustration 11.2)**.

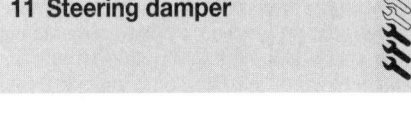

● Check the action of the steering and the damper after installation. The damper is not adjustable.

12 Rear suspension linkage

Removal

1 Remove the bottom fairing panel (see Chapter 8).

2 Support the motorcycle on its centrestand if fitted, on an auxiliary stand that does not take the weight through any part of the rear suspension, or by using a hoist – axle stands positioned under the frame bottom section on each side work well. Position a support under the rear wheel or swingarm so that it does not drop when the suspension linkage is detached from the shock absorber, but also making sure that the weight of the machine is off the rear suspension so that the shock is not compressed. Make a note of which side the bolts go in from, and make a note of which way round the linkage arm fits.

3 Unscrew the nut and withdraw the bolt securing the linkage rods to the swingarm and swing the rods down **(see illustration)**.

4 If required unscrew the nut and withdraw the bolt securing the linkage rods to the linkage arm and remove the rods.

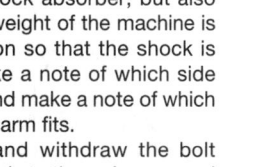

5 Unscrew the nut and withdraw the bolt securing the bottom of the shock absorber to the linkage arm, then swing the arm down **(see illustration)**.

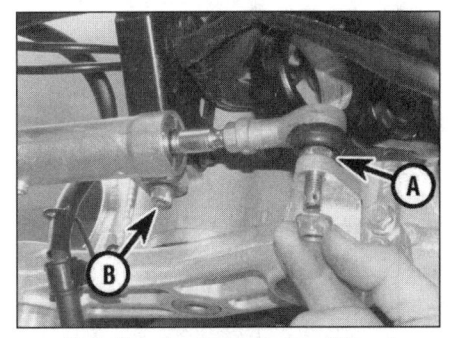

11.2 Counter-hold the hex (A) and unscrew the nut and the bolt (B)

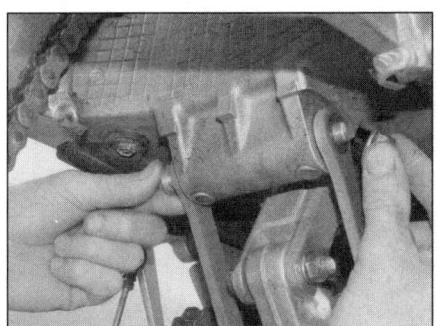

12.3 Unscrew the nut, withdraw the bolt and swing the rods down

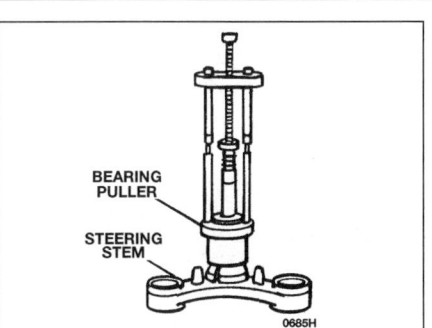

12.5 Unscrew the nut, withdraw the bolt and swing the linkage arm down

6

6•14 Frame, suspension and final drive

12.6a Unscrew the nut (arrowed) . . .

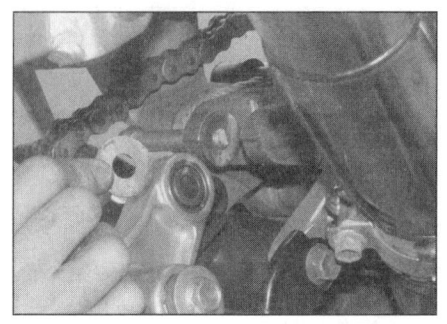

12.6b . . . then withdraw the bolt and remove the linkage arm, noting the washers

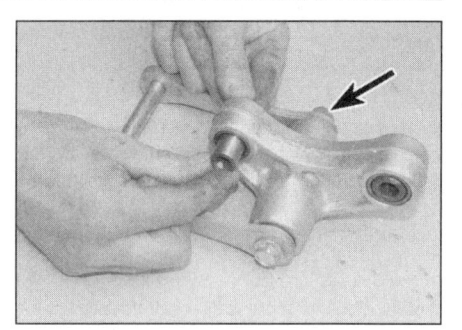

12.7a Detach the rods by unscrewing the nut (arrowed) and withdrawing the bolt, then remove the spacers and check the components as described

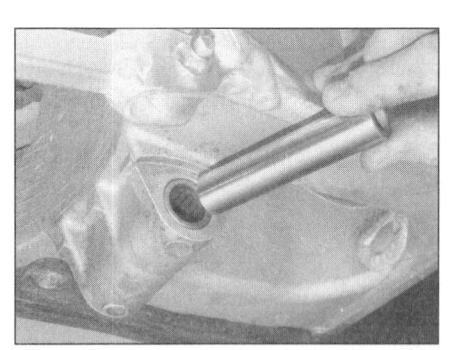

12.7b Withdraw the spacer and check the bearings in the linkage rod pivot on the swingarm as well

12.12 Do not forget to fit the washers with the linkage arm

6 Unscrew the nut and withdraw the bolt securing the linkage arm to the frame and remove the arm, noting the washers that fit between the arm and the frame **(see illustrations)**.

Inspection

7 If not already done unscrew the nut and withdraw the bolt securing the linkage rods to the linkage arm and remove the rods **(see illustration)**. Withdraw the spacers from the linkage arm and from the linkage rod pivot in the swingarm, noting the difference in sizes **(see illustration)**. Thoroughly clean all components, paying attention to the needle bearings, removing all traces of dirt, corrosion and grease.
8 Inspect all components closely, looking for obvious signs of wear such as heavy scoring, or for damage such as cracks or distortion. Slip each spacer back into its bearing and check that there is not an excessive amount of freeplay between the two components. Replace any worn or damaged components with new ones as required.
9 Check the condition of the needle roller bearings. Refer to *Tools and Workshop Tips* (Section 5) in the Reference section for information on bearings.
10 Worn bearings can be drifted out of their bores, but note that removal will destroy them; obtain new bearings before you start. Press or draw the new bearings into their bores – do not drive them in. In the absence of a press, a suitable drawbolt tool can be made up as described in *Tools and Workshop Tips* in the Reference section. Where the needle bearings have an integral seal, make sure the side with the seal is on the outside. In all cases make sure the marked side of the bearing is on the outside.
11 Lubricate the needle bearings and spacers with multi-purpose grease **(see illustrations 12.7a and b)**. Install the spacers.

Installation

12 Installation is the reverse of removal, noting the following points.
● Apply multi-purpose grease to the linkage pivot points.
● Do not forget to fit the washers between the linkage arm and the frame **(see illustration)**.
● Leave all nuts and bolts loose until all are installed, then tighten them to the torque settings specified at the beginning of the Chapter.

13 Rear shock absorber

Removal

1 Remove the bottom fairing panel (see Chapter 8), the fuel tank (see Chapter 4), and the battery (see Chapter 9).
2 Support the motorcycle on its centrestand if fitted, on an auxiliary stand that does not take the weight through any part of the rear suspension, or by using a hoist – axle stands positioned under the frame bottom section on each side work well. Position a support under the rear wheel or swingarm so that it does not drop when the shock absorber is removed, but also making sure that the weight of the machine is off the rear suspension so that the shock is not compressed. Make a note of which side the bolts go in from, and make a note of which way round the shock absorber fits.
3 Unscrew the nut and withdraw the bolt securing the linkage rods to the swingarm and swing the rods down. Note that there is no need to do this if you are using spanners to remove the shock absorber; if you are using a socket, or if you have a torque wrench for tightening on installation, the rods restrict access **(see illustration 12.3)**.
4 Unscrew the nut and withdraw the bolt securing the bottom of the shock absorber to the linkage arm **(see illustration 12.5)**.
5 Unscrew the nut on the shock absorber upper mounting bolt **(see illustration)**. Support the shock absorber, then withdraw the bolt and manoeuvre the shock out of the top **(see illustration)**.

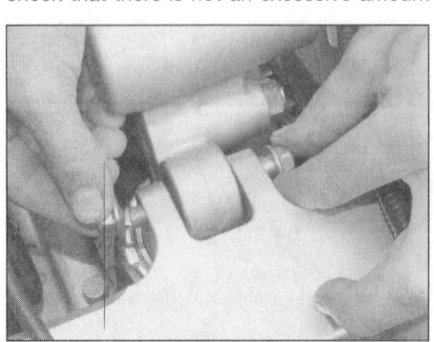

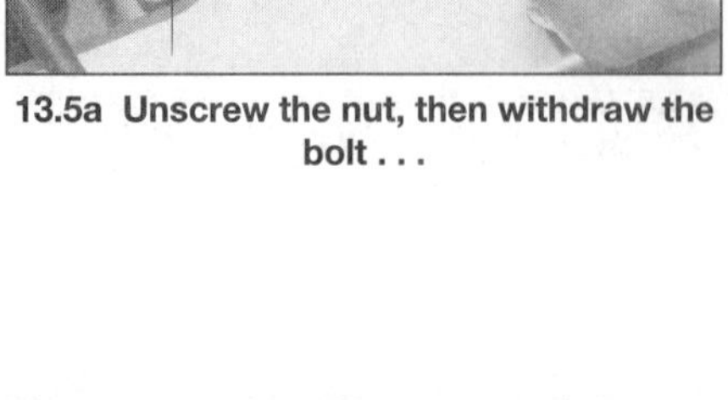

13.5a Unscrew the nut, then withdraw the bolt . . .

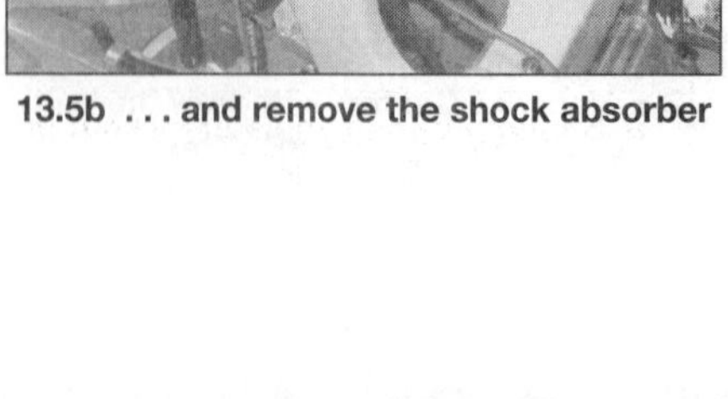

13.5b . . . and remove the shock absorber

Frame, suspension and final drive 6•15

Inspection

6 Inspect the shock absorber for obvious physical damage and the coil spring for looseness, cracks or signs of fatigue.
7 Inspect the rod for signs of bending, pitting and oil leakage **(see illustration)**.
8 Inspect the pivot hardware at the top and bottom for wear or damage **(see illustration)**.
9 Individual components are not available for the shock absorber, although it may be worth checking with a suspension specialist whether the unit can be rebuilt. Take the unit to a Suzuki dealer or suspension specialist for safe disposal.

Installation

10 Installation is the reverse of removal, noting the following points.
- Apply multi-purpose grease to the shock absorber pivot points.
- Leave all nuts and bolts loose until all are installed, then tighten them to the torque settings specified at the beginning of the Chapter.

14 Suspension adjustment

Front suspension

1 The front forks are adjustable for spring pre-load, rebound damping, and compression damping.
2 Spring pre-load is adjusted using a suitable spanner on the adjuster flats on the top of the forks **(see illustration)**. The amount of pre-load is indicated by lines on the adjuster. There are eight lines. The standard position is with the 5th line just visible above the top bolt hex. Turn the adjuster clockwise to increase pre-load and anti-clockwise to decrease it. Always make sure both adjusters are set equally.
3 Rebound damping is adjusted using a screwdriver in the slot in the adjuster protruding from the pre-load adjuster **(see illustration)**. The amount of damping is indicated by the number of clicks when turned anti-clockwise from the fully screwed-in position. The standard position is three clicks out. Turn the adjuster clockwise to increase damping and anti-clockwise to decrease it. To establish the current setting, turn the adjuster in (clockwise) until it stops, counting the number of clicks, then reset it as required by turning it out. Always make sure both adjusters are set equally.
4 Compression damping is adjusted using a screwdriver in the slot in the adjuster on the base of each fork **(see illustration)**. The amount of damping is indicated by the number of clicks when turned anti-clockwise from the fully screwed-in position. The standard position is nine clicks out. Turn the adjuster clockwise to increase damping and anti-clockwise to decrease it. To establish the current setting, turn the adjuster in (clockwise) until it stops, counting the number of clicks, then reset it as required by turning it out. Always make sure both adjusters are set equally.

13.7 Check the rod (arrowed) for pitting and oil traces

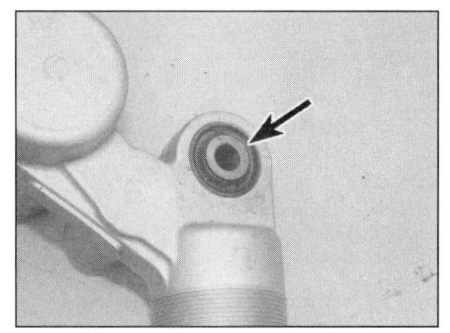

13.8 Check the bush (arrowed) in the top mount

Rear suspension

5 The shock absorber is adjustable for spring pre-load, rebound damping and compression damping.
6 Spring pre-load (spring set length) is adjusted by slackening the locknut on the top of the spring on the shock absorber using a C-spanner, then turning the adjuster nut as required **(see illustration)**. The standard set length of the spring, measured from the top of the top coil to the bottom of the bottom coil, is 183 mm. To increase pre-load set the spring length shorter, but no shorter than 180 mm. To reduce pre-load set the length longer, but no longer than 190 mm. To make the adjustment it is best to remove the shock absorber (see Section 13).
7 Rebound damping is adjusted using a screwdriver in the slot in the adjuster on the bottom of the shock absorber on the left-hand

14.2 Spring pre-load adjuster (arrowed)

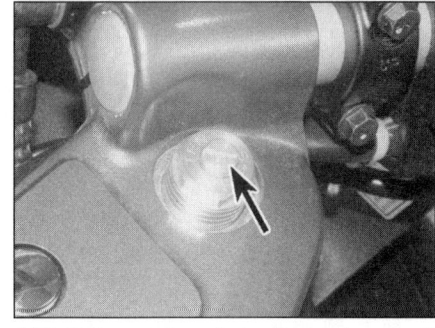

14.3 Rebound damping adjuster (arrowed)

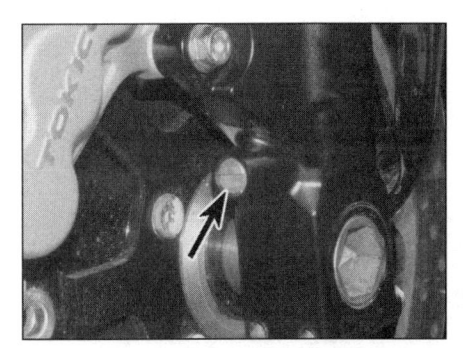

14.4 Compression damping adjuster (arrowed)

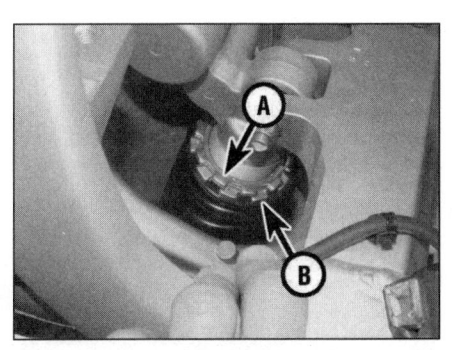

14.6a Spring pre-load adjuster locknut (A) and adjuster (B) . . .

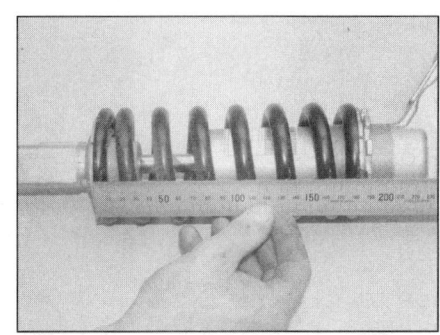

14.6b . . . always measure the spring set length when making adjustment

6•16 Frame, suspension and final drive

14.7 Rebound damping adjuster (arrowed)

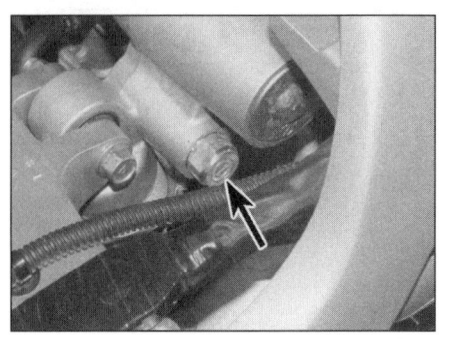

14.8 Compression damping adjuster (arrowed)

side **(see illustration)**. The amount of damping is indicated by the number of clicks when turned anti-clockwise from the fully screwed-in position. The standard position is when the punch marks align at about eleven clicks out. Turn the adjuster clockwise to increase damping and anti-clockwise to decrease it. To establish the current setting, turn the adjuster in (clockwise) until it stops, counting the number of clicks, then reset it as required by turning it out.

8 Compression damping is adjusted using a screwdriver in the slot in the adjuster on the top of the shock absorber on the left-hand side of the unit **(see illustration)**. The amount of damping is indicated by the number of turns anti-clockwise from the fully screwed-in position. The standard position is when the punch marks align at about eight clicks out. Turn the adjuster clockwise to increase damping and anti-clockwise to decrease it. To establish the current setting, turn the adjuster in (clockwise) until it stops, counting the number of clicks, then reset it as required by turning it out.

15 Swingarm removal and installation

Removal

1 Either remove the front sprocket (see Section 18) and remove the swingarm with the chain looped through it, or split the drive chain (see Section 17) and remove it first.

2 Due to the rear brake hose being routed through a closed riveted guide on the inside of the swingarm, it is necessary to either detach the hose from the rear brake caliper, and then draw the hose out of the guide (follow Step 3), or to remove the swingarm bringing the rear brake system (except the reservoir) with it (follow Step 4). The decision will depend on your reason for removing the swingarm – access to the bearings is not affected if you bring the brake system with the swingarm. Also bear in mind that whatever method you choose you will have to bleed the brake system afterwards as it is necessary to detach the reservoir hose from the master cylinder to avoid having to remove the entire rear mudguard assembly, due to the fact the hose routes through a hole which means the reservoir cannot be removed along with the rest of the system.

3 If you are detaching the brake hose, have plenty of rag to hand to catch the brake fluid from the both the caliper and the hose. Unscrew the brake hose banjo bolt and detach the hose, noting its alignment with the caliper, and immediately cover the end of the hose in rag **(see illustration)**. Now draw the hose out of the closed guide, removing the rag as you do then immediately replacing it, and raise the hose end up. Now either clamp the hose, plug it using another suitable short piece of hose fitted through the eye of the banjo union (it must be a fairly tight fit to seal it properly), block it using a suitable bolt with the old sealing washers and a capped (domed) nut, or wrap plastic foodwrap tightly around (a finger cut off a latex glove also works well), the object being to minimise fluid loss and prevent dirt entering the system. Keep the end of the hose covered in rag and if possible tie the hose so its end is above the level of the master cylinder and pointing up. Note the routing of the hose round the swingarm, and free it from the open guides **(see illustration)**. Note that new sealing washers must be used on installation of the brake hose. Unscrew the nut and withdraw the bolt securing the brake torque arm to the swingarm so that after removing the rear wheel it can be removed along with the rear brake caliper and its bracket **(see illustration)**.

> **Warning:** Brake fluid can harm your eyes and damage painted surfaces and plastic parts, so use extreme care when disconnecting the hose.

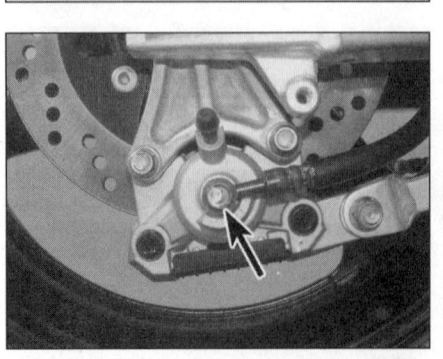

TOOL TIP

A peg spanner is required to slacken and tighten the swingarm pivot bolt locknut. If the Suzuki service tool (Pt. No. 09940-14970) is not available, a suitable one can be made by cutting up an old socket as shown so that its rim is suitably castellated (measure the width and depth of the slots in the locknut), or by brazing or welding pegs onto an old nut (see illustration 15.9). On some models (those with an internal hex on the right-hand end of the pivot bolt as opposed to an external one), you will also need a large hex bit (measure to check the size) or a nut welded onto the end of a bolt (see illustration 15.11a) to unscrew the pivot bolt.

15.3a Brake hose banjo bolt (arrowed)

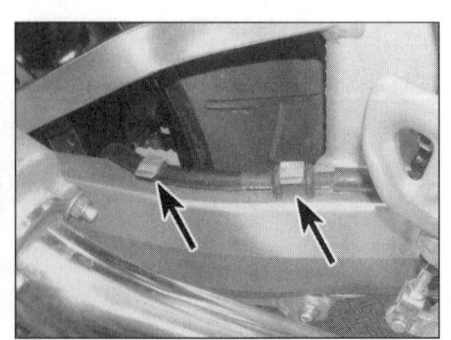

15.3b Free the hose from the guides (arrowed)

15.3c Brake torque arm nuts (arrowed)

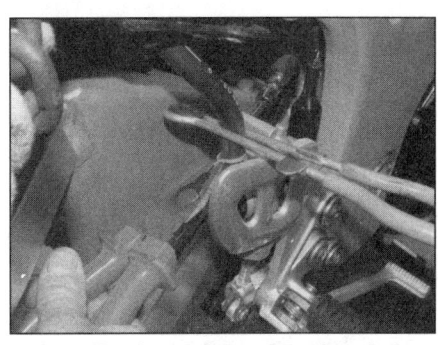

Frame, suspension and final drive 6•17

15.4a Fit a hose clamp, then detach the hose from the master cylinder . . .

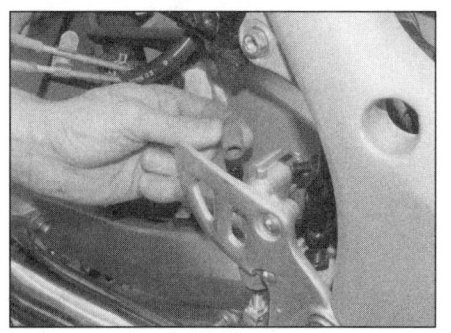

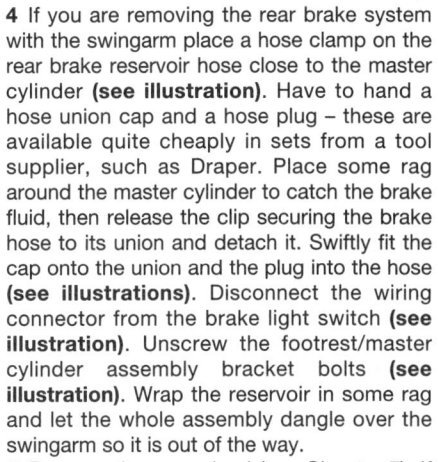

15.4b . . . and fit a cap onto the union . . .

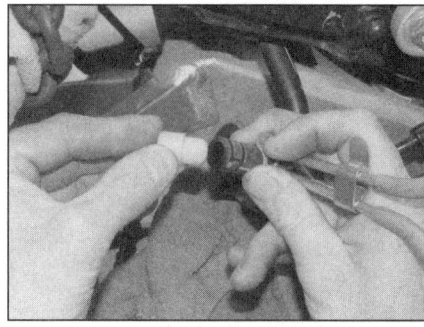

15.4c . . . and a plug into the hose

4 If you are removing the rear brake system with the swingarm place a hose clamp on the rear brake reservoir hose close to the master cylinder **(see illustration)**. Have to hand a hose union cap and a hose plug – these are available quite cheaply in sets from a tool supplier, such as Draper. Place some rag around the master cylinder to catch the brake fluid, then release the clip securing the brake hose to its union and detach it. Swiftly fit the cap onto the union and the plug into the hose **(see illustrations)**. Disconnect the wiring connector from the brake light switch **(see illustration)**. Unscrew the footrest/master cylinder assembly bracket bolts **(see illustration)**. Wrap the reservoir in some rag and let the whole assembly dangle over the swingarm so it is out of the way.

5 Remove the rear wheel (see Chapter 7). If using axle stands to support the bike, position them under the frame bottom section on each side.

6 If required undo the screws securing the chainguard to the swingarm and remove it, noting how it locates **(see illustration)**.

7 Unscrew the nut and withdraw the bolt securing the linkage rods to the swingarm and swing the rods down **(see illustration 12.3)**.

8 Remove the rear shock absorber (see Section 13).

9 Unscrew the locknut on the right-hand end of the swingarm pivot bolt using a suitable peg spanner (see **Tool Tip** above) **(see illustration)**.

10 Counter-hold the right-hand end of the pivot bolt then unscrew the nut on the left-

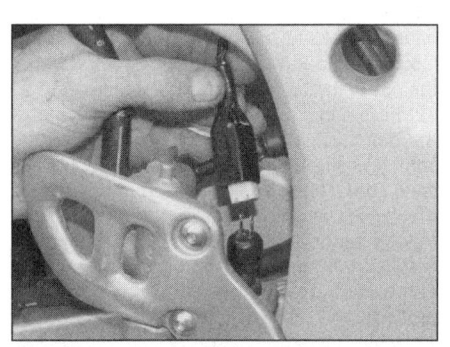

15.4d Disconnect the wiring connector

15.4e Unscrew the bolts and displace the assembly

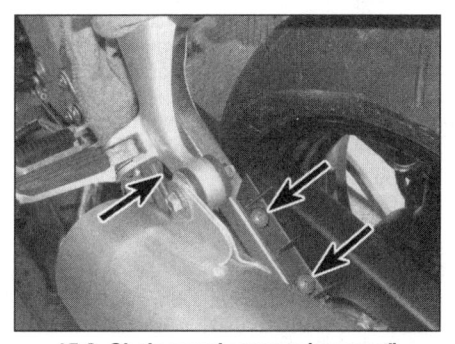

15.6 Chainguard screws (arrowed)

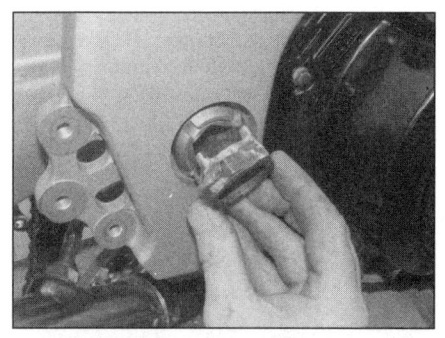

15.9 Unscrew the locknut on the right-hand side using a peg spanner . . .

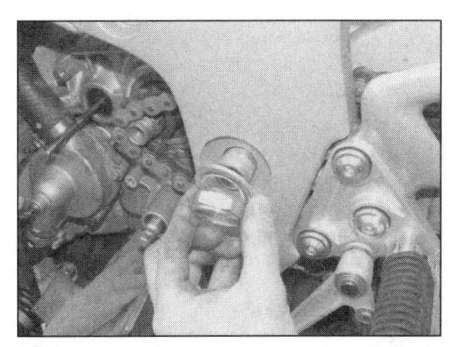

hand end and remove the washer **(see illustration)**.

11 Unscrew the pivot bolt, then support the swingarm and withdraw the bolt from the

right-hand side **(see illustrations)**. Manoeuvre the swingarm out of the frame, guiding the chain off the output shaft end if you didn't split it earlier **(see illustration 15.15)**.

15.10 . . . then unscrew the nut on the left-hand side, and remove the washer

15.11a Unscrew the pivot bolt . . .

15.11b . . . then withdraw it and remove the swingarm

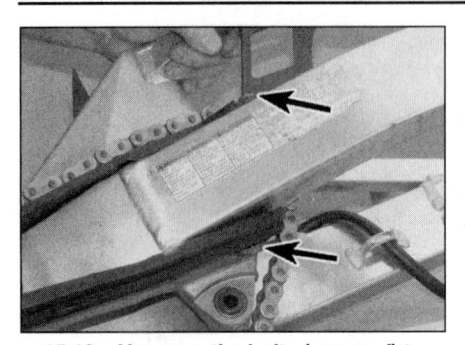

6•18 Frame, suspension and final drive

15.12a Unscrew the bolts (arrowed) to remove the chain slider

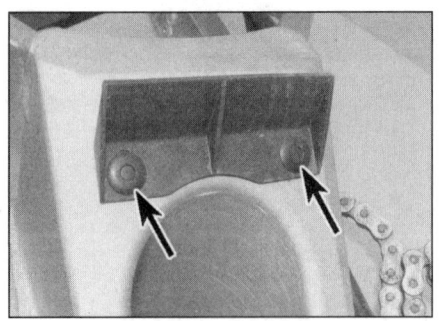

15.12b Release the trim clips (arrowed) to remove the deflector

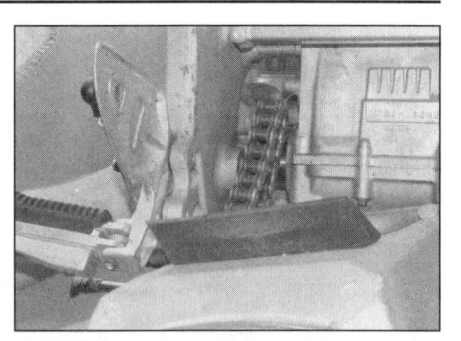

15.15 Loop the chain round the output shaft before installing the swingarm

12 If required, unscrew the bolts securing the chain slider, noting the spacers, and remove it, noting how it fits **(see illustration)**. If it is badly worn or damaged it should be replaced with a new one. Also remove the mud deflector if required – it is secured by two trim clips **(see illustration)**.

13 Clean, inspect and re-grease all pivot components as described in Section 16.

Installation

14 If removed, install the chain slider, making sure it locates correctly **(see illustration 15.12a)**. Also fit the mud deflector if removed **(see illustration 15.12b)**.

15 Offer up the swingarm and ideally have an assistant hold it in place. Loop the drive chain over the output shaft **(see illustration)**. Slide the pivot bolt in from the right-hand side and push it all the way through **(see illustration 15.11b)**. Tighten the bolt to the torque setting specified at the beginning of the Chapter.

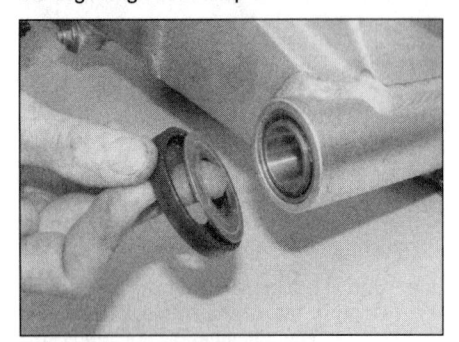

16.2a Remove the cap and washer from each side . . .

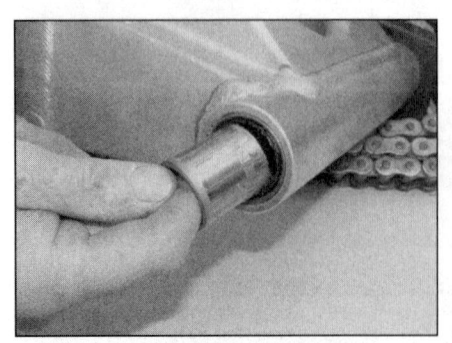

16.2b . . . then withdraw the spacers

16 Fit the nut with its washer onto the left-hand end of the bolt **(see illustration 15.10)**. Counter-hold the head of the bolt and tighten the nut to the specified torque setting.

17 Fit the locknut onto the right-hand end of the bolt and tighten it to the specified torque setting, using the peg-spanner as on removal (see *Tool Tip*) **(see illustration 15.9)**. Move the swingarm up and down and check that it moves smoothly and freely. If it is tight slacken the locknut, nut and bolt, move the arm up and down, then repeat the tightening procedure.

18 Install the shock absorber (see Section 13).

19 If removed install the chainguard **(see illustration 15.6)**.

20 Install the rear wheel (see Chapter 7).

21 If detached, locate the footrest/master cylinder assembly onto the frame and tighten the bolts to the specified torque setting **(see illustration 15.4e)**. Remove the plug from the brake reservoir hose, then remove the cap from the brake master cylinder and swiftly connect the hose **(see illustrations 15.4c, b and a)**. Secure the hose with its clip. Release the hose clamp. Connect the brake light switch wiring connector **(see illustration 15.4d)**.

22 Fit the brake torque arm onto the swingarm, then install the torque arm bolt and tighten the nut to the specified torque setting **(see illustration 15.3c)**. Route the brake hose through its closed guide. Fit the hose into its open guides **(see illustration 15.3b)**. Remove whatever plugging method you used from the end of the brake hose, then connect the hose to the caliper, using new sealing washers on each side of the union, and tighten the banjo

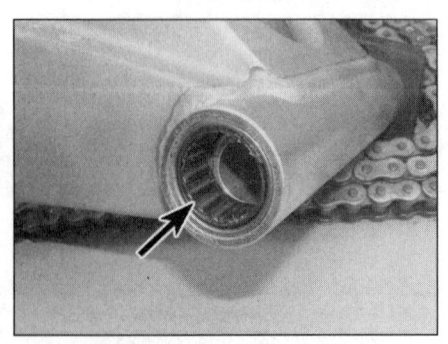

16.7 Check the bearing (arrowed) on each side as described

bolt to the torque setting specified at the beginning of the Chapter, aligning the hose as noted on removal **(see illustration 15.3a)**. Remove the brake hose clamp if used.

23 Refer to Chapter 7 and bleed the rear brake.

24 Install the drive chain or front sprocket as required (see Section 17 or 18).

25 Check and adjust the drive chain slack (see Chapter 1). Check the operation of the rear suspension and brake before taking the machine on the road.

16 Swingarm inspection, bearing check and renewal

Inspection

1 Remove the swingarm (see Section 15).

2 Remove the dust cap and thrust washer (which if stuck together may appear as one component) from each side of the swingarm pivot, then withdraw the spacers **(see illustrations)**.

3 Thoroughly clean the swingarm, removing all traces of dirt, corrosion and grease.

4 Inspect the swingarm closely, looking for obvious signs of wear such as heavy scoring, and cracks or distortion due to accident damage. Any damaged or worn component must be replaced with a new one.

5 Check the swingarm pivot bolt for straightness by rolling it on a flat surface such as a piece of plate glass (first wipe off all old grease and remove any corrosion using wire wool). If the equipment is available, place the axle in V-blocks and measure the runout using a dial gauge. If the axle is bent or the runout exceeds the limit specified, replace it with a new one.

Bearing check and renewal

6 Remove the dust cap and thrust washer (which if stuck together may appear as one component) from each side of the swingarm pivot, then withdraw the spacers **(see illustration 16.2a and b)**.

7 Clean off all old grease from the spacers and bearings. Check the surfaces on the spacers. Check the condition of the bearings – there is a needle roller bearing in each side **(see illustration)**. Slip each spacer back into

Frame, suspension and final drive 6•19

its bearing and check that there is not an excessive amount of freeplay between the two. If the bearings do not run smoothly and freely or if there is excessive freeplay, they must be replaced with new ones. Refer to *Tools and Workshop Tips* (Section 5) in the Reference section for more information on bearings.

8 Worn bearings can be drifted out of their bores, but note that removal will destroy them; new bearings should be obtained before work commences. The new bearings should be pressed or drawn into their bores rather than driven into position. In the absence of a press, a suitable drawbolt tool can be made up as described in *Tools and Workshop Tips* in the Reference section. A central spacer separates the two bearings – remove it if required, but do not forget to fit it before installing the bearings. Where the needle bearings have an integral seal, make sure the side with the seal is on the outside. In all cases make sure the marked side of the bearing is on the outside.

9 Check the condition of the washers and dust caps and replace them with new ones if they are damaged.

10 Lubricate the bearings and spacers and all other pivot components according to model with multi-purpose grease. Insert the spacers, then fit the washers and dust caps.

17 Drive chain removal and installation

Removal

Note: *The drive chain fitted to these models has a riveted-type joining link which can be disassembled using either Suzuki service tool, Pt. No. 09922-22711, or one of several commercially-available drive chain breaking/riveting tools. Such chains can be recognised by the joining link side plate's identification marks (and usually its different colour), as well as by the riveted ends of the link's two pins which look as if they have*

been deeply centre-punched, instead of peened over as with all the other pins **(see illustration 17.2)**.

⚠️ **Warning: Use ONLY the correct service tools to disassemble the riveted-type of master link – if you do not have access to such tools or do not have the skill to operate them correctly, have the chain removed by a Suzuki dealer.**

1 Remove the front sprocket cover (see Section 18). If the sprockets are being replaced with new ones, slacken the front sprocket nut before splitting the chain so that the rear brake can be used to stop the sprocket turning (see Section 18).

2 Locate the joining link in a suitable position to work on by rotating the back wheel **(see illustration)**.

3 Slacken the drive chain as described in Chapter 1.

4 Split the chain at the joining link using the chain tool, following carefully the manufacturer's operating instructions (see also Section 8 in *Tools and Workshop Tips* in the Reference Section). Remove the chain from the bike, noting its routing through the swingarm.

Installation

⚠️ **Warning: NEVER install a drive chain which uses a clip-type master (split) link. Use ONLY the correct service tools to secure the riveted-type of joining link – if you do not have access to such tools or do not have the skill to operate them correctly, have the chain installed by a Suzuki dealer.**

5 Slip the drive chain through the swingarm sections and around the front and rear sprockets, leaving the two ends in a convenient position to work on.

6 Refer to Section 8 in *Tools and Workshop Tips* in the Reference Section. Install the new joining link from the inside. Fit an O-ring onto each pin, then slide the link through from the inside and fit the other two O-rings. Install the new side plate with its identification marks facing out. Use the chain tool to press the side plate into position – on the RK chain fitted as original equipment Suzuki advise

pressing it into position so that the distance between the outer edges of the joining link and side plate are within the measurements specified at the beginning of the Chapter. Now use the chain tool to rivet the ends of the two pins.

7 After riveting, check the joining link and rivet heads for any signs of cracking. If there is any evidence of cracking, the joining link, O-rings and side plate must be replaced. On the RK chain fitted as original equipment, measure the diameter of the riveted ends in two directions and check that it is evenly riveted and within the measurements specified at the beginning of the Chapter.

8 Install the sprocket cover (see Section 18).

9 On completion, adjust and lubricate the chain following the procedures described in Chapter 1.

18 Sprocket cover and sprockets

Front sprocket cover

1 Remove the left-hand fairing side panel (see Chapter 8). Undo the screws securing the coolant reservoir and displace it from the frame – support or tie it so that it remains upright but is clear of the release cylinder **(see illustration)**. If necessary drain and remove the reservoir completely (see Chapter 1).

2 If the clutch release cylinder is being removed from the cover, refer to Chapter 2 for the necessary Steps. Note that release cylinder removal is not necessary for sprocket cover removal.

3 Unscrew the speed sensor bolt and withdraw the sensor from the cover **(see illustration)**.

4 On X models release the oil catch tank drain hose from its clamp.

5 Make an alignment mark between the gearchange shaft end and the slit in the gearchange linkage arm clamp, then unscrew the pinch bolt and slide the arm off the shaft **(see illustration 3.12)**.

6 Unscrew the front sprocket cover bolts and

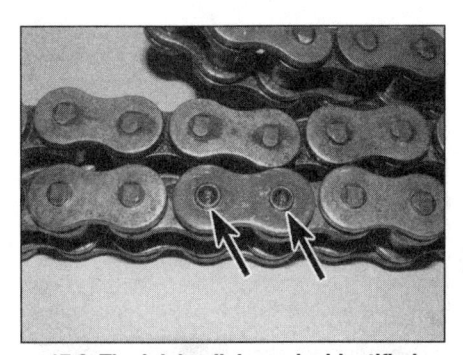

17.2 The joining link can be identified either by its different colour, or by the difference in the pin ends (arrowed)

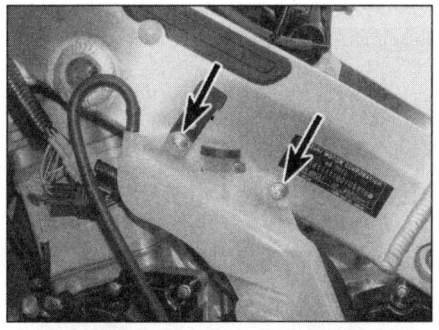

18.1 Undo the screws (arrowed) and displace the coolant reservoir

18.3 Unscrew the bolt (arrowed) and remove the speed sensor

6•20 Frame, suspension and final drive

18.6a Unscrew the bolts (arrowed) . . .

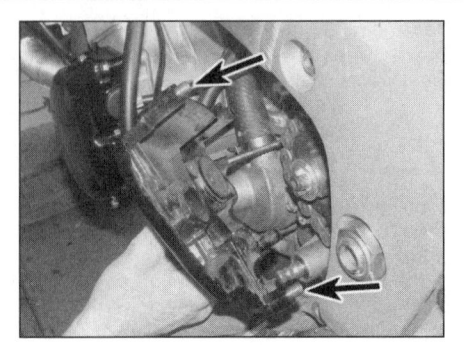

18.6b . . . and remove the cover, noting the dowels (arrowed)

18.6c Note the protective sleeve

remove the cover **(see illustrations)**. Remove the dowels if they are loose. Note the protective sleeve on the sprocket cover bottom bolt boss and remove it for safekeeping if required **(see illustration)**.

7 Where fitted, note the rubber diaphragm in the end of the clutch release cylinder and remove it for safekeeping if it is loose **(see illustration)**. Do not operate the clutch lever with the release cylinder removed.

> **HAYNES HiNT**: *Wrap some cable ties around the release cylinder piston to prevent the piston creeping out, or from being displaced should the lever be accidentally pulled in.*

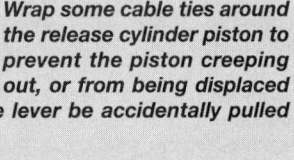

18.7 Note the rubber diaphragm

8 If required, withdraw the clutch short pushrod from the engine **(see illustration)**.
9 Installation is the reverse of removal, noting the following.
● Do not forget to fit the protective sleeve for the sprocket cover bottom bolt boss if removed **(see illustration 18.6c)**.
● Do not forget to fit the clutch pushrod if removed **(see illustration 18.8)**, and the rubber diaphragm where fitted **(see illustration 18.7)**, and make sure you align the hole in the clutch release cylinder with it when installing the cover **(see illustration 18.6b)**.
● Tighten the speed sensor bolt to the torque setting specified at the beginning of the Chapter **(see illustration 18.3)**.
● Align the slit in the gearchange linkage arm clamp with the mark made on the end of the shaft **(see illustration 3.12)**.

18.8 Withdraw the pushrod if required

Front sprocket

10 Remove the front sprocket cover (see above).
11 Counter-hold the sprocket nut then unscrew the speedometer rotor bolt and remove the rotor **(see illustration)**.
12 Engage first gear, then have an assistant hold the rear brake on hard. Unscrew the sprocket nut and remove the washer **(see illustration)**.
13 Fully slacken the drive chain as described in Chapter 1. If the rear sprocket is being removed as well, remove the rear wheel now to give full chain slack. Otherwise disengage the chain from the rear sprocket.
14 Disengage the chain from the front sprocket then slide the sprocket off the shaft **(see illustration)**.
15 Slide the new sprocket on the shaft, making sure the marked side is facing out, and fit the chain around it. Fit the chain onto the rear sprocket or install the rear wheel (see Chapter 7), then take up the slack in the chain.
16 Apply a suitable non-permanent thread locking compound to the sprocket nut threads. Fit the washer onto the shaft. Fit the nut and tighten it to the specified torque setting, with the engine in gear and holding the rear brake on hard as before **(see illustration 18.12)**.
17 Apply a suitable non-permanent thread locking compound to the speedometer rotor bolt threads. Fit the rotor and tighten the bolt

18.11 Unscrew the rotor bolt and remove the rotor

18.12 Unscrew the sprocket nut and remove the washer

18.14 Disengage the chain and remove the sprocket

Frame, suspension and final drive 6•21

18.20 Rear sprocket nuts (arrowed)

19.2 Lift the sprocket coupling out of the wheel, noting the spacer (arrowed)

19.3 Check the rubber dampers

to the specified torque setting while counter-holding the sprocket nut **(see illustration 18.11)**.
18 Install the sprocket cover. Adjust and lubricate the chain following the procedures described in Chapter 1.

> **HAYNES HiNT**: *Keep your old front sprocket as it can be used along with a holding tool to lock the transmission input shaft should you ever need to remove the clutch (see Chapter 2).*

Rear sprocket
19 Remove the rear wheel (see Chapter 7).
20 Unscrew the nuts securing the sprocket to the hub assembly **(see illustration)**. Lift the sprocket off the studs.
21 Fit the sprocket onto the hub with the stamped mark facing out. Install the nuts and tighten them evenly and in a criss-cross sequence to the torque setting specified at the beginning of the Chapter.
22 Install the rear wheel (see Chapter 7).

19 Rear sprocket coupling/rubber dampers

1 Remove the rear wheel (see Chapter 7).
Caution: Do not lay the wheel down on the disc as it could become warped. Lay the wheel on wooden blocks so that the disc is off the ground.
2 Lift the sprocket coupling away from the wheel leaving the rubber dampers in position **(see illustration)**. Note the sprocket coupling spacer. Check the coupling for cracks or any obvious signs of damage. Also check the sprocket studs for wear or damage.
3 Lift the rubber damper segments from the wheel and check them for cracks, hardening and general deterioration **(see illustration)**. Renew them as a set if necessary.
4 Procedures for the sprocket coupling bearing are described in Chapter 7.
5 Installation is the reverse of removal. Smear grease onto the inside and the ends of the sprocket coupling spacer.
6 Install the rear wheel (see Chapter 7).

Notes

Chapter 7
Brakes, wheels and tyres

Contents

Brake discs	4	Rear brake caliper	6
Brake fluid level check	see Daily (pre-ride) checks	Rear brake master cylinder	8
Brake light switches	see Chapter 9	Rear brake pads	3
Brake pad wear check	see Chapter 1	Rear wheel	14
Brake hoses and unions	9	Tyre fitting	16
Brake system bleeding	10	Tyre pressure, tread depth and condition	see Daily (pre-ride) checks
Brake system check	see Chapter 1	Wheel check	see Chapter 1
Front brake calipers	5	Wheel bearing check	see Chapter 1
Front brake master cylinder	7	Wheel bearing replacement	15
Front brake pads	2	Wheel alignment check	12
Front wheel	13	Wheel inspection and repair	11
General information	1		

Degrees of difficulty

Easy, suitable for novice with little experience	Fairly easy, suitable for beginner with some experience	Fairly difficult, suitable for competent DIY mechanic	Difficult, suitable for experienced DIY mechanic	Very difficult, suitable for expert DIY or professional

Specifications

Brakes

Brake fluid type	DOT 4
Disc minimum thickness (front and rear)	
Standard	4.8 to 5.2 mm
Service limit	4.5 mm
Disc maximum runout (front and rear)	0.3 mm
Caliper bore ID	
Front	
Lower	24.000 to 24.076 mm
Middle and upper	27.000 to 27.076 mm
Rear	38.180 to 38.256 mm
Caliper piston OD	
Front	
Lower	23.925 to 23.975 mm
Middle and upper	26.920 to 26.970 mm
Rear	38.098 to 38.148 mm
Master cylinder bore ID	
Front	15.870 to 15.913 mm
Rear	12.700 to 12.743 mm
Master cylinder piston OD	
Front	15.827 to 15.854 mm
Rear	12.657 to 12.684 mm

7•2 Brakes, wheels and tyres

Wheels
Rim size
- Front .... 17 x MT 3.5
- Rear .... 17 x MT 6.0

Wheel rim runout (max)
- Axial (side-to-side) .... 2.0 mm
- Radial (out-of-round) .... 2.0 mm

Wheel axle runout (max) .... 0.25 mm

Tyres
Tyre pressures .... 42 psi (2.9 Bar) front and rear

Tyre tread depth (min recommended)
- Front .... 1.6 mm
- Rear .... 2.0 mm

Tyre sizes*
- Front 120/70-ZR17 (58W)
- Rear 190/50-ZR17 (73W)

*Refer to the owners handbook, the tyre information label on the swingarm, or your dealer for approved tyre brands.

Torque wrench settings
Bleed valves	7.5 Nm
Brake hose banjo bolts	23 Nm
Brake torque arm nuts	
Front (swingarm) mount	28 Nm
Rear (caliper bracket) mount	35 Nm
Front brake caliper body joining bolts	21 Nm
Front brake caliper mounting bolts	39 Nm
Front brake disc bolts	23 Nm
Front brake master cylinder clamp bolts	10 Nm
Front wheel axle clamp bolts	23 Nm
Front wheel axle	100 Nm
Rear axle nut	100 Nm
Rear brake caliper body joining bolts	30 Nm
Rear brake caliper mounting bolts	26 Nm
Rear brake disc bolts	35 Nm
Rear brake master cylinder mounting bolts	10 Nm

1 General information

All models are fitted with 17-inch cast alloy wheels designed for tubeless tyres only. Both front and rear brakes are hydraulically operated disc brakes.

The front brake is a twin disc with six-piston opposed calipers. The rear brake is a single disc with a two-piston opposed caliper.

Caution: *Do not disassemble components unless absolutely necessary. If a hydraulic brake line is loosened, the system must be bled. Do not use solvents on internal brake components. Solvents will cause the seals to swell and distort. Use only clean brake fluid for cleaning. Use care when working with brake fluid as it can injure your eyes and it will damage painted surfaces and plastic parts.*

2 Front brake pads

⚠️ **Warning: The dust created by the brake system may contain asbestos, which is harmful to your health. Never blow it out with compressed air and don't inhale any of it. An approved filtering mask should be worn when working on the brakes. Do not, under any circumstances, use petroleum-based solvents to clean brake parts. Use clean brake fluid only.**

Note: *If the pad pins have not been previously greased and have not been removed for a while, they could well be very difficult to withdraw. If this is the case, they will have to be driven out using a suitable drift or punch. To do this you will have to remove the caliper (see Section 4), as otherwise the shock could distort the disc. If you apply penetrating fluid this will help, but make sure none gets on the pads or discs.*

1 Unscrew the two bolts securing the pad spring and remove the spring **(see illustration)**.

2.1 Unscrew the bolts and remove the pad spring

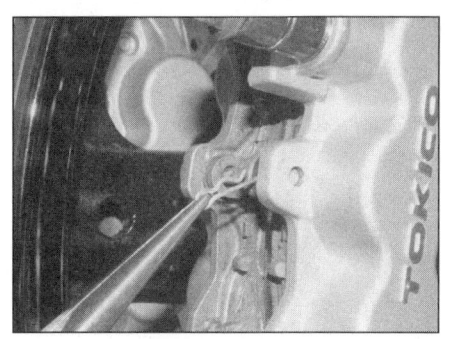

Brakes, wheels and tyres 7•3

2.2a Remove the R-clip . . .

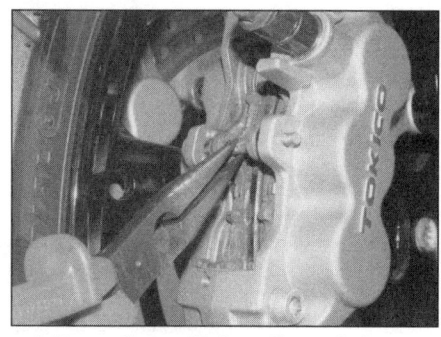

2.2b . . . then withdraw the pad pin . . .

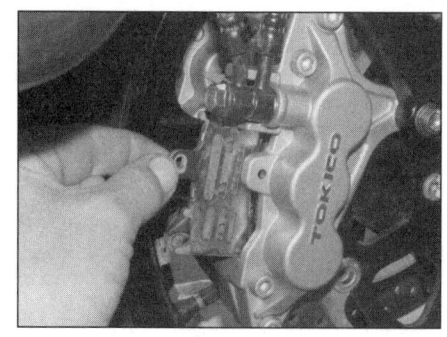

2.2c . . . and lift the pads out

2 Remove the R-clip from the end of the pad retaining pin, then withdraw the pad pin **(see illustrations)**. Remove the pads from the caliper, noting how they fit **(see illustration)**.

3 If new pads are being installed, or if you want to check that none of the pistons are seized in their caliper, unscrew the caliper mounting bolts and slide the caliper off the disc – it is much easier to push the pistons back into the caliper with it displaced **(see illustration)**. Free the brake hose from its guide and/or clip (according to side) to give more freedom of movement if required **(see illustration 5.3)**.

4 Inspect the surface of each pad for contamination and check whether the friction material has worn beyond its service limit (see Chapter 1). If either pad is worn to or beyond the service limit, is fouled with oil or grease, or is heavily scored or damaged by dirt and debris, replace the pads in both calipers with new ones. Note that it is extremely difficult to effectively degrease the friction material; if the pads are contaminated in any way new ones must be fitted. Also check whether either pad has worn unevenly, which is indicative of a seized piston (see Step 8).

5 If the pads are in good condition clean them carefully, using a fine wire brush which is completely free of oil and grease to remove all traces of road dirt and corrosion. Using a pointed instrument, clean out the grooves in the friction material and dig out any embedded particles of foreign matter. Any areas of glazing can be removed using emery cloth. Spray with a dedicated brake cleaner to remove any dust. It is also worth spraying the inside of the caliper to remove any dust there, and also to spray the discs.

6 Check the condition of the brake disc (see Section 4).

7 Remove all traces of corrosion from the pad pin. If corrosion is excessive, or the pin is damaged in any way, replace it with a new one.

8 Clean around the exposed section of each piston to remove any dirt or debris that could cause the seals to be damaged. If new pads are being fitted, now push the pistons all the way back into the caliper to create room for them; if the old pads are still serviceable but you want to check that none of the pistons are seized in their bores push them in a little way. To push the pads back use finger pressure or a piece of wood as leverage, or place the old pads back in the caliper and use a metal bar or a screwdriver inserted between them, or use grips and a piece of wood, rag or card to protect the caliper body. Alternatively obtain a proper piston-pushing tool from a good tool supplier **(see illustration)**. It may be necessary to remove the master cylinder reservoir cover, plate and diaphragm and siphon out some fluid (see *Daily (pre-ride) checks*). If the pistons are difficult to push back, remove the bleed valve cap, then attach a length of clear hose to the bleed valve and place the open end in a suitable container, then open the valve and try again **(see illustrations 10.5a and c)**. Take great care not to draw any air into the system. If in doubt, bleed the brakes afterwards (see Section 10). If any of the pistons appear seized, first block or hold the other pistons using wood or cable ties (see Section 5), then apply the brake lever and check whether the piston in question moves at all. If it moves out but can't be pushed back in the chances are there is some hidden corrosion stopping it. If it doesn't move at all, or to fully clean and inspect the pistons, disassemble the caliper and overhaul it (see Section 5).

9 If displaced slide the caliper onto the disc **(see illustration 2.3)**. Install the caliper mounting bolts and tighten them to the torque setting specified at the beginning of the Chapter. Fit the brake hose into its guide if removed **(see illustration 5.3)**.

10 Lightly smear the back and sides of the pad backing material (where it contacts the caliper body) with copper-based grease, making sure that none gets on the friction material. Also smear the pad pin and the surfaces on the underside of the pad spring that contact the protrusions on the top of each pad.

11 Insert the pads into the caliper so that the friction material of each pad faces the disc **(see illustration)**. Install the pad retaining pin

2.3 Unscrew the bolts and slide the caliper off the disc

2.8 Using a dedicated tool to press the pistons back

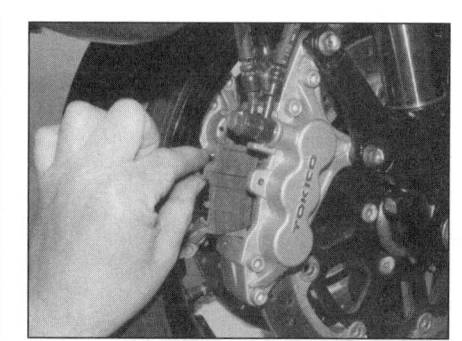

2.11a Insert the pads . . .

7•4 Brakes, wheels and tyres

with the hole for the R-clip on the outside (see illustration). Make sure it passes through the hole in each pad, and secure it with the R-clip, using a new one if necessary (see illustration).
12 Fit the pad spring and secure it with the bolts (see illustration 2.1).
13 Top up the master cylinder reservoir if necessary (see *Daily (pre-ride) checks*), and refit the diaphragm, plate and reservoir cover.
14 Operate the brake lever several times to bring the pads into contact with the disc. Check the operation of the front brake before riding the motorcycle.

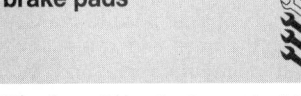

2.11b . . . then slide the pad pin all the way in . . .

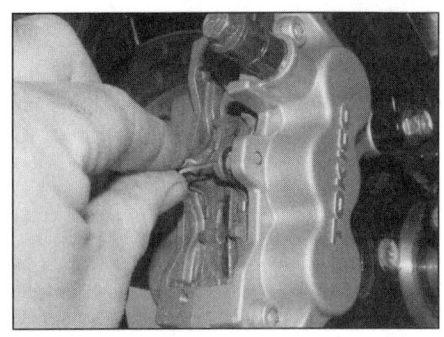

2.11c . . . and secure it with the R-clip

3 Rear brake pads

Warning: *The dust created by the brake system may contain asbestos, which is harmful to your health. Never blow it out with compressed air and don't inhale any of it. An approved filtering mask should be worn when working on the brakes. Do not, under any circumstances, use petroleum-based solvents to clean brake parts. Use clean brake fluid only.*

Note: *If the pad pins have not been previously greased and have not been removed for a while, they could well be very difficult to withdraw. If this is the case, they will have to be driven out using a suitable drift or punch.*

To do this you will have to remove the caliper (see Section 4), as otherwise the shock could distort the disc. If you apply penetrating fluid this will help, but make sure none gets on the pads or discs.
1 Slacken the caliper mounting bolts, then unscrew the nut and withdraw the bolt securing the torque arm to the caliper (see illustrations). Unscrew the caliper mounting bolts and slide the caliper off the disc (see illustration 3.14).
2 Prise off the brake pad cover using a flat-bladed screwdriver (see illustration).
3 Remove the pad pin retaining clip, noting how its ends fit through the holes in the pad pins (see illustration).
4 Withdraw the pad pins from the caliper using a suitable pair of pliers and remove the pad springs, noting how they fit (see illustration).

5 Withdraw the pads from the caliper body (see illustration). Note the shim on the back of each pad – if new pads are being installed, remove the old shims and keep them in case the new ones don't come with them fitted.
6 Inspect the surface of each pad for contamination and check whether the friction material has worn beyond its service limit (see Chapter 1). If either pad is worn to or beyond the service limit, is fouled by oil or grease, or is heavily scored or damaged by dirt and debris, replace the pads with new ones. Note that it is extremely difficult to effectively degrease the friction material; if the pads are contaminated in any way new ones must be fitted. Also check whether the pads have worn unevenly, which is indicative of a seized piston (see Step 10).
7 If the pads are in good condition clean them carefully, using a fine wire brush which is

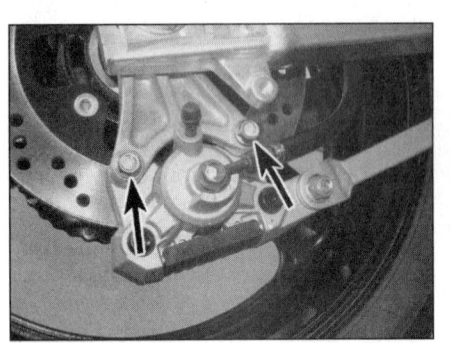

3.1a Caliper mounting bolts (arrowed)

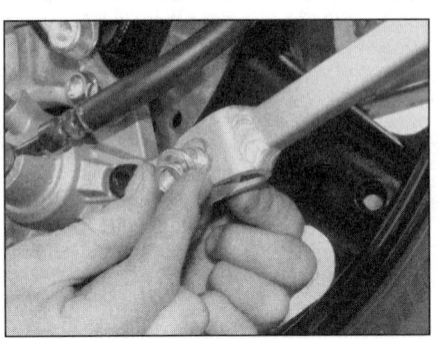

3.1b Unscrew the brake torque arm nut and remove the bolt

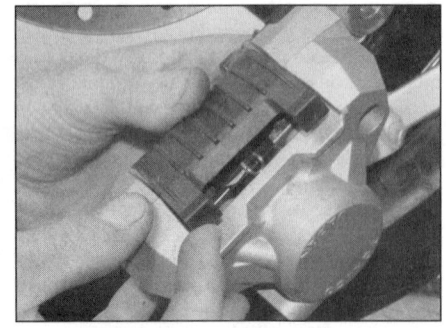

3.2 Remove the pad cover . . .

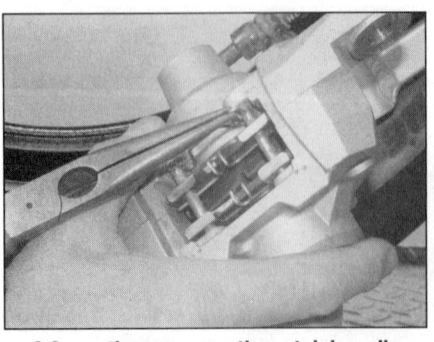

3.3 . . . then remove the retaining clip

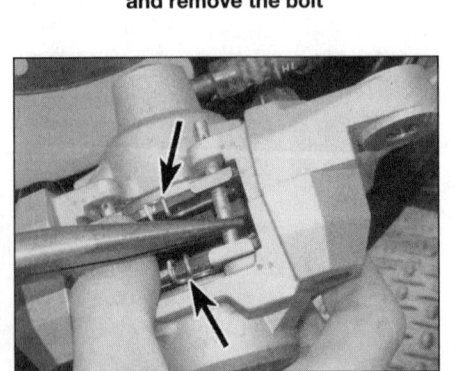

3.4 Withdraw the pins and remove the springs (arrowed) . . .

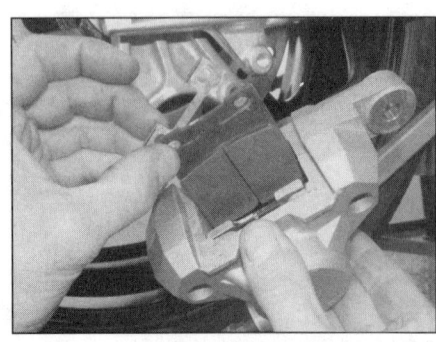

3.5 . . . and the pads

Brakes, wheels and tyres 7•5

completely free of oil and grease to remove all traces of road dirt and corrosion. Using a pointed instrument, clean out the grooves in the friction material and dig out any embedded particles of foreign matter. Any areas of glazing can be removed using emery cloth. Spray with a dedicated brake cleaner to remove any dust. It is also worth spraying the inside of the caliper to remove any dust there, and also to spray the discs.

8 Check the condition of the brake disc (see Section 4).

9 Remove all traces of corrosion from the pad pins. If corrosion is excessive, or the pins are damaged in any way, replace them with new ones.

10 Clean around the exposed section of each piston to remove any dirt or debris that could cause the seals to be damaged. Now push the pistons back into the caliper – if new pads are being fitted you need to push them all the way in to create room for them; if the old pads are still serviceable push them in a little way, not only because it makes installation easier, but also because it serves as a check that neither of the pistons are seized in their bores. To push the pads back use finger pressure or a piece of wood as leverage, or place the old pads back in the caliper and use a metal bar or a screwdriver inserted between them, or use grips and a piece of wood, rag or card to protect the caliper body. Alternatively obtain a proper piston-pushing tool from a good tool supplier **(see illustration)**. It may be necessary to remove the master cylinder reservoir cover and diaphragm and siphon out some fluid (see *Daily (pre-ride) checks*). If the pistons are difficult to push back, remove the bleed valve cap, then attach a length of clear hose to the bleed valve and place the open end in a suitable container, then open the valve and try again **(see illustrations 10.5b and d)**. Take great care not to draw any air into the system. If in doubt, bleed the brakes afterwards (see Section 10). If either piston appears seized, first block or hold the other piston using wood or cable ties (see Section 6), then apply the brake pedal and check whether the piston moves at all. If it moves out but can't be pushed back in the chances are there is some hidden corrosion stopping it. If it doesn't move at all, or to fully clean and inspect the pistons, disassemble the caliper and overhaul it (see Section 6).

11 Lightly smear the back and the sides of the pad backing material (where it contacts the caliper body) with copper-based grease, making sure that none gets on the friction material. Also smear the pad pins.

12 Fit the shim onto the back of each pad so that its open edge faces forwards when installed in the caliper **(see illustration)**.

13 Insert the pads into the caliper so that the friction material of each pad is facing the disc **(see illustration 3.5)**. Slide one pad pin, with its holed end on the outside, through the caliper and the holes in the pads **(see illustration)**. Fit the pad springs, locating one end under the installed pad pin and onto the edge of the friction material, and fitting the central hooked section onto the bottom edge of the pad backing **(see illustration)**. Press down on the free end of the outer pad spring and slide the other pad pin over the spring end. Now press down on the inner spring end and slide the pin the rest of the way through **(see illustration)**. Secure the pins with the retaining clip, making sure that its ends fit through the holes in the pad pins – if necessary rotate the pad pins to align their holes correctly **(see illustration)**. Install the pad cover **(see illustration 3.2)**.

14 Slide the caliper onto the brake disc, making sure the pads sit squarely on either side **(see illustration)**. Install the caliper mounting bolts and tighten them to the torque setting specified at the beginning of the Chapter.

15 Top up the master cylinder reservoir if necessary (see *Daily (pre-ride) checks*), then refit the diaphragm and reservoir cover.

16 Operate the brake pedal several times to bring the pads into contact with the disc. Check the operation of the rear brake before riding the motorcycle.

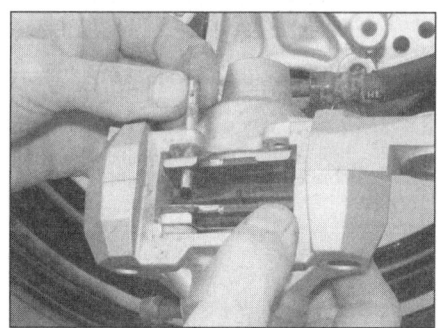

3.10 You can push the pistons back using grips or a dedicated tool as shown

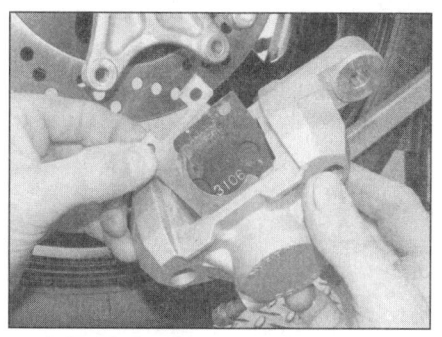

3.12 Fit the shims onto the pads as described and shown

3.13a Slide one pin through both pads

3.13b Fit the springs, then slide the other pin over one spring . . .

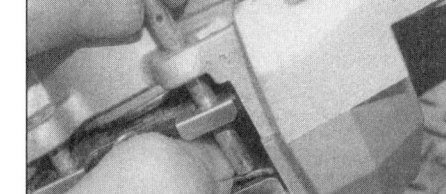

3.13c . . . then the other . . .

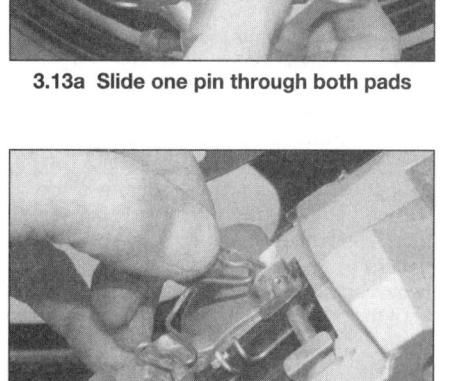

3.13d . . . and fit the clip

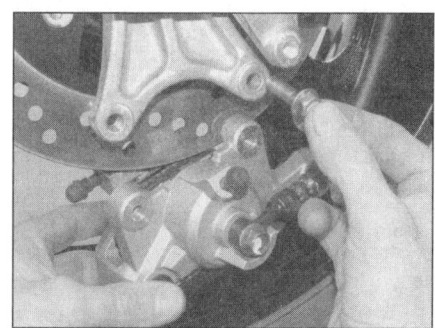

3.14 Slide the caliper onto the disc and tighten the bolts to the specified torque

7•6 Brakes, wheels and tyres

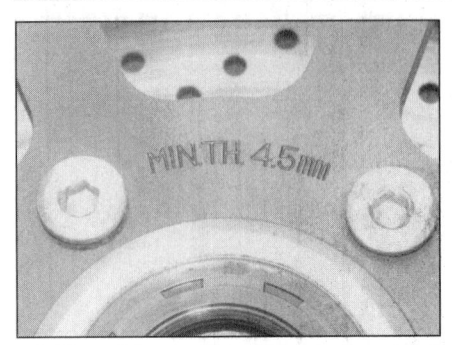

4.3 The minimum disc thickness is marked on the disc

4.5a Front disc bolts (arrowed)

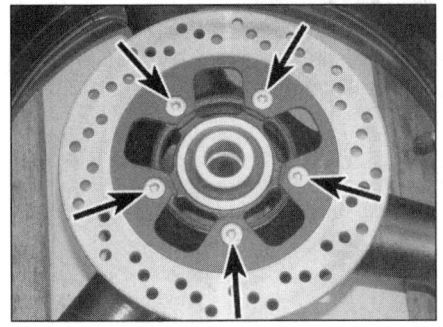

4.5b Rear disc bolts (arrowed)

4 Brake discs

Warning: *The dust created by the brake system may contain asbestos, which is harmful to your health. Never blow it out with compressed air and don't inhale any of it. An approved filtering mask should be worn when working on the brakes. Do not, under any circumstances, use petroleum-based solvents to clean brake parts. Use clean brake fluid only.*

Inspection

1 Visually inspect the surface of each disc for score marks and other damage. Light scratches are normal after use and won't affect brake operation, but deep grooves and heavy score marks will reduce braking efficiency and accelerate pad wear. If a disc is badly grooved it must be machined or replaced with a new one.

2 To check disc runout, position the bike on its centrestand or an auxiliary stand so that the wheel being checked is off the ground. Mount a dial gauge to a fork leg or on the swingarm, according to wheel, with the plunger on the gauge touching the surface of the disc about 10 mm (1/2 in) from the outer edge. Rotate the wheel and watch the gauge needle, comparing the reading with the limit listed in the Specifications at the beginning of the Chapter. If the runout is greater than the service limit, check the wheel bearings for play (see Chapter 1). If the bearings are worn, replace them with new ones (see Section 15) and repeat this check. It is also worth removing the disc (see below) and checking for built-up corrosion (see Steps 5 and 6) as this will cause runout. If the runout is still excessive, the disc will have to be replaced with a new one.

3 The disc must not be allowed to wear down to a thickness less than the service limit listed in this Chapter's Specifications and as sometimes marked on the disc itself **(see illustration)**. Check the thickness of the disc using a micrometer. If the thickness of the disc is less than the service limit, it must be replaced with a new one.

Removal

4 Remove the wheel (see Section 13 or 14). **Caution:** *Do not lay the wheel down and allow it to rest on the disc – the disc could become warped. Set the wheel on wood blocks so the disc doesn't support the weight of the wheel.*

5 Mark the relationship of the disc to the wheel, so it can be installed in the same position. Unscrew the disc retaining bolts, loosening them a little at a time in a criss-cross pattern to avoid distorting the disc, then remove the disc from the wheel **(see illustrations)**.

Installation

Note: *If either front disc is damaged warped or worn, always replace both discs as a pair. Always fit new brake pads when fitting new discs.*

6 Before installing the disc, make sure there is no dirt or corrosion where the disc seats on the hub, particularly right in the angle of the seat, as this will not allow the disc to sit flat when it is bolted down and it will appear to be warped when checked or when using the brake.

7 Install the disc on the wheel, making sure any directional arrow is on the outside and pointing in the direction of normal (i.e. forward) wheel rotation. Also note any R or L marking on the front discs that denotes on which side of the wheel it must be mounted. Align the previously applied matchmarks (if you're reinstalling the original disc).

8 Apply a suitable non-permanent thread locking compound to the threads of the disc bolts, and tighten them evenly in a criss-cross pattern to the torque setting specified at the beginning of the Chapter. Clean off all grease from the brake disc(s) using acetone or brake system cleaner. If a new brake disc has been installed, remove any protective coating from its working surfaces.

9 Install the wheel (see Section 13 or 14).

10 Operate the brake lever and pedal several times to bring the pads into contact with the disc. Check the operation of the brakes carefully before riding the bike.

5 Front brake calipers

Warning: *The dust created by the brake pads may contain asbestos, which is harmful to your health. Never blow it out with compressed air and don't inhale any of it. An approved filtering mask should be worn when working on the brakes. If a caliper indicates the need for an overhaul (usually due to leaking fluid or sticky operation), all old brake fluid should be flushed from the system. Do not, under any circumstances, use petroleum-based solvents to clean brake parts. Use clean brake fluid only. Use care when working with brake fluid as it can injure your eyes and it will damage painted surfaces and plastic parts – cover these with rag. Disassembly, overhaul and reassembly of the calipers must be done in a spotlessly clean work area to avoid contamination and possible failure of the hydraulic system components.*

Note: *If the entire front brake system is being overhauled (i.e. master cylinder as well as calipers), or if you intend to change the brake fluid as part of the caliper overhaul (which is advisable), drain the brake fluid completely from the system after displacing the pistons from the caliper (see Section 10), as opposed to retaining the old fluid within it by blocking the hose as described (Step 4).*

1 If the caliper is leaking fluid, or if the brake pads are wearing unevenly, or the pistons do not move smoothly or are tight or stuck in their bores, then caliper overhaul is required.

2 Before disassembling the caliper, read through the entire procedure and make sure that you have the correct seal kit. Also, you will need some new DOT 4 brake fluid, and some clean rags.

Removal

3 If the caliper is being displaced from the fork legs to enable wheel removal, there is no need to detach the brake hose, just free the

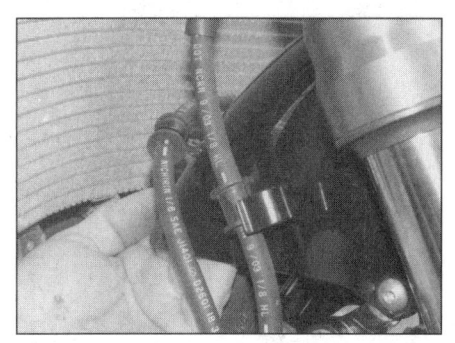

Brakes, wheels and tyres 7•7

5.3 Release the hose from the open guide (right-hand side only) and on each side free the closed guide from the mudguard

5.4 Slacken or unscrew the brake hose banjo bolt as required

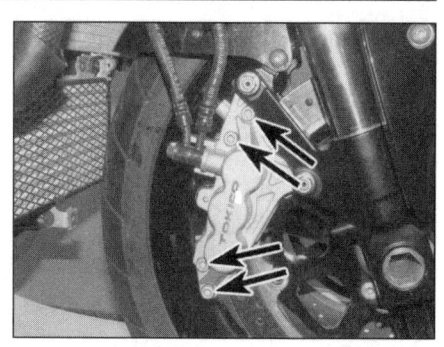

5.5 Caliper body joining bolts (arrowed)

hose from its guide and/or clip on the mudguard **(see illustration)**.

4 If the caliper is being overhauled, slacken the brake hose banjo bolt then retighten it lightly, enough to prevent fluid leakage **(see illustration)**. The bike's hydraulic system can then be used to force the pistons out of the body once the pads have been removed. If the caliper is being completely removed but not overhauled, unscrew the brake hose banjo bolt and detach the hose(s), noting the alignment with the caliper. Discard the sealing washers as new ones must be used on installation. Either clamp each hose, plug it using another suitable short piece of hose fitted through the eye of the banjo union (a tight fit is necessary for a good seal), block it using a suitable bolt with sealing washers and a capped (domed) nut, or wrap some plastic foodwrap tightly around (a finger cut off a latex glove also works well), the object being to minimise fluid loss and prevent dirt entering the system. Whatever you do, also cover the end of the hose in rag, just in case.

5 If the caliper body is to be split into its halves for overhaul, slacken the caliper body joining bolts now and retighten them lightly **(see illustration)**.

6 If the caliper is being overhauled, remove the brake pads (see Section 2).

7 Unscrew the caliper mounting bolts and slide the caliper off the disc **(see illustration)**. Free the brake hose from its guide and/or clip (according to side) to give more freedom of movement if required and not already done **(see illustration 5.3)**.

Overhaul

8 Clean the exterior of the caliper and around the pistons with denatured alcohol or brake system cleaner, making sure all grit and dirt is removed.

9 Displace the pistons as far as possible from the caliper body by pumping them out using the brake lever. A good way to do this is to cable-tie or hold a thin piece of sheet steel across all three pistons on one side, then pump the brake lever until the pistons on the other side are almost in the middle of the caliper – do not displace them any further as you need them to remain in their bores **(see illustration)**. Now cable-tie or hold the almost-displaced pistons in the same way and pump the lever until the other three meet the first three in the middle, with the piece of steel separating them **(see illustration)**. If a suitable piece of steel is not available make sure all pistons are displaced evenly by blocking or cable-tying ones that move further than others, so that all six pistons are eventually equally displaced – cable ties (readily available from a number of accessory outlets) can be used on individual pistons. If you find that a piston is seized, block all the others so that the hydraulic system acts on the seized piston alone – this should be sufficient to displace it. If not, then you can use compressed air directed into the fluid inlet once the hose has been detached. Alternatively wait until the caliper halves have been separated (Step 10), then place the caliper half piston-down on the bench and

5.7 Unscrew the bolts and slide the caliper off the disc

apply the compressed air which should then lift the caliper off the piston. Take care to apply the compressed air gradually and progressively, starting with a fairly low pressure, until the piston is displaced.

⚠ **Warning: Use only low air pressure, otherwise the pistons may be forcibly expelled and cause damage or injury. Never place your fingers in front of the pistons in an attempt to catch or protect them when applying compressed air, as serious injury could result.**

10 Refer to Step 4 and detach the hydraulic hose(s) from the caliper, blocking or plugging them as described. Tip all the residual brake fluid from the caliper into a suitable container or onto a wad of rag, which you should then throw away **(see illustration)**. Unscrew the caliper body joining bolts and separate the

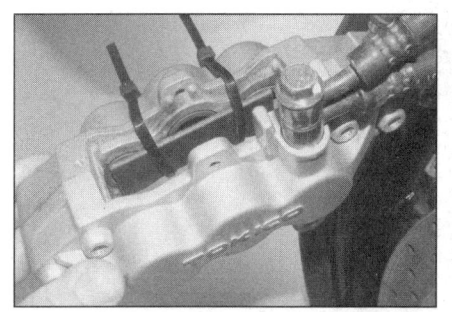

5.9a Use cable ties and a piece of steel as shown and displace the pistons as described . . .

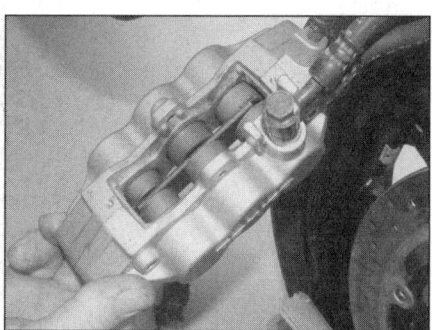

5.9b . . . until both sets meet in the middle

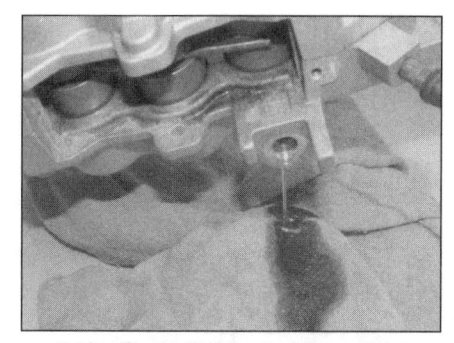

5.10a Tip the fluid out of the caliper

7

7•8 Brakes, wheels and tyres

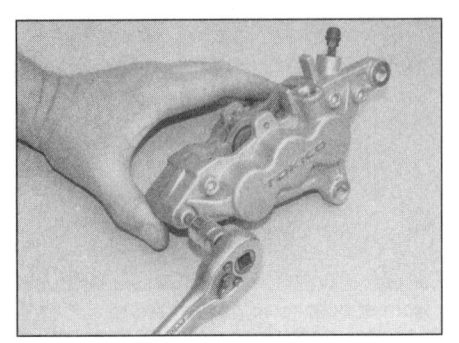

5.10b Unscrew the bolts . . .

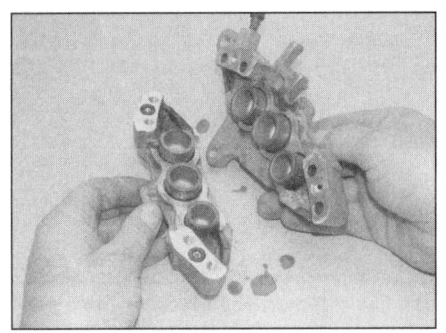

5.10c . . . and separate the halves

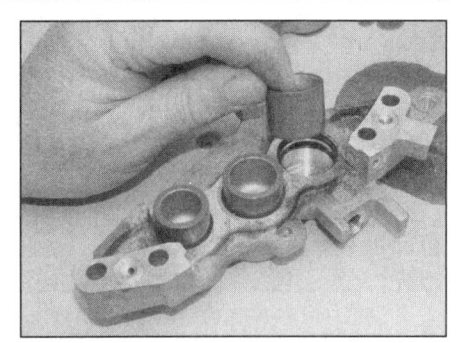

5.10d Remove the pistons . . .

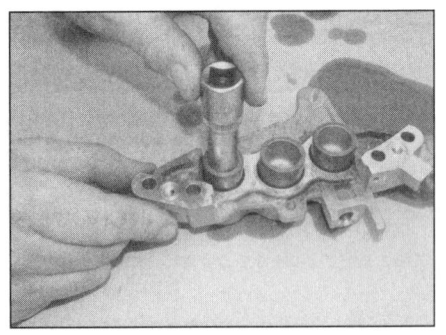

5.10e . . . using a bar as shown to jiggle them out if necessary

5.10f Discard the caliper O-rings as new ones must be used

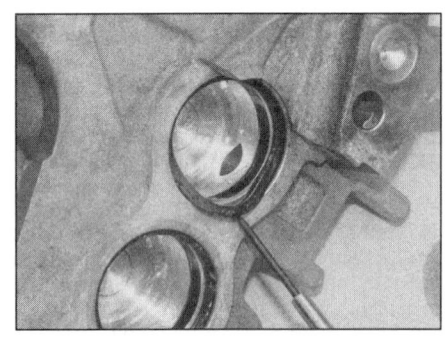

5.11 Remove the dust seals . . .

body halves **(see illustrations)**. Remove the pistons from each half – you should be able to pick them out by hand, but if necessary use a suitably sized piece of wooden dowel or a socket and/or extension bar inserted in the piston to jiggle it while simultaneously pulling it out with your hands **(see illustrations)**. Grips can be used only if they are sufficiently covered in tape so that there is no possibility of scoring the pistons. Mark each piston head and caliper body with a felt marker to ensure that the pistons can be matched to their original bores on reassembly. Note that two sizes of piston are used (see Specifications). Remove the caliper O-rings from whichever body half they are in and discard them as new ones must be used **(see illustration)**.

Caution: Do not try to remove the pistons by levering them out.

11 Remove the dust seal from each caliper bore using a wooden or plastic tool **(see illustration)**. Discard them as new ones must be used on installation. If a metal tool is being used, take great care not to damage the bores.
12 Remove and discard the piston seals in the same way **(see illustration)**.
13 Clean the pistons and bores, paying attention to the seal grooves, with clean brake fluid of the specified type. If compressed air is available, use it to dry the parts thoroughly (make sure it's filtered and unlubricated).

Caution: Do not, under any circumstances, use a petroleum-based solvent to clean brake parts.

14 Inspect the caliper bores and pistons for signs of corrosion, nicks and burrs and loss of plating. If surface defects are present, either fit new pistons or obtain an entire new caliper assembly as required. If the necessary measuring equipment is available, compare the dimensions of the pistons and bores to those specified at the beginning of the Chapter. If the caliper is in bad shape the master cylinder should also be checked.
15 Lubricate the new piston seals with clean brake fluid and fit them in their grooves in the caliper bores **(see illustrations)**. Note that two sizes of bore and piston are used (see Specifications), and care must therefore be taken to ensure that the correct size seals are fitted to the correct bores. The same

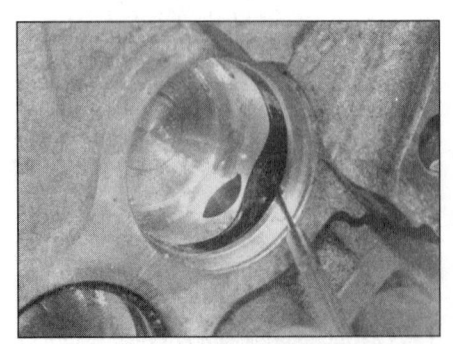

5.12 . . . and the piston seals

5.15a Lubricate the new seals with clean fluid

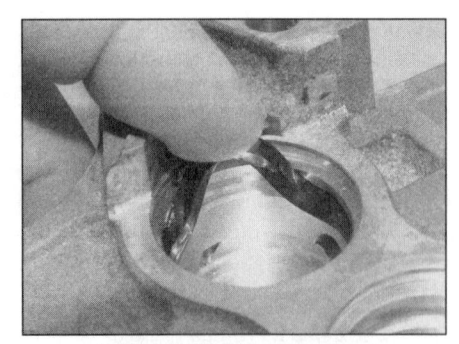

5.15b Fit the piston seal . . .

Brakes, wheels and tyres 7•9

applies when fitting the new dust seals and pistons.

16 Lubricate the new dust seals with clean brake fluid and fit them in their grooves in the caliper bores **(see illustration)**.

17 Lubricate the pistons with clean brake fluid and install them closed-end first into the caliper bores **(see illustrations)**. Using your thumbs, push the pistons all the way in, making sure they enter the bore squarely **(see illustration)**.

18 Lubricate the new caliper O-rings with clean brake fluid and fit them into their recesses in the caliper body **(see illustration)**. Join the two halves of the caliper together, making sure that the O-rings stay correctly seated **(see illustration)**. Install the joining bolts and tighten them to the torque setting specified at the beginning of the Chapter **(see illustrations)**. If it is not possible to tighten the bolts fully at this stage, tighten them as much as possible, then tighten them fully once the caliper has been installed.

Installation

19 If necessary, push the pistons a little way back into the caliper (see Section 2, Step 8). If removed, install the brake pads (see Section 2 – you can do this after the caliper has been installed if preferred).

20 Slide the caliper onto the brake disc, making sure the pads sit squarely on either side **(see illustration 5.7)**. Install the caliper mounting bolts and tighten them to the torque setting specified at the beginning of the Chapter.

21 If the caliper has been overhauled and the body joining bolts have not yet been tightened, tighten them now to the specified torque setting **(see illustration 5.5)**.

22 If removed, connect the brake hose(s) to the caliper, using new sealing washers on each side of the fitting(s) **(see illustration 5.4)**. Align the hose(s) as noted on removal. Tighten the banjo bolt to the torque setting specified at the beginning of the Chapter. Top up the master cylinder reservoir with DOT 4 brake fluid (see *Daily (pre-ride) checks*) and bleed the hydraulic system as described in Section 10.

23 Fit the brake hose(s) into its guide and/or clip(s) **(see illustration 5.3)**.

24 Check that there are no leaks and thoroughly test the operation of the front brake before riding the motorcycle.

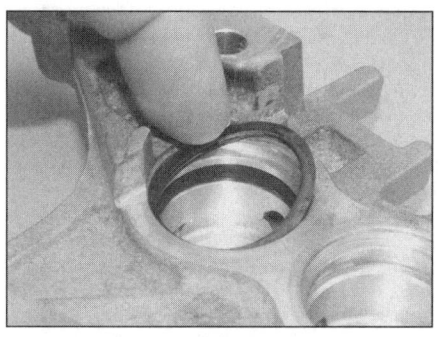

6 Rear brake caliper

Warning: The dust created by the brake pads may contain asbestos, which is harmful to your health. Never blow it out with compressed air and don't inhale any of it. An approved filtering mask should be worn when working on the brakes. If a caliper indicates the need for an overhaul (usually due to leaking fluid or sticky operation), all old brake fluid should be flushed from the system. Do not, under any circumstances, use petroleum-based solvents to clean brake parts. Use clean brake fluid only. Use care when working with brake fluid as it can injure your eyes and it will damage painted surfaces and plastic parts – cover these with rag. Disassembly, overhaul and reassembly of the caliper must be done in a spotlessly clean work area to avoid contamination and possible failure of the hydraulic system components.

5.16 . . . followed by the dust seal

5.17a Lubricate each piston . . .

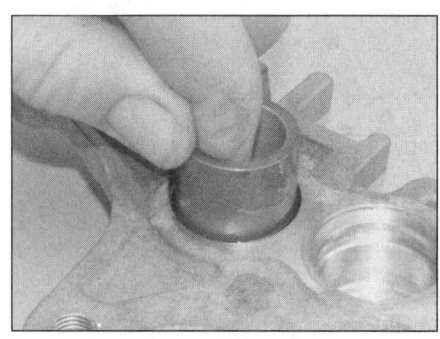

5.17b . . . then fit it into the bore . . .

5.17c . . . and push it all the way in

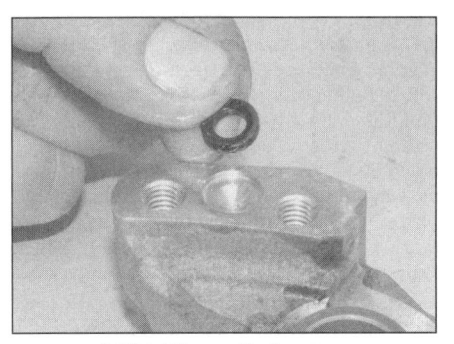

5.18a Fit new O-rings . . .

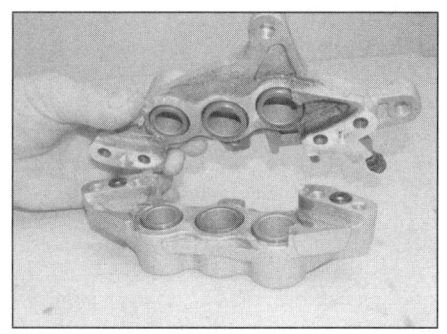

5.18b . . . then join the caliper halves . . .

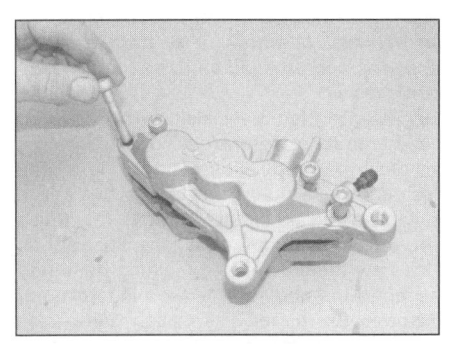

5.18c . . . install the bolts . . .

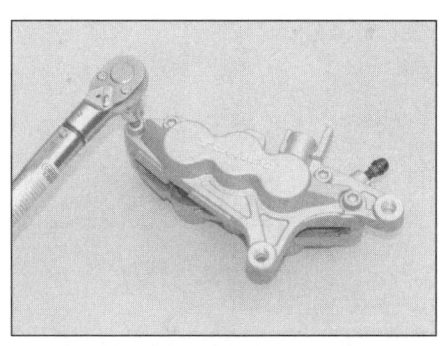

5.18d . . . and tighten them to the specified torque

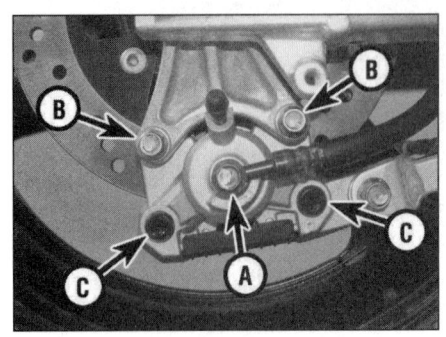

7•10 Brakes, wheels and tyres

6.3 Brake hose banjo bolt (A), caliper body joining bolts (C), caliper mounting bolts (B)

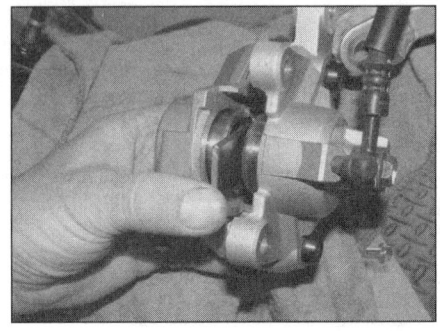

Note: *If the entire rear brake system is being overhauled (i.e. master cylinder as well as caliper), or if you intend to change the brake fluid as part of the caliper overhaul (which is advisable), drain the brake fluid completely from the system after displacing the pistons from the caliper (see Section 10), as opposed to retaining the old fluid within it by blocking the hose as described (Step 3).*

1 If the caliper is leaking fluid, or if the brake pads are wearing unevenly, or the pistons do not move smoothly or are tight or stuck in their bores, then caliper overhaul is required.

2 Before disassembling the caliper, read through the entire procedure and make sure that you have the correct seal kit. Also, you will need some new DOT 4 brake fluid, and some clean rags.

Removal

3 If the caliper is being overhauled, slacken the brake hose banjo bolt then retighten it lightly, enough to prevent fluid leakage **(see illustration)**. The bike's hydraulic system can then be used to force the pistons out of the body once the pads have been removed. If the caliper is being completely removed but not overhauled, unscrew the brake hose banjo bolt and detach the hose, noting the alignment with the caliper. Discard the sealing washers as new ones must be used on installation. Either clamp the hose, plug it using another suitable short piece of hose fitted through the eye of the banjo union (a tight fit is necessary for a good seal), block it using a suitable bolt with sealing washers and a capped (domed) nut, or wrap some plastic foodwrap tightly around (a finger cut off a latex glove also works well), the object being to minimise fluid loss and prevent dirt entering the system. Whatever you do, also cover the end of the hose in rag, just in case.

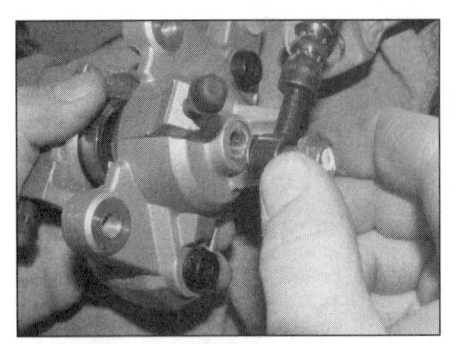

6.9 Use cable ties and/or a piece of steel as shown and displace the pistons as described until both meet in the middle

6.10a Detach the brake hose...

6.10b ...and tip the fluid out of the caliper

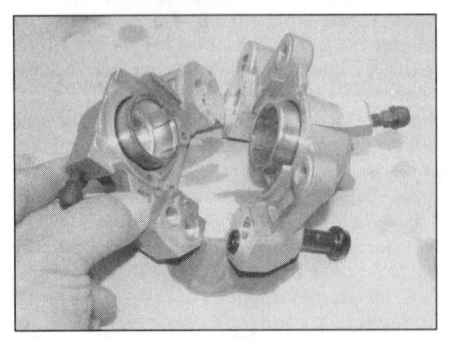

6.10c Unscrew the bolts and separate the halves

6.10d Remove the pistons...

4 If the caliper body is to be split into its halves for overhaul, slacken the caliper body joining bolts at this stage and retighten them lightly **(see illustration 6.3)**.

5 Slacken the caliper mounting bolts, then unscrew the nut and withdraw the bolt securing the torque arm to the caliper **(see illustrations 6.3 and 3.1b)**.

6 Unscrew the caliper mounting bolts and slide the caliper off the disc.

7 If the caliper is being overhauled, remove the brake pads (see Section 3).

Overhaul

8 Clean the exterior of the caliper and around the pistons with denatured alcohol or brake system cleaner, making sure all grit and dirt is removed.

9 Displace the pistons as far as possible from the caliper body by pumping them out using the brake pedal. A good way to do this is to cable-tie or hold a thin piece of sheet steel across the piston on one side, then pump the brake pedal until the piston on the other side is almost in the middle of the caliper – do not displace it any further as you need it to remain in its bore. Now cable-tie the almost-displaced piston in the same way and pump the pedal until the other one meets the first one in the middle, with the piece of steel separating them **(see illustration)**. If a suitable piece of steel is not available make sure the pistons are displaced evenly by blocking or cable-tying the one that moves further than other, so that both pistons are eventually equally displaced – cable ties are readily available in a number of outlets. If you find that a piston is seized, and the hydraulic system is not sufficient to displace it even with the other piston blocked, then you can use compressed air directed into the fluid inlet once the hose has been detached, again with the other piston blocked. Alternatively wait until the caliper halves have been separated (Step 10), then place the caliper half piston-down on the bench and apply the compressed air which should then lift the caliper off the piston. Take care to apply the compressed air gradually and progressively, starting with a fairly low pressure, until the piston is displaced.

⚠ **Warning:** *Use only low air pressure, otherwise the piston may be forcibly expelled and cause damage or injury. Never place your fingers in front of the piston in an attempt to catch or protect it when applying compressed air, as serious injury could result.*

10 Refer to Step 3 and detach the hydraulic hose from the caliper, blocking or plugging it as described **(see illustration)**. Tip all the residual brake fluid from the caliper into a suitable container or onto a wad of rag, which you should then throw away **(see illustration)**. Unscrew the caliper body joining bolts and separate the body halves **(see illustration)**. Remove the piston from each half – you should be able to pick them out by hand **(see illustration)**, but if necessary use a suitably

Brakes, wheels and tyres 7•11

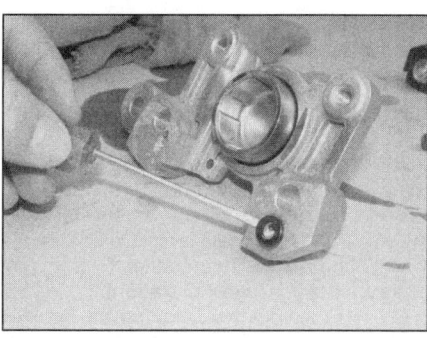

6.10e . . . and discard the caliper O-ring

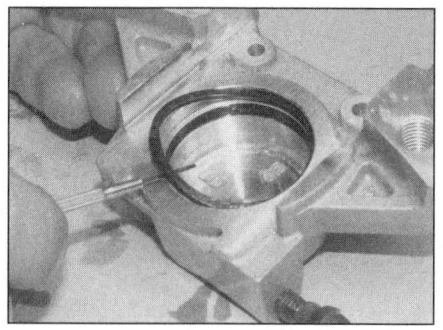

6.11 Remove the dust seals . . .

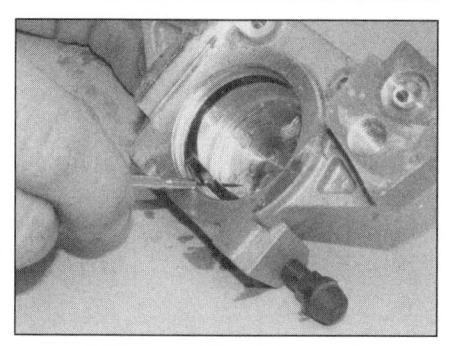

6.12 . . . and the piston seals

6.15a Lubricate the new seals with clean fluid

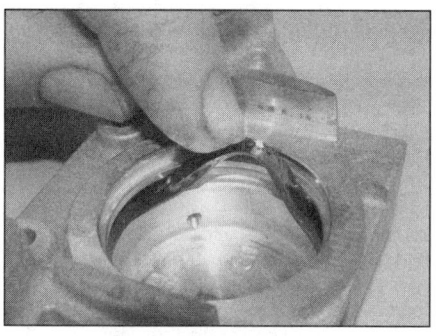

6.15b Fit the piston seal . . .

6.16 . . . followed by the dust seal

sized piece of wooden dowel or a socket and/or extension bar inserted in the piston to jiggle it while simultaneously pulling it out with your hands **(see illustration 5.10e)**. Grips can be used only if they are sufficiently covered in tape so that there is no possibility of scoring the pistons. Mark each piston head and caliper body with a felt marker to ensure that the pistons can be matched to their original bores on reassembly. Remove the caliper O-ring from whichever body half it is in and discard it as a new one must be used **(see illustration)**.

Caution: Do not try to remove the pistons by levering them out.

11 Remove the dust seal from each caliper bore using a wooden or plastic tool **(see illustration)**. Discard them as new ones must be used on installation. If a metal tool is being used, take great care not to damage the bores.

12 Remove and discard the piston seals in the same way **(see illustration)**.

13 Clean the pistons and bores, paying attention to the seal grooves, with clean brake fluid of the specified type. If compressed air is available, use it to dry the parts thoroughly (make sure it's filtered and unlubricated).

Caution: Do not, under any circumstances, use a petroleum-based solvent to clean brake parts.

14 Inspect the caliper bores and pistons for signs of corrosion, nicks and burrs and loss of plating. If surface defects are present, either fit new pistons or obtain an entire new caliper assembly as required. If the necessary measuring equipment is available, compare the dimensions of the pistons and bores to those specified at the beginning of the Chapter. If the caliper is in bad shape the master cylinder should also be checked.

15 Lubricate the new piston seals with clean brake fluid and fit them in their grooves in the caliper bores as shown **(see illustrations)**.

16 Lubricate the new dust seals with clean brake fluid and fit them in their grooves in the caliper bores **(see illustration)**.

17 Lubricate the pistons with clean brake fluid and install them closed-end first into the caliper bores **(see illustration)**. Using your thumbs, push the pistons all the way in, making sure they enter the bore squarely **(see illustration)**.

18 Lubricate the new caliper O-ring with clean brake fluid and fit it into its recess in the caliper body **(see illustration)**. Join the two halves of the caliper together, making sure that the

6.17a Lubricate each piston . . .

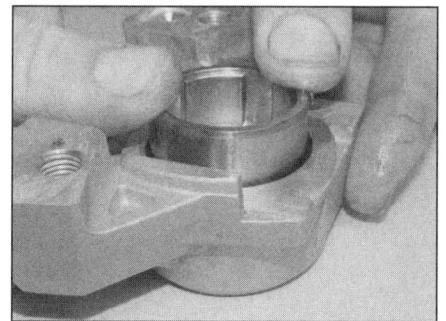

6.17b . . . then fit it into the bore and push it all the way in

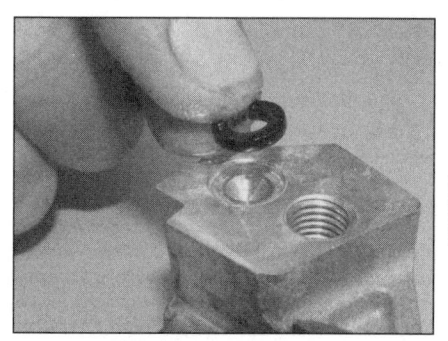

6.18a Fit a new O-ring . . .

7•12 Brakes, wheels and tyres

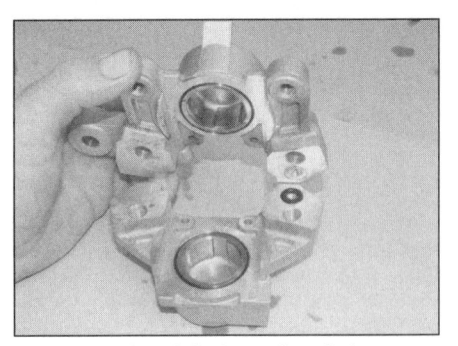

6.18b ... then join the caliper halves, ...

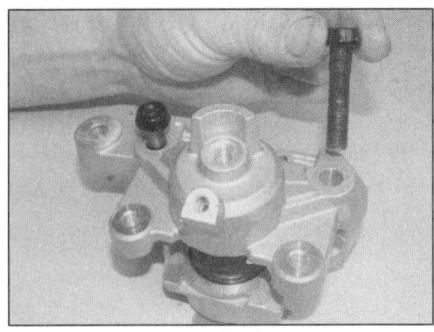

6.18c ... install the bolts, and tighten them to the specified torque

O-ring stays correctly seated **(see illustration)**. Install the joining bolts and tighten them to the torque setting specified at the beginning of the Chapter **(see illustration)**. If it is not possible to tighten the bolts fully at this stage, tighten them as much as possible, then tighten them fully once the caliper has been installed.

Installation

19 If necessary, push the pistons a little way back into the caliper (see Section 3, Step 10). If removed, install the brake pads (see Section 3).
20 If the caliper has just been displaced, slide it onto the disc, making sure the pads sit squarely on either side **(see illustration 3.14)**. Install the caliper mounting bolts and the torque arm bolt and nut and tighten them to the torque settings specified at the beginning of the Chapter **(see illustrations 6.3 and 3.1b)**.
21 If the caliper has been overhauled and the body joining bolts have not yet been tightened, tighten them now to the specified torque setting **(see illustration 6.3)**.
22 If removed, connect the brake hose to the caliper, using new sealing washers on each side of the fitting. Align the hose as noted on removal **(see illustration 6.3)**. Tighten the banjo bolt to the torque setting specified at the beginning of the Chapter. Top up the master cylinder reservoir with DOT 4 brake fluid (see *Daily (pre-ride) checks*) and bleed the hydraulic system as described in Section 10.
23 Check that there are no leaks and thoroughly test the operation of the rear brake before riding the motorcycle.

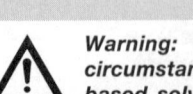

7 Front brake master cylinder

⚠ **Warning:** *Do not, under any circumstances, use petroleum-based solvents to clean brake parts. Use clean brake fluid only.* Use care when working with brake fluid as it can injure your eyes and it will damage painted surfaces and plastic parts – cover surrounding components with rag and wipe up any spills immediately and wash the area with soap and water. Disassembly, overhaul and reassembly of the brake master cylinder must be done in a spotlessly clean work area to avoid contamination and possible failure of the hydraulic system components.

Note: *If the entire front brake system is being overhauled (i.e. calipers as well as master cylinder), or if you intend to change the brake fluid as part of the master cylinder overhaul (which is advisable), drain the fluid completely from the system (after displacing the pistons from the caliper if applicable) (see Section 10), as opposed to retaining the old fluid within it by blocking the hose as described (Step 6).*

1 If the master cylinder is leaking fluid, or if the lever does not produce a firm feel when the brake is applied, and bleeding the brakes does not help (see Section 10), and the hydraulic hoses and unions are all in good condition, then master cylinder overhaul is recommended.
2 Before disassembling the master cylinder, read through the entire procedure and make sure that you have the correct rebuild kit. Also, you will need some new DOT 4 brake fluid, some clean rags and internal circlip pliers. **Note:** *To prevent damage to the paint from spilled brake fluid, always cover the fuel tank when working on the master cylinder.*

Removal

Note: *If the master cylinder is being displaced from the handlebar and not being removed completely or overhauled, follow Steps 4 and 7 only.*

3 Remove the front brake lever (see Chapter 6).
4 Disconnect the wiring connector from the brake light switch **(see illustration)**.
5 Loosen then lightly re-tighten the screws holding the reservoir cover in place **(see illustration)**.
6 If the master cylinder is just being displaced and not completely removed or overhauled, do not detach the brake hose. If the master cylinder is being completely removed or overhauled, unscrew the brake hose banjo bolt and detach the hose from the master cylinder, noting its alignment **(see illustration)**. Discard the sealing washers as new ones must be used on installation. Either clamp the hose, plug it using another suitable short piece of hose fitted through the eye of the banjo union (it must be a fairly tight fit to seal it properly), block it using a suitable bolt with sealing washers and a capped (domed) nut, or wrap plastic foodwrap tightly around (a finger cut off a latex glove also works well), the object being to minimise fluid loss and prevent dirt entering the system. Whatever you do, also cover the end of the hose in rag, just in case.

Caution: Do not tip the master cylinder or brake fluid will run out.

7 Unscrew the master cylinder clamp bolts, then lift the master cylinder and reservoir away from the handlebar **(see illustration)**.

7.4 Disconnect the wiring connector (arrowed)

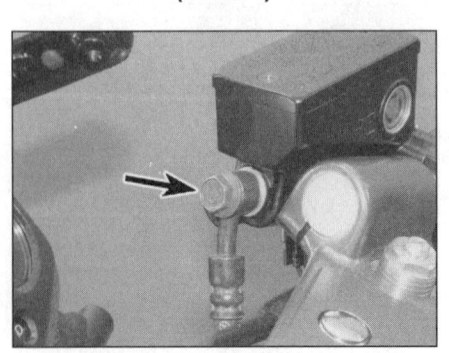

7.5 Slacken the cover screws

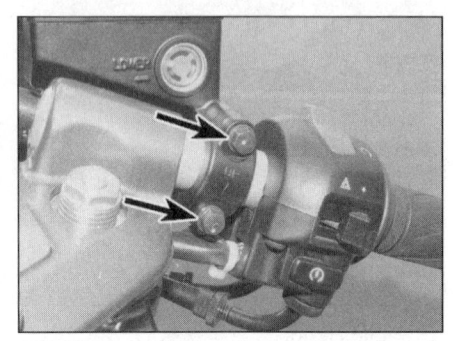

7.6 Brake hose banjo bolt (arrowed)

7.7 Master cylinder clamp bolts (arrowed)

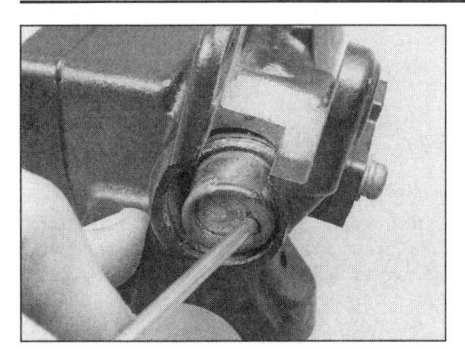

Brakes, wheels and tyres 7•13

7.10 Remove the boot from the end of the piston . . .

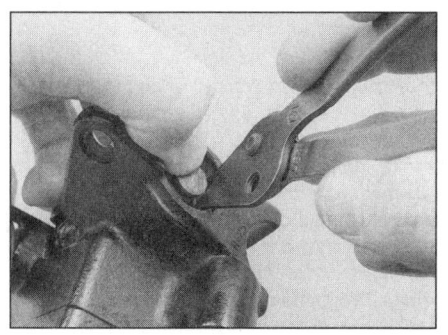

7.11a . . . then push the piston in and remove the circlip

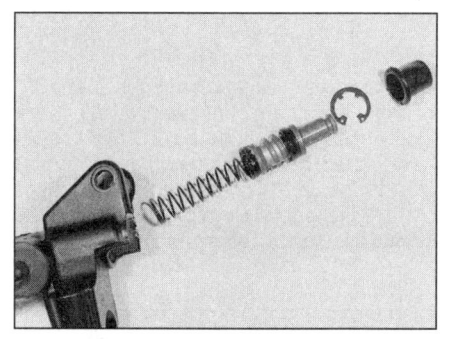

7.11b Note the layout of the components

8 Remove the reservoir cover, diaphragm plate and rubber diaphragm. If the system hasn't been drained, tip the brake fluid from the reservoir into a suitable container. Wipe any remaining fluid out of the reservoir with a clean rag.

9 If required undo the brake light switch screw and remove the switch, noting how it fits.

Overhaul

10 Carefully remove the dust boot from the end of the master cylinder and from around the piston, noting how it locates **(see illustration)**.

11 Push the piston in and, using circlip pliers, remove the circlip from its groove in the master cylinder and slide out the piston assembly and the spring, noting how they fit **(see illustration)**. If they are difficult to remove, apply low pressure compressed air to the fluid outlet. Lay the parts out in order as you remove them to prevent confusion during reassembly **(see illustration)**.

12 Clean all parts with clean brake fluid. If compressed air is available, use it to dry the parts thoroughly (make sure it's filtered and unlubricated).

Caution: Do not, under any circumstances, use a petroleum-based solvent to clean brake parts.

13 Check the master cylinder bore for corrosion, scratches, nicks and score marks. If the necessary measuring equipment is available, compare the diameters of the piston and bore to those specified at the beginning of the Chapter. If damage or wear is evident,

the master cylinder must be replaced with a new one. If the master cylinder is in poor condition, then the calipers should be checked as well. Check that the fluid inlet and outlet ports in the master cylinder are clear.

14 The dust boot, circlip, piston, seal, cup and spring are included in the rebuild kit. Use all of the new parts, regardless of the apparent condition of the old ones. Assemble and install them according to the layout of the old ones – locate the protrusion on the inside of the cup into the narrow end of the spring so they fit together **(see illustration 7.11b)**.

15 Lubricate the cup, seal and piston with clean brake fluid.

16 Slide the spring into the master cylinder, with the wide end of the spring going in first, then insert piston assembly. Make sure the lips on the cup and seal do not turn inside out when they enter the bore. Depress the piston and install the new circlip, making sure that it locates in the groove in the master cylinder.

17 Apply some silicone grease to the inside of the rubber dust boot, then install it, making sure it is seated properly in the groove in the master cylinder and around the piston.

18 Inspect the reservoir rubber diaphragm and replace it with a new one it if it is damaged or deteriorated.

Installation

19 If removed, locate the brake light switch on the underside of the master cylinder and secure it with the screw.

20 Attach the master cylinder to the handlebar and fit the clamp with the UP marking facing up, aligning the mating

surfaces with the punch mark on the top of the handlebar **(see illustrations)**. Tighten the top bolt first, then the bottom bolt, to the torque setting specified at the beginning of the Chapter.

21 If detached connect the brake hose to the master cylinder, using new sealing washers on each side of the union, and aligning the hose as noted on removal **(see illustration 7.6)**. Tighten the banjo bolt to the torque setting specified at the beginning of the Chapter.

22 Connect the brake light switch wiring **(see illustration 7.4)**. Install the brake lever (see Chapter 6).

23 Fill the fluid reservoir with new DOT 4 brake fluid as described in *Daily (pre-ride) checks*. Refer to Section 10 of this Chapter and bleed the air from the system.

24 Fit the rubber diaphragm, making sure it is correctly seated, the diaphragm plate and the cover onto the reservoir. Tighten the cover screws.

25 Check the operation of the front brake and brake light before riding the motorcycle.

8 Rear brake master cylinder

Warning: Do not, under any circumstances, use petroleum-based solvents to clean brake parts. Use clean brake fluid only. Use care when working with brake fluid as it can injure your eyes and it will damage painted surfaces and plastic parts – cover surrounding components with rag. Disassembly, overhaul and reassembly of the brake master cylinder must be done in a spotlessly clean work area to avoid contamination and possible failure of the hydraulic system components.

Note: If the entire rear brake system is being overhauled (i.e. caliper as well as master cylinder), or if you intend to change the brake fluid as part of the master cylinder overhaul (which is advisable), drain the brake fluid completely from the system (after displacing the pistons from the caliper if applicable) (see Section 10), as opposed to retaining the old

7.20a Fit the master cylinder onto the handlebar . . .

7.20b . . . aligning the clamp mating surfaces with the punch mark (arrowed)

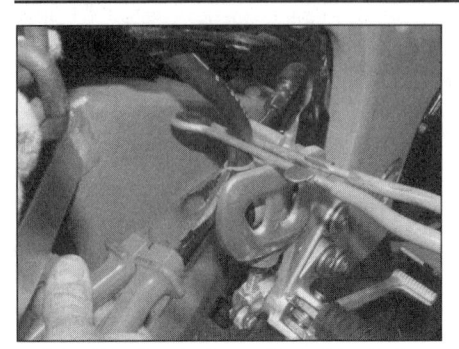

7•14 Brakes, wheels and tyres

8.4a Fit a hose clamp, then detach the hose from the master cylinder...

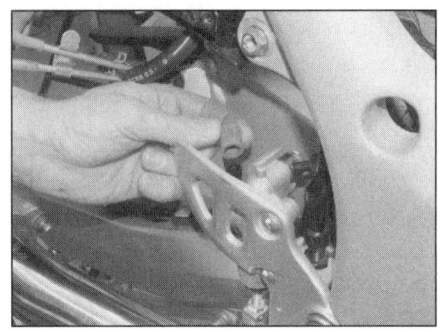

8.4b ... and fit a cap onto the union ...

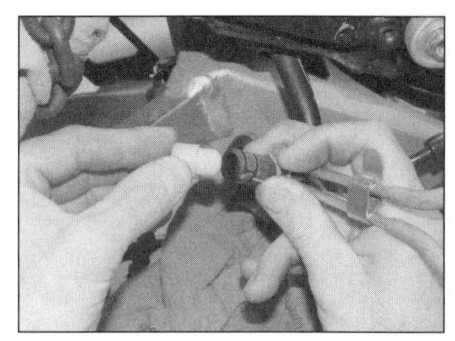

8.4c ... and a plug into the hose

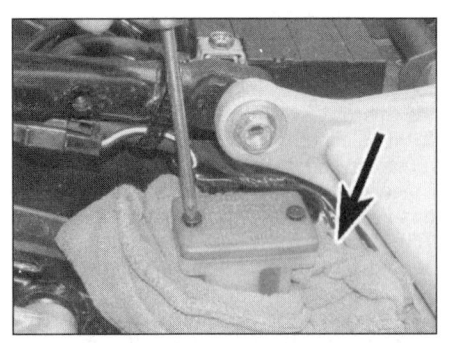

8.5 Slacken the cover screws, then unscrew the mounting bolt (arrowed)

8.6 Brake hose banjo bolt (arrowed)

fluid within it by blocking the hose as described (Step 6).

1 If the master cylinder is leaking fluid, or if the pedal does not produce a firm feel when the brake is applied, and bleeding the brakes does not help (see Section 10), and the hydraulic hoses and unions are all in good condition, then master cylinder overhaul is recommended.

2 Before disassembling the master cylinder, read through the entire procedure and make sure that you have the correct rebuild kit. Also, you will need some new DOT 4 brake fluid, some clean rags and internal circlip pliers. **Note:** *To prevent damage to the paint from spilled brake fluid, always cover the surrounding components when working on the master cylinder.*

Removal

3 Remove the seat cowling (see Chapter 8).
4 Place a hose clamp on the rear brake reservoir hose close to the master cylinder **(see illustration)**. Have to hand a hose union cap and a hose plug – these are available quite cheaply in sets from tool suppliers, such as Draper. Place some rag around the master cylinder to catch the brake fluid, then release the clamp securing the brake hose to its union and detach it. Swiftly fit the cap onto the union and the plug into the hose **(see illustrations)**.
5 If required, loosen then lightly re-tighten the screws holding the reservoir cover in place **(see illustration)**. Remove the clamp from the reservoir hose, then unscrew the bolt securing the reservoir and draw the hose up through the hole in the mudguard. Remove the reservoir cover and diaphragm and tip the contents of the reservoir and hose into a suitable container. Wipe any remaining fluid out with a clean rag. Inspect the reservoir hose for cracks or splits and replace it with a new one if necessary.
6 If the master cylinder is just being displaced and not completely removed or overhauled, do not disconnect the brake hose. If the master cylinder is being completely removed or overhauled, unscrew the brake hose banjo bolt and detach the hose from the master cylinder, noting its alignment **(see illustration)**. Discard the sealing washers as new ones must be used on installation. Either clamp the hose, plug it using another suitable short piece of hose fitted through the eye of the banjo union (it must be a fairly tight fit to seal it properly), block it using a suitable bolt with sealing washers and a capped (domed) nut, or wrap plastic foodwrap tightly around (a finger cut off a latex glove also works well), the object being to minimise fluid loss and prevent dirt entering the system. Whatever you do, also cover the end of the hose in rag, just in case.
7 Remove the split pin and washer from the clevis pin securing the brake pedal to the master cylinder pushrod, then withdraw the clevis pin and separate the pedal from the pushrod **(see illustration)**.
8 Unscrew the two bolts securing the master cylinder to the bracket and remove the master cylinder **(see illustration)**.

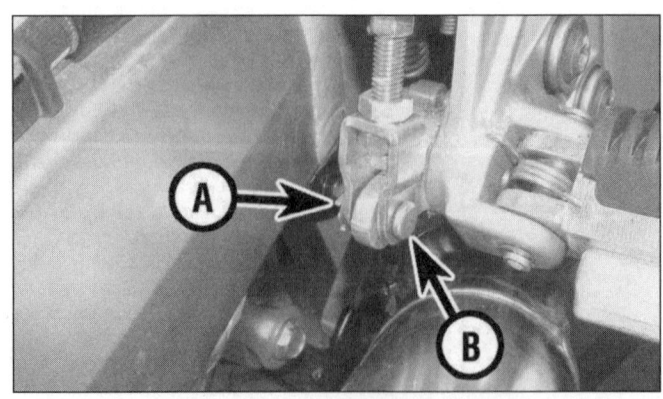

8.7 Remove the split pin and washer (A), then withdraw the clevis pin (B)

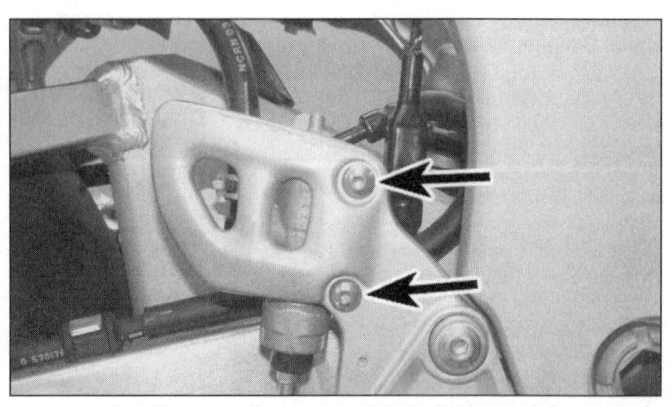

8.8 Master cylinder mounting bolts (arrowed)

Brakes, wheels and tyres 7•15

Overhaul

9 If required, mark the position of the clevis locknut on the pushrod, then slacken the locknut and thread the clevis off the pushrod **(see illustration)**.

10 Dislodge the rubber dust boot from the base of the master cylinder and from around the pushrod, noting how it locates, and slide it down the pushrod.

11 Push the pushrod in and, using circlip pliers, remove the circlip from its groove in the master cylinder and slide out the pushrod, piston assembly and the spring, noting how they fit. If they are difficult to remove, apply low pressure compressed air to the fluid outlet. Lay the parts out in the proper order to prevent confusion during reassembly.

12 If required, undo the screw securing the fluid reservoir hose union and detach it from the master cylinder. Discard the O-ring as a new one must be used.

13 Clean all of the parts with clean brake fluid. If compressed air is available, use it to dry the parts thoroughly (make sure it's filtered and unlubricated).

Caution: Do not, under any circumstances, use a petroleum-based solvent to clean brake parts.

14 Check the master cylinder bore for corrosion, scratches, nicks and score marks. If the necessary measuring equipment is available, compare the diameters of the piston and bore to those specified at the beginning of the Chapter. If damage or wear is evident, the master cylinder must be replaced with a new one. If the master cylinder is in poor condition, then the caliper should be checked as well.

15 The dust boot, circlip, piston, seal, cup and spring are included in the rebuild kit. Use all of the new parts, regardless of the apparent condition of the old ones. Assemble and install them according to the layout of the old ones – locate the protrusion on the inside of the cup into the narrow end of the spring so they fit together.

16 Lubricate the cup, seal and piston with clean brake fluid.

17 Slide the spring into the master cylinder, with the wide end of the spring going in first, then insert piston assembly. Make sure the lips on the cup and seal do not turn inside out when they enter the bore.

18 Apply some silicone grease to the end of the pushrod and fit it into the master cylinder. Depress the pushrod, then install the new circlip, making sure it is properly seated in the groove.

19 Install the rubber dust boot, making sure it is seated properly in the groove in the master cylinder and around the pushrod.

20 If removed, fit a new O-ring onto the fluid reservoir hose union, then fit the union into the master cylinder and secure it with its screw.

21 If removed, thread the clevis locknut and the clevis onto the master cylinder pushrod end. Position the clevis as noted on removal, then tighten the locknut against the clevis.

Installation

22 Fit the master cylinder onto its bracket and tighten the bolts to the torque setting specified at the beginning of the Chapter **(see illustration 8.8)**.

23 Align the brake pedal with the master cylinder pushrod clevis, then slide in the clevis pin, fit the washer and secure it using a new split pin **(see illustration 8.7)**.

24 Connect the brake hose to the master cylinder, using new sealing washers on each side of the union. Align the hose as noted on removal and tighten the banjo bolt to the specified torque setting **(see illustration 8.6)**.

25 If removed install the reservoir and tighten its bolt **(see illustration 8.5)**. Connect the reservoir hose to the union on the master cylinder and secure it with the clip **(see illustration 8.4a)**. Check that the hose is secure at the reservoir end as well. If the clips have weakened, use new ones.

26 Fill the fluid reservoir with new DOT 4 brake fluid (see *Daily (pre-ride) checks*) and bleed the system following the procedure in Section 10.

27 Install the seat cowling (see Chapter 8).

28 Check the operation of the brake and brake light carefully before riding the motorcycle.

9 Brake hoses and unions

Inspection

1 Check brake hose condition regularly and replace the hoses at the specified interval (see Chapter 1).

2 Twist and flex the hoses while looking for

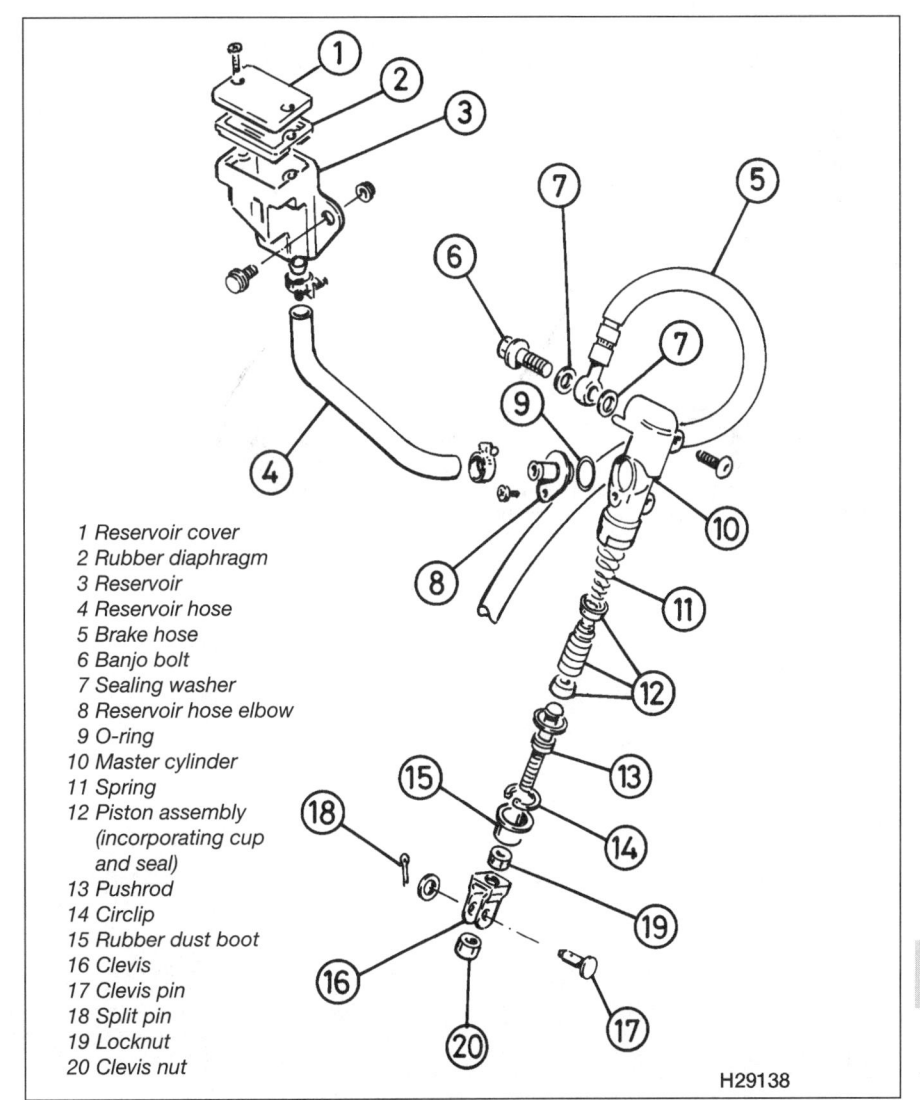

1 Reservoir cover
2 Rubber diaphragm
3 Reservoir
4 Reservoir hose
5 Brake hose
6 Banjo bolt
7 Sealing washer
8 Reservoir hose elbow
9 O-ring
10 Master cylinder
11 Spring
12 Piston assembly (incorporating cup and seal)
13 Pushrod
14 Circlip
15 Rubber dust boot
16 Clevis
17 Clevis pin
18 Split pin
19 Locknut
20 Clevis nut

8.9 Rear brake master cylinder components

7•16 Brakes, wheels and tyres

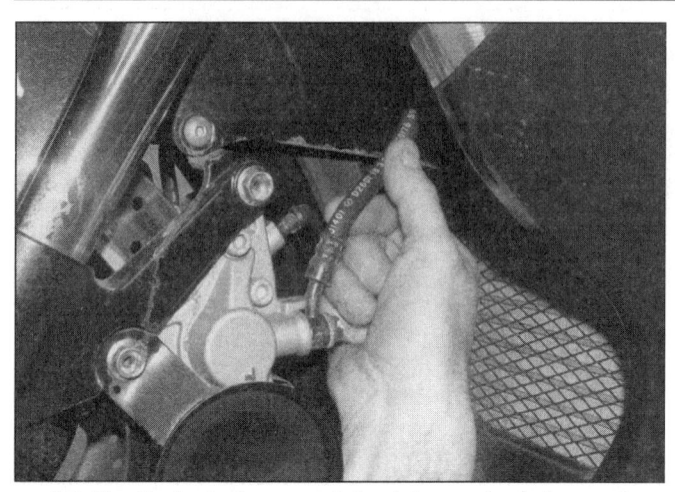

9.2 Flex the brake hoses and check for cracks, bulges and leaking fluid

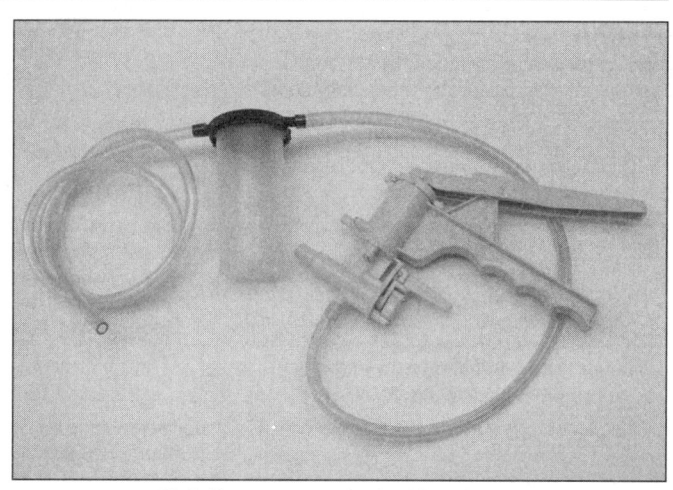

10.0 Vacuum-type brake bleeding kit

cracks, bulges and seeping fluid **(see illustration)**. Check extra carefully around the areas where the hoses connect with the banjo fittings, as these are common areas for hose failure.

3 Inspect the banjo union fittings connected to the brake hoses. If the fittings are rusted, scratched or cracked, replace them with new ones.

Replacement

4 The brake hoses have banjo union fittings on each end. Cover the surrounding area with plenty of rags and unscrew the banjo bolt at each end of the hose, noting its alignment **(see illustrations 5.4, 6.3, 7.6, 8.6)**. Free the hoses from any clips or guides and remove them. Discard the sealing washers as new ones must be used.

5 Position the new hose, making sure it isn't twisted or otherwise strained, and abut the tab on the hose union with the lug on the component casting, where present. Otherwise align the hose as noted on removal. Install the hose banjo bolts using new sealing washers on both sides of the unions. Tighten the banjo bolts to the torque setting specified at the beginning of this Chapter.

6 Make sure the hoses are correctly aligned and routed clear of all moving components. Flush the old brake fluid from the system, refill with new DOT 4 brake fluid (see *Daily (pre-ride) checks*) and bleed the air from the system (see Section 10). Check the operation of the brakes carefully before riding the motorcycle.

10 Brake system bleeding

Note: *If required use a commercially available vacuum-type brake bleeding tool. If bleeding the system using the conventional method does not work sufficiently well, it is advisable to obtain a bleeder and repeat the procedure detailed below, following the manufacturers instructions for using the tool* **(see illustration)**.

⚠ *Warning: Use care when working with brake fluid as it can injure your eyes and it will damage painted surfaces and plastic parts.*

Bleeding

1 Bleeding the brakes is simply the process of removing all the air bubbles from the brake fluid reservoirs, the hoses and the brake calipers. Bleeding is necessary whenever a brake system hydraulic connection is loosened, when a component or hose is replaced, or when a master cylinder or caliper is overhauled. Leaks in the system may also allow air to enter, but leaking brake fluid will reveal their presence and warn you of the need for repair.

2 To bleed the brakes, you will need some new DOT 4 brake fluid, a length of clear vinyl or plastic tubing, a small container partially filled with clean brake fluid, some rags and a ring spanner to fit the brake caliper bleed valves.

3 Cover the any body panels and other

10.5a Remove the dust cap from the caliper bleed valve

10.5b To bleed the brakes you need a spanner to fit on the bleed valve, a short section of clear tubing, and a clear container half-filled with brake fluid

Brakes, wheels and tyres 7•17

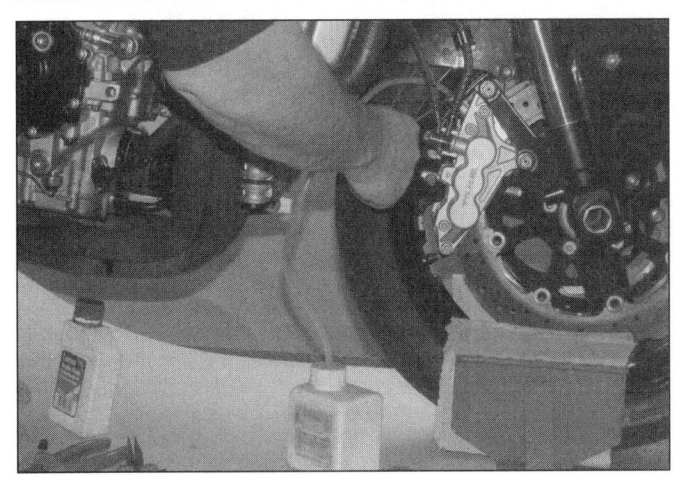

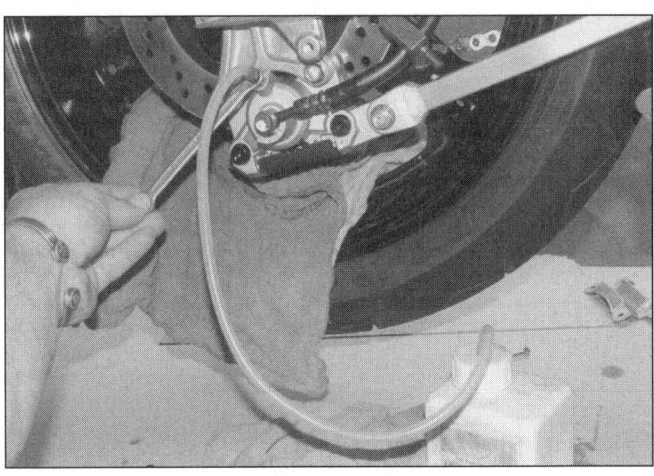

10.5c Bleeding the front brake

10.5d Bleeding the rear brake

painted components as required to prevent damage in the event that brake fluid is spilled. To access the rear master cylinder reservoir remove the seat cowling (see Chapter 8).

4 Remove the reservoir cover, diaphragm plate (front reservoir only), and diaphragm (see *Daily (pre-ride) checks*) and slowly pump the brake lever or pedal a few times, until no air bubbles can be seen floating up from the holes in the bottom of the reservoir. Doing this bleeds the air from the master cylinder end of the line. Loosely refit the reservoir cover or cap.

5 Pull the dust cap off the bleed valve on the caliper **(see illustration)**. Attach one end of the clear vinyl or plastic tubing to the bleed valve and submerge the other end in the brake fluid in the container **(see illustrations)**.

6 Check the fluid level in the reservoir – do not allow it to drop below the lower mark during the bleeding process.

7 Carefully pump the brake lever or pedal three or four times and hold it in (front) or down (rear) while opening the caliper bleed valve. When the valve is opened, brake fluid will flow into the clear tubing and the lever will move toward the handlebar or the pedal will move down.

8 Retighten the bleed valve, then release the brake lever or pedal gradually. Repeat the process until no air bubbles are visible in the brake fluid leaving the caliper and the lever or pedal is firm when applied. On completion, disconnect the bleeding equipment, then tighten the bleed valve to the torque setting specified at the beginning of the chapter and install the dust cap. Note that there are two bleed valves on the rear caliper.

9 Install the diaphragm, plate (front reservoir), and cover. Wipe up any spilled brake fluid and check that there are no fluid leaks.

Changing the fluid

10 Changing the brake fluid is a similar process to bleeding the brakes and requires the same materials, plus a suitable tool for siphoning the fluid out of the hydraulic

HAYNES HiNT
If it's not possible to produce a firm feel to the lever or pedal the fluid my be aerated. Let the brake fluid in the system stabilise for a few hours and then repeat the procedure when the tiny bubbles in the system have settled out. Also check to make sure that there are no 'high-spots' in the brake hose in which an air bubble can become trapped – this will occur most often in an incorrectly mounted hose union, but can also arise through bleeding the brakes while some of the brake system components are at such an angle to encourage this. Reversing the angle or displacing and moving the offending component around will normally dislodge any trapped air.

reservoir (such as a syringe, though if one isn't available it is no problem to displace the reservoir and tip the fluid out as described in Section 7 or 8). Ensure that your container is large enough to take all the old fluid when it is flushed out of the system.

11 Follow Steps 3, 4 and 5, but after removing the reservoir cap or cover, diaphragm plate, and diaphragm siphon or tip the old fluid out of the reservoir. Fill the reservoir with new brake fluid, then follow Step 7.

12 Retighten the bleed valve, then release the brake lever or pedal gradually. Keep the reservoir topped-up with new fluid to above the LOWER level at all times or air may enter the system and greatly increase the length of the task. Repeat the process until new fluid can be seen emerging from the bleed valve.

HAYNES HiNT
Old brake fluid is invariably much darker in colour than new fluid, making it easy to see when all old fluid has been expelled from the system.

13 Disconnect the hose, then tighten the bleed valve to the specified torque setting and install the dust cap.

14 Top-up the reservoir, install the diaphragm, plate (front reservoir), and cover. Wipe up any spilled brake fluid and check the entire system for leaks.

15 Check the operation of the brakes before riding the motorcycle.

Draining the system for overhaul

16 Draining the brake fluid is again a similar process to bleeding the brakes. The quickest and easiest way is to use a commercially available vacuum-type brake bleeding tool (see **Note** above) – follow the manufacturer's instructions. Otherwise follow the procedure described above for changing the fluid, but quite simply do not put any new fluid into the reservoir.

11 Wheel inspection and repair

1 Position the motorcycle on its centrestand or an auxiliary stand, so that the wheel being checked is raised off the ground. Clean the wheels thoroughly to remove mud and dirt that may interfere with the inspection procedure or mask defects. Make a general check of the wheels (see Chapter 1) and tyres (see *Daily (pre-ride) checks*).

2 To check axial (side-to-side) runout, attach a dial gauge to the fork slider or the swingarm and position its stem against the side of the rim **(see illustration overleaf)**. Spin the wheel slowly and check the amount of runout at the rim. To accurately check radial (out of round) runout with the dial gauge, remove the wheel from the machine, and the tyre from the wheel. With the axle clamped in a vice and the dial gauge positioned on the top of the rim, rotate the wheel and check the runout.

3 An easier, though slightly less accurate, method is to attach a stiff wire pointer to the

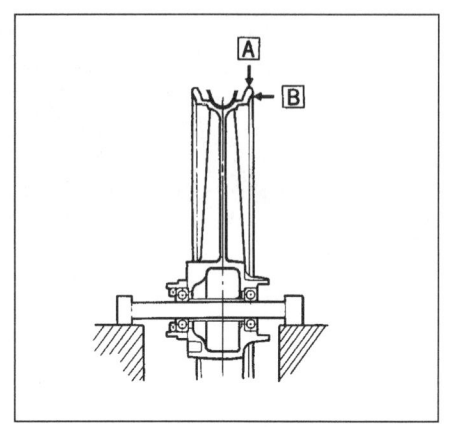

7•18 Brakes, wheels and tyres

11.2 Check the wheel for radial (out-of-round) runout (A) and axial (side-to-side) runout (B)

fork slider or the swingarm and position the end a fraction of an inch from the wheel (where the wheel and tyre join). If the wheel is true, the distance from the pointer to the rim will be constant as the wheel is rotated. **Note:** *If wheel runout is excessive, check the wheel bearings and axle very carefully before replacing.*

4 Visually inspect the wheels for cracks, flat spots on the rim, and other damage. Look very closely for dents in the area where the tyre bead contacts the rim. Dents in this area may prevent complete sealing of the tyre against the rim, which leads to deflation of the tyre over a period of time.

5 If damage is evident, or if runout in either direction is excessive, the wheel will have to be replaced with a new one. Never attempt to repair a damaged cast alloy wheel.

12 Wheel alignment check

1 Misalignment of the wheels, which may be due to a bent frame or fork yokes, can cause strange and possibly serious handling problems. If the frame or yokes are at fault, repair by a frame specialist or replacement with new parts are the only alternatives.

2 To check the alignment you will need an assistant, a length of string or a perfectly straight piece of wood and a ruler. A plumb bob or other suitable weight will also be required.

3 Place the bike on an auxiliary stand on level ground, so the bike is upright. If possible measure the width of both tyres at their widest points. Subtract the smaller measurement from the larger measurement, then divide the difference by two. The result is the amount of offset that should exist between the front and rear tyres on both sides.

4 If a string is used, have your assistant hold one end of it about halfway between the floor and the rear axle, touching the rear sidewall of the tyre.

5 Run the other end of the string forward and pull it tight so that it is roughly parallel to the floor **(see illustration)**. Slowly bring the string into contact with the front sidewall of the rear tyre, then turn the front wheel until it is parallel with the string. Measure the distance from the front tyre sidewall to the string.

6 Repeat the procedure on the other side of the motorcycle. The distance from the front tyre sidewall to the string should be equal on both sides, and equal to the amount of offset if calculated earlier.

7 As previously mentioned, a perfectly straight length of wood or metal bar may be substituted for the string **(see illustration)**. The procedure is the same.

8 If the front-to-back alignment is correct, the wheels still may be out of alignment vertically.

9 Using a plumb bob, or other suitable weight, and a length of string, check the rear wheel to make sure it is vertical. To do this, hold the string against the tyre upper sidewall and allow the weight to settle just off the floor. When the string touches both the upper and lower tyre sidewalls and is perfectly straight, the wheel is vertical. If it is not, place thin spacers under one leg of the stand until it is.

10 Once the rear wheel is vertical, check the front wheel in the same manner. If both wheels are not perfectly vertical, the frame and/or major suspension components are bent.

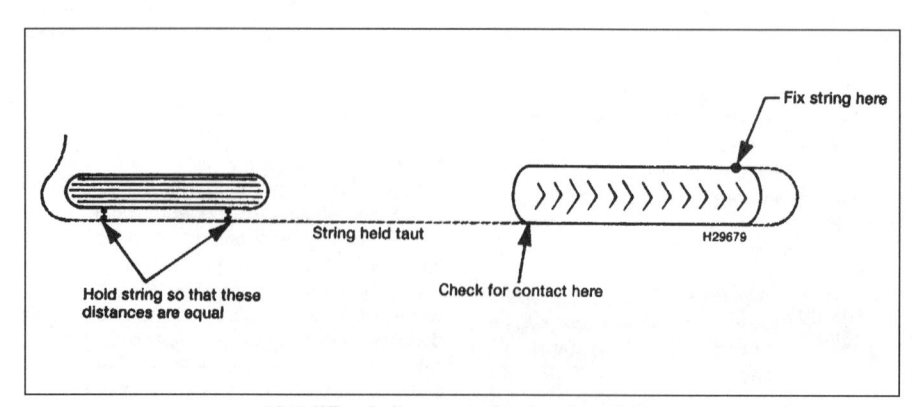

13 Front wheel

Removal

Note: *On K2 models onward a 24 mm hex bit is needed to unscrew the axle – this size bit may not be readily available from your average tool shop, in which case you will need to contact a commercial tool supplier. Alternatively Suzuki can provide one under part number 09900-18740, or you can weld a 24 mm nut onto the end of a bolt (as shown in illustration 13.2b).*

1 Displace the brake calipers (see Section 5). Support the calipers with a cable tie or a bungee cord so that no strain is placed on the hydraulic hoses. There is no need to disconnect the hoses from the calipers. **Note:** *Do not operate the front brake lever with the calipers removed.*

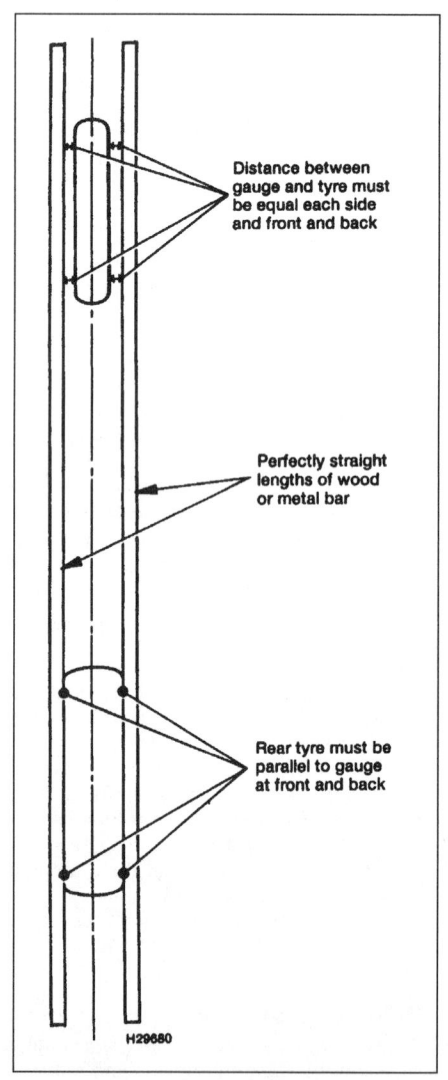

12.5 Wheel alignment check using string

12.7 Wheel alignment check using a straight-edge

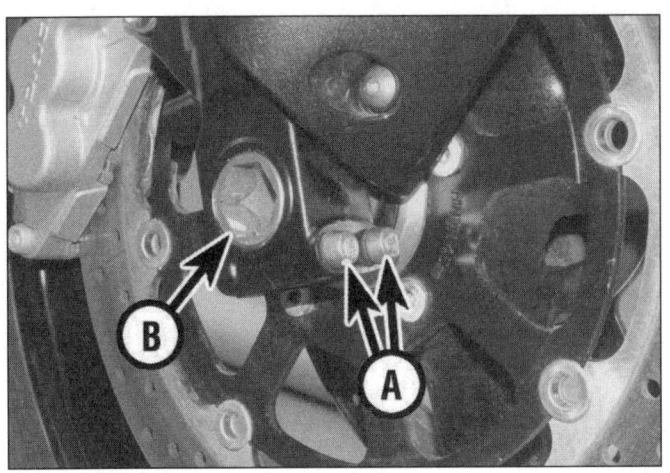

Brakes, wheels and tyres 7•19

13.2a Slacken the axle clamp bolts (A), then unscrew the axle (B)

13.2b Special tool made for the internal hex on later models

2 Slacken the axle clamp bolts on the bottom of the right-hand fork, then slacken the axle **(see illustrations)**.
3 Position the motorcycle on its centrestand (if fitted) or on an auxiliary stand, so that the front wheel is raised off the ground – if using a jack under the engine remove the fairing side panels first if necessary, and do not support the bike through the exhaust system. Note that for the wheel to clear the mudguard the wheel must be sufficiently raised, otherwise you have to remove the mudguard before removing the wheel (see Chapter 8). Always make sure the motorcycle is properly supported.
4 Support the wheel, then unscrew and withdraw the axle from the right-hand side, using a drift to tap it out if necessary, and carefully lower the wheel **(see illustration)**.
Caution: Don't lay the wheel down and allow it to rest on a disc – the disc could become warped. Set the wheel on wood blocks so the disc doesn't support the weight of the wheel.
5 Check that the axle is straight by rolling it on a flat surface such as a piece of plate glass (first wipe off all old grease and remove any corrosion using wire wool). If the equipment is available, place the axle in V-blocks and check for runout using a dial gauge. If the axle is bent, replace it with a new one.
6 Check the condition of the bearing seals and bearings (see Section 15).

Installation

7 Apply a smear of grease to the axle and the bearing seals.
8 Manoeuvre the wheel into position between the forks, making sure the directional arrows on the tyre and wheel are pointing in the normal direction of rotation (check both to make sure they concur, especially if you have just had a new tyre fitted – the tyre could have been fitted the wrong way round) **(see illustration)**.
9 Lift the wheel into place and slide the axle in from the right-hand side **(see illustration 13.4)**. Tighten the axle lightly **(see illustration 13.2b)**. Check that the wheel spins freely.
10 Install the brake calipers (see Section 5). Now tighten the axle to the torque setting specified at the beginning of the Chapter.
11 Apply the front brake a few times to bring the pads back into contact with the discs. Move the motorcycle off its stand, apply the front brake and pump the front forks a few times to settle all components in position.
12 Now tighten the axle clamp bolts on the bottom of the right-hand fork to the specified torque setting **(see illustration 13.2a)**.
13 Check for correct operation of the brakes before riding the motorcycle.

14 Rear wheel

Removal

1 Position the motorcycle on its centrestand or an auxiliary stand so that the rear wheel is off the ground. It is advisable to place a block in front of the front wheel, or better still to tie the front brake lever to the handlebar so that the front wheel is locked. Note that if the wheel is being removed as part of the swingarm removal procedure, do not use a

13.4 Withdraw the axle and remove the wheel

13.8 Make sure the wheel is installed with the arrow pointing in the direction of forward rotation

7•20 Brakes, wheels and tyres

14.2 Slacken the nut (arrowed)

14.3 Unscrew the axle nut and remove the washer where fitted and the chain adjuster block

paddock type stand that supports the bike via the swingarm – instead use axle stands positioned under the main frame (below the swingarm pivot points) as shown in the swingarm removal Section 6 in Chapter 6.

2 Slacken the nut on the brake torque arm front bolt **(see illustration)**.

3 Where fitted, remove the split pin locking the nut on the right-hand end of the axle. Discard it as a new one must be used. Unscrew the axle nut and where fitted remove the washer (generally if there is a split pin securing the nut, the nut won't have a separate washer) **(see illustration)**. Remove the chain adjuster block, noting how it fits.

4 Support the wheel (a good way to do this is

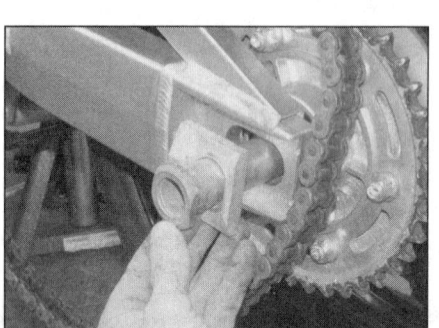

14.4 Withdraw the axle and disengage the chain

to slide your foot partway under it) then tap the axle out from the right-hand end and withdraw it along with the adjuster block, noting how it passes through the caliper bracket **(see illustration)**. Disengage the chain from the sprocket, then draw the wheel back so the disc is clear of the caliper, then lower the wheel and remove it.

5 Note the spacer in the seal in each side of the wheel and remove them for safekeeping if required (for example to access the bearings), noting which fits where **(see illustration 14.11)**.

Caution: Do not lay the wheel down and allow it to rest on the disc – it could become warped. Lay the tyre on blocks of wood, or stand the wheel upright. Do not operate the brake pedal with the wheel removed.

6 Check that the axle is straight by rolling it on a flat surface such as a piece of plate glass (first wipe off all old grease and remove any corrosion using wire wool). If the equipment is available, place the axle in V-blocks and check for runout using a dial gauge. If the axle is bent, replace it with a new one.

7 Check the condition of the grease seals and wheel bearings (see Section 15), and of the final drive coupling dampers (see Chapter 6).

Installation

8 If you have had a new tyre fitted make sure

the directional arrows point in the direction of normal rotation – you never know, it may have been fitted the wrong way round.

9 Push the pistons a little way back into the brake caliper using hand pressure or a piece of wood on the pads as leverage.

10 Thread the chain adjuster bolt locknuts up the bolts, then thread the bolts into the swingarm – it is easier to install the wheel axle when there is no tension on the chain.

11 Apply a thin coat of grease to the lips of each bearing seal, to the inside and the inner faces of the spacers where they contact the seals, and to the axle. Fit the spacers into the wheel **(see illustration)**.

12 Slide the left-hand side adjuster block onto the axle, making sure its cut-out side faces the axle head.

13 Loop the chain over the end of the swingarm. Pivot the brake caliper and bracket down on the torque arm as far as it will go without straining the hose.

14 Move the wheel into position and support it with your foot or a block while you fit the drive chain around the sprocket **(see illustration)**. Move the wheel in line with the swingarm holes. Pivot the caliper and bracket up onto the brake disc, making sure the pads sit squarely on each side of the disc and the bracket bore is aligned with the wheel and swingarm **(see illustration)**. Make sure the spacers remain correctly in place in the wheel.

14.11 Fit the spacer into each side of the wheel

14.14a Fit the chain around the sprocket . . .

14.14b . . . and locate the caliper onto the disc and the bracket between the wheel and swingarm

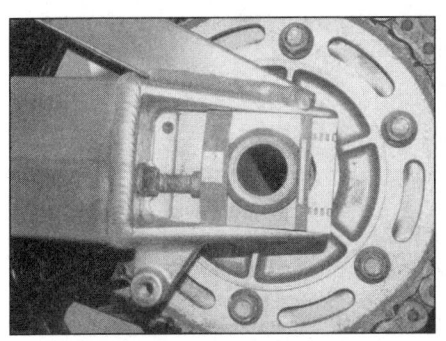

Brakes, wheels and tyres 7•21

14.15 Locate the chain adjuster block and axle head as shown

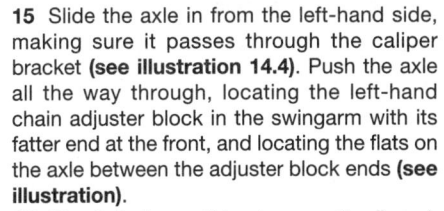

15.3 Lever out the seal on each side

15.5 Knock out the bearings using a drift

15 Slide the axle in from the left-hand side, making sure it passes through the caliper bracket **(see illustration 14.4)**. Push the axle all the way through, locating the left-hand chain adjuster block in the swingarm with its fatter end at the front, and locating the flats on the axle between the adjuster block ends **(see illustration)**.

16 Check that everything is correctly aligned, then fit the left-hand side adjuster block with its flanged end at the front, the washer (where fitted) and the axle nut, but do not tighten it yet **(see illustration 14.3)**.

17 Adjust the chain slack as described in Chapter 1.

18 Tighten the axle nut to the torque setting specified at the beginning of the Chapter. Where removed, fit a new split pin into the axle to lock the nut.

19 Tighten the front torque arm bolt nut to the torque setting specified at the beginning of the Chapter **(see illustration 14.2)**.

20 Operate the brake pedal several times to bring the pads into contact with the disc. Check the operation of the rear brake carefully before riding the bike.

15 Wheel bearing replacement

Note: *Before removing the bearings (but having removed the seals etc as required to access the bearings), refer to* Tools and Workshop Tips *in the Reference Section and check them to see if new ones are needed – however good their apparent condition, once the bearings have been driven out of the wheel they should be replaced with new ones rather than being reused, as the impact on the inner race when driving them out will damage them. Always replace the wheel bearings in sets. Never replace the bearings individually. Avoid using a high pressure cleaner on the wheel bearing area.*

Front wheel bearings

1 Remove the wheel (see Section 13).
2 Set the wheel on blocks so as not to allow the weight to rest on the brake disc.

3 Lever out the bearing seal on one side of the wheel using a seal hook or flat-bladed screwdriver, taking care not to damage the rim of the hub **(see illustration)**. Turn the wheel over and remove the other seal. Discard the seals as new ones must be used.

> **HAYNES HiNT** *Position a piece of wood against the wheel to prevent the screwdriver shaft damaging it when levering the grease seal out.*

4 Refer to *Tools and Workshop Tips* (Section 5 in the Reference Section) and check the bearings as described.

5 If the bearings are worn, remove them as follows: lay the wheel on the blocks with its left-hand side facing down. Insert a metal rod (preferably a brass drift punch) through the centre of the upper bearing and locate it on the rim of the lower bearing, pushing the spacer aside to expose it. Tap evenly around the rim to drive the bearing from the hub **(see illustration)**. The spacer should drop out once the bearing is free.

6 If it proves difficult or impossible to get your drift to purchase on the rim of the bearing, remove it using a knife-edged puller with slide-hammer attachment, or a driver with knife-edge attachment. Two such tools are available from Suzuki, pt. nos. 09921-20220 (puller), and 09944-60210 (driver).

7 Lay the wheel on its other side so that the remaining bearing faces down. Drive or pull the bearing out of the wheel.

8 Thoroughly clean the hub area of the wheel. First install the new left-hand bearing into its recess in the hub, with the marked or sealed side facing outwards. Using the old bearing, a bearing driver or a socket large enough to contact the outer race of the bearing only, drive it in until it's completely seated **(see illustration)**. Do not drive the bearing in against its inner race.

9 Turn the wheel over and install the bearing spacer. Drive the right-hand side bearing into place as described above.

10 Apply a smear of lithium based grease to the lips of the new seals, then press them into the wheel, using a seal or bearing driver or a suitable socket to drive it into place if necessary **(see illustration)**. As the seals sit flush with the top surface of their housing, using a piece of wood as shown will automatically set them flush without the risk of setting them too deep and having to lever them out again.

11 Clean off all grease from the brake discs using acetone or brake system cleaner then install the wheel (see Section 13).

Rear wheel bearings

12 Remove the rear wheel (see Section 14). Set the wheel on blocks, disc side down, making sure the disc is off the work surface.
13 Lift the sprocket coupling out of the wheel, noting how it fits **(see illustration)**. Remove the coupling spacer from the wheel if

15.8 A socket can be used to drive in the bearing

15.10 Press or drive the seal into the wheel – using a piece of wood as shown automatically sets the seal flush

7•22 Brakes, wheels and tyres

15.13a Lift the sprocket coupling out of the wheel...

15.13b ...and remove the spacer

15.20 A socket can be used to drive in the bearings

it didn't come away with the coupling **(see illustration)**.

14 Turn the wheel over so the brake disc is facing up. Lever out the bearing seal using a seal hook or flat-bladed screwdriver, taking care not to damage the rim of the hub (see **Haynes Hint** above) **(see illustration 15.3)**. Discard the seal as a new one must be used.

15 Refer to *Tools and Workshop Tips* (Section 5 in the Reference Section) and check the bearings as described.

16 If the bearings are worn, remove them as follows: lay the wheel on the blocks with its left-hand side facing down. Insert a metal rod (preferably a brass drift punch) through the centre of the upper bearing and locate it on the rim of the lower bearing, pushing the spacer aside to expose it. Tap evenly around the rim to drive the bearing from the hub **(see illustration 15.5)**. The spacer should drop out once the bearing is free.

17 If it proves difficult or impossible to get your drift to purchase on the rim of the bearing, remove it using a knife-edged puller with slide hammer attachment, or a driver with knife-edge attachment. Two such tools are available from Suzuki, pt. nos. 09921-20220 (puller), and 09944-60210 (driver).

18 Lay the wheel on its other side so that the remaining bearing faces down. Drive or pull the bearing out of the wheel.

19 Thoroughly clean the hub area of the wheel. First install the right-hand bearing into its recess in the hub, with the marked or sealed side facing outwards. Using the old bearing, a bearing driver or a socket large enough to contact the outer race of the bearing only, drive it in squarely until it's completely seated **(see illustration 15.8)**. Do not drive the bearing in against its inner race.

20 Turn the wheel over and install the bearing spacer. Drive the left-hand side bearing into place as described above **(see illustration)**.

21 Apply a smear of grease to the lips of the new grease seal, then press it into the right-hand side of the wheel, using a seal or bearing driver, a suitable socket or a flat piece of wood to drive it into place if necessary **(see illustration 15.10)**.

22 Clean off all grease from the brake disc using acetone or brake system cleaner.

23 Smear the sprocket coupling spacer ends and inside with grease. Fit the spacer into the wheel bearing **(see illustration 15.13b)**.

24 Fit the sprocket coupling into the wheel, making sure the coupling spacer locates correctly **(see illustration 15.13a)**.

25 Install the wheel (see Section 14).

Sprocket coupling bearing

26 Remove the rear wheel (see Section 14). Set the wheel on blocks, disc side down, making sure the disc is off the work surface.

27 Lift the sprocket coupling out of the wheel, noting how it fits **(see illustration 15.13a)**. Remove the spacer from the coupling if it didn't stay in the wheel **(see illustration 15.13b)**.

28 Lever out the bearing seal on the outside of the coupling using a seal hook or flat-bladed screwdriver, taking care not to damage the rim of the hub (see **Haynes Hint** above) **(see illustration)**. Discard the seal as a new one must be used.

29 Refer to *Tools and Workshop Tips* (Section 5 in the Reference Section) and check the bearing as described.

30 If the bearing is worn support the coupling on blocks of wood and drive the bearing out from the inside using a bearing driver or socket **(see illustration)**.

31 Thoroughly clean the bearing recess then install the bearing into the outside of the coupling, with the marked or sealed side facing out. Using the old bearing, a bearing driver or a socket large enough to contact the outer race of the bearing only, drive it in until it is completely seated **(see illustration)**. Do not drive the bearing in against its inner race.

32 Apply a smear of grease to the lips of the new seal, then press it into the coupling, using a seal or bearing driver, a suitable socket or a flat piece of wood to drive it into place if necessary **(see illustration)**.

15.28 Lever out the grease seal

15.30 Drive the bearing out from the inside

15.31 A socket can be used to drive in the bearing

15.32 Using a piece of wood as shown automatically sets the seal flush

Brakes, wheels and tyres 7•23

33 Check the sprocket coupling/rubber dampers (see Chapter 6).
34 Smear the sprocket coupling spacer ends and inside with grease. Fit the spacer into the wheel bearing.
35 Fit the sprocket coupling into the wheel, making sure the coupling spacer locates correctly.
36 Install the wheel (see Section 14).

16 Tyre fitting

General information
1 The wheels fitted to all models are designed to take tubeless tyres only. Tyre sizes are given in the Specifications at the beginning of this chapter.
2 Refer to the *Daily (pre-ride) checks* listed at the beginning of this manual for tyre maintenance.

Fitting new tyres
3 When selecting new tyres, refer to the tyre information label on the swingarm and the tyre options listed in the owners handbook. Ensure that front and rear tyre types are compatible, the correct size and correct speed rating; if necessary seek advice from a Suzuki dealer or tyre fitting specialist **(see illustration)**.

4 It is recommended that tyres are fitted by a motorcycle tyre specialist rather than attempted in the home workshop. This is particularly relevant in the case of tubeless tyres because the force required to break the seal between the wheel rim and tyre bead is substantial, and is usually beyond the capabilities of an individual working with normal tyre levers. Additionally, the specialist will be able to balance the wheels after tyre fitting.
5 Note that punctured tubeless tyres can in some cases be repaired. Such repairs must only be carried out by a motorcycle tyre fitting specialist. Suzuki specify not to exceed 50 mph (80 kmh) for the first 24 hours after a repair, and 80 mph (130 kmh) thereafter.

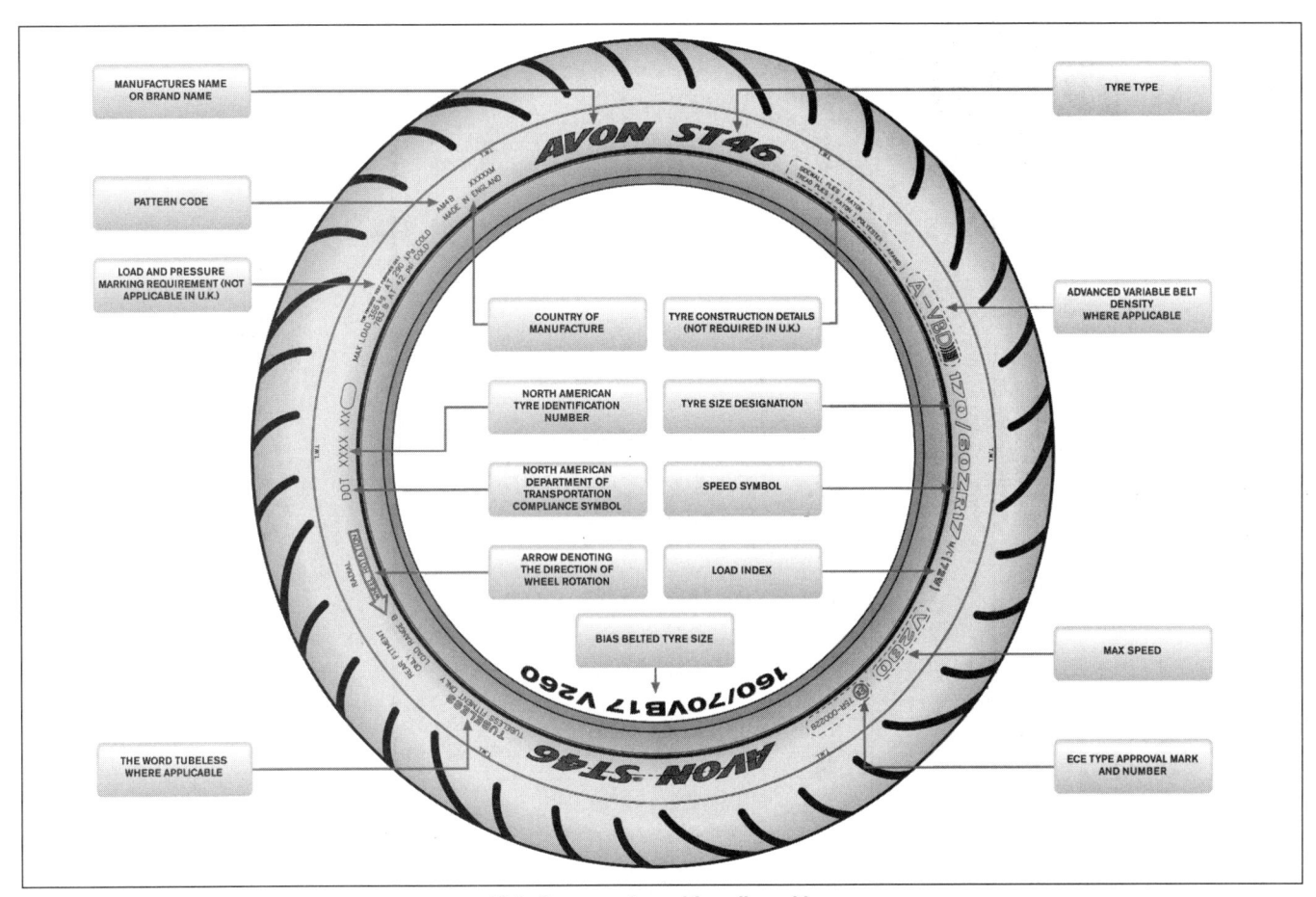

16.3 Common tyre sidewall markings

Notes

Chapter 8
Bodywork

Contents

Fairing and bodypanels 4
Front mudguard 5
General information 1
Seats 2
Rear view mirrors 3

Degrees of difficulty

| Easy, suitable for novice with little experience | Fairly easy, suitable for beginner with some experience | Fairly difficult, suitable for competent DIY mechanic | Difficult, suitable for experienced DIY mechanic | Very difficult, suitable for expert DIY or professional |

1 General information

This Chapter covers the procedures necessary to remove and install the body parts. Since many service and repair operations require the removal of body parts, the procedures are grouped here and referred to from other Chapters.

In the case of damage to the body parts, it is usually necessary to remove the broken component and replace it with a new (or used) one. The material that the body panels are composed of doesn't lend itself to conventional repair techniques. There are however some shops that specialise in 'plastic welding' and a range of DIY plastic repair kits available.

When attempting to remove any body panel, first study it closely, noting any fasteners and associated fittings, to be sure of returning everything to its correct place on installation. In some cases the aid of an assistant will be required when removing panels, to help avoid the risk of damage to paintwork. Once the evident fasteners have been removed, try to withdraw the panel as described but DO NOT FORCE IT – if it will not release, check that all fasteners have been removed and try again. Where a panel engages another by means of tabs, be careful not to break the tab or its mating slot or to damage the paintwork. Remember that a few moments of patience at this stage will save you a lot of money in replacing broken fairing panels!

When installing a body panel, first study it closely, noting any fasteners and associated fittings removed with it, to be sure of returning everything to its correct place. Check that all fasteners are in good condition, including all trim nuts or clips and damping/rubber mounts; any of these must be replaced if faulty before the panel is reassembled. Check also that all mounting brackets are straight and repair or replace them if necessary before attempting to install the panel. Where assistance was required to remove a panel, make sure your assistant is on hand to install it. Tighten the fasteners securely, but be careful not to overtighten any of them or the panel may break (not always immediately) due to the uneven stress.

Where trim clips are used, first identify which type they are – there are three main types. If the centre portion is flush with the body rim, push the centre in to release the clip, then draw the whole clip out of the panel **(see illustration)**. Reset the clip by pushing the inner end through the body so the top of the centre portion now protrudes from the rim. Fit the body into the

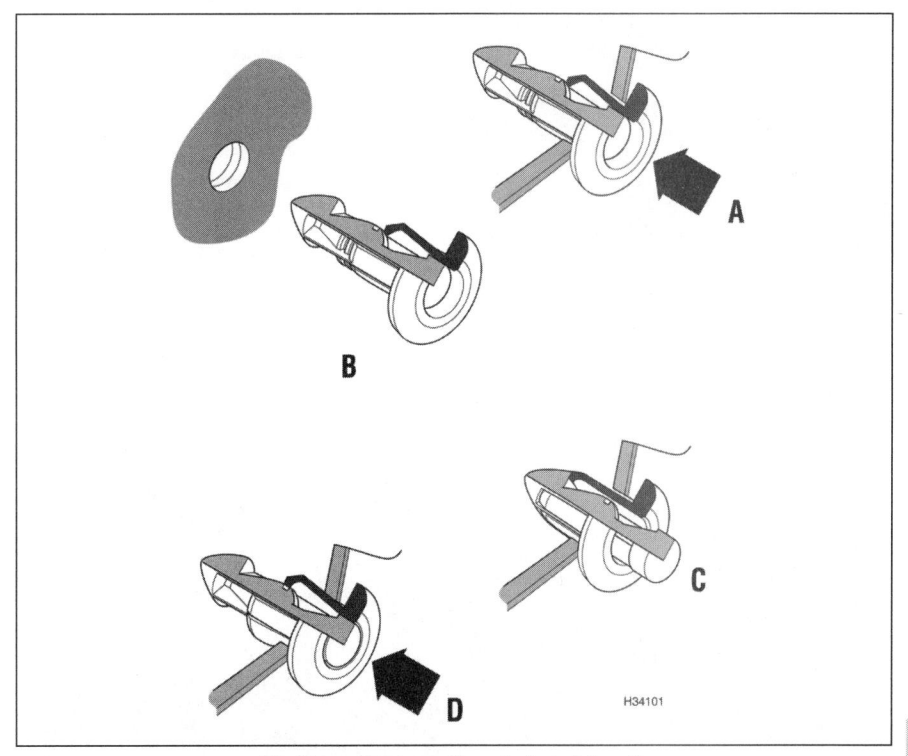

1.1 Removing a centre-pin type trim clip

To remove, push the centre pin in (A) to allow the clip body to be withdrawn from the panel (B). To install, depress the clip pawls to extend the centre pin and insert into the panel (C), then press the centre pin in flush with the body of the clip to lock it in place (D)

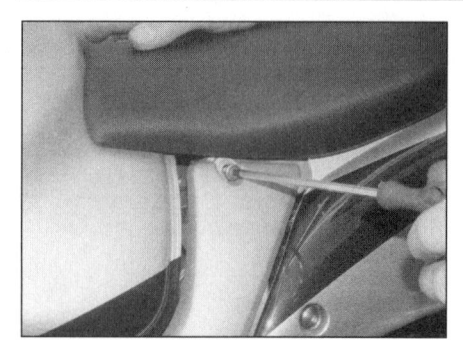

8•2 Bodywork

2.1a Unscrew the bolt on each side . . .

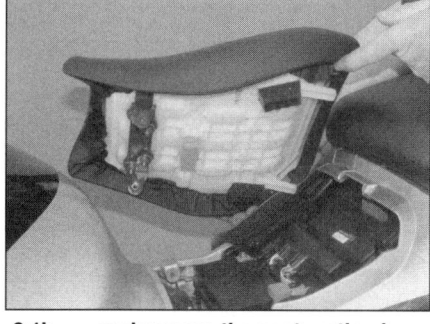

2.1b . . . and remove the seat, noting how the tabs locate under the hooks

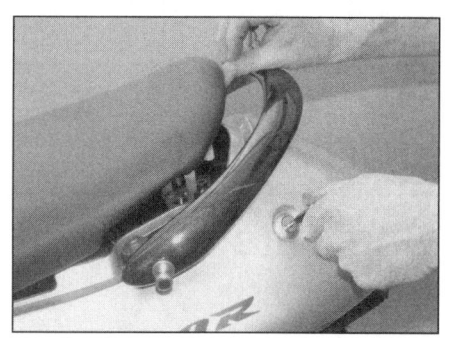

2.2a Turn the key to release the seat . . .

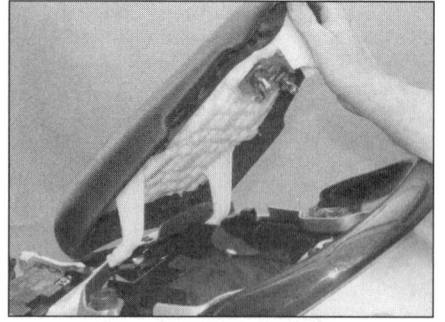

2.2b . . . noting how it locates

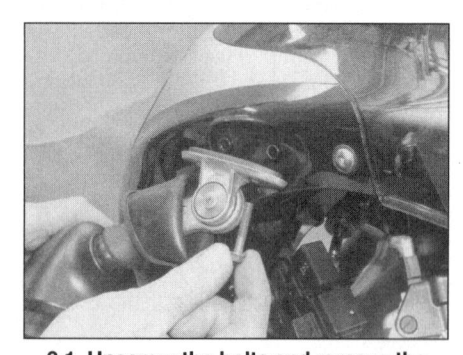

3.1 Unscrew the bolts and remove the mirror

panel, then lock it by pushing the centre into the body until they are flush. If the centre portion has a Phillips cross in the head, or if the centre portion protrudes from the body, to release them unscrew or pull out the centre of the clip, then pull the body of the clip out of the panel. When installing them, fit the body of the clip into the panel then push the centre into the body. As they are made of plastic, the threads on the screw-type ones easily become worn in which case the centres may not unscrew. If this happens, lever the centre out of the body using a small screwdriver and replace the trim clip with a new one.

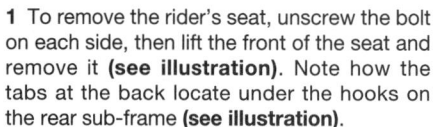

2 Seats

Removal

1 To remove the rider's seat, unscrew the bolt on each side, then lift the front of the seat and remove it **(see illustration)**. Note how the tabs at the back locate under the hooks on the rear sub-frame **(see illustration)**.
2 To remove the passenger's seat, insert the ignition key into the seat lock on the left-hand side and turn it clockwise to release the seat, then lift the back and remove it **(see illustration)**. Note how the tabs at the front locate under the hook on the rear sub-frame **(see illustration)**.

Installation

3 Installation is the reverse of removal. Push down on the back of the passenger seat to engage the latch.

3 Rear view mirrors

1 Pull the rubber boot of the mirror base. Unscrew the two bolts and remove the mirror **(see illustration)**.
2 Installation is the reverse of removal.

4 Fairing and body panels

Fairing bottom panel

1 Undo the four screws, then release the bottom panel from the fairing side panels and remove it **(see illustration)**. Check the condition of the rubber mounts and replace them with new ones if they are damaged, deformed or deteriorated.
2 Installation is the reverse of removal.

Fairing side panels

3 Undo the screw securing the underside at the back to the fairing bottom panel **(see illustration 4.1)**.
4 Release the trim clip securing the top trim section to the frame **(see illustration)**. Undo the screw securing the top trim section to the cockpit trim panel.

4.1 Bottom panel screws (arrowed)

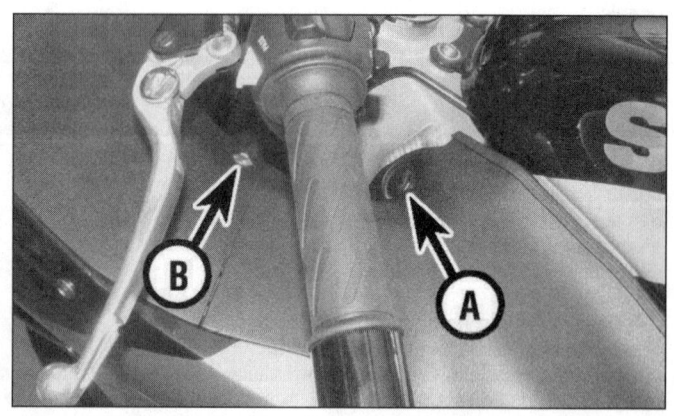

4.4 Release the trim clip (A) and undo the screw (B)

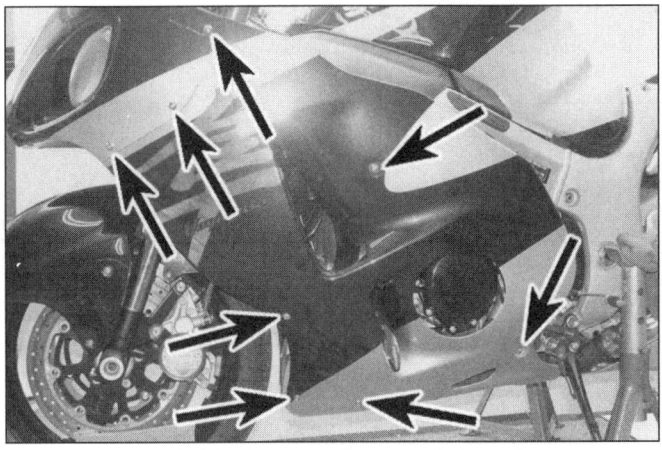

Bodywork 8•3

4.5 Fairing side panel screws (arrowed)

4.6 Release the trim clip (arrowed)

5 Undo the three screws securing the panel to the fairing **(see illustration)**.

6 Release and remove the trim clip securing the inner section to the access panel on the underside of the fairing **(see illustration)**.

7 Undo the five screws securing the fairing side panel to the frame and the centre section **(see illustration 4.5)** – note that if you are removing both sides there is no need to remove the second from front bolt on the bottom as it threads into the bracket joining the two panels, which will simply come away with the second panel.

8 Carefully pull the top trim section up to release the peg from the grommet, then remove the panel, noting how engages with the fairing and cockpit trim **(see illustration)**.

9 To remove the centre section that fits between the two panels, undo the three screws securing it – if the side panels have not been removed also undo the screws securing the centre panel to them **(see illustration)**.

10 Installation is the reverse of removal.

Cockpit trim panels

11 Undo the screw securing the cockpit trim panel to the top trim section on the fairing side panel **(see illustration 4.4)**.

12 Release the trim clip securing the panel to the fairing **(see illustration)**.

13 Undo the screw securing the two sections together in the middle **(see illustration)**.

14 Lift the panel up off the instruments and remove it **(see illustration)**.

15 Installation is the reverse of removal.

Fairing

16 Remove the rear view mirrors (see Section 3).

17 Remove the cockpit trim panels (see above).

18 Disconnect the headlight assembly wiring connector **(see illustration)**.

19 Release the trim clips securing the access panel to the underside of the fairing and

4.8 Release the peg on the trim section (arrowed) from the grommet and remove the panel

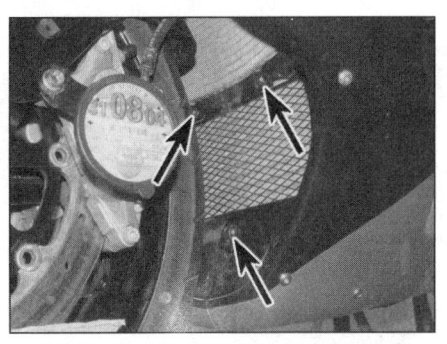

4.9 Centre section screws (arrowed)

4.12 Release the trim clip ...

4.13 ... then undo the screw (arrowed) ...

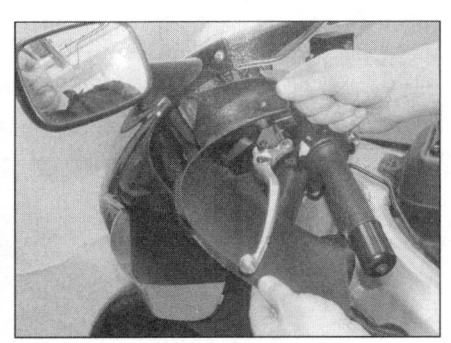

4.14 ... and remove the panel

4.18 Disconnect the wiring connector

8•4 Bodywork

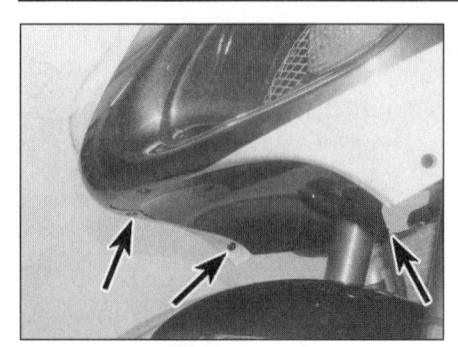

4.19a Release the three trim clips (arrowed) on each side . . .

4.19b . . . and remove the panel

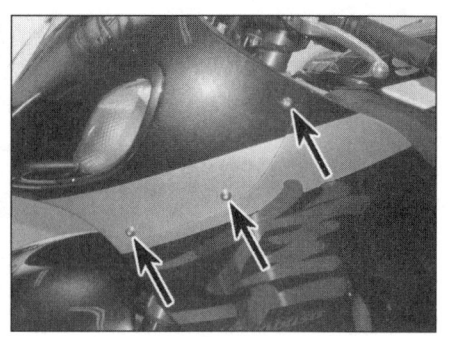

4.20 Undo the screws (arrowed) . . .

remove the panel – although this is not essential for fairing removal, it makes installation easier later **(see illustrations)**.
20 Undo the three screws securing the fairing to each fairing side panel **(see illustration)**.
21 Carefully draw the fairing forwards off its stay, spreading the ears to release it from the mirror mounts, and remove it **(see illustration)**. If you feel there is not enough flex to get the fairing off the mirror mounts, remove the windshield. Note the rubber pads that fit between the fairing and the mirror mounts on the stay.
22 Installation is the reverse of removal. Make sure the air ducts locate over the mesh covers in the intakes, and the pegs on the headlight locate in the grommets **(see illustrations)**.

Seat cowling

23 Remove both seats (see Section 2).
24 Unscrew the four bolts securing the passenger grab-rail and remove it, noting the arrangement of any collars, washers and grommets **(see illustration)**.
25 Release the seat lock outer cable from its

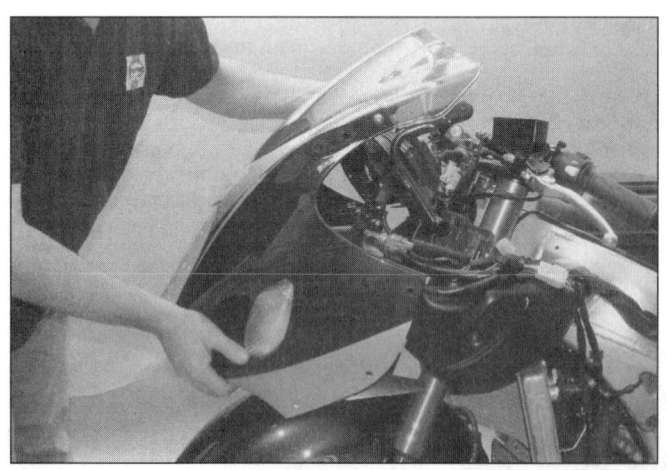

4.21 . . . and remove the fairing

4.22a Make sure the air ducts locate over the mesh . . .

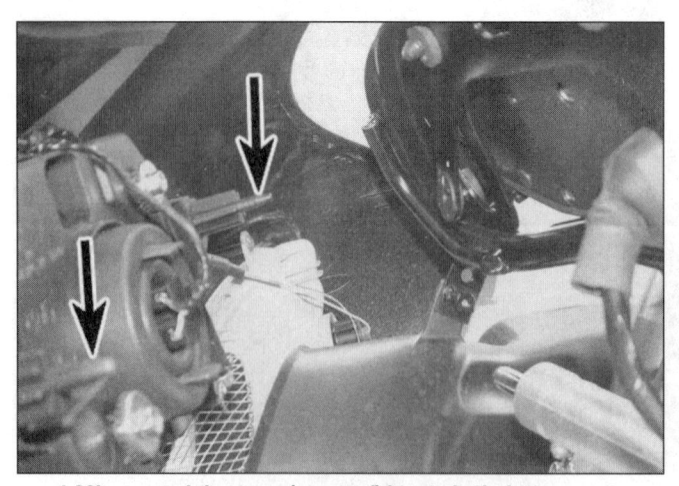

4.22b . . . and the pegs (arrowed) locate in their grommets

4.24 Unscrew the bolts and remove the grab-rail

Bodywork 8•5

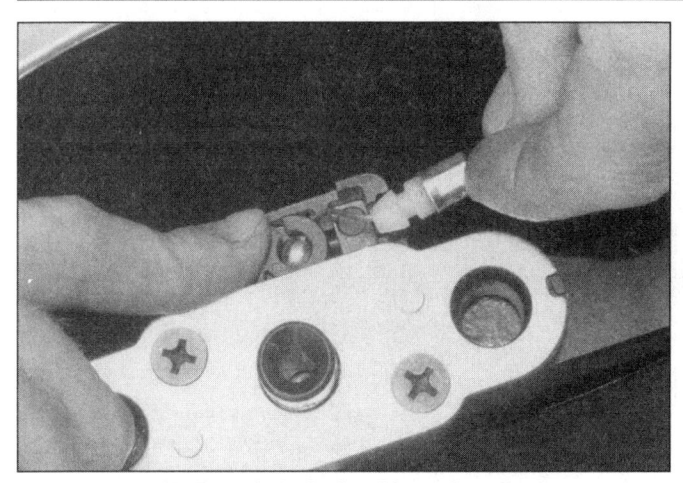

4.25 Detach the lock cable as described

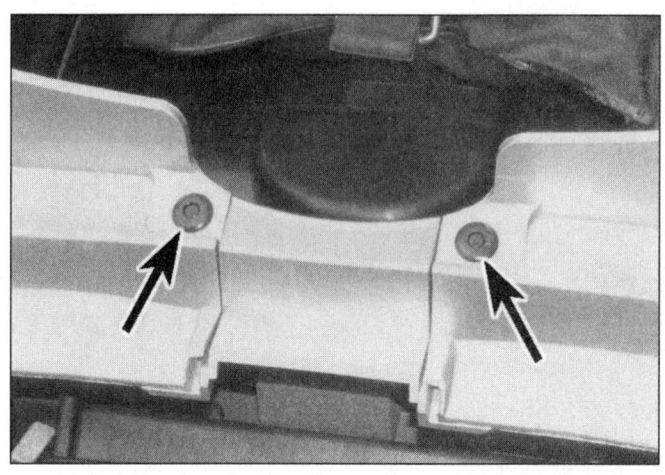

4.26 Release the trim clips (arrowed) and remove the middle section

holder and detach the inner cable end from the latch **(see illustration)**.
26 Release and remove the trim clips securing the middle section and remove it **(see illustration)**.
27 Where fitted remove the cap from each bungee hook bolt **(see illustration)**.
28 Release the trim clips and undo the screws securing the cowling **(see illustration)**. Lift the back of the cowling up on the left and displace it forwards slightly, then disconnect the tail light wiring connector **(see illustration)**.
29 Carefully draw the cowling back off the bike and remove it **(see illustration)**.
30 Installation is the reverse of removal.

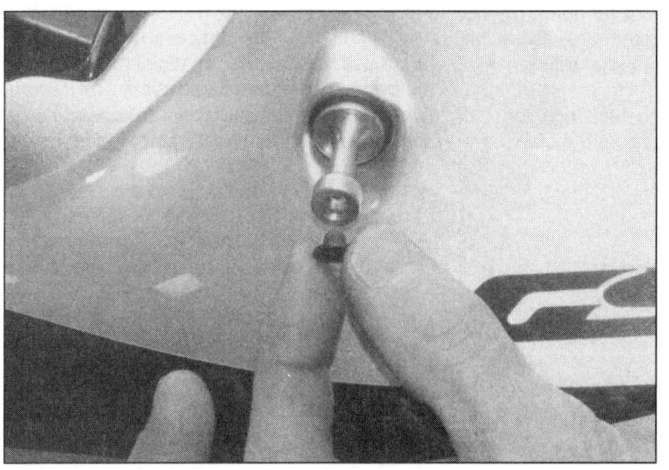

4.27 Remove the caps from the bungee hook bolts

4.28a Release the trim clips and undo the screws (arrowed – according to model) . . .

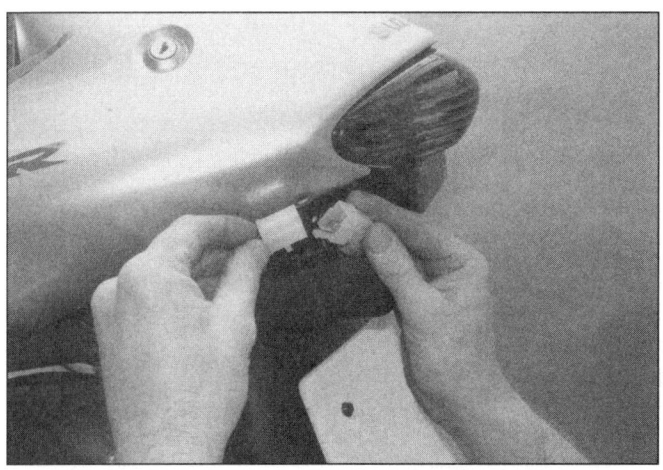

4.28b . . . then disconnect the wiring connector . . .

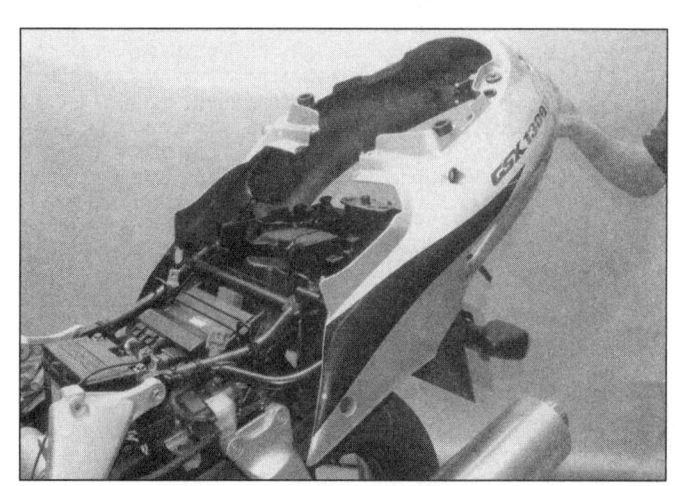

4.29 . . . and remove the seat cowling

8•6 Bodywork

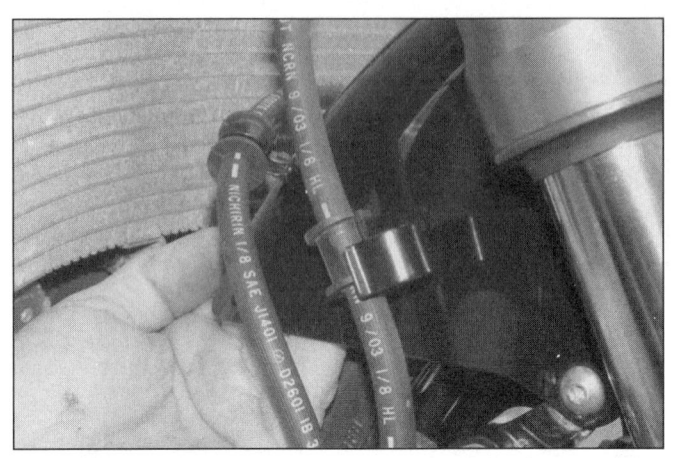

5.1 Free the brake hose from the open guide and release the clips securing the closed guides

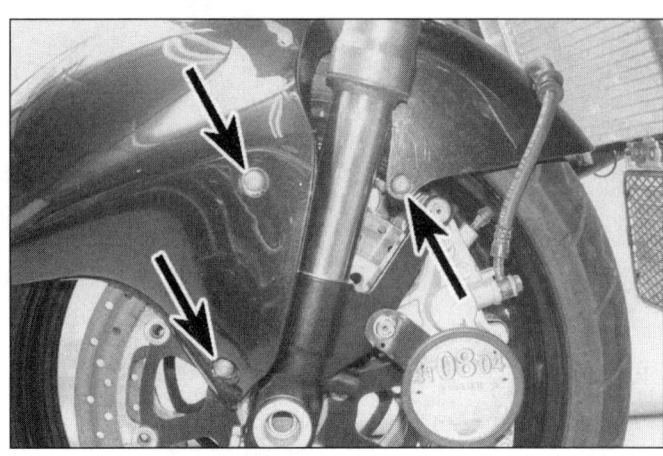

5.2 Unscrew the bolts (arrowed) on each side . . .

5.3 . . . and remove the mudguard, making sure the hose guide clears the fork

5 Front mudguard

1 Free the brake hose from its guide on the right-hand side **(see illustration)**. Release the brake hose clips from the mudguard.
2 Unscrew the bolts securing the mudguard **(see illustration)** – due to their position the bolts are prone to seizing, so if they feel tight when unscrewing them, do not force them; spray some penetrating lubricant around them and work them carefully back and forth to free them up.
3 Carefully remove the mudguard, squeezing the sides together and twisting it so that the hose guide clears the fork, and taking care not to scratch the top on the brake hose guide on the bottom yoke **(see illustration)**.
4 Installation is the reverse of removal. Apply some copper grease to the bolt threads.

Chapter 9
Electrical system

Contents

Alternator	29
Battery charging	4
Battery removal and maintenance	3
Brake light switches	14
Brake/tail/licence plate light bulb renewal	9
Charging system	28
Clutch switch	21
Diodes	22
Electrical system fault finding	2
Fuel pump and relay	see Chapter 4
Fuses	5
Gear position switch	see Chapter 4
General information	1
Handlebar switches	19
Headlight aim	see Chapter 1
Headlight assembly	8
Headlight bulb and sidelight bulb renewal	7
Horn	23
Ignition (main) switch	18
Ignition system components	see Chapter 5
Instrument and warning light LEDs	17
Instrument cluster removal and installation	15
Instrument check and renewal	16
Lighting system check	6
Oil pressure switch	24
Regulator/rectifier	30
Sidestand switch and relay	20
Starter motor check and overhaul	27
Starter motor removal and installation	26
Starter relay	25
Tail light assembly	10
Turn signal bulb renewal	12
Turn signal circuit check	11
Turn signal removal	13

Degrees of difficulty

Easy, suitable for novice with little experience	Fairly easy, suitable for beginner with some experience	Fairly difficult, suitable for competent DIY mechanic	Difficult, suitable for experienced DIY mechanic	Very difficult, suitable for expert DIY or professional

Specifications

Battery
Type	YT12A-BS
Capacity	12 V, 10 Ah
Current leakage	3 mA (max)
Charging time	5 to 10 hours @ 1.0 to 1.2 A

Charging system
Alternator stator coil resistance	0.2 to 0.4 ohms
Alternator output (max)	approx. 400 W at 5000 rpm
Unregulated voltage output (no-load, cold engine)	min. 65 V (ac) at 5000 rpm
Regulated voltage	13.5 to 15.0 V at 5000 rpm

Starter relay
Resistance .... 3 to 5 ohms

Fuses
Main .... 30 A
Headlight (high beam) .... 15 A
Headlight (low beam) .... 15 A
Turn signal .... 15 A
Ignition .... 15 A
Fuel pump relay .... 10 A
Fan motor .... 10 A

Bulbs
Headlight
  Main (HI) beam .... 60 W halogen
  Dipped (LO) beam .... 55 W halogen
Sidelight (European models) .... 5 W
License plate light .... 5 W
Brake/tail light .... 21/5 W x 2
Turn signal lights .... 21 W x 4
Warning lights and instrument lights .... LED

Torque settings
Alternator cover bolts .... 10 Nm
Alternator rotor bolt .... 120 Nm
Alternator stator bolts .... 10 Nm
Crankshaft position sensor bolts .... 5.5 Nm
Footrest bracket bolts .... 26 Nm
Oil pressure switch .... 14 Nm
Speed sensor bolt .... 4.5 Nm

1 General information

All models have a 12-volt electrical system charged by a three-phase alternator with a separate regulator/rectifier.

The regulator maintains the charging system output within the specified range to prevent overcharging, and the rectifier converts the ac (alternating current) output of the alternator to dc (direct current) to power the lights and other components and to charge the battery. The alternator rotor is mounted on the left-hand end of the crankshaft.

The starter motor is mounted on the right-hand side of the crankcase behind the cylinder block. The starting system includes the battery, the starter relay, the starter motor, and the various switches and wires. Some of the switches (sidestand switch, clutch switch and gear position switch) are part of the safety interlock circuit, which cuts the ignition if the sidestand is extended whilst the engine is running and in gear, or if a gear is selected whilst the engine is running and the sidestand is extended. It also prevents the engine from being started unless the clutch lever is pulled in, and if the engine is in gear while the sidestand is down. The engine can be started in gear as long as the sidestand is up and the clutch is pulled in.

Note: *Keep in mind that electrical parts, once purchased, cannot be returned. To avoid unnecessary expense, make very sure the faulty component has been positively identified before buying a replacement part.*

2 Electrical system fault finding

Warning: To prevent the risk of short circuits, the ignition (main) switch must always be OFF and the battery negative (–) terminal should be disconnected before any of the bike's other electrical components are disturbed. Don't forget to reconnect the terminal securely once work is finished or if battery power is needed for circuit testing.

1 A typical electrical circuit consists of an electrical component, the switches, relays, etc. related to that component and the wiring and connectors that link the component to the battery and the frame. To aid in locating a problem in any electrical circuit, and to guide you with the wiring colour codes and connectors, refer to the *Wiring Diagram* for your model at the end of this Chapter.

2 Before tackling any troublesome electrical circuit, first study the wiring diagram (see end of Chapter) thoroughly to get a complete picture of what makes up that individual circuit. Trouble spots, for instance, can often be narrowed down by noting if other components related to that circuit are operating properly or not. If several components or circuits fail at one time, chances are the fault lies in the fuse or earth (ground) connection, as several circuits often are routed through the same fuse and earth (ground) connections.

3 Electrical problems often stem from simple causes, such as loose or corroded connections or a blown fuse. Prior to any electrical fault finding, always visually check the condition of the fuse, wires and connections in the problem circuit. Intermittent failures can be especially frustrating, since you can't always duplicate the failure when it's convenient to test. In such situations, a good practice is to clean all connections in the affected circuit, whether or not they appear to be good. All of the connections and wires should also be wiggled to check for looseness which can cause intermittent failure.

4 If testing instruments are going to be utilised, use the wiring diagram to plan where you will make the necessary connections in order to accurately pinpoint the trouble spot.

5 The basic tools needed for electrical fault finding include a battery and bulb test circuit or a continuity tester, a test light, and a jumper wire. A multimeter capable of reading volts, ohms and amps is a very useful alternative and performs the functions of all of the above, and is necessary for performing more extensive tests and checks where specific voltage, current or resistance values are needed.

HAYNES HiNT *Refer to Fault Finding Equipment in the Reference section for details of how to use electrical test equipment.*

Electrical system 9•3

3.2 Negative terminal (A), positive terminal (B)

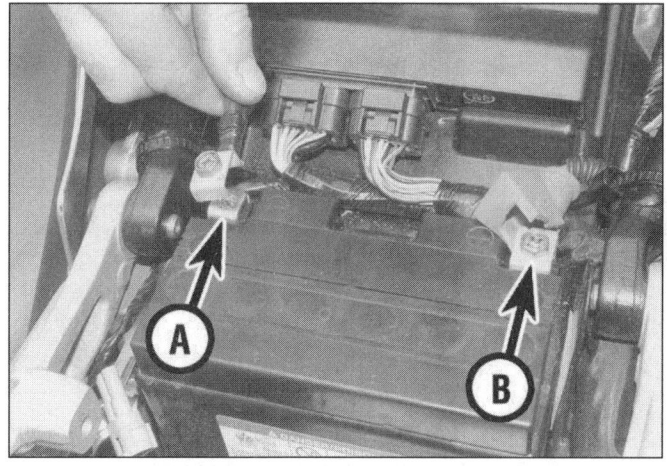

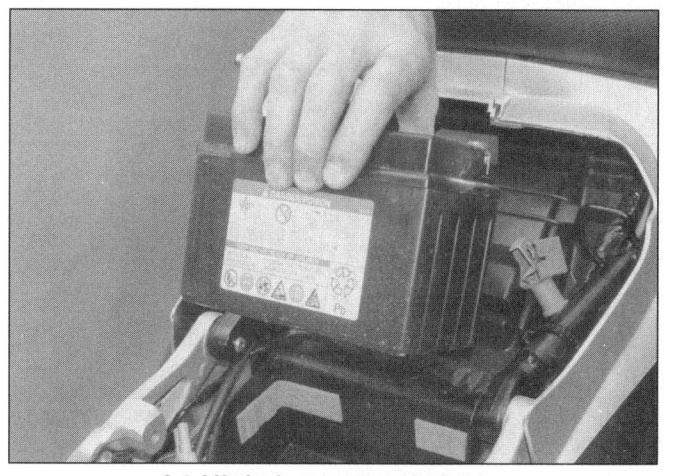

3.4 Lift the battery out of its holder

3 Battery removal and maintenance

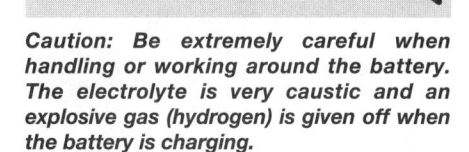

Caution: Be extremely careful when handling or working around the battery. The electrolyte is very caustic and an explosive gas (hydrogen) is given off when the battery is charging.

Removal and installation

1 Remove the rider's seat (see Chapter 8).
2 Unscrew the negative (–) terminal bolt and disconnect the lead from the battery **(see illustration)**.
3 Lift the insulating over off the positive (+) terminal, then unscrew the bolt and disconnect the lead.
4 Remove the battery from the bike **(see illustration)**.
5 Before installing the battery, clean the terminals and lead ends with a wire brush or knife, and emery paper.
6 Installation is the reverse of removal. When you reconnect the leads, connect the positive (+) terminal first.

> **HAYNES HiNT** *Battery corrosion can be kept to a minimum by applying a layer of petroleum jelly or battery terminal (dielectric) grease to the terminals after the cables have been connected. Do not use normal lubricating grease.*

Inspection and maintenance

7 All models are fitted with a sealed MF (maintenance free) battery. **Note:** *Do not attempt to remove the battery caps to check the electrolyte level or battery specific gravity. Removal will damage the caps, resulting in electrolyte leakage and battery damage. However the following checks should be regularly performed – remove the battery first (see above).*

8 Check that the battery terminals and leads are clean. If corrosion is evident, clean the terminals and lead ends with a wire brush or knife, and emery paper. On installation apply a thin coat of petroleum jelly or dielectric grease to the connections to slow further corrosion.
9 Keep the battery case clean to prevent current leakage, which can discharge the battery over a period of time (especially when it sits unused). Wash the outside of the case with a solution of baking soda and water. Rinse the battery thoroughly, then dry it.
10 Look for cracks in the case and replace the battery with a new one if any are found. If acid has been spilled on the frame or battery box, neutralise it with a baking soda and water solution, dry it thoroughly, then touch up any damaged paint.
11 If the motorcycle sits unused for long periods of time, refer to Section 4 and charge the battery once every month to six weeks.
12 Assess the condition of the battery by measuring the voltage across the battery terminals – connect the voltmeter positive (+) probe to the battery positive (+) terminal, and the negative (–) probe to the battery negative (–) terminal. When fully charged there should be 12.6 volts (or more) present. If the voltage falls below 12.3 volts remove the battery (see above) and recharge it as described in Section 4.

4 Battery charging

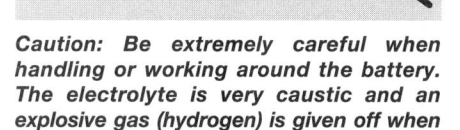

Caution: Be extremely careful when handling or working around the battery. The electrolyte is very caustic and an explosive gas (hydrogen) is given off when the battery is charging.

1 Your charger must be rated for 12 volts. Remove the battery (see Section 3). If not already done, refer to Section 3, Step 12, and check the open circuit voltage of the battery.
2 Connect the charger to the battery, making sure that the positive (+) lead on the charger is connected to the positive (+) terminal on the battery, and the negative (–) lead is connected to the negative (–) terminal. The battery should be charged at the rate and for the time specified at the beginning of the Chapter, or until the voltage across the terminals reaches 12.8V (allow the battery to stabilise for 30 minutes after charging before taking a voltage reading). Exceeding this can cause the battery to overheat, buckling the plates and rendering it useless. Few owners will have access to an expensive current controlled charger, so if a normal domestic charger is used check that after a possible initial peak, the charge rate falls to a reasonable level – if that level is more than specified, then reduce the charging time accordingly **(see illustration)**. If the battery becomes hot during charging **stop**. Further charging will cause damage. **Note:** *In emergencies the battery can be charged at a higher rate of around 5.0 amps, for a period of 1 hour. However, this is not recommended and the low amp charge is by far the safer method of charging the battery.*
3 If the recharged battery discharges rapidly when left disconnected it is likely that an internal short caused by physical damage or

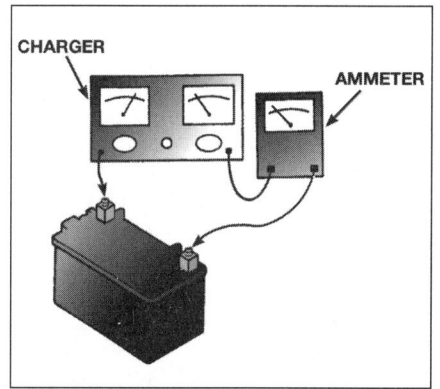

4.2 If the charger doesn't have an ammeter built in, connect one in series as shown. DO NOT connect the ammeter between the battery terminals or it will be ruined

9•4 Electrical system

5.1a Fusebox (arrowed)

5.1b Unclip the lid to access the fuses

5.2a Remove the relay cover . . .

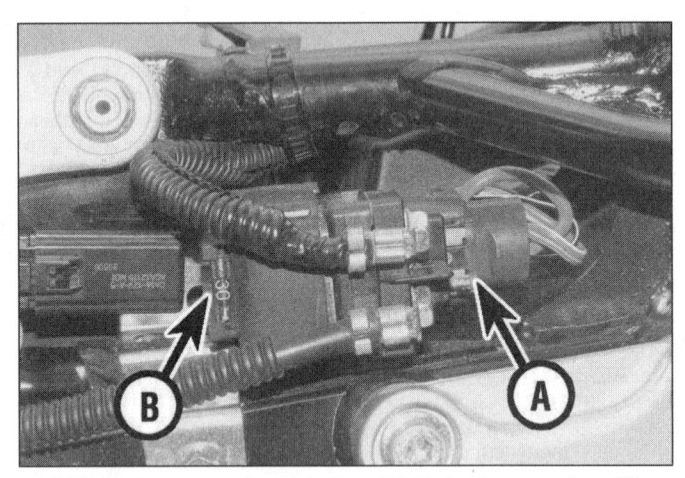

5.2b . . . to access the main fuse (A). Note the spare fuse (B)

sulphation has occurred. A new battery will be required. A sound item will tend to lose its charge at about 1% per day.

4 Install the battery (see Section 3).

5 If the motorcycle sits unused for long periods of time, charge the battery once every month to six weeks and leave it disconnected.

5 Fuses

1 The electrical system is protected by fuses of different ratings. All the fuses except the main fuse are housed in the fusebox, which is under the left-hand cockpit trim panel **(see illustration)** – remove the panel for access (see Chapter 8), then open the fusebox lid **(see illustration)**.

2 The main fuse is housed in the starter relay, which is behind the seat cowling on the left-hand side – remove the seat cowling for access (see Chapter 8), then remove the relay cover **(see illustrations)**.

3 The fuses can be removed and checked visually. If you can't pull the fuse out with your fingertips, use a suitable pair of pliers. A blown fuse is easily identified by a break in the element **(see illustration)**, or can be tested for continuity using an ohmmeter or continuity tester – if there is no continuity, it has blown. Each fuse is clearly marked with its rating and must only be replaced by a fuse of the same rating. There is a spare fuse of each rating. If a spare is used, always replace it with a new one so that a spare of each rating is carried on the bike at all times.

⚠ *Warning: Never put in a fuse of a higher rating or bridge the terminals with any other substitute, however temporary it may be. Serious damage may be done to the circuit, or a fire may start.*

4 If a fuse blows, be sure to check the wiring circuit very carefully for evidence of a short-circuit. Look for bare wires and chafed, melted or burned insulation. If the fuse is renewed before the cause is located, the new fuse will blow immediately.

5 Occasionally a fuse will blow or cause an open-circuit for no obvious reason. Corrosion of the fuse ends and fusebox terminals may occur and cause poor fuse contact. If this happens, remove the corrosion with a wire brush or emery paper, then spray the fuse end and terminals with electrical contact cleaner.

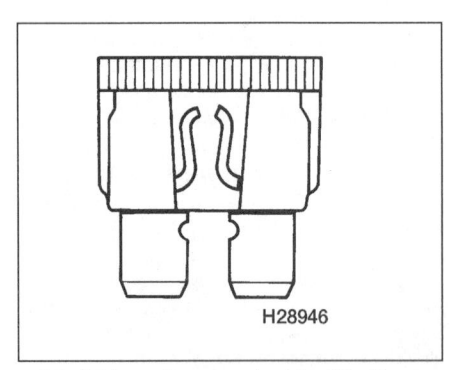

5.3 A blown fuse can be identified by a break in its element

Electrical system 9•5

6 Lighting system check

1 The battery provides power for operation of the headlight, sidelight (where fitted), tail light, brake light, turn signals and instrument cluster lights. If none of the lights operate, always check battery voltage before proceeding. Low battery voltage indicates either a faulty battery or a defective charging system. Refer to Section 3 for battery checks and Section 28 for charging system tests. Also check the fuses (see Section 5). When checking for a blown filament in a bulb, it is advisable to back up a visual check with a continuity test of the filament as it is not always apparent that a bulb has blown. When testing for continuity, remember that on tail light and turn signal bulbs it is often the metal body of the bulb which is the ground or earth, and make sure when testing a dual filament tail light bulb that you are testing the correct filament, and if in doubt test them both. A definitive way of testing a bulb is to connect it directly to a fully charged 12 volt battery using suitable jumper wires, and to see whether it comes on or not. Note that if there is more than one problem at the same time, it is likely to be a fault relating to a multi-function component, such as one of the fuses governing more than one circuit, or the ignition switch.

Headlight

2 If a headlight fails to work, check the bulb, the bulb terminals and the wiring connector first (see Section 7), then the fuse (see Section 5), then check for battery voltage at the yellow wire terminal on the supply side of the headlight wiring connector for the HI beam, and/or the white wire terminal on the supply side of the headlight wiring connector for the LO beam, with the ignition switch ON and light switch ON (where fitted), and the HI/LO beam switch set appropriately. If voltage is present, check for continuity between the black/white wire terminal and earth (ground). If there is no continuity, check the earth (ground) circuit for an open or poor connection.

3 If no voltage is indicated, check the wiring and connectors between the headlight, light switches and the ignition switch, then check the switches themselves.

Sidelight

4 On models equipped with a sidelight, if it fails to work, check the bulb, the bulb terminals and the wiring connector first (see Section 7), then check for battery voltage at the brown wire terminal on the supply side of the sidelight wiring connector, with the ignition switch in the P (park) position. If voltage is present, check for continuity between the wiring connector terminals on the sidelight side of the connector and the corresponding terminals in the bulbholder. If voltage and continuity are present, check for continuity between the black/white wire terminal on the supply side of the sidelight wiring connector and earth (ground). If there is no continuity, check the earth (ground) circuit for an open or poor connection.

5 If no voltage is indicated, check the wiring and connectors between the sidelight and the ignition switch, then check the ignition switch itself.

Tail light

6 If a tail light bulb fails to work, check the bulb, the bulb terminals and the wiring connectors first (see Section 9), then the fuse (see Section 5), then check for battery voltage at the brown wire terminal on the supply side of the tail light main wiring connector, with the ignition switch ON and light switch ON (where fitted). If voltage is present, check for continuity between the wiring connector terminals on the tail light side of the connector and the corresponding terminals in the bulbholder. If continuity is present, check for continuity between the black/white wire terminal on the supply side of the tail light wiring connector and earth (ground). If there is no continuity, check the earth (ground) circuit for an open or poor connection.

7 If no voltage is indicated, check the wiring and connectors between the tail light, the light switch and the ignition switch, then check the switches themselves.

Brake light

8 If a brake light fails to work, check the bulb, the bulb terminals and the wiring connector first (see Section 9), then the signal fuse, then check for battery voltage at the white/black wire terminal on the supply side of the main tail light wiring connector, with the ignition switch ON and the brake lever or pedal applied. If voltage is present, check for continuity between the wiring connector terminals on the tail light side of the connector and the corresponding terminals in the bulbholder. If continuity is present, check for continuity between the black/white wire terminal on the supply side of the tail light wiring connector and earth (ground). If there is no continuity, check the earth (ground) circuit for an open or poor connection.

9 If no voltage is indicated, check the brake light switches (see Section 14), then the wiring and connectors between the tail light and the switches.

Instrument and warning lights

10 See Section 17.

Turn signal lights

11 If one light fails to work, check the bulb and the bulb terminals first, then the wiring connectors (see Section 12). If none of the turn signals work, first check the signal fuse (see Section 5).

12 If the fuse is good, see Section 11 for the turn signal circuit check.

7 Headlight bulb and sidelight bulb renewal

Note: *The headlight bulbs are of the quartz-halogen type. Do not touch the bulb glass as skin acids will shorten the bulb's service life. If the bulb is accidentally touched, it should be wiped carefully when cold with a rag soaked in methylated spirit and dried before fitting.*

⚠ **Warning:** *Allow the bulb time to cool before removing it if the headlight has just been on.*

Headlight

1 Remove the access panel from the underside of the fairing (see Chapter 8).
2 To change the dipped (LO) beam bulb (the upper bulb), disconnect the wiring connector, then remove the rubber dust cover **(see illustrations)**. Release the bulb retaining clip

7.2a Disconnect the headlight wiring connector . . .

7.2b . . . and remove the dust cover

7.2c Release the retaining clip . . .

9•6 Electrical system

7.2d ... and remove the bulb

7.2e Pull the bulb off the holder

then remove the bulb **(see illustrations)**. Pull the bulb out of the bulbholder **(see illustration)**. If access is too restricted from below the fairing, remove the cockpit trim panels (see Chapter 8), and the instrument cluster (see Section 15) and access the bulb from the top.

3 To change the main (HI) beam bulb (the lower bulb), twist the bulbholder to release it from the headlight **(see illustration)**. Disconnect the wiring connector **(see illustration)**.

4 Fit the new bulb in a reverse order, bearing in mind the information in the **Note** above. Make sure the bulb locates correctly.

5 Fit the dipped (LO) beam bulb dust cover with the 'TOP' mark at the top **(see illustration 7.2b)**.

6 Check the operation of the headlight.
7 Install the fairing access panel or instrument cluster and cockpit trim panels as required.

> **HAYNES HINT** *Always use a paper towel or dry cloth when handling new bulbs to prevent injury if the bulb should break and to increase bulb life.*

Sidelight

8 Remove the access panel from the underside of the fairing (see Chapter 8).
9 Pull the bulbholder out of the headlight, then remove the bulb **(see illustrations)**. Fit the new bulb in the bulbholder, then fit the bulbholder into the headlight, making sure it correctly seated. Check the operation of the sidelight.
10 Install the access panel (see Chapter 8).

7.3a Release the bulb from the headlight ...

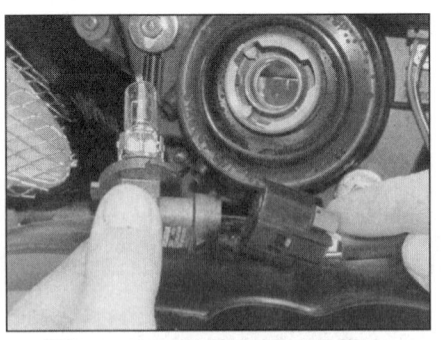

7.3b ... then disconnect the wiring connector

7.9a Withdraw the bulbholder ...

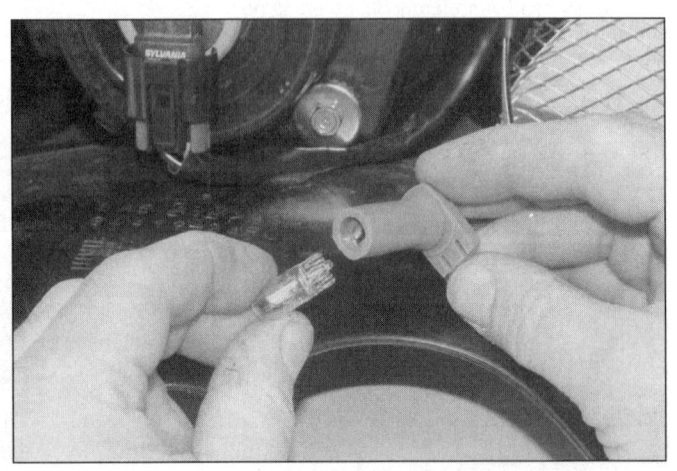

7.9b ... then carefully pull the bulb out of the holder

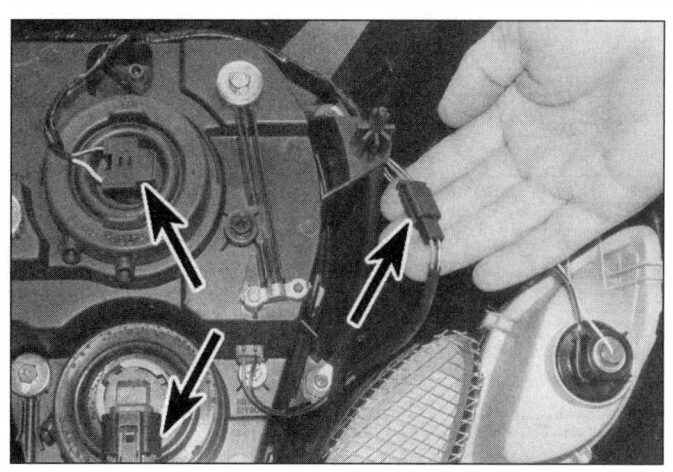

Electrical system 9•7

8.2 Disconnect the wiring connectors (arrowed) . . .

8.3 . . . then undo the screws (arrowed) and remove the headlight from the fairing

8 Headlight assembly

Removal

1 Remove the fairing (see Chapter 8).
2 Disconnect the headlight wiring connectors, and where fitted the sidelight wiring connector (or alternatively pull the sidelight bulbholder out of the headlight) – see Section 7 **(see illustration)**. Free the wiring from any clips and ties on the headlight, noting its routing.
3 Undo the four screws securing the headlight and remove it **(see illustration)**.
4 Check the rubber mounts for damage, deformation and deterioration and replace them with new ones if necessary.

Installation

5 Installation is the reverse of removal. Make sure all the wiring is correctly routed, connected and secured. Check the operation of the headlight and sidelight where fitted, and of the turn signals. Check the headlight aim (see Chapter 1).

9 Brake/tail/licence plate light bulb renewal

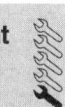

Brake/tail light

1 Undo the two lens screws and remove the lens **(see illustrations)**. Note the rubber seal between the lens and the tail light and replace it with a new one if it is damaged, deformed or deteriorated.
2 Push the bulb into the holder and twist it anti-clockwise to remove it **(see illustration)**.
3 Check the socket terminals for corrosion and clean them if necessary. Line up the pins of the new bulb with the slots in the socket, then push the bulb in and turn it clockwise until it locks into place. **Note:** *The pins on the bulb are offset so it can only be installed one way. It is a good idea to use a paper towel or dry cloth when handling the new bulb to prevent injury if the bulb should break and to increase bulb life.*
4 Make sure the rubber seal is correctly seated **(see illustration)**, then install the lens – do not overtighten the screws as it is easy to either strip the threads in the lugs or to crack the lens.

Licence plate light

5 Undo the two cover screws and remove the cover **(see illustration)**.

9.1a Undo the screws . . .

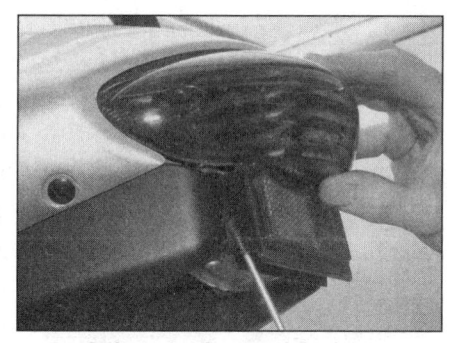

9.1b . . . and remove the lens

9.2 Push the bulb in, then twist it anti-clockwise to release it

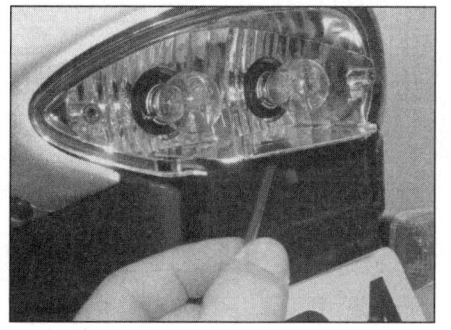

9.4 Make sure the seal is seated in its groove

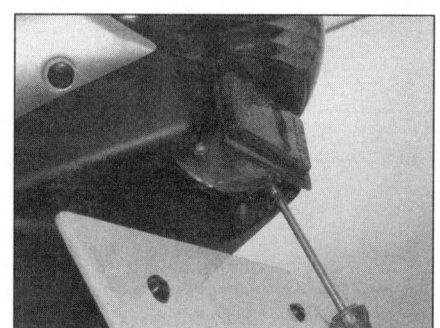

9.5 Undo the screws and remove the cover . . .

9•8 Electrical system

6 Pull the bulb out of the holder **(see illustration)**.
7 Check the socket terminals for corrosion and clean them if necessary. Line up the bulb with the socket and push it into place.
8 Install the cover – do not overtighten the screws as it is easy to strip the threads in the lugs.

10 Tail light assembly

Removal

1 Remove the seat cowling (see Chapter 8).
2 Twist the bulbholders anti-clockwise and withdraw them **(see illustrations)**.
3 Undo the screws securing the tail light and remove it from the back **(see illustration)**.
4 If required undo the screws securing the outer bulbholder plates and remove them, the cushions and the inner plates, noting how they locate. Replace the cushions with new ones if they are damaged, deformed or deteriorated.
5 If required undo the screws securing the tail light bracket in the seat cowling and remove it.

Installation

6 Installation is the reverse of removal. Check the operation of the tail light and the brake light.

11 Turn signal circuit check

1 Most turn signal problems are the result of a burned out bulb or a corroded socket. This is especially true when the turn signals function properly in one direction, but fail to flash in the other direction. Check the bulbs and the sockets (see Section 12) and the wiring connectors. Also, check the signal fuse (see Section 5) and the switch (see Section 19).
2 The battery provides power for operation of the turn signal lights, so if they do not operate, also check the battery voltage. Low battery voltage indicates either a faulty battery or a defective charging system. Refer to Section 3 for battery checks and Section 28 for charging system tests.
3 If the bulbs, sockets, connectors, fuse, switch and battery are good, check the turn signal relay – to access the relay remove the left-hand cockpit trim panel (see Chapter 8). The relay is integrated with the sidestand switch relay and diodes in one unit.
4 Pull the relay/diode unit off its connector **(see illustration)**. Check for battery voltage at the orange/green wire terminal (X to K2

9.6 . . . then remove the bulb

10.2a Release the tail light bulbholders . . .

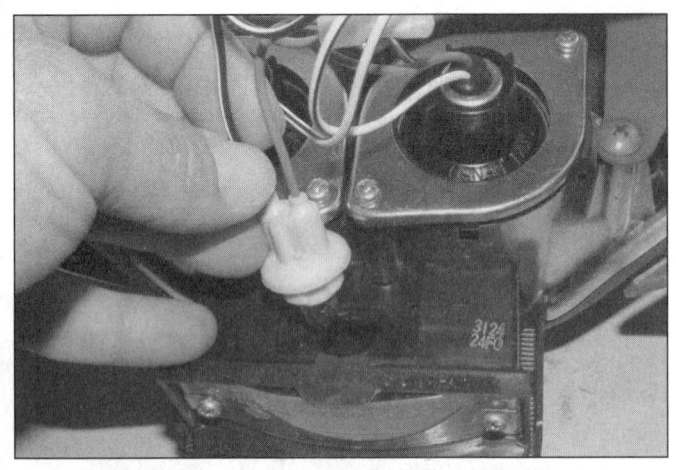

10.2b . . . and the licence plate light bulbholder . . .

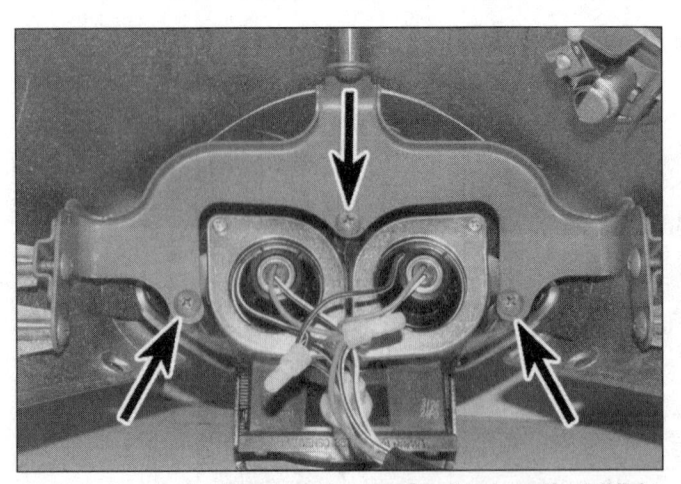

10.3 . . . then undo the screws (arrowed) and remove the tail light

11.4 Unit houses turn signal relay, sidestand relay and diodes (arrowed)

Electrical system 9•9

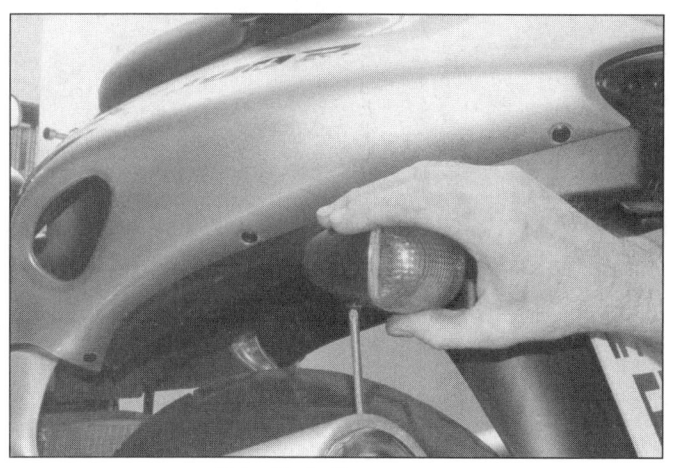

12.2a Undo the screw . . .

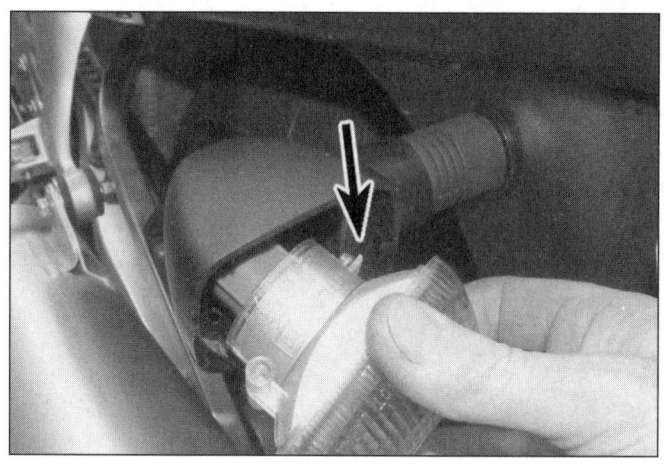

12.2b . . . and remove the lens/bulb assembly, noting the tab (arrowed)

models) or brown wire terminal (K3-on models) on the connector with the ignition ON. Connect the positive (+) probe of the meter to the terminal and the negative (–) to the frame or engine. Turn the ignition OFF when the check is complete and plug the relay back in.

5 If no power was present at the relay, check the wiring from the relay to the ignition (main) switch for continuity.

6 If power was present at the relay, now check for battery voltage at the light blue wire terminal from the relay with the relay connected, the ignition switch ON and the turn signal switch ON to either side. Connect the positive (+) probe of the meter to the terminal and the negative (–) to the frame or engine. Turn the ignition OFF when the check is complete. If no power was present the relay is probably faulty.

7 As Suzuki provide no test data for the relay, it can only be checked by substituting it with a known good one. If power was present, use the appropriate wiring diagram at the end of this Chapter and check the wiring between the relay, turn signal switch and turn signal lights for continuity.

12 Turn signal bulb renewal

1 To access the front turn signal bulbs remove the access panel from the underside of the fairing (see Chapter 8).

2 To access a rear turn signal bulb undo the screw securing the lens/bulbholder assembly and remove it, noting how the tab locates **(see illustrations)**.

3 Turn the bulbholder anti-clockwise and withdraw it from the lens, then push the bulb into the holder and twist it anti-clockwise to remove it **(see illustrations)**.

4 Check the socket terminals for corrosion and clean them if necessary. Line up the pins of the new bulb with the slots in the socket, then push the bulb in and turn it clockwise until it locks into place.

5 Fit the bulbholder back into the lens and turn it clockwise, making sure it is securely held.

6 At the front install the access panel.

7 At the rear fit the lens/bulbholder assembly back into the housing, making sure the tab locates correctly, then install the screw.

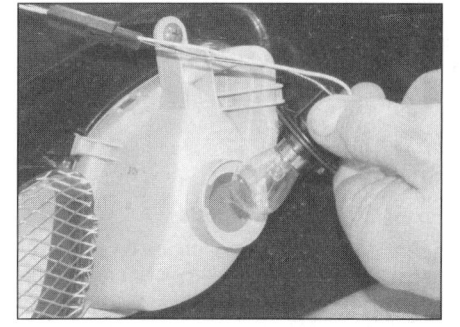

12.3a Release the bulbholder . . .

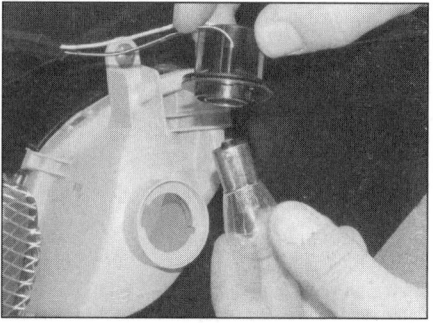

12.3b . . . and remove the bulb – front turn signal

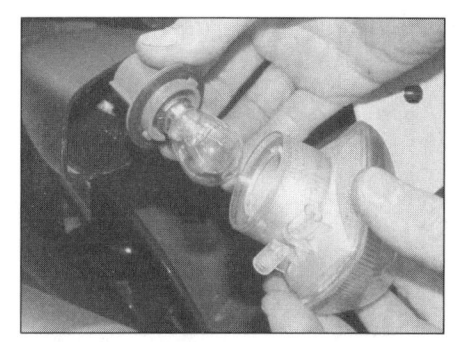

12.3c Release the bulbholder . . .

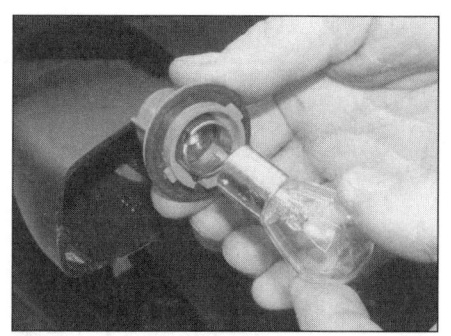

12.3d . . . and remove the bulb – rear turn signal

13 Turn signal removal and installation

Removal

Front

1 Remove the fairing (see Chapter 8).

2 Either disconnect the turn signal wiring connector or turn the bulbholder anti-

9•10 Electrical system

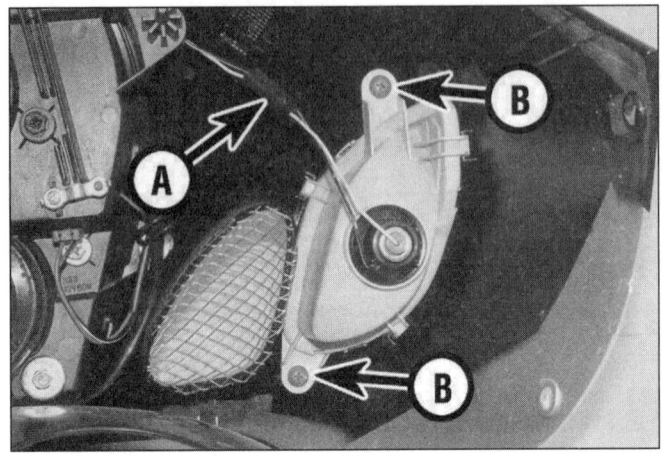

13.2 Front turn signal wiring connector (A) and mounting screws (B)

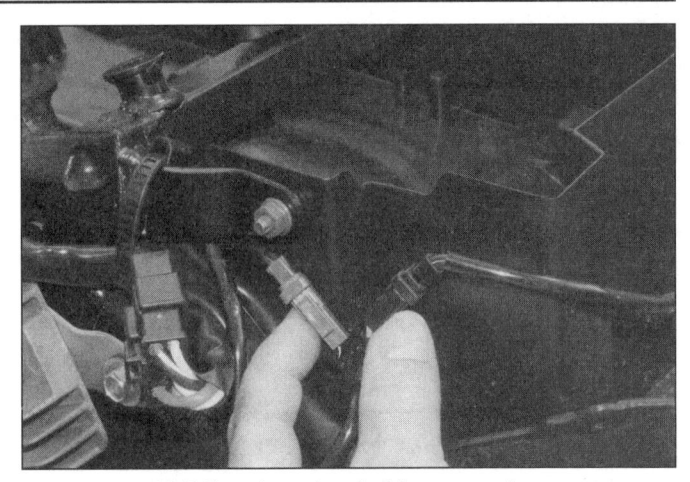

13.5 Rear turn signal wiring connectors

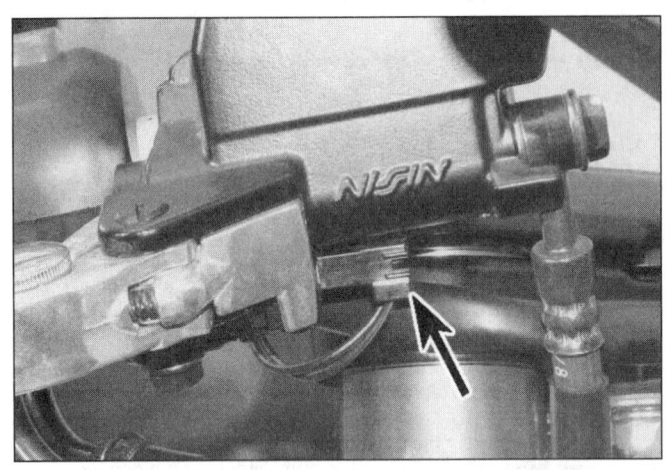

14.2 Front brake switch wiring connector (arrowed)

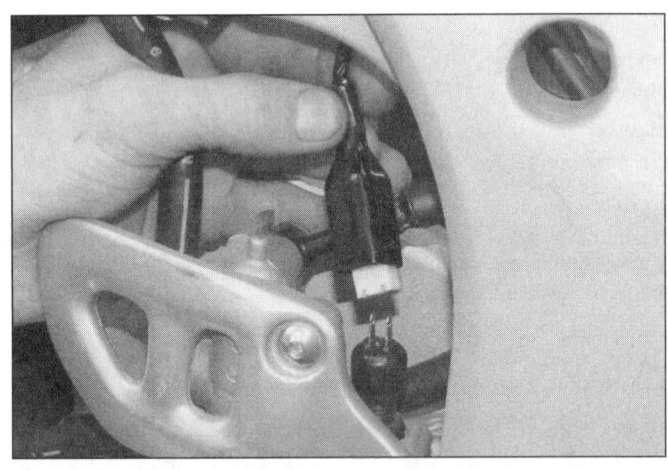

14.3 Disconnect the wiring connector from the switch

clockwise and withdraw it from the lens **(see illustration or 12.3a)**.

3 Undo the two screws securing the turn signal and remove it.

Rear

4 Remove the seat cowling (see Chapter 8).
5 Trace the wiring back from the turn signal and disconnect it at the connector **(see illustration)**.
6 Unscrew the nut securing the turn signal on the inside of the rear mudguard, and remove the washer. Withdraw the turn signal from the mudguard, noting the spacer.

Installation

7 Installation is the reverse of removal. Make sure the wiring is correctly routed and securely connected. Check the operation of the turn signals.

14 Brake light switches

Circuit check

1 Before checking the switches, check the brake light circuit (see Section 6, Step 8).

2 The front brake light switch is mounted on the underside of the brake master cylinder. Disconnect the wiring connector from the switch **(see illustration)**. Using a continuity tester, connect the probes to the terminals of the switch. With the brake lever at rest, there should be no continuity. With the brake lever applied, there should be continuity. If the switch does not behave as described, replace it with a new one.
3 The rear brake light switch is mounted on the inside of the rider's right-hand footrest bracket above the brake pedal. Disconnect the wiring connector from the switch **(see illustration)**. Using a continuity tester, connect the probes to the terminals on the switch. With the brake pedal at rest, there should be no continuity. With the brake pedal applied, there should be continuity. If the switch does not behave as described, replace it with a new one.
4 If the switches are good, check for voltage at the black/red wire terminal (front brake switch) or the orange/green wire terminal (rear brake switch) on the connector with the ignition switch ON – there should be battery voltage. If there's no voltage present, check the wiring between the switch and the ignition switch (see the *Wiring Diagrams* at the end of this Chapter). If there is voltage, check the wiring and connectors between the switch and the brake light bulbs.

Switch renewal

Front brake light switch

5 The switch is mounted on the underside of the brake master cylinder. Disconnect the wiring connector from the switch **(see illustration 14.2)**.
6 Remove the single screw securing the switch to the bottom of the master cylinder and remove the switch **(see illustration)**.

14.6 Front brake switch mounting screw (arrowed)

Electrical system 9•11

14.9a If required unscrew the bolts and displace the bracket

14.9b Hold the nut (arrowed) and unscrew the switch

7 Installation is the reverse of removal. The switch isn't adjustable.

Rear brake light switch

8 The switch is mounted on the inside of the rider's right-hand footrest bracket above the brake pedal. Disconnect the wiring connector from the switch **(see illustration 14.3)**.

9 If access to the switch is too restricted, unscrew the bolts securing the footrest bracket and displace it **(see illustration)**. Detach the lower end of the switch spring from the brake pedal, then unscrew and remove the switch, holding the adjuster nut to prevent it turning if required **(see illustration)**.

10 Installation is the reverse of removal. Make sure the brake light is activated just before the rear brake pedal takes effect. If adjustment is necessary, hold the switch and turn the adjuster nut on the switch body until the brake light is activated when required. If displaced, tighten the footrest bracket bolts to the torque setting specified at the beginning of the Chapter.

15 Instrument cluster removal and installation

Removal

1 For best access remove the fairing (see Chapter 8), though it is possible to remove the instrument cluster by just removing the cockpit trim panels, and if required the windshield (see Chapter 8).

2 Disconnect the instrument cluster wiring connector – do this after displacing the instrument cluster if you haven't removed the fairing **(see illustration)**.

3 Unscrew the two bolts then lift the instrument cluster off, noting how the pegs on the top locate in the grommets **(see illustrations)**. Note the spacers in the grommets for the bottom mounts.

Installation

4 Installation is the reverse of removal. Check the rubber mounting grommets for cracks and deterioration and replace them with new ones if necessary.

15.2 Disconnect the wiring connector . . .

15.3a . . . then unscrew the bolts (arrowed) . . .

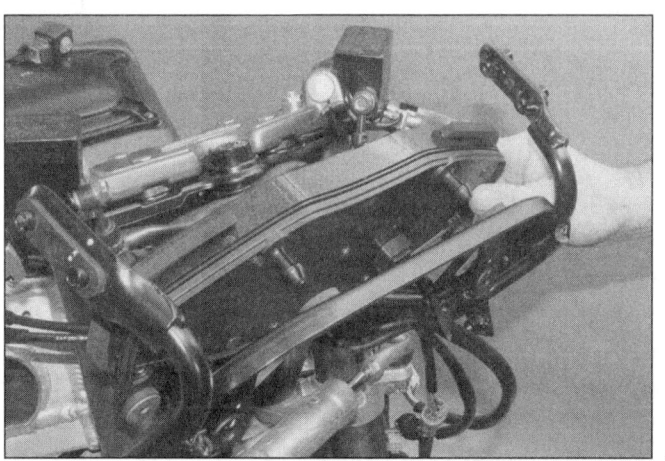

15.3b . . . and remove the instruments, noting how the pegs locate

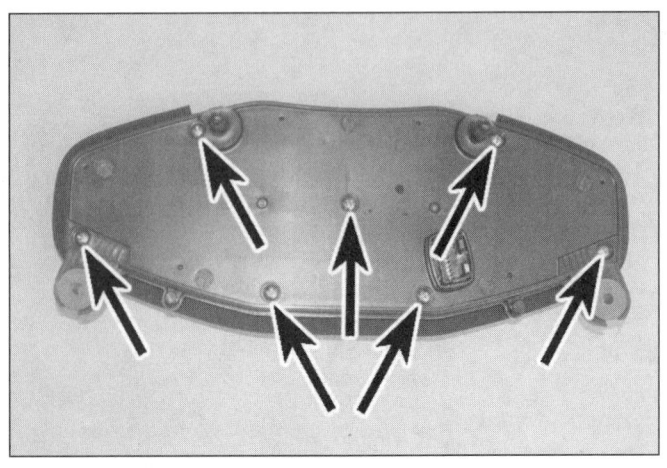

9•12 Electrical system

16.5a Undo the screws (arrowed) . . .

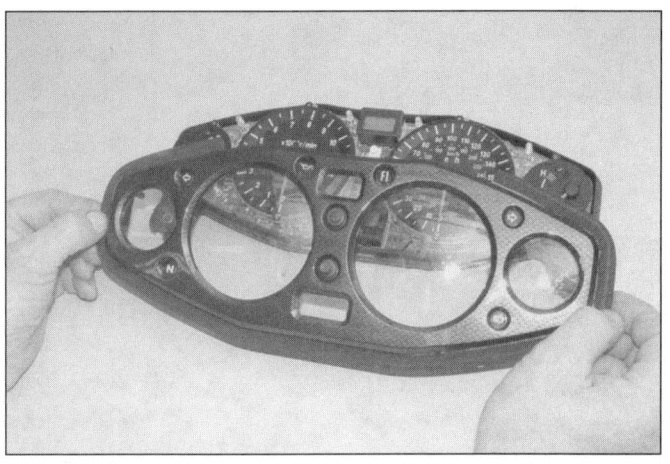

16.5b . . . then turn the assembly over and remove the front cover . . .

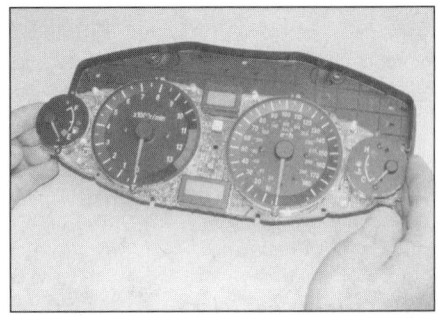

16.5c . . . and the instrument panel/PCB

16 Instrument check and renewal

Note: *The individual instruments and LEDs are integral with the instrument panel printed circuit board (PCB) – separate components for the PCB are not available, but the PCB is available separately from the cover and housing. This Section does not fully describe the function and display characteristics of the instrument cluster – refer to the Suzuki owners handbook for this.*

General check

1 When the ignition switch is turned ON, the fuel, oil, temperature and FI (fuel injection) LEDs should light for two seconds, all LCD display segments should come on for two seconds, and the needle on each gauge (speedo, tacho, fuel and temperature), should swing round the dial or up the gauge and back to its rest position. This serves as a functionality check of the instrument cluster. If this fails to happen, first check that the wiring connector has not become disconnected (see Section 15). If that is OK, and the battery, fuses and wiring between the ignition switch and the instrument cluster are all good, the instrument cluster PCB may have a fault – take the cluster to a Suzuki dealer for further assessment.

2 If, for example when it is extremely cold, the needles on the gauges do not return to their rest point, they can be reset as follows: turn the ignition OFF. Press the function switch (the bottom button in the middle) down and hold it, then turn the ignition switch ON. Within 3 to 5 seconds of turning the ignition ON release the function button. Then press the function button twice quickly and release it, then turn the ignition switch OFF, making sure the whole procedure does not take more than 10 seconds.

Speedometer and speed sensor

Check

3 If the speedometer, odometer or trip meter fail to work, take the motorcycle to a Suzuki dealer for assessment. Special equipment is needed to check the operation of the speedometer and the speed sensor.

Removal and installation

4 Remove the instrument cluster (see Section 15).
5 Undo the screws on the back of the instrument cluster **(see illustration)**. Hold the front and rear covers together and turn the cluster over. Lift the front cover off **(see illustration)**. Carefully lift the instrument panel/PCB out **(see illustration)**. Further dismantling is not possible.
6 To remove the speed sensor, remove the left-hand fairing side panel (see Chapter 8), then trace the wiring from the sensor in the front sprocket cover and disconnect it at the connector **(see illustration)**. Unscrew the bolt securing the sensor to the sprocket cover and withdraw it **(see illustration)**. If required,

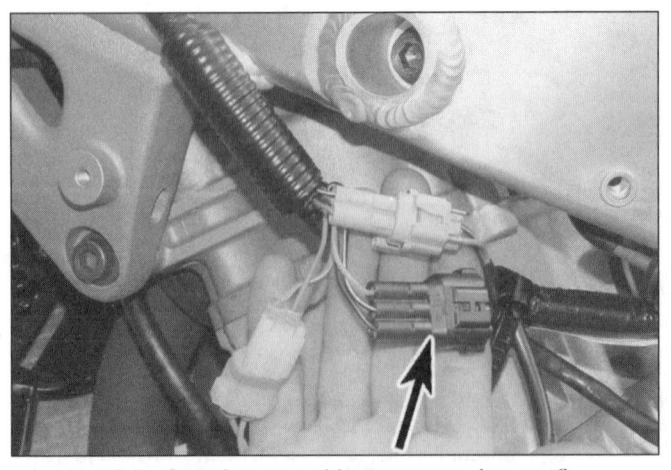

16.6a Speed sensor wiring connector (arrowed)

16.6b Speed sensor bolt (arrowed)

remove the sprocket cover and check the condition of the speed sensor rotor (see Chapter 6).
7 Installation is the reverse of removal. Tighten the sensor bolt to the torque setting specified at the beginning of the Chapter.

Tachometer

Check

8 Suzuki provides no data for testing the tachometer. If the tachometer fails to work, take the motorcycle to a Suzuki dealer for assessment.

Removal and installation

9 Remove the instrument cluster (see Section 15). Remove the instrument panel/PCB from the case (see Step 5).

Coolant temperature gauge and warning light

Check

10 Ensure that the engine coolant temperature (ECT) sensor is working correctly (see Chapter 3, Section 4 and Chapter 4 Section 12). Special equipment is needed to check the operation of the LED and LCD display circuits. If any of the circuits fail to work, take the motorcycle to a Suzuki dealer for assessment. Note that if the ignition switch is ON but the engine kill switch is in the OFF position, the temperature gauge will read H, the LED will come on and the LCD will display CHEC – this is not a malfunction, just the gauge indicating it is receiving no signal from the ECM. Turn the kill switch to RUN to reset.

Removal and installation

11 Remove the instrument cluster (see Section 15). Remove the instrument panel/PCB from the case (see Step 5).

Oil pressure warning light

Check

12 When the ignition is first turned ON and before the engine is started, the oil warning LED should come on. When the engine is started it should extinguish. This is part of the instrument's self checking procedure.
13 If the LED does not come on, remove the right-hand fairing side panel (see Chapter 8). Turn the ignition OFF and disconnect the wiring connector from the oil pressure switch (see Section 24). Turn the ignition ON and earth (ground) the wiring connector on the crankcase – the warning LED should come on. If the LED does not come on, first check the wire between the oil pressure switch and instrument cluster wiring connector for continuity. If that is good check the main earth connections between the engine and the battery. If that is good the instrument panel should be replaced with a new one.

14 If the warning LED comes on when the engine is running, stop the engine immediately and check the oil level, and if necessary the pressure (see Chapter 1). If the LED coming on is not due to low oil level or low oil pressure, disconnect the oil pressure switch wiring connector (see Section 24), then turn the ignition ON; the display and light should be out. If they are on, the wire between the switch and instrument cluster must be earthed (grounded) at some point.

Removal and installation

15 Remove the instrument cluster (see Section 15). Remove the instrument panel/PCB from the case (see Step 5).

Fuel level gauge and warning light

Check

16 If the gauge does not work or the LED does not come on, first ensure that the fuel level sensor is working correctly (see Chapter 4 Section 6). If it is, do not yet fit it back into the fuel tank.
17 Now check the wiring from the fuel level sensor wiring connector to the instrument cluster for continuity.
18 If continuity is shown, connect the sensor to the wiring connector. With the sensor float in its lowest (empty) position the gauge needle should be on E and the LED should be on. Carefully raise the float to its highest (full) position – the gauge needle should be on F and the LED should be out.
19 If the display does not read as it should, replace the instrument panel/PCB with a new one.

Removal and installation

20 Remove the instrument cluster (see Section 15). Remove the instrument panel/PCB from the case (see Step 5).

17 Instrument and warning light LEDs

Note: All instrument and warning illumination is by LED. If an LED fails the instrument panel/PCB must be replaced with a new one.
1 Remove the instrument cluster (See Section 15).
2 Undo the screws on the back of the instrument cluster **(see illustration 16.5a)**. Hold the front and rear covers together and turn the cluster over. Lift the front cover off. Carefully lift the instrument panel/PCB out and replace it with a new one **(see illustrations 16.5b and c)**. Further dismantling is not possible.
3 Installation is the reverse of removal.

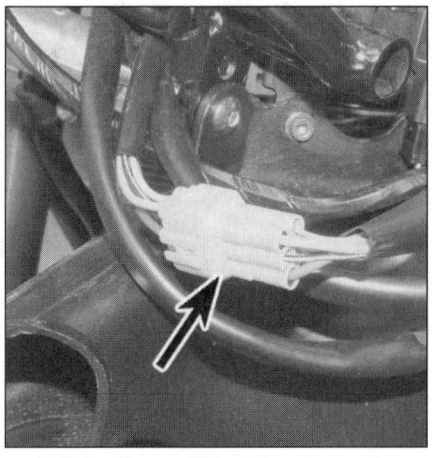

18.2 Ignition switch wiring connector (arrowed)

18 Ignition (main) switch

Warning: To prevent the risk of short circuits, remove the rider's seat and disconnect the battery negative (–) lead before making any ignition (main) switch checks.

Check

1 Remove the left-hand cockpit trim panel (see Chapter 8).
2 Trace the wiring from the base of the ignition switch and disconnect it at the connector **(see illustration)** – if access is too restricted remove the left-hand fairing side panel or the fairing as required.
3 Make the checks on the switch side of the connector. Using an ohmmeter or a continuity tester, check the continuity of the connector terminal pairs (see the *Wiring Diagrams* at the end of this Chapter). Continuity should exist between the terminals connected by a solid line on the diagram when the switch key is turned to the indicated position.
4 If the switch fails any of the tests, replace it with a new one.

Removal

5 Remove the fairing (see Chapter 8), and for best access the instrument cluster (see Section 15).
6 Trace the wiring from the base of the ignition switch and disconnect it at the connector **(see illustration 18.2)** – if access is too restricted remove the left-hand fairing side panel or the fairing as required. Release the wiring from any clips and ties and feed it through to the switch, noting its routing.
7 Security Torx bolts are used to mount the ignition switch to the underside of the top yoke, and they require a special Torx bit to unscrew them – these are readily available from any good tool dealer. Unscrew the two bolts, turning the handlebars as required to

9•14 Electrical system

18.7 Ignition switch bolts (arrowed)

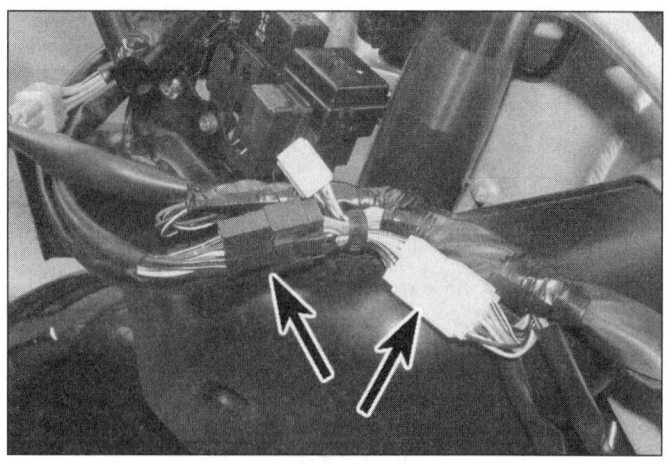

19.4 Handlebar switch wiring connectors (arrowed)

provide best access for your tools **(see illustration)**. If access is still too restricted, refer to Chapter 6, Sections 5 and 9 and remove the top yoke.

Installation

8 Installation is the reverse of removal. Apply a suitable non-permanent thread locking compound to the bolts. Make sure wiring is correctly routed and the connector securely connected.

19 Handlebar switches

Check

1 Generally speaking, the switches are reliable and trouble-free. Most troubles, when they do occur, are caused by dirty or corroded contacts, but wear and breakage of internal parts is a possibility that should not be overlooked. If breakage does occur, the entire switch and related wiring harness will have to be replaced with a new one, as individual parts are not available.
2 The switches can be checked for continuity using an ohmmeter or a continuity test light. Make sure the ignition is switched OFF.
3 To access the switch wiring connectors, remove the left-hand cockpit trim panel (see Chapter 8).
4 Trace the wiring from the switch housing being checked and disconnect it at the connector **(see illustration)**. Make the checks on the switch side of the connectors.
5 Check for continuity between the terminals of the switch connector with the switch in the various positions (i.e. switch off – no continuity, switch on – continuity) – see the *wiring diagrams* at the end of this Chapter. Continuity should exist between the terminals connected by a solid line on the diagram when the switch is in the indicated position.
6 If the continuity check indicates a problem

exists, displace the switch housing (see below) and spray the switch contacts with electrical contact cleaner (there is no need to remove the switch completely). If they are accessible, the contacts can be scraped clean with a knife or polished with crocus cloth. If switch components are damaged or broken, it should be obvious when the switch is disassembled.

Removal

7 If the switch is to be removed from the bike, rather than just displaced from the handlebar, remove the left-hand cockpit trim panel (see Chapter 8). Trace the wiring from the switch housing being removed and disconnect it at the connector **(see illustration 19.4)**. Work back along the harness, freeing it from all clips and ties, and feed it to the switch, noting its routing.
8 Disconnect the wiring connectors from the brake light switch (if removing the right-hand switch) or the clutch switch (if removing the left-hand switch) **(see illustration 14.2 or 21.2)**.
9 Refer to Chapter 4 for removal of the throttle cables and/or fast idle cable, which involves detaching the switch housing from the handlebars.

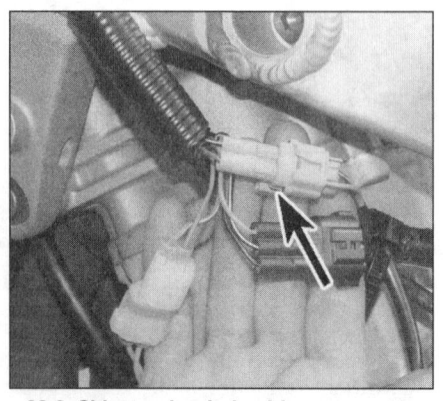

20.2 Sidestand switch wiring connector (arrowed)

Installation

10 Installation is the reverse of removal. Make sure the wiring connectors are correctly routed and securely connected. Refer to Chapter 4 for installation of the throttle cables and fast idle cable.

20 Sidestand switch and relay

Sidestand switch

1 The sidestand switch is mounted on the sidestand bracket. The switch is part of the safety circuit which prevents or stops the engine running if the transmission is in gear whilst the sidestand is down, and prevents the engine from starting if the transmission is in gear unless the sidestand is up and the clutch lever is pulled in.
2 To access the wiring connector, remove the left-hand fairing side panel (see Chapter 8). Trace the wiring from the switch and disconnect it at the connector **(see illustration)**.
3 Check the operation of the switch using a multimeter set to the diode testing function – make sure the multimeter batteries are good. Connect the positive (+) probe to the green wire terminal on the switch side of the connector and the negative (–) probe to the black/white wire terminal. With the sidestand up there should be 0.4 to 0.6 volts; with the stand down there should be 1.4 to 1.5 volts (but note that this figure may vary according the output voltage of the meter you are using – the voltage given is the output voltage of the meter used by Suzuki, Pt. No. 09900-25008).
4 If the switch does not perform as expected, check that the fault is not caused by a sticking switch plunger due to the ingress of road dirt; spray the switch with a water dispersant aerosol. If the switch still does not work it is defective and must be replaced with a new one.

Electrical system 9•15

20.7 Sidestand switch bolt (arrowed)

5 If the switch is good, check the sidestand relay (Steps 11 to 13) and diodes (Section 22). Also check the wiring between the various components (see *Wiring Diagrams* at the end of this book).

6 To remove the switch, first disconnect the wiring connector (see Step 2). Feed the wiring back to the switch noting its routing and freeing it from any clips or ties.

7 Unscrew the bolt securing the switch to the sidestand and remove the switch, noting how it locates **(see illustration)**.

8 Fit the new switch onto the bracket, locating the lug in the hole. Apply a suitable non-permanent thread locking compound to the bolt threads.

9 Make sure the wiring is correctly routed up to the connector and retained by any clips and ties. Reconnect the wiring connector.

10 Install the fairing side panel (see Chapter 8).

Sidestand relay

11 If the sidestand switch and wiring are good, the sidestand relay may be at fault. To access the relay remove the left-hand cockpit trim panel (see Chapter 8). The relay is integrated with the turn signal relay and diodes in one unit **(see illustration 11.4)**.

12 Pull the relay/diode unit off its connector. Using an ohmmeter or continuity tester, check for continuity between the D and E terminals on the relay **(see illustration)**. There should be no continuity (infinite resistance). Now use jumper wires to connect the positive (+) terminal of a 12V battery to the D terminal on the relay and the negative (–) battery terminal to the C relay terminal, and again check for continuity between the D and E terminals. There should now be continuity (zero resistance). If either of the above conditions do not exist, install a new relay.

13 If the relay is good (and the sidestand switch has been checked – see above), check the other components in the starter safety circuit (clutch switch, gear position switch and diodes) as described in the relevant sections of this Chapter, or Chapter 4 for the gear position switch. If all components are good,

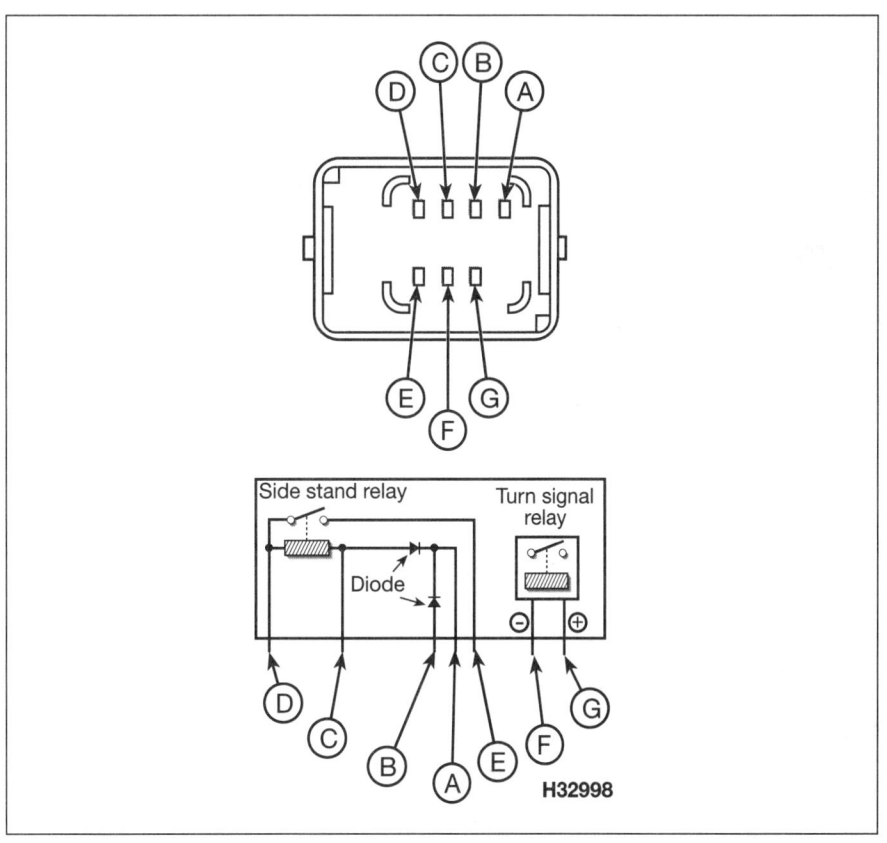

20.12 Sidestand/turn signal relay and diode unit terminal identification

check the wiring between the various components (see the *wiring diagrams* at the end of this book).

Removal and installation

14 Remove the left-hand cockpit trim panel (see Chapter 8). Unplug the relay/diode unit from its connector **(see illustration 11.4)**. Install the new unit and check the operation of the sidestand switch and safety circuit.

21 Clutch switch

Check

1 The clutch switch is mounted on the front of the clutch master cylinder. The switch is part of the safety circuit which prevents or stops the engine running if the transmission is in gear whilst the sidestand is down, and prevents the engine from starting if the transmission is in gear unless the sidestand is up and the clutch lever is pulled in. The switch isn't adjustable.

2 To check the switch, disconnect the wiring connectors **(see illustration)**. Connect the probes of an ohmmeter or a continuity test light to the two switch terminals. With the clutch lever pulled in, continuity should be indicated. With the clutch lever out, no continuity (infinite resistance) should be indicated.

3 If the switch is good, check the other components in the starter safety circuit (sidestand switch and relay, gear position switch and diodes) as described in the relevant sections of this Chapter, or Chapter 4 for the gear position switch. If all components are good, check the wiring between the various components (see the *wiring diagrams* at the end of this book).

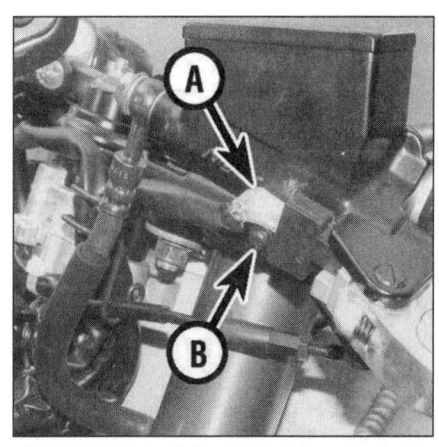

21.2 Clutch switch wiring connectors (A) and mounting screw (B)

9•16 Electrical system

Renewal

4 The clutch switch is mounted on the underside of the clutch master cylinder.
5 Disconnect the wiring connectors **(see illustration 21.2)**, then undo the screw and detach the switch.
6 Installation is the reverse of removal.

22 Diodes

1 The diodes are part of the safety circuit which prevents or stops the engine running if the transmission is in gear whilst the sidestand is down, and prevents the engine from starting if the transmission is in gear unless the sidestand is up and the clutch lever is pulled in. The diodes are integrated with the sidestand relay and turn signal relay in one unit – remove the left-hand cockpit trim panel to access it (see Chapter 8).
2 Pull the relay/diode unit off its connector **(see illustration 11.4)**. Using an ohmmeter or continuity tester, connect the positive (+) probe to C terminal of the diode and the negative (–) probe to A terminal of the diode – there should be 0.4 to 0.6 volts **(see illustration 20.12)**. Now reverse the probes – there should be 1.4 to 1.5 volts (but note that this figure may vary according the output voltage of the meter you are using – the voltage given is the output voltage of the meter used by Suzuki, Pt. No. 09900-25008). Repeat the tests between B terminal and A terminal. The same results should be achieved. If it doesn't behave as stated, install a new relay/diode unit.
3 If the diodes are good, check the other components in the starter safety circuit (clutch switch, gear position switch, sidestand switch and relay) as described in the relevant sections of this Chapter, or Chapter 4 for the gear position switch. If all components are good, check the wiring between the various components (see the *wiring diagrams* at the end of this book).

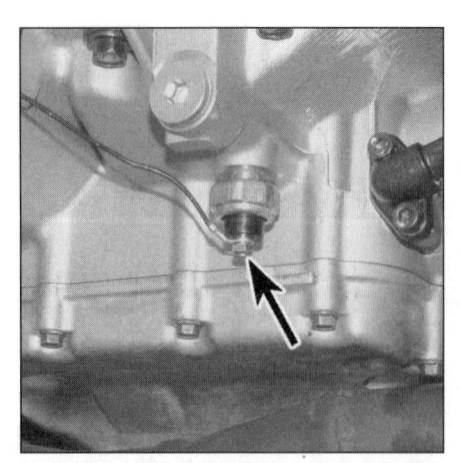

24.3 Undo the screw (arrowed) and detach the lead

23 Horn

Check

1 If the horn doesn't work, first check the signal fuse (see Section 5) and the battery (see Section 3).
2 The horn is mounted above the radiator – remove a fairing side panel for best access (see Chapter 8).
3 Unplug the wiring connectors from the horn. Using two jumper wires, apply battery voltage (12 volts) directly to the terminals on the horn. If the horn doesn't sound, replace it with a new one.
4 If the horn sounds, check for battery voltage at the orange wire terminal with the ignition ON. If there is voltage check the black and black/blue wire between the horn and the horn switch for continuity, then if the wiring is good check the switch (see Section 19). If the switch is good check for continuity to earth in the black/white wire from the switch (see *Wiring Diagrams* at the end of this Chapter).
5 If there was no voltage at the orange wire terminal check the wiring and connectors between the ignition (main) switch, the fusebox and the horn and repair it as necessary (see *Wiring Diagrams* at the end of this Chapter).

Renewal

6 The horn is mounted above the radiator – remove a fairing side panel for best access (see Chapter 8).
7 Unplug the wiring connectors from the horn. Unscrew the bolts securing the horn and remove it from the bike.
8 Install the horn and tighten the bolts. Connect the wiring connectors then check the horn works.

24 Oil pressure switch

Check

1 When the ignition is first turned ON and before the engine is started, the oil warning LED should come on. When the engine is started it should extinguish. If it comes on whilst the engine is running, stop the engine immediately and carry out an oil level check, and if necessary a pressure check, as described in Chapter 1. If the oil pressure warning does not come on when the ignition is turned on, check the display (see Section 16).
2 The oil pressure switch is screwed into the right-hand side of the crankcase. Remove the right-hand fairing side panel (see Chapter 8).
3 Undo the screw and detach the wiring connector from the switch **(see illustration)**.

Turn the ignition ON and check for voltage at the wiring connector. If there is no voltage check the wiring between the switch and the instrument cluster for continuity (see *Wiring Diagrams* at the end of this Chapter). If there is voltage, earth (ground) the connector on the crankcase and check that the oil warning LED comes on. If it does, the switch is faulty. If not, check the main earth connections between the engine and the battery.
4 Now touch the connector to the terminal on the switch and check that the oil warning LED comes on. If the display and warning light do not come on, the switch is faulty and a new one must be fitted.

Removal

5 Remove the right-hand fairing side panel (see Chapter 8). Drain the engine oil (see Chapter 1).
6 Undo the screw and detach the wiring connector from the switch.
7 Unscrew the switch and withdraw it from the crankcase.

Installation

8 Apply a suitable sealant (Suzuki-Bond 1215 or equivalent) to the threads near the switch body, then install it in the crankcase and tighten it to the torque setting specified at the beginning of the Chapter.
9 Attach the wiring connector and tighten the screw **(see illustration 24.3)**.
10 Fill the engine with the correct type and quantity of oil as described in Chapter 1. Start the engine and check that there are no leaks around the switch.
11 Install the right-hand fairing side panel (see Chapter 8).

25 Starter relay

Check

1 If the starter circuit is faulty, first check the main fuse (see Section 5).
2 The starter relay is behind the seat cowling on the left-hand side – remove the seat cowling for access (see Chapter 8).
3 Disconnect the battery negative (–) lead (see Section 3). Remove the plastic cover on the top of the relay **(see illustration)**. Unscrew the bolt securing the starter motor lead to its terminal and disconnect the lead **(see illustration)**; position the lead away from the relay terminal. Reconnect the battery negative (–) lead. With the ignition switch ON, the engine kill switch in the RUN position, the transmission in neutral and the clutch pulled in, press the starter switch. The relay should be heard to click. If not, switch off the ignition, then remove the relay as described below and test it as follows.
4 Set a multimeter to the ohms x 1 scale and connect it across the relay's starter motor and

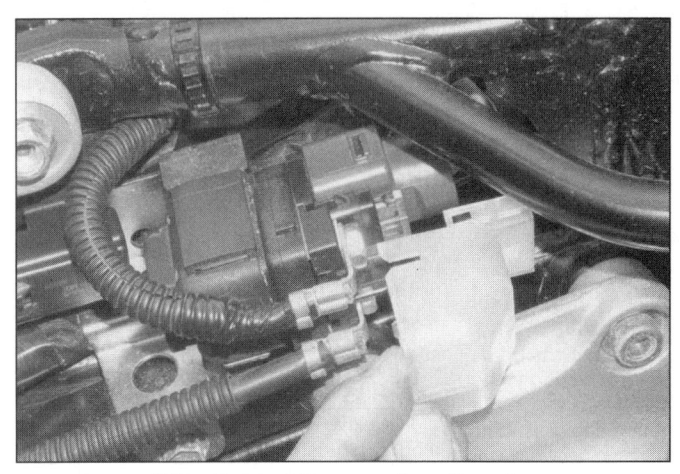

Electrical system 9•17

25.3a Remove the cover from the relay

25.3b Starter motor lead (A) and battery lead (B)

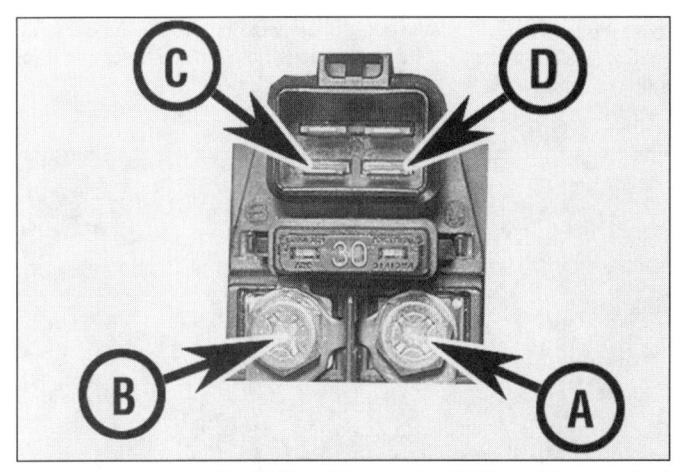

25.4a Starter motor lead (A) and battery lead (B), positive terminal (C) and negative terminal (D)

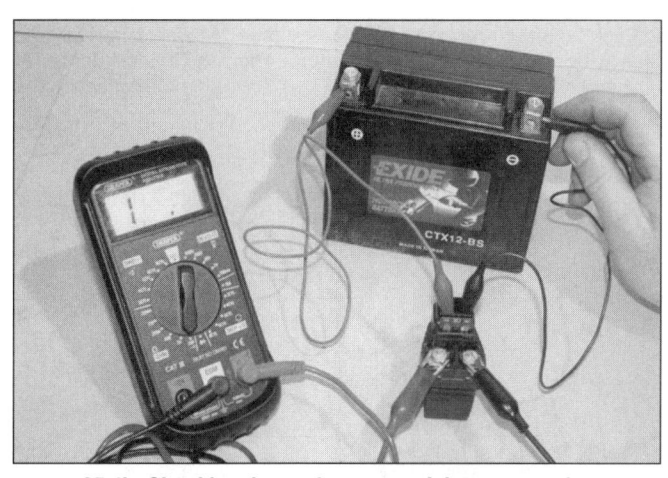

25.4b Checking the performance of the starter relay

battery lead terminals **(see illustration)**. Using a fully-charged 12 volt battery and two insulated jumper wires, connect the positive (+) terminal of the battery to the positive (C) terminal of the relay, and the negative (–) terminal to the negative (D) terminal **(see illustration)**. At this point the relay should be heard to click and the multimeter read 0 ohms (continuity). If this is the case the relay is proved good. If the relay does not click when battery voltage is applied and indicates no continuity (infinite resistance) across its terminals, it is faulty and must be replaced with a new one.

5 To check the internal resistance of the relay, use a multimeter set to the ohms x 1 scale and connect the probes to the positive and negative terminals of the relay **(see illustration)**. The resistance reading obtained should be as specified at the beginning of the Chapter.

6 If the relay is good, check for battery voltage between the yellow/green and the black/yellow wire terminals on the relay wiring connector with the ignition ON, the kill switch in the RUN position, the clutch lever pulled in and the starter button pressed. If voltage is present, check the other components in the starter circuit as described in the relevant sections of this Chapter. If no voltage was present or if all components are good, check the wiring and connectors between the various components (see the *wiring diagrams* at the end of this book).

Removal and installation

7 The starter relay is behind the seat cowling on the left-hand side – remove the seat cowling for access (see Chapter 8).

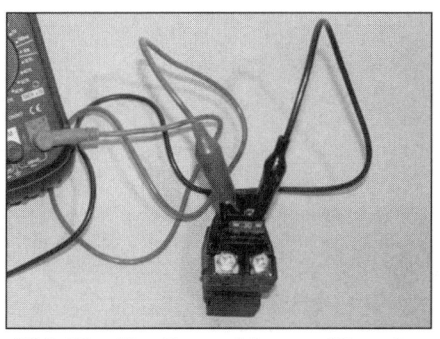

8 Disconnect the battery terminals, remembering to disconnect the negative (–) terminal first (see Section 3).

9 Remove the plastic cover on the top of the relay **(see illustration 25.3a)**. Unscrew the two bolts securing the starter motor and battery leads to the relay and detach the leads **(see illustration 25.3b)**. Displace the relay from its mount and disconnect the wiring connector **(see illustration)**. If you are fitting a new relay remove the main and spare fuses

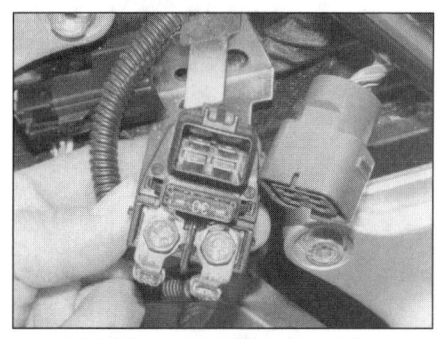

25.5 Checking the resistance of the relay

25.9 Disconnect the relay wiring connector

9•18 Electrical system

from the old relay and fit them to the new one, or keep them as spares if the new one is already fitted with them.

10 Installation is the reverse of removal. Make sure the terminal bolts are tight. Connect the negative (–) lead last when reconnecting the battery.

26 Starter motor removal and installation

Removal

1 Remove the rider's seat and disconnect the battery negative (–) lead (see Section 3). The starter motor is mounted on the right-hand side of the crankcase behind the cylinder block – raise or remove the fuel tank (see Chapter 8).

2 Peel back the rubber terminal cover **(see illustration)**. Unscrew the nut securing the lead and detach it.

3 Unscrew the two bolts securing the starter motor, noting the earth lead secured by the rear bolt **(see illustration)**. Draw the starter motor out of the crankcase and remove it from the machine **(see illustration)**.

4 Remove the O-ring on the end of the starter motor and discard it as a new one must be used.

Installation

5 Fit a new O-ring onto the end of the starter motor, making sure it is seated in its groove, and smear it with grease **(see illustration)**.

6 Manoeuvre the motor into position and slide it into the crankcase. Ensure that the starter motor teeth mesh correctly. Install the mounting bolts and tighten them, not forgetting the earth lead.

7 Connect the lead to the starter motor and secure it with the nut. Make sure the rubber cover is correctly seated over the terminal.

8 Connect the battery negative (–) lead. Install the fuel tank (see Chapter 8).

27 Starter motor check and overhaul

Check

1 Remove the starter motor (see Section 26). Cover the body in some rag and clamp the motor in a soft-jawed vice – do not overtighten it.

2 Using a fully-charged 12 volt battery and two insulated jumper wires, connect the positive (+) terminal of the battery to the protruding terminal on the starter motor, and the negative (–) terminal to one of the motor's mounting lugs. At this point the starter motor should spin. If this is the case the motor is proved good, though it is worth disassembling it and checking it if you suspect it of not working properly under load. If the motor does not spin, disassemble it for inspection.

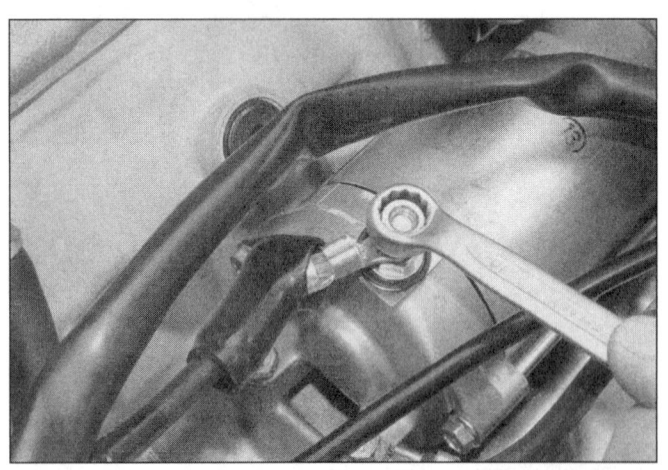

26.2 Pull back the rubber cover and unscrew the terminal nut

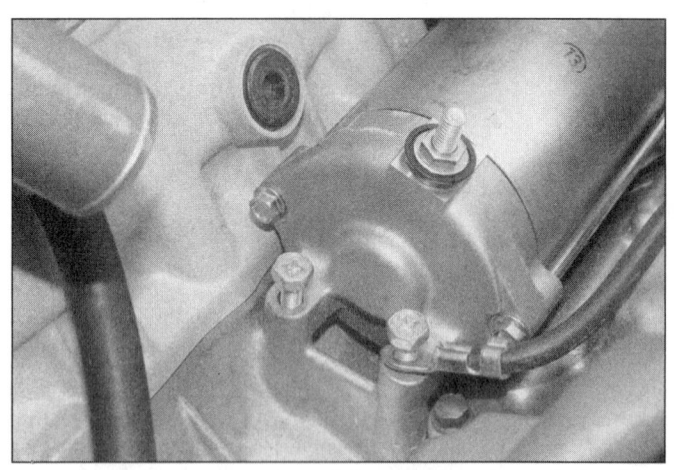

26.3a Unscrew the bolts (arrowed), noting the earth lead . . .

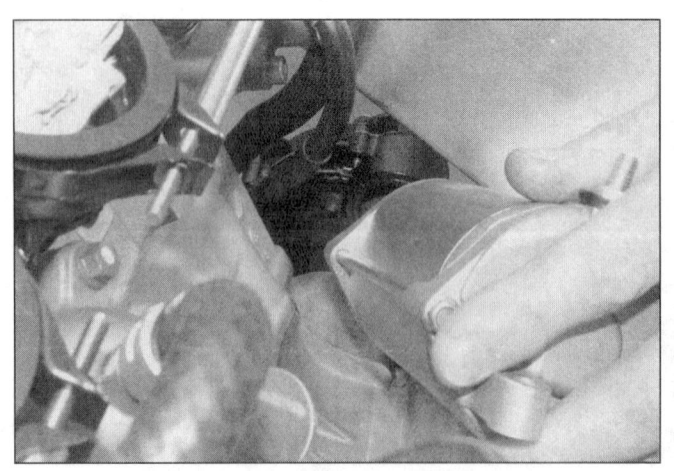

26.3b . . . and remove the starter motor

26.5 Fit a new O-ring

Electrical system 9•19

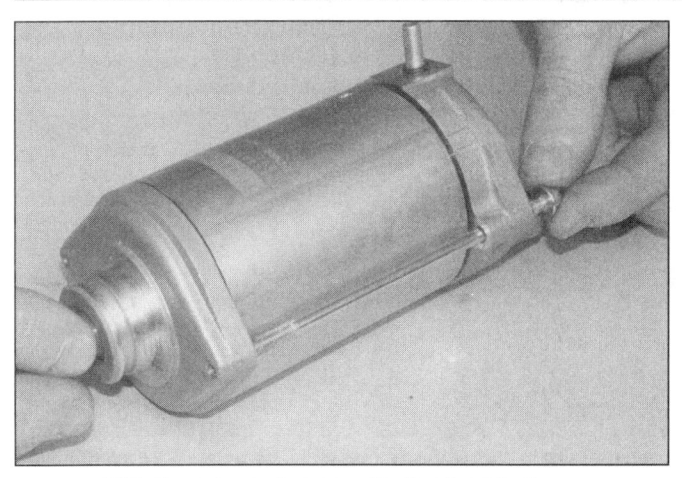

27.6 Unscrew and remove the two long bolts . . .

27.7 . . . and remove the front cover

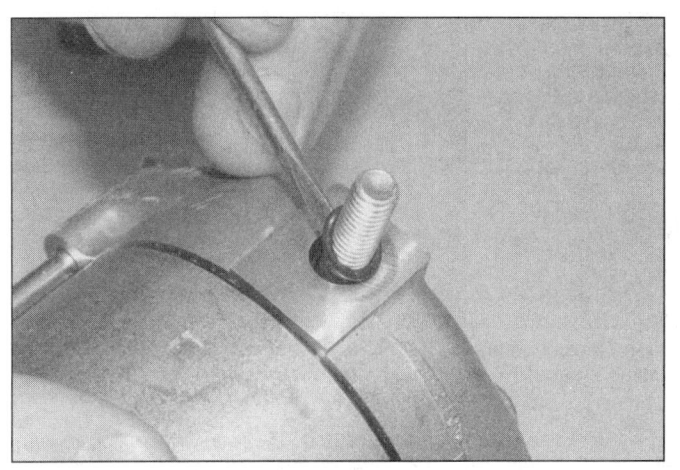

27.10 Remove the O-ring from the bolt

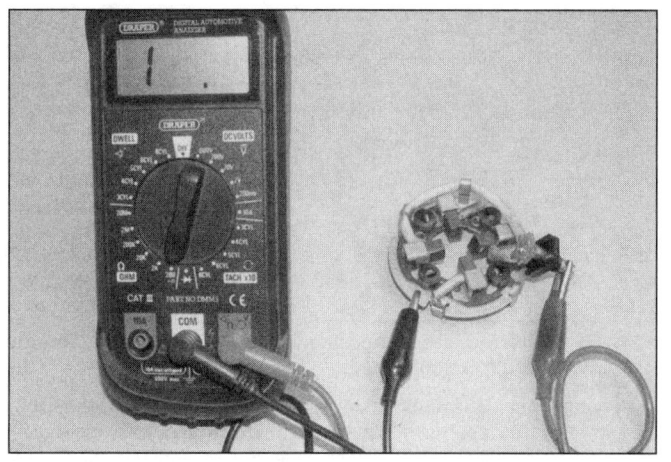

27.11 Check there is no continuity between the bolt and the plate

3 Check for continuity between the terminal bolt and the rear cover – there should be no continuity (infinite resistance).

Disassembly

Note: *Before disassembling the motor, spray some penetrating fluid around the front cover bolt threads and holes.*

4 Remove the starter motor (see Section 26).
5 Note any alignment marks between the main housing and the front and rear covers, or make your own if they aren't clear.
6 Unscrew the two long bolts and withdraw them from the starter motor **(see illustration)**.
7 Wrap some insulating tape around the teeth on the end of the starter motor shaft – this will protect the oil seal from damage as the front cover is removed. Remove the front cover from the motor **(see illustration)**. Remove the sealing ring from the cover or main housing and discard it as a new one must be used **(see illustration 27.21b)**. Remove the tabbed washer from the cover **(see illustration 27.21a)**. Slide the shim(s) off the shaft **(see illustration 27.20a)**.
8 Remove the rear cover from the motor, bringing the brushplate with it. Remove the sealing ring from the cover or main housing and discard it as a new one must be used.
9 Withdraw the armature from the main housing, noting that you will have to pull it out against the attraction of the magnets.
10 Unscrew the terminal nut and remove it along with the insulator bush and the O-ring **(see illustration 27.20c)**, which you may have to carefully dig out from around the base of the terminal bolt **(see illustration)**. Remove the brushplate from the rear cover, noting how it locates, drawing the terminal bolt out of the cover as you do. Remove the insulator piece from the terminal bolt if required. Check the condition of the O-ring and replace it with a new one if it is damaged, deformed or deteriorated.

Inspection

11 The parts of the starter motor that are most likely to require attention are the brushes. Suzuki provide no minimum length specification, but if the brushes are obviously short (less than 5 mm), cracked, chipped, or otherwise damaged, replace the brushplate assembly with a new one. Also check the brush springs. Check there is no continuity between the terminal bolt and brushplate – if there is replace the assembly with a new one **(see illustration)**.
12 Inspect the commutator bars on the armature for scoring, scratches and discoloration. The commutator can be cleaned and polished with crocus cloth, but do not use sandpaper or emery paper. After cleaning, wipe away any residue with a cloth soaked in electrical system cleaner or denatured alcohol. Check that the insulating Mica is below the surface of the commutator bars **(see illustration)**. If there is little or no undercut, scrape the Mica away until the undercut is as shown.
13 Using an ohmmeter or a continuity test light, check for continuity between the

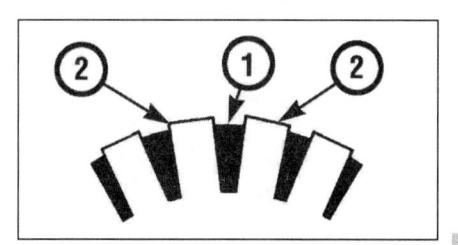

27.12 Check the Mica (1) is below the commutator bars (2)

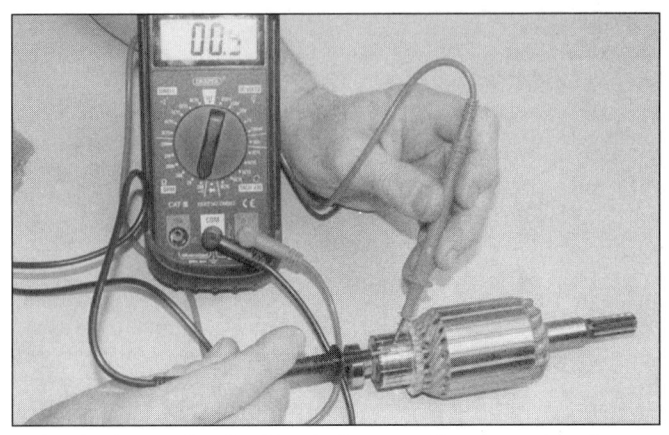

9•20 Electrical system

27.13a Continuity should exist between the commutator bars

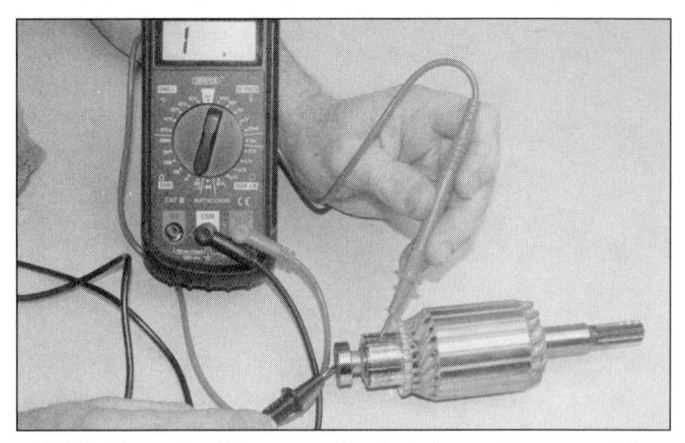

27.13b There should be no continuity between the commutator bars and the armature shaft

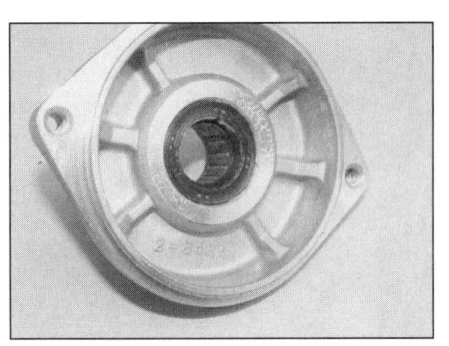

27.15a Check the oil seal and bearing in the front cover . . .

27.15b . . . and the bearing (arrowed) on the shaft

27.18 Slide the brush plate onto the commutator, locating the brush ends on the bars

commutator bars **(see illustration)**. Continuity should exist between each bar and all of the others. Also, check for continuity between the commutator bars and the armature shaft **(see illustration)**. There should be no continuity (infinite resistance) between the commutator and the shaft. If the checks indicate otherwise, replace the starter motor with a new one (the armature is not listed separately).

14 Check the front end of the armature shaft for worn, cracked, chipped and broken teeth.

15 Inspect the front and rear covers for signs of cracks or wear. Check the oil seal and bearing in the front cover, and the bearing on the rear end of the shaft for wear and damage **(see illustrations)**. None of those components are available individually.

16 Inspect the magnets in the main housing and the housing itself for cracks.

17 Inspect the insulator bush, insulator piece and O-ring, and the sealing rings for signs of damage, deformation and deterioration and replace them with new ones if necessary.

Reassembly

18 Slide the brushplate onto the commutator – you will need to press the brushes back into their housings so they do not snag **(see illustration)**.

19 Fit the insulator piece and O-ring onto the terminal bolt. Insert the terminal bolt in the cover then locate the brushplate, making sure the bearing on the end of the armature shaft locates in the cover, and the brushplate tab locates in its cut-out **(see illustrations)**.

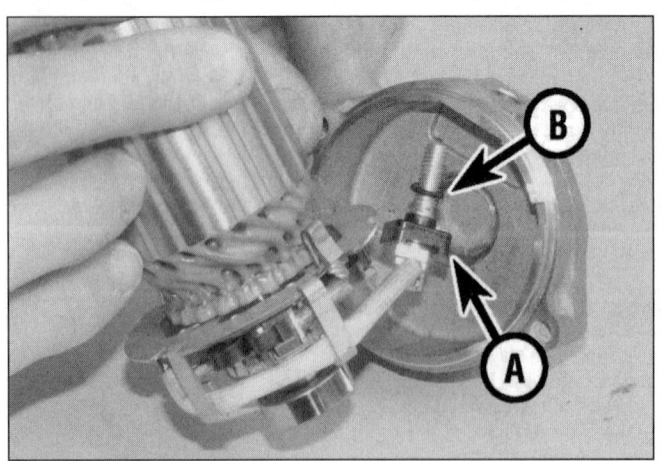

27.19a Fit the insulator (A) and O-ring (B) onto the bolt, then fit the rear cover . . .

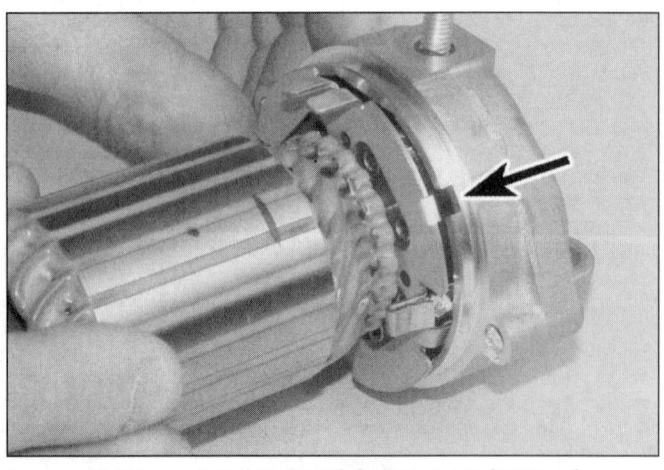

27.19b . . . locating the tab in its cut-out (arrowed)

Electrical system 9•21

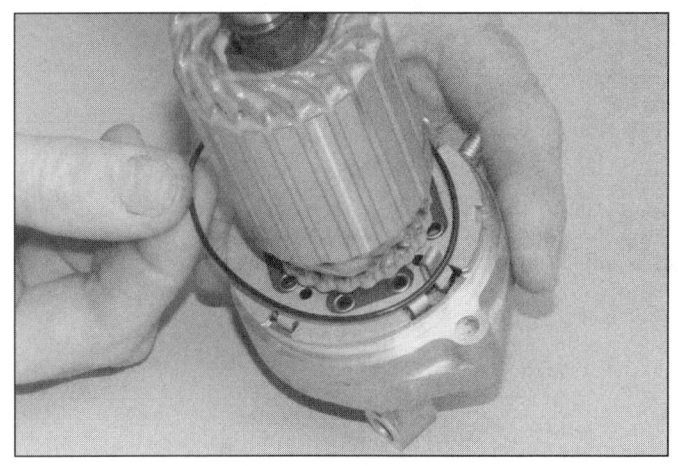

27.19c Fit a new sealing ring

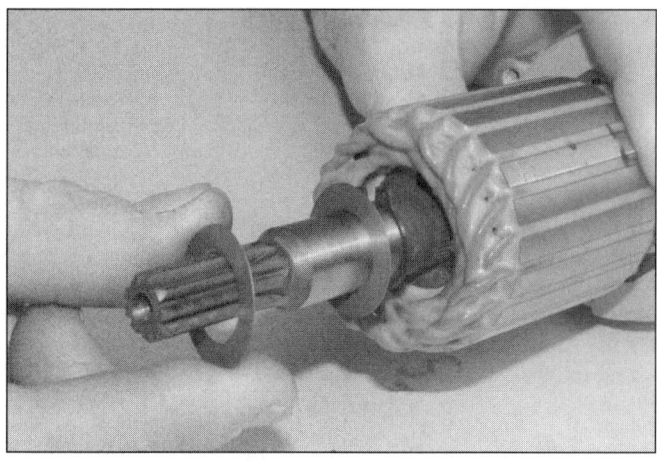

27.20a Slide the shim(s) onto the shaft . . .

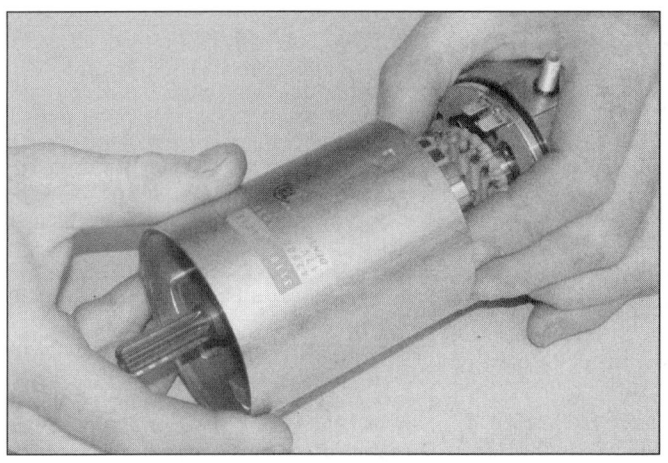

27.20b . . . then carefully fit the housing over the armature

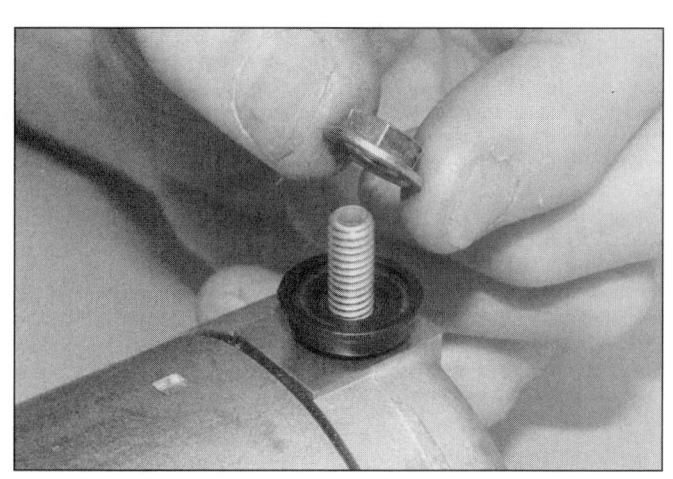

27.20c Fit the bush and the nut onto the bolt

Fit the rear cover sealing ring **(see illustration)**.
20 Slide the shim(s) onto the shaft **(see illustration)**. Slide the main housing over the armature and onto the rear cover, noting that the magnets will forcibly draw the cover on, or alternatively try to draw the armature out of the cover **(see illustration)**. Grasp each component securely and control the action, taking care not to get your fingers jammed between the housing and the cover. Fit the bush and the nut onto the terminal bolt **(see illustration)**.
21 Apply a smear of grease to the lips of the front cover oil seal, then fit the tabbed washer **(see illustration)**. Fit the front cover sealing ring **(see illustration)**. Install the cover, aligning the marks made on removal **(see illustration 27.7)**. Remove the protective tape from the shaft end.
22 Check the alignment marks made on removal

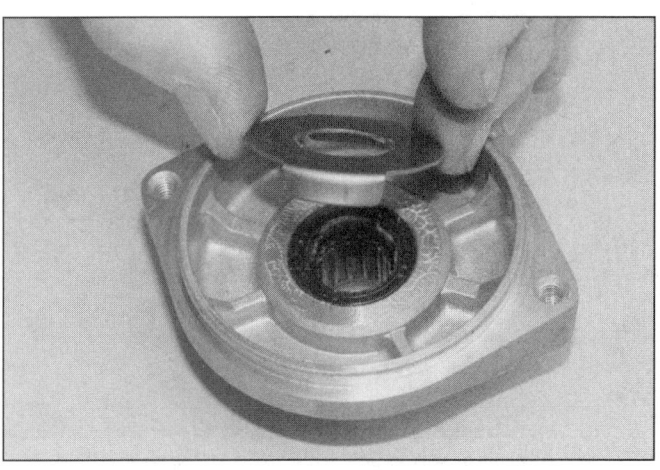

27.21a Fit the tabbed washer onto the cover . . .

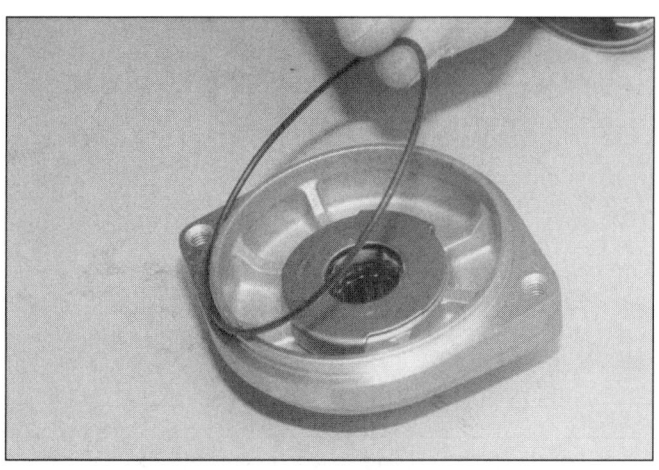

27.21b . . . then fit a new sealing ring

9•22 Electrical system

are correctly aligned, then install the long bolts and tighten them **(see illustration 27.6)**.
23 Install the starter motor (see Section 26).

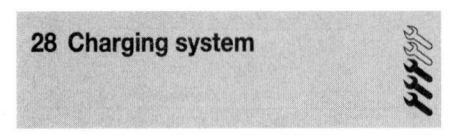

28 Charging system

General information and precautions

1 If the performance of the charging system is suspect, the system as a whole should be checked first, followed by testing of the individual components. **Note:** *Before beginning the checks, make sure the battery is fully charged and that all system connections are clean and tight.*
2 Checking the output of the charging system and the performance of the various components within the charging system requires the use of a multimeter (with voltage, current and resistance checking facilities).
3 When making the checks, follow the procedures carefully to prevent incorrect connections or short circuits, as irreparable damage to electrical system components may result if short circuits occur.
4 If a multimeter is not available, the job of checking the charging system should be left to a Suzuki dealer or automotive electrician.
5 If the charging system of the machine is thought to be faulty, perform the following checks.

Leakage test

Caution: Always connect an ammeter in series, never in parallel with the battery, otherwise it will be damaged. Do not turn the ignition ON or operate the starter motor when the ammeter is connected – a sudden surge in current will blow the meter's fuse.

6 Remove the rider's seat (see Chapter 8).
7 Make sure the ignition switch is OFF. Disconnect the lead from the battery negative (–) terminal **(see illustration 3.2)**.
8 Set the multimeter to the Amps function and connect its negative (–) probe to the battery negative (–) terminal, and positive (+) probe to the disconnected negative (–) lead **(see illustration)**. Always set the meter to a high amps range initially and then bring it down to the mA (milli Amps) range; if there is a high current flow in the circuit it may blow the meter's fuse.
9 No current flow should be indicated. If current leakage is indicated (greater than 3 mA), there is a short circuit in the wiring. Using the wiring diagrams at the end of this Chapter, systematically disconnect individual electrical components, checking the meter each time until the source is identified.
10 If no leakage is indicated, disconnect the meter and connect the negative (–) lead to the battery, tightening it securely.

Output test

11 Start the engine and warm it up to normal operating temperature. Remove the rider's seat (see Chapter 8).
12 To check the regulated voltage output, allow the engine to idle and connect a multimeter set to the 0 to 20 volts DC scale (voltmeter) across the terminals of the battery (positive (+) lead to battery positive (+) terminal, negative (–) lead to battery negative (–) terminal) (see Section 3) **(see illustration 3.2)**. Slowly increase the engine speed to 5000 rpm and note the reading obtained. The regulated voltage should be as specified at the beginning of the Chapter. If the voltage is outside these limits, check the alternator and the regulator/rectifier (see Sections 29 and 30).

> **HAYNES HiNT** *Clues to a faulty regulator are constantly blowing bulbs, with brightness varying considerably with engine speed, and battery overheating.*

29 Alternator

Check

1 Raise the fuel tank (see Chapter 4).
2 Trace the alternator wiring back from the alternator cover on the left-hand side of the engine and disconnect it at the connector with three yellow wires **(see illustration)**.
3 Using a multimeter set to the ohms x 1 (ohmmeter) scale measure the stator coil winding resistance by connecting the probes between each of the yellow wire terminal pairs on the alternator side of the connector, taking a total of three readings. Also check for continuity between each terminal and ground (earth). If the stator coil windings are in good condition the three readings should be within the range shown in the Specifications at the start of this Chapter and there should be no continuity (infinite resistance) between any of the terminals and ground (earth). If not, check the fault is not due to damaged wiring between the connector and stator. If the wiring and connectors are good, the alternator stator coil assembly is at fault and must be replaced with a new one.

Removal

4 Drain the engine oil (see Chapter 1). Remove the left-hand fairing side panel (see Chapter 8).

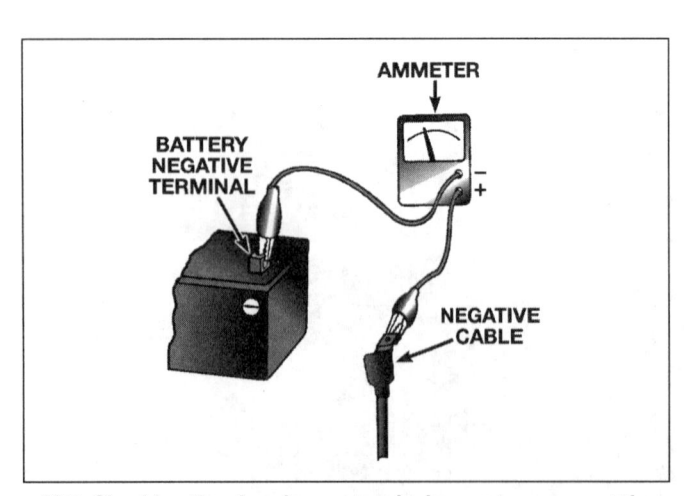

28.8 Checking the charging system leakage rate – connect the meter as shown

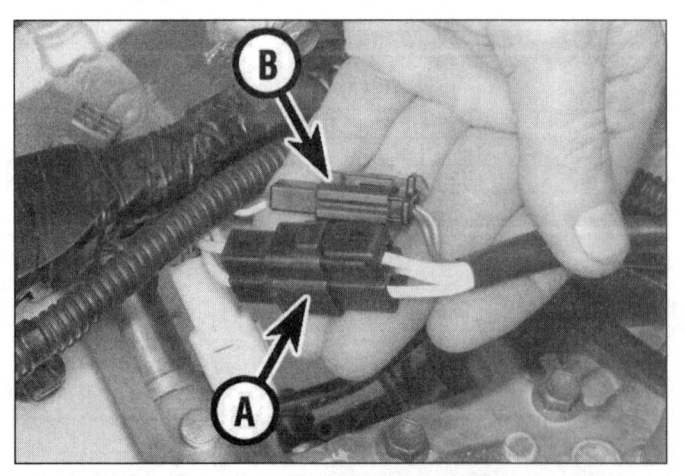

29.2 Alternator wiring connector (A), CKP sensor wiring connector (B)

Electrical system 9•23

29.7 Alternator cover bolts (arrowed)

29.8 Counter-hold the rotor boss and unscrew the bolt in its centre

29.9 Thread the puller into the rotor until the rotor is displaced – use a bar inserted into the puller for extra leverage if required

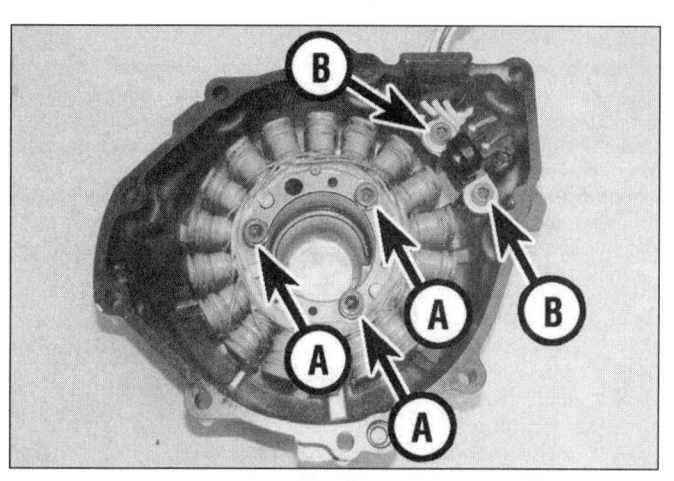

29.10 Stator bolts (A), CKP sensor bolts (B)

5 Raise the fuel tank (see Chapter 4).
6 Trace the alternator and crankshaft position sensor wiring back from the alternator cover on the left-hand side of the engine and disconnect it at the connectors (see illustration 29.2). Free the wiring from its ties and guides and feed it through to the alternator cover, noting its routing.
7 Working in a criss-cross pattern, unscrew the alternator cover bolts, on K2 (2002) models onward noting the wiring clamp (see illustration). Remove the cover, noting that it will be restrained by the pull of the rotor magnets, and be prepared to catch any residual oil (see illustration 29.14b). Note that there is a leverage point on the bottom of the cover if it is difficult to displace. Never lever between the cover and crankcase mating surfaces as you could score them and cause a leak. Discard the gasket as a new one must be used. Remove the dowels for safekeeping if they are loose.
8 Counter-hold the alternator rotor using a 32 mm open spanner on the rotor boss and unscrew the rotor bolt (see illustration).

9 To remove the rotor from the shaft it is necessary to use a rotor puller, either the Suzuki service tool (Pt. No. 09930-30450) or a commercial available equivalent from a motorcycle dealer. Thread the rotor puller into the centre of the rotor and turn it until the rotor is displaced from the shaft, holding the rotor as described above to prevent the engine turning (see illustration). Remove the Woodruff key from its slot in the crankcase if it is loose (see illustration 29.12).
10 If required unscrew the bolts securing the stator and the crankshaft position sensor in the cover (see illustration). Free the wiring grommet from its cut-out and remove the stator assembly.

Installation

11 Fit the stator and crankshaft position sensor into the cover, then route the wiring to the cut-out (see illustrations 29.10). Apply a suitable non-permanent thread locking compound to the threads of the stator and CKP sensor bolts, and tighten them to the appropriate torque setting specified at the beginning of the Chapter. Apply a suitable sealant to the wiring grommet, then press it into the cut-out in the cover.
12 Clean the tapered end of the crankshaft and the corresponding mating surface on the inside of the rotor with a suitable solvent. Fit the Woodruff key into its slot in the crankshaft if removed (see illustration). Make sure that

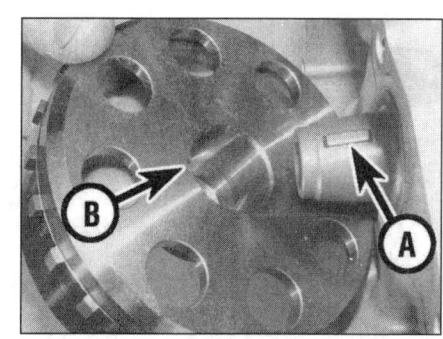

29.12 Check that the Woodruff key (A) is in its slot, then slide the rotor onto the shaft, aligning the cut-out (B) with the key

9•24 Electrical system

29.13a Install the bolt with its washer . . .

29.13b . . . and tighten it to the specified torque

no metal objects have attached themselves to the magnets on the inside of the rotor. Slide the rotor onto the shaft, making sure the groove on the inside is aligned with and fits over the Woodruff key. Make sure the Woodruff key does not become dislodged.

13 Install the rotor bolt with its washer and tighten it to the torque setting specified at the beginning of the Chapter, using the method employed on removal to prevent the rotor from turning **(see illustrations)**.

14 Apply a suitable sealant to the mating surface of the cover around each crankcase joint. Fit the dowels into the crankcase if removed, then fit a new cover gasket onto them **(see illustration)**. Install the alternator cover, making sure it locates onto the dowels **(see illustration)** – take care not to trap your fingers or damage the gasket as the cover is drawn into place by the pull of the magnets. Tighten the cover bolts evenly in a criss-cross sequence to the specified torque setting, on K2 (2002) models onward not forgetting the wiring clamp with the bolt in the 10 o'clock position **(see illustration 29.7)**.

15 Reconnect the wiring at the connectors, making sure it is correctly routed, and secure it with any clips or ties previously released.

16 Replenish the engine oil (see Chapter 1).

17 Lower the fuel tank (see Chapter 4). Install the left-hand fairing side panel (see Chapter 8).

30 Regulator/rectifier

Check

1 Remove the rider's seat and disconnect the battery negative (–) lead (see Section 3).

2 Remove the seat cowling (see Chapter 8) – the regulator/rectifier is mounted on the left-hand side of the rear sub-frame **(see illustration 30.6)**.

3 Disconnect the regulator/rectifier wiring connector. Using a multimeter set to the diode testing function, measure the voltage between the various terminals on the regulator/rectifier side of the wiring connectors as shown in the table **(see illustration)**. **Note:** *Depending on the output voltage of the multimeter used for the test, the results may vary from the specified figures. However, as long as the variance is constant, the test will give an indication of the condition of the regulator/rectifier. If the readings do not compare closely with those shown in the table, have the regulator/rectifier tested by a Suzuki dealer.*

4 If the regulator/rectifier appears to be good, check the wiring between the battery, regulator/rectifier and alternator, and the wiring connectors (see *Wiring Diagrams* at the end of this book).

Removal and installation

5 Remove the rider's seat and disconnect the

29.14a Locate the new gasket onto the dowels . . .

29.14b . . . then install the cover

Electrical system 9•25

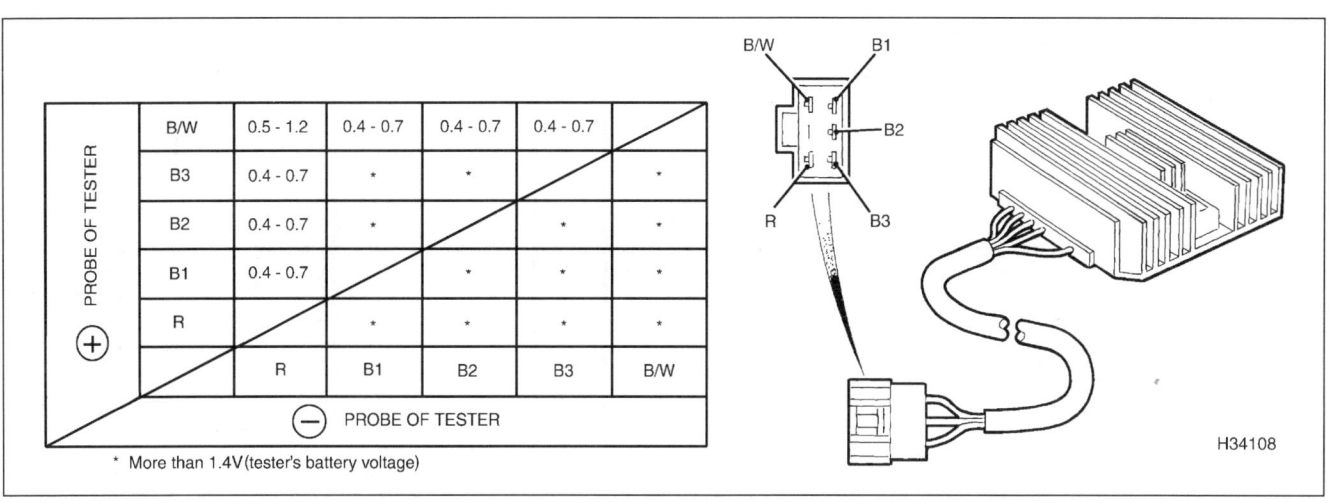

	B/W	0.5 - 1.2	0.4 - 0.7	0.4 - 0.7	0.4 - 0.7	
PROBE OF TESTER (+)	B3	0.4 - 0.7	*	*		*
	B2	0.4 - 0.7	*		*	*
	B1	0.4 - 0.7		*	*	*
	R		*	*	*	*
		R	B1	B2	B3	B/W

(−) PROBE OF TESTER

* More than 1.4V (tester's battery voltage)

30.3 Regulator/rectifier test data and terminal identification

battery negative (−) lead (see Section 3).
6 Remove the seat cowling (see Chapter 8) – the regulator/rectifier is mounted on the left-hand side of the rear sub-frame **(see illustration)**.
7 Disconnect the regulator/rectifier wiring connector, and free the wiring from the cable tie (where fitted).
8 Unscrew the three bolts securing the regulator/rectifier and remove it. Note the collars in the rubber grommets. Check the condition of the grommets and replace them with new ones if they are damaged, deformed or deteriorated. If required separate the regulator/rectifier from its bracket by unscrewing the nuts and removing the bolts.
9 Install the new unit in reverse order and connect the wiring connector.
10 Install the seat cowling (see Chapter 8). Reconnect the battery negative lead (−) (see Section 3).

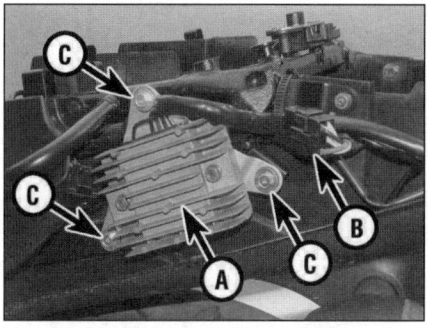

30.6 Regulator/rectifier (A), wiring connector (B) and mounting bolts (C)

9•26 Wiring diagrams

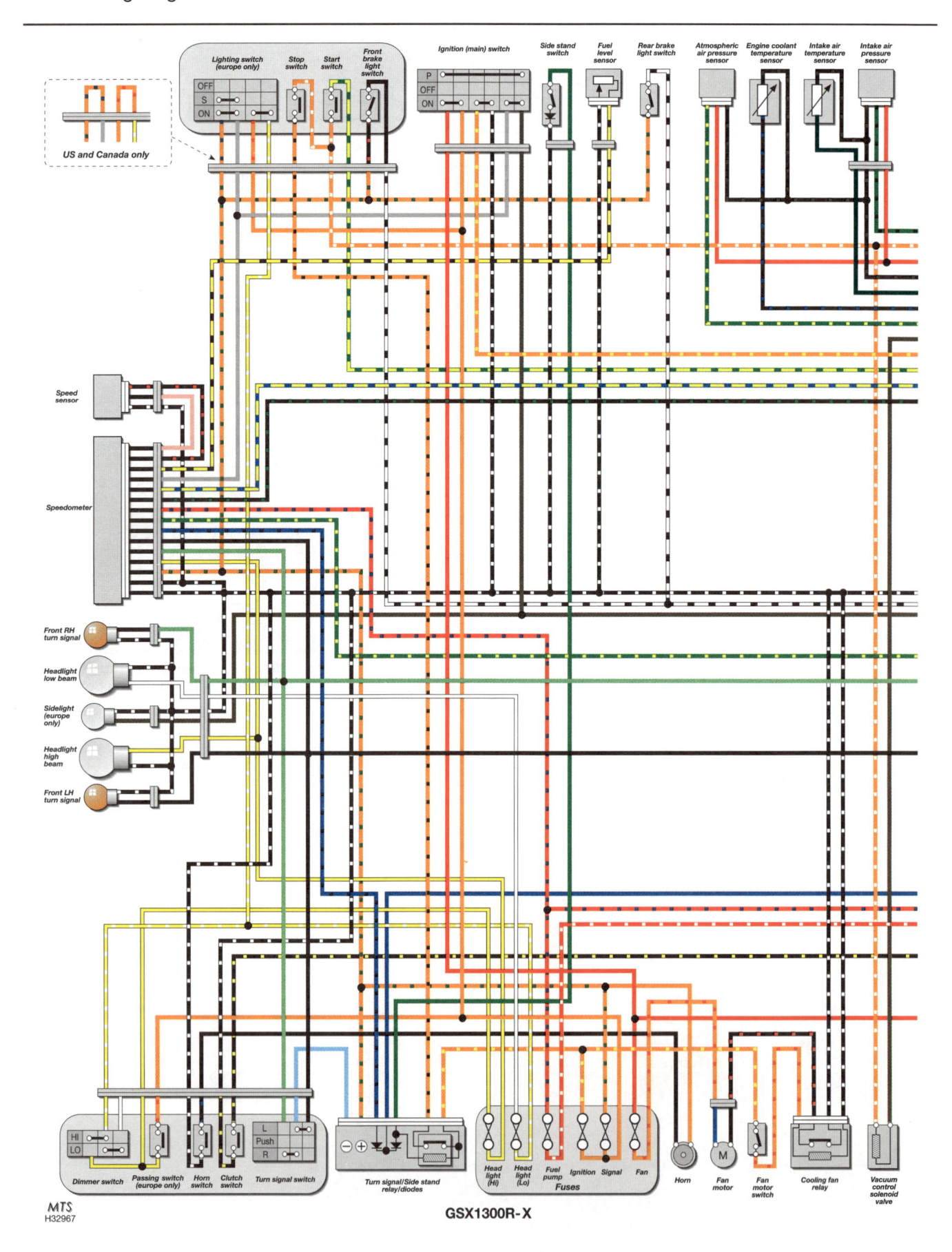

Wiring diagrams 9•27

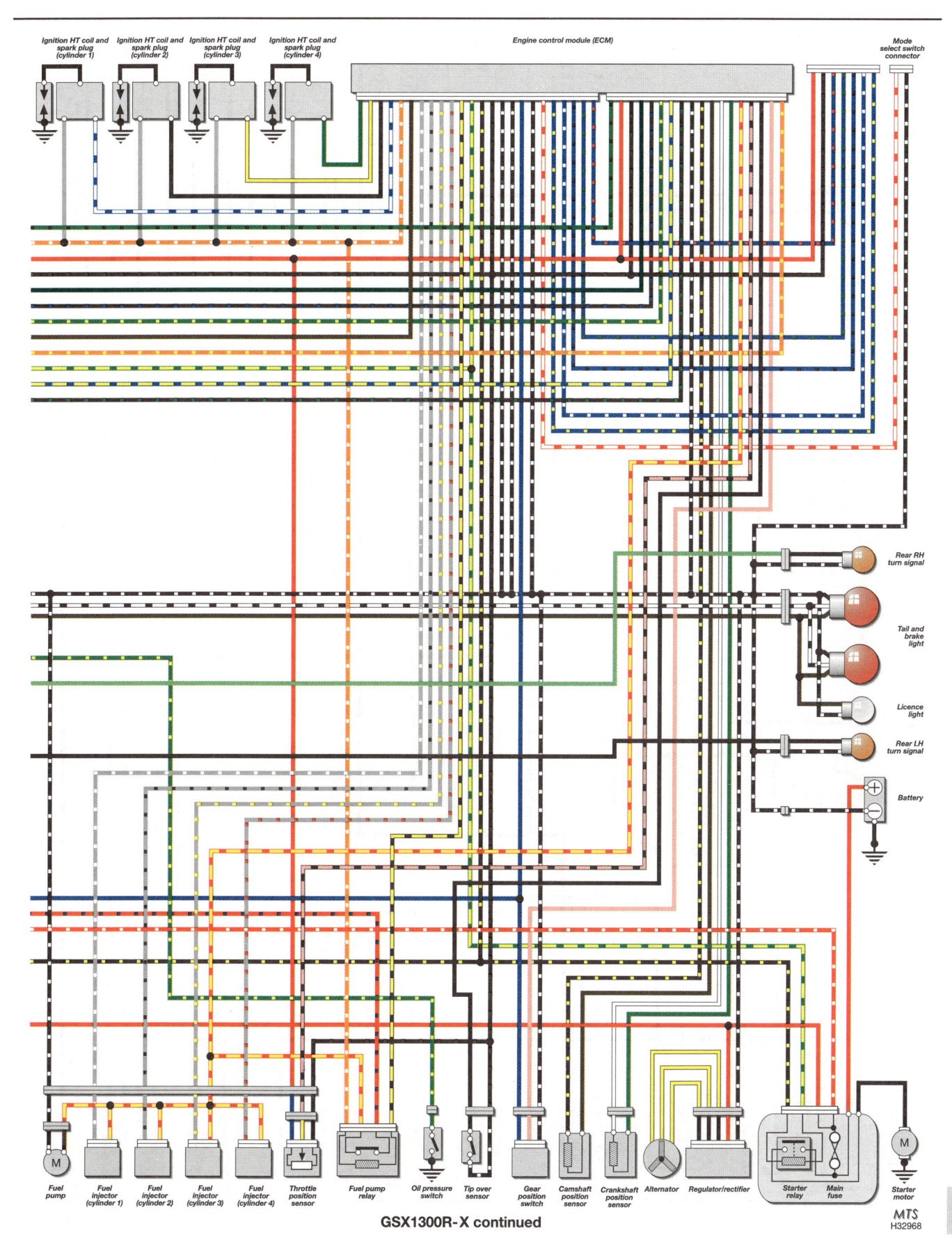

GSX1300R-X continued

9•28 Wiring diagrams

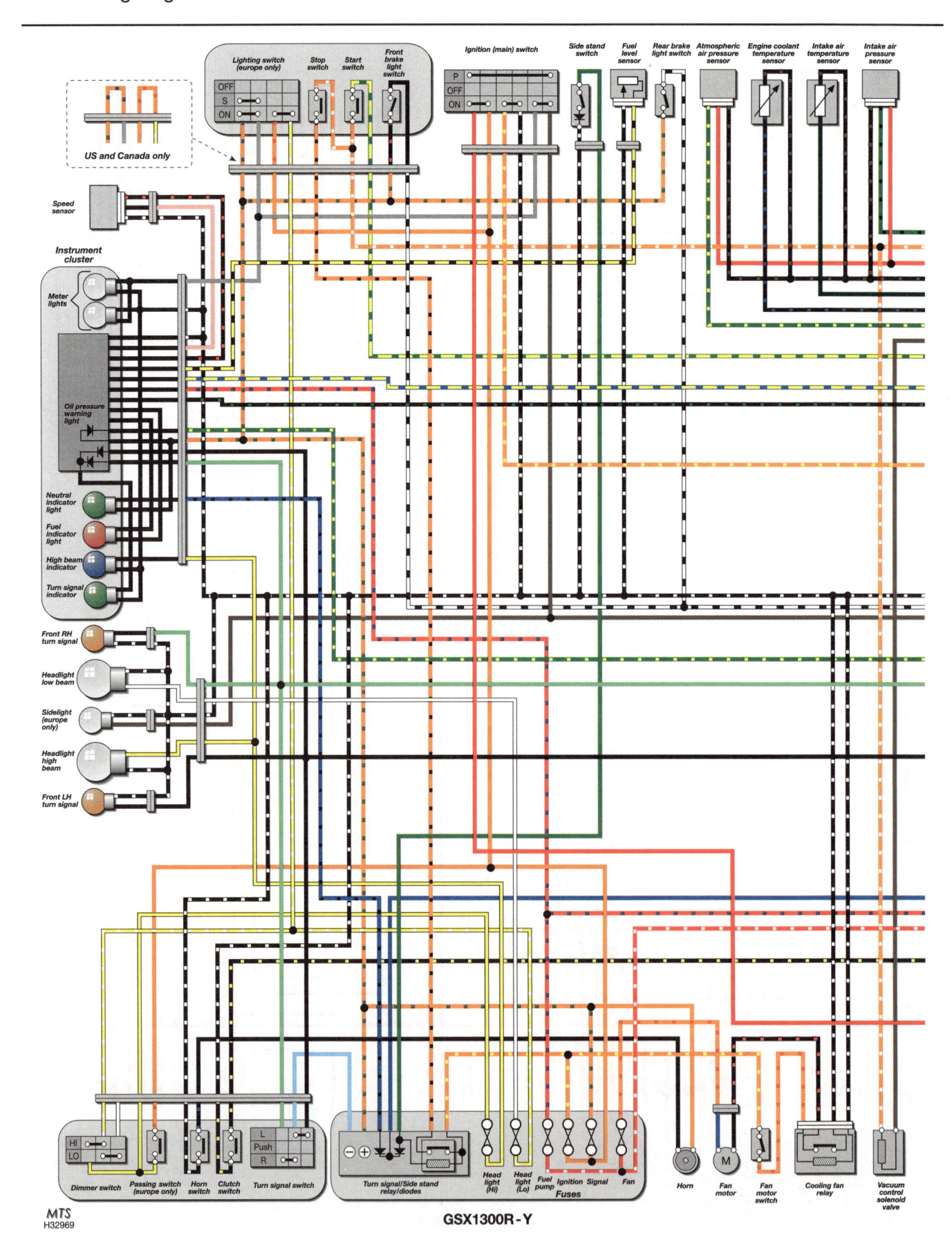

GSX1300R-Y

Wiring diagrams 9•29

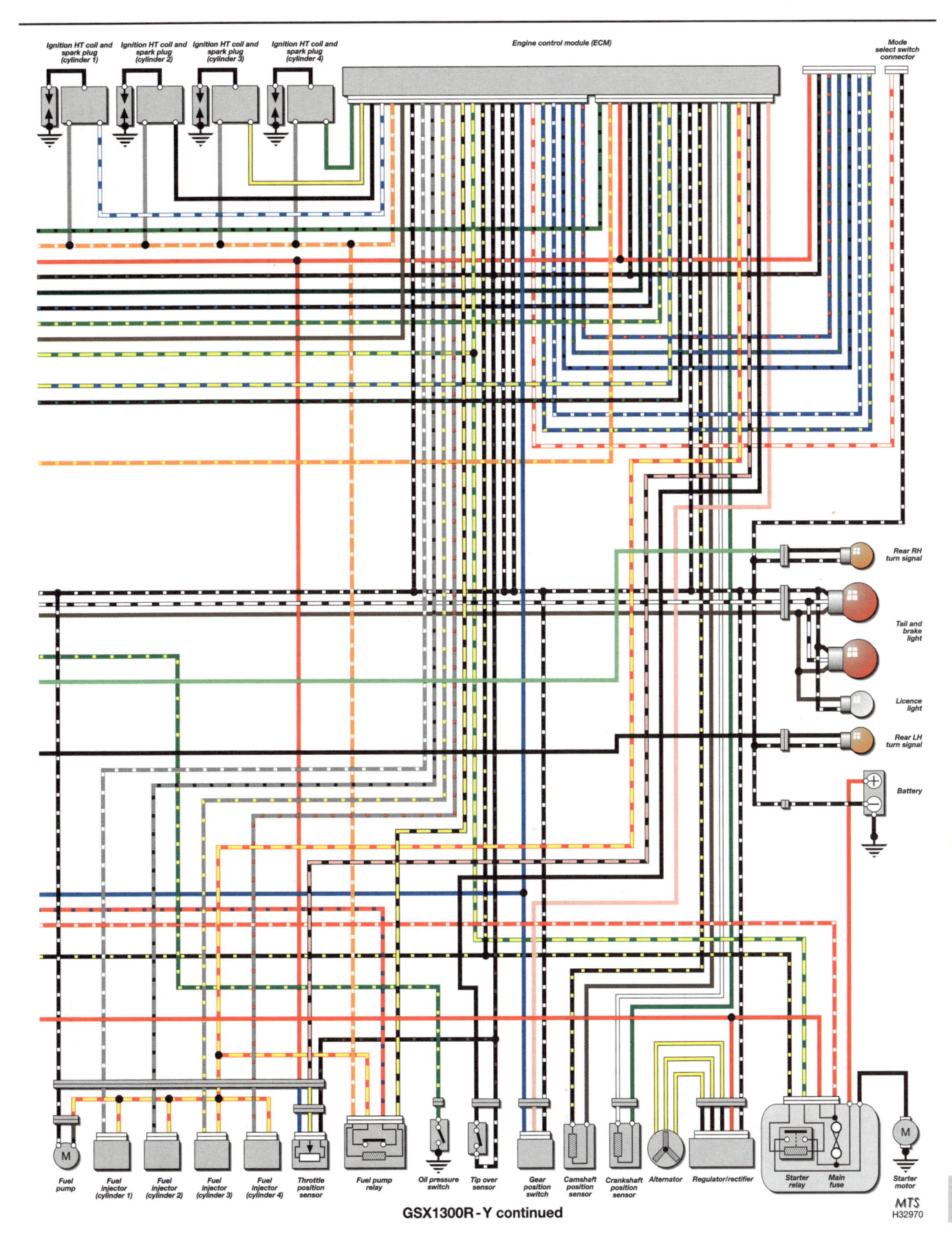

GSX1300R - Y continued

9•30 Wiring diagrams

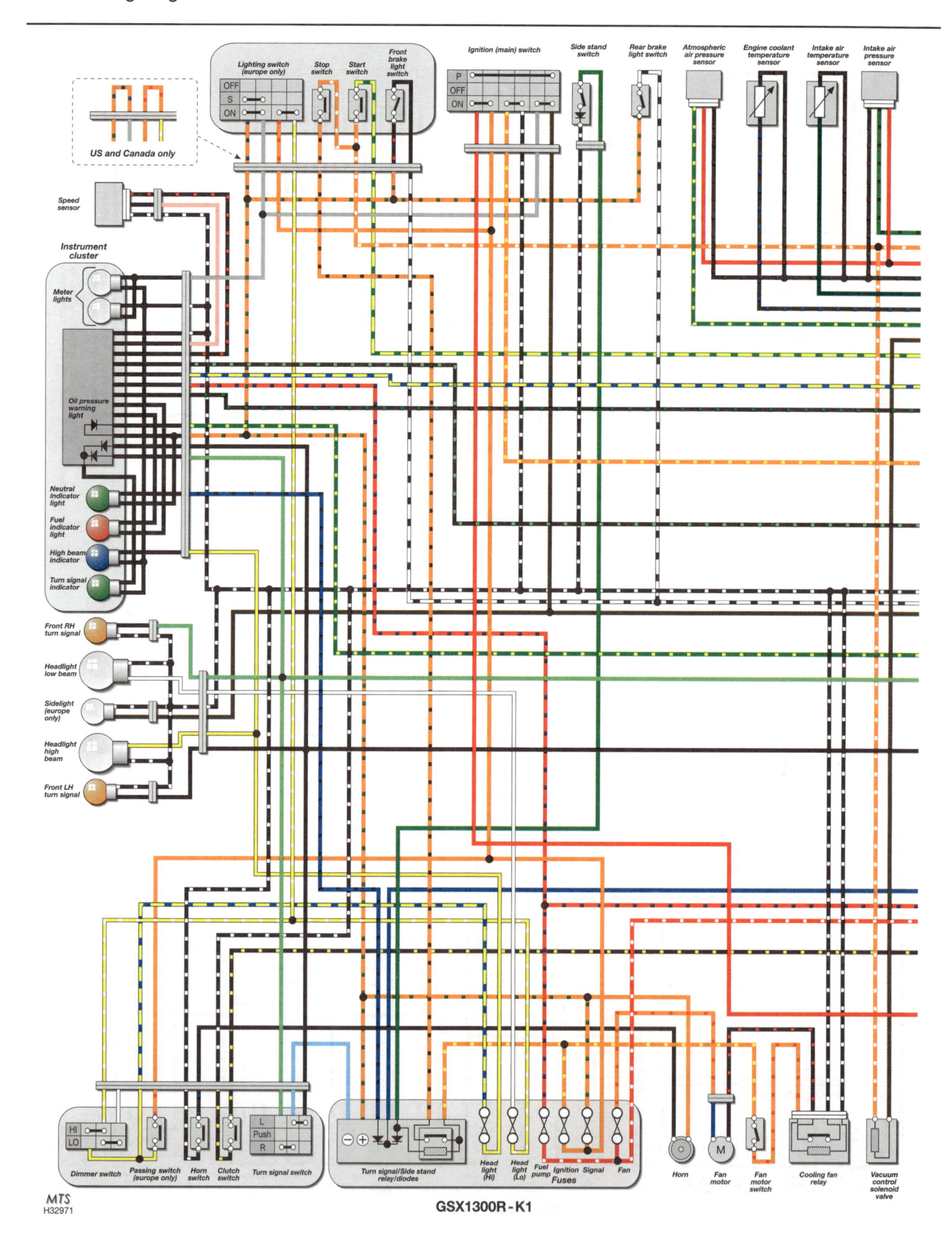

Wiring diagrams 9•31

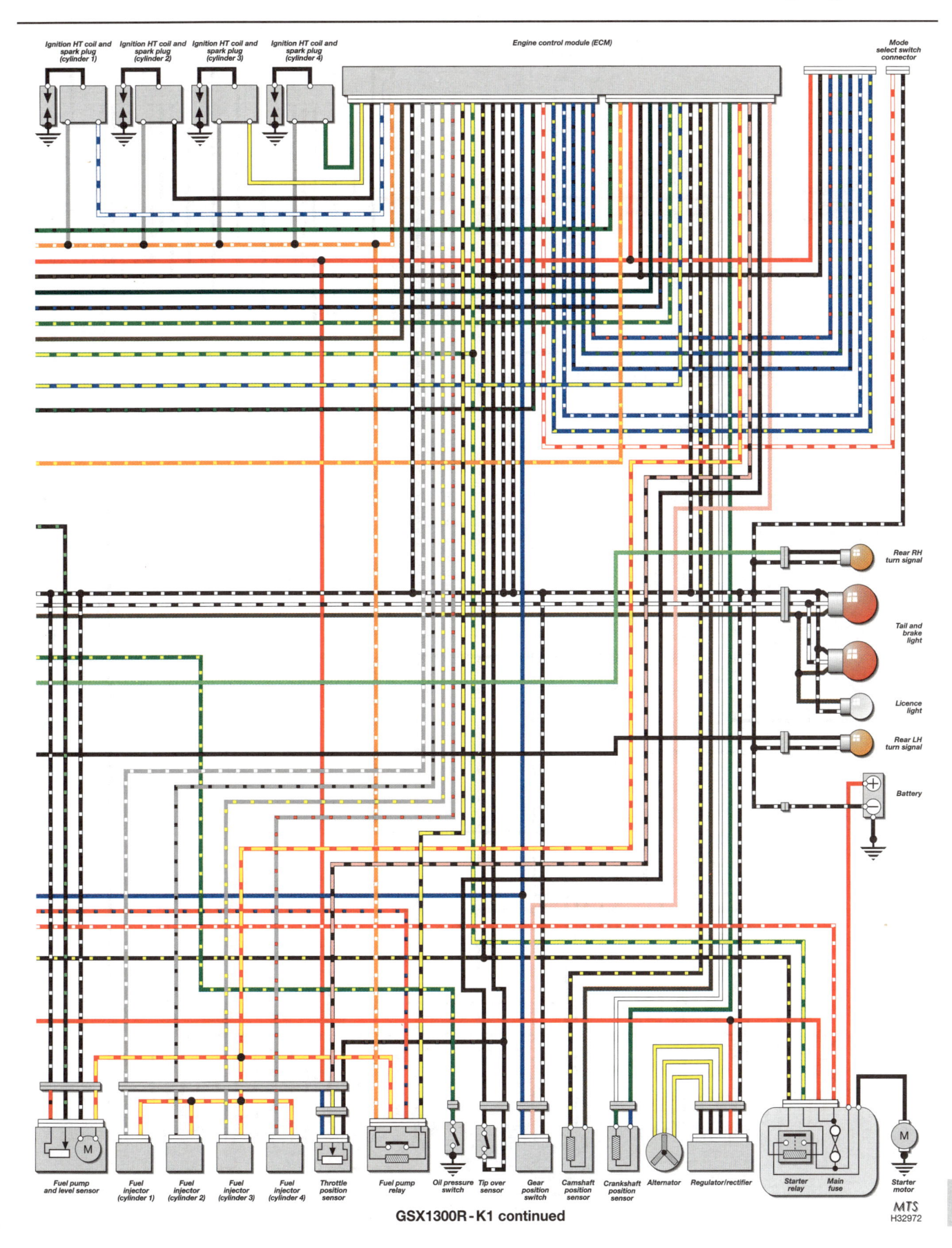

GSX1300R - K1 continued

9•32 Wiring diagrams

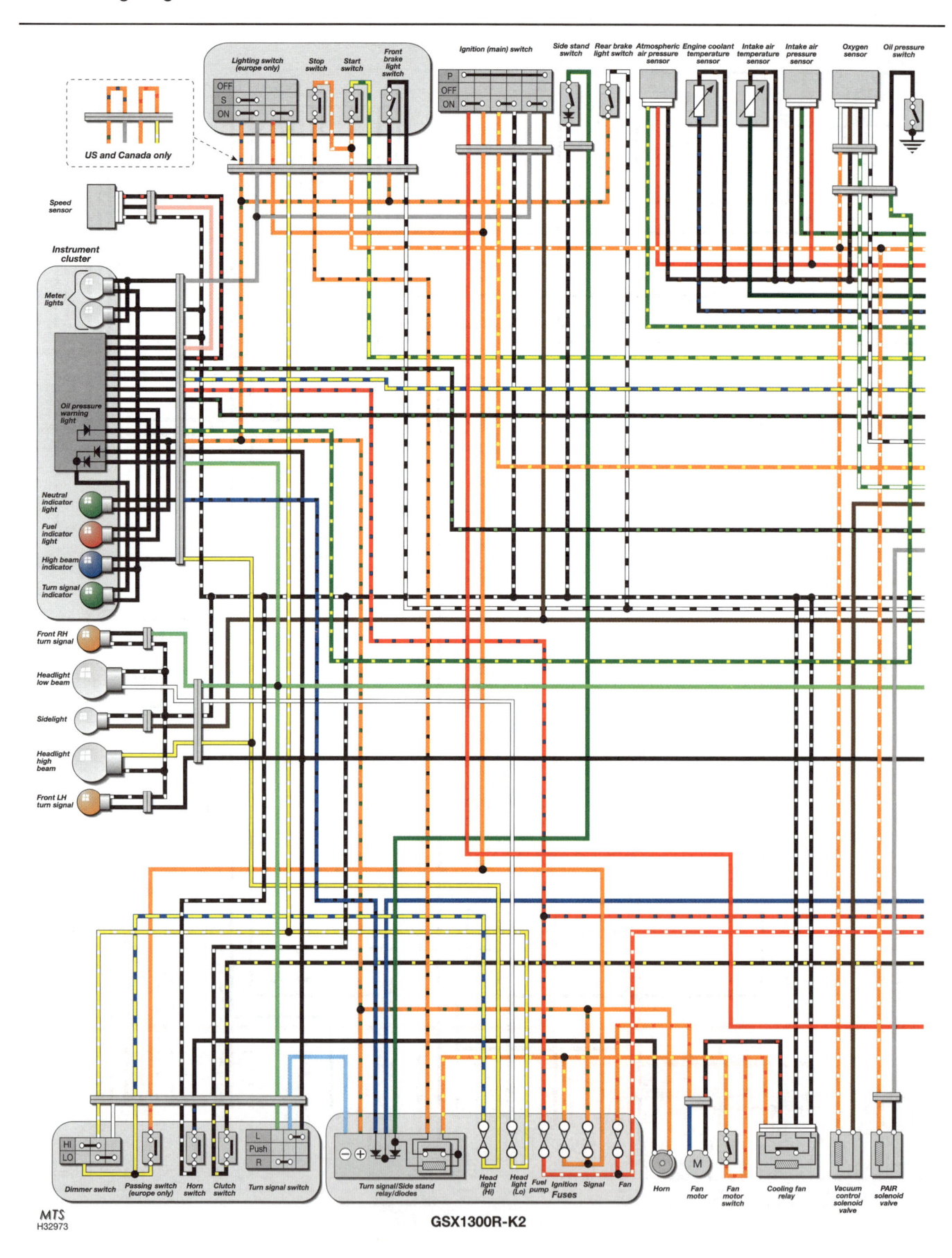

GSX1300R-K2

Wiring diagrams 9•33

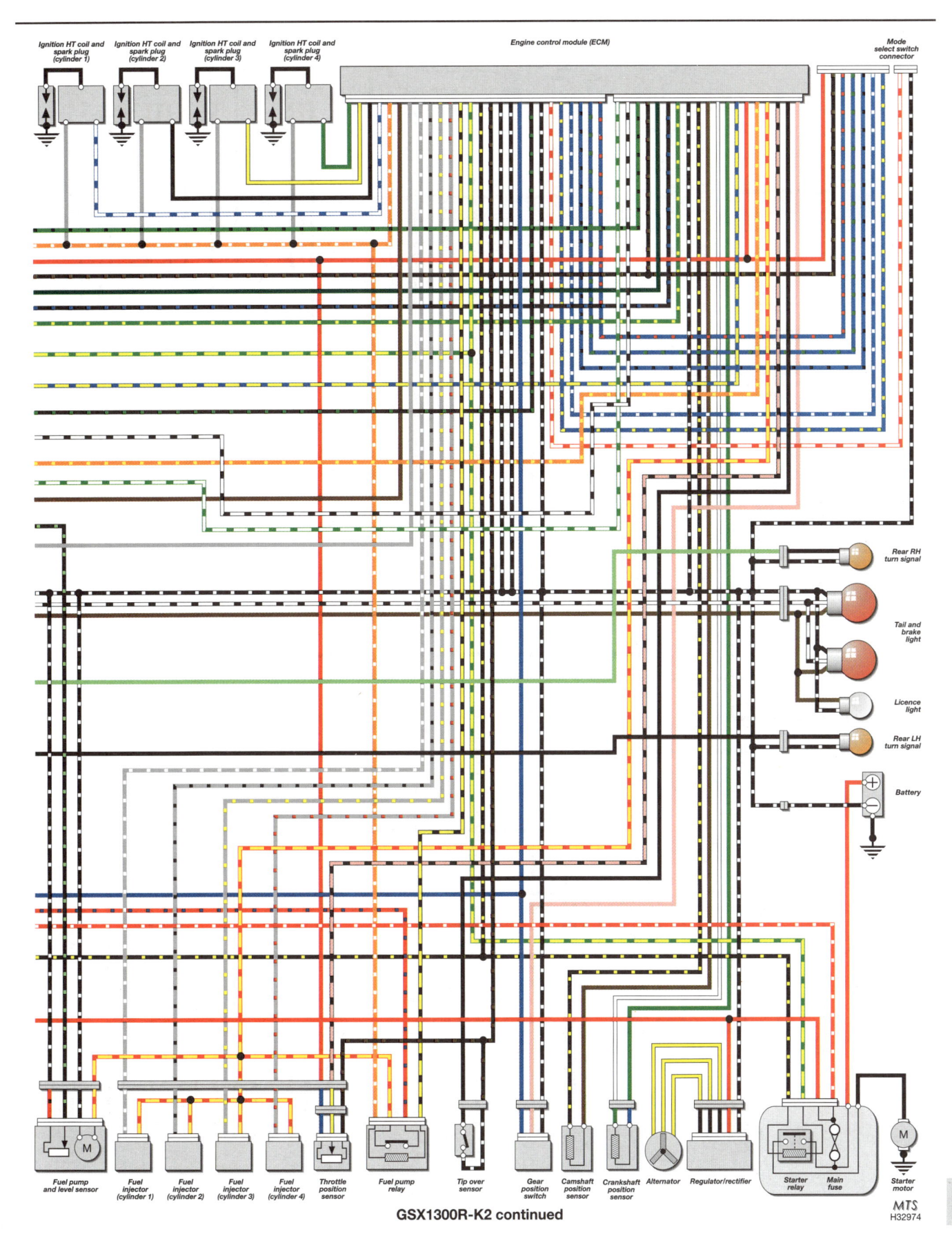

GSX1300R-K2 continued

9•34 Wiring diagrams

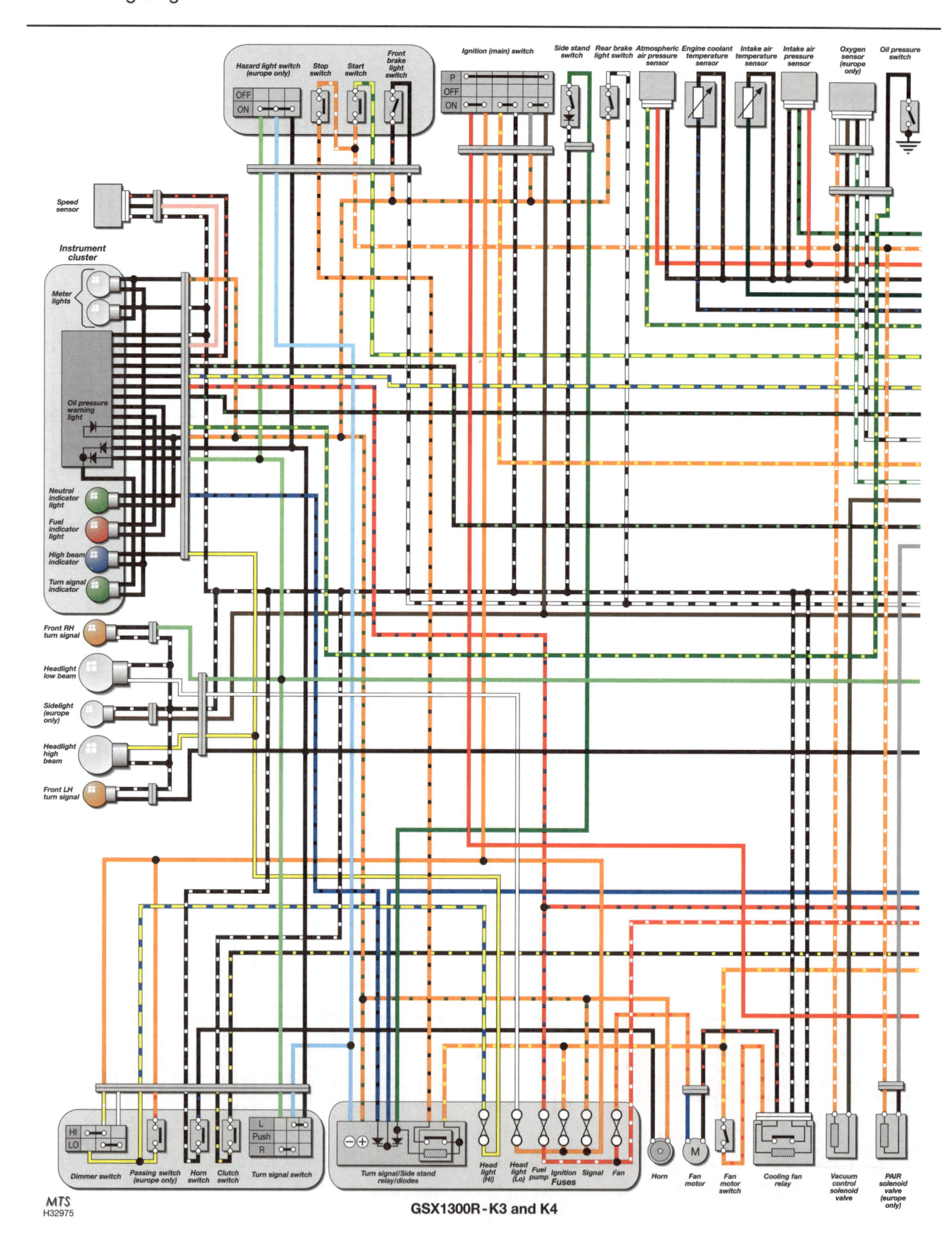

Wiring diagrams 9•35

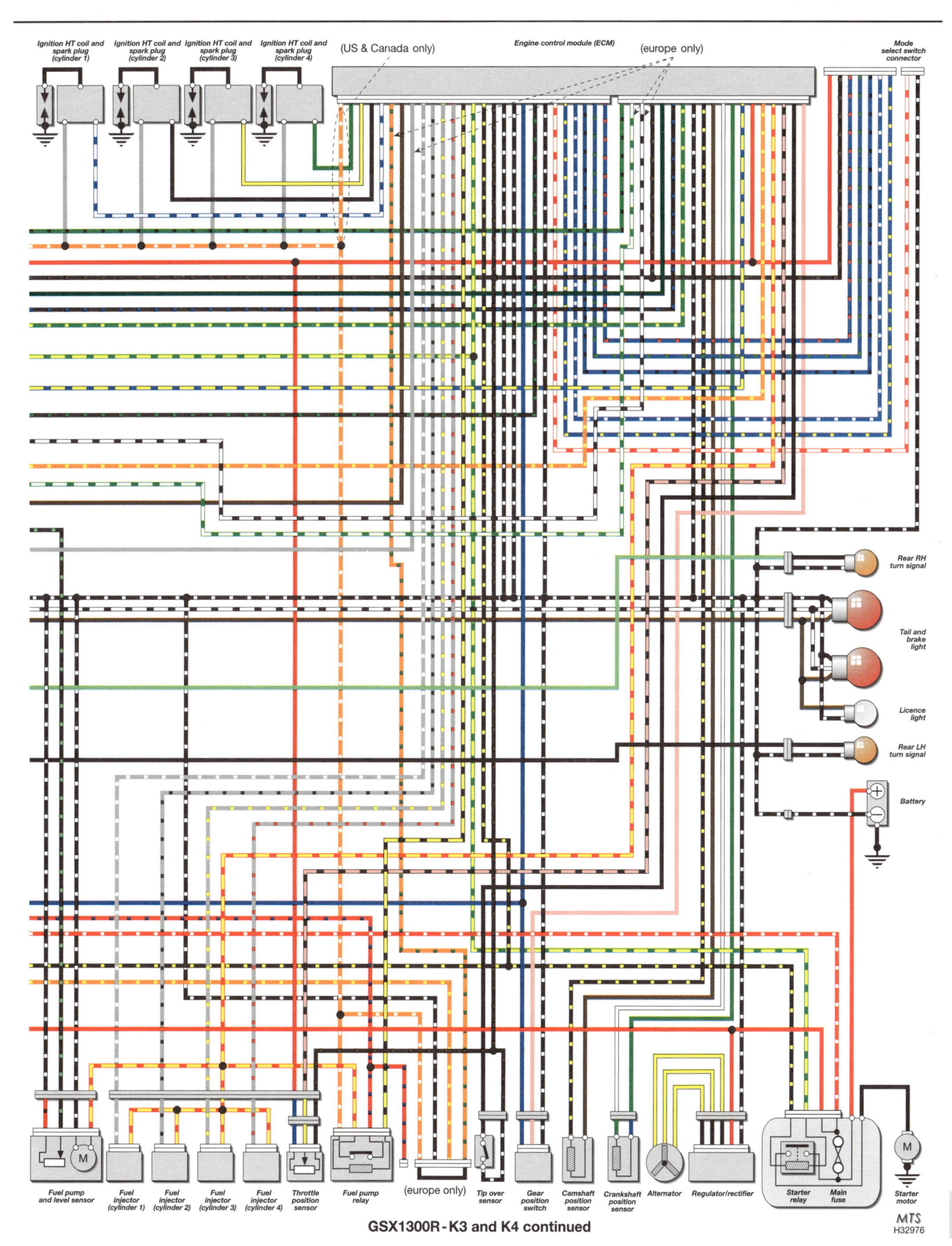

GSX1300R - K3 and K4 continued

Reference

Tools and Workshop Tips — REF•2
- Building up a tool kit and equipping your workshop ● Using tools ● Understanding bearing, seal, fastener and chain sizes and markings ● Repair techniques

Security — REF•20
- Locks and chains ● U-locks ● Disc locks ● Alarms and immobilisers ● Security marking systems ● Tips on how to prevent bike theft

Lubricants and fluids — REF•23
- Engine oils ● Transmission (gear) oils ● Coolant/anti-freeze ● Fork oils and suspension fluids ● Brake/clutch fluids ● Spray lubes, degreasers and solvents

Conversion Factors — REF•26
- Formulae for conversion of the metric (SI) units used throughout the manual into Imperial measures

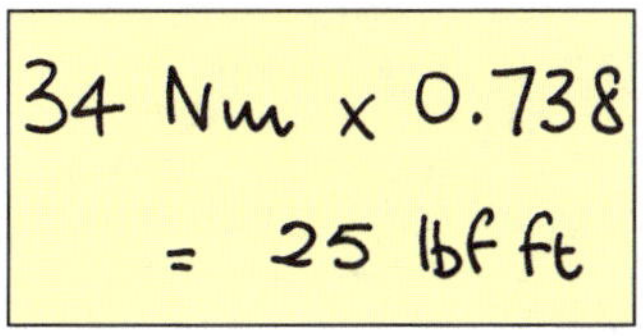

34 Nm × 0.738 = 25 lbf ft

MOT Test Checks — REF•27
- A guide to the UK MOT test ● Which items are tested ● How to prepare your motorcycle for the test and perform a pre-test check

Storage — REF•31
- How to prepare your motorcycle for going into storage and protect essential systems ● How to get the motorcycle back on the road

Fault Finding — REF•34
- Common faults and their likely causes ● How to check engine cylinder compression ● How to make electrical tests and use test meters

Index — REF•47

REF•2 Tools and Workshop Tips

Buying tools

A toolkit is a fundamental requirement for servicing and repairing a motorcycle. Although there will be an initial expense in building up enough tools for servicing, this will soon be offset by the savings made by doing the job yourself. As experience and confidence grow, additional tools can be added to enable the repair and overhaul of the motorcycle. Many of the specialist tools are expensive and not often used so it may be preferable to hire them, or for a group of friends or motorcycle club to join in the purchase.

As a rule, it is better to buy more expensive, good quality tools. Cheaper tools are likely to wear out faster and need to be renewed more often, nullifying the original saving.

> **Warning: To avoid the risk of a poor quality tool breaking in use, causing injury or damage to the component being worked on, always aim to purchase tools which meet the relevant national safety standards.**

The following lists of tools do not represent the manufacturer's service tools, but serve as a guide to help the owner decide which tools are needed for this level of work. In addition, items such as an electric drill, hacksaw, files, soldering iron and a workbench equipped with a vice, may be needed. Although not classed as tools, a selection of bolts, screws, nuts, washers and pieces of tubing always come in useful.

For more information about tools, refer to the Haynes *Motorcycle Workshop Practice TechBook* (Bk. No. 3470).

Manufacturer's service tools

Inevitably certain tasks require the use of a service tool. Where possible an alternative tool or method of approach is recommended, but sometimes there is no option if personal injury or damage to the component is to be avoided. Where required, service tools are referred to in the relevant procedure.

Service tools can usually only be purchased from a motorcycle dealer and are identified by a part number. Some of the commonly-used tools, such as rotor pullers, are available in aftermarket form from mail-order motorcycle tool and accessory suppliers.

Maintenance and minor repair tools

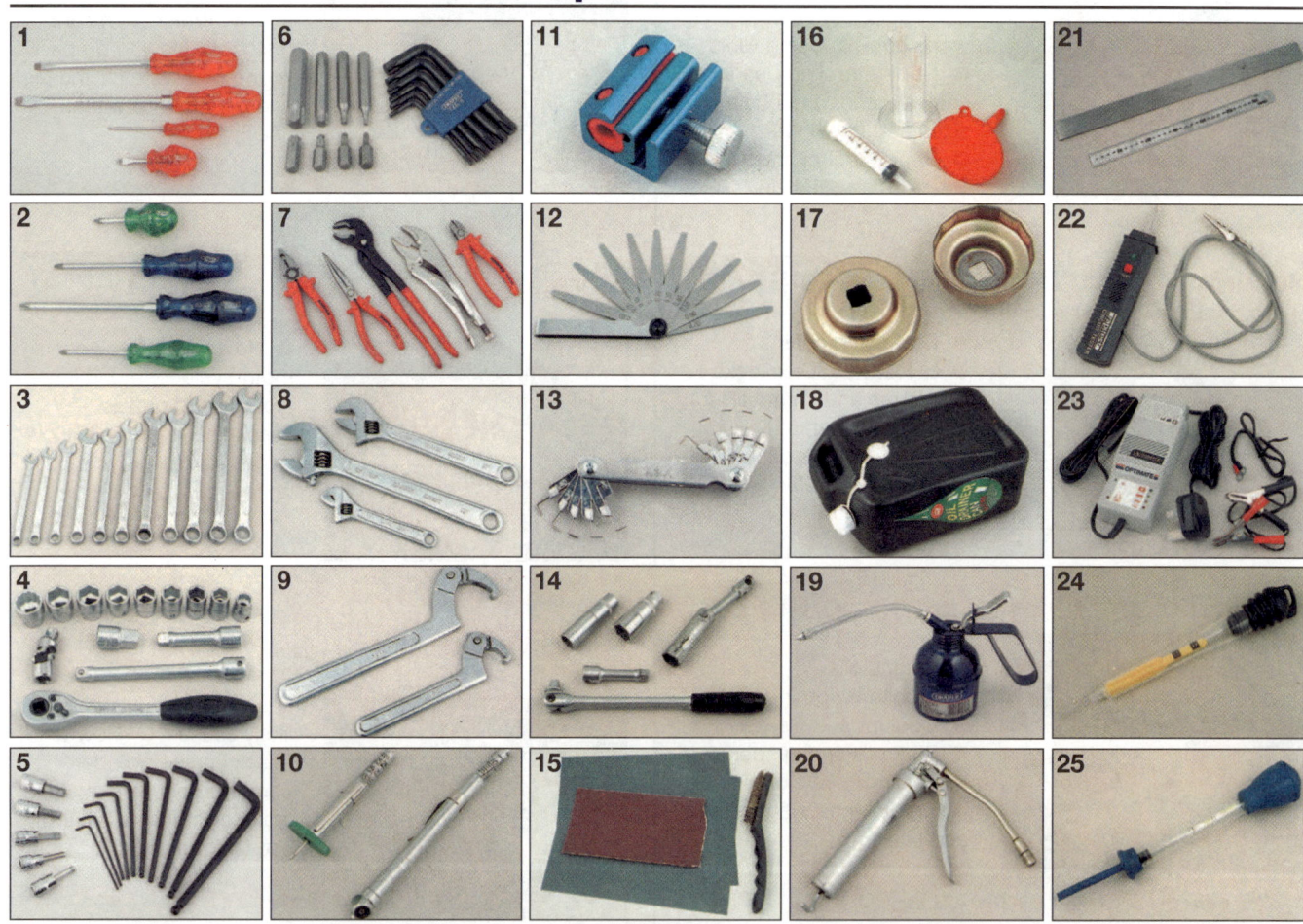

1. Set of flat-bladed screwdrivers
2. Set of Phillips head screwdrivers
3. Combination open-end and ring spanners
4. Socket set (3/8 inch or 1/2 inch drive)
5. Set of Allen keys or bits
6. Set of Torx keys or bits
7. Pliers, cutters and self-locking grips (Mole grips)
8. Adjustable spanners
9. C-spanners
10. Tread depth gauge and tyre pressure gauge
11. Cable oiler clamp
12. Feeler gauges
13. Spark plug gap measuring tool
14. Spark plug spanner or deep plug sockets
15. Wire brush and emery paper
16. Calibrated syringe, measuring vessel and funnel
17. Oil filter adapters
18. Oil drainer can or tray
19. Pump type oil can
20. Grease gun
21. Straight-edge and steel rule
22. Continuity tester
23. Battery charger
24. Hydrometer (for battery specific gravity check)
25. Anti-freeze tester (for liquid-cooled engines)

Tools and Workshop Tips REF•3

Repair and overhaul tools

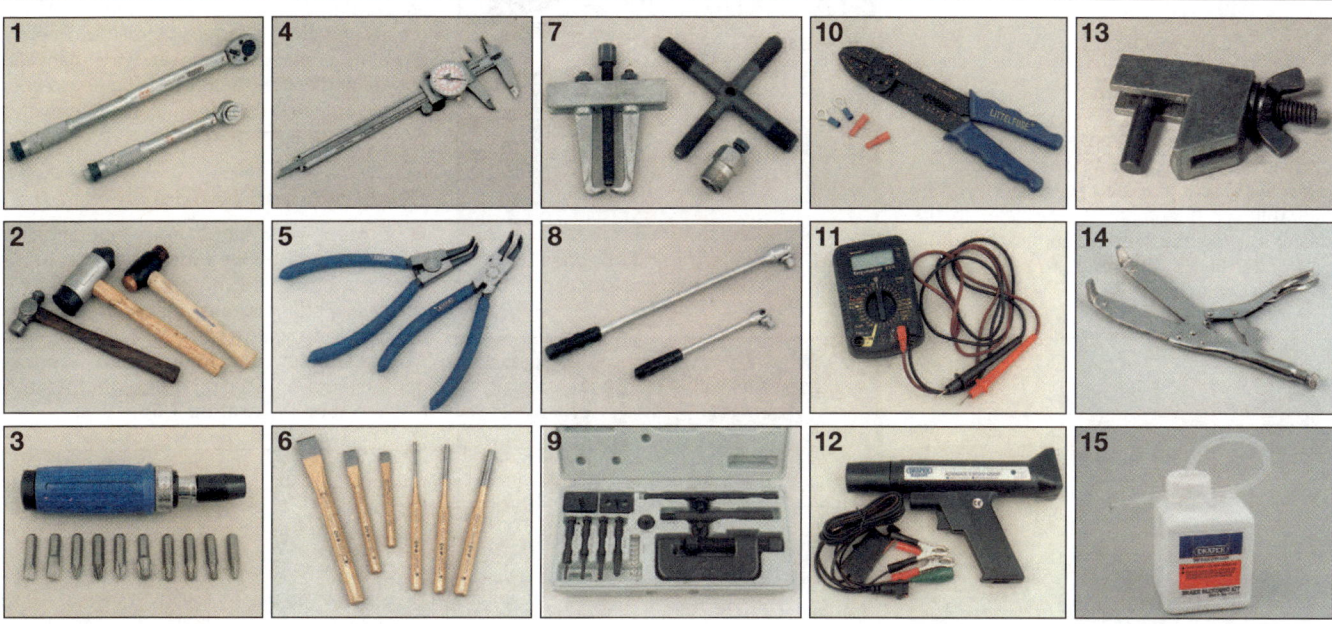

1 Torque wrench (small and mid-ranges)
2 Conventional, plastic or soft-faced hammers
3 Impact driver set
4 Vernier gauge
5 Circlip pliers (internal and external, or combination)
6 Set of cold chisels and punches
7 Selection of pullers
8 Breaker bars
9 Chain breaking/ riveting tool set
10 Wire stripper and crimper tool
11 Multimeter (measures amps, volts and ohms)
12 Stroboscope (for dynamic timing checks)
13 Hose clamp (wingnut type shown)
14 Clutch holding tool
15 One-man brake/clutch bleeder kit

Specialist tools

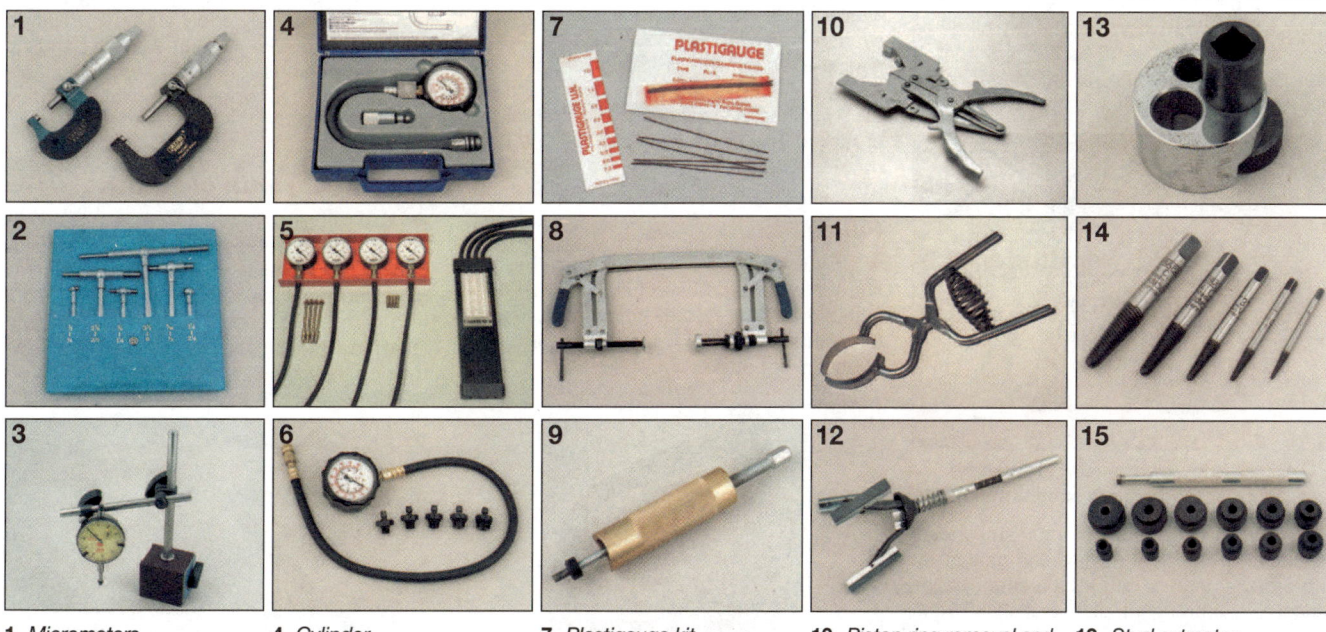

1 Micrometers (external type)
2 Telescoping gauges
3 Dial gauge
4 Cylinder compression gauge
5 Vacuum gauges (left) or manometer (right)
6 Oil pressure gauge
7 Plastigauge kit
8 Valve spring compressor (4-stroke engines)
9 Piston pin drawbolt tool
10 Piston ring removal and installation tool
11 Piston ring clamp
12 Cylinder bore hone (stone type shown)
13 Stud extractor
14 Screw extractor set
15 Bearing driver set

REF•4 Tools and Workshop Tips

1 Workshop equipment and facilities

The workbench

● Work is made much easier by raising the bike up on a ramp - components are much more accessible if raised to waist level. The hydraulic or pneumatic types seen in the dealer's workshop are a sound investment if you undertake a lot of repairs or overhauls (see illustration 1.1).

1.3 This auxiliary stand attaches to the swingarm pivot

1.1 Hydraulic motorcycle ramp

1.4 Always use a block of wood between the engine and jack head when supporting the engine in this way

● If raised off ground level, the bike must be supported on the ramp to avoid it falling. Most ramps incorporate a front wheel locating clamp which can be adjusted to suit different diameter wheels. When tightening the clamp, take care not to mark the wheel rim or damage the tyre - use wood blocks on each side to prevent this.
● Secure the bike to the ramp using tie-downs (see illustration 1.2). If the bike has only a sidestand, and hence leans at a dangerous angle when raised, support the bike on an auxiliary stand.

1.2 Tie-downs are used around the passenger footrests to secure the bike

● Auxiliary (paddock) stands are widely available from mail order companies or motorcycle dealers and attach either to the wheel axle or swingarm pivot (see illustration 1.3). If the motorcycle has a centrestand, you can support it under the crankcase to prevent it toppling whilst either wheel is removed (see illustration 1.4).

Fumes and fire

● Refer to the Safety first! page at the beginning of the manual for full details. Make sure your workshop is equipped with a fire extinguisher suitable for fuel-related fires (Class B fire - flammable liquids) - it is not sufficient to have a water-filled extinguisher.
● Always ensure adequate ventilation is available. Unless an exhaust gas extraction system is available for use, ensure that the engine is run outside of the workshop.
● If working on the fuel system, make sure the workshop is ventilated to avoid a build-up of fumes. This applies equally to fume build-up when charging a battery. Do not smoke or allow anyone else to smoke in the workshop.

Fluids

● If you need to drain fuel from the tank, store it in an approved container marked as suitable for the storage of petrol (gasoline) (see illustration 1.5). Do not store fuel in glass jars or bottles.

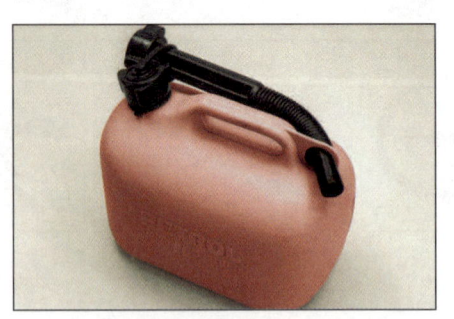

1.5 Use an approved can only for storing petrol (gasoline)

● Use proprietary engine degreasers or solvents which have a high flash-point, such as paraffin (kerosene), for cleaning off oil, grease and dirt - never use petrol (gasoline) for cleaning. Wear rubber gloves when handling solvent and engine degreaser. The fumes from certain solvents can be dangerous - always work in a well-ventilated area.

Dust, eye and hand protection

● Protect your lungs from inhalation of dust particles by wearing a filtering mask over the nose and mouth. Many frictional materials still contain asbestos which is dangerous to your health. Protect your eyes from spouts of liquid and sprung components by wearing a pair of protective goggles (see illustration 1.6).

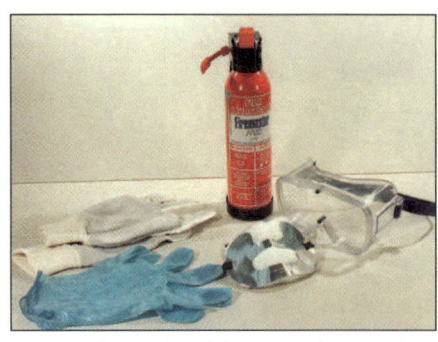

1.6 A fire extinguisher, goggles, mask and protective gloves should be at hand in the workshop

● Protect your hands from contact with solvents, fuel and oils by wearing rubber gloves. Alternatively apply a barrier cream to your hands before starting work. If handling hot components or fluids, wear suitable gloves to protect your hands from scalding and burns.

What to do with old fluids

● Old cleaning solvent, fuel, coolant and oils should not be poured down domestic drains or onto the ground. Package the fluid up in old oil containers, label it accordingly, and take it to a garage or disposal facility. Contact your local authority for location of such sites or ring the oil care hotline.

Note: It is antisocial and illegal to dump oil down the drain. To find the location of your local oil recycling bank, call this number free.

OIL CARE
OIL BANK LINE
0800 66 33 66
www.oilbankline.org.uk

In the USA, note that any oil supplier must accept used oil for recycling.

Tools and Workshop Tips

2 Fasteners - screws, bolts and nuts

Fastener types and applications

Bolts and screws

- Fastener head types are either of hexagonal, Torx or splined design, with internal and external versions of each type **(see illustrations 2.1 and 2.2)**; splined head fasteners are not in common use on motorcycles. The conventional slotted or Phillips head design is used for certain screws. Bolt or screw length is always measured from the underside of the head to the end of the item **(see illustration 2.11)**.

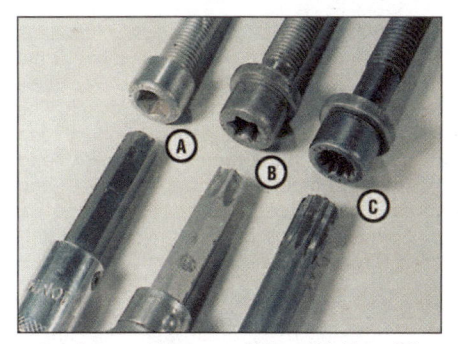

2.1 Internal hexagon/Allen (A), Torx (B) and splined (C) fasteners, with corresponding bits

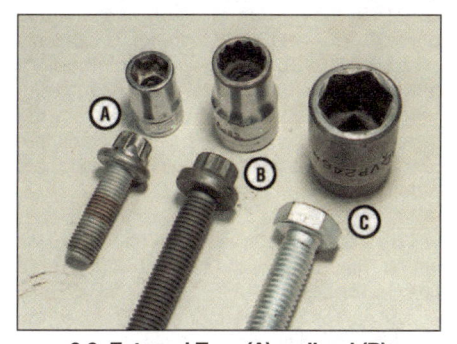

2.2 External Torx (A), splined (B) and hexagon (C) fasteners, with corresponding sockets

- Certain fasteners on the motorcycle have a tensile marking on their heads, the higher the marking the stronger the fastener. High tensile fasteners generally carry a 10 or higher marking. Never replace a high tensile fastener with one of a lower tensile strength.

Washers (see illustration 2.3)

- Plain washers are used between a fastener head and a component to prevent damage to the component or to spread the load when torque is applied. Plain washers can also be used as spacers or shims in certain assemblies. Copper or aluminium plain washers are often used as sealing washers on drain plugs.

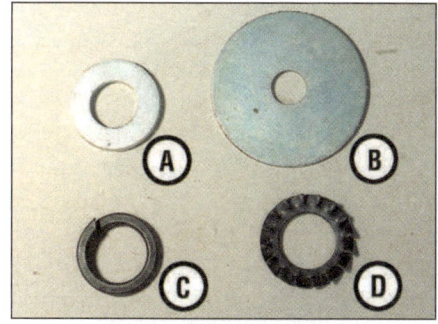

2.3 Plain washer (A), penny washer (B), spring washer (C) and serrated washer (D)

- The split-ring spring washer works by applying axial tension between the fastener head and component. If flattened, it is fatigued and must be renewed. If a plain (flat) washer is used on the fastener, position the spring washer between the fastener and the plain washer.
- Serrated star type washers dig into the fastener and component faces, preventing loosening. They are often used on electrical earth (ground) connections to the frame.
- Cone type washers (sometimes called Belleville) are conical and when tightened apply axial tension between the fastener head and component. They must be installed with the dished side against the component and often carry an OUTSIDE marking on their outer face. If flattened, they are fatigued and must be renewed.
- Tab washers are used to lock plain nuts or bolts on a shaft. A portion of the tab washer is bent up hard against one flat of the nut or bolt to prevent it loosening. Due to the tab washer being deformed in use, a new tab washer should be used every time it is disturbed.
- Wave washers are used to take up endfloat on a shaft. They provide light springing and prevent excessive side-to-side play of a component. Can be found on rocker arm shafts.

Nuts and split pins

- Conventional plain nuts are usually six-sided **(see illustration 2.4)**. They are sized by thread diameter and pitch. High tensile nuts carry a number on one end to denote their tensile strength.

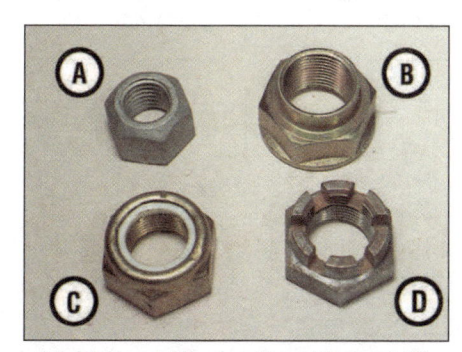

2.4 Plain nut (A), shouldered locknut (B), nylon insert nut (C) and castellated nut (D)

- Self-locking nuts either have a nylon insert, or two spring metal tabs, or a shoulder which is staked into a groove in the shaft - their advantage over conventional plain nuts is a resistance to loosening due to vibration. The nylon insert type can be used a number of times, but must be renewed when the friction of the nylon insert is reduced, ie when the nut spins freely on the shaft. The spring tab type can be reused unless the tabs are damaged. The shouldered type must be renewed every time it is disturbed.
- Split pins (cotter pins) are used to lock a castellated nut to a shaft or to prevent slackening of a plain nut. Common applications are wheel axles and brake torque arms. Because the split pin arms are deformed to lock around the nut a new split pin must always be used on installation - always fit the correct size split pin which will fit snugly in the shaft hole. Make sure the split pin arms are correctly located around the nut **(see illustrations 2.5 and 2.6)**.

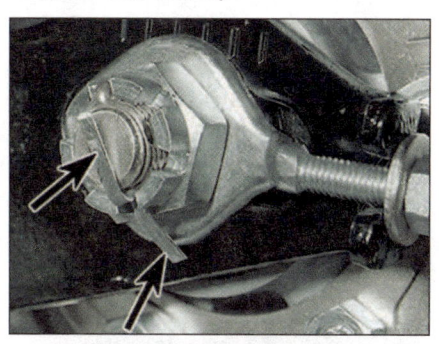

2.5 Bend split pin (cotter pin) arms as shown (arrows) to secure a castellated nut

2.6 Bend split pin (cotter pin) arms as shown to secure a plain nut

Caution: If the castellated nut slots do not align with the shaft hole after tightening to the torque setting, tighten the nut until the next slot aligns with the hole - never slacken the nut to align its slot.

- R-pins (shaped like the letter R), or slip pins as they are sometimes called, are sprung and can be reused if they are otherwise in good condition. Always install R-pins with their closed end facing forwards **(see illustration 2.7)**.

REF•6 Tools and Workshop Tips

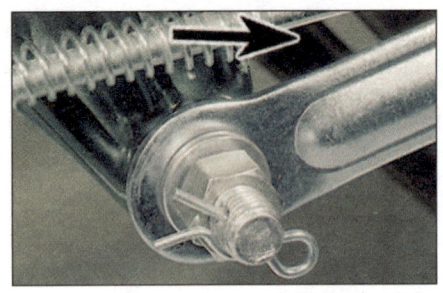

2.7 Correct fitting of R-pin. Arrow indicates forward direction

Circlips (see illustration 2.8)

● Circlips (sometimes called snap-rings) are used to retain components on a shaft or in a housing and have corresponding external or internal ears to permit removal. Parallel-sided (machined) circlips can be installed either way round in their groove, whereas stamped circlips (which have a chamfered edge on one face) must be installed with the chamfer facing away from the direction of thrust load **(see illustration 2.9)**.

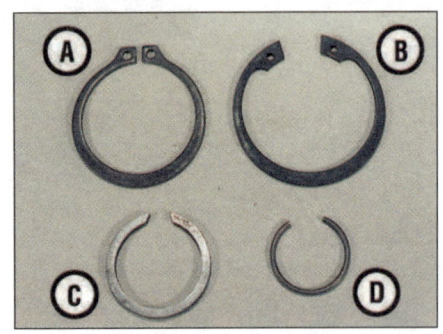

2.8 External stamped circlip (A), internal stamped circlip (B), machined circlip (C) and wire circlip (D)

● Always use circlip pliers to remove and install circlips; expand or compress them just enough to remove them. After installation, rotate the circlip in its groove to ensure it is securely seated. If installing a circlip on a splined shaft, always align its opening with a shaft channel to ensure the circlip ends are well supported and unlikely to catch **(see illustration 2.10)**.

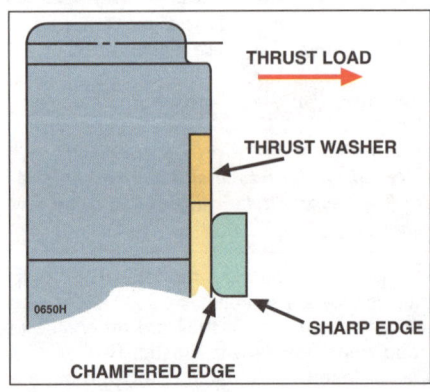

2.9 Correct fitting of a stamped circlip

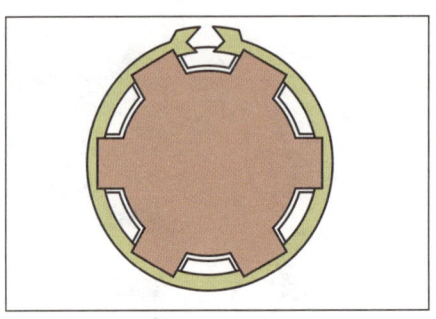

2.10 Align circlip opening with shaft channel

● Circlips can wear due to the thrust of components and become loose in their grooves, with the subsequent danger of becoming dislodged in operation. For this reason, renewal is advised every time a circlip is disturbed.

● Wire circlips are commonly used as piston pin retaining clips. If a removal tang is provided, long-nosed pliers can be used to dislodge them, otherwise careful use of a small flat-bladed screwdriver is necessary. Wire circlips should be renewed every time they are disturbed.

Thread diameter and pitch

● Diameter of a male thread (screw, bolt or stud) is the outside diameter of the threaded portion **(see illustration 2.11)**. Most motorcycle manufacturers use the ISO (International Standards Organisation) metric system expressed in millimetres, eg M6 refers to a 6 mm diameter thread. Sizing is the same for nuts, except that the thread diameter is measured across the valleys of the nut.

● Pitch is the distance between the peaks of the thread **(see illustration 2.11)**. It is expressed in millimetres, thus a common bolt size may be expressed as 6.0 x 1.0 mm (6 mm thread diameter and 1 mm pitch). Generally pitch increases in proportion to thread diameter, although there are always exceptions.

● Thread diameter and pitch are related for conventional fastener applications and the accompanying table can be used as a guide. Additionally, the AF (Across Flats), spanner or socket size dimension of the bolt or nut **(see illustration 2.11)** is linked to thread and pitch specification. Thread pitch can be measured with a thread gauge **(see illustration 2.12)**.

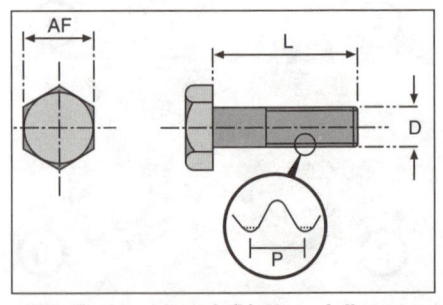

2.11 Fastener length (L), thread diameter (D), thread pitch (P) and head size (AF)

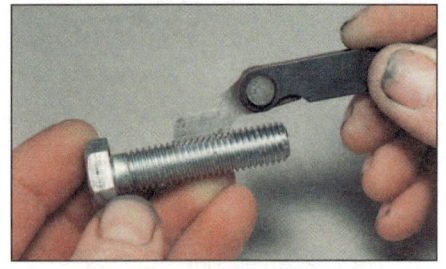

2.12 Using a thread gauge to measure pitch

AF size	Thread diameter x pitch (mm)
8 mm	M5 x 0.8
8 mm	M6 x 1.0
10 mm	M6 x 1.0
12 mm	M8 x 1.25
14 mm	M10 x 1.25
17 mm	M12 x 1.25

● The threads of most fasteners are of the right-hand type, ie they are turned clockwise to tighten and anti-clockwise to loosen. The reverse situation applies to left-hand thread fasteners, which are turned anti-clockwise to tighten and clockwise to loosen. Left-hand threads are used where rotation of a component might loosen a conventional right-hand thread fastener.

Seized fasteners

● Corrosion of external fasteners due to water or reaction between two dissimilar metals can occur over a period of time. It will build up sooner in wet conditions or in countries where salt is used on the roads during the winter. If a fastener is severely corroded it is likely that normal methods of removal will fail and result in its head being ruined. When you attempt removal, the fastener thread should be heard to crack free and unscrew easily - if it doesn't, stop there before damaging something.

● A smart tap on the head of the fastener will often succeed in breaking free corrosion which has occurred in the threads **(see illustration 2.13)**.

● An aerosol penetrating fluid (such as WD-40) applied the night beforehand may work its way down into the thread and ease removal. Depending on the location, you may be able to make up a Plasticine well around the fastener head and fill it with penetrating fluid.

2.13 A sharp tap on the head of a fastener will often break free a corroded thread

Tools and Workshop Tips REF•7

- If you are working on an engine internal component, corrosion will most likely not be a problem due to the well lubricated environment. However, components can be very tight and an impact driver is a useful tool in freeing them **(see illustration 2.14)**.

2.14 Using an impact driver to free a fastener

- Where corrosion has occurred between dissimilar metals (eg steel and aluminium alloy), the application of heat to the fastener head will create a disproportionate expansion rate between the two metals and break the seizure caused by the corrosion. Whether heat can be applied depends on the location of the fastener - any surrounding components likely to be damaged must first be removed **(see illustration 2.15)**. Heat can be applied using a paint stripper heat gun or clothes iron, or by immersing the component in boiling water - wear protective gloves to prevent scalding or burns to the hands.

2.15 Using heat to free a seized fastener

- As a last resort, it is possible to use a hammer and cold chisel to work the fastener head unscrewed **(see illustration 2.16)**. This will damage the fastener, but more importantly extreme care must be taken not to damage the surrounding component.

Caution: Remember that the component being secured is generally of more value than the bolt, nut or screw - when the fastener is freed, do not unscrew it with force, instead work the fastener back and forth when resistance is felt to prevent thread damage.

2.16 Using a hammer and chisel to free a seized fastener

Broken fasteners and damaged heads

- If the shank of a broken bolt or screw is accessible you can grip it with self-locking grips. The knurled wheel type stud extractor tool or self-gripping stud puller tool is particularly useful for removing the long studs which screw into the cylinder mouth surface of the crankcase or bolts and screws from which the head has broken off **(see illustration 2.17)**. Studs can also be removed by locking two nuts together on the threaded end of the stud and using a spanner on the lower nut **(see illustration 2.18)**.

2.17 Using a stud extractor tool to remove a broken crankcase stud

2.18 Two nuts can be locked together to unscrew a stud from a component

- A bolt or screw which has broken off below or level with the casing must be extracted using a screw extractor set. Centre punch the fastener to centralise the drill bit, then drill a hole in the fastener **(see illustration 2.19)**. Select a drill bit which is approximately half to three-quarters the

2.19 When using a screw extractor, first drill a hole in the fastener . . .

diameter of the fastener and drill to a depth which will accommodate the extractor. Use the largest size extractor possible, but avoid leaving too small a wall thickness otherwise the extractor will merely force the fastener walls outwards wedging it in the casing thread.

- If a spiral type extractor is used, thread it anti-clockwise into the fastener. As it is screwed in, it will grip the fastener and unscrew it from the casing **(see illustration 2.20)**.

2.20 . . . then thread the extractor anti-clockwise into the fastener

- If a taper type extractor is used, tap it into the fastener so that it is firmly wedged in place. Unscrew the extractor (anti-clockwise) to draw the fastener out.

Warning: Stud extractors are very hard and may break off in the fastener if care is not taken - ask an engineer about spark erosion if this happens.

- Alternatively, the broken bolt/screw can be drilled out and the hole retapped for an oversize bolt/screw or a diamond-section thread insert. It is essential that the drilling is carried out squarely and to the correct depth, otherwise the casing may be ruined - if in doubt, entrust the work to an engineer.
- Bolts and nuts with rounded corners cause the correct size spanner or socket to slip when force is applied. Of the types of spanner/socket available always use a six-point type rather than an eight or twelve-point type - better grip

REF•8 Tools and Workshop Tips

2.21 Comparison of surface drive ring spanner (left) with 12-point type (right)

is obtained. Surface drive spanners grip the middle of the hex flats, rather than the corners, and are thus good in cases of damaged heads (see illustration 2.21).

• Slotted-head or Phillips-head screws are often damaged by the use of the wrong size screwdriver. Allen-head and Torx-head screws are much less likely to sustain damage. If enough of the screw head is exposed you can use a hacksaw to cut a slot in its head and then use a conventional flat-bladed screwdriver to remove it. Alternatively use a hammer and cold chisel to tap the head of the fastener around to slacken it. Always replace damaged fasteners with new ones, preferably Torx or Allen-head type.

HAYNES HiNT

A dab of valve grinding compound between the screw head and screwdriver tip will often give a good grip.

Thread repair

• Threads (particularly those in aluminium alloy components) can be damaged by overtightening, being assembled with dirt in the threads, or from a component working loose and vibrating. Eventually the thread will fail completely, and it will be impossible to tighten the fastener.

• If a thread is damaged or clogged with old locking compound it can be renovated with a thread repair tool (thread chaser) (see illustrations 2.22 and 2.23); special thread

2.22 A thread repair tool being used to correct an internal thread

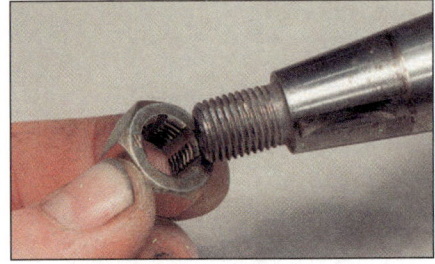

2.23 A thread repair tool being used to correct an external thread

chasers are available for spark plug hole threads. The tool will not cut a new thread, but clean and true the original thread. Make sure that you use the correct diameter and pitch tool. Similarly, external threads can be cleaned up with a die or a thread restorer file (see illustration 2.24).

2.24 Using a thread restorer file

• It is possible to drill out the old thread and retap the component to the next thread size. This will work where there is enough surrounding material and a new bolt or screw can be obtained. Sometimes, however, this is not possible - such as where the bolt/screw passes through another component which must also be suitably modified, also in cases where a spark plug or oil drain plug cannot be obtained in a larger diameter thread size.

• The diamond-section thread insert (often known by its popular trade name of Heli-Coil) is a simple and effective method of renewing the thread and retaining the original size. A kit can be purchased which contains the tap, insert and installing tool (see illustration 2.25). Drill out the damaged thread with the size drill specified (see illustration 2.26). Carefully retap the thread (see illustration 2.27). Install the

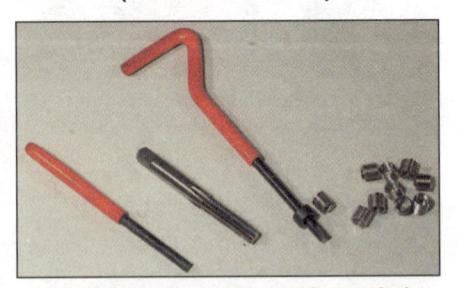

2.25 Obtain a thread insert kit to suit the thread diameter and pitch required

2.26 To install a thread insert, first drill out the original thread . . .

2.27 . . . tap a new thread . . .

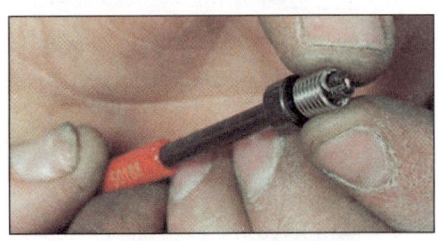

2.28 . . . fit insert on the installing tool . . .

2.29 . . . and thread into the component . . .

2.30 . . . break off the tang when complete

insert on the installing tool and thread it slowly into place using a light downward pressure (see illustrations 2.28 and 2.29). When positioned between a 1/4 and 1/2 turn below the surface withdraw the installing tool and use the break-off tool to press down on the tang, breaking it off (see illustration 2.30).

• There are epoxy thread repair kits on the market which can rebuild stripped internal threads, although this repair should not be used on high load-bearing components.

Tools and Workshop Tips   REF•9

Thread locking and sealing compounds

● Locking compounds are used in locations where the fastener is prone to loosening due to vibration or on important safety-related items which might cause loss of control of the motorcycle if they fail. It is also used where important fasteners cannot be secured by other means such as lockwashers or split pins.

● Before applying locking compound, make sure that the threads (internal and external) are clean and dry with all old compound removed. Select a compound to suit the component being secured - a non-permanent general locking and sealing type is suitable for most applications, but a high strength type is needed for permanent fixing of studs in castings. Apply a drop or two of the compound to the first few threads of the fastener, then thread it into place and tighten to the specified torque. Do not apply excessive thread locking compound otherwise the thread may be damaged on subsequent removal.

● Certain fasteners are impregnated with a dry film type coating of locking compound on their threads. Always renew this type of fastener if disturbed.

● Anti-seize compounds, such as copper-based greases, can be applied to protect threads from seizure due to extreme heat and corrosion. A common instance is spark plug threads and exhaust system fasteners.

3 Measuring tools and gauges

Feeler gauges

● Feeler gauges (or blades) are used for measuring small gaps and clearances **(see illustration 3.1)**. They can also be used to measure endfloat (sideplay) of a component on a shaft where access is not possible with a dial gauge.

● Feeler gauge sets should be treated with care and not bent or damaged. They are etched with their size on one face. Keep them clean and very lightly oiled to prevent corrosion build-up.

3.1 Feeler gauges are used for measuring small gaps and clearances - thickness is marked on one face of gauge

● When measuring a clearance, select a gauge which is a light sliding fit between the two components. You may need to use two gauges together to measure the clearance accurately.

Micrometers

● A micrometer is a precision tool capable of measuring to 0.01 or 0.001 of a millimetre. It should always be stored in its case and not in the general toolbox. It must be kept clean and never dropped, otherwise its frame or measuring anvils could be distorted resulting in inaccurate readings.

● External micrometers are used for measuring outside diameters of components and have many more applications than internal micrometers. Micrometers are available in different size ranges, eg 0 to 25 mm, 25 to 50 mm, and upwards in 25 mm steps; some large micrometers have interchangeable anvils to allow a range of measurements to be taken. Generally the largest precision measurement you are likely to take on a motorcycle is the piston diameter.

● Internal micrometers (or bore micrometers) are used for measuring inside diameters, such as valve guides and cylinder bores. Telescoping gauges and small hole gauges are used in conjunction with an external micrometer, whereas the more expensive internal micrometers have their own measuring device.

External micrometer

Note: *The conventional analogue type instrument is described. Although much easier to read, digital micrometers are considerably more expensive.*

● Always check the calibration of the micrometer before use. With the anvils closed (0 to 25 mm type) or set over a test gauge (for

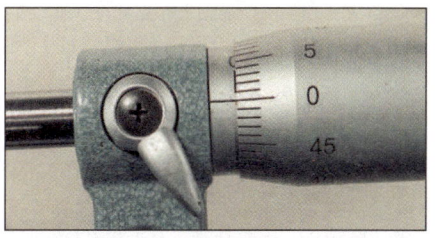

3.2 Check micrometer calibration before use

the larger types) the scale should read zero **(see illustration 3.2)**; make sure that the anvils (and test piece) are clean first. Any discrepancy can be adjusted by referring to the instructions supplied with the tool. Remember that the micrometer is a precision measuring tool - don't force the anvils closed, use the ratchet (4) on the end of the micrometer to close it. In this way, a measured force is always applied.

● To use, first make sure that the item being measured is clean. Place the anvil of the micrometer (1) against the item and use the thimble (2) to bring the spindle (3) lightly into contact with the other side of the item **(see illustration 3.3)**. Don't tighten the thimble down because this will damage the micrometer - instead use the ratchet (4) on the end of the micrometer. The ratchet mechanism applies a measured force preventing damage to the instrument.

● The micrometer is read by referring to the linear scale on the sleeve and the annular scale on the thimble. Read off the sleeve first to obtain the base measurement, then add the fine measurement from the thimble to obtain the overall reading. The linear scale on the sleeve represents the measuring range of the micrometer (eg 0 to 25 mm). The annular scale

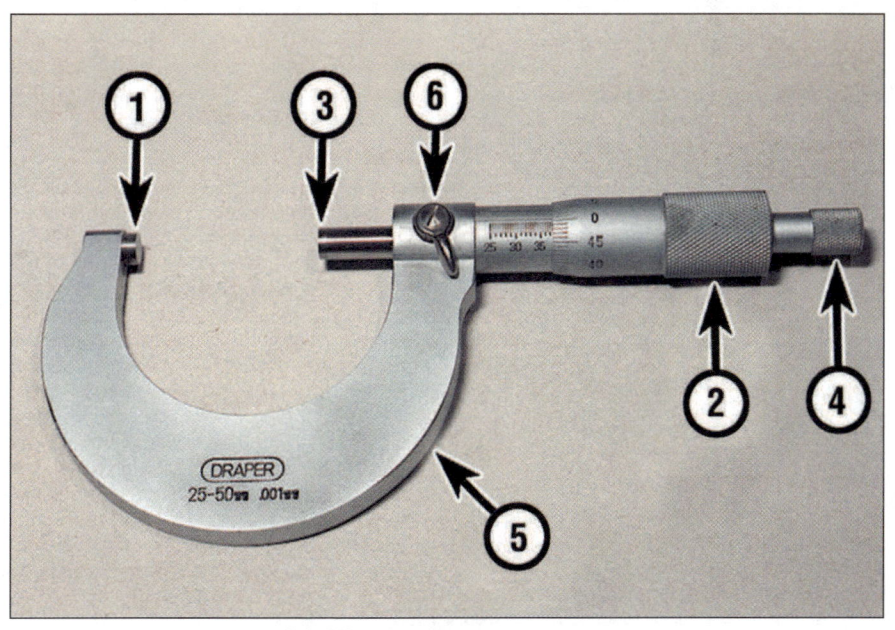

3.3 Micrometer component parts

1 Anvil	3 Spindle	5 Frame
2 Thimble	4 Ratchet	6 Locking lever

REF•10 Tools and Workshop Tips

on the thimble will be in graduations of 0.01 mm (or as marked on the frame) - one full revolution of the thimble will move 0.5 mm on the linear scale. Take the reading where the datum line on the sleeve intersects the thimble's scale. Always position the eye directly above the scale otherwise an inaccurate reading will result.

In the example shown the item measures 2.95 mm **(see illustration 3.4)**:

Linear scale	2.00 mm
Linear scale	0.50 mm
Annular scale	0.45 mm
Total figure	**2.95 mm**

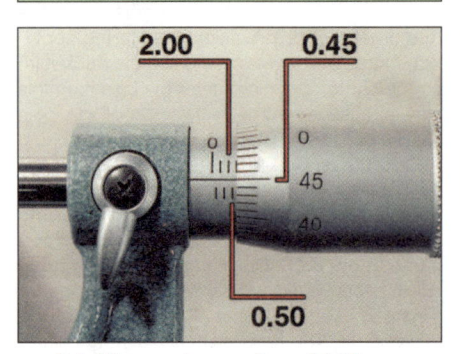

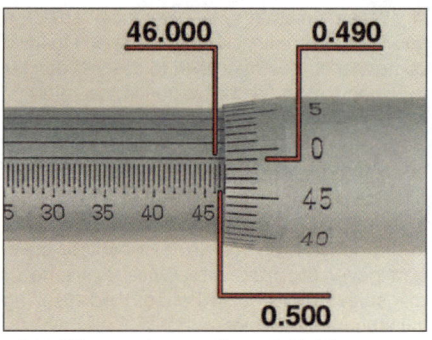

3.5 Micrometer reading of 46.99 mm on linear and annular scales . . .

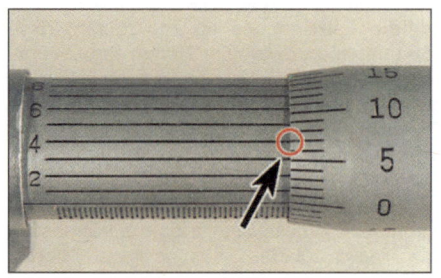

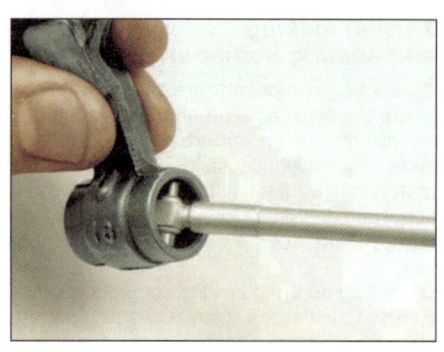

3.7 Expand the telescoping gauge in the bore, lock its position . . .

3.4 Micrometer reading of 2.95 mm

3.6 . . . and 0.004 mm on vernier scale

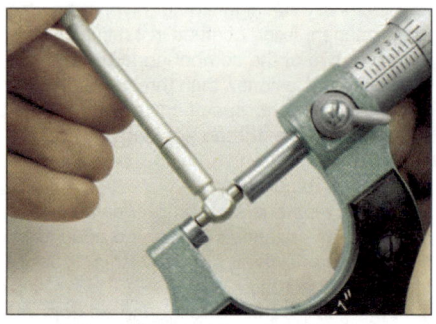

3.8 . . . then measure the gauge with a micrometer

Most micrometers have a locking lever (6) on the frame to hold the setting in place, allowing the item to be removed from the micrometer.
● Some micrometers have a vernier scale on their sleeve, providing an even finer measurement to be taken, in 0.001 increments of a millimetre. Take the sleeve and thimble measurement as described above, then check which graduation on the vernier scale aligns with that of the annular scale on the thimble **Note:** *The eye must be perpendicular to the scale when taking the vernier reading - if necessary rotate the body of the micrometer to ensure this.* Multiply the vernier scale figure by 0.001 and add it to the base and fine measurement figures.

In the example shown the item measures 46.994 mm **(see illustrations 3.5 and 3.6)**:

Linear scale (base)	46.000 mm
Linear scale (base)	00.500 mm
Annular scale (fine)	00.490 mm
Vernier scale	00.004 mm
Total figure	**46.994 mm**

Internal micrometer

● Internal micrometers are available for measuring bore diameters, but are expensive and unlikely to be available for home use. It is suggested that a set of telescoping gauges and small hole gauges, both of which must be used with an external micrometer, will suffice for taking internal measurements on a motorcycle.
● Telescoping gauges can be used to measure internal diameters of components. Select a gauge with the correct size range, make sure its ends are clean and insert it into the bore. Expand the gauge, then lock its position and withdraw it from the bore **(see illustration 3.7)**. Measure across the gauge ends with a micrometer **(see illustration 3.8)**.
● Very small diameter bores (such as valve guides) are measured with a small hole gauge. Once adjusted to a slip-fit inside the component, its position is locked and the gauge withdrawn for measurement with a micrometer **(see illustrations 3.9 and 3.10)**.

Vernier caliper

Note: *The conventional linear and dial gauge type instruments are described. Digital types are easier to read, but are far more expensive.*
● The vernier caliper does not provide the precision of a micrometer, but is versatile in being able to measure internal and external diameters. Some types also incorporate a depth gauge. It is ideal for measuring clutch plate friction material and spring free lengths.
● To use the conventional linear scale vernier, slacken off the vernier clamp screws (1) and set its jaws over (2), or inside (3), the item to be measured **(see illustration 3.11)**. Slide the jaw into contact, using the thumbwheel (4) for fine movement of the sliding scale (5) then tighten the clamp screws (1). Read off the main scale (6) where the zero on the sliding scale (5) intersects it, taking the whole number to the left of the zero; this provides the base measurement. View along the sliding scale and select the division which

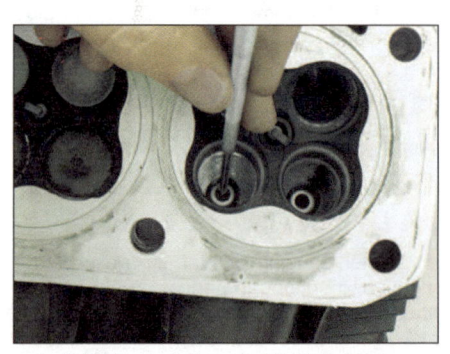

3.9 Expand the small hole gauge in the bore, lock its position . . .

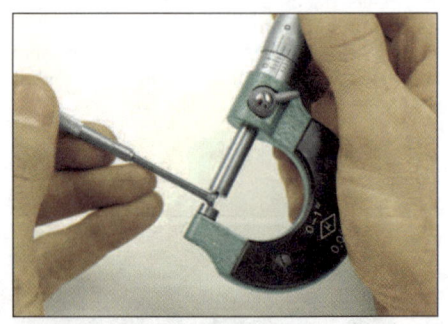

3.10 . . . then measure the gauge with a micrometer

lines up exactly with any of the divisions on the main scale, noting that the divisions usually represents 0.02 of a millimetre. Add this fine measurement to the base measurement to obtain the total reading.

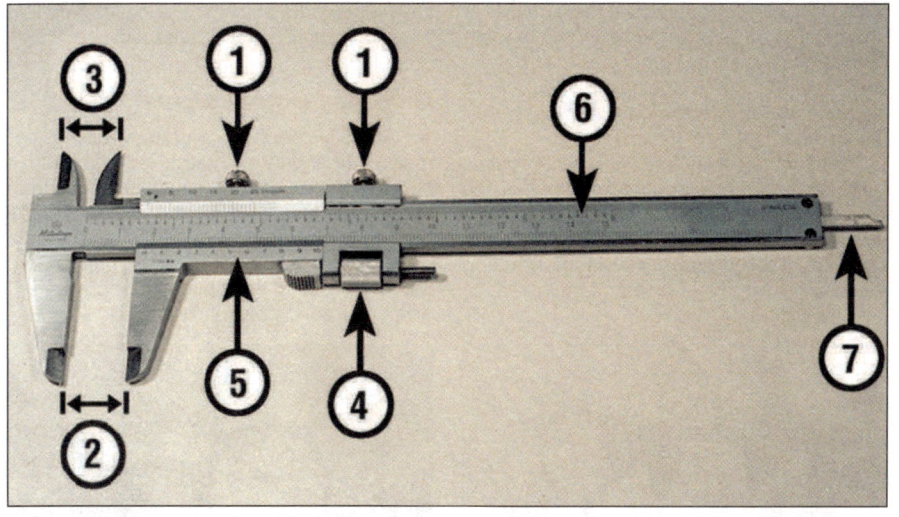

Tools and Workshop Tips   REF•11

Plastigauge

● Plastigauge is a plastic material which can be compressed between two surfaces to measure the oil clearance between them. The width of the compressed Plastigauge is measured against a calibrated scale to determine the clearance.

● Common uses of Plastigauge are for measuring the clearance between crankshaft journal and main bearing inserts, between crankshaft journal and big-end bearing inserts, and between camshaft and bearing surfaces. The following example describes big-end oil clearance measurement.

● Handle the Plastigauge material carefully to prevent distortion. Using a sharp knife, cut a length which corresponds with the width of the bearing being measured and place it carefully across the journal so that it is parallel with the shaft **(see illustration 3.15)**. Carefully install both bearing shells and the connecting rod. Without rotating the rod on the journal tighten its bolts or nuts (as applicable) to the specified torque. The connecting rod and bearings are then disassembled and the crushed Plastigauge examined.

3.11 Vernier component parts (linear gauge)

1 Clamp screws
2 External jaws
3 Internal jaws
4 Thumbwheel
5 Sliding scale
6 Main scale
7 Depth gauge

In the example shown the item measures 55.92 mm **(see illustration 3.12)**:

Base measurement	55.00 mm
Fine measurement	00.92 mm
Total figure	**55.92 mm**

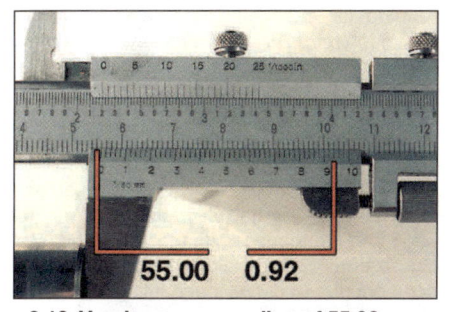

● Some vernier calipers are equipped with a dial gauge for fine measurement. Before use, check that the jaws are clean, then close them fully and check that the dial gauge reads zero. If necessary adjust the gauge ring accordingly. Slacken the vernier clamp screw (1) and set its jaws over (2), or inside (3), the item to be measured **(see illustration 3.13)**. Slide the jaws into contact, using the thumbwheel (4) for fine movement. Read off the main scale (5) where the edge of the sliding scale (6) intersects it, taking the whole number to the left of the zero; this provides the base measurement. Read off the needle position on the dial gauge (7) scale to provide the fine measurement; each division represents 0.05 of a millimetre. Add this fine measurement to the base measurement to obtain the total reading.

In the example shown the item measures 55.95 mm **(see illustration 3.14)**:

3.12 Vernier gauge reading of 55.92 mm

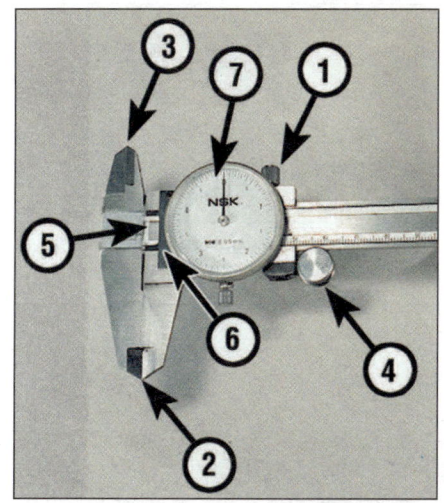

3.15 Plastigauge placed across shaft journal

● Using the scale provided in the Plastigauge kit, measure the width of the material to determine the oil clearance **(see illustration 3.16)**. Always remove all traces of Plastigauge after use using your fingernails.

Caution: Arriving at the correct clearance demands that the assembly is torqued correctly, according to the settings and sequence (where applicable) provided by the motorcycle manufacturer.

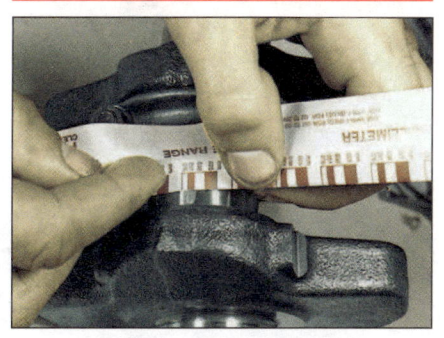

Base measurement	55.00 mm
Fine measurement	00.95 mm
Total figure	**55.95 mm**

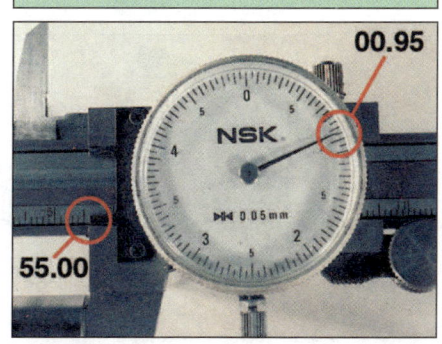

3.13 Vernier component parts (dial gauge)

1 Clamp screw
2 External jaws
3 Internal jaws
4 Thumbwheel
5 Main scale
6 Sliding scale
7 Dial gauge

3.14 Vernier gauge reading of 55.95 mm

3.16 Measuring the width of the crushed Plastigauge

REF•12 Tools and Workshop Tips

Dial gauge or DTI (Dial Test Indicator)

- A dial gauge can be used to accurately measure small amounts of movement. Typical uses are measuring shaft runout or shaft endfloat (sideplay) and setting piston position for ignition timing on two-strokes. A dial gauge set usually comes with a range of different probes and adapters and mounting equipment.
- The gauge needle must point to zero when at rest. Rotate the ring around its periphery to zero the gauge.
- Check that the gauge is capable of reading the extent of movement in the work. Most gauges have a small dial set in the face which records whole millimetres of movement as well as the fine scale around the face periphery which is calibrated in 0.01 mm divisions. Read off the small dial first to obtain the base measurement, then add the measurement from the fine scale to obtain the total reading.

In the example shown the gauge reads 1.48 mm **(see illustration 3.17)**:

Base measurement	1.00 mm
Fine measurement	0.48 mm
Total figure	**1.48 mm**

3.17 Dial gauge reading of 1.48 mm

- If measuring shaft runout, the shaft must be supported in vee-blocks and the gauge mounted on a stand perpendicular to the shaft. Rest the tip of the gauge against the centre of the shaft and rotate the shaft slowly whilst watching the gauge reading **(see illustration 3.18)**. Take several measurements along the length of the shaft and record the maximum gauge reading as the amount of runout in the shaft. **Note:** *The reading obtained will be total runout at that point - some manufacturers specify that the runout figure is halved to compare with their specified runout limit.*
- Endfloat (sideplay) measurement requires that the gauge is mounted securely to the surrounding component with its probe touching the end of the shaft. Using hand pressure, push and pull on the shaft noting the maximum endfloat recorded on the gauge **(see illustration 3.19)**.

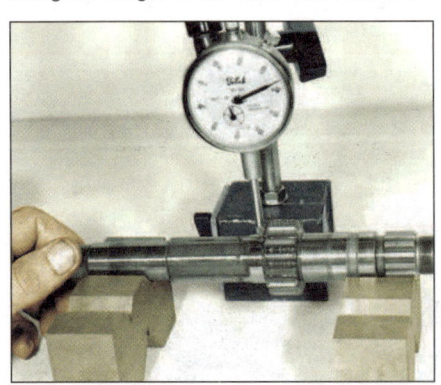

3.18 Using a dial gauge to measure shaft runout

3.19 Using a dial gauge to measure shaft endfloat

- A dial gauge with suitable adapters can be used to determine piston position BTDC on two-stroke engines for the purposes of ignition timing. The gauge, adapter and suitable length probe are installed in the place of the spark plug and the gauge zeroed at TDC. If the piston position is specified as 1.14 mm BTDC, rotate the engine back to 2.00 mm BTDC, then slowly forwards to 1.14 mm BTDC.

Cylinder compression gauges

- A compression gauge is used for measuring cylinder compression. Either the rubber-cone type or the threaded adapter type can be used. The latter is preferred to ensure a perfect seal against the cylinder head. A 0 to 300 psi (0 to 20 Bar) type gauge (for petrol/gasoline engines) will be suitable for motorcycles.
- The spark plug is removed and the gauge either held hard against the cylinder head (cone type) or the gauge adapter screwed into the cylinder head (threaded type) **(see illustration 3.20)**. Cylinder compression is measured with the engine turning over, but not running - carry out the compression test as described in *Fault Finding Equipment*. The gauge will hold the reading until manually released.

3.20 Using a rubber-cone type cylinder compression gauge

Oil pressure gauge

- An oil pressure gauge is used for measuring engine oil pressure. Most gauges come with a set of adapters to fit the thread of the take-off point **(see illustration 3.21)**. If the take-off point specified by the motorcycle manufacturer is an external oil pipe union, make sure that the specified replacement union is used to prevent oil starvation.

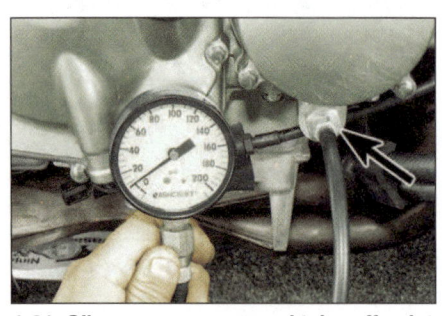

3.21 Oil pressure gauge and take-off point adapter (arrow)

- Oil pressure is measured with the engine running (at a specific rpm) and often the manufacturer will specify pressure limits for a cold and hot engine.

Straight-edge and surface plate

- If checking the gasket face of a component for warpage, place a steel rule or precision straight-edge across the gasket face and measure any gap between the straight-edge and component with feeler gauges **(see illustration 3.22)**. Check diagonally across the component and between mounting holes **(see illustration 3.23)**.

3.22 Use a straight-edge and feeler gauges to check for warpage

3.23 Check for warpage in these directions

Tools and Workshop Tips REF•13

- Checking individual components for warpage, such as clutch plain (metal) plates, requires a perfectly flat plate or piece or plate glass and feeler gauges.

4 Torque and leverage

What is torque?
- Torque describes the twisting force about a shaft. The amount of torque applied is determined by the distance from the centre of the shaft to the end of the lever and the amount of force being applied to the end of the lever; distance multiplied by force equals torque.
- The manufacturer applies a measured torque to a bolt or nut to ensure that it will not slacken in use and to hold two components securely together without movement in the joint. The actual torque setting depends on the thread size, bolt or nut material and the composition of the components being held.
- Too little torque may cause the fastener to loosen due to vibration, whereas too much torque will distort the joint faces of the component or cause the fastener to shear off. Always stick to the specified torque setting.

Using a torque wrench
- Check the calibration of the torque wrench and make sure it has a suitable range for the job. Torque wrenches are available in Nm (Newton-metres), kgf m (kilograms-force metre), lbf ft (pounds-feet), lbf in (inch-pounds). Do not confuse lbf ft with lbf in.
- Adjust the tool to the desired torque on the scale (see illustration 4.1). If your torque wrench is not calibrated in the units specified, carefully convert the figure (see *Conversion Factors*). A manufacturer sometimes gives a torque setting as a range (8 to 10 Nm) rather than a single figure - in this case set the tool midway between the two settings. The same torque may be expressed as 9 Nm ± 1 Nm. Some torque wrenches have a method of locking the setting so that it isn't inadvertently altered during use.

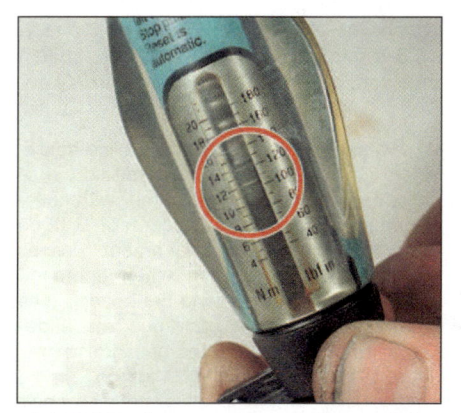

4.1 Set the torque wrench index mark to the setting required, in this case 12 Nm

- Install the bolts/nuts in their correct location and secure them lightly. Their threads must be clean and free of any old locking compound. Unless specified the threads and flange should be dry - oiled threads are necessary in certain circumstances and the manufacturer will take this into account in the specified torque figure. Similarly, the manufacturer may also specify the application of thread-locking compound.
- Tighten the fasteners in the specified sequence until the torque wrench clicks, indicating that the torque setting has been reached. Apply the torque again to double-check the setting. Where different thread diameter fasteners secure the component, as a rule tighten the larger diameter ones first.
- When the torque wrench has been finished with, release the lock (where applicable) and fully back off its setting to zero - do not leave the torque wrench tensioned. Also, do not use a torque wrench for slackening a fastener.

Angle-tightening
- Manufacturers often specify a figure in degrees for final tightening of a fastener. This usually follows tightening to a specific torque setting.
- A degree disc can be set and attached to the socket (see illustration 4.2) or a protractor can be used to mark the angle of movement on the bolt/nut head and the surrounding casting (see illustration 4.3).

4.2 Angle tightening can be accomplished with a torque-angle gauge . . .

4.3 . . . or by marking the angle on the surrounding component

Loosening sequences
- Where more than one bolt/nut secures a component, loosen each fastener evenly a little at a time. In this way, not all the stress of the joint is held by one fastener and the components are not likely to distort.
- If a tightening sequence is provided, work in the REVERSE of this, but if not, work from the outside in, in a criss-cross sequence (see illustration 4.4).

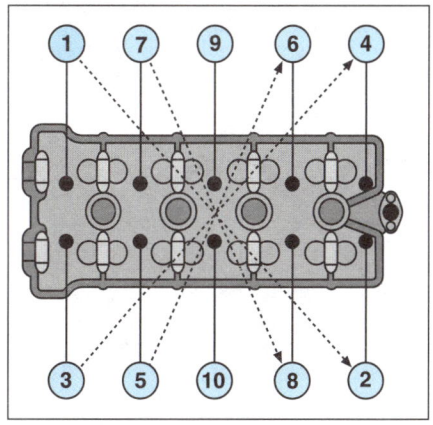

4.4 When slackening, work from the outside inwards

Tightening sequences
- If a component is held by more than one fastener it is important that the retaining bolts/nuts are tightened evenly to prevent uneven stress build-up and distortion of sealing faces. This is especially important on high-compression joints such as the cylinder head.
- A sequence is usually provided by the manufacturer, either in a diagram or actually marked in the casting. If not, always start in the centre and work outwards in a criss-cross pattern (see illustration 4.5). Start off by securing all bolts/nuts finger-tight, then set the torque wrench and tighten each fastener by a small amount in sequence until the final torque is reached. By following this practice,

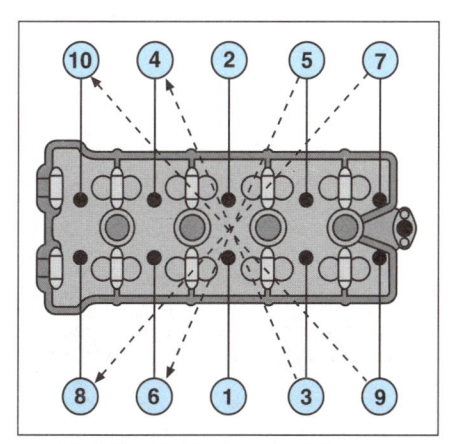

4.5 When tightening, work from the inside outwards

REF•14 Tools and Workshop Tips

the joint will be held evenly and will not be distorted. Important joints, such as the cylinder head and big-end fasteners often have two- or three-stage torque settings.

Applying leverage

● Use tools at the correct angle. Position a socket wrench or spanner on the bolt/nut so that you pull it towards you when loosening. If this can't be done, push the spanner without curling your fingers around it **(see illustration 4.6)** - the spanner may slip or the fastener loosen suddenly, resulting in your fingers being crushed against a component.

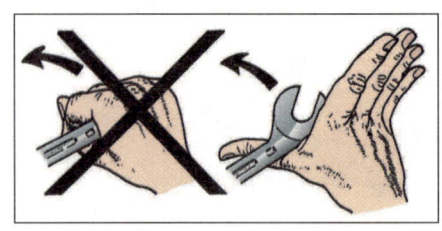

4.6 If you can't pull on the spanner to loosen a fastener, push with your hand open

● Additional leverage is gained by extending the length of the lever. The best way to do this is to use a breaker bar instead of the regular length tool, or to slip a length of tubing over the end of the spanner or socket wrench.
● If additional leverage will not work, the fastener head is either damaged or firmly corroded in place (see *Fasteners*).

5 Bearings

Bearing removal and installation
Drivers and sockets

● Before removing a bearing, always inspect the casing to see which way it must be driven out - some casings will have retaining plates or a cast step. Also check for any identifying markings on the bearing and if installed to a certain depth, measure this at this stage. Some roller bearings are sealed on one side - take note of the original fitted position.
● Bearings can be driven out of a casing using a bearing driver tool (with the correct size head) or a socket of the correct diameter. Select the driver head or socket so that it contacts the outer race of the bearing, not the balls/rollers or inner race. Always support the casing around the bearing housing with wood blocks, otherwise there is a risk of fracture. The bearing is driven out with a few blows on the driver or socket from a heavy mallet. Unless access is severely restricted (as with wheel bearings), a pin-punch is not recommended unless it is moved around the bearing to keep it square in its housing.

● The same equipment can be used to install bearings. Make sure the bearing housing is supported on wood blocks and line up the bearing in its housing. Fit the bearing as noted on removal - generally they are installed with their marked side facing outwards. Tap the bearing squarely into its housing using a driver or socket which bears only on the bearing's outer race - contact with the bearing balls/rollers or inner race will destroy it **(see illustrations 5.1 and 5.2)**.
● Check that the bearing inner race and balls/rollers rotate freely.

5.1 Using a bearing driver against the bearing's outer race

5.2 Using a large socket against the bearing's outer race

Pullers and slide-hammers

● Where a bearing is pressed on a shaft a puller will be required to extract it **(see illustration 5.3)**. Make sure that the puller clamp or legs fit securely behind the bearing and are unlikely to slip out. If pulling a bearing off a gear shaft for example, you may have to locate the puller behind a gear pinion if there is no access to the race and draw the gear pinion off the shaft as well **(see illustration 5.4)**.

5.3 This bearing puller clamps behind the bearing and pressure is applied to the shaft end to draw the bearing off

> **Caution: Ensure that the puller's centre bolt locates securely against the end of the shaft and will not slip when pressure is applied. Also ensure that puller does not damage the shaft end.**

5.4 Where no access is available to the rear of the bearing, it is sometimes possible to draw off the adjacent component

● Operate the puller so that its centre bolt exerts pressure on the shaft end and draws the bearing off the shaft.
● When installing the bearing on the shaft, tap only on the bearing's inner race - contact with the balls/rollers or outer race with destroy the bearing. Use a socket or length of tubing as a drift which fits over the shaft end **(see illustration 5.5)**.

5.5 When installing a bearing on a shaft use a piece of tubing which bears only on the bearing's inner race

● Where a bearing locates in a blind hole in a casing, it cannot be driven or pulled out as described above. A slide-hammer with knife-edged bearing puller attachment will be required. The puller attachment passes through the bearing and when tightened expands to fit firmly behind the bearing **(see illustration 5.6)**. By operating the slide-hammer part of the tool the bearing is jarred out of its housing **(see illustration 5.7)**.
● It is possible, if the bearing is of reasonable weight, for it to drop out of its housing if the casing is heated as described opposite. If this

Tools and Workshop Tips REF•15

5.6 Expand the bearing puller so that it locks behind the bearing . . .

5.7 . . . attach the slide hammer to the bearing puller

method is attempted, first prepare a work surface which will enable the casing to be tapped face down to help dislodge the bearing - a wood surface is ideal since it will not damage the casing's gasket surface. Wearing protective gloves, tap the heated casing several times against the work surface to dislodge the bearing under its own weight **(see illustration 5.8)**.

5.8 Tapping a casing face down on wood blocks can often dislodge a bearing

● Bearings can be installed in blind holes using the driver or socket method described above.

Drawbolts

● Where a bearing or bush is set in the eye of a component, such as a suspension linkage arm or connecting rod small-end, removal by drift may damage the component. Furthermore, a rubber bushing in a shock absorber eye cannot successfully be driven out of position. If access is available to a engineering press, the task is straightforward. If not, a drawbolt can be fabricated to extract the bearing or bush.

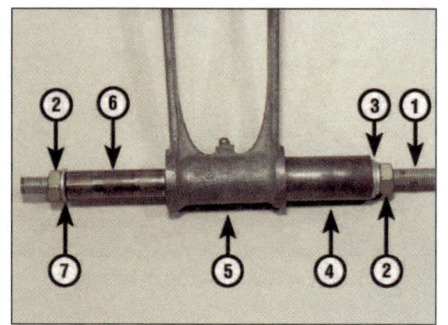

5.9 Drawbolt component parts assembled on a suspension arm

1 Bolt or length of threaded bar
2 Nuts
3 Washer (external diameter greater than tubing internal diameter)
4 Tubing (internal diameter sufficient to accommodate bearing)
5 Suspension arm with bearing
6 Tubing (external diameter slightly smaller than bearing)
7 Washer (external diameter slightly smaller than bearing)

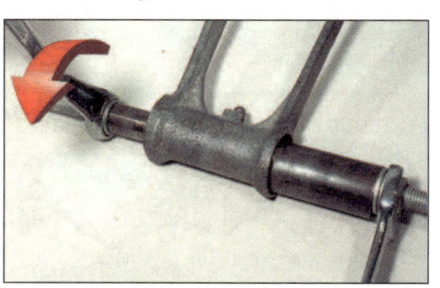

5.10 Drawing the bearing out of the suspension arm

● To extract the bearing/bush you will need a long bolt with nut (or piece of threaded bar with two nuts), a piece of tubing which has an internal diameter larger than the bearing/bush, another piece of tubing which has an external diameter slightly smaller than the bearing/bush, and a selection of washers **(see illustrations 5.9 and 5.10)**. Note that the pieces of tubing must be of the same length, or longer, than the bearing/bush.
● The same kit (without the pieces of tubing) can be used to draw the new bearing/bush back into place **(see illustration 5.11)**.

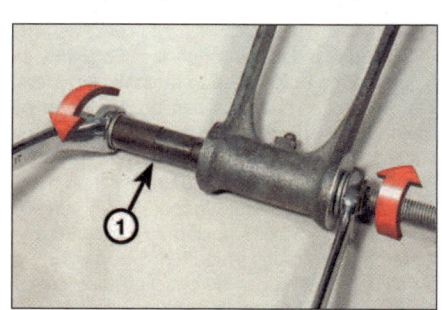

5.11 Installing a new bearing (1) in the suspension arm

Temperature change

● If the bearing's outer race is a tight fit in the casing, the aluminium casing can be heated to release its grip on the bearing. Aluminium will expand at a greater rate than the steel bearing outer race. There are several ways to do this, but avoid any localised extreme heat (such as a blow torch) - aluminium alloy has a low melting point.
● Approved methods of heating a casing are using a domestic oven (heated to 100°C) or immersing the casing in boiling water **(see illustration 5.12)**. Low temperature range localised heat sources such as a paint stripper heat gun or clothes iron can also be used **(see illustration 5.13)**. Alternatively, soak a rag in boiling water, wring it out and wrap it around the bearing housing.

> ⚠ **Warning: All of these methods require care in use to prevent scalding and burns to the hands. Wear protective gloves when handling hot components.**

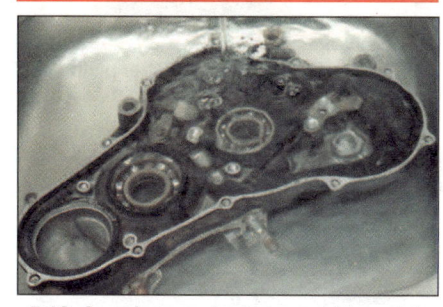

5.12 A casing can be immersed in a sink of boiling water to aid bearing removal

5.13 Using a localised heat source to aid bearing removal

● If heating the whole casing note that plastic components, such as the neutral switch, may suffer - remove them beforehand.
● After heating, remove the bearing as described above. You may find that the expansion is sufficient for the bearing to fall out of the casing under its own weight or with a light tap on the driver or socket.
● If necessary, the casing can be heated to aid bearing installation, and this is sometimes the recommended procedure if the motorcycle manufacturer has designed the housing and bearing fit with this intention.

REF•16 Tools and Workshop Tips

● Installation of bearings can be eased by placing them in a freezer the night before installation. The steel bearing will contract slightly, allowing easy insertion in its housing. This is often useful when installing steering head outer races in the frame.

Bearing types and markings

● Plain shell bearings, ball bearings, needle roller bearings and tapered roller bearings will all be found on motorcycles (see illustrations 5.14 and 5.15). The ball and roller types are usually caged between an inner and outer race, but uncaged variations may be found.

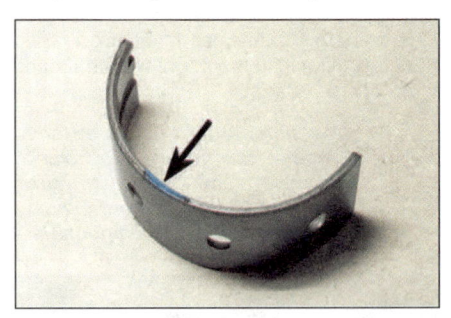

5.14 Shell bearings are either plain or grooved. They are usually identified by colour code (arrow)

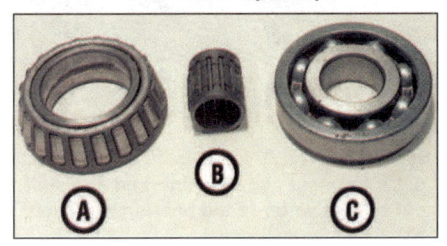

5.15 Tapered roller bearing (A), needle roller bearing (B) and ball journal bearing (C)

● Shell bearings (often called inserts) are usually found at the crankshaft main and connecting rod big-end where they are good at coping with high loads. They are made of a phosphor-bronze material and are impregnated with self-lubricating properties.

● Ball bearings and needle roller bearings consist of a steel inner and outer race with the balls or rollers between the races. They require constant lubrication by oil or grease and are good at coping with axial loads. Taper roller bearings consist of rollers set in a tapered cage set on the inner race; the outer race is separate. They are good at coping with axial loads and prevent movement along the shaft - a typical application is in the steering head.

● Bearing manufacturers produce bearings to ISO size standards and stamp one face of the bearing to indicate its internal and external diameter, load capacity and type (see illustration 5.16).

● Metal bushes are usually of phosphor-bronze material. Rubber bushes are used in suspension mounting eyes. Fibre bushes have also been used in suspension pivots.

5.16 Typical bearing marking

Bearing fault finding

● If a bearing outer race has spun in its housing, the housing material will be damaged. You can use a bearing locking compound to bond the outer race in place if damage is not too severe.

● Shell bearings will fail due to damage of their working surface, as a result of lack of lubrication, corrosion or abrasive particles in the oil (see illustration 5.17). Small particles of dirt in the oil may embed in the bearing material whereas larger particles will score the bearing and shaft journal. If a number of short journeys are made, insufficient heat will be generated to drive off condensation which has built up on the bearings.

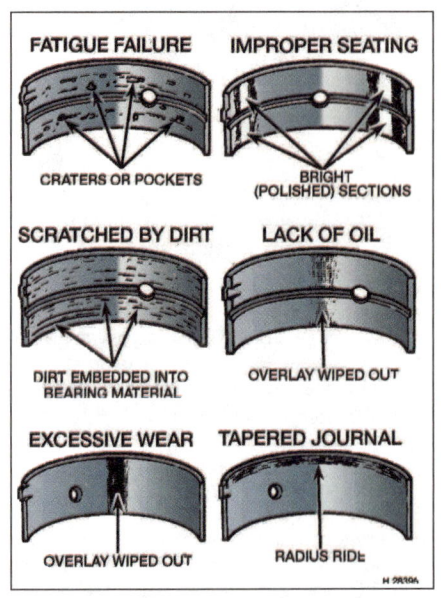

5.17 Typical bearing failures

● Ball and roller bearings will fail due to lack of lubrication or damage to the balls or rollers. Tapered-roller bearings can be damaged by overloading them. Unless the bearing is sealed on both sides, wash it in paraffin (kerosene) to remove all old grease then allow it to dry. Make a visual inspection looking to dented balls or rollers, damaged cages and worn or pitted races (see illustration 5.18).

● A ball bearing can be checked for wear by listening to it when spun. Apply a film of light oil to the bearing and hold it close to the ear - hold the outer race with one hand and spin the inner race with the other hand (see illustration 5.19). The bearing should be almost silent when spun; if it grates or rattles it is worn.

5.18 Example of ball journal bearing with damaged balls and cages

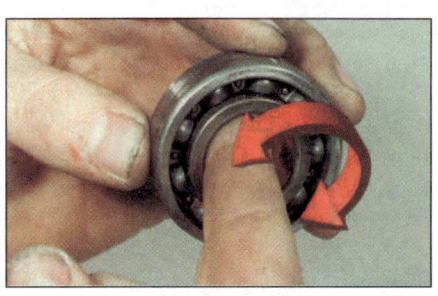

5.19 Hold outer race and listen to inner race when spun

6 Oil seals

Oil seal removal and installation

● Oil seals should be renewed every time a component is dismantled. This is because the seal lips will become set to the sealing surface and will not necessarily reseal.

● Oil seals can be prised out of position using a large flat-bladed screwdriver (see illustration 6.1). In the case of crankcase seals, check first that the seal is not lipped on the inside, preventing its removal with the crankcases joined.

6.1 Prise out oil seals with a large flat-bladed screwdriver

● New seals are usually installed with their marked face (containing the seal reference code) outwards and the spring side towards the fluid being retained. In certain cases, such as a two-stroke engine crankshaft seal, a double lipped seal may be used due to there being fluid or gas on each side of the joint.

Tools and Workshop Tips REF•17

- Use a bearing driver or socket which bears only on the outer hard edge of the seal to install it in the casing - tapping on the inner edge will damage the sealing lip.

Oil seal types and markings

- Oil seals are usually of the single-lipped type. Double-lipped seals are found where a liquid or gas is on both sides of the joint.
- Oil seals can harden and lose their sealing ability if the motorcycle has been in storage for a long period - renewal is the only solution.
- Oil seal manufacturers also conform to the ISO markings for seal size - these are moulded into the outer face of the seal **(see illustration 6.2)**.

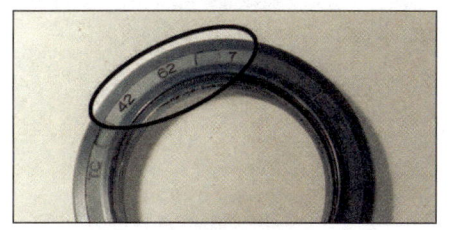

6.2 These oil seal markings indicate inside diameter, outside diameter and seal thickness

7 Gaskets and sealants

Types of gasket and sealant

- Gaskets are used to seal the mating surfaces between components and keep lubricants, fluids, vacuum or pressure contained within the assembly. Aluminium gaskets are sometimes found at the cylinder joints, but most gaskets are paper-based. If the mating surfaces of the components being joined are undamaged the gasket can be installed dry, although a dab of sealant or grease will be useful to hold it in place during assembly.
- RTV (Room Temperature Vulcanising) silicone rubber sealants cure when exposed to moisture in the atmosphere. These sealants are good at filling pits or irregular gasket faces, but will tend to be forced out of the joint under very high torque. They can be used to replace a paper gasket, but first make sure that the width of the paper gasket is not essential to the shimming of internal components. RTV sealants should not be used on components containing petrol (gasoline).
- Non-hardening, semi-hardening and hard setting liquid gasket compounds can be used with a gasket or between a metal-to-metal joint. Select the sealant to suit the application: universal non-hardening sealant can be used on virtually all joints; semi-hardening on joint faces which are rough or damaged; hard setting sealant on joints which require a permanent bond and are subjected to high temperature and pressure. **Note:** *Check first if the paper gasket has a bead of sealant impregnated in its surface before applying additional sealant.*
- When choosing a sealant, make sure it is suitable for the application, particularly if being applied in a high-temperature area or in the vicinity of fuel. Certain manufacturers produce sealants in either clear, silver or black colours to match the finish of the engine. This has a particular application on motorcycles where much of the engine is exposed.
- Do not over-apply sealant. That which is squeezed out on the outside of the joint can be wiped off, whereas an excess of sealant on the inside can break off and clog oilways.

Breaking a sealed joint

- Age, heat, pressure and the use of hard setting sealant can cause two components to stick together so tightly that they are difficult to separate using finger pressure alone. Do not resort to using levers unless there is a pry point provided for this purpose **(see illustration 7.1)** or else the gasket surfaces will be damaged.
- Use a soft-faced hammer **(see illustration 7.2)** or a wood block and conventional hammer to strike the component near the mating surface. Avoid hammering against cast extremities since they may break off. If this method fails, try using a wood wedge between the two components.

Caution: If the joint will not separate, double-check that you have removed all the fasteners.

7.1 If a pry point is provided, apply gently pressure with a flat-bladed screwdriver

7.2 Tap around the joint with a soft-faced mallet if necessary - don't strike cooling fins

Removal of old gasket and sealant

- Paper gaskets will most likely come away complete, leaving only a few traces stuck on

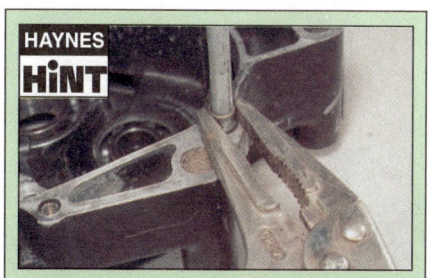

HAYNES HINT

Most components have one or two hollow locating dowels between the two gasket faces. If a dowel cannot be removed, do not resort to gripping it with pliers - it will almost certainly be distorted. Install a close-fitting socket or Phillips screwdriver into the dowel and then grip the outer edge of the dowel to free it.

the sealing faces of the components. It is imperative that all traces are removed to ensure correct sealing of the new gasket.

- Very carefully scrape all traces of gasket away making sure that the sealing surfaces are not gouged or scored by the scraper **(see illustrations 7.3, 7.4 and 7.5)**. Stubborn deposits can be removed by spraying with an aerosol gasket remover. Final preparation of

7.3 Paper gaskets can be scraped off with a gasket scraper tool . . .

7.4 . . . a knife blade . . .

7.5 . . . or a household scraper

REF•18 Tools and Workshop Tips

7.6 Fine abrasive paper is wrapped around a flat file to clean up the gasket face

7.7 A kitchen scourer can be used on stubborn deposits

8.1 Tighten the chain breaker to push the pin out of the link . . .

8.2 . . . withdraw the pin, remove the tool . . .

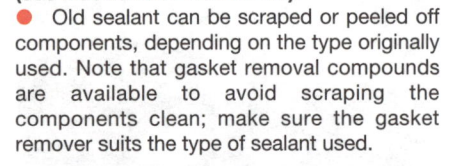

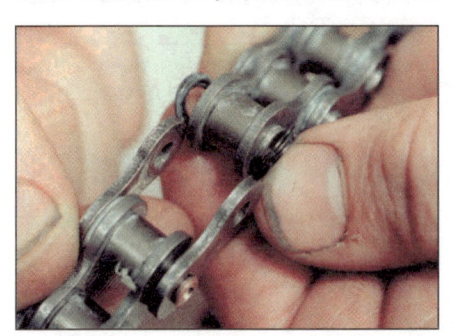

8.3 . . . and separate the chain link

8.4 Insert the new soft link, with O-rings, through the chain ends . . .

8.5 . . . install the O-rings over the pin ends . . .

8.6 . . . followed by the sideplate

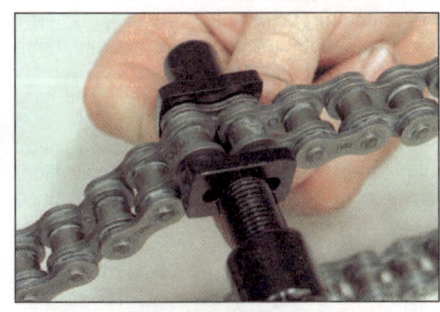

8.7 Push the sideplate into position using a clamp

the gasket surface can be made with very fine abrasive paper or a plastic kitchen scourer **(see illustrations 7.6 and 7.7)**.

● Old sealant can be scraped or peeled off components, depending on the type originally used. Note that gasket removal compounds are available to avoid scraping the components clean; make sure the gasket remover suits the type of sealant used.

8 Chains

Breaking and joining final drive chains

● Drive chains for all but small bikes are continuous and do not have a clip-type connecting link. The chain must be broken using a chain breaker tool and the new chain securely riveted together using a new soft rivet-type link. Never use a clip-type connecting link instead of a rivet-type link, except in an emergency. Various chain breaking and riveting tools are available, either as separate tools or combined as illustrated in the accompanying photographs - read the instructions supplied with the tool carefully.

> ⚠ **Warning: The need to rivet the new link pins correctly cannot be overstressed - loss of control of the motorcycle is very likely to result if the chain breaks in use.**

● Rotate the chain and look for the soft link. The soft link pins look like they have been deeply centre-punched instead of peened over like all the other pins **(see illustration 8.9)** and its sideplate may be a different colour. Position the soft link midway between the sprockets and assemble the chain breaker tool over one of the soft link pins **(see illustration 8.1)**. Operate the tool to push the pin out through the chain **(see illustration 8.2)**. On an O-ring chain, remove the O-rings **(see illustration 8.3)**. Carry out the same procedure on the other soft link pin.

> **Caution: Certain soft link pins (particularly on the larger chains) may require their ends to be filed or ground off before they can be pressed out using the tool.**

● Check that you have the correct size and strength (standard or heavy duty) new soft link - do not reuse the old link. Look for the size marking on the chain sideplates **(see illustration 8.10)**.

● Position the chain ends so that they are engaged over the rear sprocket. On an O-ring chain, install a new O-ring over each pin of the link and insert the link through the two chain ends **(see illustration 8.4)**. Install a new O-ring over the end of each pin, followed by the sideplate (with the chain manufacturer's marking facing outwards) **(see illustrations 8.5 and 8.6)**. On an unsealed chain, insert the link through the two chain ends, then install the sideplate with the chain manufacturer's marking facing outwards.

● Note that it may not be possible to install the sideplate using finger pressure alone. If using a joining tool, assemble it so that the plates of the tool clamp the link and press the sideplate over the pins **(see illustration 8.7)**. Otherwise, use two small sockets placed over

Tools and Workshop Tips   REF•19

8.8 Assemble the chain riveting tool over one pin at a time and tighten it fully

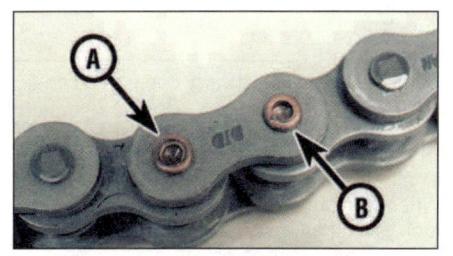

8.9 Pin end correctly riveted (A), pin end unriveted (B)

the rivet ends and two pieces of the wood between a G-clamp. Operate the clamp to press the sideplate over the pins.
● Assemble the joining tool over one pin (following the maker's instructions) and tighten the tool down to spread the pin end securely **(see illustrations 8.8 and 8.9)**. Do the same on the other pin.

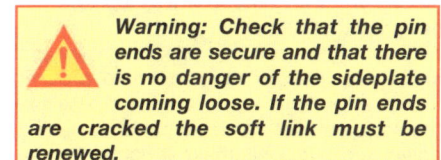

> **Warning:** Check that the pin ends are secure and that there is no danger of the sideplate coming loose. If the pin ends are cracked the soft link must be renewed.

Final drive chain sizing

● Chains are sized using a three digit number, followed by a suffix to denote the chain type **(see illustration 8.10)**. Chain type is either standard or heavy duty (thicker sideplates), and also unsealed or O-ring/X-ring type.
● The first digit of the number relates to the pitch of the chain, ie the distance from the centre of one pin to the centre of the next pin **(see illustration 8.11)**. Pitch is expressed in eighths of an inch, as follows:

8.10 Typical chain size and type marking

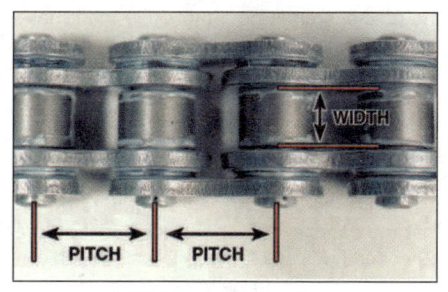

8.11 Chain dimensions

> Sizes commencing with a 4 (eg 428) have a pitch of 1/2 inch (12.7 mm)
> Sizes commencing with a 5 (eg 520) have a pitch of 5/8 inch (15.9 mm)
> Sizes commencing with a 6 (eg 630) have a pitch of 3/4 inch (19.1 mm)

● The second and third digits of the chain size relate to the width of the rollers, again in imperial units, eg the 525 shown has 5/16 inch (7.94 mm) rollers **(see illustration 8.11)**.

9 Hoses

Clamping to prevent flow

● Small-bore flexible hoses can be clamped to prevent fluid flow whilst a component is worked on. Whichever method is used, ensure that the hose material is not permanently distorted or damaged by the clamp.
a) A brake hose clamp available from auto accessory shops **(see illustration 9.1)**.
b) A wingnut type hose clamp **(see illustration 9.2)**.

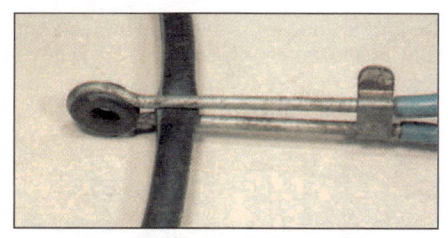

9.1 Hoses can be clamped with an automotive brake hose clamp . . .

9.2 . . . a wingnut type hose clamp . . .

c) Two sockets placed each side of the hose and held with straight-jawed self-locking grips **(see illustration 9.3)**.
d) Thick card each side of the hose held between straight-jawed self-locking grips **(see illustration 9.4)**.

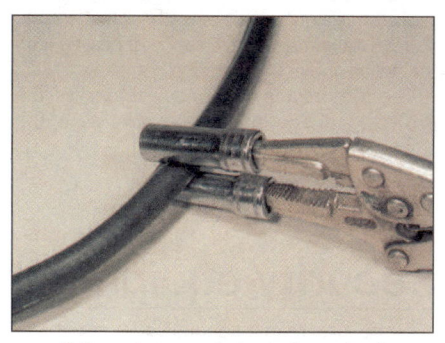

9.3 . . . two sockets and a pair of self-locking grips . . .

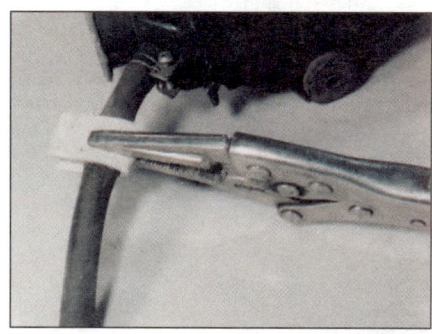

9.4 . . . or thick card and self-locking grips

Freeing and fitting hoses

● Always make sure the hose clamp is moved well clear of the hose end. Grip the hose with your hand and rotate it whilst pulling it off the union. If the hose has hardened due to age and will not move, slit it with a sharp knife and peel its ends off the union **(see illustration 9.5)**.
● Resist the temptation to use grease or soap on the unions to aid installation; although it helps the hose slip over the union it will equally aid the escape of fluid from the joint. It is preferable to soften the hose ends in hot water and wet the inside surface of the hose with water or a fluid which will evaporate.

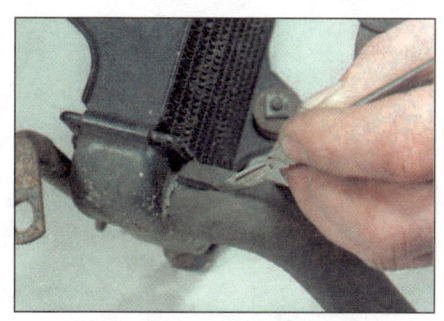

9.5 Cutting a coolant hose free with a sharp knife

REF•20 Security

Introduction

In less time than it takes to read this introduction, a thief could steal your motorcycle. Returning only to find your bike has gone is one of the worst feelings in the world. Even if the motorcycle is insured against theft, once you've got over the initial shock, you will have the inconvenience of dealing with the police and your insurance company.

The motorcycle is an easy target for the professional thief and the joyrider alike and the official figures on motorcycle theft make for depressing reading; on average a motorcycle is stolen every 16 minutes in the UK!

Motorcycle thefts fall into two categories, those stolen 'to order' and those taken by opportunists. The thief stealing to order will be on the look out for a specific make and model and will go to extraordinary lengths to obtain that motorcycle. The opportunist thief on the other hand will look for easy targets which can be stolen with the minimum of effort and risk.

Whilst it is never going to be possible to make your machine 100% secure, it is estimated that around half of all stolen motorcycles are taken by opportunist thieves. Remember that the opportunist thief is always on the look out for the easy option: if there are two similar motorcycles parked side-by-side, they will target the one with the lowest level of security. By taking a few precautions, you can reduce the chances of your motorcycle being stolen.

Security equipment

There are many specialised motorcycle security devices available and the following text summarises their applications and their good and bad points.

Once you have decided on the type of security equipment which best suits your needs, we recommended that you read one of the many equipment tests regularly carried out by the motorcycle press. These tests compare the products from all the major manufacturers and give impartial ratings on their effectiveness, value-for-money and ease of use.

No one item of security equipment can provide complete protection. It is highly recommended that two or more of the items described below are combined to increase the security of your motorcycle (a lock and chain plus an alarm system is just about ideal). The more security measures fitted to the bike, the less likely it is to be stolen.

Lock and chain

Pros: *Very flexible to use; can be used to secure the motorcycle to almost any immovable object. On some locks and chains, the lock can be used on its own as a disc lock (see below).*

Cons: *Can be very heavy and awkward to carry on the motorcycle, although some types will be supplied with a carry bag which can be strapped to the pillion seat.*

● Heavy-duty chains and locks are an excellent security measure **(see illustration 1)**. Whenever the motorcycle is parked, use the lock and chain to secure the machine to a solid, immovable object such as a post or railings. This will prevent the machine from being ridden away or being lifted into the back of a van.

● When fitting the chain, always ensure the chain is routed around the motorcycle frame or swingarm **(see illustrations 2 and 3)**. Never merely pass the chain around one of the wheel rims; a thief may unbolt the wheel and lift the rest of the machine into a van, leaving you with just the wheel! Try to avoid having excess chain free, thus making it difficult to use cutting tools, and keep the chain and lock off the ground to prevent thieves attacking it with a cold chisel. Position the lock so that its lock barrel is facing downwards; this will make it harder for the thief to attack the lock mechanism.

1 Ensure the lock and chain you buy is of good quality and long enough to shackle your bike to a solid object

2 Pass the chain through the bike's frame, rather than just through a wheel . . .

3 . . . and loop it around a solid object

Security REF•21

U-locks

Pros: *Highly effective deterrent which can be used to secure the bike to a post or railings. Most U-locks come with a carrier which allows the lock to be easily carried on the bike.*

Cons: *Not as flexible to use as a lock and chain.*

● These are solid locks which are similar in use to a lock and chain. U-locks are lighter than a lock and chain but not so flexible to use. The length and shape of the lock shackle limit the objects to which the bike can be secured **(see illustration 4)**.

Disc locks

Pros: *Small, light and very easy to carry; most can be stored underneath the seat.*

Cons: *Does not prevent the motorcycle being lifted into a van. Can be very embarrassing if you forget to remove the lock before attempting to ride off!*

● Disc locks are designed to be attached to the front brake disc. The lock passes through one of the holes in the disc and prevents the wheel rotating by jamming against the fork/brake caliper **(see illustration 5)**. Some are equipped with an alarm siren which sounds if the disc lock is moved; this not only acts as a theft deterrent but also as a handy reminder if you try to move the bike with the lock still fitted.

● Combining the disc lock with a length of cable which can be looped around a post or railings provides an additional measure of security **(see illustration 6)**.

Alarms and immobilisers

Pros: *Once installed it is completely hassle-free to use. If the system is 'Thatcham' or 'Sold Secure-approved', insurance companies may give you a discount.*

Cons: *Can be expensive to buy and complex to install. No system will prevent the motorcycle from being lifted into a van and taken away.*

● Electronic alarms and immobilisers are available to suit a variety of budgets. There are three different types of system available: pure alarms, pure immobilisers, and the more expensive systems which are combined alarm/immobilisers **(see illustration 7)**.

● An alarm system is designed to emit an audible warning if the motorcycle is being tampered with.

● An immobiliser prevents the motorcycle being started and ridden away by disabling its electrical systems.

● When purchasing an alarm/immobiliser system, check the cost of installing the system unless you are able to do it yourself. If the motorcycle is not used regularly, another consideration is the current drain of the system. All alarm/immobiliser systems are powered by the motorcycle's battery; purchasing a system with a very low current drain could prevent the battery losing its charge whilst the motorcycle is not being used.

U-locks can be used to secure the bike to a solid object – ensure you purchase one which is long enough

A typical disc lock attached through one of the holes in the disc

A disc lock combined with a security cable provides additional protection

A typical alarm/immobiliser system

REF•22 Security

Indelible markings can be applied to most areas of the bike – always apply the manufacturer's sticker to warn off thieves

Chemically-etched code numbers can be applied to main body panels . . .

. . . again, always ensure that the kit manufacturer's sticker is applied in a prominent position

Security marking kits

Pros: *Very cheap and effective deterrent. Many insurance companies will give you a discount on your insurance premium if a recognised security marking kit is used on your motorcycle.*

Cons: *Does not prevent the motorcycle being stolen by joyriders.*

● There are many different types of security marking kits available. The idea is to mark as many parts of the motorcycle as possible with a unique security number **(see illustrations 8, 9 and 10)**. A form will be included with the kit to register your personal details and those of the motorcycle with the kit manufacturer. This register is made available to the police to help them trace the rightful owner of any motorcycle or components which they recover should all other forms of identification have been removed. Always apply the warning stickers provided with the kit to deter thieves.

Ground anchors, wheel clamps and security posts

Pros: *An excellent form of security which will deter all but the most determined of thieves.*

Cons: *Awkward to install and can be expensive.*

● Whilst the motorcycle is at home, it is a good idea to attach it securely to the floor or a solid wall, even if it is kept in a securely locked garage. Various types of ground anchors, security posts and wheel clamps are available for this purpose **(see illustration 11)**. These security devices are either bolted to a solid concrete or brick structure or can be cemented into the ground.

Permanent ground anchors provide an excellent level of security when the bike is at home

Security at home

A high percentage of motorcycle thefts are from the owner's home. Here are some things to consider whenever your motorcycle is at home:

✔ Where possible, always keep the motorcycle in a securely locked garage. Never rely solely on the standard lock on the garage door, these are usual hopelessly inadequate. Fit an additional locking mechanism to the door and consider having the garage alarmed. A security light, activated by a movement sensor, is also a good investment.

✔ Always secure the motorcycle to the ground or a wall, even if it is inside a securely locked garage.

✔ Do not regularly leave the motorcycle outside your home, try to keep it out of sight wherever possible. If a garage is not available, fit a motorcycle cover over the bike to disguise its true identity.

✔ It is not uncommon for thieves to follow a motorcyclist home to find out where the bike is kept. They will then return at a later date. Be aware of this whenever you are returning home on your motorcycle. If you suspect you are being followed, do not return home, instead ride to a garage or shop and stop as a precaution.

✔ When selling a motorcycle, do not provide your home address or the location where the bike is normally kept. Arrange to meet the buyer at a location away from your home. Thieves have been known to pose as potential buyers to find out where motorcycles are kept and then return later to steal them.

Security away from the home

As well as fitting security equipment to your motorcycle here are a few general rules to follow whenever you park your motorcycle.

✔ Park in a busy, public place.
✔ Use car parks which incorporate security features, such as CCTV.
✔ At night, park in a well-lit area, preferably directly underneath a street light.
✔ Engage the steering lock.
✔ Secure the motorcycle to a solid, immovable object such as a post or railings with an additional lock. If this is not possible, secure the bike to a friend's motorcycle. Some public parking places provide security loops for motorcycles.
✔ Never leave your helmet or luggage attached to the motorcycle. Take them with you at all times.

Lubricants and fluids

A wide range of lubricants, fluids and cleaning agents is available for motor-cycles. This is a guide as to what is available, its applications and properties.

Four-stroke engine oil

● Engine oil is without doubt the most important component of any four-stroke engine. Modern motorcycle engines place a lot of demands on their oil and choosing the right type is essential. Using an unsuitable oil will lead to an increased rate of engine wear and could result in serious engine damage. Before purchasing oil, always check the recommended oil specification given by the manufacturer. The manufacturer will state a recommended 'type or classification' and also a specific 'viscosity' range for engine oil.

● The oil 'type or classification' is identified by its API (American Petroleum Institute) rating. The API rating will be in the form of two letters, e.g. SG. The S identifies the oil as being suitable for use in a petrol (gasoline) engine (S stands for spark ignition) and the second letter, ranging from A to J, identifies the oil's performance rating. The later this letter, the higher the specification of the oil; for example API SG oil exceeds the requirements of API SF oil. **Note:** *On some oils there may also be a second rating consisting of another two letters, the first letter being C, e.g. API SF/CD. This rating indicates the oil is also suitable for use in a diesel engines (the C stands for compression ignition) and is thus of no relevance for motorcycle use.*

● The 'viscosity' of the oil is identified by its SAE (Society of Automotive Engineers) rating. All modern engines require multigrade oils and the SAE rating will consist of two numbers, the first followed by a W, e.g. 10W/40. The first number indicates the viscosity rating of the oil at low temperatures (W stands for winter – tested at –20°C) and the second number represents the viscosity of the oil at high temperatures (tested at 100°C). The lower the number, the thinner the oil. For example an oil with an SAE 10W/40 rating will give better cold starting and running than an SAE 15W/40 oil.

● As well as ensuring the 'type' and 'viscosity' of the oil match the recommendations, another consideration to make when buying engine oil is whether to purchase a standard mineral-based oil, a semi-synthetic oil (also known as a synthetic blend or synthetic-based oil) or a fully-synthetic oil. Although all oils will have a similar rating and viscosity, their cost will vary considerably; mineral-based oils are the cheapest, the fully-synthetic oils the most expensive with the semi-synthetic oils falling somewhere in-between. This decision is very much up to the owner, but it should be noted that modern synthetic oils have far better lubricating and cleaning qualities than traditional mineral-based oils and tend to retain these properties for far longer. Bearing in mind the operating conditions inside a modern, high-revving motorcycle engine it is highly recommended that a fully synthetic oil is used. The extra expense at each service could save you money in the long term by preventing premature engine wear.

● As a final note always ensure that the oil is specifically designed for use in motorcycle engines. Engine oils designed primarily for use in car engines sometimes contain additives or friction modifiers which could cause clutch slip on a motorcycle fitted with a wet-clutch.

Two-stroke engine oil

● Modern two-stroke engines, with their high power outputs, place high demands on their oil. If engine seizure is to be avoided it is essential that a high-quality oil is used. Two-stroke oils differ hugely from four-stroke oils. The oil lubricates only the crankshaft and piston(s) (the transmission has its own lubricating oil) and is used on a total-loss basis where it is burnt completely during the combustion process.

● The Japanese have recently introduced a classification system for two-stroke oils, the JASO rating. This rating is in the form of two letters, either FA, FB or FC – FA is the lowest classification and FC the highest. Ensure the oil being used meets or exceeds the recommended rating specified by the manufacturer.

● As well as ensuring the oil rating matches the recommendation, another consideration to make when buying engine oil is whether to purchase a standard mineral-based oil, a semi-synthetic oil (also known as a synthetic blend or synthetic-based oil) or a fully-synthetic oil. The cost of each type of oil varies considerably; mineral-based oils are the cheapest, the fully-synthetic oils the most expensive with the semi-synthetic oils falling somewhere in-between. This decision is very much up to the owner, but it should be noted that modern synthetic oils have far better lubricating properties and burn cleaner than traditional mineral-based oils. It is therefore recommended that a fully synthetic oil is used. The extra expense could save you money in the long term by preventing premature engine wear, engine performance will be improved, carbon deposits and exhaust smoke will be reduced.

REF•24 Lubricants and fluids

● Always ensure that the oil is specifically designed for use in an injector system. Many high quality two-stroke oils are designed for competition use and need to be pre-mixed with fuel. These oils are of a much higher viscosity and are not designed to flow through the injector pumps used on road-going two-stroke motorcycles.

Transmission (gear) oil

● On a two-stroke engine, the transmission and clutch are lubricated by their own separate oil bath which must be changed in accordance with the Maintenance Schedule.
● Although the engine and transmission units of most four-strokes use a common lubrication supply, there are some exceptions where the engine and gearbox have separate oil reservoirs and a dry clutch is used.
● Motorcycle manufacturers will either recommend a monograde transmission oil or a four-stroke multigrade engine oil to lubricate the transmission.
● Transmission oils, or gear oils as they are often called, are designed specifically for use in transmission systems. The viscosity of these oils is represented by an SAE number, but the scale of measurement applied is different to that used to grade engine oils. As a rough guide a SAE90 gear oil will be of the same viscosity as an SAE50 engine oil.

Shaft drive oil

● On models equipped with shaft final drive, the shaft drive gears are will have their own oil supply. The manufacturer will state a recommended 'type or classification' and also a specific 'viscosity' range in the same manner as for four-stroke engine oil.
● Gear oil classification is given by the number which follows the API GL (GL standing for gear lubricant) rating, the higher the number, the higher the specification of the oil, e.g. API GL5 oil is a higher specification than API GL4 oil. Ensure the oil meets or exceeds the classification specified and is of the correct viscosity. The viscosity of gear oils is also represented by an SAE number but the scale of measurement used is different to that used to grade engine oils. As a rough guide an SAE90 gear oil will be of the same viscosity as an SAE50 engine oil.
● If the use of an EP (Extreme Pressure) gear oil is specified, ensure the oil purchased is suitable.

Fork oil and suspension fluid

● Conventional telescopic front forks are hydraulic and require fork oil to work. To ensure the forks function correctly, the fork oil must be changed in accordance with the Maintenance Schedule.
● Fork oil is available in a variety of viscosities, identified by their SAE rating; fork oil ratings vary from light (SAE 5) to heavy (SAE 30). When purchasing fork oil, ensure the viscosity rating matches that specified by the manufacturer.
● Some lubricant manufacturers also produce a range of high-quality suspension fluids which are very similar to fork oil but are designed mainly for competition use. These fluids may have a different viscosity rating system which is not to be confused with the SAE rating of normal fork oil. Refer to the manufacturer's instructions if in any doubt.

Brake and clutch fluid

● All disc brake systems and some clutch systems are hydraulically operated. To ensure correct operation, the hydraulic fluid must be changed in accordance with the Maintenance Schedule.
● Brake and clutch fluid is classified by its DOT rating with most motorcycle manufacturers specifying DOT 3 or 4 fluid. Both fluid types are glycol-based and can be mixed together without adverse effect; DOT 4 fluid exceeds the requirements of DOT 3 fluid. Although it is safe to use DOT 4 fluid in a system designed for use with DOT 3 fluid, never use DOT 3 fluid in a system which specifies the use of DOT 4 as this will adversely affect the system's performance. The type required for the system will be marked on the fluid reservoir cap.
● Some manufacturers also produce a DOT 5 hydraulic fluid. DOT 5 hydraulic fluid is silicone-based and is not compatible with the glycol-based DOT 3 and 4 fluids. Never mix DOT 5 fluid with DOT 3 or 4 fluid as this will seriously affect the performance of the hydraulic system.

Coolant/antifreeze

● When purchasing coolant/antifreeze, always ensure it is suitable for use in an aluminium engine and contains corrosion inhibitors to prevent possible blockages of the internal coolant passages of the system. As a general rule, most coolants are designed to be used neat and should not be diluted whereas antifreeze can be mixed with distilled water to provide a coolant solution of the required strength. Refer to the manufacturer's instructions on the bottle.
● Ensure the coolant is changed in accordance with the Maintenance Schedule.

Chain lube

● Chain lube is an aerosol-type spray lubricant specifically designed for use on motorcycle final drive chains. Chain lube has two functions, to minimise friction between the final drive chain and sprockets and to prevent corrosion of the chain. Regular use of a good-quality chain lube will extend the life of the drive chain and sprockets and thus maximise the power being transmitted from the transmission to the rear wheel.
● When using chain lube, always allow some time for the solvents in the lube to evaporate before riding the motorcycle. This will minimise the amount of lube which will

Lubricants and fluids REF•25

'fling' off from the chain when the motorcycle is used. If the motorcycle is equipped with an 'O-ring' chain, ensure the chain lube is labelled as being suitable for use on 'O-ring' chains.

Degreasers and solvents

● There are many different types of solvents and degreasers available to remove the grime and grease which accumulate around the motorcycle during normal use. Degreasers and solvents are usually available as an aerosol-type spray or as a liquid which you apply with a brush. Always closely follow the manufacturer's instructions and wear eye protection during use. Be aware that many solvents are flammable and may give off noxious fumes; take adequate precautions when using them (see Safety First!).

● For general cleaning, use one of the many solvents or degreasers available from most motorcycle accessory shops. These solvents are usually applied then left for a certain time before being washed off with water.

Brake cleaner is a solvent specifically designed to remove all traces of oil, grease and dust from braking system components. Brake cleaner is designed to evaporate quickly and leaves behind no residue.

Carburettor cleaner is an aerosol-type solvent specifically designed to clear carburettor blockages and break down the hard deposits and gum often found inside carburettors during overhaul.

Contact cleaner is an aerosol-type solvent designed for cleaning electrical components. The cleaner will remove all traces of oil and dirt from components such as switch contacts or fouled spark plugs and then dry, leaving behind no residue.

Gasket remover is an aerosol-type solvent designed for removing stubborn gaskets from engine components during overhaul. Gasket remover will minimise the amount of scraping required to remove the gasket and therefore reduce the risk of damage to the mating surface.

Spray lubricants

● Aerosol-based spray lubricants are widely available and are excellent for lubricating lever pivots and exposed cables and switches. Try to use a lubricant which is of the dry-film type as the fluid evaporates, leaving behind a dry-film of lubricant. Lubricants which leave behind an oily residue will attract dust and dirt which will increase the rate of wear of the cable/lever.

● Most lubricants also act as a moisture dispersant and a penetrating fluid. This means they can also be used to 'dry out' electrical components such as wiring connectors or switches as well as helping to free seized fasteners.

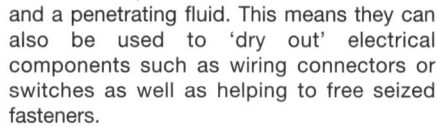

Greases

● Grease is used to lubricate many of the pivot-points. A good-quality multi-purpose grease is suitable for most applications but some manufacturers will specify the use of specialist greases for use on components such as swingarm and suspension linkage bushes. These specialist greases can be purchased from most motorcycle (or car) accessory shops; commonly specified types include molybdenum disulphide grease, lithium-based grease, graphite-based grease, silicone-based grease and high-temperature copper-based grease.

Gasket sealing compounds

● Gasket sealing compounds can be used in conjunction with gaskets, to improve their sealing capabilities, or on their own to seal metal-to-metal joints. Depending on their type, sealing compounds either set hard or stay relatively soft and pliable.

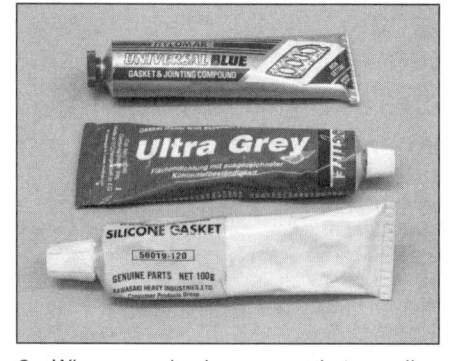

● When purchasing a gasket sealing compound, ensure that it is designed specifically for use on an internal combustion engine. General multi-purpose sealants available from DIY stores may appear visibly similar but they are not designed to withstand the extreme heat or contact with fuel and oil encountered when used on an engine (see 'Tools and Workshop Tips' for further information).

Thread locking compound

● Thread locking compounds are used to secure certain threaded fasteners in position to prevent them from loosening due to vibration. Thread locking compounds can be purchased from most motorcycle (and car) accessory shops. Ensure the threads of the both components are completely clean and dry before sparingly applying the locking compound (see 'Tools and Workshop Tips' for further information).

Fuel additives

● Fuel additives which protect and clean the fuel system components are widely available. These additives are designed to remove all traces of deposits that build up on the carburettors/injectors and prevent wear, helping the fuel system to operate more efficiently. If a fuel additive is being used, check that it is suitable for use with your motorcycle, especially if your motorcycle is equipped with a catalytic converter.

● Octane boosters are also available. These additives are designed to improve the performance of highly-tuned engines being run on normal pump-fuel and are of no real use on standard motorcycles.

Conversion Factors

Length (distance)
Inches (in)	x 25.4	= Millimetres (mm)	x 0.0394	=	Inches (in)
Feet (ft)	x 0.305	= Metres (m)	x 3.281	=	Feet (ft)
Miles	x 1.609	= Kilometres (km)	x 0.621	=	Miles

Volume (capacity)
Cubic inches (cu in; in³)	x 16.387	= Cubic centimetres (cc; cm³)	x 0.061	=	Cubic inches (cu in; in³)
Imperial pints (Imp pt)	x 0.568	= Litres (l)	x 1.76	=	Imperial pints (Imp pt)
Imperial quarts (Imp qt)	x 1.137	= Litres (l)	x 0.88	=	Imperial quarts (Imp qt)
Imperial quarts (Imp qt)	x 1.201	= US quarts (US qt)	x 0.833	=	Imperial quarts (Imp qt)
US quarts (US qt)	x 0.946	= Litres (l)	x 1.057	=	US quarts (US qt)
Imperial gallons (Imp gal)	x 4.546	= Litres (l)	x 0.22	=	Imperial gallons (Imp gal)
Imperial gallons (Imp gal)	x 1.201	= US gallons (US gal)	x 0.833	=	Imperial gallons (Imp gal)
US gallons (US gal)	x 3.785	= Litres (l)	x 0.264	=	US gallons (US gal)

Mass (weight)
Ounces (oz)	x 28.35	= Grams (g)	x 0.035	=	Ounces (oz)
Pounds (lb)	x 0.454	= Kilograms (kg)	x 2.205	=	Pounds (lb)

Force
Ounces-force (ozf; oz)	x 0.278	= Newtons (N)	x 3.6	=	Ounces-force (ozf; oz)
Pounds-force (lbf; lb)	x 4.448	= Newtons (N)	x 0.225	=	Pounds-force (lbf; lb)
Newtons (N)	x 0.1	= Kilograms-force (kgf; kg)	x 9.81	=	Newtons (N)

Pressure
Pounds-force per square inch (psi; lbf/in²; lb/in²)	x 0.070	= Kilograms-force per square centimetre (kgf/cm²; kg/cm²)	x 14.223	=	Pounds-force per square inch (psi; lbf/in²; lb/in²)
Pounds-force per square inch (psi; lbf/in²; lb/in²)	x 0.068	= Atmospheres (atm)	x 14.696	=	Pounds-force per square inch (psi; lbf/in²; lb/in²)
Pounds-force per square inch (psi; lbf/in²; lb/in²)	x 0.069	= Bars	x 14.5	=	Pounds-force per square inch (psi; lbf/in²; lb/in²)
Pounds-force per square inch (psi; lbf/in²; lb/in²)	x 6.895	= Kilopascals (kPa)	x 0.145	=	Pounds-force per square inch (psi; lbf/in²; lb/in²)
Kilopascals (kPa)	x 0.01	= Kilograms-force per square centimetre (kgf/cm²; kg/cm²)	x 98.1	=	Kilopascals (kPa)
Millibar (mbar)	x 100	= Pascals (Pa)	x 0.01	=	Millibar (mbar)
Millibar (mbar)	x 0.0145	= Pounds-force per square inch (psi; lbf/in²; lb/in²)	x 68.947	=	Millibar (mbar)
Millibar (mbar)	x 0.75	= Millimetres of mercury (mmHg)	x 1.333	=	Millibar (mbar)
Millibar (mbar)	x 0.401	= Inches of water (inH$_2$O)	x 2.491	=	Millibar (mbar)
Millimetres of mercury (mmHg)	x 0.535	= Inches of water (inH$_2$O)	x 1.868	=	Millimetres of mercury (mmHg)
Inches of water (inH$_2$O)	x 0.036	= Pounds-force per square inch (psi; lbf/in²; lb/in²)	x 27.68	=	Inches of water (inH$_2$O)

Torque (moment of force)
Pounds-force inches (lbf in; lb in)	x 1.152	= Kilograms-force centimetre (kgf cm; kg cm)	x 0.868	=	Pounds-force inches (lbf in; lb in)
Pounds-force inches (lbf in; lb in)	x 0.113	= Newton metres (Nm)	x 8.85	=	Pounds-force inches (lbf in; lb in)
Pounds-force inches (lbf in; lb in)	x 0.083	= Pounds-force feet (lbf ft; lb ft)	x 12	=	Pounds-force inches (lbf in; lb in)
Pounds-force feet (lbf ft; lb ft)	x 0.138	= Kilograms-force metres (kgf m; kg m)	x 7.233	=	Pounds-force feet (lbf ft; lb ft)
Pounds-force feet (lbf ft; lb ft)	x 1.356	= Newton metres (Nm)	x 0.738	=	Pounds-force feet (lbf ft; lb ft)
Newton metres (Nm)	x 0.102	= Kilograms-force metres (kgf m; kg m)	x 9.804	=	Newton metres (Nm)

Power
Horsepower (hp)	x 745.7	= Watts (W)	x 0.0013	=	Horsepower (hp)

Velocity (speed)
Miles per hour (miles/hr; mph)	x 1.609	= Kilometres per hour (km/hr; kph)	x 0.621	=	Miles per hour (miles/hr; mph)

Fuel consumption*
Miles per gallon (mpg)	x 0.354	= Kilometres per litre (km/l)	x 2.825	=	Miles per gallon (mpg)

Temperature

Degrees Fahrenheit = (°C x 1.8) + 32   Degrees Celsius (Degrees Centigrade; °C) = (°F - 32) x 0.56

*It is common practice to convert from miles per gallon (mpg) to litres/100 kilometres (l/100km), where mpg x l/100 km = 282

MOT Test Checks REF•27

About the MOT Test

In the UK, all vehicles more than three years old are subject to an annual test to ensure that they meet minimum safety requirements. A current test certificate must be issued before a machine can be used on public roads, and is required before a road fund licence can be issued. Riding without a current test certificate will also invalidate your insurance.

For most owners, the MOT test is an annual cause for anxiety, and this is largely due to owners not being sure what needs to be checked prior to submitting the motorcycle for testing. The simple answer is that a fully roadworthy motorcycle will have no difficulty in passing the test.

This is a guide to getting your motorcycle through the MOT test. Obviously it will not be possible to examine the motorcycle to the same standard as the professional MOT tester, particularly in view of the equipment required for some of the checks. However, working through the following procedures will enable you to identify any problem areas before submitting the motorcycle for the test.

It has only been possible to summarise the test requirements here, based on the regulations in force at the time of printing. Test standards are becoming increasingly stringent, although there are some exemptions for older vehicles. More information about the MOT test can be obtained from the HMSO publications, *How Safe is your Motorcycle* and *The MOT Inspection Manual for Motorcycle Testing*.

Many of the checks require that one of the wheels is raised off the ground. If the motorcycle doesn't have a centre stand, note that an auxiliary stand will be required. Additionally, the help of an assistant may prove useful.

Certain exceptions apply to machines under 50 cc, machines without a lighting system, and Classic bikes - if in doubt about any of the requirements listed below seek confirmation from an MOT tester prior to submitting the motorcycle for the test.

Check that the frame number is clearly visible.

HAYNES HiNT *If a component is in borderline condition, the tester has discretion in deciding whether to pass or fail it. If the motorcycle presented is clean and evidently well cared for, the tester may be more inclined to pass a borderline component than if the motorcycle is scruffy and apparently neglected.*

Electrical System

Lights, turn signals, horn and reflector

✔ With the ignition on, check the operation of the following electrical components. **Note:** *The electrical components on certain small-capacity machines are powered by the generator, requiring that the engine is run for this check.*

a) Headlight and tail light. Check that both illuminate in the low and high beam switch positions.
b) Position lights. Check that the front position (or sidelight) and tail light illuminate in this switch position.
c) Turn signals. Check that all flash at the correct rate, and that the warning light(s) function correctly. Check that the turn signal switch works correctly.
d) Hazard warning system (where fitted). Check that all four turn signals flash in this switch position.
e) Brake stop light. Check that the light comes on when the front and rear brakes are independently applied. Models first used on or after 1st April 1986 must have a brake light switch on each brake.
f) Horn. Check that the sound is continuous and of reasonable volume.

✔ Check that there is a red reflector on the rear of the machine, either mounted separately or as part of the tail light lens.
✔ Check the condition of the headlight, tail light and turn signal lenses.

Headlight beam height

✔ The MOT tester will perform a headlight beam height check using specialised beam setting equipment **(see illustration 1)**. This equipment will not be available to the home mechanic, but if you suspect that the headlight is incorrectly set or may have been maladjusted in the past, you can perform a rough test as follows.
✔ Position the bike in a straight line facing a brick wall. The bike must be off its stand, upright and with a rider seated. Measure the height from the ground to the centre of the headlight and mark a horizontal line on the wall at this height. Position the motorcycle 3.8 metres from the wall and draw a vertical line up the wall central to the centreline of the motorcycle. Switch to dipped beam and check that the beam pattern falls slightly lower than the horizontal line and to the left of the vertical line **(see illustration 2)**.

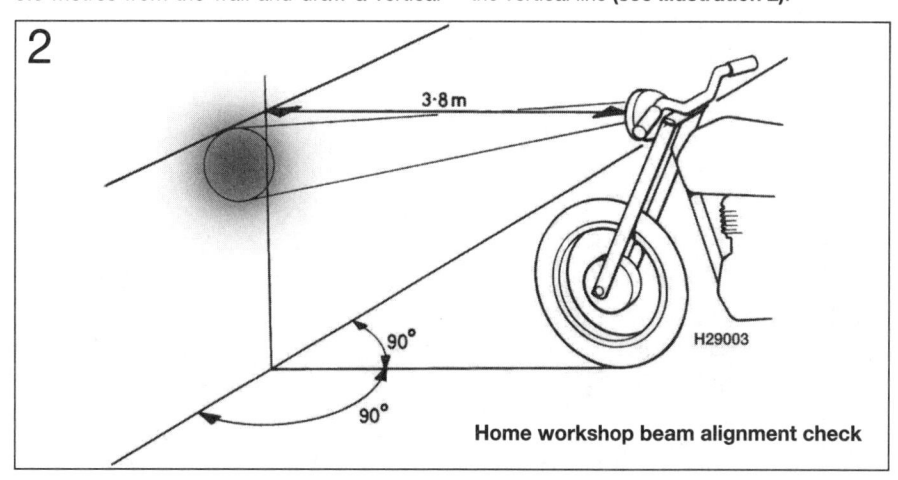

Headlight beam height checking equipment

Home workshop beam alignment check

REF•28 MOT Test Checks

Exhaust System and Final Drive

Exhaust

✔ Check that the exhaust mountings are secure and that the system does not foul any of the rear suspension components.
✔ Start the motorcycle. When the revs are increased, check that the exhaust is neither holed nor leaking from any of its joints. On a linked system, check that the collector box is not leaking due to corrosion.
✔ Note that the exhaust decibel level ("loudness" of the exhaust) is assessed at the discretion of the tester. If the motorcycle was first used on or after 1st January 1985 the silencer must carry the BSAU 193 stamp, or a marking relating to its make and model, or be of OE (original equipment) manufacture. If the silencer is marked NOT FOR ROAD USE, RACING USE ONLY or similar, it will fail the MOT.

Final drive

✔ On chain or belt drive machines, check that the chain/belt is in good condition and does not have excessive slack. Also check that the sprocket is securely mounted on the rear wheel hub. Check that the chain/belt guard is in place.
✔ On shaft drive bikes, check for oil leaking from the drive unit and fouling the rear tyre.

Steering and Suspension

Steering

✔ With the front wheel raised off the ground, rotate the steering from lock to lock. The handlebar or switches must not contact the fuel tank or be close enough to trap the rider's hand. Problems can be caused by damaged lock stops on the lower yoke and frame, or by the fitting of non-standard handlebars.
✔ When performing the lock to lock check, also ensure that the steering moves freely without drag or notchiness. Steering movement can be impaired by poorly routed cables, or by overtight head bearings or worn bearings. The tester will perform a check of the steering head bearing lower race by mounting the front wheel on a surface plate, then performing a lock to lock check with the weight of the machine on the lower bearing **(see illustration 3)**.
✔ Grasp the fork sliders (lower legs) and attempt to push and pull on the forks **(see illustration 4)**. Any play in the steering head bearings will be felt. Note that in extreme cases, wear of the front fork bushes can be misinterpreted for head bearing play.
✔ Check that the handlebars are securely mounted.
✔ Check that the handlebar grip rubbers are secure. They should by bonded to the bar left end and to the throttle cable pulley on the right end.

Front suspension

✔ With the motorcycle off the stand, hold the front brake on and pump the front forks up and down **(see illustration 5)**. Check that they are adequately damped.
✔ Inspect the area above and around the front fork oil seals **(see illustration 6)**. There should be no sign of oil on the fork tube (stanchion) nor leaking down the slider (lower leg). On models so equipped, check that there is no oil leaking from the anti-dive units.
✔ On models with swingarm front suspension, check that there is no freeplay in the linkage when moved from side to side.

Rear suspension

✔ With the motorcycle off the stand and an assistant supporting the motorcycle by its handlebars, bounce the rear suspension **(see illustration 7)**. Check that the suspension components do not foul on any of the cycle parts and check that the shock absorber(s) provide adequate damping.

3 Front wheel mounted on a surface plate for steering head bearing lower race check

4 Checking the steering head bearings for freeplay

5 Hold the front brake on and pump the front forks up and down to check operation

6 Inspect the area around the fork dust seal for oil leakage (arrow)

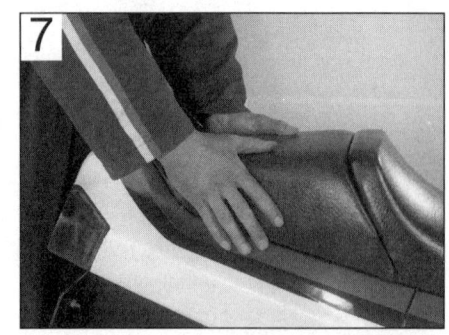

7 Bounce the rear of the motorcycle to check rear suspension operation

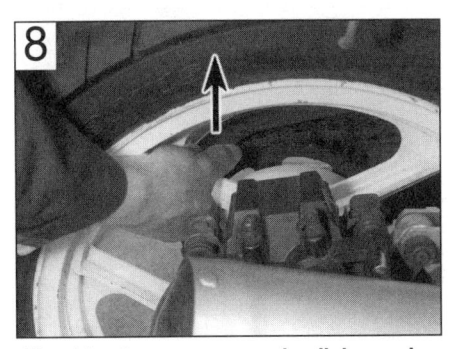

MOT Test Checks REF•29

Checking for rear suspension linkage play

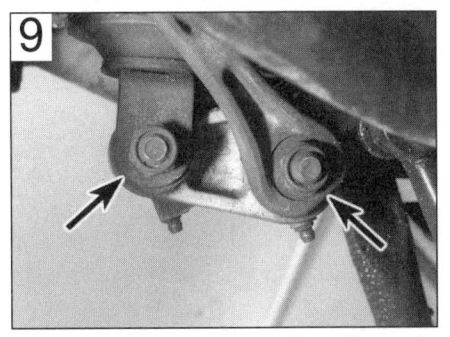

Worn suspension linkage pivots (arrows) are usually the cause of play in the rear suspension

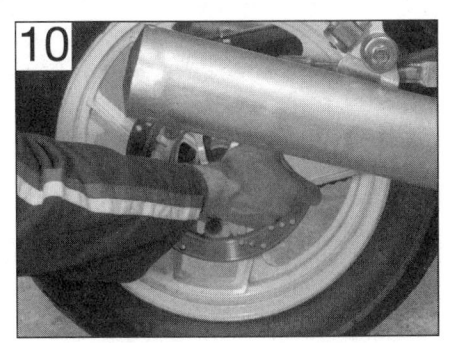

Grasp the swingarm at the ends to check for play in its pivot bearings

✔ Visually inspect the shock absorber(s) and check that there is no sign of oil leakage from its damper. This is somewhat restricted on certain single shock models due to the location of the shock absorber.

✔ With the rear wheel raised off the ground, grasp the wheel at the highest point and attempt to pull it up **(see illustration 8)**. Any play in the swingarm pivot or suspension linkage bearings will be felt as movement. **Note:** *Do not confuse play with actual suspension movement.* Failure to lubricate suspension linkage bearings can lead to bearing failure **(see illustration 9)**.

✔ With the rear wheel raised off the ground, grasp the swingarm ends and attempt to move the swingarm from side to side and forwards and backwards - any play indicates wear of the swingarm pivot bearings **(see illustration 10)**.

Brakes, Wheels and Tyres

Brakes

✔ With the wheel raised off the ground, apply the brake then free it off, and check that the wheel is about to revolve freely without brake drag.

✔ On disc brakes, examine the disc itself. Check that it is securely mounted and not cracked.

✔ On disc brakes, view the pad material through the caliper mouth and check that the pads are not worn down beyond the limit **(see illustration 11)**.

✔ On drum brakes, check that when the brake is applied the angle between the operating lever and cable or rod is not too great **(see illustration 12)**. Check also that the operating lever doesn't foul any other components.

✔ On disc brakes, examine the flexible hoses from top to bottom. Have an assistant hold the brake on so that the fluid in the hose is under pressure, and check that there is no sign of fluid leakage, bulges or cracking. If there are any metal brake pipes or unions, check that these are free from corrosion and damage. Where a brake-linked anti-dive system is fitted, check the hoses to the anti-dive in a similar manner.

✔ Check that the rear brake torque arm is secure and that its fasteners are secured by self-locking nuts or castellated nuts with split-pins or R-pins **(see illustration 13)**.

✔ On models with ABS, check that the self-check warning light in the instrument panel works.

✔ The MOT tester will perform a test of the motorcycle's braking efficiency based on a calculation of rider and motorcycle weight. Although this cannot be carried out at home, you can at least ensure that the braking systems are properly maintained. For hydraulic disc brakes, check the fluid level, lever/pedal feel (bleed of air if its spongy) and pad material. For drum brakes, check adjustment, cable or rod operation and shoe lining thickness.

Wheels and tyres

✔ Check the wheel condition. Cast wheels should be free from cracks and if of the built-up design, all fasteners should be secure. Spoked wheels should be checked for broken, corroded, loose or bent spokes.

✔ With the wheel raised off the ground, spin the wheel and visually check that the tyre and wheel run true. Check that the tyre does not foul the suspension or mudguards.

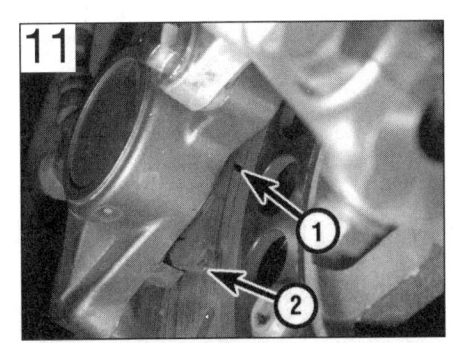

Brake pad wear can usually be viewed without removing the caliper. Most pads have wear indicator grooves (1) and some also have indicator tangs (2)

On drum brakes, check the angle of the operating lever with the brake fully applied. Most drum brakes have a wear indicator pointer and scale.

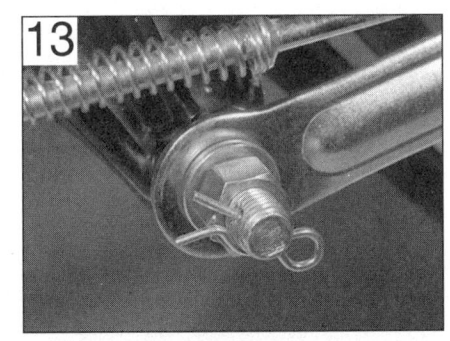

Brake torque arm must be properly secured at both ends

REF•30 MOT Test Checks

Check for wheel bearing play by trying to move the wheel about the axle (spindle)

Checking the tyre tread depth

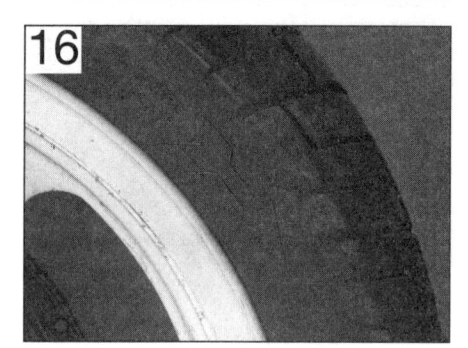

Tyre direction of rotation arrow can be found on tyre sidewall

Castellated type wheel axle (spindle) nut must be secured by a split pin or R-pin

Two straightedges are used to check wheel alignment

✔ With the wheel raised off the ground, grasp the wheel and attempt to move it about the axle (spindle) **(see illustration 14)**. Any play felt here indicates wheel bearing failure.
✔ Check the tyre tread depth, tread condition and sidewall condition **(see illustration 15)**.
✔ Check the tyre type. Front and rear tyre types must be compatible and be suitable for road use. Tyres marked NOT FOR ROAD USE, COMPETITION USE ONLY or similar, will fail the MOT.
✔ If the tyre sidewall carries a direction of rotation arrow, this must be pointing in the direction of normal wheel rotation **(see illustration 16)**.
✔ Check that the wheel axle (spindle) nuts (where applicable) are properly secured. A self-locking nut or castellated nut with a split-pin or R-pin can be used **(see illustration 17)**.
✔ Wheel alignment is checked with the motorcycle off the stand and a rider seated. With the front wheel pointing straight ahead, two perfectly straight lengths of metal or wood and placed against the sidewalls of both tyres **(see illustration 18)**. The gap each side of the front tyre must be equidistant on both sides. Incorrect wheel alignment may be due to a cocked rear wheel (often as the result of poor chain adjustment) or in extreme cases, a bent frame.

General checks and condition

✔ Check the security of all major fasteners, bodypanels, seat, fairings (where fitted) and mudguards.
✔ Check that the rider and pillion footrests, handlebar levers and brake pedal are securely mounted.
✔ Check for corrosion on the frame or any load-bearing components. If severe, this may affect the structure, particularly under stress.

Sidecars

A motorcycle fitted with a sidecar requires additional checks relating to the stability of the machine and security of attachment and swivel joints, plus specific wheel alignment (toe-in) requirements. Additionally, tyre and lighting requirements differ from conventional motorcycle use. Owners are advised to check MOT test requirements with an official test centre.

Storage REF•31

Preparing for storage

Before you start

If repairs or an overhaul is needed, see that this is carried out now rather than left until you want to ride the bike again.

Give the bike a good wash and scrub all dirt from its underside. Make sure the bike dries completely before preparing for storage.

Engine

● Remove the spark plug(s) and lubricate the cylinder bores with approximately a teaspoon of motor oil using a spout-type oil can **(see illustration 1)**. Reinstall the spark plug(s). Crank the engine over a couple of times to coat the piston rings and bores with oil. If the bike has a kickstart, use this to turn the engine over. If not, flick the kill switch to the OFF position and crank the engine over on the starter **(see illustration 2)**. If the nature on the ignition system prevents the starter operating with the kill switch in the OFF position, remove the spark plugs and fit them back in their caps; ensure that the plugs are earthed (grounded) against the cylinder head when the starter is operated **(see illustration 3)**.

⚠ *Warning: It is important that the plugs are earthed (grounded) away from the spark plug holes otherwise there is a risk of atomised fuel from the cylinders igniting.*

HAYNES HiNT *On a single cylinder four-stroke engine, you can seal the combustion chamber completely by positioning the piston at TDC on the compression stroke.*

● Drain the carburettor(s) otherwise there is a risk of jets becoming blocked by gum deposits from the fuel **(see illustration 4)**.

● If the bike is going into long-term storage, consider adding a fuel stabiliser to the fuel in the tank. If the tank is drained completely, corrosion of its internal surfaces may occur if left unprotected for a long period. The tank can be treated with a rust preventative especially for this purpose. Alternatively, remove the tank and pour half a litre of motor oil into it, install the filler cap and shake the tank to coat its internals with oil before draining off the excess. The same effect can also be achieved by spraying WD40 or a similar water-dispersant around the inside of the tank via its flexible nozzle.

● Make sure the cooling system contains the correct mix of antifreeze. Antifreeze also contains important corrosion inhibitors.

● The air intakes and exhaust can be sealed off by covering or plugging the openings. Ensure that you do not seal in any condensation; run the engine until it is hot,

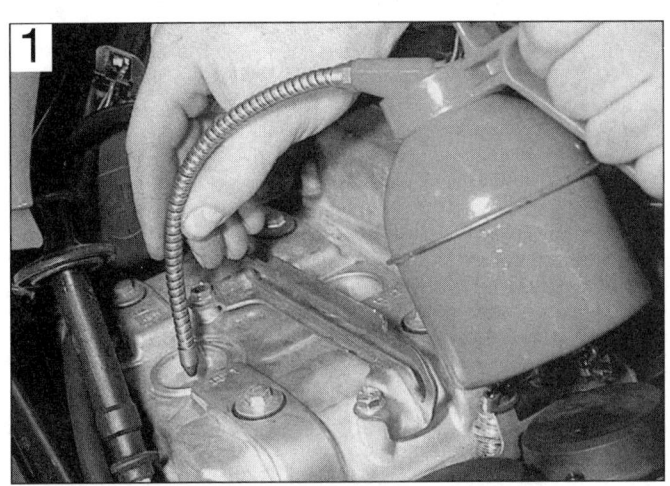

1 Squirt a drop of motor oil into each cylinder

2 Flick the kill switch to OFF . . .

3 . . . and ensure that the metal bodies of the plugs (arrows) are earthed against the cylinder head

4 Connect a hose to the carburettor float chamber drain stub (arrow) and unscrew the drain screw

REF•32 Storage

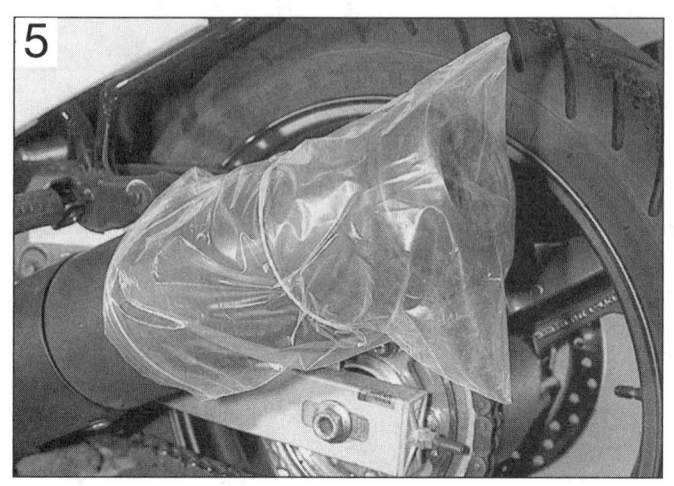

Exhausts can be sealed off with a plastic bag

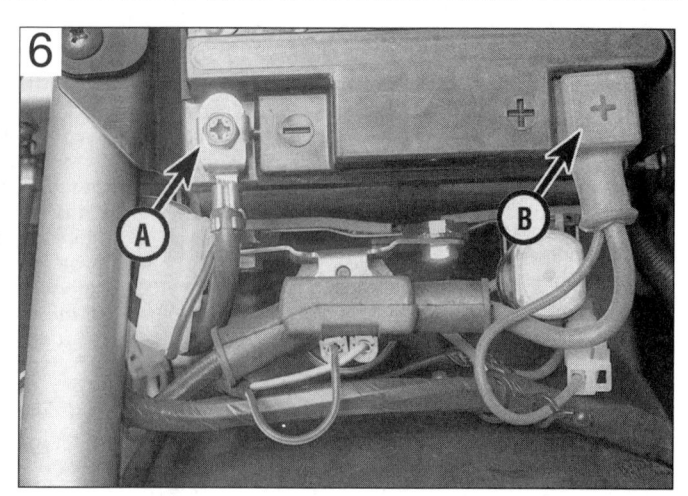

Disconnect the negative lead (A) first, followed by the positive lead (B)

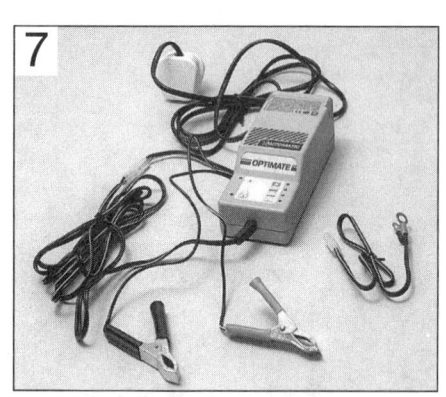

Use a suitable battery charger - this kit also assess battery condition

then switch off and allow to cool. Tape a piece of thick plastic over the silencer end(s) **(see illustration 5)**. Note that some advocate pouring a tablespoon of motor oil into the silencer(s) before sealing them off.

Battery

● Remove it from the bike - in extreme cases of cold the battery may freeze and crack its case **(see illustration 6)**.

● Check the electrolyte level and top up if necessary (conventional refillable batteries). Clean the terminals.
● Store the battery off the motorcycle and away from any sources of fire. Position a wooden block under the battery if it is to sit on the ground.
● Give the battery a trickle charge for a few hours every month **(see illustration 7)**.

Tyres

● Place the bike on its centrestand or an auxiliary stand which will support the motorcycle in an upright position. Position wood blocks under the tyres to keep them off the ground and to provide insulation from damp. If the bike is being put into long-term storage, ideally both tyres should be off the ground; not only will this protect the tyres, but will also ensure that no load is placed on the steering head or wheel bearings.
● Deflate each tyre by 5 to 10 psi, no more or the beads may unseat from the rim, making subsequent inflation difficult on tubeless tyres.

Pivots and controls

● Lubricate all lever, pedal, stand and footrest pivot points. If grease nipples are fitted to the rear suspension components, apply lubricant to the pivots.
● Lubricate all control cables.

Cycle components

● Apply a wax protectant to all painted and plastic components. Wipe off any excess, but don't polish to a shine. Where fitted, clean the screen with soap and water.
● Coat metal parts with Vaseline (petroleum jelly). When applying this to the fork tubes, do not compress the forks otherwise the seals will rot from contact with the Vaseline.
● Apply a vinyl cleaner to the seat.

Storage conditions

● Aim to store the bike in a shed or garage which does not leak and is free from damp.
● Drape an old blanket or bedspread over the bike to protect it from dust and direct contact with sunlight (which will fade paint). This also hides the bike from prying eyes. Beware of tight-fitting plastic covers which may allow condensation to form and settle on the bike.

Getting back on the road

Engine and transmission

● Change the oil and replace the oil filter. If this was done prior to storage, check that the oil hasn't emulsified - a thick whitish substance which occurs through condensation.
● Remove the spark plugs. Using a spout-type oil can, squirt a few drops of oil into the cylinder(s). This will provide initial lubrication as the piston rings and bores comes back into contact. Service the spark plugs, or fit new ones, and install them in the engine.

● Check that the clutch isn't stuck on. The plates can stick together if left standing for some time, preventing clutch operation. Engage a gear and try rocking the bike back and forth with the clutch lever held against the handlebar. If this doesn't work on cable-operated clutches, hold the clutch lever back against the handlebar with a strong elastic band or cable tie for a couple of hours **(see illustration 8)**.
● If the air intakes or silencer end(s) were blocked off, remove the bung or cover used.
● If the fuel tank was coated with a rust

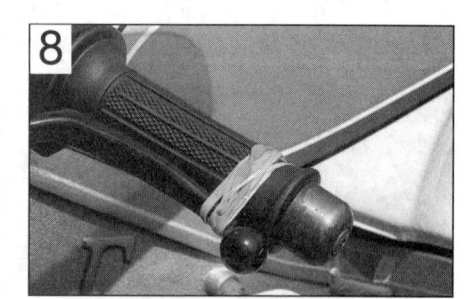

Hold clutch lever back against the handlebar with elastic bands or a cable tie

Storage

preventative, oil or a stabiliser added to the fuel, drain and flush the tank and dispose of the fuel sensibly. If no action was taken with the fuel tank prior to storage, it is advised that the old fuel is disposed of since it will go off over a period of time. Refill the fuel tank with fresh fuel.

Frame and running gear

- Oil all pivot points and cables.
- Check the tyre pressures. They will definitely need inflating if pressures were reduced for storage.
- Lubricate the final drive chain (where applicable).
- Remove any protective coating applied to the fork tubes (stanchions) since this may well destroy the fork seals. If the fork tubes weren't protected and have picked up rust spots, remove them with very fine abrasive paper and refinish with metal polish.
- Check that both brakes operate correctly. Apply each brake hard and check that it's not possible to move the motorcycle forwards, then check that the brake frees off again once released. Brake caliper pistons can stick due to corrosion around the piston head, or on the sliding caliper types, due to corrosion of the slider pins. If the brake doesn't free after repeated operation, take the caliper off for examination. Similarly drum brakes can stick due to a seized operating cam, cable or rod linkage.
- If the motorcycle has been in long-term storage, renew the brake fluid and clutch fluid (where applicable).
- Depending on where the bike has been stored, the wiring, cables and hoses may have been nibbled by rodents. Make a visual check and investigate disturbed wiring loom tape.

Battery

- If the battery has been previously removal and given top up charges it can simply be reconnected. Remember to connect the positive cable first and the negative cable last.
- On conventional refillable batteries, if the battery has not received any attention, remove it from the motorcycle and check its electrolyte level. Top up if necessary then charge the battery. If the battery fails to hold a charge and a visual checks show heavy white sulphation of the plates, the battery is probably defective and must be renewed. This is particularly likely if the battery is old. Confirm battery condition with a specific gravity check.
- On sealed (MF) batteries, if the battery has not received any attention, remove it from the motorcycle and charge it according to the information on the battery case - if the battery fails to hold a charge it must be renewed.

Starting procedure

- If a kickstart is fitted, turn the engine over a couple of times with the ignition OFF to distribute oil around the engine. If no kickstart is fitted, flick the engine kill switch OFF and the ignition ON and crank the engine over a couple of times to work oil around the upper cylinder components. If the nature of the ignition system is such that the starter won't work with the kill switch OFF, remove the spark plugs, fit them back into their caps and earth (ground) their bodies on the cylinder head. Reinstall the spark plugs afterwards.
- Switch the kill switch to RUN, operate the choke and start the engine. If the engine won't start don't continue cranking the engine - not only will this flatten the battery, but the starter motor will overheat. Switch the ignition off and try again later. If the engine refuses to start, go through the fault finding procedures in this manual. **Note:** *If the bike has been in storage for a long time, old fuel or a carburettor blockage may be the problem. Gum deposits in carburettors can block jets - if a carburettor cleaner doesn't prove successful the carburettors must be dismantled for cleaning.*
- Once the engine has started, check that the lights, turn signals and horn work properly.
- Treat the bike gently for the first ride and check all fluid levels on completion. Settle the bike back into the maintenance schedule.

REF•34 Fault Finding

This Section provides an easy reference-guide to the more common faults that are likely to afflict your machine. Obviously, the opportunities are almost limitless for faults to occur as a result of obscure failures, and to try and cover all eventualities would require a book. Indeed, a number have been written on the subject.

Successful troubleshooting is not a mysterious 'black art' but the application of a bit of knowledge combined with a systematic and logical approach to the problem. Approach any troubleshooting by first accurately identifying the symptom and then checking through the list of possible causes, starting with the simplest or most obvious and progressing in stages to the most complex.

Take nothing for granted, but above all apply liberal quantities of common sense.

The main symptom of a fault is given in the text as a major heading below which are listed the various systems or areas which may contain the fault. Details of each possible cause for a fault and the remedial action to be taken are given, in brief, in the paragraphs below each heading. Further information should be sought in the relevant Chapter.

1 Engine doesn't start or is difficult to start
- ☐ Starter motor doesn't rotate
- ☐ Starter motor rotates but engine does not turn over
- ☐ Starter works but engine won't turn over (seized)
- ☐ No fuel flow
- ☐ Engine flooded
- ☐ No spark or weak spark
- ☐ Compression low
- ☐ Stalls after starting
- ☐ Rough idle

2 Poor running at low speed
- ☐ Spark weak
- ☐ Fuel/air mixture incorrect
- ☐ Compression low
- ☐ Poor acceleration

3 Poor running or no power at high speed
- ☐ Firing incorrect
- ☐ Fuel/air mixture incorrect
- ☐ Compression low
- ☐ Knocking or pinking
- ☐ Miscellaneous causes

4 Overheating
- ☐ Engine overheats
- ☐ Firing incorrect
- ☐ Fuel/air mixture incorrect
- ☐ Compression too high
- ☐ Engine load excessive
- ☐ Lubrication inadequate
- ☐ Miscellaneous causes

5 Clutch problems
- ☐ Clutch slipping
- ☐ Clutch not disengaging completely

6 Gearchange problems
- ☐ Doesn't go into gear, or lever doesn't return
- ☐ Jumps out of gear
- ☐ Overselects

7 Abnormal engine noise
- ☐ Knocking or pinking
- ☐ Piston slap or rattling
- ☐ Valve noise
- ☐ Other noise

8 Abnormal driveline noise
- ☐ Clutch noise
- ☐ Transmission noise
- ☐ Final drive noise

9 Abnormal frame and suspension noise
- ☐ Front end noise
- ☐ Rear suspension noise
- ☐ Brake noise

10 Oil pressure warning light comes on
- ☐ Engine lubrication system
- ☐ Electrical system

11 Excessive exhaust smoke
- ☐ White smoke
- ☐ Black smoke
- ☐ Brown smoke

12 Poor handling or stability
- ☐ Handlebar hard to turn
- ☐ Handlebar shakes or vibrates excessively
- ☐ Handlebar pulls to one side
- ☐ Poor shock absorbing qualities

13 Braking problems
- ☐ Brakes are spongy, don't hold
- ☐ Brake lever or pedal pulsates
- ☐ Brakes drag

14 Electrical problems
- ☐ Battery dead or weak
- ☐ Battery overcharged

Fault Finding   REF•35

1 Engine doesn't start or is difficult to start

Starter motor doesn't rotate
- [ ] Engine kill switch OFF.
- [ ] Fuse blown. Check main fuse and ignition circuit fuse (Chapter 9).
- [ ] Battery voltage low. Check and recharge battery (Chapter 9).
- [ ] Starter motor defective. Make sure the wiring to the starter is secure. Make sure the starter relay clicks when the start button is pushed. If the relay clicks, then the fault is in the wiring or motor.
- [ ] Starter relay faulty. Check it according to the procedure in Chapter 9.
- [ ] Starter button not contacting. The contacts could be wet, corroded or dirty. Disassemble and clean the switch (Chapter 9).
- [ ] Wiring open or shorted. Check all wiring connections and harnesses to make sure that they are dry, tight and not corroded. Also check for broken or frayed wires that can cause a short to ground (earth) (see wiring diagram, Chapter 9).
- [ ] Ignition (main) switch defective. Check the switch according to the procedure in Chapter 9. Replace the switch with a new one if it is defective.
- [ ] Engine kill switch defective. Check for wet, dirty or corroded contacts. Clean or replace the switch as necessary (Chapter 9).
- [ ] Faulty gear position switch, sidestand switch or clutch switch. Check the wiring to each switch and the switch itself according to the procedures in Chapter 9. Also check the diodes.

Starter motor rotates but engine does not turn over
- [ ] Starter clutch defective. Inspect and repair or replace (Chapter 2).
- [ ] Damaged idle/reduction or starter gears. Inspect and renew the damaged parts (Chapter 2).

Starter works but engine won't turn over (seized)
- [ ] Seized engine caused by one or more internally damaged components. Failure due to wear, abuse or lack of lubrication. Damage can include seized valves, followers, camshafts, pistons, crankshaft, connecting rod bearings, or transmission gears or bearings. Refer to Chapter 2 for engine disassembly.

No fuel flow
- [ ] No fuel in tank.
- [ ] Fuel tank breather hose obstructed.
- [ ] Fuel pump assembly filter/strainer clogged. Remove the pump and clean or renew the filter and/or strainer (Chapters 1 and 4).
- [ ] Fuel hose clogged or pinched through incorrect routing. Remove the fuel tank and check the hoses (Chapters 4 and 1).
- [ ] Faulty fuel pump relay. Check the relay (see Chapter 4).
- [ ] Fuel pump faulty. Check the fuel pump pressure (Chapter 4).

Engine flooded
- [ ] Faulty pressure regulator – if it is stuck closed there could be excessive pressure in the fuel rail. Check as described in Chapter 4.
- [ ] Injector(s) stuck open, allowing a constant flow of fuel into the engine. Check as described in Chapter 4.
- [ ] Starting technique incorrect. When the engine is cold, use the fast idle lever on the handlebar and no throttle. When the engine is warm use a small amount of throttle.

No spark or weak spark
- [ ] Engine kill switch turned to the OFF position.
- [ ] Battery voltage low. Check and recharge the battery as necessary (Chapter 9).
- [ ] Spark plugs dirty, defective or worn out. Locate reason for fouled plugs using spark plug condition chart and follow the plug maintenance procedures (Chapter 1).
- [ ] Spark plug caps/ignition coils faulty or not making good contact over the spark plugs. Check condition. Replace if cracks or deterioration are evident (Chapter 5).
- [ ] ECM defective. Check the unit, referring to Chapter 5 or 4 for details.
- [ ] Crankshaft position sensor defective. Check the unit, referring to Chapter 4 for details.
- [ ] Ignition or kill switch shorted. This is usually caused by water, corrosion, damage or excessive wear. The switches can be disassembled and cleaned with electrical contact cleaner. If cleaning does not help, renew the switches (Chapter 9).
- [ ] Wiring shorted or broken between:
    a)   Ignition (main) switch and engine kill switch (or blown fuse)
    b)   ECM and engine kill switch
    c)   ECM and ignition coils
    d)   ECM and crankshaft position sensor
- [ ] Make sure that all wiring connections are clean, dry and tight. Look for chafed and broken wires (Chapters 4, 5 and 9).

Compression low
- [ ] Spark plugs loose. Remove the plugs and inspect their threads. Reinstall and tighten to the specified torque (Chapter 1).
- [ ] Cylinder head not sufficiently tightened down. If the cylinder head is suspected of being loose, then there's a chance that the gasket or head is damaged if the problem has persisted for any length of time. The head bolts should be tightened to the proper torque in the correct sequence (Chapter 2).
- [ ] Incorrect valve clearance. This means that the valve is not closing completely and compression pressure is leaking past the valve. Check and adjust the valve clearances (Chapter 1).
- [ ] Cylinder and/or piston worn. Excessive wear will cause compression pressure to leak past the rings. This is usually accompanied by worn rings as well. A top-end overhaul is necessary (Chapter 2).
- [ ] Piston rings worn, weak, broken, or sticking. Broken or sticking piston rings usually indicate a lubrication or fuelling problem that causes excess carbon deposits or seizures to form on the pistons and rings. Top-end overhaul is necessary (Chapter 2).
- [ ] Piston ring-to-groove clearance excessive. This is caused by excessive wear of the piston ring lands. Piston replacement is necessary (Chapter 2).
- [ ] Cylinder head gasket damaged. If the head is allowed to become loose, or if excessive carbon build-up on the piston crown and combustion chamber causes extremely high compression, the head gasket may leak. Re-torquing the head is not always sufficient to restore the seal, so gasket renewal is necessary (Chapter 2).
- [ ] Cylinder head warped. This is caused by overheating or improperly tightened head bolts. Machine shop resurfacing or head replacement is necessary (Chapter 2).
- [ ] Valve spring broken or weak. Caused by component failure or wear; the springs must be renewed (Chapter 2).
- [ ] Valve not seating properly. This is caused by a bent valve (from over-revving or improper valve adjustment), burned valve or seat (improper fuelling) or an accumulation of carbon deposits on the seat (from fuelling or lubrication problems). The valves must be cleaned and/or renewed and the seats serviced if possible (Chapter 2).

1 Engine doesn't start or is difficult to start (continued)

Stalls after starting

- [ ] Ignition malfunction. See Chapter 5.
- [ ] Fuel injection system malfunction. See Chapter 4.
- [ ] Fuel contaminated. The fuel can be contaminated with either dirt or water, or can change chemically if the machine is allowed to sit for several months or more. Drain the tank and fuel rail (Chapter 4). Also check that the fuel flows freely and is not being restricted.
- [ ] Fuel pump assembly filter/strainer clogged. Remove the pump and clean or renew the filter and/or strainer (Chapters 1 and 4).
- [ ] Fuel hose clogged or pinched through incorrect routing. Remove the fuel tank and check the hoses (Chapters 4 and 1).
- [ ] Fuel pump faulty – perform a pressure check (see Chapter 4).
- [ ] Intake air leak. Check for loose throttle body-to-intake manifold connections, loose or missing vacuum gauge adapter blanking caps or hoses (Chapter 4).
- [ ] Engine idle speed incorrect (see Chapter 1). Also check the fast idle system (See Chapter 4).

Rough idle

- [ ] Ignition malfunction. See Chapter 5.
- [ ] Idle speed incorrect. See Chapter 1.
- [ ] Throttle bodies not synchronised. Adjust with vacuum gauge or manometer set as described in Chapter 1.
- [ ] Throttle body or fuel injection system malfunction. See Chapter 4.
- [ ] Fuel contaminated. The fuel can be contaminated with either dirt or water, or can change chemically if the machine is allowed to sit for several months or more. Drain the tank and fuel rail (Chapter 4).
- [ ] Intake air leak. Check for loose throttle body-to-intake manifold connections, loose or missing vacuum take-off point blanking caps or hoses (Chapter 4).
- [ ] Air filter clogged. Clean or renew the air filter element (Chapter 1).

2 Poor running at low speeds

Spark weak

- [ ] Battery voltage low. Check and recharge battery (Chapter 9).
- [ ] Spark plugs fouled, defective or worn out. Refer to Chapter 1 for spark plug maintenance.
- [ ] Incorrect spark plugs. Wrong type, heat range or cap configuration. Check and install correct plugs listed in Chapter 1.
- [ ] ECM defective. Check the unit, referring to Chapter 4 for details.
- [ ] Crankshaft position sensor defective. See Chapter 4.
- [ ] Ignition HT coils/spark plug caps defective or not making good contact with spark plugs. See Chapter 5.

Fuel/air mixture incorrect

- [ ] Fuel injection system malfunction (see Chapter 4).
- [ ] Fuel injector clogged (see Chapter 4).
- [ ] Fuel pump or pressure regulator faulty (see Chapter 4).
- [ ] Throttle body intake manifolds loose. Check for cracks, breaks, tears or loose clamps. Renew the rubber intake manifold joints if split or perished.
- [ ] Air filter clogged, poorly sealed or missing (Chapter 1).
- [ ] Air filter housing poorly sealed. Look for cracks, holes or loose clamps and renew or repair defective parts.
- [ ] Fuel tank breather hose obstructed.

Compression low

- [ ] Spark plugs loose. Remove the plugs and inspect their threads. Reinstall and tighten to the specified torque (Chapter 1).
- [ ] Cylinder head not sufficiently tightened down. If the cylinder head is suspected of being loose, then there's a chance that the gasket and head are damaged if the problem has persisted for any length of time. The head bolts should be tightened to the proper torque in the correct sequence (Chapter 2).
- [ ] Incorrect valve clearance. This means that the valve is not closing completely and compression pressure is leaking past the valve. Check and adjust the valve clearances (Chapter 1).
- [ ] Cylinder and/or piston worn. Excessive wear will cause compression pressure to leak past the rings. This is usually accompanied by worn rings as well. A top-end overhaul is necessary (Chapter 2).
- [ ] Piston rings worn, weak, broken, or sticking. Broken or sticking piston rings usually indicate a lubrication or fuelling problem that causes excess carbon deposits or seizures to form on the pistons and rings. Top-end overhaul is necessary (Chapter 2).
- [ ] Piston ring-to-groove clearance excessive. This is caused by excessive wear of the piston ring lands. Piston renewal is necessary (Chapter 2).
- [ ] Cylinder head gasket damaged. If the head is allowed to become loose, or if excessive carbon build-up on the piston crown and combustion chamber causes extremely high compression, the head gasket may leak. Retorquing the head is not always sufficient to restore the seal, so gasket renewal is necessary (Chapter 2).
- [ ] Cylinder head warped. This is caused by overheating or improperly tightened head bolts. Machine shop resurfacing or head renewal is necessary (Chapter 2).
- [ ] Valve spring broken or weak. Caused by component failure or wear; the springs must be renewed (Chapter 2).
- [ ] Valve not seating properly. This is caused by a bent valve (from over-revving or improper valve adjustment), burned valve or seat (improper fuelling) or an accumulation of carbon deposits on the seat (from fuelling, lubrication problems). The valves must be cleaned and/or renewed and the seats serviced if possible (Chapter 2).

Poor acceleration

- [ ] Throttle bodies leaking or dirty. Overhaul them (Chapter 4).
- [ ] Fuel injection system malfunction, faulty fuel pump, or pressure regulator – see Chapter 4.
- [ ] Fuel pump assembly filter/strainer clogged. Remove the pump and clean or renew the filter and/or strainer (Chapters 1 and 4).
- [ ] Fuel hose clogged or pinched through incorrect routing. Remove the fuel tank and check the hoses (Chapters 4 and 1).
- [ ] Timing not advancing. The CKP sensor or ECM may be defective. If so, they must be renewed, as they can't be repaired. Check them (see Chapter 4).
- [ ] Throttle bodies not synchronised. Adjust them with a vacuum gauge set or manometer as described in Chapter 1.
- [ ] Engine oil viscosity too high. Using a heavier oil than that recommended in Chapter 1 can damage the oil pump or lubrication system and cause drag on the engine.
- [ ] Brakes dragging. Usually caused by debris which has entered the brake piston seals, or from a warped disc or bent axle. Repair as necessary (Chapter 7).

Fault Finding REF•37

3 Poor running or no power at high speed

Firing incorrect
- ☐ Air filter restricted. Clean or renew filter (Chapter 1).
- ☐ Spark plugs fouled, defective or worn out. See Chapter 1 for spark plug maintenance.
- ☐ Incorrect spark plugs. Wrong type, heat range or cap configuration. Check and install correct plugs listed in Chapter 1.
- ☐ ECM defective. See Chapter 4.
- ☐ Ignition HT coils/spark plug caps defective or not making good contact with spark plugs. See Chapter 5.

Fuel/air mixture incorrect
- ☐ Fuel injection system malfunction (see Chapter 4).
- ☐ Fuel injector clogged (see Chapter 4).
- ☐ Fuel pump or pressure regulator faulty (see Chapter 4).
- ☐ Throttle body intake manifolds loose. Check for cracks, breaks, tears or loose clamps. Renew the rubber intake manifold joints if split or perished.
- ☐ Air filter clogged, poorly sealed or missing (Chapter 1).
- ☐ Air filter housing poorly sealed. Look for cracks, holes or loose clamps and renew or repair defective parts.
- ☐ Fuel tank breather hose obstructed.

Compression low
- ☐ Spark plugs loose. Remove the plugs and inspect their threads. Reinstall and tighten to the specified torque (Chapter 1).
- ☐ Cylinder head not sufficiently tightened down. If the cylinder head is suspected of being loose, then there's a chance that the gasket and head are damaged if the problem has persisted for any length of time. The head bolts should be tightened to the proper torque in the correct sequence (Chapter 2).
- ☐ Incorrect valve clearance. This means that the valve is not closing completely and compression pressure is leaking past the valve. Check and adjust the valve clearances (Chapter 1).
- ☐ Cylinder and/or piston worn. Excessive wear will cause compression pressure to leak past the rings. This is usually accompanied by worn rings as well. A top-end overhaul is necessary (Chapter 2).
- ☐ Piston rings worn, weak, broken, or sticking. Broken or sticking piston rings usually indicate a lubrication problem that causes excess carbon deposits or seizures to form on the pistons and rings. A top-end overhaul is necessary (Chapter 2).
- ☐ Piston ring-to-groove clearance excessive. This is caused by excessive wear of the piston ring lands. Piston renewal is necessary (Chapter 2).
- ☐ Cylinder head gasket damaged. If the head is allowed to become loose, or if excessive carbon build-up on the piston crown and combustion chamber causes extremely high compression, the head gasket may leak. Retorquing the head is not always sufficient to restore the seal, so gasket renewal is necessary (Chapter 2).
- ☐ Cylinder head warped. This is caused by overheating or improperly tightened head bolts. Machine shop resurfacing or head renewal is necessary (Chapter 2).
- ☐ Valve spring broken or weak. Caused by component failure or wear; the springs must be renewed (Chapter 2).
- ☐ Valve not seating properly. This is caused by a bent valve (from over-revving or improper valve adjustment), burned valve or seat (improper fuelling) or an accumulation of carbon deposits on the seat (from fuelling or lubrication problems). The valves must be cleaned and/or renewed and the seats serviced if possible (Chapter 2).

Knocking or pinking
- ☐ Carbon build-up in combustion chamber. Use of a fuel additive that will dissolve the adhesive bonding the carbon particles to the crown and chamber is the easiest way to remove the build-up. Otherwise, the cylinder head will have to be removed and decarbonised (Chapter 2).
- ☐ Incorrect or poor quality fuel. Old or improper grades of fuel can cause detonation. This causes the piston to rattle, thus the knocking or pinking sound. Drain old fuel and always use the recommended fuel grade.
- ☐ Spark plug heat range incorrect. Uncontrolled detonation indicates the plug heat range is too hot. The plug in effect becomes a glow plug, raising cylinder temperatures. Install the proper heat range plug (Chapter 1).
- ☐ Improper air/fuel mixture. This will cause the cylinders to run hot, which leads to detonation. Clogged injectors or an air leak can cause this imbalance. See Chapter 4.

Miscellaneous causes
- ☐ Fuel pump assembly filter/strainer clogged. Remove the pump and clean or renew the filter and/or strainer (Chapters 1 and 4).
- ☐ Fuel hose clogged or pinched through incorrect routing. Remove the fuel tank and check the hoses (Chapters 4 and 1).
- ☐ Throttle valve doesn't open fully. Adjust the throttle grip freeplay (Chapter 1).
- ☐ Clutch slipping. May be caused by loose or worn clutch components. Refer to Chapter 2 for clutch overhaul procedures.
- ☐ Timing not advancing – faulty ECM.
- ☐ Engine oil viscosity too high. Using a heavier oil than the one recommended in Chapter 1 can damage the oil pump or lubrication system and cause drag on the engine.
- ☐ Brakes dragging. Usually caused by debris which has entered the brake piston seals, or from a warped disc or bent axle. Repair as necessary.

REF•38 Fault Finding

4 Overheating

Engine overheats
- ☐ Coolant level low. Check and add coolant (Chapter 1).
- ☐ Leak in cooling system. Check cooling system hoses and radiator for leaks and other damage. Repair or renew parts as necessary (Chapter 3).
- ☐ Thermostat sticking open or closed. Test as described in Chapter 3.
- ☐ Faulty radiator cap. Remove the cap and have it pressure tested by a dealer.
- ☐ Coolant passages clogged. Drain and flush the entire system, then refill with fresh coolant (Chapter 1).
- ☐ Water pump defective. Remove the pump and check the components (Chapter 3).
- ☐ Clogged radiator fins. Clean them by blowing compressed air through the fins from the rear side of the radiator.
- ☐ Cooling fan motor or fan motor switch fault (Chapter 3).

Firing incorrect
- ☐ Spark plugs fouled, defective or worn out. See Chapter 1 for spark plug maintenance.
- ☐ Incorrect spark plugs.
- ☐ ECM defective (Chapter 4).
- ☐ Crankshaft position sensor faulty (Chapter 4).
- ☐ Faulty HT ignition coils/spark plug caps (Chapter 5).

Fuel/air mixture incorrect
- ☐ Fuel injection system malfunction (see Chapter 4).
- ☐ Fuel injector clogged (see Chapter 4).
- ☐ Fuel pump or pressure regulator faulty (see Chapter 4).
- ☐ Throttle body intake manifolds loose. Check for cracks, breaks, tears or loose clamps. Renew the rubber intake manifold joints if split or perished.
- ☐ Air filter clogged, poorly sealed or missing (Chapter 1).
- ☐ Air filter housing poorly sealed. Look for cracks, holes or loose clamps and renew or repair defective parts.
- ☐ Fuel tank breather hose obstructed.

Compression too high
- ☐ Carbon build-up in combustion chamber. Use of a fuel additive that will dissolve the adhesive bonding the carbon particles to the piston crown and chamber is the easiest way to remove the build-up. Otherwise, the cylinder head will have to be removed and decarbonised (Chapter 2).

Engine load excessive
- ☐ Clutch slipping. Can be caused by damaged, loose or worn clutch components. Refer to Chapter 2 for overhaul procedures.
- ☐ Engine oil level too high. The addition of too much oil will cause pressurisation of the crankcase and inefficient engine operation. Check Specifications and drain to proper level (Chapter 1 and *Daily (pre-ride) checks*).
- ☐ Engine oil viscosity too high. Using a heavier oil than the one recommended in Chapter 1 can damage the oil pump or lubrication system as well as cause drag on the engine.
- ☐ Brakes dragging. Usually caused by debris which has entered the brake piston seals, or from a warped disc or bent axle. Repair as necessary.

Lubrication inadequate
- ☐ Engine oil level too low. Friction caused by intermittent lack of lubrication or from oil that is overworked can cause overheating. The oil provides a definite cooling function in the engine. Check the oil level (Chapter 1).
- ☐ Poor quality engine oil or incorrect viscosity or type. Oil is rated not only according to viscosity but also according to type. Some oils are not rated high enough for use in this engine. Check the Specifications section and change to the correct oil (Chapter 1).
- ☐ Worn oil pump – check the oil pressure (Chapter 1).

Miscellaneous causes
- ☐ Modification to exhaust system. Most aftermarket exhaust systems cause the engine to run leaner, which make them run hotter.

5 Clutch problems

Clutch slipping
- ☐ Clutch master or release cylinder faulty (Chapter 4).
- ☐ Friction plates worn or warped. Overhaul the clutch assembly (Chapter 2).
- ☐ Plain plates warped (Chapter 2).
- ☐ Clutch springs broken or weak. Old or heat-damaged (from slipping clutch) springs should be replaced with new ones (Chapter 2).
- ☐ Clutch release mechanism defective. Replace any defective parts (Chapter 2).
- ☐ Clutch centre or housing unevenly worn. This causes improper engagement of the plates. Renew the damaged or worn parts (Chapter 2).

Clutch not disengaging completely
- ☐ Clutch master or release cylinder faulty, or system requires bleeding (Chapter 4).
- ☐ Clutch plates warped or damaged. This will cause clutch drag, which in turn will cause the machine to creep. Overhaul the clutch assembly (Chapter 2).
- ☐ Clutch spring tension uneven. Usually caused by a sagged or broken spring. Check and renew the springs as a set (Chapter 2).
- ☐ Engine oil deteriorated. Old, thin, worn out oil will not provide proper lubrication for the plates, causing the clutch to drag. Renew the oil and filter (Chapter 1).
- ☐ Engine oil viscosity too high. Using a heavier oil than recommended in Chapter 1 can cause the plates to stick together, putting a drag on the engine. Change to the correct weight oil (Chapter 1).
- ☐ Clutch housing spacer seized on gearbox input shaft. Lack of lubrication, severe wear or damage can cause the spacer to seize on the shaft. Overhaul of the clutch, and perhaps transmission, may be necessary to repair the damage (Chapter 2).
- ☐ Clutch release mechanism defective (Chapter 2).
- ☐ Loose clutch centre nut. Causes housing and centre misalignment putting a drag on the engine. Engagement adjustment continually varies. Overhaul the clutch assembly (Chapter 2).

Fault Finding   REF•39

6 Gearchange problems

Doesn't go into gear or lever doesn't return
- [ ] Clutch not disengaging. See above.
- [ ] Selector fork(s) bent or seized. Often caused by dropping the machine or from lack of lubrication. Overhaul the transmission (Chapter 2).
- [ ] Gear(s) stuck on shaft. Most often caused by a lack of lubrication or excessive wear in transmission bearings and bushings. Overhaul the transmission (Chapter 2).
- [ ] Selector drum binding. Caused by lubrication failure or excessive wear. Renew the drum and bearing (Chapter 2).
- [ ] Gearchange lever return spring weak or broken (Chapter 2).
- [ ] Gearchange lever broken. Splines stripped out of lever or shaft, caused by allowing the lever to get loose or from accident damage. Renew necessary parts (Chapter 2).
- [ ] Gearchange mechanism stopper arm broken or worn. Full engagement and rotary movement of selector drum results. Renew the arm (Chapter 2).
- [ ] Stopper arm spring broken. Allows arm to float, causing sporadic shift operation. Renew spring (Chapter 2).

Jumps out of gear
- [ ] Selector fork(s) worn. Overhaul the transmission (Chapter 2).
- [ ] Gear groove(s) worn. Overhaul the transmission (Chapter 2).
- [ ] Gear dogs or dog slots worn or damaged. The gears should be inspected and renewed if necessary.

Overselects
- [ ] Stopper arm spring weak or broken (Chapter 2).
- [ ] Gearchange shaft return spring post broken or distorted (Chapter 2).

7 Abnormal engine noise

Knocking or pinking
- [ ] Carbon build-up in combustion chamber. Use of a fuel additive that will dissolve the adhesive bonding the carbon particles to the piston crown and chamber is the easiest way to remove the build-up. Otherwise, the cylinder head will have to be removed and decarbonised (Chapter 2).
- [ ] Incorrect or poor quality fuel. Old or improper fuel can cause detonation. This causes the pistons to rattle, thus the knocking or pinking sound. Drain the old fuel and always use the recommended grade fuel (Chapter 4).
- [ ] Spark plug heat range incorrect. Uncontrolled detonation indicates that the plug heat range is too hot. The plug in effect becomes a glow plug, raising cylinder temperatures. Install the proper heat range plug (Chapter 1).
- [ ] Improper fuel/air mixture. This will cause the cylinders to run hot and lead to detonation. Clogged injectors or an air leak can cause this imbalance. See Chapter 4.

Piston slap or rattling
- [ ] Cylinder-to-piston clearance excessive. Caused by improper assembly. Inspect and overhaul top-end parts (Chapter 2).
- [ ] Connecting rod bent. Caused by over-revving, trying to start a badly flooded engine or from ingesting a foreign object into the combustion chamber. Renew the damaged parts (Chapter 2).
- [ ] Piston pin or piston pin bore worn or seized from wear or lack of lubrication. Renew damaged parts (Chapter 2).
- [ ] Piston ring(s) worn, broken or sticking. Overhaul the top-end (Chapter 2).
- [ ] Piston seizure damage. Usually from lack of lubrication or overheating. Renew the pistons and bore the cylinders, as necessary (Chapter 2).
- [ ] Connecting rod small or big-end clearance excessive. Caused by excessive wear or lack of lubrication. Renew worn parts.

Valve noise
- [ ] Incorrect valve clearances. Adjust the clearances by referring to Chapter 1.
- [ ] Valve spring broken or weak. Check and renew weak valve springs (Chapter 2).
- [ ] Camshaft or cylinder head worn or damaged. Lack of lubrication at high rpm is usually the cause of damage. Insufficient oil or failure to change the oil at the recommended intervals are the chief causes. Since there are no replaceable bearings in the head, the head and camshaft holders will have to be renewed if there is excessive wear or damage (Chapter 2).

Other noise
- [ ] Cylinder head gasket leaking.
- [ ] Exhaust pipe leaking at cylinder head connection. Caused by improper fit of pipe or loose exhaust flange. All exhaust fasteners should be tightened evenly and carefully. Failure to do this will lead to a leak.
- [ ] Crankshaft runout excessive. Caused by a bent crankshaft (from over-revving) or damage from an upper cylinder component failure. Can also be attributed to dropping the machine on either of the crankshaft ends.
- [ ] Engine mounting bolts loose. Tighten all engine mount bolts (Chapter 2).
- [ ] Crankshaft bearings worn (Chapter 2).
- [ ] Cam chain tensioner defective, cam chain or guide blades worn. Check according to the procedure in Chapter 2.

8 Abnormal driveline noise

Clutch noise
- [ ] Clutch housing/friction plate clearance excessive (Chapter 2).
- [ ] Loose or damaged clutch pressure plate and/or bolts (Chapter 2).

Transmission noise
- [ ] Bearings worn. Also includes the possibility that the shafts are worn. Overhaul the transmission (Chapter 2).
- [ ] Gears worn or chipped (Chapter 2).
- [ ] Metal chips jammed in gear teeth. Probably pieces from a broken clutch, gear or selector mechanism that were picked up by the gears. This will cause early bearing failure (Chapter 2).
- [ ] Engine oil level too low. Causes a howl from transmission. Also affects engine power and clutch operation (Chapter 1).

Final drive noise
- [ ] Chain not adjusted properly (Chapter 1).
- [ ] Front or rear sprocket loose. Tighten fasteners (Chapter 6).
- [ ] Sprockets worn. Renew sprockets (Chapter 6).
- [ ] Rear sprocket warped. Renew sprockets (Chapter 6).
- [ ] Rubber dampers in rear wheel hub worn. Check and renew (Chapter 7).

9 Abnormal frame and suspension noise

Front end noise

- ☐ Low fluid level or improper viscosity oil in forks. This can sound like spurting and is usually accompanied by irregular fork action (Chapter 6).
- ☐ Spring weak or broken. Makes a clicking or scraping sound. Fork oil, when drained, will have a lot of metal particles in it (Chapter 6).
- ☐ Steering head bearings loose or damaged. Clicks when braking. Check and adjust or replace as necessary (Chapters 1 and 6).
- ☐ Fork yokes loose. Make sure all clamp pinch bolts are tightened to the specified torque (Chapter 6).
- ☐ Fork tube bent. Good possibility if machine has been dropped. Replace tube with a new one (Chapter 6).
- ☐ Front axle bolt or axle clamp bolts loose. Tighten them to the specified torque (Chapter 7).
- ☐ Loose or worn wheel bearings. Check and renew as necessary (Chapter 7).

Rear suspension noise

- ☐ Fluid level incorrect. Indicates a leak caused by defective seal. Shock will be covered with oil. Renew shock or seek advice on repair from a Suzuki dealer or suspension specialist (Chapter 6).
- ☐ Defective shock absorber with internal damage – this is in the body of the shock and can't be remedied. The shock must be replaced with a new one or rebuilt by a suspension specialist.
- ☐ Bent or damaged shock body. Replace with a new one (Chapter 6).
- ☐ Loose or worn suspension linkage or swingarm components. Check and renew as necessary (Chapter 6).

Brake noise

- ☐ Squeal caused by pad shim not installed or positioned correctly (where fitted) (Chapter 7).
- ☐ Squeal caused by dust on brake pads. Usually found in combination with glazed pads. Clean using brake cleaning solvent (Chapter 7).
- ☐ Contamination of brake pads. Oil, brake fluid or dirt causing brake to chatter or squeal. Replace pads (Chapter 7).
- ☐ Pads glazed. Renew the pads (Chapter 7).
- ☐ Disc warped. Can cause a chattering, clicking or intermittent squeal. Usually accompanied by a pulsating lever and uneven braking. Renew the disc (Chapter 7).
- ☐ Loose or worn wheel bearings. Check (Chapter 1) and renew (Chapter 7) as necessary.

10 Oil pressure warning light comes on

Engine lubrication system

- ☐ Engine oil pump defective, blocked oil strainer gauze or failed relief valve. Carry out an oil pressure check (Chapter 1).
- ☐ Engine oil level low. Inspect for leak or other problem causing low oil level and add recommended oil (*Daily (pre-ride) checks*).
- ☐ Engine oil viscosity too low. Very old, thin oil or an improper weight of oil used in the engine. Change to correct oil (Chapter 1).
- ☐ Camshaft or journals worn. Excessive wear causing drop in oil pressure. Measure oil clearance (Chapter 2). Abnormal wear could be caused by oil starvation at high rpm from low oil level or improper weight or type of oil (Chapter 1).
- ☐ Crankshaft and/or bearings worn. Same problems as above. Measure connecting rod and main bearing oil clearance (Chapter 2).

Electrical system

- ☐ Oil pressure switch defective. Check the switch according to the procedure in Chapter 9. Replace it if it is defective.
- ☐ Oil pressure warning light circuit defective. Check for pinched, shorted, disconnected or damaged wiring (Chapter 9).

11 Excessive exhaust smoke

White smoke

- ☐ Piston oil ring worn. The ring may be broken or damaged, causing oil from the crankcase to be pulled past the piston into the combustion chamber. Replace the rings with new ones (Chapter 2).
- ☐ Cylinders worn, cracked, or scored. Caused by overheating or oil starvation. The cylinder block will require renewal.
- ☐ Valve oil seal damaged or worn. Replace oil seals with new ones (Chapter 2).
- ☐ Valve guide worn. Perform a complete valve job (Chapter 2).
- ☐ Engine oil level too high, which causes the oil to be forced past the rings. Drain oil to the proper level (Chapter 1).
- ☐ Head gasket broken between oil return and cylinder. Causes oil to be pulled into the combustion chamber. Renew the head gasket and check the head for warpage (Chapter 2).
- ☐ Abnormal crankcase pressurisation, which forces oil past the rings. Clogged breather is usually the cause.

Black smoke

- ☐ Fuel injection system malfunction (see Chapter 4).
- ☐ Air filter clogged (Chapter 1).

Brown smoke

- ☐ Fuel injection system malfunction (see Chapter 4).
- ☐ Faulty fuel pump or pressure regulator (see Chapter 4).
- ☐ Air filter poorly sealed or not installed (Chapter 1).

Fault Finding REF•41

12 Poor handling or stability

Handlebars hard to turn
- [ ] Steering head bearing adjuster nut too tight. Check adjustment as described in Chapter 1.
- [ ] Bearings damaged. Roughness can be felt as the bars are turned from side-to-side. Renew bearings and races (Chapter 6).
- [ ] Races dented or worn. Denting results from wear in only one position (e.g., straight ahead), from a collision or hitting a pothole or from dropping the machine. Renew bearings (Chapter 6).
- [ ] Steering stem lubrication inadequate. Causes are grease getting hard from age or being washed out by high pressure car washes. Disassemble steering head and repack bearings with fresh grease (Chapter 6).
- [ ] Steering stem bent. Caused by a collision, hitting a pothole or by dropping the machine. Renew damaged part. Don't try to straighten the steering stem (Chapter 6).
- [ ] Front tyre air pressure too low (Chapter 1).
- [ ] Faulty steering damper (Chapter 6).

Handlebar shakes or vibrates excessively
- [ ] Tyres worn or out of balance (Chapter 7).
- [ ] Swingarm bearings worn. Renew worn bearings (Chapter 6).
- [ ] Wheel rim(s) warped or damaged. Inspect wheels for runout (Chapter 7).
- [ ] Wheel bearings worn. Worn front or rear wheel bearings can cause poor tracking. Worn front bearings will cause wobble (Chapter 7).
- [ ] Handlebar holder or bridge bolts loose (Chapter 6).
- [ ] Fork yoke bolts loose. Tighten them to the specified torque (Chapter 6).
- [ ] Engine mounting bolts loose. Will cause excessive vibration with increased engine rpm (Chapter 2).

Handlebar pulls to one side
- [ ] Frame bent. Definitely suspect this if the machine has been dropped. May or may not be accompanied by cracking near the bend. Renew the frame (Chapter 6).
- [ ] Wheels out of alignment. Caused by improper location of axle spacers or from bent steering stem or frame (Chapter 6).
- [ ] Swingarm bent or twisted from accident damage. Renew the swingarm (Chapter 6).
- [ ] Steering stem bent. Caused by impact damage or by dropping the motorcycle. Renew the steering stem (Chapter 6).
- [ ] Fork tube bent. Disassemble the forks and renew the damaged parts (Chapter 6).
- [ ] Fork oil level uneven. Check and add or drain as necessary (Chapter 6).

Poor shock absorbing qualities
- [ ] Too hard:
    a) Fork oil level excessive (Chapter 6).
    b) Fork oil viscosity too high. Use a lighter oil (see the Specifications in Chapter 6).
    c) Fork tube bent. Causes a harsh, sticking feeling (Chapter 6).
    d) Rear shock absorber shaft or body bent or damaged (Chapter 6).
    e) Fork internal damage (Chapter 6).
    f) Shock absorber internal damage.
    g) Tyre pressure too high (Chapter 1).
    h) Incorrect adjustment settings (Chapter 6).
- [ ] Too soft:
    a) Fork or shock oil insufficient and/or leaking (Chapter 6).
    b) Fork oil level too low (Chapter 6).
    c) Fork oil viscosity too light (Chapter 6).
    d) Fork springs weak or broken (Chapter 6).
    e) Shock absorber internal damage or leakage (Chapter 6).
    f) Incorrect adjustment settings (Chapter 6).

13 Braking problems

Brakes are spongy, or lack power
- [ ] Air in brake line. Caused by inattention to master cylinder fluid level or by leakage. Locate problem and bleed brakes (Chapter 7).
- [ ] Pads or discs worn (Chapters 1 and 7).
- [ ] Brake fluid leak. See paragraph 1.
- [ ] Contaminated pads. Caused by contamination with oil, grease, brake fluid, etc. Renew pads (Chapter 7). Clean disc thoroughly with brake cleaner (Chapter 7).
- [ ] Brake fluid deteriorated. Fluid is old or contaminated. Drain system, replenish with new fluid and bleed the system (Chapter 7).
- [ ] Master cylinder internal parts worn or damaged causing fluid to bypass (Chapter 7).
- [ ] Master cylinder bore scratched by foreign material or broken spring. Repair or renew master cylinder (Chapter 7).

Brake lever or pedal pulsates
- [ ] Disc warped. Renew disc (Chapter 7).
- [ ] Wheel axle bent. Renew axle (Chapter 7).
- [ ] Brake caliper bolts loose (Chapter 7).
- [ ] Wheel warped or otherwise damaged (Chapter 7).
- [ ] Wheel bearings damaged or worn (Chapters 1 and 7).

Brakes drag
- [ ] Master cylinder piston seized. Caused by wear or damage to piston or cylinder bore (Chapter 7).
- [ ] Lever balky or stuck. Check pivot and lubricate (Chapter 7).
- [ ] Brake caliper piston seized in bore. Caused by wear or ingestion of dirt past deteriorated seal (Chapter 7).
- [ ] Brake pad damaged. Renew pads (Chapter 7).
- [ ] Pads improperly installed (Chapter 7).

14 Electrical problems

Battery dead or weak

- [ ] Battery faulty. Caused by sulphated plates which are shorted through sedimentation. Also, broken battery terminal making only occasional contact (Chapter 9).
- [ ] Battery cables making poor contact (Chapter 9).
- [ ] Load excessive. Caused by addition of high wattage lights or other electrical accessories.
- [ ] Ignition (main) switch defective. Switch either grounds (earths) internally or fails to shut off system. Renew the switch (Chapter 9).
- [ ] Regulator/rectifier defective (Chapter 9).
- [ ] Alternator stator coil open or shorted (Chapter 9).
- [ ] Wiring faulty. Wiring grounded (earthed) or connections loose in ignition, charging or lighting circuits (Chapter 9).

Battery overcharged

- [ ] Regulator/rectifier defective. Overcharging is noticed when battery gets excessively warm (Chapter 9).
- [ ] Battery defective. Replace battery with a new one (Chapter 9).
- [ ] Battery amperage too low, wrong type or size. Install manufacturer's specified amp-hour battery to handle charging load (Chapter 9).

Fault Finding Equipment REF•43

Checking engine compression

● Low compression will result in exhaust smoke, heavy oil consumption, poor starting and poor performance. A compression test will provide useful information about an engine's condition and if performed regularly, can give warning of trouble before any other symptoms become apparent.
● A compression gauge will be required, along with an adapter to suit the spark plug hole thread size. Note that the screw-in type gauge/adapter set up is preferable to the rubber cone type.
● Before carrying out the test, first check the valve clearances as described in Chapter 1.

1 Run the engine until it reaches normal operating temperature, then stop it and remove the spark plug(s), taking care not to scald your hands on the hot components.
2 Install the gauge adapter and compression gauge in No. 1 cylinder spark plug hole **(see illustration 1)**.

Screw the compression gauge adapter into the spark plug hole, then screw the gauge into the adapter

3 On kickstart-equipped motorcycles, make sure the ignition switch is OFF, then open the throttle fully and kick the engine over a couple of times until the gauge reading stabilises.
4 On motorcycles with electric start only, the procedure will differ depending on the nature of the ignition system. Flick the engine kill switch (engine stop switch) to OFF and turn the ignition switch ON; open the throttle fully and crank the engine over on the starter motor for a couple of revolutions until the gauge reading stabilises. If the starter will not operate with the kill switch OFF, turn the ignition switch OFF and refer to the next paragraph.
5 Install the plugs back in their caps and arrange the plug electrodes so that their metal bodies are earthed (grounded) against the cylinder head; this is essential to prevent damage to the ignition system **(see illustration 2)**. Position the plugs well away from the plug holes otherwise there is a risk of

All spark plugs must be earthed (grounded) against the cylinder head

atomised fuel escaping from the plug holes and igniting. As a safety precaution, cover the cylinder head cover with rag and disconnect the fuel pump wiring connector (see Chapter 4). Turn the ignition switch and kill switch ON, open the throttle fully and crank the engine over on the starter motor for a couple of revolutions until the gauge reading stabilises.
6 After one or two revolutions the pressure should build up to a maximum figure and then stabilise. Take a note of this reading and on multi-cylinder engines repeat the test on the remaining cylinders.
7 The correct pressures are given in Chapter 1 Specifications. If the results fall within the specified range and on multi-cylinder engines all are relatively equal, the engine is in good condition. If there is a marked difference between the readings, or if the readings are lower than specified, inspection of the top-end components will be required.
8 Low compression pressure may be due to worn cylinder bores, pistons or rings, failure of the cylinder head gasket, worn valve seals, or poor valve seating.
9 To distinguish between cylinder/piston wear and valve leakage, pour a small quantity of oil into the bore to temporarily seal the piston rings, then repeat the compression tests **(see illustration 3)**. If the readings show

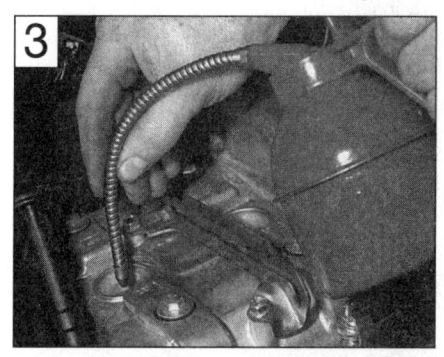

Bores can be temporarily sealed with a squirt of motor oil

a noticeable increase in pressure this confirms that the cylinder bore, piston, or rings are worn. If, however, no change is indicated, the cylinder head gasket or valves should be examined.
10 High compression pressure indicates excessive carbon build-up in the combustion chamber and on the piston crown. If this is the case the cylinder head should be removed and the deposits removed. Note that excessive carbon build-up is less likely with the used on modern fuels.

Checking battery open-circuit voltage

⚠ *Warning: The gases produced by the battery are explosive - never smoke or create any sparks in the vicinity of the battery. Never allow the electrolyte to contact your skin or clothing - if it does, wash it off and seek immediate medical attention.*

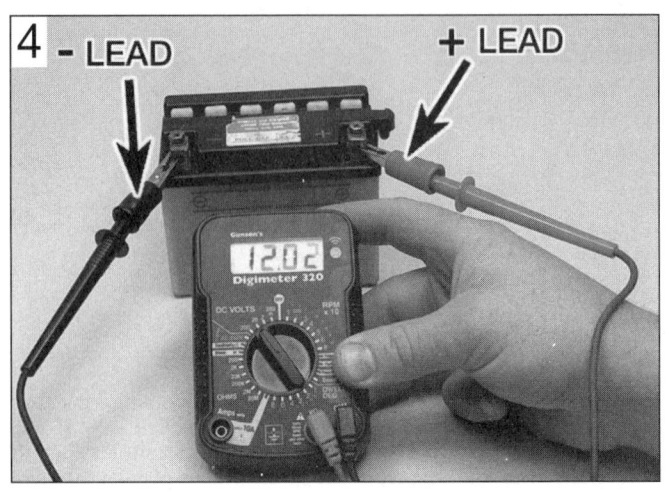

REF•44 Fault Finding Equipment

Measuring open-circuit battery voltage

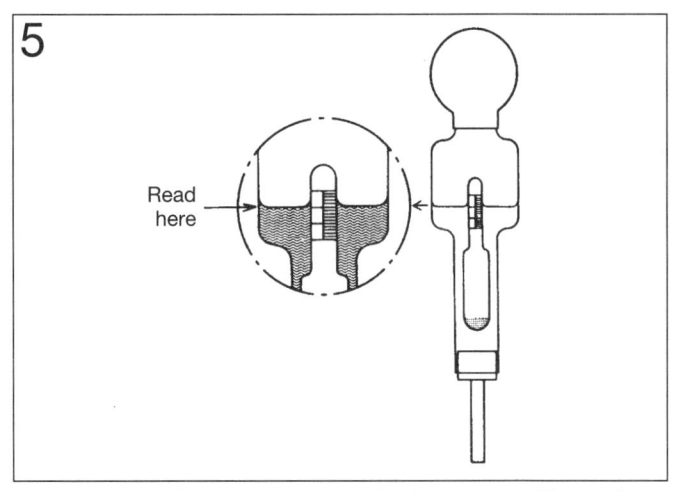

Float-type hydrometer for measuring battery specific gravity

- Before any electrical fault is investigated the battery should be checked.
- You'll need a dc voltmeter or multimeter to check battery voltage. Check that the leads are inserted in the correct terminals on the meter, red lead to positive (+ve), black lead to negative (-ve). Incorrect connections can damage the meter.
- A sound fully-charged 12 volt battery should produce between 12.3 and 12.6 volts across its terminals (12.8 volts for a maintenance-free battery). On machines with a 6 volt battery, voltage should be between 6.1 and 6.3 volts.

1 Set a multimeter to the 0 to 20 volts dc range and connect its probes across the battery terminals. Connect the meter's positive (+ve) probe, usually red, to the battery positive (+ve) terminal, followed by the meter's negative (-ve) probe, usually black, to the battery negative terminal (-ve) **(see illustration 4)**.

2 If battery voltage is low (below 10 volts on a 12 volt battery or below 4 volts on a six volt battery), charge the battery and test the voltage again. If the battery repeatedly goes flat, investigate the motorcycle's charging system.

Checking battery specific gravity (SG)

⚠ **Warning: The gases produced by the battery are explosive - never smoke or create any sparks in the vicinity of the battery. Never allow the electrolyte to contact your skin or clothing - if it does, wash it off and seek immediate medical attention.**

- The specific gravity check gives an indication of a battery's state of charge.
- A hydrometer is used for measuring specific gravity. Make sure you purchase one which has a small enough hose to insert in the aperture of a motorcycle battery.
- Specific gravity is simply a measure of the electrolyte's density compared with that of water. Water has an SG of 1.000 and fully-charged battery electrolyte is about 26% heavier, at 1.260.
- Specific gravity checks are not possible on maintenance-free batteries. Testing the open-circuit voltage is the only means of determining their state of charge.

1 To measure SG, remove the battery from the motorcycle and remove the first cell cap. Draw some electrolyte into the hydrometer and note the reading **(see illustration 5)**. Return the electrolyte to the cell and install the cap.

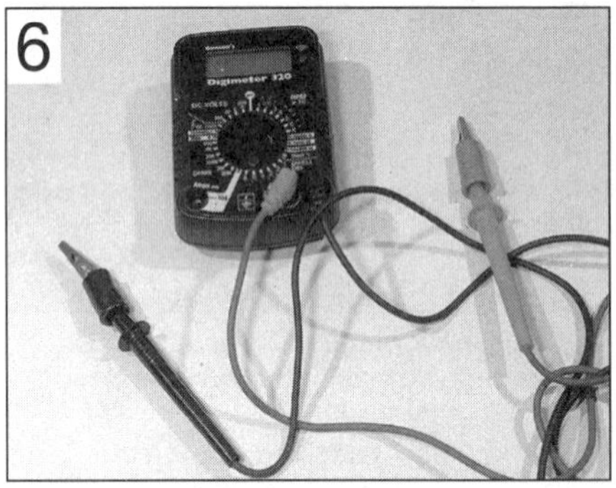

2 The reading should be in the region of 1.260 to 1.280. If SG is below 1.200 the battery needs charging. Note that SG will vary with temperature; it should be measured at 20°C (68°F). Add 0.007 to the reading for every 10°C above 20°C, and subtract 0.007 from the reading for every 10°C below 20°C. Add 0.004 to the reading for every 10°F above 68°F, and subtract 0.004 from the reading for every 10°F below 68°F.

3 When the check is complete, rinse the hydrometer thoroughly with clean water.

Checking for continuity

- The term continuity describes the uninterrupted flow of electricity through an electrical circuit. A continuity check will determine whether an **open-circuit** situation exists.
- Continuity can be checked with an ohmmeter, multimeter, continuity tester or battery and bulb test circuit **(see illustrations 6, 7 and 8)**.

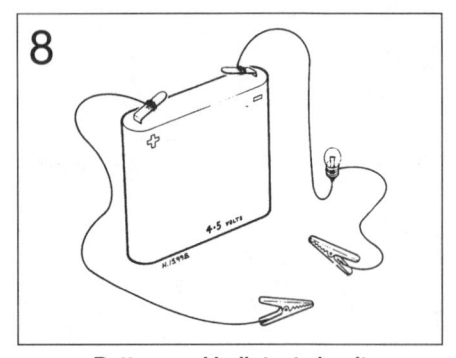

Digital multimeter can be used for all electrical tests

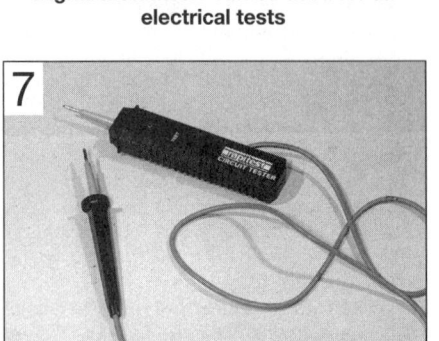

Battery-powered continuity tester

Battery and bulb test circuit

Fault Finding Equipment   REF•45

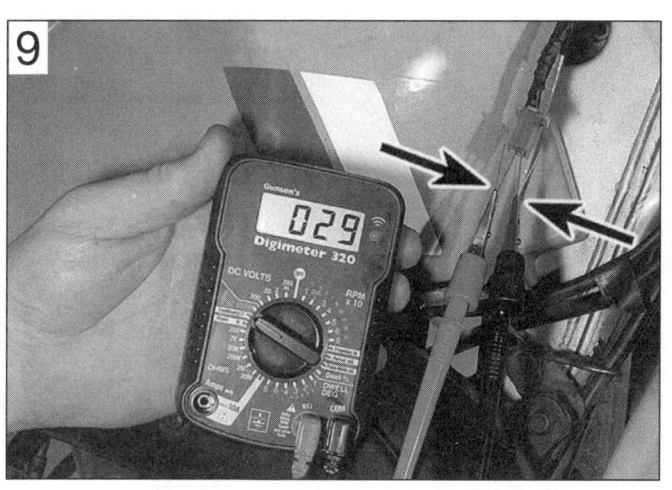

Continuity check of front brake light switch using a meter - note split pins used to access connector terminals

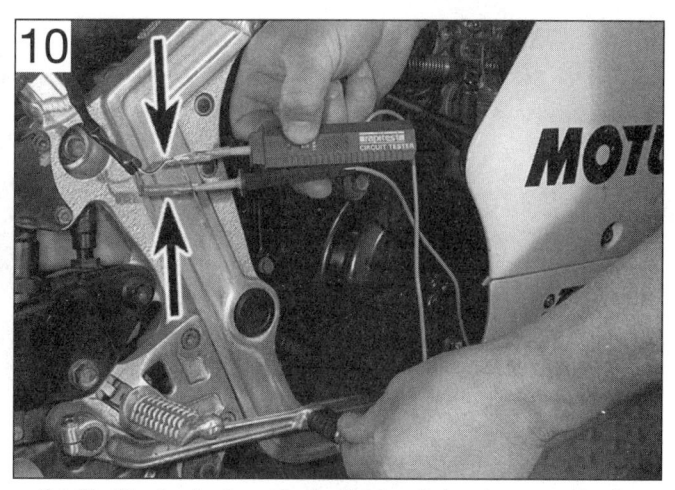

Continuity check of rear brake light switch using a continuity tester

● All of these instruments are self-powered by a battery, therefore the checks are made with the ignition OFF.
● As a safety precaution, always disconnect the battery negative (-ve) lead before making checks, particularly if ignition switch checks are being made.
● If using a meter, select the appropriate ohms scale and check that the meter reads infinity (∞). Touch the meter probes together and check that meter reads zero; where necessary adjust the meter so that it reads zero.
● After using a meter, always switch it OFF to conserve its battery.

Switch checks

1 If a switch is at fault, trace its wiring up to the wiring connectors. Separate the wire connectors and inspect them for security and condition. A build-up of dirt or corrosion here will most likely be the cause of the problem - clean up and apply a water dispersant such as WD40.

2 If using a test meter, set the meter to the ohms x 10 scale and connect its probes across the wires from the switch **(see illustration 9)**. Simple ON/OFF type switches, such as brake light switches, only have two wires whereas combination switches, like the ignition switch, have many internal links. Study the wiring diagram to ensure that you are connecting across the correct pair of wires. Continuity (low or no measurable resistance - 0 ohms) should be indicated with the switch ON and no continuity (high resistance) with it OFF.

3 Note that the polarity of the test probes doesn't matter for continuity checks, although care should be taken to follow specific test procedures if a diode or solid-state component is being checked.

4 A continuity tester or battery and bulb circuit can be used in the same way. Connect its probes as described above **(see illustration 10)**. The light should come on to indicate continuity in the ON switch position, but should extinguish in the OFF position.

Wiring checks

● Many electrical faults are caused by damaged wiring, often due to incorrect routing or chaffing on frame components.
● Loose, wet or corroded wire connectors can also be the cause of electrical problems, especially in exposed locations.

1 A continuity check can be made on a single length of wire by disconnecting it at each end and connecting a meter or continuity tester across both ends of the wire **(see illustration 11)**.

2 Continuity (low or no resistance - 0 ohms) should be indicated if the wire is good. If no continuity (high resistance) is shown, suspect a broken wire.

Checking for voltage

● A voltage check can determine whether current is reaching a component.
● Voltage can be checked with a dc voltmeter, multimeter set on the dc volts scale, test light or buzzer **(see illustrations 12 and 13)**. A meter has the advantage of being able to measure actual voltage.
● When using a meter, check that its leads are inserted in the correct terminals on the meter, red to positive (+ve), black to negative (-ve). Incorrect connections can damage the meter.
● A voltmeter (or multimeter set to the dc volts scale) should always be connected in parallel (across the load). Connecting it in series will not harm the meter, but the reading will not be meaningful.
● Voltage checks are made with the ignition ON.

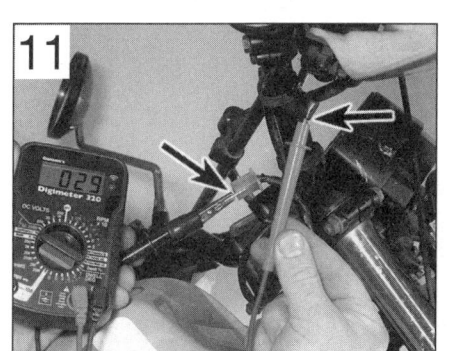

Continuity check of front brake light switch sub-harness

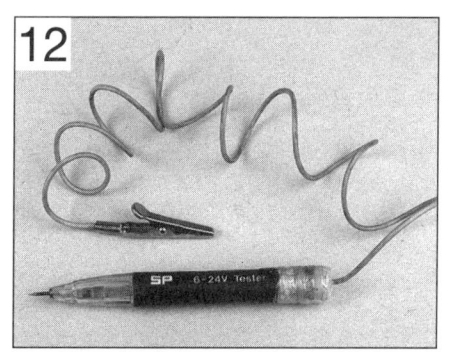

A simple test light can be used for voltage checks

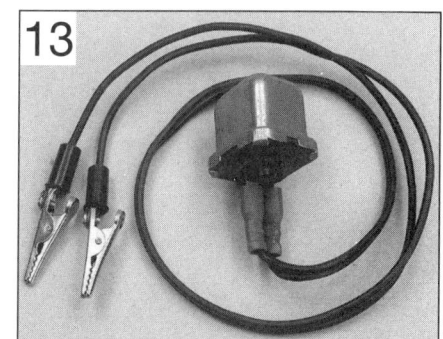

A buzzer is useful for voltage checks

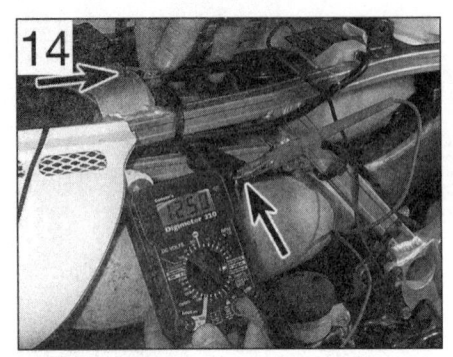

Fault Finding Equipment

Checking for voltage at the rear brake light power supply wire using a meter . . .

1 First identify the relevant wiring circuit by referring to the wiring diagram at the end of this manual. If other electrical components share the same power supply (ie are fed from the same fuse), take note whether they are working correctly - this is useful information in deciding where to start checking the circuit.

2 If using a meter, check first that the meter leads are plugged into the correct terminals on the meter (see above). Set the meter to the dc volts function, at a range suitable for the battery voltage. Connect the meter red probe (+ve) to the power supply wire and the black probe to a good metal earth (ground) on the motorcycle's frame or directly to the battery negative (-ve) terminal **(see illustration 14)**. Battery voltage should be shown on the meter

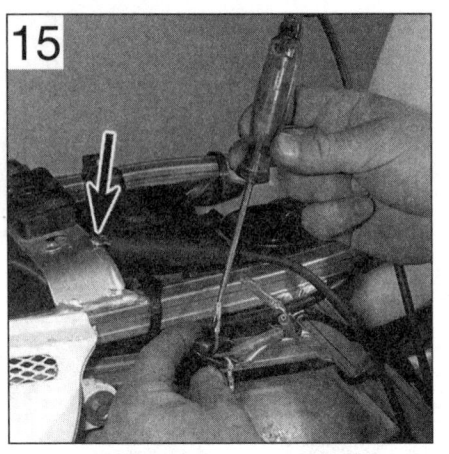

. . . or a test light - note the earth connection to the frame (arrow)

with the ignition switched ON.

3 If using a test light or buzzer, connect its positive (+ve) probe to the power supply terminal and its negative (-ve) probe to a good earth (ground) on the motorcycle's frame or directly to the battery negative (-ve) terminal **(see illustration 15)**. With the ignition ON, the test light should illuminate or the buzzer sound.

4 If no voltage is indicated, work back towards the fuse continuing to check for voltage. When you reach a point where there is voltage, you know the problem lies between that point and your last check point.

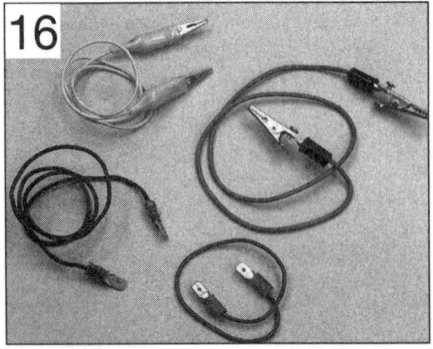

Checking the earth (ground)

● Earth connections are made either directly to the engine or frame (such as sensors, neutral switch etc. which only have a positive feed) or by a separate wire into the earth circuit of the wiring harness. Alternatively a short earth wire is sometimes run directly from the component to the motorcycle's frame.

● Corrosion is often the cause of a poor earth connection.

● If total failure is experienced, check the security of the main earth lead from the negative (-ve) terminal of the battery and also the main earth (ground) point on the wiring harness. If corroded, dismantle the connection and clean all surfaces back to bare metal.

1 To check the earth on a component, use an insulated jumper wire to temporarily bypass its earth connection **(see illustration 16)**. Connect one end of the jumper wire between the earth terminal or metal body of the component and the other end to the motorcycle's frame.

2 If the circuit works with the jumper wire installed, the original earth circuit is faulty. Check the wiring for open-circuits or poor connections. Clean up direct earth connections, removing all traces of corrosion and remake the joint. Apply petroleum jelly to the joint to prevent future corrosion.

Tracing a short-circuit

● A short-circuit occurs where current shorts to earth (ground) bypassing the circuit components. This usually results in a blown fuse.

● A short-circuit is most likely to occur where the insulation has worn through due to wiring chafing on a component, allowing a direct path to earth (ground) on the frame.

1 Remove any bodypanels necessary to access the circuit wiring.

2 Check that all electrical switches in the circuit are OFF, then remove the circuit fuse and connect a test light, buzzer or voltmeter (set to the dc scale) across the fuse terminals. No voltage should be shown.

3 Move the wiring from side to side whilst observing the test light or meter. When the test light comes on, buzzer sounds or meter shows voltage, you have found the cause of the short. It will usually shown up as damaged or burned insulation.

4 Note that the same test can be performed on each component in the circuit, even the switch.

A selection of jumper wires for making earth (ground) checks

Index

Note: *References throughout this index are in the form - "Chapter number" • "Page number"*

A

Air control valve system – 4.10
Air filter
 check and cleaning – 1.7
 renewal – 1.19
Air filter housing – 4.9
Alternator – 9.22
Atmospheric pressure (AP) sensor – 4.14

B

Balancer shaft – 2.46
Battery
 charging – 9.3
 check – 1.25
 removal and maintenance – 9.3
 specifications – 9.1
Bleeding
 brake – 7.16
 clutch – 2.38
Body panels – 8.2
Brake
 bleeding – 7.16
 calipers – 7.6, 7.9
 discs – 7.6
 fluid change – 1.22
 fluid level check – 0.12
 hoses and unions – 1.24, 7.15
 master cylinders – 7.12, 7.13
 pads – 1.14, 7.2, 7.4
 seal renewal – 1.25
 specifications – 7.1
 system check – 1.14
Brake light
 bulb – 9.7
 check – 9.5
 switches – 1.14, 9.10
Bulbs
 brake/tail light – 9.7
 headlight – 9.5
 licence plate light – 9.9
 sidelight – 9.6
 turn signals – 9.9
 wattages – 9.2

C

Cable
 fast idle – 1.11, 4.21
 lubrication – 1.15
 throttle – 1.11, 4.19
Calipers – 7.6, 7.9
Catalytic converter – 4.25
Cam chain, guides and blades – 2.17
Cam chain tensioner – 2.16
Camshaft position (CMP) sensor – 4.13
Camshafts and followers – 2.12
Centrestand – 6.3
Chain (cam) – 2.17
Chain (drive) – 0.15, 1.6, 1.13, 6.19
Charging system – 9.1, 9.22
Clutch
 bleeding – 2.38
 check – 1.12
 fluid change – 1.22
 fluid level check – 0.13
 hose renewal – 1.24
 lever – 6.5
 master cylinder – 2.34
 overhaul – 2.28
 release cylinder – 2.36
 seal renewal – 1.25
 specifications – 2.3
Clutch switch – 9.15
Colour code – 0.9
Coolant
 change – 1.22
 level check – 0.14
Coolant temperature gauge and warning light – 9.13
Cooling system
 check – 1.12
 coolant temperature sensor (ECT) – 3.3, 4.14
 fan, fan switch and relay – 3.2
 hoses and unions – 3.7
 pressure cap – 1.13, 3.2
 radiator – 3.5
 thermostat – 3.4
 water pump – 3.6
Connecting rods – 2.52, 2.54
Conversion factors – REF.26

REF•48 Index

Crankcases – 2.48, 2.50
Crankshaft – 2.52
Crankshaft position (CKP) sensor – 4.13
Cylinder block – 2.24
Cylinder compression check – 1.24
Cylinder head – 2.19, 2.20

D

Dimensions – 0.16
Diodes – 9.16
Discs – 7.6
Drive chain
    check, adjustment, cleaining and lubrication – 0.15, 1.6
    removal and installation – 6.19
    wear check – 1.13

E

Engine
    balancer shaft – 2.46
    cam chain, guides and blades – 2.17
    cam chain tensioner – 2.16
    camshafts and followers – 2.12
    connecting rods – 2.54
    crankcases – 2.48, 2.50
    crankshaft – 2.52
    cylinder block – 2.24
    cylinder compression check – 1.24
    cylinder head – 2.19, 2.20
    idle speed check – 1.10, 4.22
    oil and filter change – 1.19
    oil change – 1.9
    oil cooler – 2.11
    oil level check – 0.11
    oil pressure check – 1.24
    oil pump – 2.38
    oil sump, strainer and pressure regulator – 2.45
    main and connecting rod bearings – 2.52
    piston rings – 2.27
    pistons – 2.25
    removal and installation – 2.7
    running-in procedure – 2.65
    specifications – 0.16, 1.2, 2.1
    sprocket cover – 6.19
    starter clutch – 2.42
    valve clearance check – 1.20
    valve cover – 2.11
    valves – 2.20
Engine control module (ECM) – 5.3
Engine coolant temperature (ECT) sensor – 3.3, 4.14
Engine number – 0.9
EVAP (emission control system) – 4.25
Exhaust system – 4.22

F

Fairing – 8.2
Fan, fan switch and relay – 3.2
Fast idle cable
    check and adjustment – 1.11
    renewal – 4.21

Fast idle speed – 4.22
Fault codes – 4.11
Fault finding – 4.11, 9.2, REF.34 *et seq*
Filter
    air – 1.7, 1.19
    fuel – 1.9, 4.6
    oil – 1.19
Footrests – 6.2
Frame – 6.2
Frame number – 0.9
Front brake
    calipers – 7.6
    discs – 7.6
    lever – 6.5
    master cylinder – 7.12
    pads – 7.2
Front brake light switch – 9.10
Front forks
    adjustment – 6.15
    check – 1.18
    oil change – 1.25, 6.6
    overhaul – 6.8
    removal and installation – 6.5
Front mudguard – 8.5
Front wheel
    bearings – 1.25, 7.21
    removal and installation – 7.18
Fuel injection system
    description – 4.11
    fault finding – 4.11
    fuel injectors – 4.15, 4.18
    fuel rail – 4.18
    sensors – 4.13
    throttle bodies – 1.16, 4.16
Fuel level gauge and warning light – 9.13
Fuel level sensor – 4.8
Fuel supply system
    check – 1.9
    filter and strainer – 4.6
    hose renewal – 1.24
    pressure check – 4.5
    pressure regulator – 4.9
    pump and relay – 4.5, 4.6
    specifications – 4.1
    tank – 4.3
Fuses – 9.2, 9.4

G

Gear position (GP) sensor – 4.15
Gearchange lever – 6.2
Gearchange mechanism – 2.40
Gearshafts – 2.57

H

Handlebar switches – 9.14
Handlebars – 6.4
Headlight
    aim check – 1.26
    bulb – 9.5
    check – 9.5
    unit – 9.7
Horn – 9.16
HT coils – 5.3

Index

I

Idle speed check – 1.10, 4.22
Ignition (main) switch – 9.13
Ignition system
    check – 5.2
    engine control module (ECM) – 5.3
    HT coils – 5.3
Injector (fuel) – 4.15, 4.18
Instruments – 9.11, 9.12, 9.13
Intake air control valve system – 4.10
Intake air pressure (IAP) sensor – 4.13
Intake air temperature (IAT) sensor – 4.14

L

Legal check – 0.15
Levers
    clutch and front brake – 6.4
    gearchange – 6.3
Licence light bulb – 9.7
Lighting system – 9.5
Lubricants – 1.2, REF.23

M

Main bearings – 2.52
Maintenance schedule – 1.3
Master cylinder
    clutch – 2.34
    front brake – 7.12
    rear brake – 7.13
Mirrors – 8.2
Model development – 0.17
MOT test checks – REF.27
Mudguard (front) – 8.5

O

Oil (engine)
    change – 1.9, 1.19
    level check – 0.11
Oil (front forks) – 1.25,
Oil cooler – 2.11
Oil pump – 2.38
Oil pressure check – 1.24
Oil pressure switch – 9.16
Oil pressure warning light – 9.13
Oil recommendations – 1.2
Oil sump, strainer and pressure regulator – 2.45
Oxygen sensor – 4.16

P

Pads (brake) – 1.14, 7.2, 7.4
PAIR (Pulse secondary AIR) system – 4.24
Piston rings – 2.27
Pistons – 2.25
Pre-ride checks – 0.11 *et seq*

Pressure cap (radiator) – 1.13
Pressure check
    fuel – 4.5
    oil – 1.24
    tyre – 0.15
Pressure regulator
    fuel – 4.9
    oil – 2.45
Pump
    fuel – 4.6
    oil – 2.38
    water – 3.6

R

Radiator – 3.5
Radiator pressure cap – 1.13, 3.2
Rear brake
    caliper – 7.9
    disc – 7.6
    master cylinder – 7.13
    pads – 7.4
    pedal height adjustment – 1.14
    pedal removal and installation – 6.3
Rear brake light switch – 1.14, 9.11
Rear suspension
    bearing re-greasing – 1.25
    check – 1.18
    linkage – 6.13
    shock absorber – 6.14
    swingarm – 6.16, 6.18
Rear view mirrors – 8.2
Rear wheel
    bearings – 1.25, 7.21
    removal and installation – 7.19
Regulator/rectifier – 9.24
Relay
    cooling fan – 3.2
    fuel pump – 4.5
    starter – 9.16
    turn signal/sidestand – 9.8
Release cylinder (clutch) – 2.36
Routine maintenance – 1.1 *et seq*

S

Safety – 0.10, 0.15
Seat cowling – 8.4
Seats – 8.2
Security – REF.20
Selector drum and forks – 2.64
Shock absorber (rear)
    adjustment – 6.15
    removal and installation – 6.14
Sidelight
    bulb – 9.6
    check – 9.5
Sidestand – 1.25, 6.3
Sidestand switch and relay – 9.14
Silencers – 4.22
Spark plug
    check and gap adjustment – 1.8
    renewal – 1.16

Index

Specifications
  brakes – 7.1
  clutch – 2.3
  cooling system – 3.1
  electrical system – 9.1
  engine – 0.16, 1.2, 2.1
  final drive – 6.1
  fuel system – 4.1
  general – 0.17
  ignition system – 5.1
  maintenance – 1.2
  suspension – 6.1
  transmission – 2.5
  wheels – 7.2
Speedometer and speed sensor – 9.12
Sprockets
  coupling bearing – 7.22
  coupling/rubber dampers – 6.21
  removal and installation – 6.19
  wear check – 1.13
Starter clutch – 2.42
Starter interlock circuit – 1.25
Starter motor – 9.18
Starter relay – 9.16
Steering check – 0.15
Steering damper – 6.13
Steering head bearings
  check and adjustment – 1.17
  re-greasing – 1.25
  renewal – 6.12
Steering stem – 6.10
Storage – REF.31
Suspension
  adjustment – 6.15
  check – 0.15, 1.18
  front forks – 6.5, 6.6, 6.8
  rear shock – 6.14
Swingarm
  bearing check – 1.18, 6.18
  bearing re-greasing – 1.25
  bearing renewal – 6.18
  removal and installation – 6.16

T

Tachometer – 9.13

Tail light
  bulb – 9.7
  check – 9.5
  unit – 9.8
Tank (fuel) – 4.3
Thermostat – 3.4
Throttle cable
  check and adjustment – 1.11
  renewal – 4.19
Throttle body
  overhaul – 4.16
  synchronisation – 1.16
Throttle position (TP) sensor – 4.13
Tip-over (TO) sensor – 4.15
Tools – REF.2
Torque settings – 1.2, 2.5, 3.1, 4.2, 5.1, 6.2, 7.2, 9.2
Transmission
  gearshafts – 2.57
  selector drum and forks – 2.64
  specifications – 2.5
Turn signals
  bulbs – 9.9
  check and relay – 9.5, 9.8
  units – 9.9
Tyre
  fitting – 7.23
  pressure and tread check – 0.15
  sizes – 7.2

V

Valve clearance check – 1.20
Valve cover – 2.11
Valves – 2.20

W

Water pump – 3.6
Weights – 0.16
Wheel
  alignment – 7.18
  bearings – 1.25, 7.21
  check – 1.15
  inspection and repair – 7.17
  removal and installation – 7.18, 7.19
  sizes – 7.2
Wiring diagrams – 9.26 *et seq*

Haynes Motorcycle Manuals – The Complete List

Title	Book No
BMW 2-valve Twins (70 - 96)	♦ 0249
BMW K100 & 75 2-valve Models (83 - 96)	♦ 1373
BMW R850, 1100 & 1150 4-valve Twins (93 - 04)	♦ 3466
BSA Bantam (48 - 71)	0117
BSA Unit Singles (58 - 72)	0127
BSA Pre-unit Singles (54 - 61)	0326
BSA A7 & A10 Twins (47 - 62)	0121
BSA A50 & A65 Twins (62 - 73)	0155
DUCATI 600, 750 & 900 2-valve V-Twins (91 - 96)	♦ 3290
Ducati MK III & Desmo Singles (69 - 76)	◊ 0445
Ducati 748, 916 & 996 4-valve V-Twins (94 - 01)	♦ 3756
GILERA Runner, DNA, Stalker & Ice (97 - 04)	4163
HARLEY-DAVIDSON Sportsters (70 - 03)	♦ 2534
Harley-Davidson Big Twins (73 - on)	2536
Harley-Davidson Twin Cam 88 (99 - 03)	♦ 2478
HONDA NB, ND, NP & NS50 Melody (81 - 85)	◊ 0622
Honda NE/NB50 Vision & SA50 Vision Met-in (85 - 95)	◊ 1278
Honda MB, MBX, MT & MTX50 (80 - 93)	0731
Honda C50, C70 & C90 (67 - 99)	0324
Honda XR80R & XR100R (85 - 04)	2218
Honda XL/XR 80, 100, 125, 185 & 200 2-valve Models (78 - 87)	0566
Honda H100 & H100S Singles (80 - 92)	◊ 0734
Honda CB/CD125T & CM125C Twins (77 - 88)	◊ 0571
Honda CG125 (76 - 00)	◊ 0433
Honda NS125 (86 - 93)	3056
Honda MBX/MTX125 & MTX200 (83 - 93)	◊ 1132
Honda CD/CM185 200T & CM250C 2-valve Twins (77 - 85)	0572
Honda XL/XR 250 & 500 (78 - 84)	0567
Honda XR250L, XR250R & XR400R (86 - 03)	2219
Honda CB250 & CB400N Super Dreams (78 - 84)	◊ 0540
Honda CR Motocross Bikes (86 - 01)	2222
Honda CBR400RR Fours (88 - 99)	◊ ♦ 3552
Honda VFR400 (NC30) & RVF400 (NC35) V-Fours (89 - 98)	◊ ♦ 3496
Honda CB500 (93 - 01)	◊ ♦ 3753
Honda CB400 & CB550 Fours (73 - 77)	0262
Honda CX/GL500 & 650 V-Twins (78 - 86)	0442
Honda CBX550 Four (82 - 86)	◊ 0940
Honda XL600R & XR600R (83 - 00)	2183
Honda XL600/650V Transalp & XRV750 Africa Twin (87 - 02)	◊ 3919
Honda CBR600F1 & 1000F Fours (87 - 96)	♦ 1730
Honda CBR600F2 & F3 Fours (91 - 98)	♦ 2070
Honda CBR600F4 (99 - 02)	♦ 3911
Honda CB600F Hornet (98 - 02)	◊ ♦ 3915
Honda CB650 sohc Fours (78 - 84)	0665
Honda NTV600 Revere, NTV650 & NT650V Deauville (88 - 01)	◊ 3243
Honda Shadow VT600 & 750 (USA) (88 - 03)	2312
Honda CB750 sohc Four (69 - 79)	0131
Honda V45/65 Sabre & Magna (82 - 88)	0820
Honda VFR750 & 700 V-Fours (86 - 97)	♦ 2101
Honda VFR800 V-Fours (97 - 01)	♦ 3703
Honda CB750 & CB900 dohc Fours (78 - 84)	0535
Honda VTR1000 (FireStorm, Super Hawk) & XL1000V (Varadero) (97 - 00)	♦ 3744
Honda CBR900RR FireBlade (92 - 99)	♦ 2161
Honda CBR900RR FireBlade (00 - 03)	♦ 4060
Honda CBR1100XX Super Blackbird (97 - 02)	♦ 3901
Honda ST1100 Pan European V-Fours (90 - 01)	♦ 3384
Honda Shadow VT1100 (USA) (85 - 98)	2313
Honda GL1000 Gold Wing (75 - 79)	0309
Honda GL1100 Gold Wing (79 - 81)	0669
Honda Gold Wing 1200 (USA) (84 - 87)	2199

Title	Book No
Honda Gold Wing 1500 (USA) (88 - 00)	2225
KAWASAKI AE/AR 50 & 80 (81 - 95)	1007
Kawasaki KC, KE & KH100 (75 - 99)	1371
Kawasaki KMX125 & 200 (86 - 02)	◊ 3046
Kawasaki 250, 350 & 400 Triples (72 - 79)	0134
Kawasaki 400 & 440 Twins (74 - 81)	0281
Kawasaki 400, 500 & 550 Fours (79 - 91)	0910
Kawasaki EN450 & 500 Twins (Ltd/Vulcan) (85 - 04)	2053
Kawasaki EX & ER500 (GPZ500S & ER-5) Twins (87 - 99)	♦ 2052
Kawasaki ZX600 (Ninja ZX-6, ZZ-R600) Fours (90 - 00)	♦ 2146
Kawasaki ZX-6R Ninja Fours (95 - 02)	♦ 3541
Kawasaki ZX600 (GPZ600R, GPX600R, Ninja 600R & RX) & ZX750 (GPX750R, Ninja 750R) Fours (85 - 97)	♦ 1780
Kawasaki 650 Four (76 - 78)	0373
Kawasaki Vulcan 700/750 & 800 (85 - 01)	♦ 2457
Kawasaki 750 Air-cooled Fours (80 - 91)	0574
Kawasaki ZR550 & 750 Zephyr Fours (90 - 97)	♦ 3382
Kawasaki ZX750 (Ninja ZX-7 & ZXR750) Fours (89 - 96)	♦ 2054
Kawasaki Ninja ZX-7R & ZX-9R (ZX750P, ZX900B/C/D/E) (94 - 00)	♦ 3721
Kawasaki 900 & 1000 Fours (73 - 77)	0222
Kawasaki ZX900, 1000 & 1100 Liquid-cooled Fours (83 - 97)	♦ 1681
MOTO GUZZI 750, 850 & 1000 V-Twins (74 - 78)	0339
MZ ETZ Models (81 - 95)	◊ 1680
NORTON 500, 600, 650 & 750 Twins (57 - 70)	0187
Norton Commando (68 - 77)	0125
PEUGEOT Speedfight, Trekker & Vivacity (96 - 02)	◊ 3920
PIAGGIO (Vespa) Scooters (91 - 03)	3492
SUZUKI GT, ZR & TS50 (77 - 90)	0799
Suzuki TS50X (84 - 00)	◊ 1599
Suzuki 100, 125, 185 & 250 Air-cooled Trail bikes (79 - 89)	0797
Suzuki GP100 & 125 Singles (78 - 93)	◊ 0576
Suzuki GS, GN, GZ & DR125 Singles (82 - 99)	◊ 0888
Suzuki 250 & 350 Twins (68 - 78)	0120
Suzuki GT250X7, GT200X5 & SB200 Twins (78 - 83)	◊ 0469
Suzuki GS/GSX250, 400 & 450 Twins (79 - 85)	0736
Suzuki GS500 Twin (89 - 02)	♦ 3238
Suzuki GS550 (77 - 82) & GS750 Fours (76 - 79)	0363
Suzuki GS/GSX550 4-valve Fours (83 - 88)	1133
Suzuki SV650 (99 - 02)	♦ 3912
Suzuki GSX-R600 & 750 (96 - 00)	♦ 3553e
Suzuki GSX-R600 (01 - 02), GSX-R750 (00 - 02) & GSX-R1000 (01 - 02)	♦ 3986e
Suzuki GSF600 & 1200 Bandit Fours (95 - 04)	♦ 3367
Suzuki GS850 Fours (78 - 88)	0536
Suzuki GS1000 Four (77 - 79)	0484
Suzuki GSX-R750, GSX-R1100 (85 - 92), GSX600F, GSX750F, GSX1100F (Katana) Fours (88 - 96)	♦ 2055
Suzuki GSX600/750F & GSX750 (98 - 02)	♦ 3987
Suzuki GS/GSX1000, 1100 & 1150 4-valve Fours (79 - 88)	0737
Suzuki TL1000S/R & DL1000 V-Strom (97 - 04)	♦ 4083
Suzuki GSX1300R Hayabusa (99 - 04)	♦ 4184
TRIUMPH Tiger Cub & Terrier (52 - 68)	0414
Triumph 350 & 500 Unit Twins (58 - 73)	0137
Triumph Pre-Unit Twins (47 - 62)	0251
Triumph 650 & 750 2-valve Unit Twins (63 - 83)	0122
Triumph Trident & BSA Rocket 3 (69 - 75)	0136
Triumph Fuel Injected Triples (97 - 00)	♦ 3755
Triumph Triples & Fours (carburettor engines) (91 - 99)	♦ 2162
VESPA P/PX125, 150 & 200 Scooters (78 - 03)	0707
Vespa Scooters (59 - 78)	0126
YAMAHA DT50 & 80 Trail Bikes (78 - 95)	◊ 0800
Yamaha T50 & 80 Townmate (83 - 95)	◊ 1247
Yamaha YB100 Singles (73 - 91)	◊ 0474

Title	Book No
Yamaha RS/RXS100 & 125 Singles (74 - 95)	0331
Yamaha RD & DT125LC (82 - 87)	◊ 0887
Yamaha TZR125 (87 - 93) & DT125R (88 - 02)	◊ 1655
Yamaha TY50, 80, 125 & 175 (74 - 84)	◊ 0464
Yamaha XT & SR125 (82 - 02)	◊ 1021
Yamaha Trail Bikes (81 - 00)	2350
Yamaha 250 & 350 Twins (70 - 79)	0040
Yamaha XS250, 360 & 400 sohc Twins (75 - 84)	0378
Yamaha RD250 & 350LC Twins (80 - 82)	0803
Yamaha RD350 YPVS Twins (83 - 95)	1158
Yamaha RD400 Twin (75 - 79)	0333
Yamaha XT, TT & SR500 Singles (75 - 83)	0342
Yamaha XZ550 Vision V-Twins (82 - 85)	0821
Yamaha FJ, FZ, XJ & YX600 Radian (84 - 92)	2100
Yamaha XJ600S (Diversion, Seca II) & XJ600N Fours (92 - 03)	♦ 2145
Yamaha YZF600R Thundercat & FZS600 Fazer (96 - 03)	♦ 3702
Yamaha YZF-R6 (98 - 02)	♦ 3900
Yamaha 650 Twins (70 - 83)	0341
Yamaha XJ650 & 750 Fours (80 - 84)	0738
Yamaha XS750 & 850 Triples (76 - 85)	0340
Yamaha TDM850, TRX850 & XTZ750 (89 - 99)	◊ ♦ 3540
Yamaha YZF750R & YZF1000R Thunderace (93 - 00)	♦ 3720
Yamaha FZR600, 750 & 1000 Fours (87 - 96)	♦ 2056
Yamaha XV (Virago) V-Twins (81 - 03)	♦ 0802
Yamaha XVS650 & 1100 Dragstar/V-Star (97 - 04)	♦ 4195
Yamaha XJ900F Fours (83 - 94)	♦ 3239
Yamaha XJ900S Diversion (94 - 01)	♦ 3739
Yamaha YZF-R1 (98 - 01)	♦ 3754
Yamaha FJ1100 & 1200 Fours (84 - 96)	♦ 2057
Yamaha XJR1200 & 1300 (95 - 03)	♦ 3981
Yamaha V-Max (85 - 03)	♦ 4072
ATVs	
Honda ATC70, 90, 110, 185 & 200 (71 - 85)	0565
Honda TRX300 Shaft Drive ATVs (88 - 00)	2125
Honda TRX300EX & TRX400EX ATVs (93 - 04)	2318
Honda Foreman 400 and 450 ATVs (95 - 02)	2465
Kawasaki Bayou 220/250/300 & Prairie 300 ATVs (86 - 03)	2351
Polaris ATVs (85 - 97)	2302
Polaris ATVs (98 - 03)	2508
Yamaha YFS200 Blaster ATV (88 - 98)	2317
Yamaha YFB250 Timberwolf ATVs (92 - 00)	2217
Yamaha YFM350 & YFM400 (ER and Big Bear) ATVs (87 - 03)	2126
Yamaha Banshee and Warrior ATVs (87 - 03)	2314
ATV Basics	10450
TECHBOOK SERIES	
Motorcycle Basics TechBook (2nd Edition)	3515
Motorcycle Electrical TechBook (3rd Edition)	3471
Motorcycle Fuel Systems TechBook	3514
Motorcycle Maintenance TechBook	4071
Motorcycle Workshop Practice TechBook (2nd Edition)	3470
GENERAL MANUALS	
Twist and Go (automatic transmission) Scooters Service and Repair Manual	4082

◊ = not available in the USA   ♦ = Superbike

The manuals on this page are available through good motorcycle dealers and accessory shops.
In case of difficulty, contact: **Haynes Publishing**
(UK) +44 1963 442030   (USA) +1 805 498 6703
(FR) +33 1 47 17 66 29   (SV) +46 18 124016
(Australia/New Zealand) +61 3 9763 8100

MCL17.10/04

Preserving Our Motoring Heritage

The Model J Duesenberg Derham Tourster. Only eight of these magnificent cars were ever built – this is the only example to be found outside the United States of America

Almost every car you've ever loved, loathed or desired is gathered under one roof at the Haynes Motor Museum. Over 300 immaculately presented cars and motorbikes represent every aspect of our motoring heritage, from elegant reminders of bygone days, such as the superb Model J Duesenberg to curiosities like the bug-eyed BMW Isetta. There are also many old friends and flames. Perhaps you remember the 1959 Ford Popular that you did your courting in? The magnificent 'Red Collection' is a spectacle of classic sports cars including AC, Alfa Romeo, Austin Healey, Ferrari, Lamborghini, Maserati, MG, Riley, Porsche and Triumph.

A Perfect Day Out

Each and every vehicle at the Haynes Motor Museum has played its part in the history and culture of Motoring. Today, they make a wonderful spectacle and a great day out for all the family. Bring the kids, bring Mum and Dad, but above all bring your camera to capture those golden memories for ever. You will also find an impressive array of motoring memorabilia, a comfortable 70 seat video cinema and one of the most extensive transport book shops in Britain. The Pit Stop Cafe serves everything from a cup of tea to wholesome, home-made meals or, if you prefer, you can enjoy the large picnic area nestled in the beautiful rural surroundings of Somerset.

John Haynes O.B.E., Founder and Chairman of the museum at the wheel of a Haynes Light 12.

The 1936 490cc sohc-engined International Norton – well known for its racing success

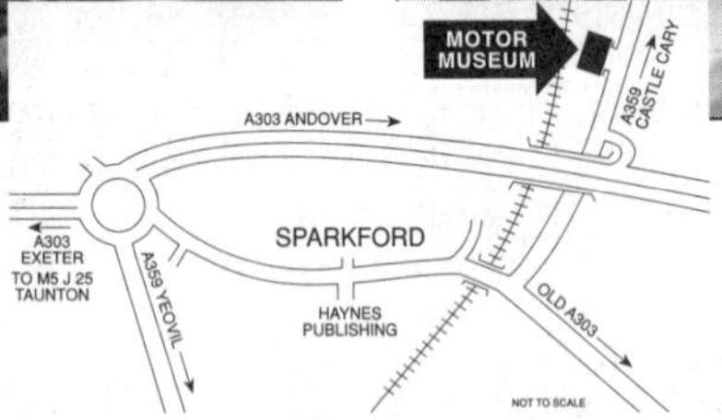

The Museum is situated on the A359 Yeovil to Frome road at Sparkford, just off the A303 in Somerset. It is about 40 miles south of Bristol, and 25 minutes drive from the M5 intersection at Taunton.
Open 9.30am - 5.30pm (10.00am - 4.00pm Winter) 7 days a week, *except Christmas Day, Boxing Day and New Years Day*
Special rates available for schools, coach parties and outings Charitable Trust No. 292048